Fourth Edition

Cambridge Preparation for the TOEFL® Test

Jolene Gear • Robert Gear

CAMBRIDGE UNIVERSITY PRESS
Cambridge, New York, Melbourne, Madrid, Cape Town, Singapore,
São Paulo, Delhi, Dubai, Tokyo, Mexico City

Cambridge University Press
32 Avenue of the Americas, New York, NY 10013–2473, USA

www.cambridge.org
Information on this title: www.cambridge.org/9780521755849

First published 2006
10th printing 2011

Printed in the United States of America

A catalog record of this publication is available from the British Library.

Library of Congress Cataloging-in-Publication Data

Gear, Jolene
Cambridge preparation for the TOEFL test / Jolene Gear and Robert Gear.–4th ed.
p.cm.
Includes index.
ISBN 978-0-521-75584-9 (pbk)
1. Test of English as a Foreign Language–Study guides. 2. English language–Textbooks for foreign speakers. 3. English language–Examinations–Study guides. I. Title: Preparation for the TOEFL test. II. Gear, Robert. III. Title.

PE1128.G35 2006
428.0076–dc22

2006042613

ISBN 978-0-521-75584-9 paperback with CD-ROM (Windows®, Mac®)
ISBN 978-0-521-75585-6 audio CDs
ISBN 978-0-521-75586-3 audio cassettes
ISBN 978-0-521-75587-0 pack consisting of book, CD-ROM (Windows®, Mac®), and audio CDs
ISBN 978-0-521-75588-7 CD-ROM (Windows®, Mac®)

Book design, layout services, and art direction: Adventure House, NYC
Audio production: Richard LePage & Associates, Paul Ruben Productions
All photography: © Frank Veronsky

Acknowledgments

We would like to thank the many people who made the publication of the Fourth Edition of this book possible. Our deepest appreciation goes to Jane Mairs, Jeff Chen, and the entire editorial team including Liane Carita, Carol Cassidy, Karen Davy, Molly Forster, John Freitas, Jill Ginsburg, Paul Heacock, Louisa Hellegers, Lisa Hutchins, Penny Laporte, Nina Metzner, Diana Nam, Heather Otrando, Kathleen O'Reilly, Carlos Rountree, Mary Sandre, Karen Shimoda, and Jennifer Wilkin for the advice, patience, understanding, and professionalism that they demonstrated throughout the process of bringing the manuscript into print.

Our gratitude also goes to the following members of the production and marketing teams for their combined efforts and painstaking care in the preparation of this edition: Cindee Howard, Jill Freshney, Heather McCarron, Sandra Pike, Tracy van Staalduinen, Heather Gray, Carine Mitchell, Bruno Paul, Tom Price, and Howard Siegelman.

Thanks also goes to Wendy Asplin of the University of Washington, Trevor Bryan, Mohamed Errihani of the University of Illinois, Richard Moore of the University of Washington, and Deborah Smith of the Centro Español de Nuevas Profesiones, La Coruna, Spain, for their insights and recommendations, and to Monica Snow of the American Language Program, California State University, Fullerton, for providing sample essays for the CD-ROM portion of the project. A special word of thanks also goes to the Oulu University Language Centre at Oulu, Finland, and the Sultan Qaboos University English Language Centre for providing office and library facilities.

The following production companies provided an invaluable service in helping to bring the edition to completion:

Adventure House, NYC
Cole Communications, Inc.
Onomatopoeia, Inc.
Paul Ruben Productions
Richard LePage & Associates
Frank Veronsky

We gratefully acknowledge permission to use the following materials:

Page 159; Exercise R3, reading passage for example. Article about mounties was originally published on the Royal Canadian Mounted Police Internet site. RCMP/GRC © 1996–1999.

Page 160-161; Reading Mini-test 1, reading passage for questions 1–4. This article was adapted from the Web site of the Rubber Pavements Association and used with its permission.

Pages 163-164; Reading Mini-test 1, reading passage for questions 13–16. The reading on resolutions is adapted from Stuart Sutherland, *Irrationality: Why We Don't Think Straight*, copyright © 1992 by Stuart Sutherland. Printed by permission of Rutgers University Press and Constable Publishers.

Pages 215-216; Reading Mini-test 4, reading passage for questions 10–13. The reading on interviewing is adapted from Stuart Sutherland, *Irrationality: Why We Don't Think Straight*, copyright © 1992 by Stuart Sutherland. Printed by permission of Rutgers University Press and Constable Publishers.

Page 220; Exercise R23, question 2. The talk about the fossil record is used by permission of the *Skeptical Inquirer* magazine.

Page 221; Exercise R23, question 4. The talk in an economics class is a summary of Chapter 2 in Richard J. Maybury, *Whatever Happened to Penny Candy?* published by Bluestocking Press, PO Box 2030, Dept. TL, Placerville, CA 95667-1014, USA, and is used with permission of the author and publisher.

Pages 422; Exercise W 37. The talk about the "War of the Worlds" radio broadcast is used by permission of the *Skeptical Inquirer* magazine.

TOEFL IBT test materials are reprinted by permission of Educational Testing Service, the copyright owner. However, the test questions and any other testing information are provided in their entirety by Cambridge University Press. No endorsement of this publication by Educational Testing Service should be inferred.

TOEFL iBT test materials selected from TOEFL iBT Tips, Educational Testing Service, 2005. Reprinted by permission of Educational Testing Service, the copyright owner. However, the test questions and any other testing information are provided in their entirety by Cambridge University Press. No endorsement of this publication by Educational Testing Service should be inferred.

Contents

To the Student

ABOUT THE BOOK

Cambridge Preparation for the TOEFL® Test, Fourth Edition, helps you build the skills necessary to successfully answer the questions and complete the tasks on the TOEFL® iBT test. It also thoroughly familiarizes you with the TOEFL test format and teaches test-taking strategies to help you improve your scores.

The book and its accompanying CD-ROM, which features seven practice tests, may be used as a classroom text or for self-study. An extensive audio program is available on audio cassette or audio CD.

In addition to helping you prepare for the TOEFL iBT test, this book and CD-ROM will give you the opportunity to develop skills that will help you succeed in your academic work.

IMPORTANT FEATURES OF THIS PROGRAM

- An **Introduction** that describes the sections of the TOEFL test and how they are scored, and offers tips for taking the TOEFL test successfully.
- A thorough **explanation** of how to answer questions on the test.
- A comprehensive **Table of Contents** that identifies the focus of every exercise in the book.
- An accompanying **CD-ROM** that features seven complete practice tests in the TOEFL iBT format.
- A **Diagnostic Test** that helps you pinpoint your weaknesses in English and then directs you to the exercises that will strengthen those areas. You may take this test on the CD-ROM (Test 1) or as a paper test in this book.
- A **Building Supporting Skills** section that provides help in note taking, paraphrasing and summarizing, increasing your vocabulary, improving your pronunciation, reviewing grammar, and developing learner strategies such as setting goals and organizing a study schedule.
- Test-taking **strategies** for each of the four sections of the TOEFL test: Reading, Listening, Speaking, and Writing.
- **Exercises** that isolate and gradually build specific skills needed for success on the TOEFL test.
- **Mini-tests** that use the TOEFL iBT test format and allow you to check your mastery of a particular set of skills.
- **Section Practice Tests** in the TOEFL iBT format at the end of the Reading, Listening, Speaking, and Writing sections. Each of these tests measures whether you have mastered the skills in that section. These Section Practice Tests are combined to form one complete practice test on the CD-ROM (Test 2).

- Two full-length **Practice Tests** at the end of the book, which give you further practice with the TOEFL test format and test-taking strategies. The answer keys to these Practice Tests direct you to exercises that will help you strengthen the areas that are causing you difficulties. These tests appear on the CD-ROM as Tests 3 and 4.
- An explanatory **Answer Key** that gives reasons for correct and incorrect answers for exercises and tests and refers you to relevant skill-building exercises.
- **Checklists** for evaluating your responses to essay questions and speaking questions.
- **Cassettes** or **audio CDs** that include all of the listening material for the exercises and Practice Tests in the book. As planned for the actual TOEFL iBT test, speakers with different English accents are used occasionally in the Practice Tests to give you the opportunity to hear a variety of native accents.
- Complete **Audio Scripts** of all of the listening material in the audio program. The scripts aid you in checking your answers by allowing you to compare your responses with what you actually heard.
- An **Index** that allows you to easily locate exercises that build specific skills (for example: making inferences) or practice grammar points (for example: subject-verb agreement).
- **Cross-references** that indicate the pages where explanations or related exercises can be found.

IMPORTANT FEATURES OF THE CD-ROM

- **Seven complete practice tests**, which consist of the four tests that are found in the book (the Diagnostic Test, the combined Section Practice Tests, and Practice Tests 1 and 2) as well as three additional tests that are not included in the book. All seven tests on the CD-ROM simulate the experience of taking the TOEFL iBT test online.
- Screen **icons** and layouts designed to familiarize you with the appearance of the TOEFL iBT computer screens.
- **Two options** that give you the choice of taking each test either as a simulated TOEFL test (Test Mode) or with access to answers and explanations during or following the test (Practice Mode).
- A **bookmark option** that allows you to stop the program during a test and come back to the same place to continue later.
- A **section choice option** in Practice Mode that allows you to choose a particular test section where you may want to focus more attention.
- A **show text option** in Practice Mode that allows you to read the audio script as you listen.
- An **Answer Key** that explains the correct answers and refers you to relevant skill-building exercises in the book.
- **Scored sample essays** for all independent essay questions and **scored sample speaking responses** for all speaking questions.

HOW TO USE THE COMPLETE *CAMBRIDGE PREPARATION FOR THE TOEFL® TEST* PROGRAM

Follow these steps to get the most benefit from your TOEFL iBT test preparation:

1. Read the explanations beginning on page XXXVII (Taking the TOEFL® Test Online) and look at the example screens in the Reading, Listening, Speaking, and Writing sections of the book to learn how to answer the types of questions you will see on the TOEFL test.
2. Take the Diagnostic Test on the CD-ROM (Test 1) or the Diagnostic Test in the book beginning on page 1. This will highlight areas that you need to concentrate on so that you will not spend time studying material you already know well.
3. Take the Diagnostic Test on the CD-ROM in Practice Mode to receive instant feedback that will direct you to relevant skill-building exercises in the book. If you take the test in Test Mode, you will receive feedback after you have completed the test.

   If you take the Diagnostic Test in the book, check your answers using the Answer Key. For every wrong answer, the Answer Key will direct you to exercises that will build the skills you need in order to answer that type of question correctly.
4. Use the Building Supporting Skills section to plan your course of study and strengthen the supporting skills that will help you succeed.
5. Read the Strategies boxes at the beginning of the Reading, Listening, Speaking, and Writing sections.
6. Work through the exercises that concentrate on the skills you need to develop. Take the Mini-tests as you proceed through a section to check your progress.
7. When you have finished all the relevant exercises in a particular section, take the Section Practice Test at the end of that section or take that section of CD-ROM Test 2. For example, once you have worked through the Listening section, take the Listening Section Practice Test in the book or do the Listening Section of Test 2 on the CD-ROM.
8. Take Practice Test 1 in the book or on the CD-ROM (Test 3). You may want to take it halfway through your course of study to confirm your progress. If you take the test in the book, check your answers using the Answer Key. The Answer Key will direct you to exercises in the book that will help you build the skills you need in order to answer that type of question correctly. On the CD-ROM, you will receive the same answer feedback in Practice Mode.
9. Take Practice Test 2 (CD-ROM Test 4) later in your course of study, or, if you are taking only the book tests, leave it to take as a final check before taking the actual TOEFL test.
10. If you are using the CD-ROM, take CD-ROM Tests 5, 6, and 7 in Test Mode as final preparation for the timed TOEFL test.

Important Notes

It is not necessary to do every exercise in this book in preparation for the TOEFL test. Concentrate on the exercises addressing your weaknesses as indicated by the Diagnostic Test and the Practice Tests. Moreover, it is not necessary to complete all of the items within an exercise. If you discover that an exercise is too easy for you, go on to an exercise that is more challenging.

When taking a test on the CD-ROM in Test Mode, you have a fixed amount of time in which to complete the Reading and Listening sections, but you can move through individual questions at your own pace. In order to complete all the questions within the time limit, pace yourself by paying attention to the number of questions and time remaining. In the Speaking and Writing sections, you will be given a fixed amount of time to organize and respond to each task, as on the TOEFL test.

On the cassettes and audio CDs, the Listening section of the Practice Tests and the Listening Mini-tests give you 10 seconds to answer each question. If you need more time, pause the cassette or audio CD.

In the Speaking section of the Practice Tests, pause the cassette or audio CD while you record your response. In the Writing sections, stop the cassette or audio CD player while you write your essays.

The audio program for the skill-building exercises gives you 10 seconds to answer multiple choice and short-answer questions. For exercises in which you write or speak an answer for each item, pause the cassette or audio CD while you write.

The following chart shows the relationship of the CD-ROM tests to the tests in the book.

CD-ROM Test	Corresponding Book Test
Test 1	Diagnostic Test
Test 2	Section Practice Tests combined
Test 3	Practice Test 1
Test 4	Practice Test 2
Test 5	(CD-ROM only)
Test 6	(CD-ROM only)
Test 7	(CD-ROM only)

BEFORE YOU BEGIN

Before you use this book, take the Diagnostic Test, which is Test 1 on the CD-ROM that accompanies this book. You can also take the Diagnostic Test in this book.

Taking the Diagnostic Test on the computer

If you have access to a computer on which to use the CD-ROM, it is suggested that you take the Diagnostic Test (Test 1) on the computer. This will allow you to experience a simulation of the actual TOEFL iBT test. If you are unsure of TOEFL test procedures, read Taking the TOEFL® Test Online on pages XXXVII–XLII.

Before taking a test on the computer, arrange to have a quiet place where you will not be disturbed for the duration of the test. The Diagnostic Test will take approximately three hours.

The CD-ROM will pace you through the test and provide you with an approximate score for the Reading and Listening sections. After you have finished the test, you can see a list of the questions that you answered incorrectly. For each incorrect answer, you will be referred to a section of the book that will help you answer questions of this type. For example, you may see, "See Exercises L9–L12."

During the Listening section of the actual test, you may not go back to check your work or change your answers. However, you may go back to review your work in the Reading section before time runs out.

Taking the Diagnostic Test on paper

If you do not have access to a computer, take the Diagnostic Test on pages 1–38 in this book. The presentation of the questions in this book is similar to the way they will look on the computer screen. Before taking one of the tests, make the following preparations:

1. Arrange to have a quiet room where you will not be disturbed for the duration of the test. The Diagnostic Test will take approximately three hours.
2. Bring the following items: a cassette or CD player; the cassette or CD that contains the Diagnostic Test; two sharpened black-lead pencils with erasers; and a watch, a clock, or a timer. You will also need a device for recording your speaking responses.
3. Bring extra paper if you do not want to write in the book. You will also need paper on which to take notes and to respond to the writing tasks.

When you have completed the test, check your answers against the Answer Key that starts on page 525. If you chose a wrong answer, the Answer Key will tell you which exercises in the book will help you improve in that area. For example, you may see, "See Exercises L9–L12."

To the Teacher

- The skills that your students practice in this book will help them be successful not only on the TOEFL test, but in their academic work in general.
- The Diagnostic Test will show you the areas that your students need to concentrate on the most. Do not feel that every exercise, or all items within an exercise, must be completed.
- You may want to encourage your students to take some of the CD-ROM practice tests using Test Mode, which simulates the test conditions that they will experience during the actual online test, and some using Practice Mode, which gives students the option of checking each answer and receiving feedback while working through the test.
- The audio program for the skill-building exercises gives students 10 seconds to answer multiple choice and short-answer questions. If students need more time, pause the cassette or audio CD. For all exercises in which students write or speak, pause the cassette or audio CD while they respond.

  In the Practice Tests, the Listening section questions give students 10 seconds to choose an answer. If they need more time, pause the cassette or audio CD. For the Speaking and Writing sections of the Practice Tests, pause or stop the audio program while students respond to each question.
- Use the exercises in the four Building Skills sections (Reading, Listening, Speaking, and Writing) to build skills in other areas. For example:

  Your students will encounter unfamiliar vocabulary throughout the Reading, Listening, Speaking, and Writing sections. Some of these words will be useful to learn in order to improve not only reading and listening skills but also to build vocabulary for use in the Speaking and Writing sections. Help students identify which of the words are useful and which may never be encountered again.

  Making inferences, drawing conclusions, and identifying topics are important skills to acquire for success in all test sections.

  Understanding the grammatical structure of a sentence is important for reading and listening comprehension as well as for using these structures for writing or speaking fluently.

  The formats of Listening lectures, Reading passages, and spoken and written responses are similar; that is, they all begin with an introduction that includes the topic, continue with ideas that support the topic, and end with a conclusion.
- In class, focus on areas that most of your students are having trouble understanding, as indicated by the Diagnostic Test. Homework assignments can be individualized so that each student can focus on his or her specific areas of difficulty.
- Stress to your students that all English language experience is useful in studying for the TOEFL test. In addition to the exercises in the book, you may wish to assign related homework or in-class activities. Watching a debate or interview on TV or listening to a talk show on the radio gives students the opportunity to hear speakers who are not following a script. Taking notes while listening to an online lecture or while reading articles in an English-language newspaper or magazine is also a useful assignment.

Introduction to the TOEFL® Test

REASONS FOR TAKING THE TOEFL TEST

The Test of English as a Foreign Language (TOEFL) is an examination that is administered by the Educational Testing Service (ETS) and is used to evaluate a nonnative English speaker's proficiency in the English language. Many North American colleges and universities, as well as a large number of institutions, agencies, and programs, ask for official TOEFL test scores during the admissions process. An acceptable score on the TOEFL test depends on the specific requirements of the particular institution or agency involved.

Requirements vary from institution to institution. You should check with the institutions or agencies you are applying to for their specific requirements. To be admitted to a North American college or university, you will probably need a TOEFL iBT score of 53 to 80 (a TOEFL paper-test score of 475 to 550 or a TOEFL computer-test score of 153 to 213). Although some colleges will accept students with a score under 45 (a paper-test score of 450 or computer-test score of 133), usually those students are required to enroll in remedial classes or in ESL classes as part of their course of study. Other colleges and universities will require a higher score of 100+ (600+ on the paper test or 250+ on the computer test). This score is frequently required for students who wish to work at the graduate level.

A few colleges and universities do not require nonnative English-speaking students to take the TOEFL test. They may, however, have their own English proficiency exam that students are required to take. Because these exams test the same skills as the TOEFL test, preparing yourself for the TOEFL test is a good way to prepare for any English proficiency exam.

Until the TOEFL iBT test has become available worldwide, whether you take the Internet-based, computer-based, or paper-based TOEFL test will depend on where you live or the circumstances under which you are taking the test. You should find out which test you will be taking so that you can become familiar with that particular test format and requirements.

For practice test materials and information about the paper-based and the computer-based TOEFL test, see *Cambridge Preparation for the TOEFL® Test*, Third Edition.

TAKING THE TOEFL iBT TEST

The TOEFL iBT test will be administered on fixed dates in a network of secure Internet-based test centers. Most areas where the test is offered will have 30 to 40 administrations per year, but the number will vary based on the number of test-takers and test center capacity.

Most colleges accept only the official score report received directly from ETS. When you register for the test, you may designate up to four institutions you would like your scores to be sent to. These may be modified until 10:00 p.m. on the day before the test. You may also order additional score reports. Your scores will be sent to you and to your designated recipients 15 business days after you take the test.

Plan on being at the test center for up to five hours. The total time for taking the TOEFL iBT test is about four hours. Remember that in addition to the actual test-taking time, time is needed for checking identification, following the score reporting procedures, taking the 10-minute break, etc.

Unlike the computer-based and paper-based tests, you can take the TOEFL iBT test as many times as it is given. However, colleges and universities usually consider only the most recent score. ETS keeps records of scores for two years. You will probably have to take the test again if your score report is more than two years old.

The TOEFL® Information and Registration Bulletin

The TOEFL® *Information and Registration Bulletin* is available at many educational advising centers, colleges, universities, and libraries. The *Bulletin* includes the necessary registration forms and the instructions for completing the forms, as well as information concerning methods of payment, special services, identification requirements, testing sites, and refund policy. Be sure to request the correct *Bulletin* for the test you are taking (Internet, computer, or paper). To receive the *Bulletin*, write to:

TOEFL Services
Educational Testing Service
P.O. Box 6151
Princeton, NJ 08541-6151
USA

Fax: 609-771-7500

E-mail: toefl@ets.org

If you have access to the Internet, you can download the *Bulletin* from the ETS Web site: http://www.ets.org/toefl

Test center information will be posted on the TOEFL Web site and updated regularly. You can register for the test online, by phone, or by mail.

TOEFL iBT FORMAT AND SCORING

Test format

The format of each of the four sections of the TOEFL iBT test is outlined in the chart below. Keep in mind that some test-takers will receive more Reading passages, and some will receive more Listening passages. You will not know ahead of time which test you will receive.

TOEFL iBT Test Format

Section	Number of Passages	Number of Tasks, or Questions Per Passage	Answering Time
Reading	3–5	12–14	60–100 minutes
Listening	4–6 lectures 2–3 conversations	6 5	60–90 minutes
Speaking		6	20 minutes
Writing		2	50 minutes

Scoring information

Each section of the TOEFL iBT test is scored separately. The number of points received for each section is converted to a scaled score of 0–30, for a combined total possible score of 120, as shown below.

Reading	0–30
Listening	0–30
Speaking	0–30
Writing	0–30
Total Score	**0–120**

Calculating scores for Practice Tests

Follow the guidelines below to calculate your scores for the Practice Tests in this book. The rubrics for scoring the Speaking and Writing sections of these tests are the rubrics used by ETS. The guidelines for scoring the Reading and Listening sections are a simplified version of the scoring system used by ETS. Note that the actual scores for each TOEFL test administered by ETS are adjusted slightly based on the raw scores received by the students who took the test.

Reading and Listening sections

In the Reading and Listening sections, most questions are worth one point. Chart and summary questions are worth more than one point. The test will indicate the number of points for questions that are worth more than one point. To calculate your score for chart or summary questions, use the charts below.

Chart Questions	
Number of Correct Matches	Number of Points
0	0
1	0
2	1
3	1
4	2
5	2
6	3
7	4

Summary Questions	
Number of Correct Matches	Number of Points
0	0
1	0
2	1
3	2

To calculate your score in the Reading and Listening sections, total the number of points for all your correct answers in each section, calculate the percentage correct, and find your converted scores in the chart below.

For example, if you received 38 points out of a possible total of 42 points in the Reading section, you would divide 38 by 42 to get 90 percent. Look at the chart to find the range that includes 90 percent. Your converted scaled score is 27.

If you had 24 points out of a possible 25 in the Listening section, you would divide 24 by 25 to get 96 percent. Look at the chart to find the range that includes 96 percent. Your converted scaled score is 29.

Converting Reading and Listening scores to scaled scores

Correct Answer Percentages	Converted Scores
98.3 – 100%	30
95 – 98.2%	29
91.7 – 94.9%	28
88.3 – 91.6%	27
85 – 88.2%	26
81.7 – 84.9%	25
78.3 – 81.6%	24
75 – 78.2%	23
71.7 – 74.9%	22
68.3 – 71.6%	21
65 – 68.2%	20
61.7 – 64.9%	19
58.3 – 61.6%	18
55 – 58.2%	17
51.7 – 54.9%	16
48.3 – 51.6%	15

Correct Answer Percentages	Converted Scores
45 – 48.2%	14
41.7 – 44.9%	13
38.3 – 41.6%	12
35 – 38.2%	11
31.7 – 34.9%	10
28.3 – 31.6%	9
25 – 28.2%	8
21.7 – 24.9%	7
18.3 – 21.6%	6
15 – 18.2%	5
11.7 – 14.9%	4
8.3 – 11.6%	3
5 – 8.2%	2
1.7 – 4.9%	1
0 – 1.6%	0

Speaking and Writing sections

Each Speaking task is worth 4 points and each Writing task is worth 5 points. The rubrics below show the ETS scoring standards for the independent and integrated tasks in the Speaking and Writing sections. Use these rubrics to calculate raw scores for your speaking and writing responses. The ETS scorers who evaluate the Speaking and Writing sections of the TOEFL iBT test follow these rubrics as well.

TOEFL iBT Test
Independent Speaking Rubrics (Scoring Standards)

Score	General Description	Delivery	Language Use	Topic Development
4	The response fulfills the demands of the task, with at most minor lapses in completeness. It is highly intelligible and exhibits sustained, coherent discourse. A response at this level is characterized by all of the following:	Generally well-paced flow (fluid expression). Speech is clear. It may include minor lapses or minor difficulties with pronunciation or intonation patterns, which do not affect overall intelligibility.	The response demonstrates effective use of grammar and vocabulary. It exhibits a fairly high degree of automaticity with good control of basic and complex structures (as appropriate). Some minor (or systematic) errors are noticeable but do not obscure meaning.	Response is sustained and sufficient to the task. It is generally well developed and coherent; relationships between ideas are clear (or clear progression of ideas).
3	The response addresses the task appropriately but may fall short of being fully developed. It is generally intelligible and coherent, with some fluidity of expression, though it exhibits some noticeable lapses in the expression of ideas. A response at this level is characterized by at least two of the following:	Speech is generally clear, with some fluidity of expression, though minor difficulties with pronunciation, intonation, or pacing are noticeable and may require listener effort at times (though overall intelligibility is not significantly affected).	The response demonstrates fairly automatic and effective use of grammar and vocabulary and fairly coherent expression of relevant ideas. Response may exhibit some imprecise or inaccurate use of vocabulary or grammatical structures or be somewhat limited in the range of structures used. This may affect overall fluency, but it does not seriously interfere with the communication of the message.	Response is mostly coherent and sustained and conveys relevant ideas/information. Overall development is somewhat limited and usually lacks elaboration or specificity. Relationships between ideas may at times not be immediately clear.
2	The response addresses the task, but development of the topic is limited. It contains intelligible speech, although problems with delivery and/or overall coherence occur; meaning may be obscured in places. A response at this level is characterized by at least two of the following:	Speech is basically intelligible, though listener effort is needed because of unclear articulation, awkward intonation, or choppy rhythm/pace; meaning may be obscured in places.	The response demonstrates limited range and control of grammar and vocabulary. These limitations often prevent full expression of ideas. For the most part, only basic sentence structures are used successfully and spoken with fluidity. Structures and vocabulary may express mainly simple (short) and/or general propositions, with simple or unclear connections made among them (serial listing, conjunction, juxtaposition).	The response is connected to the task, though the number of ideas presented or the development of ideas is limited. Mostly basic ideas are expressed with limited elaboration (details and support). At times relevant substance may be vaguely expressed or repetitious. Connections of ideas may be unclear.

Score	General Description	Delivery	Language Use	Topic Development
1	The response is very limited in content and/ or coherence or is only minimally connected to the task, or speech is largely unintelligible. A response at this level is characterized by at least two of the following:	Consistent pronunciation, stress, and intonation difficulties cause considerable listener effort; delivery is choppy, fragmented, or telegraphic; frequent pauses and hesitations.	Range and control of grammar and vocabulary severely limit (or prevent) expression of ideas and connections among ideas. Some low-level responses may rely heavily on practiced or formulaic expressions.	Limited relevant content is expressed. The response generally lacks substance beyond expression of very basic ideas. Speaker may be unable to sustain speech to complete the task and may rely heavily on repetition of the prompt.
0	Speaker makes no attempt to respond OR response is unrelated to the topic.			

TOEFL iBT Test
Integrated Speaking Rubrics (Scoring Standards)

Score	General Description	Delivery	Language Use	Topic Development
4	The response fulfills the demands of the task, with at most minor lapses in completeness. It is highly intelligible and exhibits sustained, coherent discourse. A response at this level is characterized by all of the following:	Speech is generally clear, fluid, and sustained. It may include minor lapses or minor difficulties with pronunciation or intonation. Pace may vary at times as the speaker attempts to recall information. Overall intelligibility remains high.	The response demonstrates good control of basic and complex grammatical structures that allow for coherent, efficient (automatic) expression of relevant ideas. Contains generally effective word choice. Though some minor (or systematic) errors or imprecise use may be noticeable, they do not require listener effort (or obscure meaning).	The response presents a clear progression of ideas and conveys the relevant information required by the task. It includes appropriate detail, though it may have minor errors or minor omissions.
3	The response addresses the task appropriately but may fall short of being fully developed. It is generally intelligible and coherent, with some fluidity of expression, though it exhibits some noticeable lapses in the expression of ideas. A response at this level is characterized by at least two of the following:	Speech is generally clear, with some fluidity of expression, but it exhibits minor difficulties with pronunciation, intonation, or pacing and may require some listener effort at times. Overall intelligibility remains good, however.	The response demonstrates fairly automatic and effective use of grammar and vocabulary and fairly coherent expression of relevant ideas. Response may exhibit some imprecise or inaccurate use of vocabulary or grammatical structures or be somewhat limited in the range of structures used. Such limitations do not seriously interfere with the communication of the message.	The response is sustained and conveys relevant information required by the task. However, it exhibits some incompleteness, inaccuracy, lack of specificity with respect to content, or choppiness in the progression of ideas.

Score	General Description	Delivery	Language Use	Topic Development
2	The response is connected to the task, though it may be missing some relevant information or contain inaccuracies. It contains some intelligible speech, but at times problems with intelligibility and/or over-all coherence may obscure meaning. A response at this level is characterized by at least two of the following:	Speech is clear at times, though it exhibits problems with pronunciation, intonation, or pacing and so may require significant listener effort. Speech may not be sustained at a consistent level throughout. Problems with intelligibility may obscure meaning in places (but not throughout).	The response is limited in the range and control of vocabulary and grammar demonstrated (some complex structures may be used, but they typically contain errors). This results in limited or vague expression of relevant ideas and imprecise or inaccurate connections. Automaticity of expression may only be evident at the phrasal level.	The response conveys some relevant information but is clearly incomplete or inaccurate. It is incomplete if it omits key ideas, makes vague reference to key ideas, or demonstrates limited development of important information. An inaccurate response demonstrates misunderstanding of key ideas from the stimulus. Typically, ideas expressed may not be well connected or cohesive so that familiarity with the stimulus is necessary to follow what is being discussed.
1	The response is very limited in content or coherence or is only minimally connected to the task. Speech may be largely unintelligible. A response at this level is characterized by at least two of the following:	Consistent pronunciation and intonation problems cause considerable listener effort and frequently obscure meaning. Delivery is choppy, fragmented, or telegraphic. Speech contains frequent pauses and hesitations.	Range and control of grammar and vocabulary severely limit (or prevent) expression of ideas and connections among ideas. Some very low-level responses may rely on isolated words or short utterances to communicate ideas.	The response fails to provide much relevant content. Ideas that are expressed are often inaccurate, limited to vague utterances, or repetitions (including repetition of prompt).
0	Speaker makes no attempt to respond OR response is unrelated to the topic.			

TOEFL iBT Test
Independent Writing Rubrics (Scoring Standards)

Score	Task Description
5	**An essay at this level largely accomplishes all of the following:** • effectively addresses the topic and task • is well organized and well developed, using clearly appropriate explanations, exemplifications, and/or details • displays unity, progression, and coherence • displays consistent facility in the use of language, demonstrating syntactic variety, appropriate word choice, and idiomaticity, though it may have minor lexical or grammatical errors
4	**An essay at this level largely accomplishes all of the following:** • addresses the topic and task well, though some points may not be fully elaborated • is generally well organized and well developed, using appropriate and sufficient explanations, exemplifications, and/or details • displays unity, progression, and coherence, though it may contain occasional redundancy, digression, or unclear connections • displays facility in the use of language, demonstrating syntactic variety and range of vocabulary, though it will probably have occasional noticeable minor errors in structure, word form, or use of idiomatic language that do not interfere with meaning
3	**An essay at this level is marked by one or more of the following:** • addresses the topic and task using somewhat developed explanations, exemplifications, and/or details • displays unity, progression, and coherence, though connection of ideas may be occasionally obscured • may demonstrate inconsistent facility in sentence formation and word choice that may result in lack of clarity and occasionally obscure meaning • may display accurate but limited range of syntactic structures and vocabulary
2	**An essay at this level may reveal one or more of the following weaknesses:** • limited development in response to the topic and task • inadequate organization or connection of ideas • inappropriate or insufficient exemplifications, explanations, or details to support or illustrate generalizations in response to the task • a noticeably inappropriate choice of words or word forms • an accumulation of errors in sentence structure and/or usage
1	**An essay at this level is seriously flawed by one or more of the following weaknesses:** • serious disorganization or underdevelopment • little or no detail, or irrelevant specifics, or questionable responsiveness to the task • serious and frequent errors in sentence structure or usage
0	**An essay at this level** merely copies words from the topic, rejects the topic or is otherwise not connected to the topic, is written in a foreign language, consists of keystroke characters, or is blank.

TOEFL iBT Test
Integrated Writing Rubrics (Scoring Standards)

Score	Task Description
5	A response at this level successfully selects the important information from the lecture and coherently and accurately presents this information in relation to the relevant information presented in the reading. The response is well organized, and occasional language errors that are present do not result in inaccurate or imprecise presentation of content or connections.
4	A response at this level is generally good in selecting the important information from the lecture and in coherently and accurately presenting this information in relation to the relevant information in the reading, but it may have minor omission, inaccuracy, vagueness, or imprecision of some content from the lecture or in connection to points made in the reading. A response is also scored at this level if it has more frequent or noticeable minor language errors, as long as such usage and grammatical structures do not result in anything more than an occasional lapse of clarity or in the connection of ideas.
3	A response at this level contains some important information from the lecture and conveys some relevant connection to the reading, but it is marked by one or more of the following: • Although the overall response is definitely oriented to the task, it conveys only vague, global, unclear, or somewhat imprecise connection of the points made in the lecture to points made in the reading. • The response may omit one major key point made in the lecture. • Some key points made in the lecture or the reading, or connections between the two, may be incomplete, inaccurate, or imprecise. • Errors of usage and/or grammar may be more frequent or may result in noticeably vague expressions or obscured meanings in conveying ideas and connections.
2	A response at this level contains some relevant information from the lecture, but it is marked by significant language difficulties or by significant omission or inaccuracy of important ideas from the lecture or in the connections between the lecture and the reading. A response at this level is marked by one or more of the following: • The response significantly misrepresents or completely omits the overall connection between the lecture and the reading. • The response significantly omits or significantly misrepresents important points made in the lecture. • The response contains language errors or expressions that largely obscure connections or meaning at key junctures or that would likely obscure understanding of key ideas for a reader not already familiar with the reading and the lecture.
1	A response at this level is marked by one or more of the following: • The response provides little or no meaningful or relevant coherent content from the lecture. • The language level of the response is so low that it is difficult to derive meaning.
0	A response at this level merely copies sentences from the reading, rejects the topic or is otherwise not connected to the topic, is written in a foreign language, consists of keystroke characters, or is blank.

Converting rubric scores to scaled scores for Speaking and Writing

After you have evaluated your speaking and writing tasks, find your scaled scores as described below.

Add your six scores for the speaking tasks and divide by 6. This will give you your mean score for speaking. Then look at the chart below to find the scaled score for that mean. For example, if you scored 4 on three of your speaking tasks, 3 on two tasks and 2 on one task, you would add 4 + 4 + 4 + 3 + 3 + 2 to get 20. Divide 20 by 6 to get 3.33. Look at the chart below and find 3.33 in the Speaking Rubric Mean column. Your scaled score would be 26.

Add your two scores for the writing tasks and divide that score by 2. This will give you your mean score for writing. For example, if you scored a 5 on one writing task and a 4 on the other, add 5 + 4 to get 9. Divide 9 by 2 to get 4.5. Then look at the chart below to find 4.5 in the Writing Rubric Mean column. Your scaled score would be 28.

TOEFL® iBT Test
Converting Rubric Scores to Scaled Scores

Speaking Rubric Mean	Scaled Score
4.00	30
3.83	29
3.66	28
3.50	27
3.33	26
3.16	24
3.00	23
2.83	22
2.66	20
2.50	19
2.33	18
2.16	15
2.00	14
1.83	13
1.66	11
1.50	10
1.33	9
1.16	8
1.00	6
	5
	4
	3
	1
	0

Writing Rubric Mean	Scaled Score
5.00	30
4.75	29
4.50	28
4.25	27
4.00	25
3.75	24
3.50	22
3.25	21
3.00	20
2.75	18
2.50	17
2.25	15
2.00	14
1.75	12
1.50	11
1.25	10
1.00	8
	7
	5
	4
	0

Example score calculation

The chart below shows the calculations for the scores that were used as examples in this section.

iBT Example Calculation

Section	Score	Mean Score	Converted Score
Reading	38 ÷ 42 = 90%		27
Listening	24 ÷ 25 = 96%		29
Speaking			
task 1	4		
task 2	3		
task 3	3		
task 4	4		
task 5	4		
task 6	2		
Total divided by 6	20 ÷ 6	3.33	26
Writing			
task 1	5		
task 2	4		
Total divided by 2	9 ÷ 2	4.5	28
		TOEFL score	110

Photocopy the following worksheet for calculating your scores for the Diagnostic Test, Section Tests, and Practice Tests.

Worksheet for calculating your scores

Section	Score	Mean Score	Converted Score
Reading	÷ = %		
Listening	÷ = %		
Speaking			
task 1			
task 2			
task 3			
task 4			
task 5			
task 6			
Total divided by 6			
Writing			
task 1			
task 2			
Total divided by 2			
		TOEFL score	

Total score comparisons with other versions of the TOEFL test

The charts below show the total score comparisons for the Internet-based, computer-based, and paper-based versions of the TOEFL test.

TOEFL Total Score Comparisons

Score Comparison		
Internet Total	**Computer Total**	**Paper Total**
120	300	677
120	297	673
119	293	670
118	290	667
117	287	660–663
116	283	657
114–115	280	650–653
113	277	647
111–112	273	640–643
110	270	637
109	267	630–633
106–108	263	623–627
105	260	617–620
103–104	257	613
101–102	253	607–610
100	250	600–603
98–99	247	597
96–97	243	590–593
94–95	240	587
92–93	237	580–583
90–91	233	577
88–89	230	570–573
86–87	227	567
84–85	223	563
83	220	557–560
81–82	217	553
79–80	213	550
77–78	210	547
76	207	540–543
74–75	203	537
72–73	200	533
71	197	527–530
69–70	193	523
68	190	520
66–67	187	517

Score Comparison (continued)		
Internet Total	**Computer Total**	**Paper Total**
65	183	513
64	180	507–510
62–63	177	503
61	173	500
59–60	170	497
58	167	493
57	163	487–490
56	160	483
54–55	157	480
53	153	477
52	150	470–473
51	147	467
49–50	143	463
48	140	460
47	137	457
45–46	133	450–453
44	130	447
43	127	443
41–42	123	437–440
40	120	433
39	117	430
38	113	423–427
36–37	110	420
35	107	417
34	103	410–413
33	100	407
32	97	400–403
30–31	93	397
29	90	390–393
28	87	387
26–27	83	380–383
25	80	377
24	77	370–373
23	73	363–367
22	70	357–360

Score Comparison (continued)		
Internet Total	**Computer Total**	**Paper Total**
21	67	353
19–20	63	347–350
18	60	340–343
17	57	333–337
16	53	330
15	50	323–327
14	47	317–320
13	43	313
12	40	310
11	37	310
9	33	310

Score Comparison (continued)		
Internet Total	**Computer Total**	**Paper Total**
8	30	310
7	27	310
6	23	310
5	20	310
4	17	310
3	13	310
2	10	310
1	7	310
0	3	310
0	0	310

Range Comparison

Internet-Based Test	Computer-Based Test	Paper-Based Test
111–120	273–300	640–677
96–110	243–270	590–637
79–95	213–240	550–587
65–78	183–210	513–547
53–64	153–180	477–510
41–52	123–150	437–473
30–40	93–120	397–433
19–29	63–90	347–393
9–18	33–60	310–343
0–8	0–30	310

Note: The paper-based total score does not include writing. The paper-based and computer-based total scores do not include speaking.

HOW TO TAKE THE TOEFL iBT TEST SUCCESSFULLY

Preparing for the TOEFL iBT test

1. If you do not have a sound basic knowledge of English, it is best to take English language courses before taking a TOEFL test preparation course. Preparation materials are designed to help you improve your scores through reviewing English and becoming familiar with the testing procedures and format.
2. Begin your test preparation as soon as you decide to take the exam. It will not be useful to try to learn everything the week before the exam date.
3. Study on a regular basis. Studying a small amount of material daily is more effective than studying a large amount in one sitting.
4. All English practice is helpful. Watching a movie or listening to a radio program in English is good for building your listening comprehension skills. Reading English newspaper or magazine articles will improve your reading comprehension skills. Speaking English, even with a nonnative speaker, will help you improve your speaking fluency. Systematically add new words to your vocabulary. Even though these activities are not directly related to the TOEFL test, they will help you.
5. Work carefully through the book exercises in *Cambridge Preparation for the TOEFL® Test* in the skill areas that the Diagnostic Test identifies as your weak areas. Once you have mastered the skills in your weak areas, you may want to choose other exercises to improve your strong skills even further. However, it is best to concentrate the most effort on your weaker areas.
6. Practice budgeting your time. The TOEFL test is taken under strict time limits. Effective time management is a key to doing well on the test. Learn to use your time wisely so that you can complete each section.
7. Use the CD-ROM tests or the information at the beginning of the Reading, Listening, Speaking, and Writing sections of this book to become familiar with the test format and how to answer the kinds of questions and respond to the kinds of tasks in each section.
8. Know your goal. Visit the Web site or write to the administration office of the college or university of your choice, and ask for their entrance requirements. They will confirm the minimum TOEFL score required for admission.

Taking the Internet-based test

1. The TOEFL iBT test is an Internet-based test. The actual test is delivered via the Internet at secure, official test centers. You will have your own workstation and headset and you will be able to control the volume on your headset. Test-takers cannot take the official test at home.
2. Listen and read the instructions carefully. If you do not follow the instructions correctly, you will get a computer message instructing you to go back and follow the instructions, causing you to lose valuable time.
3. Some passages in the Reading section include a word or phrase that is underlined in blue. Click on the word or phrase to see a definition or an explanation.
4. When you want to move on to the next question in the Reading section, click on **Next**. You can skip questions and go back to those in the part you are working on as long as there is time remaining. A clock at the top of the screen will show you how much

time is remaining. If you want to return to previous questions, click on **Back**. You can click on **Review** at any time, and the review screen will show you which questions you have answered and which you have not. From this review screen, you may go directly to any question you have already seen in the part of the Reading section you are working on.

5. In the Listening section, you must answer every question. After you answer, click on **Next**. Then click on **OK** to confirm your answer and go on to the next question. After you click on **OK**, you cannot return to previous questions. A clock at the top of the screen will show you how much time is remaining. The clock will not count down while you are listening to test material.
6. In the Speaking section of the test, you will answer six questions by speaking into the microphone on your headset. For each question you will be given a short time to prepare your response. A clock on the screen will show how much preparation time is remaining. When the preparation time is up, you will be told to begin your response. A clock will show how much response time is remaining. A message will appear on the screen when the response time has ended.
7. For the first writing task, you will read a passage and listen to a lecture and then type your answer to a question based on what you have read and heard. For the second writing task, you will have to type an answer to a question based on your own knowledge and experience. A clock on the screen will show how much response time is remaining for each task.

Taking the TOEFL® Test Online

You will use a computer to take the TOEFL iBT test. In the Reading and Listening sections, you will use a mouse to select the answers to the questions. For recording your speaking tasks in the Speaking section, you will use the microphone on your headset. In the Writing section, you will type your responses to the tasks using the computer keyboard.

Here is an example of a typical question on the TOEFL iBT test:

> The word " enhance " in the passage is closest in meaning to
> ○ improve
> ○ exaggerate
> ○ inform
> ○ enlist

To answer the question, use the mouse to click on the oval next to the choice that you want or on the answer text itself. As shown below, the oval will darken to show your selection. To change your answer, simply click on another answer choice.

> The word " enhance " in the passage is closest in meaning to
> ● improve
> ○ exaggerate
> ○ inform
> ○ enlist

When you are sure that you have selected the answer you want, click on the **Next** icon.

READING SECTION

In the Reading section, the reading passages appear on the right side of the screen. The questions for each passage appear on the left side of the screen. The passages are usually too long to fit on the screen all at once. To read the entire passage, scroll down the screen. You can scroll down in two ways. First, you can click on the down arrow at the bottom of the vertical scroll bar and click the mouse repeatedly (or hold the mouse button down to scroll fast). The other way to scroll down is to click on the square button within the scroll bar and drag it down.

The first time that you see a passage, the computer will not allow you to proceed to the questions until you scroll down to the bottom of the text. If you try to proceed without scrolling down, the computer will give you a message telling you to scroll down to the bottom of the passage.

In the Reading section, you can skip questions in the part you are working on and return to them later. You can also change your answers to questions that you have already answered. To do this, click on **Back** to return to previous items. Click on **Next** to go forward.

See the Reading section in this book for details on the question types you will encounter on the test as well as examples of the computer screens.

LISTENING SECTION

For the Listening section of the TOEFL iBT test, you will use a headset. Before you begin, you will hear instructions for setting the volume on your headset. You may also change the volume of your headset at any time during the listening portions of the test.

In the Listening section, you will hear conversations as well as academic discussions and classroom lectures. The conversations are introduced by the narrator. The academic discussions and classroom lectures are preceded by a screen that gives the academic subject of the talk. A narrator will tell you if the following passage is a discussion or lecture and what the course is. Pay attention to these introductions because they can help you understand what the speakers are talking about.

As you listen to the passages, you will see photographs of professors and students, and sometimes you will see illustrations or charts that help the speakers make their point. The photographs of the people are not important for answering the questions, but you should pay attention to the illustrations or charts because they can help you understand what the speakers are saying. Note that the illustrations are not visible throughout the lecture. They appear on the screen only when the speakers are referring to them.

At the end of each passage, you will be presented with a number of questions, one at a time. You may *not* go back to check your work or change your answers in the Listening section.

See the Listening section in this book for details on the question types you will encounter on the test as well as examples of the computer screens.

SPEAKING SECTION

For the Speaking section of the TOEFL iBT test, you will use the microphone on your headset. Before you begin, you will hear instructions for setting the volume on your microphone. You will answer a simple practice question while the microphone automatically adjusts to your voice tone and volume. When you have checked that the microphone is functioning correctly, the narrator will present the first task.

In the Speaking section, you will respond to two independent tasks about familiar topics and four integrated tasks. The integrated tasks consist of two reading/listening/speaking tasks and two listening/speaking tasks.

See the Speaking section in this book for details on the question types you will encounter on the test as well as examples of the computer screens.

WRITING SECTION

The Writing section consists of two tasks: an integrated task that includes a short listening and reading, and an independent task that is based on personal experience. You will need to type your response to each task on the computer.

Understanding the Writing screens

Look at the example Writing screen below.

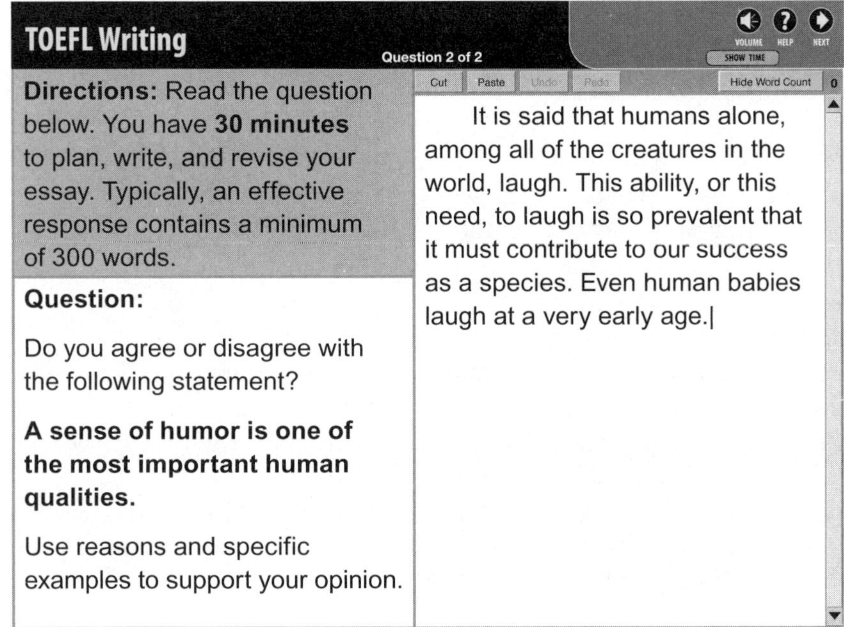

TOEFL Writing
Question 2 of 2
VOLUME HELP NEXT
SHOW TIME
Directions: Read the question below. You have 30 minutes to plan, write, and revise your essay. Typically, an effective response contains a minimum of 300 words.
Question:
Do you agree or disagree with the following statement?
A sense of humor is one of the most important human qualities.
Use reasons and specific examples to support your opinion.
Cut
Paste
Undo
Redo
Hide Word Count
0
It is said that humans alone, among all of the creatures in the world, laugh. This ability, or this need, to laugh is so prevalent that it must contribute to our success as a species. Even human babies laugh at a very early age.|

The directions for completing the task appear at the top of the screen. The question or topic you are to write about appears on the left below the directions, and the area that you will write in is on the right. In the example above, the test-taker has begun the essay. Note the small vertical line after the last word. This is called the *cursor*. On the computer, the cursor blinks constantly so that you can locate it easily. The cursor shows where you are in the text.

Using special keys on the computer keyboard

Look at the example of a typical keyboard. Moving around on the screen and typing and deleting text using special keys is explained in detail below.

Moving around on the screen

Once you have started typing your response, the writing area will fill up quickly, and you will not be able to see all of your essay at once. To see the part of your essay that is above and below the area shown, you can use the arrow keys on the keyboard or use the mouse to reposition the cursor.

Starting a new line

When typing your essay, the computer will automatically start a new line when you get to the end of a line. If you want to start a new line before you get to the right margin (for example, when you wish to start a new paragraph), press the **Enter** key. Press the **Enter** key twice if you want to leave an extra space between paragraphs.

Indenting a paragraph

If you want to indent your paragraphs (that is, leave a blank space between the left margin and the first word of a new paragraph), first press the **Enter** key to start a new line. Then press the space bar five times. This will make an appropriate indentation for your new paragraph. (*Note:* The **Tab** key on the keyboard, which is normally used to indent paragraphs, may not work on the test.)

Deleting text

To delete a small amount of text, use the **Delete** or **Backspace** key and delete one letter at a time. To delete a larger amount of text, it is faster to highlight the text and then press the **Delete** or **Backspace** key. To highlight text, place the mouse pointer at the beginning of the text. Click and hold the mouse button down as you move to the end of the text you want to delete. The text will become highlighted as you move the mouse. When you have finished highlighting the text, release the mouse button. The text will remain highlighted. Then press the **Delete** key to erase the text that you highlighted.

Using the word-processing menu

Some of the features that are available on other word-processing programs can also be used in the Writing section of the test. You can use the **Cut**, **Paste**, **Undo**, and **Redo** options to make writing on the computer easier. The use of these options is described below.

Cut and Paste

When you *cut* words or sentences from your essay, they disappear from the screen and are placed in the computer's temporary memory. When you *paste* words or sentences, they are retrieved from memory and put back into your essay. This feature is helpful when, for example, you wish to move a sentence from one place in your essay to another. The examples on the following pages show how to cut and paste.

First, highlight the text that you want to cut, as shown in the right-hand column below.

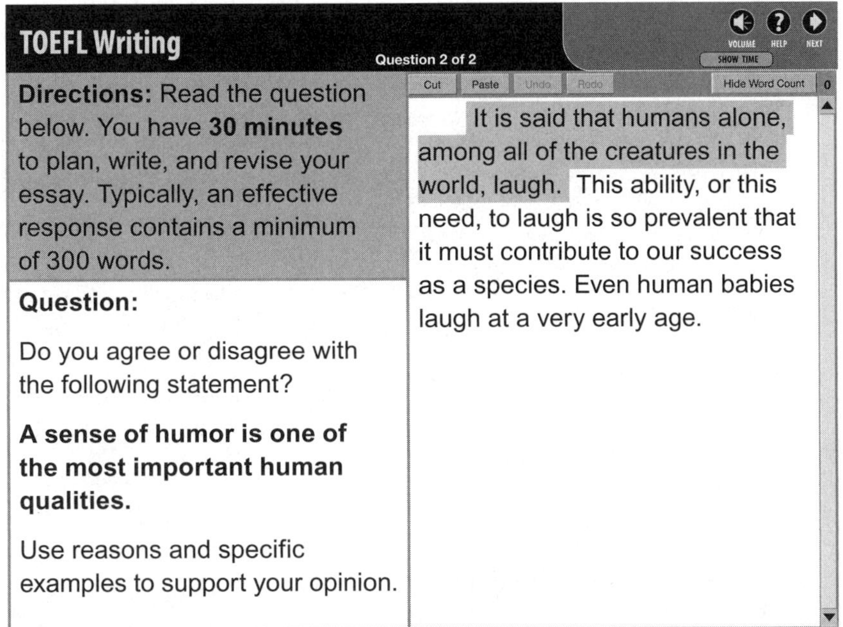
TOEFL Writing
Question 2 of 2
VOLUME HELP NEXT
SHOW TIME
Cut Paste Undo Redo
Hide Word Count 0
Directions: Read the question below. You have 30 minutes to plan, write, and revise your essay. Typically, an effective response contains a minimum of 300 words.
Question:
Do you agree or disagree with the following statement?
A sense of humor is one of the most important human qualities.
Use reasons and specific examples to support your opinion.
It is said that humans alone, among all of the creatures in the world, laugh. This ability, or this need, to laugh is so prevalent that it must contribute to our success as a species. Even human babies laugh at a very early age.

Next, click on the **Cut** button on the word-processing menu. The text will disappear, as shown below.

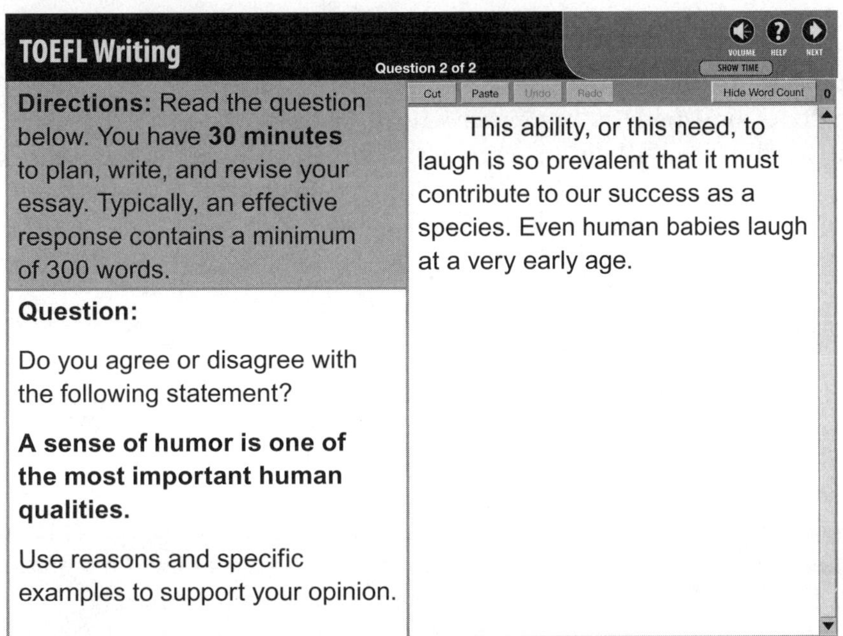
TOEFL Writing
Question 2 of 2
VOLUME HELP NEXT
SHOW TIME
Cut Paste Undo Redo
Hide Word Count 0
Directions: Read the question below. You have 30 minutes to plan, write, and revise your essay. Typically, an effective response contains a minimum of 300 words.
Question:
Do you agree or disagree with the following statement?
A sense of humor is one of the most important human qualities.
Use reasons and specific examples to support your opinion.
This ability, or this need, to laugh is so prevalent that it must contribute to our success as a species. Even human babies laugh at a very early age.

If all you want to do is cut the text, reposition the cursor and continue writing. But if you want to insert the deleted text somewhere else in your essay, you can use the **Paste** function. To insert text that you have just cut, position the mouse pointer where you want the text to appear. Click the mouse to make the blinking cursor appear in that place. Then click on the **Paste** button. The text will reappear in its new location.

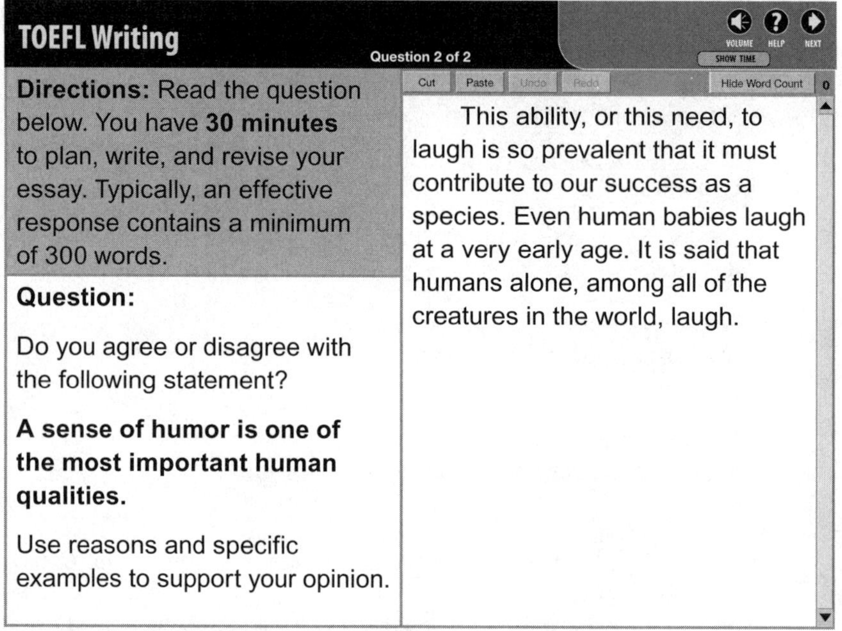
TOEFL Writing
Question 2 of 2
VOLUME HELP NEXT
SHOW TIME
Cut Paste Undo Redo
Hide Word Count
Directions: Read the question below. You have 30 minutes to plan, write, and revise your essay. Typically, an effective response contains a minimum of 300 words.
Question:
Do you agree or disagree with the following statement?
A sense of humor is one of the most important human qualities.
Use reasons and specific examples to support your opinion.
This ability, or this need, to laugh is so prevalent that it must contribute to our success as a species. Even human babies laugh at a very early age. It is said that humans alone, among all of the creatures in the world, laugh.

Undo and Redo

If you click on **Undo**, the computer will reverse your last action. If you have just typed some words, they will disappear when you click on **Undo**. If you have just cut or pasted text, that action will be reversed. Clicking on **Redo** after **Undo** will reinstate the action you just reversed. If you click on **Cut** to erase text and then click on **Undo**, the text will reappear. If you click on **Redo**, the text will disappear again.

Completing Your Essay

When you have finished your essay, click on **Next**, and then your computer will ask you to choose between **Return** and **Continue**. Be sure you have read your essay carefully before you click on **Continue**. You may not make further changes after you have clicked on **Continue**.

DIAGNOSTIC TEST

Diagnostic Test

READING SECTION

Directions

In this section, you will read three passages and answer reading comprehension questions about each passage. Most questions are worth one point, but the last question in each set is worth more than one point. The directions indicate how many points you may receive.

You have 60 minutes to read all of the passages and answer the questions. Some passages include a word or phrase followed by an asterisk (*). Go to the bottom of the page to see a definition or an explanation of these words or phrases.

Questions 1–12

Causes of Ice Ages

Geologists have shown that for about 80 percent of the past 2.5 million years, ice-age conditions have prevailed on the Earth's surface. During the past one million years, increased glacial conditions have run in cycles of approximately 100,000 years.

Many different factors may contribute to these increases in glaciation at regular intervals throughout Earth's more geologically recent history. The three most prominent factors probably relate to the amount of sunlight that reaches the Earth. This varies over time for three main reasons. First, the planet wobbles* as it spins, due to the pull of the sun and moon. Furthermore, the Earth tilts* on its axis and the degree of tilt changes over time. Finally, the orbit of the Earth around the sun is elliptical and the length of the major axis of the ellipse changes over a period of about 100,000 years. A mathematician named Milutin Milankovitch discovered in the 1930s that the pattern of insolation, or sunlight, predicted by these eccentricities in the Earth's movement matched the period of the last several eras of intense glaciation.

These Milankovitch insolation cycles were the dominant theory in ice-age research for much of the twentieth century despite the fact that the match between periods of peak insolation and most intense glaciation were not exact. For example, a cycle of 400,000 years predicted by the Milankovitch theory has never shown up in the climate records obtained through the study of microfossils deposited on the sea floor. Also, recent analysis has shown that the insolation theory predicts peaks of sunlight at intervals of 95,000 and 125,000 years. Climatological data does not support this predicted sunlight peaking. Other damaging evidence was the indication of a precisely measured sudden rise in temperature at a water-filled cave in Nevada, which preceded the increase in solar radiation that was supposed to cause it.

These and other problems with the Milankovitch cycles led some researchers to seek alternative explanations for the cyclic arrival of extended ice ages. In the 1990s, it was discovered that the orbital inclination of the Earth to the sun and planets could also be responsible for climate changes. If we imagine a flat plane with the sun in the center and the planets revolving around it, the Earth slowly moves in and out of the flat plane by a few degrees, repeating the cycle every 100,000 years. Two scientists, Muller and MacDonald, have proposed that it is this orbital inclination which is ultimately responsible for the periods of glaciation and warming. They argue that because of the oscillation, the Earth periodically travels through clouds of debris, in the form of dust and meteoroids. Such debris could reduce the amount of solar energy reaching the surface of our planet, thus plunging it into regular cold periods.

The advantage of this theory is that it is not confronted with several of the problems associated with the Milankovitch theory. In particular, the new theory fits well with the analysis of ocean sediments taken from eight locations around the world. This analysis yielded data clearly showing the peak of the last several ice ages with a period of 100,000 years and corresponding to the periods when the Earth's oscillating inclination takes it through clouds of extraterrestrial debris.

However, many researchers in this field are not yet persuaded by the inclination hypothesis. The main problem is that the amount of dust that falls to the ground when the Earth travels through space debris is relatively small – not enough to produce radical climate changes. Volcanic eruptions, for example, release much greater amounts of ash and dust and have relatively little effect on climate. Supporters have countered that the by-products created by the dust as it vaporizes on entering the atmosphere cause subtle changes to the energy levels. Nevertheless, the necessary physical proof has yet to be found to convince the skeptics.

***wobble:** to shake or move from side to side
***tilt:** to be in a sloping position

1. The word "prevailed" in the passage is closest in meaning to
   (A) ruled
   (B) existed
   (C) survived
   (D) triumphed

Geologists have shown that for about 80 percent of the past 2.5 million years, ice-age conditions have prevailed on the Earth's surface. During the past one million years, increased glacial conditions have run in cycles of approximately 100,000 years.

2. What can be inferred from paragraph 2 about the factors that contribute to glaciation?
   (A) They affect the Earth's spin.
   (B) They are geologically recent.
   (C) Only three factors relate to levels of sunlight.
   (D) Other factors than those relating to the sunlight affect ice buildup.

Paragraph 2 is marked with an arrow [➡].

➡ Many different factors may contribute to these increases in glaciation at regular intervals throughout Earth's more geologically recent history. The three most prominent factors probably relate to the amount of sunlight that reaches the Earth. This varies over time for three main reasons. First, the planet wobbles as it spins, due to the pull of the sun and moon. Furthermore, the Earth tilts on its axis and the degree of tilt changes over time. Finally, the orbit of the Earth around the sun is elliptical and the length of the major axis of the ellipse changes over a period of about 100,000 years. A mathematician named Milutin Milankovitch discovered in the 1930s that the pattern of insolation, or sunlight, predicted by these eccentricities in the Earth's movement matched the period of the last several eras of intense glaciation.

3. The phrase "these eccentricities" in the passage refers to all of the following EXCEPT
   (A) the various movements of the Earth as it spins
   (B) the degree of change in the Earth's tilt over time
   (C) the pattern of insolation matching the Earth's movement
   (D) the changing distance to the sun during the Earth's elliptical orbit

Many different factors may contribute to these increases in glaciation at regular intervals throughout Earth's more geologically recent history. The three most prominent factors probably relate to the amount of sunlight that reaches the Earth. This varies over time for three main reasons. First, the planet wobbles as it spins, due to the pull of the sun and moon. Furthermore, the Earth tilts on its axis and the degree of tilt changes over time. Finally, the orbit of the Earth around the sun is elliptical and the length of the major axis of the ellipse changes over a period of about 100,000 years. A mathematician named Milutin Milankovitch discovered in the 1930s that the pattern of insolation, or sunlight, predicted by these eccentricities in the Earth's movement matched the period of the last several eras of intense glaciation.

4. Scientists accepted the Milankovitch theory even though
   (A) the peaks of sunlight occurred at intervals of 95,000 and 125,000 years
   (B) the peaks of insolation and intense glaciation did not match
   (C) there were climate records of a 400,000-year cycle
   (D) there were microfossil deposits on the sea floor

[Refer to the full passage.]

5. In paragraph 4, why does the author suggest the image of a flat plane?
   (A) To help the reader visualize the positions and movements of the heavenly bodies
   (B) To demonstrate to the reader how the Earth orbits the sun
   (C) To support the argument that the orbital inclination increases tilting
   (D) To show how the Milankovitch theory doesn't explain the cyclical changes in climate

Paragraph 4 is marked with an arrow [➡].

➡ These and other problems with the Milankovitch cycles led some researchers to seek alternative explanations for the cyclic arrival of extended ice ages. In the 1990s, it was discovered that the orbital inclination of the Earth to the sun and planets could also be responsible for climate changes. If we imagine a flat plane with the sun in the center and the planets revolving around it, the Earth slowly moves in and out of the flat plane by a few degrees, repeating the cycle every 100,000 years. Two scientists, Muller and MacDonald, have proposed that it is this orbital inclination which is ultimately responsible for the periods of glaciation and warming. They argue that because of the oscillation, the Earth periodically travels through clouds of debris, in the form of dust and meteoroids. Such debris could reduce the amount of solar energy reaching the surface of our planet, thus plunging it into regular cold periods.

6. The word "it" in the passage refers to
   (A) such debris
   (B) solar energy
   (C) the surface
   (D) our planet

These and other problems with the Milankovitch cycles led some researchers to seek alternative explanations for the cyclic arrival of extended ice ages. In the 1990s, it was discovered that the orbital inclination of the Earth to the sun and planets could also be responsible for climate changes. If we imagine a flat plane with the sun in the center and the planets revolving around it, the Earth slowly moves in and out of the flat plane by a few degrees, repeating the cycle every 100,000 years. Two scientists, Muller and MacDonald, have proposed that it is this orbital inclination which is ultimately responsible for the periods of glaciation and warming. They argue that because of the oscillation, the Earth periodically travels through clouds of debris, in the form of dust and meteoroids. Such debris could reduce the amount of solar energy reaching the surface of our planet, thus plunging it into regular cold periods.

7. In paragraph 4, the author explains that
   (A) Milankovitch did not know about the orbital inclination of the Earth
   (B) glaciation occurs when the orbital inclination has entered a new cycle
   (C) the Earth always travels through clouds of debris after moving out of the plane by a few degrees
   (D) the amount of solar energy reaching the Earth's surface causes the changes of temperature

Paragraph 4 is marked with an arrow [➡].

➡ These and other problems with the Milankovitch cycles led some researchers to seek alternative explanations for the cyclic arrival of extended ice ages. In the 1990s, it was discovered that the orbital inclination of the Earth to the sun and planets could also be responsible for climate changes. If we imagine a flat plane with the sun in the center and the planets revolving around it, the Earth slowly moves in and out of the flat plane by a few degrees, repeating the cycle every 100,000 years. Two scientists, Muller and MacDonald, have proposed that it is this orbital inclination which is ultimately responsible for the periods of glaciation and warming. They argue that because of the oscillation, the Earth periodically travels through clouds of debris, in the form of dust and meteoroids. Such debris could reduce the amount of solar energy reaching the surface of our planet, thus plunging it into regular cold periods.

8. What problem in the Milankovitch theory was mentioned as being explained by the Muller and MacDonald theory?

   (A) The climate records obtained by studying microfossil deposits not matching his predicted cycle
   (B) The irregularities of the Earth's movements through orbital inclinations not following any pattern
   (C) The Earth's spin wobbling in relation to the Earth's oscillating inclination
   (D) The peak in the ice ages occurring at intervals between 95,000 and 125,000 years instead of 400,000

[Refer to the full passage.]

9. The word "persuaded" in the passage is closest in meaning to

   (A) convinced
   (B) discouraged
   (C) affected
   (D) challenged

However, many researchers in this field are not yet persuaded by the inclination hypothesis. The main problem is that the amount of dust that falls to the ground when the Earth travels through space debris is relatively small – not enough to produce radical climate changes. Volcanic eruptions, for example, release much greater amounts of ash and dust and have relatively little effect on climate. Supporters have countered that the by-products created by the dust as it vaporizes on entering the atmosphere cause subtle changes to the energy levels. Nevertheless, the necessary physical proof has yet to be found to convince the skeptics.

10. What problem is associated with the Muller and MacDonald theory?

   (A) The amount of debris that is released from volcanoes is proportional to the amount of interstellar dust.
   (B) The amount of ash from volcanoes and space dust that vaporizes in the atmosphere is too small.
   (C) The amount of dust entering the atmosphere is less than the amount of ash and dust released by volcanoes.
   (D) The by-products created by vaporized space dust cause relevant changes to the energy levels.

[Refer to the full passage.]

11. Look at the four squares [■] that indicate where the following sentence could be added to the passage.

When the Earth is at its furthest from the sun, less sunlight reaches the surface.

Where would the sentence best fit?

Choose the letter of the square that shows where the sentence should be added.

Many different factors may contribute to these increases in glaciation at regular intervals throughout Earth's more geologically recent history. **A** The three most prominent factors probably relate to the amount of sunlight that reaches the Earth. This varies over time for three main reasons. First, the planet wobbles as it spins, due to the pull of the sun and moon. **B** Furthermore, the Earth tilts on its axis and the degree of tilt changes over time. **C** Finally, the orbit of the Earth around the sun is elliptical and the length of the major axis of the ellipse changes over a period of about 100,000 years. **D** A mathematician named Milutin Milankovitch discovered in the 1930s that the pattern of insolation, or sunlight, predicted by these eccentricities in the Earth's movement matched the period of the last several eras of intense glaciation.

12. **Directions:** Select the appropriate phrases from the answer choices and match them to the flaws in the ice-age theories to which they relate. TWO of the answer choices will NOT be used. **This question is worth 4 points.**

Write the letters of the answer choices in the spaces where they belong. Refer to the full passage.

Answer Choices

- (A) Data of climate records not coinciding with predicted intervals of sunlight
- (B) Temperature rises occurring before the increase of sunlight
- (C) The irregularities of the Earth's movement during its orbit around the sun
- (D) The inconsistency between the periods of sunlight and glaciation
- (E) The relatively mild effect of volcanic eruptions on the climate
- (F) The orbital inclination of Earth through clouds of debris
- (G) The relatively small amount of interstellar debris reaching Earth
- (H) The lack of clear support from ocean sediment data
- (I) The lack of physical evidence in support of the effects of the inclination hypothesis

Flaws in the Milankovitch Cycles Theory

-
-
-
-

Flaws in the Muller and MacDonald Theory

-
-
-

Questions 13–26

Bird Migration

The phenomenon of seasonal bird migration has been known about for thousands of years, but it is still not fully understood by scientists. Not all birds migrate, but generally speaking the more northerly the breeding ground, the more likely is it that a species will migrate south for the winter. The main reason for this annual shifting of residence is that during the northern winters food becomes scarce and the cold temperatures make survival difficult. Some species are well adapted to these harsh conditions, but for those that aren't, moving south to warmer conditions is advantageous.

Changes in the weather can trigger the start of the journey south, although birds in the Northern Hemisphere seem to know when it is time to migrate south before the winter. In some species at least, the changes in the length of the day cause glands in the birds' bodies to secrete hormones that produce other changes, which ready the birds for the long flight south. At this time fat starts to accumulate under the skin, and this provides a store of energy for the long flight when they will be expending more calories flying than they can obtain during their brief rest stops.

In fact, bird-migration patterns are more complex than the simple pattern implied above. Birds that breed in the Southern Hemisphere migrate north to wintering grounds. Other birds travel on an approximately east-west path since milder climates can often be found in coastal areas of continental regions. Some birds find conditions more suitable at lower altitudes in a mountainous region and so migrate to lower levels in winter.

Perhaps the most mysterious and as yet not totally understood aspect of bird migration is how birds can navigate such long distances and arrive so precisely at their destination. Various possibilities exist. The most obvious explanation is that they learn the topographic* features of their route. However, it is not feasible that this method could be used for crossing larger stretches of water or very long trips across whole continents. Another possible explanation is that some birds may use magnetic fields. Scientists have actually detected tiny crystals of magnetite in the olfactory* tract of some species, and homing pigeons have been shown to follow magnetic field lines of the Earth.

A further possibility is that birds can detect the polarization patterns in sunlight. Some light waves from the sun are absorbed in the atmosphere, and some pass through. The resulting pattern of light waves forms a large bowtie-shaped image in the sky. The image has fuzzy ends and is sometimes known as Haidinger's brush after the discoverer of the effect. The image is oriented in a north and south direction and is visible at sunset. Although birds may not see this shape, they can discern gradations of polarization, which give them a kind of compass for determining directions.

Scientists believe that some birds navigate by use of star positions; this has been established with at least one species. In a series of studies, caged birds were subjected to the projection of the nighttime Northern Hemisphere inside a planetarium. All stars rotate around Polaris, the pole star, and this movement seemed to give the birds the information they needed to orientate themselves in the correct direction. However, some recent research contradicts this. Perhaps it is not the lack of movement of the pole star but rather the constellation patterns that guide them. It has also been found that when fewer stars were visible on the planetarium ceiling, the birds' sense of direction became poorer. And this, too, implies that the general star pattern does have some bearing on orientation.

The current state of research suggests that all of the above-mentioned methods probably have an influence on bird migration. Different species use one, some, or even all methods at different times and in various situations.

***topographic:** relating to the natural features of land
***olfactory:** connected with the sense of smell

13. In paragraph 1, it is understood that some birds don't migrate south in the winter because they Ⓐ already live in warmer conditions Ⓑ live in areas that have an abundant food supply Ⓒ have difficulty surviving the frigid temperatures Ⓓ are suited to the difficult conditions Paragraph 1 is marked with an arrow [➡].	➡ The phenomenon of seasonal bird migration has been known about for thousands of years, but it is still not fully understood by scientists. Not all birds migrate, but generally speaking the more northerly the breeding ground, the more likely is it that a species will migrate south for the winter. The main reason for this annual shifting of residence is that during the northern winters food becomes scarce and the cold temperatures make survival difficult. Some species are well adapted to these harsh conditions, but for those that aren't, moving south to warmer conditions is advantageous.

14. The word "those" in the passage refers to Ⓐ northern winters Ⓑ cold temperatures Ⓒ harsh conditions Ⓓ some bird species	The phenomenon of seasonal bird migration has been known about for thousands of years, but it is still not fully understood by scientists. Not all birds migrate, but generally speaking the more northerly the breeding ground, the more likely is it that a species will migrate south for the winter. The main reason for this annual shifting of residence is that during the northern winters food becomes scarce and the cold temperatures make survival difficult. Some species are well adapted to these harsh conditions, but for those that aren't, moving south to warmer conditions is advantageous.

15. According to paragraph 2, what are the results of changes in the weather? Ⓐ The change in the length of the day Ⓑ The secretion of hormones by the birds Ⓒ The expenditure of calories Ⓓ The onset of migration Paragraph 2 is marked with an arrow [➡].	➡ Changes in the weather can trigger the start of the journey south, although birds in the Northern Hemisphere seem to know when it is time to migrate south before the winter. In some species at least, the changes in the length of the day cause glands in the birds' bodies to secrete hormones that produce other changes, which ready the birds for the long flight south. At this time fat starts to accumulate under the skin, and this provides a store of energy for the long flight when they will be expending more calories flying than they can obtain during their brief rest stops.

16. The word "accumulate" in the passage is closest in meaning to Ⓐ build up Ⓑ fill in Ⓒ break up Ⓓ cut back	Changes in the weather can trigger the start of the journey south, although birds in the Northern Hemisphere seem to know when it is time to migrate south before the winter. In some species at least, the changes in the length of the day cause glands in the birds' bodies to secrete hormones that produce other changes, which ready the birds for the long flight south. At this time fat starts to accumulate under the skin, and this provides a store of energy for the long flight when they will be expending more calories flying than they can obtain during their brief rest stops.

17. All of the bird migration patterns are mentioned in the passage EXCEPT (A) the migration north from the Southern Hemisphere (B) the migration east or west toward milder climates (C) the migration from mountainous regions to lower altitudes (D) the migration from east to west towards hotter climates.	[Refer to the full passage.]

18. The word "precisely" in the passage is closest in meaning to (A) finally (B) exactly (C) entirely (D) decisively	Perhaps the most mysterious and as yet not totally understood aspect of bird migration is how birds can navigate such long distances and arrive so precisely at their destination. Various possibilities exist. The most obvious explanation is that they learn the topographic features of their route. However, it is not feasible that this method could be used for crossing larger stretches of water or very long trips across whole continents. Another possible explanation is that some birds may use magnetic fields. Scientists have actually detected tiny crystals of magnetite in the olfactory tract of some species, and homing pigeons have been shown to follow magnetic field lines of the Earth.

19. It can be inferred that polarization patterns (A) absorb sunlight (B) are tied in the center (C) are invisible at night (D) cause a magnetic force	[Refer to the full passage.]

20. Why does the author mention Haidinger's brush? (A) To understand the phenomenon (B) To describe the pattern (C) To explain what birds see (D) To define the fuzzy ends	[Refer to the full passage.]

21. The word "subjected" in the passage is closest in meaning to

(A) exposed
(B) subjugated
(C) constrained
(D) invited

Scientists believe that some birds navigate by use of star positions; this has been established with at least one species. In a series of studies, caged birds were subjected to the projection of the nighttime Northern Hemisphere inside a planetarium. All stars rotate around Polaris, the pole star, and this movement seemed to give the birds the information they needed to orientate themselves in the correct direction. However, some recent research contradicts this. Perhaps it is not the lack of movement of the pole star but rather the constellation patterns that guide them. It has also been found that when fewer stars were visible on the planetarium ceiling, the birds' sense of direction became poorer. And this, too, implies that the general star pattern does have some bearing on orientation.

22. According to paragraph 6, how do some birds navigate during the night?

(A) By using a projection of the star positions
(B) By circling around the pole star
(C) By orientating themselves using the constellations
(D) By getting their bearings from a few visible stars

Paragraph 6 is marked with an arrow [➡].

➡ Scientists believe that some birds navigate by use of star positions; this has been established with at least one species. In a series of studies, caged birds were subjected to the projection of the nighttime Northern Hemisphere inside a planetarium. All stars rotate around Polaris, the pole star, and this movement seemed to give the birds the information they needed to orientate themselves in the correct direction. However, some recent research contradicts this. Perhaps it is not the lack of movement of the pole star but rather the constellation patterns that guide them. It has also been found that when fewer stars were visible on the planetarium ceiling, the birds' sense of direction became poorer. And this, too, implies that the general star pattern does have some bearing on orientation.

23. Which of the sentences below best expresses the essential information in the highlighted sentence in the passage? Incorrect choices change the meaning in important ways or leave out essential information.

  (A) Birds needing to orientate themselves in the right direction seemed to use the information they get from the stars that rotate around Polaris.
  (B) The pole star seemed to be used by birds to get the information they needed because they were able to orientate themselves using the star's rotation in the correct direction.
  (C) Birds needing to correct the Polaris direction in which to orientate themselves seemed to use the fact that all stars rotate.
  (D) The stars rotating in the correct direction around the pole star is what seemed to give the birds the information they needed for orientating themselves to Polaris.

Scientists believe that some birds navigate by use of star positions; this has been established with at least one species. In a series of studies, caged birds were subjected to the projection of the nighttime Northern Hemisphere inside a planetarium. All stars rotate around Polaris, the pole star, and this movement seemed to give the birds the information they needed to orientate themselves in the correct direction. However, some recent research contradicts this. Perhaps it is not the lack of movement of the pole star but rather the constellation patterns that guide them. It has also been found that when fewer stars were visible on the planetarium ceiling, the birds' sense of direction became poorer. And this, too, implies that the general star pattern does have some bearing on orientation.

24. The word "this" in the passage refers to

  (A) The number of stars that were visible
  (B) The relative loss of the birds' sense of direction
  (C) The constellation patterns that guide birds
  (D) The pole star's stationary position

Scientists believe that some birds navigate by use of star positions; this has been established with at least one species. In a series of studies, caged birds were subjected to the projection of the nighttime Northern Hemisphere inside a planetarium. All stars rotate around Polaris, the pole star, and this movement seemed to give the birds the information they needed to orientate themselves in the correct direction. However, some recent research contradicts this. Perhaps it is not the lack of movement of the pole star but rather the constellation patterns that guide them. It has also been found that when fewer stars were visible on the planetarium ceiling, the birds' sense of direction became poorer. And this, too, implies that the general star pattern does have some bearing on orientation.

25. Look at the four squares [■] that indicate where the following sentence could be added to the passage.

Over short distances the birds could recognize particular landscapes such as river valleys and shapes of hills.

Where would the sentence best fit?

Choose the letter of the square that shows where the sentence should be added.

Perhaps the most mysterious and as yet not totally understood aspect of bird migration is how birds can navigate such long distances and arrive so precisely at their destination. Various possibilities exist. [A] The most obvious explanation is that they learn the topographic features of their route. [B] However, it is not feasible that this method could be used for crossing larger stretches of water or very long trips across whole continents. [C] Another possible explanation is that some birds may use magnetic fields. [D] Scientists have actually detected tiny crystals of magnetite in the olfactory tract of some species, and homing pigeons have been shown to follow magnetic field lines of the Earth.

26. **Directions:** An introductory sentence for a brief summary of the passage is provided below. Complete the summary by selecting the THREE answer choices that express the most important ideas in the passage. Some sentences do not belong in the summary because they express ideas that are not presented in the passage or are minor ideas in the passage. **This question is worth 2 points.**

Write the letters of the answer choices in the spaces where they belong.
Refer to the full passage.

Scientists have proposed several methods that birds use for orientating themselves during their seasonal migrations.

-
-
-

Answer Choices

(A) Birds not only migrate north or south depending on which hemisphere they live in, but they also migrate along coastal regions or in and out of mountainous areas.

(B) Birds' ability to detect gradations of polarization patterns in sunlight could give them a way for determining directions.

(C) Changes in both the weather and the length of day can cause the birds' bodies to make physical changes to prepare them for the long flights.

(D) The principal reason for birds to migrate is that most bird species are not adapted to the harsh winter conditions and the scarcity of food during that season.

(E) The star patterns and the way the stars rotate around the fixed position of the pole star could give birds the direction in which to navigate.

(F) Birds may use their knowledge of the features of the landscape, although this seems unlikely given the distances that birds migrate.

Questions 27–39

Radon

Radon is a radioactive gas that is invisible and odorless. It forms during the decay of uranium-238, and in decaying, itself produces solid heavy metal radioactive particles of polonium, lead, and bismuth. The parent element, uranium, is distributed in rocks and soils in many regions of the world, although usually in negligible* amounts. However, concentrations of this element occur in certain rocks, and under certain conditions it is dissolved by underground water and carried over great distances before seeping into other rocks and soils.

Since radon is a gas, it can move from the ground into the air, where it is dispersed by the winds. If it infiltrates buildings, however, it can build up over time and lead to serious health problems. In fact, the radon itself is chemically inert and so does not enter into chemical reactions with other substances. It is readily dissolved in blood and circulates through the body until it is expelled, usually before it has had time to decay. The health problems associated with radon activity arise from the radioactive products of its disintegration, mentioned above.

The products of the decay process, especially polonium-218 and polonium-214, emit radiation, which kills or damages living cells, causing genetic mutations and cancer. These radon progeny are not dispersed harmlessly like radon itself but accumulate as the radon decays. Outside the body, these solid materials can attach themselves to dust particles and surfaces throughout a building and then be inhaled. The decay products can also stick to tobacco leaves during growth and then enter the body when the tobacco is smoked. Inside the body these dangerous by-products of radon become lodged in lung tissue and the bronchial tubes. As these decay, they emit alpha and beta particles and gamma rays. Of these, the alpha particles can do the most damage since they are the bulkiest of the three and therefore cannot penetrate very far into living tissue. Because of this relative immobility, concentrations of the particle form and damage cells in the immediate area. Beta particles and gamma rays are less dangerous since they travel further and are less concentrated in the tissues.

The primary way that radon penetrates buildings is through foundations. It enters through cracks in basement floors, drains, loose-fitting pipes, and exposed soil areas. Radon also finds its way into water, although if the water is exposed to the atmosphere or agitated, the radon disperses into the air. Because of this, concentrations of this uranium daughter are not high in rivers, but water drawn from underground sources into homes can have elevated levels.

The chief health risk from inhaling radon or its daughter products is lung cancer. Scientists have concluded that exposure to this carcinogen is the second leading cause of this disease in the United States. Major scientific organizations believe it contributes to approximately 12 percent of the incidence in the United States alone. It is true that some research has cast doubt on the likelihood of residential radon accumulations contributing to cancer rates. Other larger scale studies contradict the neutral findings. For example, a recent study of 68,000 underground miners who were exposed to high levels of radon shows that they are five times more likely to die of lung cancer than the general population. Smokers, whose incidence of lung cancer is significantly higher than the nonsmoking population, are even more at risk if they are exposed to high levels of radon.

It is now possible to have buildings tested for radon accumulation. In an average home, this is about 1.3 picocuries* per liter, which is considered an acceptable although not a totally safe level. If these levels are above 4 picocuries per liter of air, then homeowners are advised to reduce the amount seeping into the living space. This can be achieved through various means including concrete sealing and the installation of active ventilation systems. It is not possible to completely eradicate traces of radon since the natural outdoors level averages 0.4 picocuries per liter, but minimizing the amount is a prudent preventative measure.

***negligible:** too small to be important
***picocurie:** a level of radiation activity

27. The phrase "this element" in the passage refers to (A) lead (B) radon (C) uranium (D) polonium	Radon is a radioactive gas that is invisible and odorless. It forms during the decay of uranium-238, and in decaying, itself produces solid heavy metal radioactive particles of polonium, lead, and bismuth. The parent element, uranium, is distributed in rocks and soils in many regions of the world, although usually in negligible amounts. However, concentrations of this element occur in certain rocks, and under certain conditions it is dissolved by underground water and carried over great distances before seeping into other rocks and soils.

28. The word "seeping" in the passage is closest in meaning to (A) leaking (B) spilling (C) releasing (D) erupting	Radon is a radioactive gas that is invisible and odorless. It forms during the decay of uranium-238, and in decaying, itself produces solid heavy metal radioactive particles of polonium, lead, and bismuth. The parent element, uranium, is distributed in rocks and soils in many regions of the world, although usually in negligible amounts. However, concentrations of this element occur in certain rocks, and under certain conditions it is dissolved by underground water and carried over great distances before seeping into other rocks and soils.

29. In paragraph 2, what can be inferred about the relationship of radon and health problems? (A) The gas has to have time to decay in order to cause health problems. (B) Since radon is chemically inert, it cannot lead to health problems. (C) As a gas, radon disperses in the wind and consequently isn't a health problem. (D) The gas has to disintegrate before it can seep into buildings. Paragraph 2 is marked with an arrow [➡].	➡ Since radon is a gas, it can move from the ground into the air, where it is dispersed by the winds. If it infiltrates buildings, however, it can build up over time and lead to serious health problems. In fact, the radon itself is chemically inert and so does not enter into chemical reactions with other substances. It is readily dissolved in blood and circulates through the body until it is expelled, usually before it has had time to decay. The health problems associated with radon activity arise from the radioactive products of its disintegration, mentioned above.

30. The word "disintegration" in the passage is closest in meaning to
    - (A) breakdown
    - (B) collapse
    - (C) corrosion
    - (D) failure

Since radon is a gas, it can move from the ground into the air, where it is dispersed by the winds. If it infiltrates buildings, however, it can build up over time and lead to serious health problems. In fact, the radon itself is chemically inert and so does not enter into chemical reactions with other substances. It is readily dissolved in blood and circulates through the body until it is expelled, usually before it has had time to decay. The health problems associated with radon activity arise from the radioactive products of its disintegration, mentioned above.

31. Health problems associated with radon are caused by
    - (A) radioactive uranium
    - (B) certain heavy metals
    - (C) decaying gases
    - (D) some chemical reactions

[Refer to the full passage.]

32. Which of the sentences below best expresses the essential information in the highlighted sentence? Incorrect choices change the meaning in important ways or leave out essential information.
    - (A) Unlike the radon, which is scattered without danger, its products accumulate as the radon disintegrates.
    - (B) Like the radon itself, the decay products are scattered safely and accumulate as the radon decays.
    - (C) Like the decaying radon, the progeny are dispersed in accumulations, which can cause harm.
    - (D) Unlike the dispersed radon, which accumulates safely, the products of decay are dangerous.

The products of the decay process, especially polonium-218 and polonium-214, emit radiation, which kills or damages living cells, causing genetic mutations and cancer. These radon progeny are not dispersed harmlessly like radon itself but accumulate as the radon decays. Outside the body, these solid materials can attach themselves to dust particles and surfaces throughout a building and then be inhaled. The decay products can also stick to tobacco leaves during growth and then enter the body when the tobacco is smoked. Inside the body these dangerous by-products of radon become lodged in lung tissue and the bronchial tubes. As these decay, they emit alpha and beta particles and gamma rays. Of these, the alpha particles can do the most damage since they are the bulkiest of the three and therefore cannot penetrate very far into living tissue. Because of this relative immobility, concentrations of the particle form and damage cells in the immediate area. Beta particles and gamma rays are less dangerous since they travel further and are less concentrated in the tissues.

33. According to paragraph 3, some products of decay cause damage because they

    (A) emit gamma rays
    (B) cannot penetrate living tissue very deeply
    (C) are highly mobile
    (D) seep into houses and form concentrations of radiation

Paragraph 3 is marked with an arrow [➡].

➡ The products of the decay process, especially polonium-218 and polonium-214, emit radiation, which kills or damages living cells, causing genetic mutations and cancer. These radon progeny are not dispersed harmlessly like radon itself but accumulate as the radon decays. Outside the body, these solid materials can attach themselves to dust particles and surfaces throughout a building and then be inhaled. The decay products can also stick to tobacco leaves during growth and then enter the body when the tobacco is smoked. Inside the body these dangerous by-products of radon become lodged in lung tissue and the bronchial tubes. As these decay, they emit alpha and beta particles and gamma rays. Of these, the alpha particles can do the most damage since they are the bulkiest of the three and therefore cannot penetrate very far into living tissue. Because of this relative immobility, concentrations of the particle form and damage cells in the immediate area. Beta particles and gamma rays are less dangerous since they travel further and are less concentrated in the tissues.

34. The phrase "uranium daughter" in the passage refers to

    (A) water
    (B) radon
    (C) particles
    (D) air

The primary way that radon penetrates buildings is through foundations. It enters through cracks in basement floors, drains, loose-fitting pipes, and exposed soil areas. Radon also finds its way into water, although if the water is exposed to the atmosphere or agitated, the radon disperses into the air. Because of this, concentrations of this uranium daughter are not high in rivers, but water drawn from underground sources into homes can have elevated levels.

35. According to the passage, all of the following are true about radon EXCEPT

    (A) it is invisible
    (B) it cannot be detected
    (C) it cannot be smelled
    (D) it is radioactive

[Refer to the full passage.]

36. It can be understood from paragraph 6 that

(A) reducing the amount of radon in your home is pointless because of the amount of radon outside

(B) even though it is possible to test buildings for radon accumulation, it is not possible to minimize the level of radiation activity

(C) the use of concrete sealing and active ventilation systems can reduce the amount of radon to an acceptable level

(D) using concrete sealing and installing active ventilation systems reduces the amount of usable living space

Paragraph 6 is marked with an arrow [➡].

➡ It is now possible to have buildings tested for radon accumulation. In an average home, this is about 1.3 picocuries per liter, which is considered an acceptable although not a totally safe level. If these levels are above 4 picocuries per liter of air, then homeowners are advised to reduce the amount seeping into the living space. This can be achieved through various means including concrete sealing and the installation of active ventilation systems. It is not possible to completely eradicate traces of radon since the natural outdoors level averages 0.4 picocuries per liter, but minimizing the amount is a prudent preventative measure.

37. The word "prudent" in the passage is closest in meaning to

(A) sensible

(B) necessary

(C) practical

(D) realistic

It is now possible to have buildings tested for radon accumulation. In an average home, this is about 1.3 picocuries per liter, which is considered an acceptable although not a totally safe level. If these levels are above 4 picocuries per liter of air, then homeowners are advised to reduce the amount seeping into the living space. This can be achieved through various means including concrete sealing and the installation of active ventilation systems. It is not possible to completely eradicate traces of radon since the natural outdoors level averages 0.4 picocuries per liter, but minimizing the amount is a prudent preventative measure.

38. Look at the four squares [■] that indicate where the following sentence could be added to the passage.

But this research has been criticized for being based on too few subjects.

Where would the sentence best fit?

Choose the letter of the square that shows where the sentence should be added.

The chief health risk from inhaling radon or its daughter products is lung cancer. [A] Scientists have concluded that exposure to this carcinogen is the second leading cause of this disease in the United States. [B] Major scientific organizations believe it contributes to approximately 12 percent of the incidence in the United States alone. It is true that some research has cast doubt on the likelihood of residential radon accumulations contributing to cancer rates. [C] Other larger scale studies contradict the neutral findings. For example, a recent study of 68,000 underground miners who were exposed to high levels of radon shows that they are five times more likely to die of lung cancer than the general population. [D] Smokers, whose incidence of lung cancer is significantly higher than the nonsmoking population, are even more at risk if they are exposed to high levels of radon.

39. **Directions:** An introductory sentence for a brief summary of the passage is provided below. Complete the summary by selecting the THREE answer choices that express the most important ideas in the passage. Some sentences do not belong in the summary because they express ideas that are not presented in the passage or are minor ideas in the passage. **This question is worth 2 points.**

Write the letters of the answer choices in the spaces where they belong. Refer to the full passage.

Radon can seep into a building, where its decay products can lead to health problems.

-
-
-

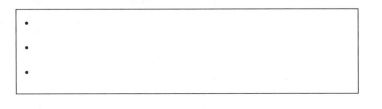

Answer Choices

(A) Although radon can enter a building in many different ways, it also escapes through cracks in the foundations.

(B) Concentrations of the radon by-products attach themselves to particles in the air inside buildings and are breathed into the lungs.

(C) People who smoke or work in mines are at greater risks of getting lung cancer that is related to alpha particles than those who work in buildings.

(D) The by-product alpha particles are too heavy to disperse through the tissues, so they accumulate in the lungs where they kill or damage lung cells.

(E) Radon does not cause lung cancer because it is chemically inert and therefore readily dissolves in the blood, where it eventually is expelled from the body.

(F) Preventative measures can be taken to reduce the amount of exposure to radon in living spaces, but it is not possible to completely eliminate the gas from the atmosphere.

LISTENING SECTION

Directions

This section measures your ability to understand conversations and lectures in English. You will hear each conversation or lecture only one time. After each conversation or lecture, you will answer some questions about it.

The questions typically ask about the main idea and supporting details. Some questions ask about a speaker's purpose or attitude. Answer the questions based on what is stated or implied by the speakers.

You may take notes while you listen. You may use your notes to help you answer the questions. Your notes will not be scored.

In some questions, you will see this icon: 🎧. This means that you will hear, but not see, part of the question.

Some questions have special directions. These directions appear in a gray box.

Most questions are worth one point. A question worth more than one point will have special instructions indicating how many points you can receive.

You will have 20 minutes to answer the questions in this section.

Now get ready to listen. You may take notes.

START ▶

Questions 1–6

Listen to part of a lecture in an American government class.

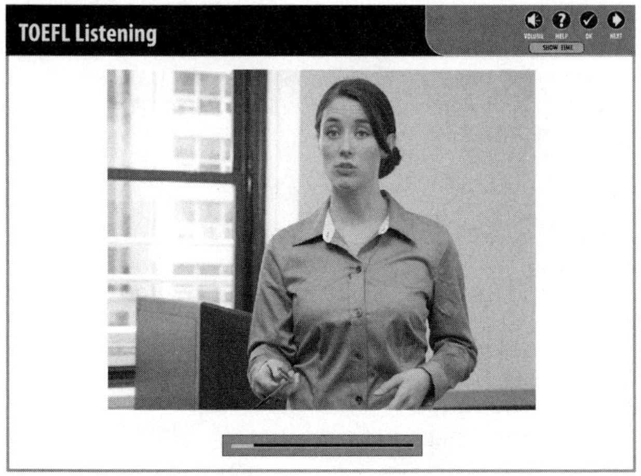

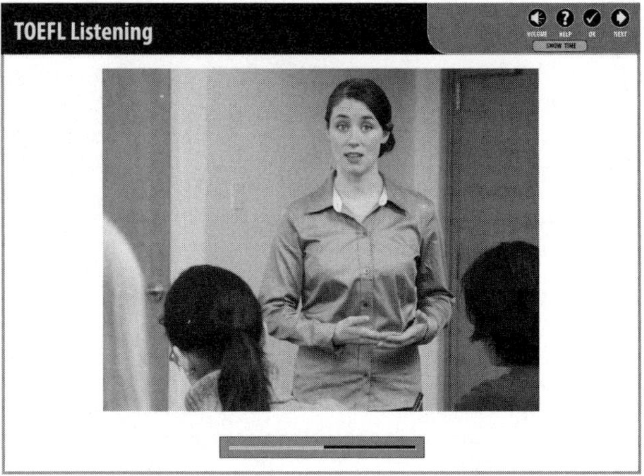

Now get ready to answer the questions. You may use your notes to help you answer.

1. What is the lecture mainly about?
   - (A) A method in Alaska for ensuring fair election results
   - (B) An important feature of the U.S. presidential election
   - (C) The essential criteria used for choosing a candidate
   - (D) A comparison of different voting systems

2. According to the professor, who becomes an elector?
   - (A) A U.S. senator or representative
   - (B) A trained member of the public
   - (C) A member of a political party
   - (D) A candidate for political office

3. Why does the professor say this: 
   - (A) To clear up a possible confusion
   - (B) To help explain the exact number of electors
   - (C) To correct something she said earlier
   - (D) To remind students of the electors' duties

4. Why does the professor use the example of Alaska in the lecture?
   - (A) To explain the number of electors each state has
   - (B) To show why states with small populations are powerful
   - (C) To remind students of the number of electors in certain states
   - (D) To develop the students' understanding of electoral politics

5. Which candidate wins the presidential election?
   - (A) The one who wins the most states
   - (B) The one who wins the biggest states
   - (C) The one who receives the most votes from the public
   - (D) The one who receives the most votes from electors

6. What does the professor mean when she says this:
   - (A) Many voters reject this system of choosing the president.
   - (B) Critics of the voting system have pointed out weaknesses.
   - (C) Students have made several objections to the voting system.
   - (D) Flaws in this voting system are not a disadvantage.

Questions 7–11

Listen to a conversation between a student and a professor.

Now get ready to answer the questions. You may use your notes to help you answer.

7. Why does the student go to see the professor?
   - (A) To apologize for arriving late
   - (B) To turn in her proposal to the professor
   - (C) To get help in analyzing her statistics
   - (D) To discuss improvements for her proposal

8. Why does the professor suggest that the student go to the Computer Center?
   - (A) To talk to Miriam at the information desk
   - (B) To get help setting up the statistical analysis
   - (C) To make changes to her statistical results
   - (D) To define her subjects' linguistic abilities

9. According to the professor, what information should the student add in her proposal?

   Choose 2 answers.
   - [A] How the analysis will be done
   - [B] How she got the statistics into a meaningful form
   - [C] How the subjects will be selected
   - [D] How she will contact the international students

10. Why does the professor say this: 
   - (A) To illustrate a flaw in the student's proposal
   - (B) To compare two language groups
   - (C) To demonstrate international students' differing linguistic levels
   - (D) To suggest the kind of test the student should give her subjects

11. What does the professor imply about the people who will decide on the grant money?
   - (A) They will not approve of her getting help in analyzing her statistics.
   - (B) They will question what stress patterns she will study.
   - (C) They will be influenced by her definition of her subjects.
   - (D) They will not understand who her subjects will be.

Questions 12–17

Listen to part of a discussion in a business correspondence class.

Now get ready to answer the questions. You may use your notes to help you answer.

12. What is the discussion mainly about?
    - (A) The procedures for sending e-mail messages in the business world
    - (B) The etiquette to use when writing a formal business letter
    - (C) The reasons for using e-mails instead of formal letters
    - (D) The types of e-mails used in the business world

13. Listen again to part of the discussion. Then answer the question.
    Why does the professor say this:
    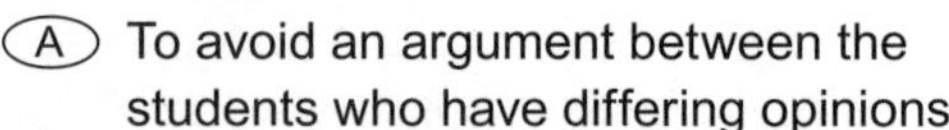
    - (A) To avoid an argument between the students who have differing opinions
    - (B) To imply that different businesses deal with mail differently
    - (C) To bring up a different situation that may have to be dealt with in business
    - (D) To indicate that most businesses have to make policy changes

14. What can be inferred about the students?
    - (A) They have come to an agreement about internal e-mail use.
    - (B) They are both experienced in using e-mail techniques.
    - (C) They frequently get annoyed with each other's way of doing things.
    - (D) They are in disagreement with the professor's solutions.

15. Listen again to part of the discussion. Then answer the question.
    Why does the professor ask this:
    - (A) She wants to go back to a previous lesson.
    - (B) She is leading the students to a different solution to the problem.
    - (C) She thinks that the students have forgotten an essential part of communication.
    - (D) She is highlighting points that the students must learn for a test.

16. According to the discussion, which way both protects customer identity and promotes customer personalization?
    - (A) Sending the customers a group message
    - (B) Writing to the customers individually
    - (C) Using the blind copy feature
    - (D) Putting all the addresses into the receiver box

17. Which of the following are valid points about messages sent to a group address instead of individual addresses?

    Choose 2 answers.

    - [A] The customer's identity is protected.
    - [B] Individual addresses are hidden.
    - [C] The message appears personal.
    - [D] The address takes a long time to type.

Questions 18–23

Listen to part of a lecture in a literature class.

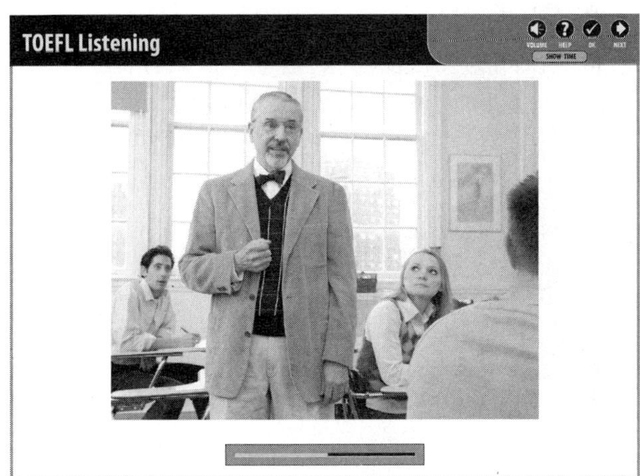

Now get ready to answer the questions. You may use your notes to help you answer.

18. What is the lecture mainly about?
    - (A) How London's life and work are contrasted
    - (B) How London's life influenced his work
    - (C) London's political writings
    - (D) London's early adventures

19. According to the professor, what effect did the absence of a father have on London?
    - (A) It affected his relationship with his mother.
    - (B) It caused him to commit crimes.
    - (C) It influenced aspects of his writing.
    - (D) It prepared him for a life of adventure.

20. What does the professor mean when he says this:
    - (A) He thinks many of the students in the class are poor.
    - (B) He is joking that some of the students may not be happy at college.
    - (C) He believes that some students are not enjoying the class.
    - (D) He is implying that some students will imitate London's behavior.

21. Why does the professor think that London read so many books?
    - (A) London wanted to learn from other writers.
    - (B) London was enrolled at a university.
    - (C) London needed to use other writers' ideas.
    - (D) London had few ways of gaining real experience.

22. What does the professor imply about London's success?
    - (A) He was immediately successful as a writer.
    - (B) He was successful only in later life.
    - (C) He worked hard to achieve success.
    - (D) He never really achieved much success.

23. What does the professor think of London's work?
    - (A) Most of London's work is excellent.
    - (B) Most of London's work is careless.
    - (C) Much of London's work is not very good.
    - (D) Much of London's work is very modern.

Questions 24–29

Listen to a discussion in an anthropology class.

Now get ready to answer the questions. You may use your notes to help you answer.

24. What is the main purpose of the lecture?
    - (A) To provide a framework for understanding early human culture
    - (B) To show how Cro-Magnon people became dominant
    - (C) To emphasize the importance of language in human evolution
    - (D) To introduce the question of the fate of the Neanderthal people

25. Why does the professor say this: 
    - (A) To remind students of a previously made point
    - (B) To check whether students are following the lecture
    - (C) To ensure that students understand a term
    - (D) To provide an example of the Neanderthal's body structure

26. Why does the professor refer to the Neanderthal's ability to make and transport fire?
    - (A) To emphasize that they were not as advanced as the Cro-Magnon
    - (B) To argue that they were sophisticated toolmakers
    - (C) To show that they were relatively unintelligent
    - (D) To support her view that they were not as backward as some people have claimed

27. What does the professor NOT mention about the Neanderthal's use of language?
    - (A) Their range of speech sounds
    - (B) The shape of their vocal tracts
    - (C) The development of their brains
    - (D) Their inability to speak

28. Indicate whether each sentence below describes Neanderthal or Cro-Magnon characteristics.

Check the correct box for each statement.

	Neanderthal	Cro-Magnon
(A) They developed tools with handles.		
(B) They used bows and arrows.		
(C) They produced unsophisticated art forms.		

29. According to the professor, why is a comparison of Neanderthal and modern human DNA useful?
    (A) To examine which diseases caused the extinction of Neanderthals
    (B) To determine whether Neanderthals interbred with the Cro-Magnon
    (C) To discover the origin of Neanderthal people
    (D) To learn how they could have survived in a severe climate

Questions 30–34

Listen to part of a conversation at a campus police station.

Now get ready to answer the questions. You may use your notes to help you answer.

30. Why did the student go to the campus police?
    (A) To report a stolen vehicle
    (B) To ask about his right of appeal
    (C) To get advice on writing a police report
    (D) To complain about the lack of handicapped parking places

31. What can be inferred about the student?
    (A) He didn't know he was parking illegally.
    (B) He lives in a student dormitory.
    (C) He uses a wheelchair.
    (D) He drives to campus.

32. Listen again to part of the conversation. Then answer the question.
    What does the officer mean when she says this:
    - (A) She is apologizing for the towing.
    - (B) She is empathizing with the student's situation.
    - (C) She regrets that the student broke the law.
    - (D) She is worried about the student's appeal.

33. Listen again to part of the conversation. Then answer the question.
    Why does the officer say this: 
    - (A) To make sure the man knows what he can do
    - (B) To give the man an excuse for breaking the rules
    - (C) To introduce the circumstances in which people appeal
    - (D) To offer the man help in writing an appeal

34. What will the student probably do?
    - (A) Write a letter of appeal
    - (B) Pay the fine immediately
    - (C) Park in the faculty parking lot
    - (D) Request a handicapped sticker

STOP ■

SPEAKING SECTION

Directions

In this section of the test, you will be able to demonstrate your ability to speak about a variety of topics. You will answer six questions by recording your response. Answer each of the questions as completely as possible.

In questions 1 and 2, you will first hear a statement or question about familiar topics. You will then speak about these topics. Your response will be scored on your ability to speak clearly and coherently about the topics.

In questions 3 and 4, you will first read a short text. You will then listen to a talk on the same topic.

You will be asked a question about what you have read and heard. You will need to combine appropriate information from the text and the talk to provide a complete answer to the question. Your response will be scored on your ability to speak clearly and coherently and on your ability to accurately convey information about what you read and heard.

In questions 5 and 6, you will listen to part of a conversation or a lecture. You will be asked a question about what you heard. Your response will be scored on your ability to speak clearly and coherently and on your ability to accurately convey information about what you heard.

You may take notes while you read and while you listen to the conversations and lectures. You may use your notes to help prepare your response.

Listen carefully to the directions for each question. For each question you will be given a short time to prepare your response. When the preparation time is up, you will be told to begin your response.

START ▶

1. Please listen carefully.

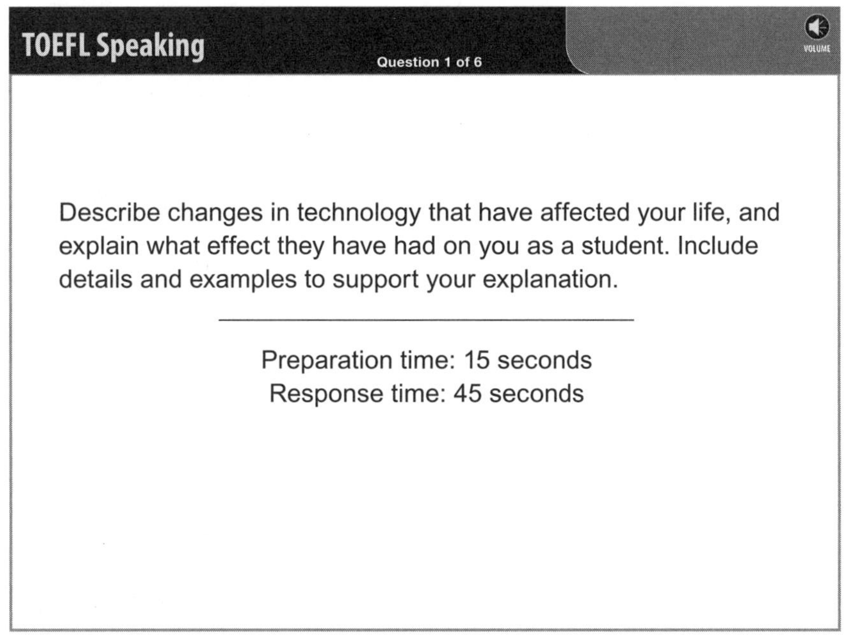
TOEFL Speaking
Question 1 of 6
VOLUME
Describe changes in technology that have affected your life, and explain what effect they have had on you as a student. Include details and examples to support your explanation.
Preparation time: 15 seconds
Response time: 45 seconds

You may begin to prepare your response after the beep.

Please begin speaking after the beep.

STOP ■

START ▶

2. Please listen carefully.

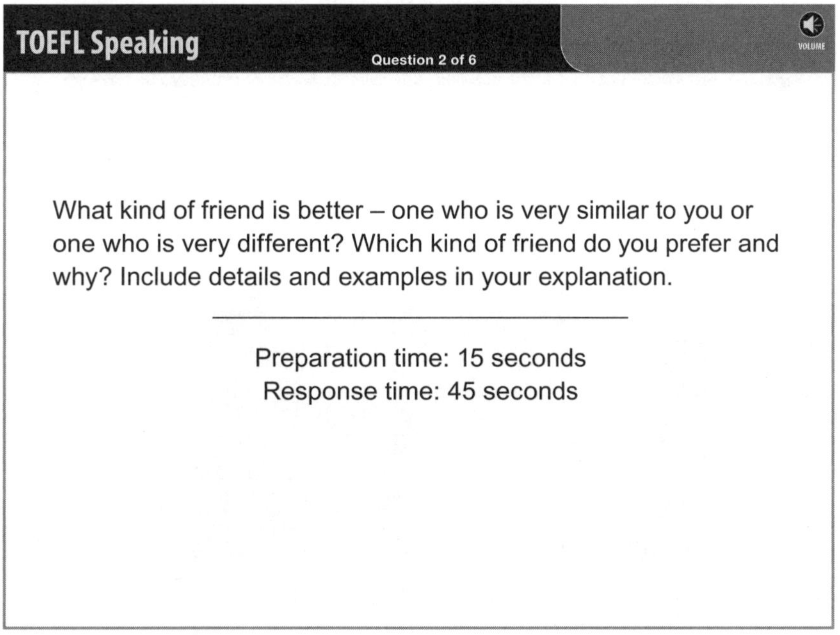
TOEFL Speaking
Question 2 of 6
VOLUME
What kind of friend is better – one who is very similar to you or one who is very different? Which kind of friend do you prefer and why? Include details and examples in your explanation.
Preparation time: 15 seconds
Response time: 45 seconds

You may begin to prepare your response after the beep.

Please begin speaking after the beep.

STOP ■

START ▶

3. Please listen carefully.

The University of the Rockies is announcing its annual job fair. Read the announcement from the Career Services Center. You will have 45 seconds to read the announcement. Begin reading now.

PAUSE II (for 45 seconds)

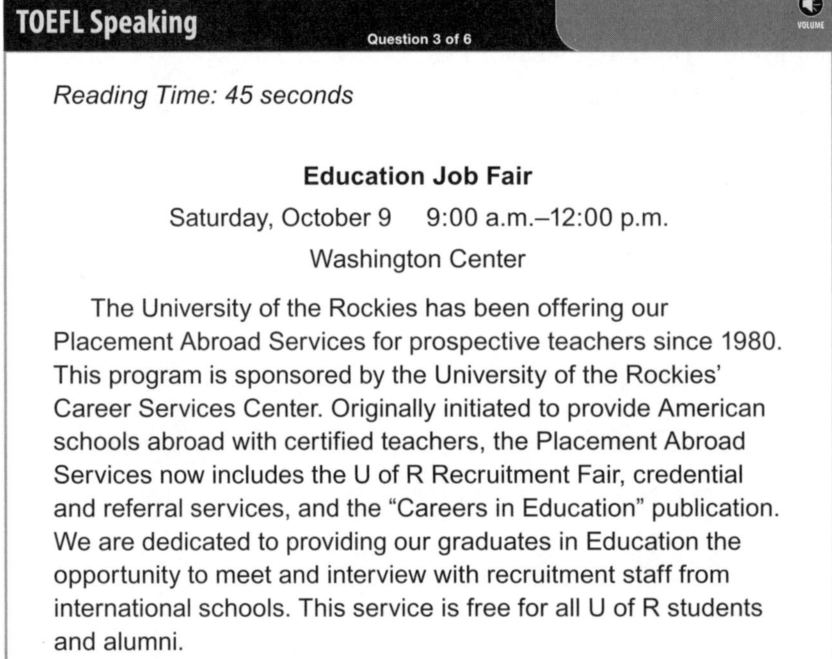

Now listen to two students as they discuss the announcement.

Now get ready to answer the question.

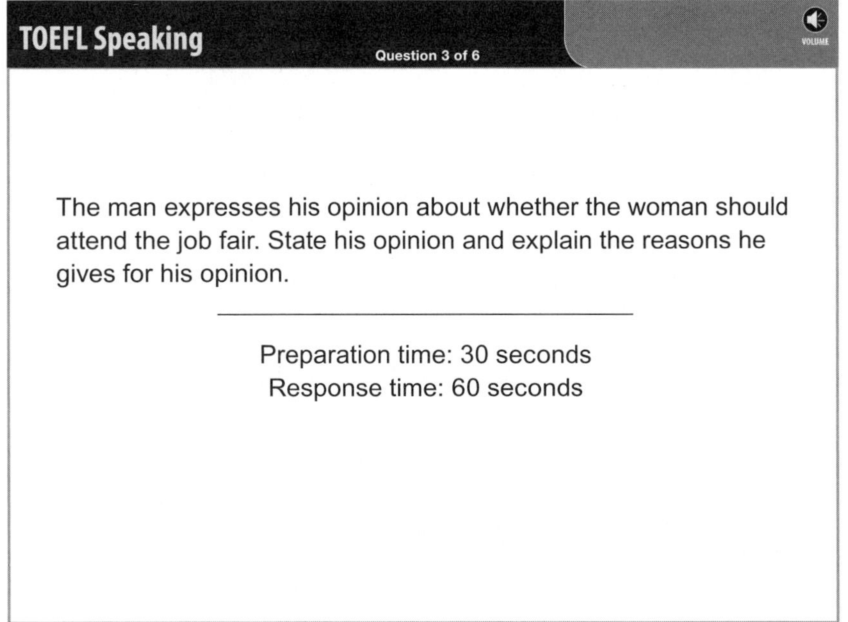

TOEFL Speaking
Question 3 of 6
VOLUME
The man expresses his opinion about whether the woman should attend the job fair. State his opinion and explain the reasons he gives for his opinion.
Preparation time: 30 seconds
Response time: 60 seconds

You may begin to prepare your response after the beep.

Please begin speaking after the beep.

STOP ■

START ▶

4. Please listen carefully.

Read the passage about misconceptions in mathematics. You have 45 seconds to read the passage. Begin reading now.

PAUSE II (for 45 seconds)

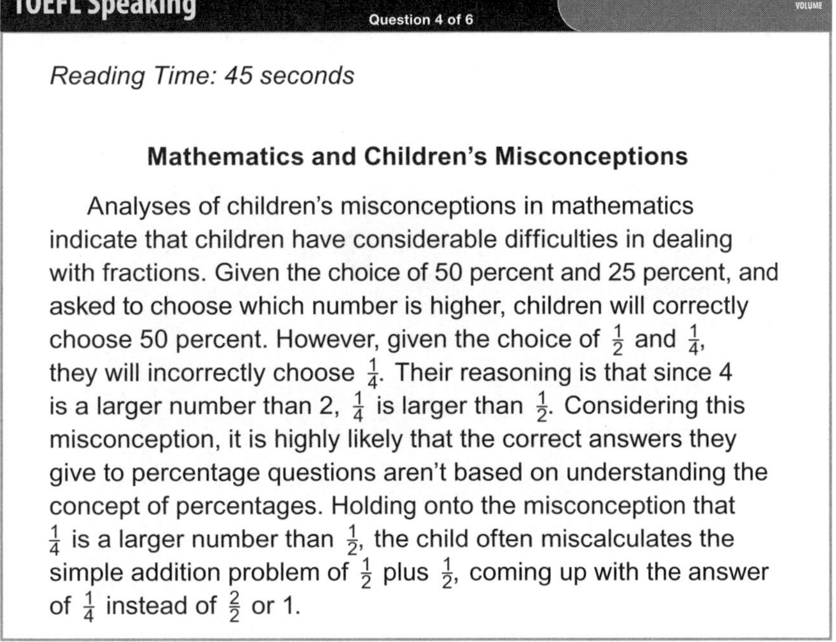

Reading Time: 45 seconds

Mathematics and Children's Misconceptions

Analyses of children's misconceptions in mathematics indicate that children have considerable difficulties in dealing with fractions. Given the choice of 50 percent and 25 percent, and asked to choose which number is higher, children will correctly choose 50 percent. However, given the choice of $\frac{1}{2}$ and $\frac{1}{4}$, they will incorrectly choose $\frac{1}{4}$. Their reasoning is that since 4 is a larger number than 2, $\frac{1}{4}$ is larger than $\frac{1}{2}$. Considering this misconception, it is highly likely that the correct answers they give to percentage questions aren't based on understanding the concept of percentages. Holding onto the misconception that $\frac{1}{4}$ is a larger number than $\frac{1}{2}$, the child often miscalculates the simple addition problem of $\frac{1}{2}$ plus $\frac{1}{2}$, coming up with the answer of $\frac{1}{4}$ instead of $\frac{2}{2}$ or 1.

Now listen to part of a lecture on this topic in a math education class.

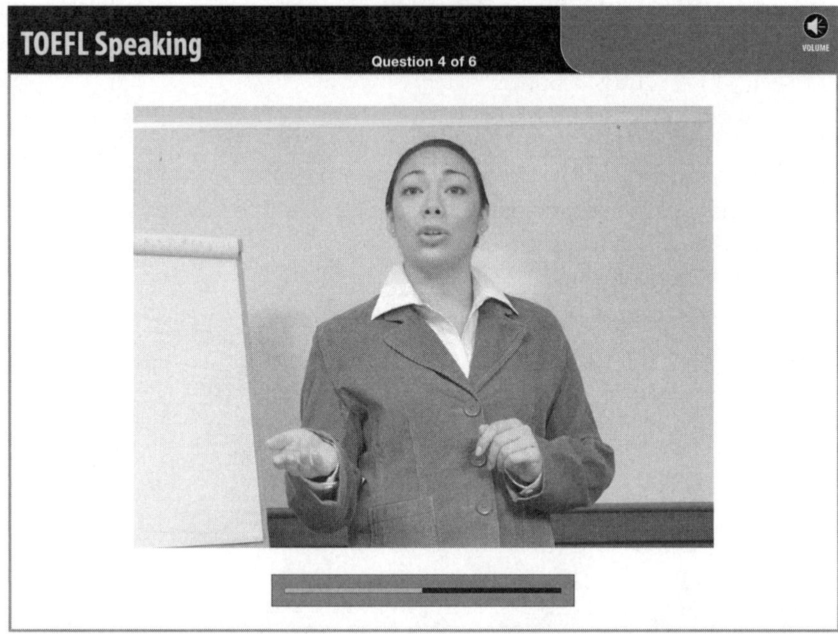

Now get ready to answer the question.

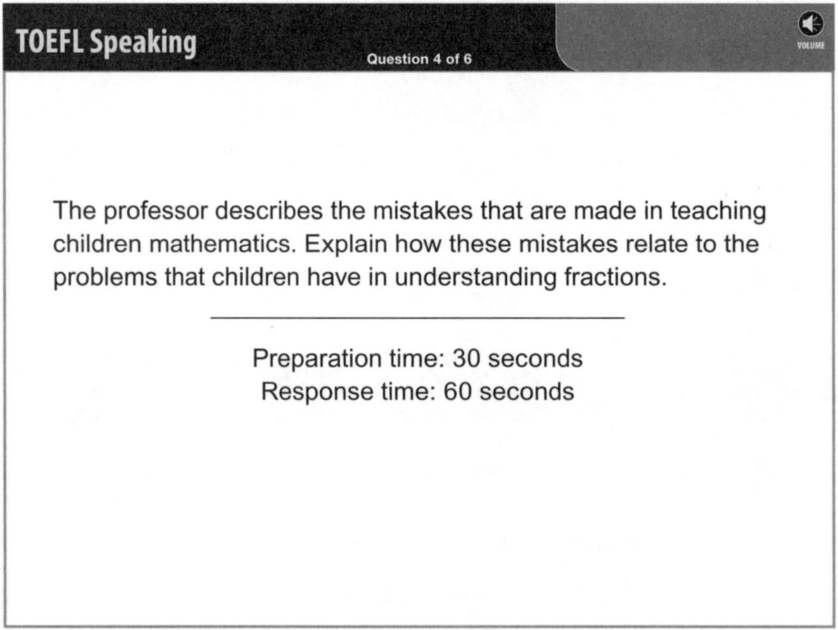

TOEFL Speaking
Question 4 of 6
VOLUME
The professor describes the mistakes that are made in teaching children mathematics. Explain how these mistakes relate to the problems that children have in understanding fractions.
Preparation time: 30 seconds
Response time: 60 seconds

You may begin to prepare your response after the beep.

Please begin speaking after the beep.

STOP ■

START ▶

5. Please listen carefully.

Listen to a conversation between two students.

Now get ready to answer the question.

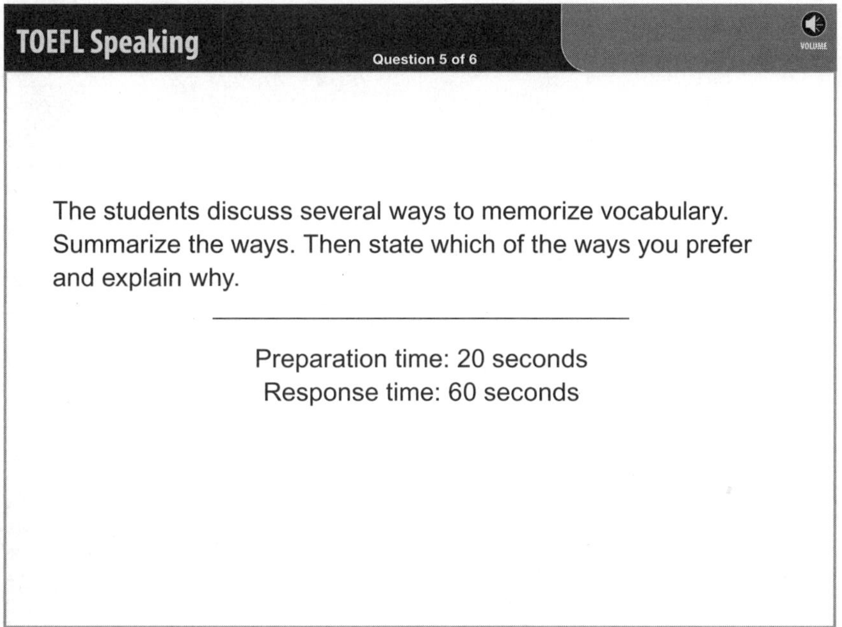

TOEFL Speaking
Question 5 of 6
VOLUME
The students discuss several ways to memorize vocabulary. Summarize the ways. Then state which of the ways you prefer and explain why.
Preparation time: 20 seconds
Response time: 60 seconds

You may begin to prepare your response after the beep.

Please begin speaking after the beep.

STOP ■

START ▶

6. Please listen carefully.

Listen to part of a lecture in an earth science class.

Now get ready to answer the question.

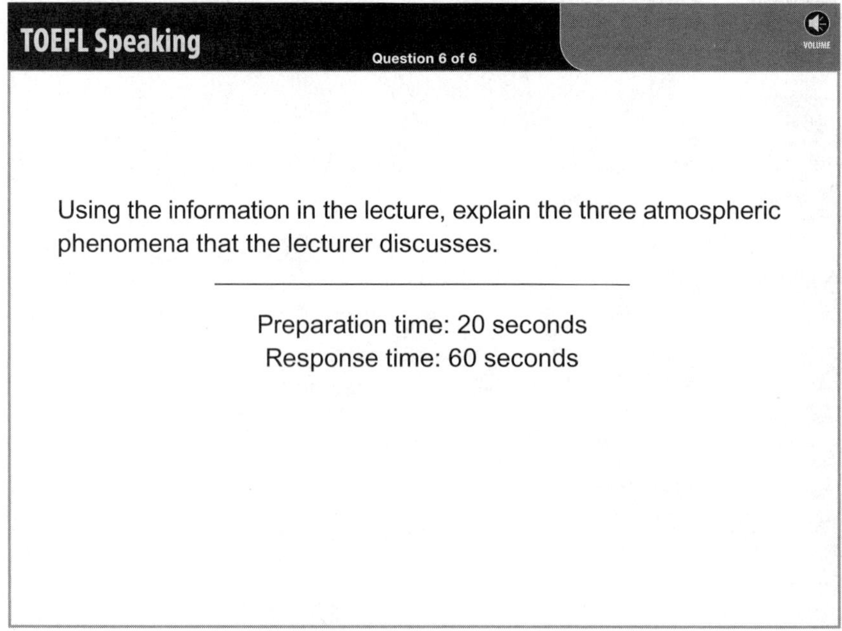

TOEFL Speaking
Question 6 of 6
VOLUME
Using the information in the lecture, explain the three atmospheric phenomena that the lecturer discusses.
Preparation time: 20 seconds
Response time: 60 seconds

You may begin to prepare your response after the beep.

Please begin speaking after the beep.

STOP ■

WRITING SECTION

Directions

This section measures your ability to use writing to communicate in an academic environment. There will be two writing tasks.

For the first writing task, you will read a passage and listen to a lecture, and then answer a question based on what you have read and heard. For the second writing task, you will answer a question based on your own knowledge and experience.

Now read the directions for the first writing task.

Writing Based on Reading and Listening

Directions

For this task, you will have three minutes to read a passage about an academic topic. You may take notes on the passage while you read. Then you will listen to a lecture about the same topic. While you listen, you may also take notes.

Then you will have 20 minutes to write a response to a question that asks you about the relationship between the lecture you heard and the reading passage. Try to answer the question as completely as possible using information from the reading passage and the lecture. The question does **not** ask you to express your personal opinion. You can refer to the reading passage again when it is time for you to write. You may use your notes to help you answer the question.

Typically, an effective response will be 150 to 225 words long. Your response will be judged on the quality of your writing and on the completeness and accuracy of the content. If you finish your response before time is up, go on to the second writing task.

On the day of the test, you will be required to type your response into a computer. Therefore, if you are taking this test in the book, practice typing your response on a computer.

INTEGRATED TASK

Directions: You have three minutes to read and take notes from the reading passage. Next, listen to the related lecture and take notes. Then write your response.

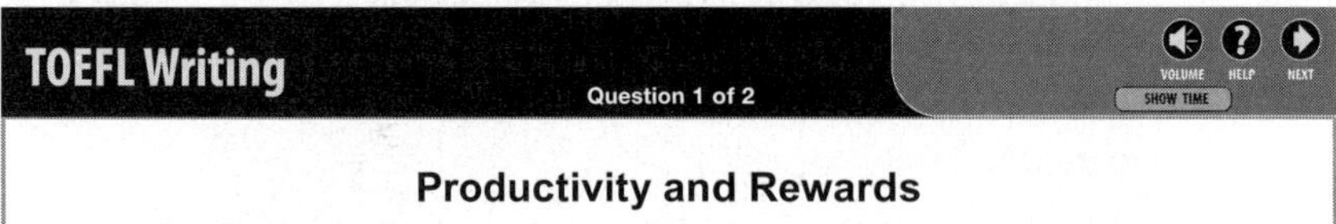

Productivity and Rewards

An important management principle is that when behavior is rewarded, it tends to be repeated. It follows that in many business enterprises, the approach to getting employees to work hard or improve productivity is to reward them with money or company stock. In addition, some enterprises use other forms of compensation such as special privileges or perhaps promotion or job reassignments or even company-paid luxury vacations and other bonuses in kind. All such rewards are usually tied in to some index of performance, which precisely calculates the relative amount of increased productivity.

Whatever the type of reward given, managerial consultants point out that the promise of such incentives improves employee attitudes, motivation, and productivity. Typical business handbooks describing compensation methods advocate giving the greatest rewards to those who perform the best. For example, a well-known academic text on incentives points out that "the closer the link between job performance and rewards, the greater the motivational effect."

Advocates of improving productivity through rewards tacitly accept that people are rather like physical bodies that require the application of some external motivating force to be set in motion. Furthermore, they argue that any such incentives must have a high perceived value to the employee and must also be perceived as within the reach of that person. If the productivity goal appears beyond the reach of the person striving for the reward, then the motivational effect will be lower and productivity may decline. But if the reward system is correctly structured, productivity experts argue, it is possible to persuade people to achieve remarkable results.

START ▶

Now listen to part of a lecture on the topic you just read about.

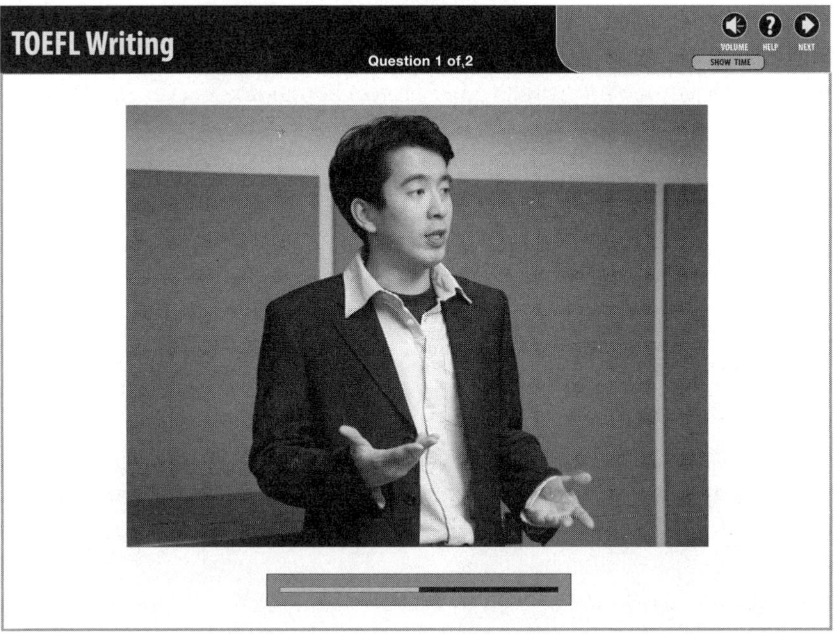

STOP ■

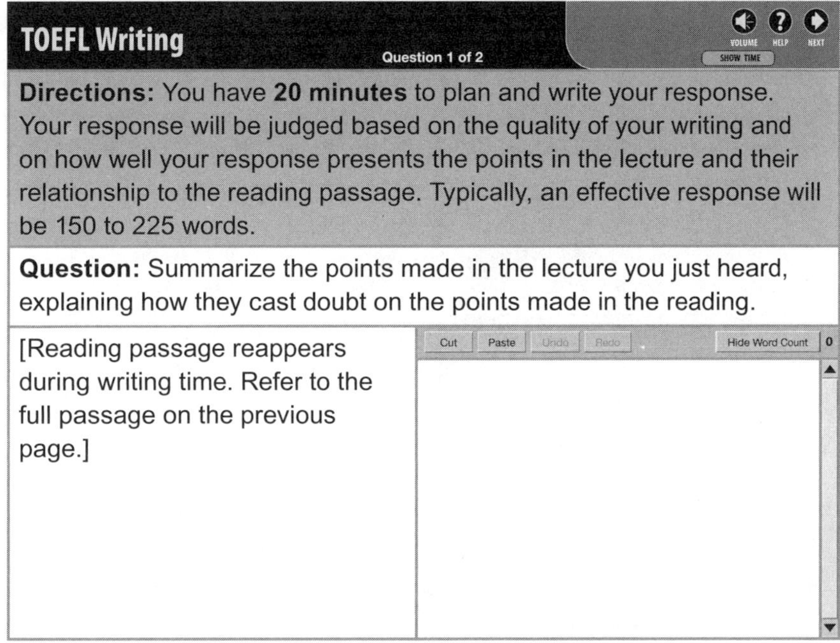

Writing Based on Knowledge and Experience

Directions

For this task, you will write an essay in response to a question that asks you to state, explain, and support your opinion on an issue. You will have 30 minutes to plan, write, and revise your essay.

Typically, an effective essay will contain a minimum of 300 words. Your essay will be judged on the quality of your writing. This includes the development of your ideas, the organization of your essay, and the quality and accuracy of the language you use to express your ideas.

On the day of the test, you will be required to type your response into a computer. Therefore, if you are taking this test in the book, practice typing your response on a computer.

INDEPENDENT WRITING TASK

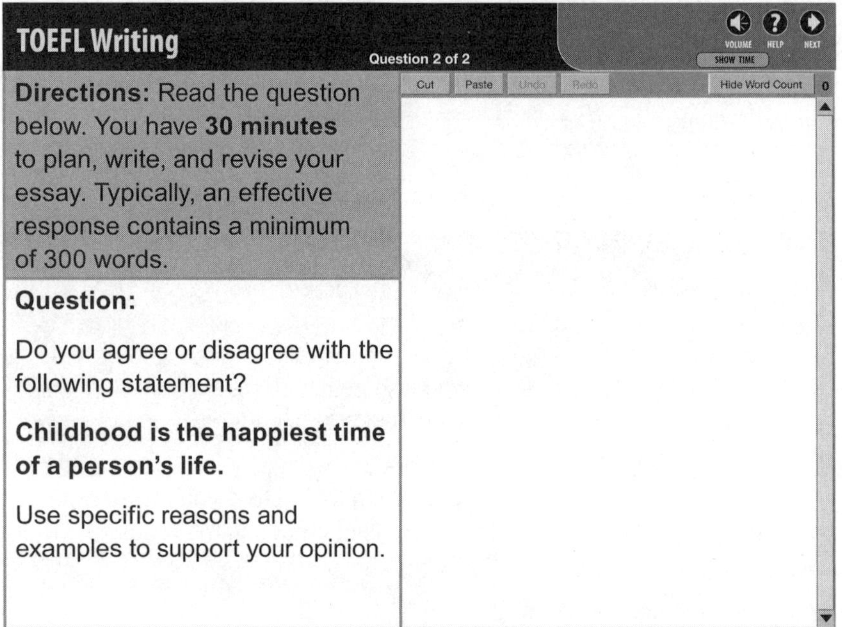

TOEFL Writing
Question 2 of 2
VOLUME HELP NEXT
SHOW TIME
Cut
Paste
Undo
Redo
Hide Word Count
0
Directions: Read the question below. You have **30 minutes** to plan, write, and revise your essay. Typically, an effective response contains a minimum of 300 words.
Question:
Do you agree or disagree with the following statement?
Childhood is the happiest time of a person's life.
Use specific reasons and examples to support your opinion.

PART 1

BUILDING SUPPORTING SKILLS

OVERVIEW

The TOEFL® iBT test directly measures your skills in reading, listening, speaking, and writing. Some supporting skills are tested indirectly. Others are not tested but will support your chances of doing well. Listed below are five categories of supporting skills you will need to develop in order to succeed on the test.

Learner strategies
You can enhance your learning by developing learner strategies. When you begin studying for the TOEFL test, it will be valuable to identify your strengths and weaknesses, analyze what motivates you, recognize your most effective learning strategies, set goals, plan a study schedule, and think about how to evaluate your progress. None of these strategies will be tested, but they will help you focus your study and do better on the test.

Note taking, paraphrasing, and summarizing
You are allowed to take notes throughout the TOEFL iBT test. Note taking is not required, but it is an important skill that will help you to focus your attention on the listening passages, remember the important points, and organize your thoughts in the integrated speaking and writing tasks. Paraphrasing and summarizing are also important skills that will help you succeed on the test.

Vocabulary
Your knowledge of vocabulary is tested in the Reading section. In addition, your ability to choose appropriate words to describe the main points and express your ideas will affect your score in the Speaking and Writing sections.

Pronunciation
The Speaking section is scored not only on how well you develop your responses but also on the clarity of your speech. Although you are not expected to have perfect native-speaker pronunciation, your ability to match English speech patterns closely will affect your score.

Grammar
There is no grammar section on the TOEFL iBT test, but how correctly and naturally you use a combination of basic and complex grammatical structures in the speaking and writing tasks will affect your score. A strong command of English grammar will also help you comprehend the material in the Reading and Listening sections.

LEARNER STRATEGIES

When you begin to study for the TOEFL test, it is worthwhile to plan your approach to preparing for the test and stick to that plan. You may want to consider the following activities.

Analyze your strengths Reflect on skills you are good at, what strengths you used to master those skills, and how you can use those strengths to reach your goals for the TOEFL test.

Identify your learning style Think about how you learn best. Use this knowledge to plan study sessions that fit your style of learning. Think of other learning styles and how they could fit into your approach to enhance your learning.

Motivate yourself Motivation refers to your desire to do something. Your motivation could be driven by external goals. For example, you may want to receive a score that will help you get into a prestigious university. Motivation can also be driven by internal goals. For example, you may want to study because you love foreign languages and want to improve your English. Think about what your motivations are for studying for the TOEFL test, and make a list. Refer to it often.

Set goals Goal-setting is an important process. You should set goals that are specific, challenging, and attainable. Set long-term goals, then come up with a list of smaller steps that lead toward attaining them. Use these steps to build a "goal map" of short-term goals that lead to your final goal.

Plan your study schedule Find time in your schedule that can be set aside for longer periods of concentrated study. Also, identify activities in your daily routine that can be combined with learning. For example, you can give 45-second speeches to yourself when you take a shower or practice thinking to yourself in English while you are commuting.

Check your progress Keep track of your progress and modify your study plans accordingly. Periodically review your goals and see if they need to be more challenging or more accessible.

Exercises LS1–LS13

Use Exercises LS1–LS13 to reflect on and develop your learning strategies.

EXERCISE LS1 *Identifying your strengths*

Think of a skill you are good at. Write it below.

I am good at ____

How do you know that you are good at the skill? Check (✓) all the reasons that apply.

I know this because

- ☐ I have won awards or prizes.
- ☐ I got a good grade in school.
- ☐ I have been praised for it.
- ☐ I was told that I was good at it by someone whose opinion I trust.
- ☐ I recognize my own ability.
- ☐ Other reasons: ____

____

EXERCISE LS2 *Analyzing your strengths*

Think about the skill you named in Exercise LS1. Write down specific activities that helped you master this skill. Write down what you did on your own and what someone else did to help you.

What I did on my own	What someone else did to help me

EXERCISE LS3 *Analyzing yourself as a teacher*

Think about a skill you learned by yourself. Write down what motivated you to learn how to do it, and the specific details of how you taught yourself. Then evaluate yourself.

1. I taught myself to ____
2. My motivation was ____

   ____
3. I taught myself in the following way(s):

   ____

   ____
4. How would I evaluate my ability in the skill that I taught myself?
   - ☐ excellent
   - ☐ good
   - ☐ average
   - ☐ poor
5. What do I base this evaluation on?

   ____

   ____

EXERCISE LS4 *Building a picture of your learning process*

Review Exercises LS1–LS2, which analyze skills you have successfully learned, and Exercise LS3, which analyzes skills you taught yourself. Then answer the questions.

1. Do I see a pattern in the way I have succeeded in mastering skills?

   ____

   ____

2. What differences are there in the ways I approach the learning process?

____

____

3. What affects my motivation?

____

____

EXERCISE LS5 *Recognizing your learning style*

For each of the four learning styles listed below, check (✓) all of the characteristics that describe you well. Then count the total number of checks for each one. Which style describes you best? Read the analysis of your learning style in the chart on the next page.

The problem solver

- ☐ I examine all parts of a task.
- ☐ I like to understand things first.
- ☐ I plan how to approach a task.
- ☐ I enjoy the challenge of difficult tasks.
- ☐ I like my work to be perfect.

_____ Total

The explorer

- ☐ I find everything interesting.
- ☐ I collect unrelated bits of information.
- ☐ I like details even though I seldom remember them.
- ☐ I have difficulty deciding what is relevant.
- ☐ I concentrate on the whole picture instead of the details.

_____ Total

The go-getter

- ☐ I tend to start in on the activity without reading instructions.
- ☐ I solve problems through trial and error.
- ☐ I like to see someone else do it first and then have the opportunity to do it myself.
- ☐ I need lots of breaks while studying because I think better when I can move around.
- ☐ I like to get on to the next activity quickly.

_____ Total

The daydreamer

- ☐ I add lots of pictures and arrows in my notes.
- ☐ I remember better if I write information down.
- ☐ I picture things in my mind.
- ☐ I work best in a quiet place.
- ☐ I think a lot about the topics.

_____ Total

Analyses of the four learning styles

	Learning strengths	Skills to be developed
The problem solver	• analytical thinking • critical thinking • organizational skills • solution-oriented	• creative thinking • stress management • working with others • risk taking
The explorer	• extensive knowledge • seeing connections • highly motivated • inventive	• time planning • priority setting • analytical thinking • sorting essential/ nonessential items
The go-getter	• quick starter • completes tasks quickly • motivator • problem solver	• time planning • creative thinking • considering alternatives • increasing concentration
The daydreamer	• reflective • gets to essence of things • successful visualizing • creative thinking	• time planning • scheduling • priority setting • distraction avoidance

EXERCISE LS6 *Reflecting on your approach to learning*

Answer the questions.

1. What tactics do I use to remember something important?

____

____

2. How do I demonstrate to myself that I have learned something?

____

____

3. How do I motivate myself?

____

____

4. What am I going to do to develop the skills I need?

____

____

5. How can I incorporate all approaches to improving the following English skills?

   Reading

____

____

Listening

Speaking

Writing

EXERCISE LS7 *Managing motivation*

Answer the questions.

1. What can I do to make an activity interesting for myself?

2. How can I build up my enthusiasm?

3. How can I avoid getting discouraged when my progress seems slow?

4. What kinds of goals can I set?

EXERCISE LS8 *Creating a learning environment*

Answer the questions.

1. At what times of the day do I feel most mentally alert (e.g., early morning, late at night)?

2. How do I deal with distractions (e.g., block them out, leave the area)?

3. What environment is most helpful for my learning (e.g., music playing in the background, total silence)?

4. What can I do to create that learning environment?

____

____

5. How can I incorporate study time into my daily schedule (e.g., set aside specific time, review things while waiting in a line)?

____

____

EXERCISE LS9 *Assessing your skills*

The charts below and on the pages that follow list the skills you need to succeed on each section of the TOEFL test. For each skill, rate yourself on a scale from 1 to 5. Check (✓) the box.

1 = poor	2 = weak	3 = average	4 = good	5 = excellent

Reading section

Think about the reading passages you completed in the Diagnostic Test as you rate yourself on each of the reading skills below.

	1	2	3	4	5
I understand the general topic of a passage.					
I understand the overall meaning of a passage.					
I understand inferences.					
I can draw conclusions.					
I understand the main ideas.					
I understand the details.					
I understand most words in context.					
I know the words that are given as choices to the vocabulary items.					
I understand the pronoun references and other phrases that refer to other parts of the passage.					
I understand long and complicated sentences.					
I am good at picking out the important parts of a passage.					
I understand how the grammar of a sentence conveys meaning.					
I can summarize a passage in my own words.					
I can complete tables based on the information in the passage.					
I understand how connecting words join the ideas between sentences.					
I can recognize restatements of the information in a passage.					
I understand the connection of ideas for inserting information.					
I recognize when information has not been included in a passage.					

Listening section

Think about the passages you heard in the Diagnostic Test as you rate yourself on each of the listening skills below.

	1	2	3	4	5
I understand the general topic of a passage.					
I understand the overall meaning of a passage.					
I understand inferences.					
I can draw conclusions.					
I understand the main ideas.					
I understand the details.					
I understand most words in context.					
I understand the pronoun references and other phrases that refer to other parts of the passage.					
I am good at picking out the important parts of a passage.					
I understand how the grammar of a sentence conveys meaning.					
I understand when the speakers use filler words like "um" and "ah."					
I understand when the speakers make mistakes that they correct.					
I understand when the speakers interrupt themselves.					
I understand when the speakers hesitate.					
I understand incomplete phrases.					
I can relate ideas throughout a passage.					

Speaking section

Think about the speaking tasks you completed in the Diagnostic Test as you rate yourself on each of the speaking skills below and on the next page.

	1	2	3	4	5
I can pronounce English consonants.					
I can pronounce combinations of consonants.					
I can pronounce English vowels.					
I can pronounce combinations of vowels.					
I can reproduce English stress patterns.					
I can reproduce English rhythms.					
I can reproduce English intonation patterns.					
I speak clearly.					
I speak at a natural speed – not too fast, not too slow.					
I organize my ideas logically.					

Speaking section *(continued)*

	1	2	3	4	5
I connect my ideas correctly.					
I use correct structures.					
I choose precise words.					
I focus on the important points.					
I show the relationships between ideas.					
I choose relevant information.					
I include appropriate details.					
I put given information into my own words.					
I answer the requirements of the tasks.					
I budget my time well.					

Writing section

Think about the writing tasks you completed in the Diagnostic Test as you rate yourself on each of the writing skills below.

	1	2	3	4	5
I organize my ideas logically.					
I connect my ideas correctly.					
I choose precise words.					
I use correct structures.					
I make my sentences concise.					
I introduce the topic.					
I focus on the important points.					
I show the relationships between ideas.					
I choose relevant information to support my ideas.					
I include appropriate details for my supporting ideas.					
I select the relevant information from the reading and listening passages.					
I put given information into my own words.					
I present the information from the passages accurately.					
I include all the important points from the passages.					
I make connections between the reading and listening passages.					
I write a concise conclusion.					
I make corrections.					
I budget my time well.					

EXERCISE LS10 *Setting goals*

Think about your English language skills, your learning style and approach to learning, the way you motivate yourself, and your ideal learning environment. Write your answers to the following questions about your goals:

1. What have I achieved so far?
2. What do I need to achieve?
3. How can I state my goals in a specific way? ("Increase my vocabulary" is not a specific goal. "Add five new words to my vocabulary every day" is a specific goal.)
4. What goals should I give priority to?
5. How can I break my long-term goals into short-term ones?
6. How am I going to break my short-term goals into small, achievable steps?
7. What time limits am I going to set on each step?
8. How will I know that I have met my short-term goals?

EXERCISE LS11 *Reviewing your goals*

Read the questions below and review the goals you wrote in Exercise LS10. Adjust your goals accordingly.

1. Have I focused on important skills to learn?
2. Have I set my goals too low? In other words, are they too easy and not challenging enough?
3. Have I set my goals too high? Are they so high that I will fail and get discouraged?
4. Are my goals accessible? (For example, you have control over a goal such as "I will practice speaking English for one hour every day," but you might not have control over a goal such as "I will practice speaking English to a native English speaker every day.")

EXERCISE LS12 *Planning your study schedule*

1. List the times during the week that you are available to study for the TOEFL test. Look at the example below.

Times during the week I can study for the TOEFL test.

Monday
8 AM – 9:30 AM
7 PM – 10 PM

Tuesday
8 AM – 9:30 AM
4 PM – 6 PM

Wednesday
8 AM – 10 AM

Thursday
4 PM – 10 PM

Friday
10 AM – 11:30 AM

Saturday
10 AM – 12 PM

Sunday
8 PM – 10 PM

2. Make a chart like the one below for each week remaining before the TOEFL test. Look at your goals and think about what you want to accomplish. Then fill in your chart for the first week.

Week of: January 8–14							
	Mon.	Tues.	Wed.	Thurs.	Fri.	Sat.	Sun.
8 AM – 10 AM	Work on Listening section in my TOEFL book.	1. Give oral summary of documentary while making breakfast. 2. Review vocabulary while on the bus.	Work on Listening section in my TOEFL book.				
10 AM – 12 PM					Meet English conversation partner at cafeteria. Give oral summary of last night's lecture.		
12 PM – 3 PM							
3 PM – 6 PM		Work on Reading section in my TOEFL book.		Attend lecture at Lyceum Hall. Take notes.			
6 PM – 10 PM	Watch documentary on English channel. Take notes. Look up unfamiliar words.			Go over notes from lecture. Look up unfamiliar words.			View English-language movie.

EXERCISE LS13 *Tracking your progress*

Look at the chart below. Make a similar chart to suit your individual needs. Use the chart to keep track of your progress.

Goal
Date work was begun
Amount of time spent on the goal
Evaluation
What I did that was successful in reaching or trying to reach this goal
What I learned that will help me in the next goal

NOTE TAKING, PARAPHRASING, AND SUMMARIZING

In addition to the four major skill areas assessed on the TOEFL test (reading, listening, speaking, and writing), there are several supplementary skills that will help you succeed on the test as well as in your academic studies. These skills – note taking, paraphrasing, and summarizing – are not directly tested on the TOEFL test, but mastering them will help you improve your score. Strategies for developing these skills are presented below.

Note taking

Note taking is an important skill for any student to develop. The average student in an American university spends 12–16 hours a week in classroom lectures and discussions. Taking notes is the most effective way to organize and remember what you hear in class, as well as what you read outside of class. Here are some reasons you will want to take notes on the TOEFL test:

- Taking notes will help you focus your attention on the content of the reading and listening passages.
- Organized notes will help you to develop a well-organized speech or essay in the time allotted.
- Writing down information will help you to remember main ideas and details.
- If you forget any details, you can refer back to your notes.

To be a good note taker, you need to develop two skills: writing notes quickly and understanding what is important in a passage. To write notes quickly, you can learn to use abbreviations and symbols, use a format, and organize ideas to show relationships clearly. To take good notes on a passage, it's important to be able to identify the topic, identify the important points, and understand the logic and the organization of the passage.

On the TOEFL iBT test, you will encounter written and spoken texts. Strategies and suggestions for taking notes from each type of passage are outlined below.

Taking notes from written texts

In order to take effective notes from a written passage, follow these steps:

1. Read the complete passage. Reread any part you don't understand.
2. Identify important information: the specific topic and main ideas.
3. Write a quick list of the important points. Use abbreviations.
4. Paraphrase the main ideas to avoid repeating exact phrases from the text.

Taking notes from spoken texts

Taking notes from spoken texts can be challenging, especially in a language that is not your own. Developing effective listening strategies will help you to overcome any anxiety, concentrate on content, and take better notes. Some strategies for effective listening are listed below:

- If you are attending a live lecture, sit at the front of the room. You will be able to hear more clearly and experience fewer distractions.
- Focus your attention on what the lecturer is saying. If you are listening to a live lecture or viewing one on a screen, do not let his or her manner of speaking distract you. Learn common ways in which native speakers hesitate, use filler phrases, and self-correct. (See Practice with Understanding Natural Speech, p. 254).
- Listen for signal words and phrases that indicate that important information is coming next. These signals help you to know when to take notes.
- Try to anticipate what the lecturer will talk about next. In this way, you can avoid getting behind and missing important details as you write.
- Try to quickly organize your notes as you write. Use one of the methods illustrated in Exercise NPS1 on p. 55 to clearly define main points versus supporting details.
- Determine how the lecture ties in with previous lectures, reading assignments, and the general subject matter. In other words, ask yourself how a lecture fits into the larger picture.

Knowing when important information is about to be presented is an essential skill in effective note taking. In the types of listening passages you will encounter on the test, listen for signals that important ideas or details are to come.

Signals in conversations In a conversation, there are several signals, or markers, you can listen for that indicate important ideas. These include:

- One speaker asking the other speaker for an explanation
- One speaker agreeing with a point made by the other speaker
- One speaker adding details to a point made by the other speaker
- One speaker disagreeing with a point made by the other speaker
- One speaker presenting information that conflicts with a point made by the other speaker

You will also need to listen for a speaker's attitude and degree of certainty. A speaker will indicate these through:

- The use of intonation and stress patterns
- The choice of words – for example, "It must be true that . . ." or "Experts say . . ."

Signals in lectures In a lecture, there are several ways in which a speaker can indicate an important point. These include:

- Saying it slower and louder, sometimes with a pause
- Repeating it
- Drawing attention to it – for example, "I want to stress that . . ." or "The crucial thing to remember is . . ."

Lecturers can indicate a new point or details by:

- Using transitions and connecting words
- Using signals – for example, "There are three reasons why . . . ," "I'd like to move on to . . . ," "Next we have . . . ," or "Most important . . ."

For a list of signal words and phrases, see Connecting Ideas Between Sentences or Paragraphs (Transition Words), p. 117.

Paraphrasing

Learning to paraphrase quickly and effectively will help you understand and remember the main points and important details from reading passages and lectures. Paraphrasing is also an important skill to use in the integrated tasks on the TOEFL iBT test. If you can paraphrase what you've heard or read, your speech or essay will be clearer and more accurate.

To paraphrase effectively, it is important to have clear notes on what you have read or heard. Look at your notes and think about how you might explain the material to someone who is unfamiliar with the topic. Then write or speak using synonyms, simplified words, and different sentence structures from the original passage to clearly explain the concepts.

To practice paraphrasing skills, follow these steps:

1. Read a text or listen to a spoken passage several times to be sure that you have fully understood the material.
2. Take abbreviated notes using one of the methods illustrated in Exercises NPS2 and NPS3 on p. 57.
3. Write full sentences in your own words to explain the concepts and details outlined in your notes.
4. Keep in mind that your audience may not be familiar with the topic. Use simplified words to paraphrase and restate the main points and supporting details.
5. Compare your version of the text or lecture with the original to make sure it is accurate. Make any adjustments and evaluate any need for improvement.

Summarizing

You will need to learn how to clearly and accurately summarize what you have read or heard in order to succeed on the TOEFL test as well as in your university studies. A summary differs from a paraphrase in that it does not present a full account of the material, but rather describes only the major points. An effective summary is concise, clear, and coherent, and much shorter than the original text.

To summarize effectively, make sure you have understood what you have read or heard and taken clear notes. If you have paraphrased the material in your notes, think about the main points and how they connect on a general level. If your notes are in outline form, look at the main categories and think about how to link them clearly without including too much detail:

To practice summarizing skills, follow these steps:

1. Read a text or listen to a spoken passage several times to make sure that you have fully understood the material.
2. Take abbreviated notes using one of the methods illustrated in Exercises NPS2 and NPS3 on p. 57.
3. Organize your notes in a way that clearly shows the hierarchy of main points versus supporting details.
4. Determine the author's or speaker's main purpose, intent, and meaning.
5. Convey the main points of the text or lecture in one or two coherent paragraphs.

Exercises NPS1–NPS10

Use Exercises NPS1–NPS10 to reflect on your note-taking strategies and to practice paraphrasing and summarizing.

EXERCISE NPS1 *Thinking about methods of note taking*

Read the lecture excerpt. Below the excerpt are examples of five different ways to organize notes on the excerpt. Check (✓) the ones that you think would be useful to you.

In the Americas, two complex societies emerged at the end of the first millennium BCE: the Mayan civilization in Mesoamerica and the Moche/Nazca states in Peru. Both these civilizations were founded on the cultivation of maize and were dominated by ceremonial centers constructed for a priestly elite. By the beginning of the second millennium CE, these states had been replaced by imperial civilizations – the Aztecs taking over the Mayan civilization and the Incas, the Moche/Nazca states.

☐ 1. Column or charting method

	Amer civs btwn 1st mil BCE & 1st mil CE	
	1. Maya – MesoAm	
		cultiv corn
		dom by cerem ctrs
	conq by Aztecs 2nd mil	
		empire dom
	2. Moche/Nazca – Peru	
		cultiv corn
		dom by cerem ctrs
	conq by Incas 2nd mil	
		empire dom

☐ 2. Outline method

A. Amer. Civ.s 1st mil BCE.
  1. Maya – MesoAm
    a. cultiv corn
    b. cerem cntrs
  2. Moche/Nazca – Peru
    a. as above
    b. "
B. Imperialist 2nd mil CE.
  1. Aztecs conq Maya
  2. Incas " M/N

☐ 3. Mind map method

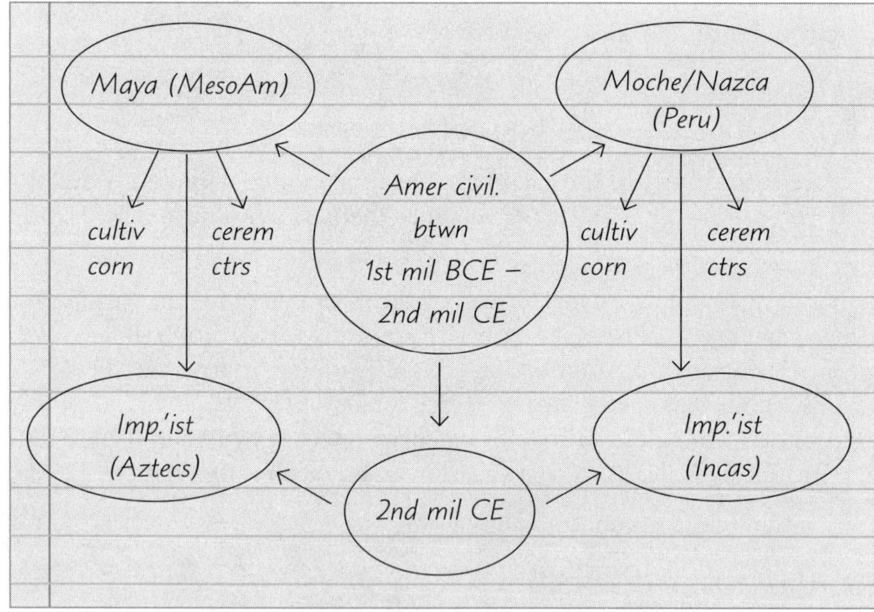

☐ 4. Pyramid method

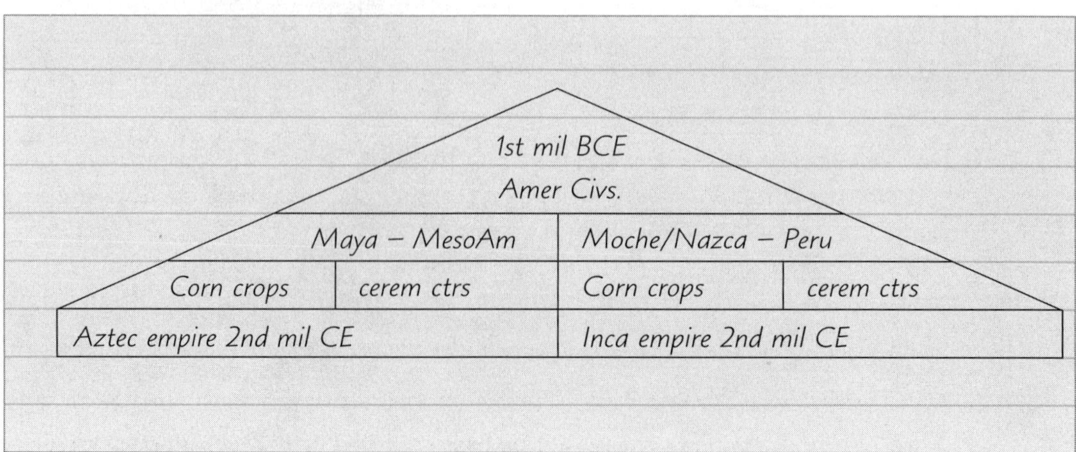

☐ 5. Flow chart method

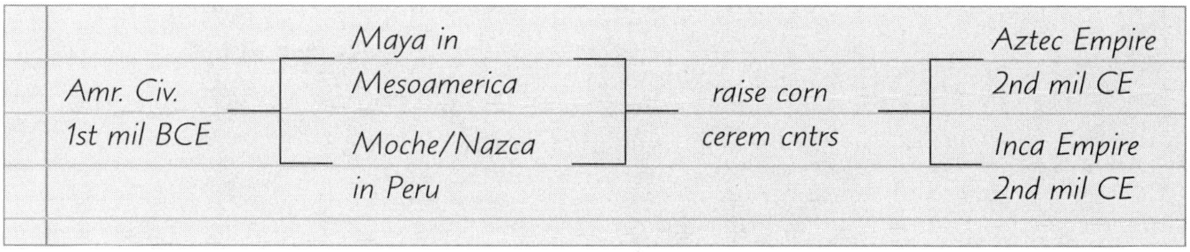

		Maya in		Aztec Empire
Amr. Civ.		Mesoamerica	raise corn	2nd mil CE
1st mil BCE		Moche/Nazca	cerem cntrs	Inca Empire
		in Peru		2nd mil CE

EXERCISE NPS2 *Using short forms*

Practice using abbreviated forms by writing your own short form of the words listed below.

department	*dpt*
percentages	*%s*
anthropologist	*anthrop.*

1. association ________________
2. World Health Organization ________________
3. for example ________________
4. lexicography ________________
5. building ________________
6. equals ________________
7. concentrated ________________
8. chapters ________________
9. developing ________________
10. without ________________

EXERCISE NPS3 *Abbreviating sentences*

Read the sentences, and write them in a shortened form.

> The decrease in the number of birds has had the effect of an increase in the insect population.
>
> *↓ # birds = ↑ bug pop*
>
> *Decrease* is represented by the arrow pointing downward. The symbol # means *number*, the symbol = means *equals* and refers to the results of the decrease in birds. *Increase* is represented by the arrow pointing upward. The word *bug* is a shorter word meaning *insect*, and *pop* is an abbreviation for *population*.

1. Ironworking probably spread to the rest of Africa via the Meroitic civilization.

   ____

2. Finely ground pigments mixed with a base such as egg yolk was the exclusive medium for painting panels in the Middle Ages.

   ____

3. Trade relations between Egypt and Africa began in 1460 BCE when Queen Hatshepsut sent her ships to the country of Punt, today's Somalia.

   ____

4. The Freedom of Information Act, passed by the U.S. Congress in 1966, gives U.S. citizens the right of access to public records.

   ____

5. In the Sonora Desert, the daytime temperatures rise to 50 degrees Celsius.

   ____

EXERCISE NPS4 *Predicting what will follow a signal word or words*

Write the kind of information you would expect to hear when a speaker uses the connecting words below.

in other words *a repetition of a previous point but said in a different way*

1. likewise ______________________________
2. therefore ______________________________
3. as an illustration ______________________________
4. granted that ______________________________
5. incidentally ______________________________
6. previously ______________________________
7. conversely ______________________________
8. furthermore ______________________________
9. above all ______________________________
10. to summarize ______________________________

EXERCISE NPS5 *Analyzing note-taking strategies*

Answer the questions.

1. How can I increase my speed in taking notes?

   ____

   ____

2. How can I organize my notes to show cause-and-effect relationships?

   ____

   ____

3. How can I organize my notes to show comparisons and contrasts in passages?

   ____

   ____

4. How can I organize my notes to indicate the reasoning for and against an argument in passages?

____

____

5. How can I organize my notes to combine the points made in the tasks that integrate reading and listening?

____

____

EXERCISE NPS6 *Taking abbreviated notes*

Read the excerpts from texts and lectures. Write abbreviated notes in the format of your choice.

Chief Washakie was the head chief of the Shoshone tribes from the mid-1800s. He earned this position through his bravery in battles and his wisdom in statesmanship. As a charismatic leader with linguistic abilities in French, English, and numerous Native American languages, Chief Washakie negotiated a treaty that protected the lands of the Shoshone people and provided them with education and health care. In 1900, after 60 years of leadership, Chief Washakie, the man known as the "Peacemaker," died. He is the only Native American chief to have been given the honor of a full military funeral by orders from the president of the United States, President McKinley.

Washakie → Shoshone chief, 1800s

Qualities → brave, wise, charismatic, multilingual

Treaty → protect lands, provide edu & health

Died → 1900, peacemaker, only Native American chief buried U.S. military honors

1. Rube Goldberg earned his degree in engineering, but a love for drawing led him into the cartooning profession. Although Goldberg's career in cartooning involved a variety of different creations, he is perhaps best known for the absurd inventions of Professor Lucifer Gorgonzola Butts. Typically, these inventions, sometimes referred to as "Rube Goldberg's inventions," consisted of outrageously complicated designs for machines that performed ridiculously simple tasks. Every year, a nationwide Rube Goldberg invention contest is sponsored by the engineering fraternity at Purdue University. University students are required to design and engineer an impractical machine to perform in less than 9 minutes a simple task using more than 20 processes. Past assignments have included designing a device that turns off an alarm clock and one that cleans and peels an apple.

____

____

____

____

____

2. When sound waves hit an object, they are reflected back. This is called an *echo*. Several species of animals use a system of emitting sounds and listening for the subsequent echoes in order to navigate or find food. This system is called *echolocation*. Echolocation makes it possible for these species to reduce their dependency on sight while hunting at night, living in dark areas such as in caves (as in the case of bats and some birds), or swimming through cloudy or dark water (as in the case of whales and dolphins).

   You may be surprised that not all whales use echolocation. Only the toothed whales, *Odontoceti*, have this capability, although baleen whales do have the apparatus for echolocation in a vestigial form, which suggests that they may have been capable of using echolocation in the past. I will go on now to discuss odontocete skull anatomy and how echolocation is achieved.

   ____

   ____

   ____

   ____

   ____

3. If scores on IQ tests are anything to go by, it seems that people are becoming more intelligent. Since the 1950s, test scores have been rising, and although many studies have been undertaken, the reasons for the rise in IQ scores remain a mystery. Factors such as the decrease in family size, improved nutrition, higher living standards, access to a better education, or a combination of these factors may account for some of the increase. Since increases have tended to be in those areas measuring abstract reason, it has been suggested that children have been stimulated by the visual effects of television and the problem-solving challenges of video games. But beyond just IQ, researchers are also beginning to study Emotional Intelligence, or EI. A person with high EI has a self-awareness that enables a better understanding of his or her own emotions and how to manage them. Furthermore, that person has the ability to be empathetic toward others. You might call this having good social skills.

   There are people with high IQs who lack emotional intelligence. However, people with emotional intelligence tend to have the capacity to keep their emotions from interfering with solving intellectual problems, and therefore, they do well on IQ tests. It has also been shown that IQ scores drop dramatically when people with low emotional intelligence have allowed negative feelings to interfere with intellectual tasks required on IQ tests.

   ____

   ____

   ____

   ____

   ____

EXERCISE NPS7 *Paraphrasing spoken and written texts*

Using your notes from Exercise NPS6, paraphrase the original texts and lectures.

The leader of the Shoshone tribes in the mid- to late 1800s was Chief Washakie. He was a brave, wise, and charismatic man who could speak many languages. He made a treaty that protected Shoshone lands and gave his people access to education and health services. When he died in 1900, he was known as the "Peacemaker," and he is the only Native American chief buried with U.S. military honors.

1. ______________________________

2. ______________________________

3. ______________________________

EXERCISE NPS8 *Summarizing spoken and written texts*

Using your notes and sentences from Exercises NPS6–NPS7, write short summaries of the original text and lectures.

Chief Washakie was a talented leader of the Shoshone tribes during the 1800s who helped protect and serve his people by negotiating a treaty for peace. At his death in 1900, he became the only Native American chief to be honored with a U.S. military funeral.

1. ______________________________

2. ____

____

____

____

3. ____

____

____

____

EXERCISE NPS9 *Determining your resources*

Read the list of resources you can use to practice taking notes, paraphrasing, and summarizing. Check (✓) the resources that are available to you.

Listening materials

- ☐ the listening and integrated skills sections of this book
- ☐ the listening and integrated skills tasks in the tests that accompany this book
- ☐ audio cassettes or CDs
- ☐ videotapes
- ☐ CD-ROMs
- ☐ DVDs
- ☐ radio programs
- ☐ TV programs
- ☐ lectures given in English
- ☐ online lectures in English

Written materials

- ☐ the reading and integrated skills sections of this book
- ☐ the reading and integrated skills tasks in the tests that accompany this book
- ☐ English-language newspapers
- ☐ English-language magazines
- ☐ English-language textbooks
- ☐ online reading material in English

EXERCISE NPS10 *Planning a study strategy*

Plan a strategy for improving your note-taking, paraphrasing, and summarizing skills.

1. The note-taking, paraphrasing, and summarizing skills I need to work on:

____

____

2. What I am going to do to improve and how I am going to do it:

____

____

3. How I am going to evaluate my progress:

____

____

VOCABULARY

The more extensive your vocabulary is, the more successful you will be on all parts of the TOEFL test. In TOEFL reading passages and lectures on the test you will encounter a wide variety of formal and academic words. Those found in conversations tend to be less academic. Also, an effective choice of words in the writing and speaking tasks will improve your score.

The best ways to expand your vocabulary are to spend as much time as you can reading and listening to English, and to make good use of reference books such as a dictionary and thesaurus. Some notes on using a dictionary and thesaurus are given here.

Using a dictionary

Invest in a good English dictionary. A good dictionary will have more information than just meanings. Look for a dictionary that includes the following information:

- The pronunciation of the word
- How the word is used grammatically, for example, whether it is a noun (*n.*), verb (*v.*), etc.
- Clear definitions
- An example of the word used in a sentence or phrase
- The origins of the word – this information can help you learn new words by giving you the meaning of the parts of the word (prefixes, roots, and suffixes)

Learn common prefixes and suffixes. Prefixes and suffixes are additions placed at the beginning and end of a root word (the base element of a word) to modify its meaning. Knowledge of these additions will help you expand your vocabulary. Consider this chart for the root word *pose,* meaning *to put or present.*

Prefix	Root word	Suffix	Meaning and example
ex- (out or from)	pose		expose: to uncover, disclose, or reveal *When the tide went out, the shells were exposed.*
im- (in, on, into, toward, or against)	pose		impose: to place upon, usually forcefully *The government is debating the possibility of imposing more taxes.*
ex-	pose	-ure (indicates a noun form)	exposure: the state of being open to and/or unprotected from a condition or influence *The exposure to the constant high level of factory noise affected his hearing.*
im-	pose	-tion (indicates a noun form)	imposition: a situation in which an unreasonable task is expected of someone *It was an imposition to ask him to pick you up from the airport 100 miles away.*

Using a thesaurus

It is easier to remember a word if you know related words. A thesaurus is a good source for finding words that are related in meaning. It may also list expressions that the words are used in.

A thesaurus can be organized in one of two ways. One type of thesaurus is organized in the same way as a dictionary: The words are in alphabetical order. The other type is organized into categories. To use this type of thesaurus, look up the word you want in the index at the back. The index entry is followed by one or more references, all of which are in some way related to the word you are looking up (although they are not necessarily synonyms). A number following each reference will direct you to a section that contains a list of synonyms. Use your dictionary to find the precise meaning of any word you are unsure of.

For example, *impose* can have the slightly different meanings *to inflict* or *to intrude*. In order to find an appropriate synonym, you will need to know which meaning is called for. Under *inflict*, you will find the synonyms *compel, oblige, force*, etc. Under *intrude*, you will find the synonyms *disturb, be a nuisance, be a burden*, etc.

Exercises V1–V10

Use Exercises V1–V10 to practice skills that will help you develop your vocabulary.

EXERCISE V1 *Identifying words to learn*

Read the following passage. Cross out any words you don't know that are specific to the fields of biology or biochemistry and that you will probably not have to understand for the test. Circle the words that you think would be useful to learn or to build on.

> Let me reiterate. There are animal cells and plant cells. Both have a cell surface membrane, but the plant cell also has a cell wall. The plant cell has a vacuole in the center of the cell that an animal cell does not have. Both animal and plant cells have a nucleus with chromosomes containing genes. The animal cell nucleus is in the cytoplasm. The plant cell nucleus is usually in the cytoplasm but can sometimes be found in the vacuole. Both animal and plant cells have mitochondria in their cytoplasm, but only plants have chloroplasts. The food stored in animal cells is glycogen granules and in plants, starch grains.

EXERCISE V2 *Learning new words*

Choose some words from the above passage to add to your vocabulary. If you already know all the words in the passage, choose words from a different passage you have read. Write each word on a different note card, and then look it up in a dictionary. On the back of the note card, write down the meaning.

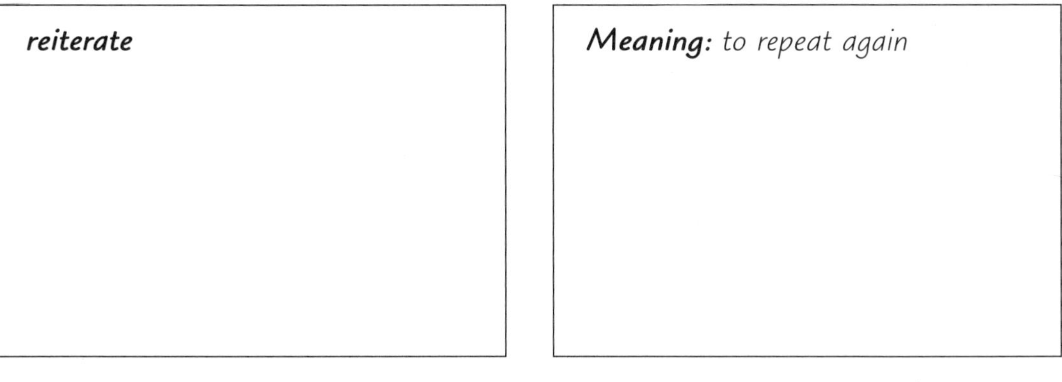

EXERCISE V3 *Adding details*

On your note card, write how the new word is pronounced. Underline the stressed syllable and add the different forms of the word.

reiterate – /riː·ɪˈ·tər·eɪt/ *verb*

reiteration – noun
reiterative – adjective
reiteratively – adverb

EXERCISE V4 *Adding related words*

On your note card, write synonyms and if possible, antonyms.

Meaning: *to repeat again*
Synonyms: *repeat*
stress

EXERCISE V5 *Adding information about the prefixes and roots*

On your note card, write the meanings of the prefix and root, if there are any. In the case of *reiterate*, the prefix *re* means *again* and the root *iterate* means *say again*. This helps you to remember that *reiterate* means *to repeat several times*.

> ***Meaning:*** *to repeat again*
> ***Synonyms:*** *repeat*
> *stress*
> ***Prefix:*** *re – again*
> ***Root:*** *iterate – to say again*

EXERCISE V6 *Thinking about synonyms*

Some words are similar in meaning but have important differences. For example, both *smolder* and *blaze* mean *to burn*. However, *smolder* means *to burn slowly without flames*, whereas *blaze* means *to burn strongly with high flames*.

Look at the synonyms that you wrote on your note cards. Write the differences in their meanings.

> ***Meaning:*** *to repeat again*
> ***Synonyms:*** *repeat – to say again*
> *stress – to emphasize*
> ***Prefix:*** *re – again*
> ***Root:*** *iterate – to say again*

EXERCISE V7 *Thinking about multiple meanings*

Some words have two or more meanings that are completely different. Look at your note cards. Identify the words that have several completely different meanings and write a sentence using each of those meanings.

> *Cell*
>
> 1. *The prisoner escaped from his cell.*
> 2. *Our body produces new blood cells.*
> 3. *Every cell in the spreadsheet was filled.*
> 4. *The solar panel that heated the water was made up of many solar cells.*
> 5. *The political movement had organized cells in various cities.*
> 6. *There is a storm cell off the coast and heading northwest.*

EXERCISE V8 *Thinking about organizing vocabulary*

Read the following ways to organize vocabulary learning. Check (✓) the one(s) that you think would be useful to you.

☐ 1. Making word maps

Here is a word map for adjectives that mean the same as *strange.*

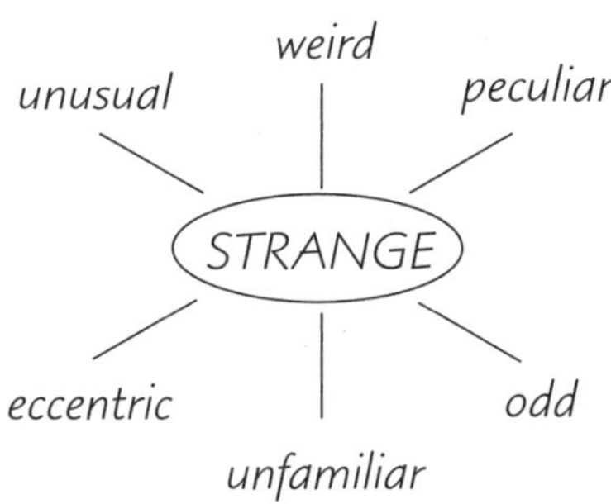

☐ 2. Making word charts

Professions

Concerning money	*Helping people*	*Working with machinery*
economist	*social worker*	*engineer*
banker	*therapist*	*mechanic*
stockbroker	*counselor*	

☐ 3. Using symbols

Write words and their opposites like this:

poor ≠ rich
destitute ≠ affluent
indigent ≠ wealthy

☐ 4. Making rhymes

To reiterate
one must restate
again and again
and again

☐ 5. Making associations

A parrot repeats phrases it has learned. We could call this bird "a reiterating parrot."

☐ 6. Drawing or visualizing

Draw a picture of one of the various meanings of a cell. If you can't draw or don't feel like drawing, picture in your mind a cell as you repeat the word.

cell =

☐ 7. Using the words in stories

Once there was a cell that was bored. It stated its boredom so often that the other cells decided to do something to stop the cell's constant reiteration . . .

☐ 8. Labeling

Write the word or words on a paper and attach it to a place where you will see it.

Post the words *My Cell* on the door to your room.

Write *reiterate* on four pieces of paper. Tape the pieces of paper above your desk.

☐ 9. Writing phrases

Make up a phrase that helps you remember the meaning of a word, using the letters of the word.

*cell: The **c**riminal **e**scaped, **l**aughing **l**oudly.*

☐ 10. Making repetition interesting

Say the word and its meaning aloud in many different ways. For example, say it as if you don't want anyone to hear you tell this secret to someone else; as if you want everyone to hear the great news; as if you are an old person with a creaky voice; as if you are a scary ghost with a haunting voice; as if you are a child; as if you are a foreigner with a different accent; or as if you are excited or depressed, etc.

EXERCISE V9 *Determining your resources*

Read the list of resources you can use to help you develop your vocabulary. Check (✓) the resources that are available to you.

Reading resources

☐ the reading passages in this book
☐ the reading passages in the tests that accompany this book
☐ English newspapers
☐ English magazines
☐ English encyclopedia entries
☐ textbooks in English
☐ a vocabulary-building textbook

Listening resources

☐ the listening passages in this book
☐ the listening passages in the tests that accompany this book
☐ audio cassettes or CDs
☐ videotapes
☐ CD-ROMs
☐ DVDs
☐ radio programs
☐ TV programs
☐ movies

Interactive resources

☐ an online dictionary
☐ Web pages
☐ online lectures

EXERCISE V10 *Planning a study strategy*

Plan a strategy for increasing your vocabulary.

1. Where I am going to find words I need:

____

____

2. How I am going to work on increasing my vocabulary:

____

____

3. How I am going to evaluate my progress:

____

____

PRONUNCIATION

Improving your pronunciation skills will help you succeed on the TOEFL test in two ways: You will improve your understanding of spoken English and do better on the tasks that involve listening, and you will improve the clarity and comprehensibility of your own speech and perform better on the Speaking tasks.

In order to improve your pronunciation skills, you should focus on three different areas of English pronunciation: individual speech sounds, stress and rhythm, and intonation. Some useful background information about these aspects of English pronunciation is given here.

Individual speech sounds

English spelling can be confusing because it does not always indicate how a word is pronounced. Some letters can be pronounced in more than one way. For example, the letter *c* can sound like the letter *k,* as in the word *carrot,* or the letter *s,* as in the word *decide.*

Also, different letters can be pronounced in the same way. For example, the sound /ʃ/ can be spelled in many different ways. All of the following words have the /ʃ/ sound: **sh**ort, musta**che**, pa**ti**ence, o**ce**an, and **s**ure.

Because English spelling is misleading, it is useful for you to learn the symbols of the International Phonetic Alphabet (IPA). This alphabet uses a different symbol for every speech sound that is made.

There are several advantages to learning the IPA symbols for English:

- You will know how to pronounce words you see in the dictionary.
- You will recognize words that are spelled the same but pronounced differently.
- You will recognize words that are spelled differently but pronounced the same.
- You will be able to practice the pronunciation as well as the meanings of vocabulary words you are trying to learn.
- You will be able to improve your pronunciation.

Consonant symbols							
/p/	pit	/v/	van	/ŋ/	ring	/ʒ/	leisure
/b/	bit	/θ/	think	/l/	leg	/tʃ/	chop
/t/	time	/ð/	that	/r/	rat	/dʒ/	jump
/d/	door	/s/	send	/w/	wet		
/k/	cat	/z/	zap	/h/	hat		
/g/	get	/m/	man	/j/	yet		
/f/	fan	/n/	nice	/ʃ/	shop		

Vowel symbols									
/ɪ/	pit	/ʌ/	luck	/i:/	meat	/eɪ/	day	/e/	bear
/e/	pet	/ʊ/	good	/u:/	too	/ɑɪ/	sky	/ə/	tour
/æ/	pat	/ə/	ago	/ɔ:/	dog	/ɔɪ/	boy	/oʊ/	go
/ɑ/	pot							/aʊ/	cow

Stress and rhythm

In English, every word has its own stress pattern or rhythm. Some syllables are given more emphasis, meaning that they are longer and stronger than others. Other syllables are reduced, or shortened. When you learn English words, it is important to learn their stress pattern as well as the individual sounds of the word. Pronouncing a word with the wrong stress pattern makes it much more difficult for listeners to understand you. For more information about stress and rhythm, see Stress Patterns, p. 311, and Rhythm Patterns, p. 312.

Intonation

Intonation refers to the melody or pitch line of a spoken utterance. Speakers of English use intonation to add an extra layer of meaning. Intonation points to the most important word in a sentence, indicates whether a sentence is a question or a statement, and tells the listener when a speaker is finished. It also helps to communicate a speaker's mood and purpose. For more information about intonation patterns, see Intonation Patterns, page 313.

Exercises P1–P8 Use Exercises P1–P8 to assess your pronunciation skills.

EXERCISE P1 *Identifying difficulties*

Read the following passage aloud and underline the words or phrases that you are uncertain how to pronounce or that you have difficulty pronouncing.

A stairway is comprised of various components that fit together to allow access from one floor of a building to another. The horizontal boards, which are the pieces actually stepped on, are called the treads. These should be sufficiently deep to enable users to place their feet down comfortably without slipping. The vertical boards that meet each tread at right angles and that raise the stairway are called the risers. These can vary in height depending on architectural requirements. On many stairways, the tread juts out a small amount over the riser and this feature is known as a nosing. The treads and risers are supported on an inclined structure called a stringer that runs flush with the sides of the staircase and presents a diagonal saw-toothed pattern when viewed from the side.

For safety, a stairway usually has a handrail on one side resting on vertical supports called balusters. Balusters and handrails together are known as banisters, and these are firmly supported at the bottom and top of the stairs by heavy posts.

Whereas these features are common to most stairway types, the actual layout of the stairway will vary depending on space and aesthetic considerations. If the stairway turns back on itself a total of 180 degrees, the landing, which is the flat area at the top of the stairs, will be twice the width of the stairs. If the stairs turn at right angles, the landing will be the width of the stairs. Perhaps the most elegant layout is called a spiral stairway. This structure usually rises around a central vertical post to which tapered treads are attached at their narrow end.

EXERCISE P2 *Analyzing difficulties*

Answer the questions about your performance in Exercise P1.

1. Which individual sounds were difficult to pronounce?

   ____

   ____

2. Which combinations of sounds were difficult to pronounce?

   ____

   ____

3. Which individual words were difficult to pronounce? Why?

   ____

   ____

4. Are there any patterns of pronunciation difficulty?

   ____

   ____

EXERCISE P3 🎧 *Analyzing speech patterns*

Read the passage silently as you listen. Then answer the questions below about the speech patterns you hear in the passage. Listen to the passage as many times as necessary to answer the questions.

START ▶

Since the seventh century, large bells have been used in cathedrals, churches, and monasteries. The greatest bell in the world is in Moscow. This famous "King of Bells" weighs about 198 tons. The next two largest bells are also located in Russia. One near St. Petersburg weighs 171 tons, and another in Moscow weighs 110 tons. Great Paul, the bell at St. Paul's in London, is the largest bell in England, but weighs a mere 17 tons.

STOP ■

1. What words or parts of words did the speaker stress (speak louder or longer)?
2. How did I know when the speaker completed a sentence?
3. When did I hear the speaker raise his voice (speak using a higher pitch)?
4. When did I hear the speaker drop his voice (speak using a lower pitch)?
5. Which words or parts of words did the speaker combine with other words or parts of words?
6. Which words or parts of words did the speaker seem to skip over?

EXERCISE P4 *Indicating speech patterns*

There are several ways to indicate speech patterns:

- Underline the words or parts of words that the speaker stresses
- Draw arrows going up or down to show where the speaker has a rise or drop in pitch
- Link words that are combined
- Cross out sounds that are dropped

Listen to the following sentence and notice how the speech patterns are indicated. Pause the audio after you have heard the sentence.

START ▶

Carnivals, with spectacular parades, masked balls, mock ceremonials, and street dancing, usually last for a week or more before Mardi Gras itself.

STOP ■

Now listen again to the passage in Exercise P3 and indicate the speech patterns using the methods above.

START ▶

Since the seventh century, large bells have been used in cathedrals, churches, and monasteries. The greatest bell in the world is in Moscow. This famous "King of Bells" weighs about 198 tons. The next two largest bells are also located in Russia. One near St. Petersburg weighs 171 tons, and another in Moscow weighs 110 tons. Great Paul, the bell at St. Paul's in London, is the largest bell in England, but weighs a mere 17 tons.

STOP ■

EXERCISE P5 *Imitating speech patterns*

Listen again to the passage in Exercise P3. Pause the audio after the first sentence, then say the sentence aloud. Try to imitate the speaker's speech patterns. Repeat with each sentence in the passage.

EXERCISE P6 🎧 *Listening to accents*

Listen again to the passage. This time you will hear it spoken three times by speakers from the United Kingdom, the United States, and Australia. Then answer the questions.

1. What are some specific words that were pronounced differently by the three speakers?

   ____

   ____

2. What individual sounds were different?

   ____

   ____

3. What features of stress, intonation, and rhythm were different?

   ____

   ____

4. Which speaker was easiest to understand? Why?

   ____

   ____

EXERCISE P7 *Determining your resources*

Read the list of resources you can use to help you sound more like a native English speaker. Check (✓) the resources that are available to you.

People

☐ an English teacher
☐ a native English speaker
☐ a friend with good English speaking skills

Listening resources

☐ the listening passages in this book
☐ a pronunciation textbook
☐ audio cassettes or CDs
☐ videotapes
☐ CD-ROMs
☐ DVDs
☐ radio programs
☐ TV programs
☐ movies
☐ lectures given in English

Interactive resources

☐ a dictionary with audio, such as the *Cambridge Dictionary of American English*
☐ an online dictionary with audio
☐ Web pages with pronunciation practice and audio
☐ computer programs
☐ online radio stations
☐ online lectures

EXERCISE P8 *Planning a study strategy*

Plan a strategy for improving your pronunciation and speech patterns.

1. The pronunciation features I need to work on:

 ____

 ____

2. What I am going to do to improve and how I am going to do it:

 ____

 ____

3. How I am going to evaluate my progress:

 ____

 ____

GRAMMAR: ASSESSING YOUR SKILLS

Although grammar is not directly tested on the TOEFL iBT test, the effective use of a variety of basic and complex structures will raise your scores in the speaking and writing sections. In addition, the more solid your understanding of grammatical structures, the more successful you will be in comprehending the reading and listening passages and responding to the tasks. Thus, a good grasp of grammatical structures will improve your overall TOEFL score.

Look at the Grammar Structures Checklist below. It lists the key topics in English grammar that students need to have a good understanding of in order to be successful in English and perform well on the TOEFL test. You will use this checklist in some of the exercises in this section. You can also use it to keep track of your progress, or you can give it to an English speaker to help you check your English usage. Make extra copies of the checklist before you begin.

Grammar Structures Checklist

☐ 1. Word forms: Confusion between forms of nouns, verbs, adjectives, and adverbs (See Grammar Review: Word Forms, p. 82.)

☐ 2. Incomplete sentences: Missing essential subject, verb, phrases, or clauses that complete the idea (See Grammar Review: Clauses and Sentence Structure, p. 87.)

☐ 3. Basic sentences: Missing parts of the sentence or incorrect word order (See Grammar Review: Word Order, p. 126.)

☐ 4. Joining parts of speech: Incorrect joining of nouns, verbs, phrases, clauses, or sentences (See Grammar Review: Parallel Structures, p. 115.)

☐ 5. Subject/verb agreement: Confusion of singular and plural use between subjects and verbs (See Subject-Verb Agreement, p. 106.)

☐ 6. Verb-tense agreement: Confusion of the verb tense and the context of time (See Verb Tenses, p. 102.)

☐ 7. Noun-clause formation: Incorrect choice of clause marker, position of clause in the sentence, noun clause as subject/verb agreement, faulty relationship to independent clause (See Noun Clauses, p. 89.)

☐ 8. Adjective-clause formation: Incorrect choice of clause marker, position of clause marker, clause marker function within clause, or faulty relationship to independent clause (See Adjective Clauses, p. 91.)

☐ 9. Reduced adjective clause: Faulty reduction of adjective clause or incorrect verb form (See Reduced Adjective Clauses, p. 93.)

☐ 10. Adverb-clause formation: Incorrect choice of clause marker, faulty relationship to independent clause (See Adverb Clauses, p. 94.)

☐ 11. Reduced adverb clause: Faulty reduction of adverb clause or incorrect verb form (See Reduced Adverb Clauses, p. 97.)

☐ 12. Nouns: Incorrect plural or singular form, or confusion of count/noncount forms (See Grammar Review: Nouns, p. 121.)

☐ 13. Pronouns: Incorrect form or ambiguous referent (See Grammar Review: Referents, p. 113.)

☐ 14. Gerunds and infinitives: Incorrect choice of gerund or infinitive (See Infinitives, p. 108, Gerunds, p. 109, and Infinitives and Gerunds, p. 110.)

☐ 15. Active/passive sentences: Incorrect use or incorrect formation (See Active and Passive Forms, p. 108.)

☐ 16. Articles: Missing articles, incorrect choice of article, or unnecessary article (See Grammar Review: Articles, p. 124.)

☐ 17. Auxiliary words and modals: Missing auxiliary verb or modal, incorrect choice or incorrect word order (See Auxiliary Verbs, p. 102, Modals, p. 107, and Grammar Review: Word Order, p. 126.)

☐ 18. Adjective and adverb modifiers: Incorrect form, order, or position in the sentence (See Grammar Review: Word Forms, p. 82, and Grammar Review: Word Order, p. 126.)

☐ 19. Comparatives and superlatives: Incorrect formation or incorrect choice (See Grammar Review: Comparisons, p. 128.)

☐ 20. Subject *there* and *it*: Missing when needed, used when unnecessary, incorrect verb agreement (See Subject-Verb Agreement, p. 106.)

☐ 21. Transition or connecting words: Not used when needed, used inappropriately, or incorrect choice (See Grammar Review: Connecting Ideas, p. 116.)

☐ 22. Prepositions: Missing when needed, used when not needed, incorrect choice (See Grammar Review: Prepositional Phrases, p. 131.)

☐ 23. Other problem areas: ____

____

____

Exercises G1–G6 Use Exercises G1–G6 to assess your grammar skills.

EXERCISE G1 *Thinking about your knowledge of grammar*

Using a copy of the Grammar Structures Checklist, check (✓) the grammar points that you consider problem areas for you. If you don't understand a term, refer to the section noted in parentheses.

EXERCISE G2 *Diagnosing grammar difficulties*

Use the following grammar quiz as a diagnostic tool. Some of the sentences contain an error. Other sentences are correct. Correct any errors that you find.

> Alpine meadows are a tranquil sight.
>
> ____________________
>
> ~~Elderly~~ sometimes need special care.
>
> *The elderly*
>
> The first sentence is correct. For the second sentence, you should write *The* before the word *elderly* because *the* is needed when an adjective is used as a noun. You could also correct this sentence by writing *Elderly people.*

1. A laser cane, which the blind find useful, sends out beams that detecting obstacles.

   ____

2. In 1918, Charles Strite invented the timer that turns off the toaster when the bread is toasted.

   ____

3. The most convincing evidence that female chimpanzees in Tanzania use the aspilia plant for medicinal purposes.

   ____

4. When adults come to night classes eager to learn has been the experience of most adult-education teachers.

   ____

5. A vending machine is a kind of robot that automatically give out candy or other items when money is inserted.

   ____

6. Apprentices sometimes fear that they must not be able to master the intricacies of their chosen craft.

   ____

7. The importance of the Chaco Canyon archaeological site is that they reveals insights into a whole civilization.

   ____

8. Arched roofs were built for a first time 2,500 years ago.

   ____

9. Because of financial restrictions, some schools cannot contemplate to stay abreast of advances in modern technology.

   ____

10. Birds that breed on high cliffs have pear-shaped eggs that roll in a tight circle. However, that makes them somewhat less likely to roll off the cliff.

    ____

11. Botulism spores, which bees carry from certain kinds of plants, have been found in jars of honey.

    ____

12. Butterfly wings have iridescent scales consist of thin, interlaced layers.

____

13. China's first emperor was buried surrounded by 7,000 life-sized clay figures of soldiers standing in battle formation along by life-sized ceramic chariots.

____

14. Christopher Columbus persuaded the Spanish monarchs Isabel and Fernando financing his expeditions to the Caribbean.

____

15. East Coker is where the Anglo-American poet T. S. Eliot buried in 1965.

____

16. Even though the team of scientists encounter snow and strong winds, they continued their excavation.

____

17. Every four years the International Olympic Committee selects that city will hold the next games.

____

18. Filming a wild animal in its habitat requires meticulous preparation, unending patience, and, at times, one must be courageous.

____

19. George Gershwin gathered motifs for his folk opera *Porgy and Bess* while lived in Charleston.

____

20. Having first domesticated for milk production, sheep were then used for wool.

____

21. John Wesley Hyatt discovered plastics by accident while cooking up a recipe for making the billiard ball.

____

22. Lucid dreamers are those people who recognize when they are dreaming and thus controlling the plot of their dreams.

____

23. Many traditional attitudes and value seem to be disappearing under the pressure of global media.

____

24. Marine excavation is a race against time, the sea, and the looters who want history's treasures for themselves.

____

25. Mice aren't really more attracted to cheese as they are to grains.

____

26. Monteverdi, who works were mainly written on commission for the private theaters of wealthy Italian nobility, wrote his final opera in 1642.

    ____

27. Most pioneers walked across the continent than rode in wagons or on horses.

    ____

28. When immersed in liquid oxygen, a magnet's pulling power is intensified.

    ____

29. Mount Rainier towers nearly three miles along sea level.

    ____

30. NASA does not quarantine space crews since returning astronauts have carried no harmful agents or living organisms.

    ____

31. Postwar women had more opportunities to find the work than they had had in the prewar days.

    ____

32. Natural oils taken from the rose and the jasmine flower are valuable ingredients of perfume.

    ____

33. New Orleans is a city which older traditions can still be seen.

    ____

34. Not until the early nineteenth century was the modern notion of the atom formulated.

    ____

35. Of all salmon species, the king salmon is the rare.

    ____

36. Only if packages are labeled properly sufferers will be able to avoid severe allergic reactions.

    ____

37. Political researchers have explained why female candidates have a difficult time raising campaign money.

    ____

38. Putrefy is caused by bacteria and not by a chemical process.

    ____

39. The diary of Samuel Pepys contains eyewitness descriptive of the Great Plague and the Great Fire of London.

    ____

40. When a hive becomes overcrowded, a swarm of bees will search for a new home.

    ____

41. Scientists must be willing to change their position when confronted with new and conflicting data as is this openness to change that allows scientific progress to be made.

42. Scissors, a Bronze Age invention remained basically unchanged to this day, consist of two blades linked by a C-shaped spring.

43. Since the discovery of the double-helix structure of DNA, geneticists have made great advances in the knowledge of life at a molecular level.

44. When telephones were first invented, many business owners refused to have them installed in their offices because were messenger services that they believed to be more efficient.

45. Sixteenth-century mariners called Bermuda the "Isle of Devils" partly because breeding seabirds are making horrid sounds in the night.

46. Small animals can survival the desert heat by finding shade during the daytime.

47. So incredible explorer John Colter's descriptions were of the Yellowstone area that people didn't believe in its existence.

48. Public lands in many parts of the West may be overgrazed as cattle, sheep, and wildlives compete for forage.

49. Studies into the effects of music suggest that it can serve as a type of drug which regulates behavior.

50. Swimmers should avoid to enter ocean areas contaminated by red tide organisms.

51. That Thomas Hardy used real locations in his novels is disguised by his having altered place names.

52. The great stone city Angkor flourished for six centuries so that it fell in 1431 and lay prey to the jungle for four long centuries.

53. The largest known gathering of bald eagles anywhere is on the Chilkat River.

54. When llamas were first brought into the Colorado wilderness, no one could have predicted how popularly the animal would become.

55. The more technical today's world becomes, the most compatible with both humans and machines language needs to be.

____

56. Though capable of walking upright, apelike Australopithecus did so only for short periods of time.

____

57. Today, *carpet* refers to floor coverings that reach from wall to wall, and therefore, *rug* refers to a piece of material that covers only one section of the floor.

____

58. What we will already learn about tornadoes has contributed to reducing the casualty rates.

____

59. Silk has been woven into luxurious tapestries, rugs, clothes, and accessories for some 4,000 years.

____

60. While large numbers of eagles have long nested in national parks, only recently the birds generating outside curiosity.

____

EXERCISE G3 *Evaluating your knowledge of grammar*

Use the Answer Keys in the back of the book to check your answers to Exercise G2. Have a fresh copy of the Grammar Structures Checklist ready. For each answer that you got wrong – whether you corrected the wrong part of a sentence, corrected a sentence that had no errors, or did not correct a sentence that had an error – identify the grammar structure involved and check it off on your checklist as something that you need to work on. Make a check for every error. It is okay to check the same grammar structure more than once.

> Alpine meadows are a tranquil sight.
>
> *Alpine meadows are tranquil sight.*
>
> Your answer is incorrect. The sentence is correct as is. You should check *Articles* on your Grammar Structures Checklist.
>
> Elderly sometimes need special ~~care~~.
>
> *special cares*
>
> Your answer is incorrect. The correct answer is *The elderly.* You should check *Articles* and *Nouns* on your Grammar Structures Checklist.

EXERCISE G4 *Analyzing problem areas*

Compare your self-assessment checklist from Exercise G1 with your diagnostic checklist from Exercise G3. Answer the questions on the following page.

1. Are there any areas that I checked as problem areas on my self-assessment but that I did correctly on the diagnostic quiz?

____

____

2. Are there any areas that I checked as problem areas on my self-assessment and that the diagnostic quiz also showed to be problem areas?

____

____

3. Are there any areas that I considered myself knowledgeable in on my self-assessment but that the diagnostic quiz showed to be problem areas?

____

____

4. How often did I identify a correct sentence as being wrong?

____

____

5. How often did I recognize that a sentence was incorrect but not know why it was incorrect?

____

____

6. What patterns of difficulty in my understanding of English grammar structures do I see in my analysis?

____

____

EXERCISE G5 *Determining your resources*

Read the list of resources you can use to help you develop your use and comprehension of basic and complex English structures. Check (✓) all of the resources that are available to you.

People

☐ an English teacher
☐ a native English speaker
☐ a friend with good English language skills

Written materials

☐ English newspapers
☐ English magazines
☐ books

Textbooks

☐ the grammar review in this book
☐ a grammar textbook
☐ a grammar handbook

Listening and viewing resources

☐ audio cassettes or CDs
☐ videotapes
☐ CD-ROMs
☐ DVDs
☐ radio programs
☐ TV programs
☐ movies

Interactive resources

☐ online interactive grammar sites
☐ Web pages
☐ Computer-Assisted Language Learning (CALL) programs

EXERCISE G6 *Planning a study strategy*

Plan a strategy for improving your grammar skills.

1. People who can help me analyze my use of English grammar structures in speaking and writing using the checklist:

   ____

   ____

2. The structures I can use confidently are:

   ____

   ____

3. The structures I need to work on are:

   ____

   ____

4. What I am going to do to improve and how I am going to do it:

   ____

   ____

5. How I am going to evaluate my progress:

   ____

   ____

GRAMMAR REVIEW: WORD FORMS

A word may have one or more related forms. Notice, for example, how the word *decide* changes form:

Noun	The **decision** was made months ago.
Verb	We **decided** to move to a larger house.
Adjective	His **decisive** action brought order to the meeting.
Adverb	She acted very **decisively**.

Nouns are used to express people, places, physical objects, concepts, and activities. They are found in the following positions:

Subject	The **doctor** came immediately.
Complement	My mother is a **doctor**.
Object	We saw the **doctor**.
	The nurse gave the file to the **doctor**.
	The nurse stood beside the **doctor**.

Verbs are used to express the action or a state of being of the subject. Verbs must agree in number and person with the subject:

Linda and Jan **jog** around the lake every day.
Carlos **was** upset with us for leaving him behind.

Adjectives are words that modify (describe) nouns. Adjectives have only one form, which is used with both singular and plural nouns. With the exception of *this/these* and *that/those,* adjectives have no singular or plural form:

ADJ N ADJ N
The **old** man was carrying several **brown paper** bags.

ADJ N ADJ N
The **heavy** books were difficult for the **little** boy to carry.

ADJ N
These heavy books belonged to his mother.

Adjectives have two positions. They usually come before the noun they describe or after a verb that links the adjective to the subject:

ADJ N ADJ N
We had a **wonderful** meal at the **new** restaurant.

N ADJ
The meal was **expensive**.

N ADJ
The restaurant is becoming very **popular**.

To determine if a word is an adjective, ask yourself whether it can answer the question "What kind of _____?" Look at the following sentence:

I was **sad** because I lost my **lace** handkerchief.

Sad answers the question "What kind of person was I?" and *lace* answers the question "What kind of handkerchief was it?" Therefore *sad* and *lace* are adjectives.

Adverbs modify verbs, adjectives, and other adverbs. Like adjectives, adverbs have no singular or plural form:

V ADV
The soldier fought **bravely**.

ADV ADJ
I am **very** fond of toffee.

ADV ADV
Jeff speaks **too quickly**.

To determine if a word is an adverb, check whether it can answer questions beginning with "How?," "When?," "Where?," or "How often?" Look at the following sentences:

The boy skipped **happily** along the road.
I went **outside**.

In the first example, *happily* answers the question "How did the boy skip?" Therefore, *happily* is an adverb. In the second example, *outside* answers the question "Where did I go?" Therefore, *outside* is an adverb.

Adverbs can be used in many different positions in the sentence:

Frequently I eat out.
I **frequently** eat out.
I eat out **frequently**.

Most adverbs are formed by adding *-ly* to the adjective form:

ADJ	ADJ
He was a **brave** soldier.	She is a **competent** driver.
ADV	ADV
He fought **bravely**.	She drives **competently**.

Some adverbs and adjectives have the same form:

deep	hard	late	low
early	high	leisurely	much
far	kindly	little	near
fast			

The adverb forms *highly, lowly, deeply, nearly, hardly,* and *lately* exist, but they have different meanings from the adverb form without *-ly*:

ADV
The seagull soared **high** above the rocks.
("*Where* did the seagull fly?" A long way above the rocks.)

ADV
The people spoke **highly** of their governor.
("*How* did the people speak?" Favorably, or with praise.)

The adverbs *warmly, hotly, coolly, coldly, presently, shortly, scarcely,* and *barely* also have different meanings from their adjective forms:

ADJ
It was a **hot** day. (The temperature was high.)

ADV
They debated the issue **hotly**. (They showed strong emotions during the debate.)

Suffixes are groups of letters placed at the end of a word to modify its meaning or change it into a different word form. They are helpful in identifying word forms:

The employ**er**'s enthusi**asm** infect**ed** all the employ**ees** equal**ly**.

-er, -or, and *-ee* are endings used for people.
-ism and *-asm* are endings used for nouns.
-ed is an ending for verbs and adjectives.
-ly is an ending for most adverbs and some adjectives.

The following chart can help you identify word forms:

Noun endings	Verb endings	Adjective endings	Adverb endings
-acy (-cy)			
-age			
-al	-al	-ial (-ical)	
-ance (-ence)			
-ant (-ent), -ant (-ent)			

Noun endings	Verb endings	Adjective endings	Adverb endings
-ate	-ate	-ate	
-ation			
-dom			
-ee			
-eer			
-en	-en	-en	
-er (-or)			
-ese		-ese	
-ess (-tress)			
-ful		-ful	
-hood			
-ian (-an)		-ian	
-ia			
-ic (-ics)		-ic	
-id			
-ide			
-in (-ine)			
-ing	-ing	-ing	
-ion			
-ism			
-ist			
-ite			
-ity			
-let (-lette)			
-ling			
-ment			
-ness			
-ocracy			
-ry (-ary, -ery)			
-ship			
-ster			
-tion (-sion)			
-tive			
-y (-ie)		-y	
	-ed	-ed	
	-er	-er	
	-ify		
	-ize		
		-able (-ible)	
		-ile	
		-ish	

Noun endings	Verb endings	Adjective endings	Adverb endings
		-ive (-ative, -itive)	
		-less	
		-like	
		-ly	-ly
		-ous (-eous, -ious)	
			-ward
			-wise

Exercise G7 Use Exercise G7 to practice your skills in using word forms correctly.

EXERCISE G7 *Checking word forms*

If the underlined word is the wrong word form, write the correct form. Write the name of the correct form in parentheses.

> Maxwell's four equations neatly summarization the behavior of electric and magnetic fields.
>
> *summarize (verb)*

1. Social interaction involves both verbal and nonverbal forms of interaction.

   ____

2. Roaches tolerant and even thrive in climatic extremes.

   ____

3. Child-development specialists have noted that cooperate games encourage self-esteem in young children.

   ____

4. Each year bees pollinate several billion dollars' worth of bee-dependent crops.

   ____

5. In folktales, the wolf usually symbols greed and rapacity.

   ____

6. Butch Cassidy was an outlaw fame for robbing trains.

   ____

7. Lack of transportation is a major impede to development in remote areas.

   ____

8. While undeniable appealing, rabbits are also known to be destructive.

   ____

9. Techniques such as aerial stereographic photography yield most of the detail on a map.

   ____

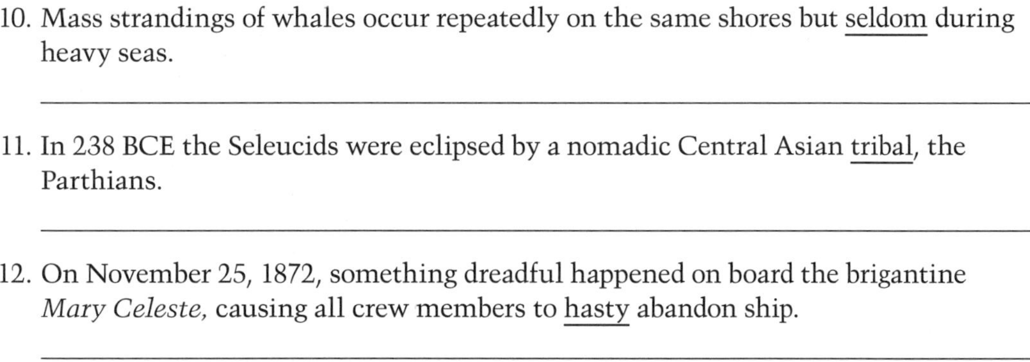

10. Mass strandings of whales occur repeatedly on the same shores but <u>seldom</u> during heavy seas.

____

11. In 238 BCE the Seleucids were eclipsed by a nomadic Central Asian <u>tribal</u>, the Parthians.

____

12. On November 25, 1872, something dreadful happened on board the brigantine *Mary Celeste*, causing all crew members to <u>hasty</u> abandon ship.

____

GRAMMAR REVIEW: CLAUSES AND SENTENCE STRUCTURE

Sentences are made up of clauses. A clause is a group of words that includes a subject and a verb.

Independent clauses

Independent clauses contain a subject and verb and convey a complete idea. Three types of sentences contain independent clauses: simple sentences, compound sentences, and complex sentences.

Simple sentences are made up of one independent clause with one subject and one verb. Read the examples below:

S V
The cat ran.

S V
Last night the fat black cat ran swiftly under the speeding blue sports car.

Compound sentences are made up of two (or sometimes more) independent clauses that are joined by a conjunction such as *and, but, or, nor,* or *yet*:

S V S V
The cat ran **and** the dog chased it.

S V S V
Kelly wanted to take the geometry course, **but** it was offered at the same time as her biochemistry lab.

S V S V
We could trade in our old car, **or** we could keep it as a second car.

Complex sentences are made up of one or more independent clauses and one or more dependent clauses. A dependent clause is an incomplete sentence. It needs to be connected to an independent clause. For more information about dependent clauses, see below:

S DEPENDENT CLAUSE V
The cat that I saw ran.

S DEPENDENT CLAUSE V
Last night, the fat black cat that I saw in the street ran under the speeding

DEPENDENT CLAUSE
blue sports car as the big shaggy dog chased after it.

Dependent clauses

Dependent clauses have a subject and a verb, but they do not form complete sentences. They must be connected to an independent clause. Look at the following dependent clauses:

S V
that she wanted

S V
when the children played with it

Both of the dependent clauses above have a subject and a verb. However, they are not complete sentences. These dependent clauses can be made into sentences if they are connected to independent clauses, as shown in the examples below:

The DVD **that she wanted** was on sale.
The toy broke **when the children played with it**.

The above sentences are now complete. In the first example, the dependent clause "that she wanted" has been connected to the independent clause "The DVD was on sale." The dependent clause gives further information; in this example, it says which DVD was on sale.

In the second example, the dependent clause "when the children played with it" has been connected to the independent clause "The toy broke." The dependent clause gives additional information; in this example, it says *who* broke the toy (the children) and *when* the toy was broken (while the children played with it).

For more information about dependent clauses, see Grammar Review: Noun, Adjective, and Adverb Clauses, p. 89.

Exercises G8–G9

Use Exercises G8–G9 to practice your skills in identifying sentence structure.

EXERCISE G8 *Identifying complete sentences*

Check (✓) the complete sentences.

1. _____ Is spreading its wings?
2. _____ The rain came suddenly.
3. _____ Swimming is an invigorating sport.
4. _____ The start of industrialization in the Midlands.

EXERCISE G9 *Identifying compound sentences*

Write *S* above the subject or subjects. Write *V* above the verb or verbs. Then write *C* in front of the compound sentences.

S V
_____ Differences among environmental groups illustrate a broad range of philosophies and tactics.

S V S V
__C__ Beethoven wrote the *Grosse Fuge* for string quartet, but he later transcribed it for piano four-hands.

1. _____ Soil is highly fertile in volcanic areas, and volcanic activity offers advantages such as geothermal energy.
2. _____ Women with very narrow pelvises are more likely to experience potentially life-threatening problems during childbirth.
3. _____ On collective farms, land, buildings, and equipment are shared, the farmers work together, and the profits are divided equally.
4. _____ Life expectancy, or the average length of an individual life, varies over time within the same community and from community to community at the same time.

GRAMMAR REVIEW: NOUN, ADJECTIVE, AND ADVERB CLAUSES

There are three kinds of dependent clauses: noun clauses, adjective clauses, and adverb clauses. Information about their structure and function is presented below.

Noun clauses

Noun clauses are dependent clauses that are introduced by a noun clause marker. Like all dependent clauses, they have a subject and a verb but are not complete sentences. Noun clauses can be used in exactly the same way as nouns. Compare the following uses of nouns and noun clauses:

Subject	Sam's **jokes** are very funny. (noun)
	What Sam says is very funny. (noun clause)
Object	The man told us the **address**. (noun)
	The man told us **where he lived**. (noun clause)
Object of a preposition	I wasn't asked about the **party**. (noun)
	I wasn't asked about **who was invited**. (noun clause)

The chart below lists noun clause markers that can introduce noun clauses, with examples.

Noun clause marker	Example
That indicates a fact.	I knew **that he had to go**.
What focuses on a fact.	Everyone was surprised at **what he brought for the picnic**.
When indicates a time.	He told us **when the plane would arrive**.
Where indicates a place.	**Where they are going on their honeymoon** is a secret.
Why indicates a reason.	She wouldn't say **why he left so early**.
Who indicates a person.	**Who sent the letter** is a mystery to me.
How many indicates a quantity.	I've lost count of **how many times I've broken my glasses**.

Noun clause marker	Example
How much indicates an amount.	He wasn't paying attention to **how much he ate**.
How indicates a manner.	He showed us **how he was going to win the race**.
Which indicates a choice.	I didn't know **which book I was supposed to read**.
**Whether* indicates two or more alternatives.	I didn't know **whether I should bring my bike or leave it at home**.
Whose indicates possession.	I never found out **whose car was parked outside our house**.
Whom indicates a person.	Sue didn't know **whom he was talking to**.
**If* indicates alternatives.	I didn't know **if I should bring my bike**.

* When used as clause markers, *if* and *whether* are interchangeable.

The noun clause marker *that* can be left out if the noun clause is the object of the sentence:

Object position Janet noticed **[that] the window was broken**.

That cannot be left out if the noun clause is the subject of the sentence:

Subject position **That he passed** is a miracle.

If a noun clause is used in the subject position, there must be a verb in the independent clause:

S (That he might fall) V (worries)

That he might fall worries me.

If a noun clause is used in the object position, there must be a subject and a verb in the independent clause:

S (Sam) V (knew) OBJECT (what he had to do)

Sam knew **what he had to do**.

Verb tenses in noun clauses

The verb tense used in a noun clause must make sense with the verb tense of the independent clause:

Correct Last week Antonio asked where we were going.

Last week indicates that the action of asking took place in the past. The verb tense *were going* indicates that the action of going could have occurred at any point in time after Antonio asked the question.

Correct Last week Antonio asked where we had gone.

Last week indicates that the action of asking took place in the past. The verb tense *had gone* indicates that the action of going occurred before Antonio asked the question.

Incorrect Last week Antonio asked where we will go.

The verb tense *will go* (future) in the noun clause does not make sense with the verb tense *asked* (past) in the independent clause.

Adjective clauses

Adjective clauses are dependent clauses that are used like adjectives to describe, identify, or give more information about nouns and indefinite pronouns (e.g., *someone, anybody,* and *everything.*) Like all dependent clauses, adjective clauses have a subject and a verb but they do not form complete sentences. Some examples are shown below:

NOUN — ADJ CLAUSE
The **house** that has the green shutters is for sale.

NOUN — ADJ CLAUSE
The **woman** whose son won the award was out of town.

PRONOUN — ADJ CLAUSE
Anybody who finishes the test early can leave.

NOUN — ADJ CLAUSE
Sam's **uncle**, who is very rich, came for a visit.

Adjective clause markers

An adjective clause is introduced by a clause marker that refers to the noun or pronoun it follows. The most common adjective clause markers are the relative pronouns *who, whom, which, whose,* and *that*:

- *Who* and *whom* are used to refer to people. *Who* is used in the subject position of a clause, and *whom* is used in the object position:

  The man **who** saw the child works nearby. (*Who* refers to the man.)
  The man **whom** we saw works nearby. (*Whom* refers to the man.)

- *Which* is used to refer to things:

  Her watch, **which** I liked, was not valuable. (*Which* refers to the watch.)

- *That* can be used to refer to either people or things:

  The man **that** was hired lives in the blue house. (*That* refers to the man.)
  The vase **that** I bought was handmade. (*That* refers to the vase.)

- *Whose* is used to refer to the person or thing that possesses something:

  The woman **whose** car broke down needs a ride. (*Whose* refers to the woman.)
  The car **whose** hood is dented belongs to that man. (*Whose* refers to the car.)

The clause markers *where, when,* and *whereby* can also be used to introduce adjective clauses:

- *Where* is used to refer to a location or the name of a location:

  The school **where** I met my husband is now closed. (*Where* refers to the location: the school.)

- *When* is used to refer to a time:

  That was the year **when** we moved to Alaska. (*When* refers to the year.)

- *Whereby* is used to refer to words indicating an agreement:

  They made a deal **whereby** she would pay for the expenses and he would complete the work by Saturday. (*Whereby* refers to the deal.)

Within adjective clauses, relative pronoun clause markers can fill the same function as nouns. They can be subjects, objects, or objects of prepositions.

ADJ CLAUSE
S V OBJ

Subject The woman **who** wrote the book has just left.

ADJ CLAUSE
OBJ S V

Object The woman **whom** I saw was in a hurry.

ADJ CLAUSE
OBJ OF PREP S V

Object of a preposition The woman to **whom** I owe a big favor lives nearby.

The clause markers *where, when,* and *whereby* take an adverb position:

ADV S V OBJ

The store **where** I bought my camera is having a sale.

Omitting clause markers

Sometimes adjective clause markers can be omitted. If the relative pronoun is the object of the adjective clause, it can be omitted:

OBJ S V

The picture **[that]** I wanted had been sold.

If the relative pronoun is the object of the preposition in the adjective clause, it can be omitted, and the preposition goes to the end of the clause:

OBJ OF PREP S V

The man for **whom** I work gave me a raise.

S V PREP

The man I work for has given me a raise.

However, if the relative pronoun is the subject of the adjective clause, it cannot be omitted:

S V

The man **who** quit forgot his papers.

The clause marker *when* can be omitted, but the relative pronoun *whose* cannot:

That was the year **[when]** the miners were on strike.

The man **whose** opinion we respect teaches at the local community college.

Where and *whereby* cannot be omitted:

That's the room **where** I was born.
The factory devised a system **whereby** we could get more overtime work.

Verb tenses in adjective clauses

Although the tenses of the adjective clause and the independent clause may differ, they must be logical together. In both of the following sentences, the verb in the adjective clause is in the past tense and the verb in the independent clause is in the present continuous tense. However, the first sentence is correct and the second one does not make sense:

Correct The man who sang at the concert last night is sitting over there.
Incorrect The bug that was killed is buzzing around my head.

In the second sentence, it is illogical for a bug to have been killed in the past and to be buzzing around now.

Reduced adjective clauses

Some adjective clauses can be reduced to phrases. Unlike a clause, a phrase is a group of words that does *not* contain both a subject and a verb.

An adjective clause can often be reduced to an adjective phrase when the relative pronoun of the adjective clause is the *subject* of the clause. Study the following examples to see how the clause is reduced. Note that the clause marker as well as the auxiliary verbs and/or the verb *be* are omitted. Any changes to the main verb depend on the voice. The *-ing* form is used for the active voice, and the *-ed* form is used for the passive voice:

1. active voice:
   - The man **who is driving** has a new car. (clause)
   - The man **driving** has a new car. (phrase)
   - The writer published a book **that contains illustrations**. (clause)
   - The writer published a book **containing illustrations**. (phrase)
2. passive voice:
   - The magazine ad, **which was printed in *Shopper's Weekly*,** showed the city skyline. (clause)
   - The magazine ad **printed in *Shopper's Weekly*** showed the city skyline. (phrase)
   - The ideas **that had been presented in the previous meeting** were discussed. (clause)
   - The ideas **presented in the previous meeting** were discussed. (phrase)
3. subject + *to be* + adjective:
   - The man **who is responsible** said the underground water had a high salt content. (clause)
   - The man **responsible** said the underground water had a high salt content. (phrase)
4. subject + *to be* + noun:
   - Her name, **which is Ann**, is easy to remember. (clause)
   - Her name, **Ann**, is easy to remember. (phrase)
5. subject + *to be* + prepositional phrase:
   - The books **that are on the table** belong to Emma. (clause)
   - The books **on the table** belong to Emma. (phrase)

A verb that is used to indicate a permanent characteristic takes the *-ing* form in an adjective phrase:

6. present:
   - The window **that overlooks** the yard is broken.
   - The window **overlooking** the yard is broken.
7. past:
   - The window **that overlooked** the yard was broken.
   - The window **overlooking** the yard was broken.

A verb that is used to indicate an ongoing activity also takes the *-ing* form:

8. present continuous:
   - The detective **who is investigating** the case has found an important clue.
   - The detective **investigating** the case has found an important clue.
9. past continuous:
   - The detective **who was investigating** the case found an important clue.
   - The detective **investigating** the case found an important clue.

Some adjective clauses cannot be reduced to an adjective phrase. When a clause marker is the object of a clausal verb, it cannot be reduced to an adjective phrase:

Correct The books **that I checked out of the library** are due today.
Incorrect The books checking out of the library are due today.

In the example above, the adjective clause cannot be shortened to "checking out of the library" because the subject *books* is not the subject for the verb *check*. Books cannot "check" themselves out.

An adjective clause beginning with *whose* cannot be reduced without a change in meaning:

The woman **whose son is blocking the entrance** works upstairs.
The woman **blocking the entrance** works upstairs.

Although the second sentence above is grammatically correct, it no longer has the same meaning as the first sentence. In the first sentence, the son is blocking the entrance. In the second sentence, the woman is blocking the entrance.

An adjective clause beginning with a clause marker that takes the adverb position cannot be reduced to an adjective phrase:

Correct The time **when Andrew arrived** was inconvenient.
Incorrect The time arriving was inconvenient.

"The time arriving was inconvenient" is incorrect because the time did not arrive; Andrew did.

Correct The house **where we grew up** was torn down.
Incorrect The house growing up was torn down.

"The house growing up was torn down" is incorrect because the house did not grow up; we did.

Adverb clauses

Adverb clauses are dependent clauses (incomplete sentences) with a subject and a verb. They function like adverbs. They may occur at the beginning of a sentence before an independent clause or at the end of a sentence after an independent clause. When they occur at the beginning, they are frequently separated from the independent clause by a comma:

Even though Ted knew the material, he failed the exam.
Ted failed the exam **even though he knew the material**.

Adverb clause markers

Below are some clause markers commonly used to introduce adverb clauses:

1. clause markers indicating time:

after	by the time	until
as	now that	when
as long as	once	whenever
as soon as	since	while
before		

   The people danced **while** the music played.
   We worked **as long as** we could.

2. clause markers indicating concessions:

although	even though	though
as much as	except that	whereas
despite the fact that	in spite of the fact that	while
even if	not that	

   Jim has a cat, **despite the fact that** he is allergic to them.
   Jenny's smile is an important factor in her success, **even if** she doesn't realize it.

3. clause markers indicating cause and effect (reason):

as	in case	so
because	since	

   We should take a first-aid kit **in case** there is an accident.
   Since Max seldom talks about himself, I didn't know he liked classical ballet.

4. clause markers indicating results:

   so that   so . . . that   such . . . that

   I like to live on campus **so that** I don't have to commute.
   The traffic was **so** heavy **that** we arrived an hour late.
   She got **such** a shock **that** she dropped the tray.

5. clause markers indicating purpose:

   in order that   so   so that

   He wrote that memo **in order that** there would be no misunderstandings.
   I bought the book **so that** I could read on the flight.

6. clause markers indicating manner:

   as   as if   as though   just as   like

   Betty looks **as if** something is wrong.
   The wind was cold yesterday **just as** it had been all week long.

7. clause markers indicating place:

   where   wherever   everywhere

   Wherever I looked, I found fingerprints.
   Everywhere he went, people admired him.

8. clause markers indicating conditions:

   even if   if only   if   provided   unless

   We can go camping with Bill **provided** we bring our own equipment.
   Lucy can't attend the meeting **unless** she finds a baby-sitter.

An adverb clause must begin with a clause marker:

When Sam arrives, we'll open the gifts.
I want to leave now **so** I'll get home early.

However, if the auxiliary word or verb in a conditional clause is *should, were,* or *had,* it is sometimes put at the beginning of the clause and the clause marker *if* is omitted:

If he had planned on going, he would have let us know.
Had he planned on going, he would have let us know.

Verb tenses in adverb clauses

As with all dependent clauses, an adverb clause must be used with an independent clause:

INDEPENDENT CLAUSE: Lenny can't work
ADV CLAUSE: until the cast is off his foot.

Lenny can't work until the cast is off his foot.

In most cases, the verb in the adverb clause has the same tense as the verb in the independent clause. The following cases are exceptions:

- clauses of time
  If a time clause refers to something that will happen, it takes the present tense:

  As soon as I **find** my shoes, we'll leave.

- clauses of reason
  If a clause of reason introduced by the markers *in case* or *just in case* refers to a possible future situation, the clause is in the simple present tense:

  I'm bringing my umbrella in case it **rains**.

- clauses of purpose
  If the verb in the independent clause is in the present or present perfect tense, one of the modals *can, may, will,* or *shall* is usually used:

  I want to learn to type so that I **can type** my own essays.

  If the verb in the independent clause is in the past tense, one of the modals *could, might, would,* or *should* is usually used:

  Margo wrote the items on a list so that we **would remember** everything.

- clauses of condition
  If a sentence concerns a common occurrence, the simple present or the present continuous tense is used in both the adverb clause and the independent clause:

  If someone **speaks** to Lily, she **turns** red.

  If a sentence concerns a common occurrence in the past, the simple past or past continuous tense is used in the adverb clause, and the simple past and a modal are used in the independent clause:

  He **couldn't sleep** unless he **got** a lot of exercise.

If a sentence concerns a possible situation in the present, the simple present or the present perfect tense is used in the adverb clause and a modal is used in the independent clause:

If you **don't believe** me, you **can ask** Mike.
If you **haven't done** any climbing before, you **should get** some professional advice.

If a sentence concerns a possible future occurrence, the simple present is used in the adverb clause and the simple future tense is used in the independent clause:

If he **goes**, I **will go** too.

If a sentence concerns an unlikely situation, the simple past is used in the adverb clause and *would, should,* or *might* is used in the independent clause:

If I **asked** for another raise, my boss **would fire** me.

If a sentence concerns something that could have happened in the past but did not happen, the past perfect tense is used in the adverb clause and *would have, could have, should have,* or *might have* is used in the independent clause:

If I **had realized** the danger at that time, I **would have taken** more precautions.

Reduced adverb clauses

Some adverb clauses can be reduced to phrases without changing their meaning. Remember that a clause contains a subject and a verb, but a phrase does not.

An adverb clause can be reduced to an adverb phrase only when the subject of the independent clause is the same as the subject of the adverb clause. Study the examples below to see how adverb clauses are reduced:

1. Time sequences with *after, before, once, since, until, when,* and *while:*

After they sang two songs, the performers did a dance. (clause)
After singing two songs, the performers did a dance. (phrase)

Before he answered the phone, he grabbed a pencil and notepad. (clause)
Before answering the phone, he grabbed a pencil and notepad. (phrase)

Once he had been challenged to play tennis, Tim wouldn't stop practicing. (clause)
Once challenged to play tennis, Tim wouldn't stop practicing. (phrase)

Since she finished studying at the university, Ellen has gone on to become a successful designer. (clause)
Since studying at the university, Ellen has gone on to become a successful designer. (phrase)

He fidgeted with his keys **until he dropped them**. (clause)
He fidgeted with his keys **until dropping them**. (phrase)

When she is working in her garden, Jan always wears a floppy hat. (clause)
When working in her garden, Jan always wears a floppy hat. (phrase)

While George was away in London, he wrote daily. (clause)
While away in London, George wrote daily. (phrase)

2. Giving reasons with *because*

When a clause introduced by *because* is reduced, *because* is omitted and the verb changes form:

Because she had always been interested in sports, Linda became an avid supporter of the team. (clause)
Having always been interested in sports, Linda became an avid supporter of the team. (phrase)

3. Clauses of concession with *although, despite, in spite of, though,* and *while*:

Although he was hurt, Jack managed to smile. (clause)
Although hurt, Jack managed to smile. (phrase)

Despite the fact that she was ill, Lisa went on stage. (clause)
Despite being ill, Lisa went on stage. (phrase)

In spite of the fact that she works long hours, Joan spends a lot of time with her family. (clause)
In spite of working long hours, Joan spends a lot of time with her family. (phrase)

Though I am capable of making cakes, I prefer to bake cookies. (clause)
Though capable of making cakes, I prefer to bake cookies. (phrase)

While I am fond of Jeff, I don't want to marry him. (clause)
While fond of Jeff, I don't want to marry him. (phrase)

The verb in a reduced adverb clause can be in one of two forms. The *-ing* form is used for the active voice, and the *-ed* form (the past participle) is used for the passive voice:

- active voice

Present tense:

When I work, I forget to eat.
When working, I forget to eat.

Past tense:

While he was studying, he heard the explosion.
While studying, he heard the explosion.

Perfect tenses:

After he had finished the book, he put it on the table.
After finishing the book, he put it on the table.
After having finished the book, he put it on the table.

- passive voice

Present tense:

The building will be used as a convention center **when it is completed**.
When completed, the building will be used as a convention center.

Past tense:

When the boy was told to go to bed, he began to cry.
When told to go to bed, the boy began to cry.

Perfect tenses:

Because the house has been remodeled, it will get more on the market.
Having been remodeled, the house will get more on the market.

When the subject of an adverb clause and the subject of the independent clause are not the same, the adverb clause cannot be reduced. Reducing the adverb clause changes the meaning:

- Same subject:
  Ever since **she** graduated, **Sue** has been working for an engineering firm. (clause)
  Ever since graduating, Sue has been working for an engineering firm. (phrase)
- Different subjects:
  After **Sue** graduated, **her parents** retired. (clause)
  (= The daughter graduated, then her parents retired.)
  After graduating, her parents retired. (phrase)
  (= Her parents graduated, then her parents retired.)

Adverb clauses, beginning with *as* or *as soon as*, cannot be reduced:

Correct As he was walking, he kept stopping to look at the flowers.
Incorrect As walking, he kept stopping to look at the flowers.

Exercises G10–G14

Use Exercises G10–G14 to build your skills in identifying and analyzing complex sentences, clauses, and phrases.

EXERCISE G10 *Analyzing complex sentences with noun clauses*

Analyze the sentences below. Follow these steps:

a. Underline the noun clause.
b. Circle the clause marker.
c. Write *IS* above the independent clause subject and *IV* above the independent clause verb.
d. Write *ds* above the dependent clause subject and *dv* above the dependent clause verb.

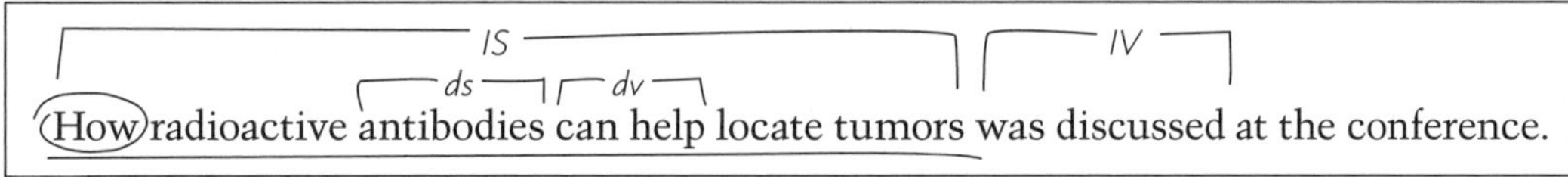

1. That rent-control laws may inhibit landlords from repairing properties is unfortunate but true.
2. Studies of newborn infants show that some perceptual processes, such as depth perception, may be inherited.
3. How glass is blown in a cylinder was demonstrated at the Stuart Crystal Factory.
4. One can easily understand why fast-food restaurants are so popular.

EXERCISE G11 *Analyzing complex sentences with adjective clauses*

Analyze the sentences below. Follow these steps:

a. Underline the adjective clause.
b. Circle the clause marker if there is one and the word the clause marker relates to.
c. Write *IS* above the independent clause subject and *IV* above the independent clause verb.
d. Write *ds* above the dependent clause subject and *dv* above the dependent clause verb – in this case, the adjective clause.

1. A species of tomato that is adapted to harsh climatic conditions has been developed.
2. The date on which Romulus founded Rome is generally considered to be 753 BCE.
3. In the Colosseum in Ancient Rome, cranes lifted cages to a level where the animals could enter the arena up a ramp.
4. The common hedgehog, which has outlived the mammoth and the saber-toothed tiger, is now threatened by automobile traffic.
5. Many English villages have churches that date back to Norman times or before.
6. Shakespeare wrote plays people have enjoyed for four centuries.
7. People who are in charge of ticket reservations warn travelers to book early during the high seasons.
8. Walt Disney was a man whose creations still bring happiness to many children.
9. Using low doses of antibiotics that don't kill bacteria only increases these germs' resistance.
10. The only U.S. president the people did not choose in a national presidential election was President Gerald Ford.

EXERCISE G12 *Identifying adjective phrases*

Check (✓) the sentences that have adjective phrases, and underline the phrases.

1. _____ Helen Keller became a role model for all people trying to overcome severe obstacles.
2. _____ The track leading into the ancient city of Petra follows a mile-long canyon that ends in front of an impressive temple carved out of the sandstone cliffs.
3. _____ Identical twins who have been raised apart have shown amazing similarities on physical, intelligence, and behavioral tests.
4. _____ The highest ruins found in the Andes have yet to be properly examined because of their inaccessibility.

EXERCISE G13 *Analyzing complex sentences with adverb clauses*

Analyze the sentences below. Follow these steps:

a. Underline the adverb clause.
b. Circle the clause marker.
c. Write *IS* above the independent clause subject and *IV* above the independent clause verb.
d. Write *ds* above the dependent clause subject and *dv* above the dependent clause verb – in this case, the adverb clause.

1. Hundreds of pandas starved to death when one of the species of bamboo on which they feed died out.
2. While the world population continues to grow, natural resources remain finite.
3. Because the ice crystals from which they form are usually hexagonal, snowflakes often have six sides.
4. Antiochus was overthrown by Rome around 34 BCE after he apparently used some of his funds to support a local rebellion backed by the Persians.
5. The Romans built raised sidewalks of stone in Pompeii so that pedestrians would not get their feet muddy.
6. Although the existence of germs was verified in about 1600, scientists did not prove the connection between germs and diseases until the mid-nineteenth century.
7. Since the search to find and document sites of Native American cave paintings was first begun, several hundred have come to light.
8. Aphrodisias continued as a Byzantine center until violent earthquakes and invasions brought its prosperity to an end.

EXERCISE G14 *Identifying adverb phrases*

Check (✓) the sentences that have adverb phrases, and underline the phrases.

1. _____ In winter, the Magdalen Islands are almost as isolated as when Cartier first discovered them.
2. _____ Once covered by thick, solid ice during the last Ice Age, the land now is one of the greatest continuous areas of dense coniferous forests in the world known as the boreal forest.
3. _____ By the time newcomers to the United States had passed through the immigration center on Ellis Island, they had been screened for certain contagious diseases.
4. _____ When building Hadrian's Wall, the Romans erected towers about every mile.

GRAMMAR REVIEW: VERBS AND VERBALS

A verb can indicate a state of being (what the subject is) or a location:

Present	**Past**
Betty **is** intelligent.	Betty **was** happy about her scores.
Robin and Donald **are** doctors.	Robin and Donald **were** students together.
Mickey **is** at work.	Mickey **was** at home yesterday.

A verb can indicate what the subject is like or what it becomes:

That child **seems** frightened.
The book **had become** obsolete.

A verb can indicate an action (what the subject is doing):

The students **will finish** in time.
My neighbor **has bought** a new car.

Auxiliary verbs

A verb may consist of a single word or of a main verb and one or more auxiliary verbs (sometimes called "helping verbs").

The following auxiliary verbs are used in *yes/no* questions and *Wh-* questions:

Auxiliary Verbs

Present	Past	Present	Past	Present	Past
will	would	have / has	had	is / am / are	was / were
can	could	do / does	did	shall	should
may	might				
must					

Where **did** Andy buy his camera?
Should I mention the problems involved?

The negative is formed by adding *not* or the ending *-n't* after the auxiliary verb:

I **can't** go home.
We **had not** yet gone to the shop.
They **aren't** going with us.

The verbs *do, have,* and *will* should not be confused with the auxiliary verbs *do, have,* and *will*:

Verbs	**Auxiliary verbs**
I do my homework right after class.	**Do** you take the bus?
The Adamses still **have** an electric typewriter.	They **have** worked for us for many years.
My grandfather **willed** us his fortune.	I **will** bring my suit to the convention.

Verb tenses

Verb tenses indicate a point in time or period of time in the past, present, or future. The verb tense in a sentence must be logical in time. Agreement between the verb tense and time markers such as *today, next year, last week,* and *now,* and between verbs in different clauses, is important. (For more information, see Noun Clauses, p. 89; Adjective Clauses, p. 91; and Adverb Clauses, p. 94.)

Verb tenses and their uses are shown in the chart below:

Tense	Used for	Example
SIMPLE PRESENT	1. a present state of affairs 2. a general fact 3. habitual actions 4. future timetables	1. My sister **lives** in Washington. 2. The sun **rises** in the east. 3. I **listen** to the radio in the mornings. 4. My flight **leaves** at 10:00.
PRESENT CONTINUOUS	1. a specific action that is occurring (right now) 2. a general activity that takes place over a period of time 3. future arrangements	1. Andrew **is watching** TV. 2. My sister **is living** in Washington. Sue's condition **is improving**. These days, I**'m taking** it easy. 3. I**'m inviting** Emma to the party on Friday.
SIMPLE PAST	1. an action or a state that began and ended at a particular time in the past 2. an action that occurred over a period of time but was completed in the past 3. an activity that took place regularly in the past	1. The mail **came** early this morning. I **was** shy in high school. 2. Dad **worked** in advertising for 10 years. 3. We **jogged** every morning before class.
PAST CONTINUOUS	1. ongoing actions that were interrupted 2. a continuous state or repeated action in the past 3. events planned in the past	1. I **was sewing** when the telephone rang. While I **was sewing**, the telephone rang. 2. She **was looking** very ill. I **was meeting** lots of people at that time. 3. Nancy **was leaving** for Chicago but had to make a last-minute cancellation.

Tense	Used for	Example
FUTURE *(going to)*	1. expressing a future intent based on a decision made in the past 2. predicting an event that is likely to happen in the future 3. predicting an event that is likely to happen based on the present conditions	1. Jim **is going to bring** his sister tonight. 2. You**'re going to pass** the test. Don't worry. 3. I don't feel well. **I'm going to faint**.
FUTURE *(will)*	1. making a decision at the time of speaking 2. predicting an event that is likely to happen in the future 3. indicating willingness to do something	1. **I'll call** you after lunch. 2. You **will pass** the test. Don't worry. 3. If I don't feel better soon, **I'll go** to the doctor.
FUTURE CONTINUOUS	1. an action that will be ongoing at a particular time in the future 2. future actions that have already been decided	1. At noon tomorrow, **I'll be taking** the children to their piano lessons. 2. **I'll be attending** law school for the next three years.
PRESENT PERFECT	1. an action or a state that happened at an unspecified time 2. an action that has recently occurred 3. an action that began in the past and continues up to the present (often used with *for* or *since*) 4. an action that happened repeatedly before now	1. He **has been** ill. I'm sorry. I **have forgotten** your name. 2. He's just **gone** to sleep. 3. Judy **has lived** in Maine all her life. **I've been** here since Monday. He's **known** her for two weeks. 4. We **have flown** across the Pacific four times. **I've failed** my driver's test twice.

Tense	Used for	Example
PRESENT PERFECT CONTINUOUS	1. an action that began in the past and has just recently ended 2. an action that began in the past and continues in the present 3. an action repeated over a period of time in the past and continuing in the present 4. a general action recently in progress (no particular time is mentioned)	1. **Have** you **been raking** the lawn? There are leaves all over your shoes. 2. Laura **has been studying** for two hours. 3. Simon **has been playing the guitar** since he was 13. 4. I'**ve been thinking** about going to college next year.
PAST PERFECT	1. a past action that occurred before another past action 2. an action that was expected to occur in the past	1. Tom **had left** hours before we got there. 2. I **had hoped** to know about the job before now.
PAST PERFECT CONTINUOUS	1. a continuous action that occurred before another past action 2. a continuous action that was expected to occur in the past	1. They **had been playing** tennis before the storm broke. His eyes hurt because he **had been reading** for eight hours. 2. I **had been expecting** his change in travel dates.
FUTURE PERFECT	an action that will be completed before a particular time in the future	By next July, my parents **will have been married** for 50 years.
FUTURE PERFECT CONTINUOUS	an action emphasizing the length of time that has occurred before a specific time in the future	By May, my father **will have been working** at the same job for 30 years.

Subject-verb agreement

The subject of a sentence must agree with the verb in person and number:

S V
Susie is working.

S V
Susie, Bill, and Albert are working.

Note the following subject-verb agreement rules:

1. A prepositional phrase does not affect the verb:

   S V
   The houses **on that street** are for sale.

   S V
   The house **with the broken steps** is for sale.

2. The following expressions do not affect the verb:

accompanied by	as well as
along with	in addition to
among	together with

   S V
   Jim, **along with his family**, is going camping.

   S V
   Jim and his family, **as well as the dog**, are going camping.

3. Subjects joined by *and* or *both . . . and . . .* take a plural verb:

   Both Jill **and** Lydia *are* leaving town.

4. When *several, many, both,* and *few* are used as pronouns, they take a plural verb:

   Several *have* already left the party.

5. When the following phrases are used, the verb agrees with the subject that is closer to the verb in the sentence:

   either . . . or
   neither . . . nor
   not only . . . but also

   Neither my sister **nor** my brothers *want* to work in an office.
   Neither my brothers **nor** my sister *wants* to work in an office.

6. The expression *a number of* (meaning *several*) is plural. The expression *the number of* is singular:

   A number of items *have* been deleted.
   The number of deleted items *is* small.

7. When a word indicating nationality refers to a language, it is singular. When it refers to the people, it is plural:

   Japanese *was* a difficult language for me to learn.
   The Japanese *are* investing heavily in Southeast Asia.

8. When clauses, infinitives, or gerunds are used as subjects, they usually take a singular verb:

   - Clauses as subjects
     What it takes *is* lots of courage.
     What those boys need *is* a good hot meal.
     Where we go *depends* on job opportunities.
     Whether it rains or not *doesn't* matter.

- Infinitives as subjects
  To fly in space *is* her dream.
  To be able to read *is* very important in today's world.

- Gerunds as subjects
  Learning a new skill *is* very satisfying.
  Answering trivia questions *is* a common pastime.

9. Sometimes a speaker wants to focus on the type of information that is expressed by an adjective. Since an adjective cannot be used in a subject position, the word *it* is used as the subject:

   S V ADJ
   It was windy and the rain beat down.

10. Sometimes a speaker wants to emphasize a noun and its relative clause. The speaker uses *it* in the subject position followed by the verb *be*:

    S V CLAUSE
    It was Tom who broke the window.

11. Sometimes a speaker wants to say that something exists or wants to mention the presence of something. The word *there* is used as the subject, and the verb agrees with the noun or noun phrase:

    S V N PHR
    There were six men in the boat.

Modals

Look at the list of modals below:

can	had better	may	must	shall	will
could	have to	might	ought to	should	would

Modals are always followed by the base form of a verb. Modals have many meanings and can be used for a variety of purposes.

Modal	Meaning
We **can** leave after 2:30.	This is within our ability.
We **could** leave after 2:30. **may** **might**	This is a possibility.
We **had better** leave after 2:30. **ought to** **should**	This is advisable.
We **have to** leave in the morning. **must**	This is a necessity.
We **will** leave in the morning. **shall**	This is our intention.
We **would** leave every morning at 8:30.	This is a past habit.
That woman **must** be the new president. I'm lost. I **must have** taken a wrong turn.	This is an assumption. This is an assumption concerning a past action.
You **can't** be hungry – you just ate! He **couldn't have** taken the book. I had it with me.	This seems like an impossibility. This seems like an impossibility.

Active and passive forms

An active sentence focuses on the person or thing doing the action. A passive sentence focuses on the person or thing affected by the action:

Active Washington Augustus Roebling finished the Brooklyn Bridge in 1883.
Passive The Brooklyn Bridge was finished in 1883.

Active Rebecca's boss had given her the assignment.
Passive Rebecca had been given the assignment.

The passive voice is formed by the verb *be* in the appropriate tense followed by the past participle of the verb.

	Active	Passive
Present	My brother **washes** our car every weekend.	Our car **is washed** every weekend.
Present continuous	My brother **is washing** our car.	Our car **is being washed**.
Simple past	My brother **washed** our car yesterday.	Our car **was washed** yesterday.
Past perfect	My brother **had** just **washed** our car before it rained.	Our car **had** just **been washed** before it rained.

Infinitives

Infinitives are verbals formed with *to* and the base form of the verb. They can be used as a noun, an adverb, or an adjective:

To eat is a necessity. (noun)
I came home **to change**. (adverb)
He always has money **to spend**. (adjective)

Some of the verbs that can be followed by an infinitive are:

afford	consent	hope	prepare	swear
agree	decide	intend	pretend	tend
appear	demand	learn	promise	threaten
arrange	deserve	manage	refuse	try
ask	desire	mean	regret	volunteer
attempt	expect	need	seem	wait
beg	fail	offer	strive	want
care	forget	plan	struggle	wish
claim	hesitate			

We *agreed* **to go** to the movies.
Laura couldn't *afford* **to buy** the ring.
Terry *volunteered* **to work** on the committee.

Some of the adjectives that can be followed by an infinitive are:

anxious	difficult	hard	ready
boring	eager	pleased	strange
common	easy	prepared	usual
dangerous	good		

I am *anxious* **to hear** from him.
We were *ready* **to leave** before the end of the movie.
It is *dangerous* **to smoke** near gasoline.

Some of the verbs that can be followed by a noun or pronoun *and* an infinitive are:

advise	convince	force	order	teach
allow	dare	hire	permit	tell
ask	encourage	instruct	persuade	urge
beg	expect	invite	remind	want
cause	forbid	need	require	warn
challenge				

He *advised* **me to buy** a newer car.
I *persuaded* **my father to lend** me the money.
I *need* **you to help me**.

Gerunds

Gerunds are nouns that are formed by adding *-ing* to the base form of the verb:

Swimming is healthy for you. (subject)
You should try **studying** more. (object)
He was suspected of **cheating**. (object of the preposition)

Some of the verbs that can be followed by a gerund are:

admit	deny	postpone	resist
advise	discuss	practice	resume
anticipate	enjoy	quit	risk
appreciate	finish	recall	suggest
avoid	keep	recommend	tolerate
can't help	mention	regret	try
consider	mind	report	understand
delay	miss	resent	

We *appreciated* his **giving** us the car.
I *finished* **writing** the report.
Lou *enjoys* **playing** tennis on weekends.

Some of the two- and three-word verbs that can be followed by gerunds are:

aid in	depend on	put off
approve of	give up	rely on
be better off	insist on	succeed in
call for	keep on	think about
confess to	look forward to	think of
count on	object to	worry about

You can *count on* his **being** there.
I *keep on* **forgetting** her name.
Sam *confessed to* **eating** all the cookies.

Some of the adjectives + prepositions that can be followed by gerunds are:

accustomed to	intent on
afraid of	interested in
capable of	successful in
fond of	tired of

Sue is *accustomed to* **working** long hours.
Edward is *interested in* **becoming** an artist.
I am *afraid of* **catching** another cold.

Some of the nouns + prepositions that can be followed by gerunds are:

choice of	method of/for
excuse for	possibility of
intention of	reason for

I have no *intention of* **driving** to Nevada.
Sean had a good *excuse for* **arriving** late.
There is a *possibility of* **flying** to Cyprus.

Infinitives and gerunds

Some of the verbs that can be followed by either an infinitive or gerund without a difference in meaning are:

begin	dread	love
can't stand	hate	prefer
continue	like	start

I *hate* **to go** shopping.
I *hate* **going** shopping.

Some of the verbs that can be followed by either an infinitive or gerund but with a difference in meaning are:

forget remember stop

I *stopped* **to buy** tomatoes. (I stopped at the store and bought tomatoes.)
I *stopped* **buying** tomatoes. (I no longer buy tomatoes.)

Adjectives that are formed from verbs

The adjective takes the present participle form when describing the actor and the past participle form when describing the receiver (the acted upon):

The teacher	amuses	the students.
(the actor)	(the action)	(the acted upon)

The teacher is do**ing** the action. Therefore, the teacher is amus**ing**:

The **amusing** teacher made the class laugh.

The students are act**ed** upon. Therefore, the students are amus**ed**:

The **amused** students were laughing in class.

Some other verbs used as adjectives are:

amaze	depress	exhaust	satisfy
annoy	disgust	fascinate	shock
astonish	embarrass	frighten	terrify
bore	excite	horrify	worry
confuse			

EXERCISES G15–G17

Use Exercises G15–G17 to practice your skills in using verbs and verbals.

EXERCISE G15 *Checking verb tenses*

If the underlined verb is incorrect, write the correct verb form in the blank.

1. Aerial photography will recently and unexpectedly revealed many historical sites.

   ____

2. Electricity using superconductivity can travel farther with greater efficiency.

   ____

3. In the future, we may have been measuring movements on the Earth's crust that are undetectable today.

   ____

4. It was not until the invention of the camera that artists correctly painted galloping horses.

   ____

5. Mice with disorders similar to human diseases have been grown from genetically engineered mouse cells.

   ____

6. Navigational errors have now been almost a thing of the past.

   ____

7. Once a crocodile has seized an animal, it is dragging the prey beneath the surface of the water.

   ____

8. Suburbs harbor an extraordinary variety of birds, insects, plants, and animals since urban sprawl began.

   ____

EXERCISE G16 *Checking subject-verb agreement*

Write *C* (correct) if the subject and verb agree. Write *I* (incorrect) if the subject and verb do not agree.

1. _____ The difference between the living conditions in the countryside and in towns has been eliminated.
2. _____ A reorganization of brain cells occurs during adolescence.
3. _____ The radiation levels from a computer display terminal is well below presently accepted standards of exposure.
4. _____ Pollution, together with water erosion, is taking its toll on the buildings.
5. _____ The exquisite decoration and the effective use of space, light, and water contributes to the Alhambra's unique beauty.

EXERCISE G17 *Choosing verb forms*

Choose the letter of the word or phrase that correctly completes the sentence.

> Remote sensing from orbiting instruments aided explorers _____ the lost city of Ubar.
>
> (A) to find
> (B) in finding
>
> You should choose *B* because the verb *aid* is used with the word *in* followed by a gerund.

1. The English Heritage members attempt _____ castles and other ancient buildings in England.
   (A) to maintain
   (B) maintaining
2. In 1970, the Canadian scientist George Kell _____ that warm water freezes more quickly than cold water.
   (A) proved
   (B) proving
3. A great deal of thought has _____ into the designing of a concert hall.
   (A) to go
   (B) been gone
4. Only through diplomatic means can a formal agreement be _____.
   (A) reaching
   (B) reached
5. The vessel that sank _____ the gold and jewels from the dowry of Catherine of Aragon.
   (A) may have been carrying
   (B) will have been carrying
6. Hollywood film producers have been regularly _____ tens of millions of dollars for a single movie.
   (A) budgeted
   (B) budgeting
7. Attempts _____ the face cards from playing cards have proved unsuccessful.
   (A) abolishing
   (B) to abolish
8. One out of every eight balloons in the world _____ at Albuquerque, New Mexico.
   (A) is launched
   (B) launched
9. For noncriminal purposes, U.S. currency _____ only if the copy is one-sided and significantly different in size.
   (A) must be copied
   (B) may be copied
10. Even though many governments disapprove of their citizens' _____ the opium poppy, the practice thrives.
    (A) cultivating
    (B) to cultivate

GRAMMAR REVIEW: REFERENTS

Pronouns and demonstrative adjectives can be used to refer to other words in a sentence. These forms are called *referents* and they agree with the word they refer to.

Pronouns

Pronouns have different forms depending on their use, as shown in the chart below.

Subject Pronoun	Object Pronoun	Possessive		Reflexive Pronoun
		Adjective	Pronoun	
I	me	my	mine	myself
you	you	your	yours	yourself
he	him	his	his	himself
she	her	her	hers	herself
it	it	its	–	itself
we	us	our	ours	ourselves
you	you	your	yours	yourselves
they	them	their	theirs	themselves

Study the following sentence:

When you see the African lions in the park, you see them in their true environment.

Both instances of *you* are in the subject position. The pronoun *them* is the object pronoun and refers to the lions. *Their* is in the possessive adjective form because the environment discussed in the sentence is that of the lions.

A possessive pronoun or adjective must agree with the word it refers to:

The little girl put on **her** hat, and the little boy put on **his**.

If the hat the girl put on belongs to the girl, the possessive adjective must agree with the word *girl*. If the hat the boy put on belongs to the boy, the possessive pronoun must agree with the word *boy*. If something in the sentence indicates that the hats they put on belong to someone else, agreement must be made between the possessive pronoun or adjective and that other person:

The boy and girl switched hats. **She** put on **his** hat and **he** put on **hers**.

Demonstrative adjectives

Demonstratives are the only adjectives that agree in number with their nouns:

Singular	**Plural**
this	these
that	those

That hat is nice.
Those hats are nice.

When there is the idea of selection, the pronoun *one* (or *ones*) often follows the demonstrative:

I want a book. I'll get **this [one]**.

If the demonstrative is followed by another adjective, *one* (or *ones*) must be used:

I want a book. I'll get this big one.

EXERCISE G18 Use Exercise G18 to practice your skills in understanding referents.

EXERCISE G18 *Understanding referents*

Write the word or phrase that the underlined words refer to.

1. The dogs must be loyal, intelligent, and calm; these qualities are what make them suitable for training to lead the blind.

   these qualities ______________________________

   them ______________________________

2. To understand ancient Egypt, scholars study its hieroglyphics and try to interpret them.

   its ______________________________

   them ______________________________

3. When Caesar and his troops invaded Britain, they anchored their transports above an area they erroneously thought was the high tidemark.

   his ______________________________

   they ______________________________

   their ______________________________

   they ______________________________

4. The prickly pear anchors itself on rocky, barren hills and in those places grows to about three meters high.

   itself ______________________________

   those places ______________________________

5. The dodo was first sighted around 1600 on Mauritius, but unfortunately this bird became extinct on that island within eighty years after that.

   this bird ______________________________

   that island ______________________________

   that ______________________________

6. In 1978, Maxie Anderson and his two partners made the first crossing of the Atlantic Ocean in their hot-air balloon.

   his ______________________________

   their ______________________________

GRAMMAR REVIEW: PARALLEL STRUCTURES

Many sentences present information in a list or series. The items in the list or series must have parallel structures. Notice how the words in the following sentences are parallel (use the same word form or phrasing):

Nouns	The children played on the **swings, slides,** and **seesaw.**
Gerunds	**Reading, writing,** and **speaking** are important skills to learn.
Infinitives	After her accident, Allie had to learn how **to speak, to walk,** and **to write** again.
Verbs	We will **run, swim,** and **play** at the beach.
Adjectives	Betty is **short, stocky,** and **vivacious.**
Adverbs	This car runs **efficiently, quietly,** and **dependably.**
Subjects	**Vendors selling postcards, artists drawing on the pavement,** and **folk singers strumming guitars** can all be seen at the summer festival in the park.
Phrases	For all her years **of triumph and tragedy, of glory and ruin, of hope and despair,** the actress was still able to draw a crowd.
Clauses	Creating a map is a compromise of **what needs to be shown, what can be shown in terms of map design,** and **what mapmakers would like to include.**

EXERCISE G19 Use Exercise G19 to practice your skills in using parallel structures.

EXERCISE G19 *Checking for parallel structure*

Write the correct form for any parallel phrase that is used incorrectly.

> Mammoth Cave is comprised of over 360 miles of connecting caverns, massive columns, and it has eroded forms that are grotesque.
>
> *grotesque eroded forms*
>
> Dartmoor sheep produce quality fleece, are comparatively prolific, and have lambs that fatten readily.
>
> ______________________
>
> You should write *grotesque eroded forms* in the first blank because a noun is needed to be parallel to the other nouns. The word *forms* is a noun, and the words *grotesque* and *eroded* are adjectives. The second sentence is correct, so you should leave the blank empty.

1. On the stones of the Sacra Via, patricians and plebeians bargained, elected officials, heard speeches, and were paying homage to pagan gods.

   ____

2. Following Charles V's death, the Louvre reverted to its former uses as a fortress, a prison, an arsenal, and a treasure-house.

   ____

3. The towering pinnacles of Bryce Canyon, the eroded valleys of the Grand Canyon, and Death Valley's parched landscape are sights the tourist will always remember.

____

4. The money raised goes directly to schooling for the children, teaching survival skills to women, and most importantly medical supplies.

____

5. The farmer explained which kinds of apples are used for cider, how they are processed, and the small bitter apples make the best cider.

____

6. Orphaned hawk chicks have been raised on a diet of liquidized mice, dog food, fish, proteins, and vitamins.

____

GRAMMAR REVIEW: CONNECTING IDEAS

Ideas must be connected within sentences and between sentences. Certain types of words and phrases smooth the flow of ideas and make sentences, paragraphs, and passages more connected and coherent. Some examples of these words and phrases and their functions within a text are outlined below.

Connecting ideas within a sentence

And joins two or more words, phrases, or clauses of similar value or equal importance:

We went swimming **and** boating.
We looked in the house **and** around the yard for the lost necklace.
We booked the flight, **and** we picked up the tickets the same day.

When *and* joins two equal subjects, the verb must be plural:

Swimming **and** boating *are* fun.

Or joins two or more words, phrases, or clauses that contain the idea of choice:

We could go swimming **or** boating.
We could look in the house **or** around the yard for the lost necklace.
We could book the flight now, **or** we could wait until tomorrow.

But shows a contrast between two or more words, phrases, or clauses:

We went swimming **but** not boating.
We didn't look in the house **but** around the yard for the lost necklace.
We booked the flight, **but** we haven't picked up the tickets.

Either is used with *or* to express alternatives:

We can **either** go to the park **or** stay home and watch TV.

Neither is used with *nor* to express negative alternatives:

He **neither** called **nor** came to visit me. (He didn't call, and he didn't visit me.)

Both is used with *and* to combine two words, phrases, or clauses:

He had **both** the time **and** the patience to be a good parent.

Connecting ideas between sentences or paragraphs (transition words)

Transitional expressions can be used to connect ideas between sentences or paragraphs. Different categories of transition words and phrases are presented below. Words in the same category are not always interchangeable.

You can use the following words as signals that additional information will follow:

additionally	first, second, third, etc.	likewise
also	following this further	moreover
and	further	not only . . . , but also . . .
and then	furthermore	not to mention
as well, as well as	in addition	or
besides, besides that	indeed	then, too
equally important	in fact	too
finally	last, lastly	what is more

You can use the following words as signals that specific examples will be given:

especially	notably
for example, an example	on this occasion
for instance	particularly, in particular
in this case, in another case	specifically
in this situation	take the case of
including	to demonstrate
namely	to illustrate, as an illustration

You can use the following words as signals to clarify information that has been presented:

I mean	that is to say	under certain circumstances
in other words	to put it another way	up to a point
in this case		

You can use the following words as signals to emphasize information that has been presented or will be presented:

above all	extremely	obviously
absolutely	forever	surprisingly
always	in any case	that is
as a matter of fact	in any event	undeniably
besides	indeed	undoubtedly
certainly	in fact	unquestionably
definitely	more importantly	without a doubt
emphatically	naturally	without reservation
even more	never	

You can use the following words as signals that a cause-and-effect relationship will be presented:

accordingly	for
as, as a result	for the simple reason that, for this reason
because, because of	hence
being that	inasmuch as
consequently, as a consequence	in that
due to (the fact that)	in view of (the fact that)

owing to (the fact that)
seeing that
since
so, so much (so) that
so that
therefore
thus

You can use the following words as signals that the information already presented will be compared or contrasted with new information:

after all
although, although this is true
at the same time
balanced against
but
compared to/with, in comparison, by comparison
conversely
for all that
however
in contrast
in the same manner/way
likewise
meanwhile
nevertheless
nonetheless
notwithstanding
on the contrary
on the other hand
similarly
still
when in fact
where
whereas
while this is true
yet

You can use the following words as signals of a time relationship:

after, after a while
afterwards
as soon as
at first, at last, at the same time
before, before long, before this
currently
during
eventually
finally
first of all, first, second, third, etc.
formerly,
immediately
immediately before, immediately following
in the end
initially
in the first place
in the future
in the meantime
last, last but not least, lastly
later
meanwhile
next
previously
simultaneously
soon, soon after
subsequently
then, and then
thereafter

You can use the following words as signals for introducing disagreement or conflict:

Making a concession or compromise about a point:

admittedly
albeit
although
at least
be that as it may
but even so
even though
given that
granted that, granting that
however
I admit that
in any event
in either event
in the event that
naturally
nevertheless
nonetheless
notwithstanding
still
though
yet

Dismissing a previous statement or argument:

all the same
besides
either way
even if
in any case
in any event
in either case
in either event
in the event that
it may appear that
rather
regardless
whatever happens
whichever

Pointing out a contradiction:

but	conversely	however	in spite of	when in fact
by way of contrast	despite	in contrast	instead	whereas

Indicating reservations:

indeed	notwithstanding
nevertheless	regardless
nonetheless	

Indicating a digression to a previous point or resuming after a digression or interruption:

anyway	at any rate	incidentally	to get back to the point
as I was saying	by the way	to change the topic	to return to the subject

Pointing out conditions:

although	if	only if	providing that
as/so long as	on (the) condition (that)	provided that	unless

You can use the following words as signals that a summary or conclusion will be presented:

accordingly	given these facts
all in all, all together	hence
as a result	in conclusion, to conclude
as I have said, as I stated, as I have shown	in short
as indicated above/earlier	on the whole
as mentioned, as I mentioned	overall
as noted earlier, as has been noted, as I have noted	since
briefly, in brief, to put it briefly	so
by and large	summing up, in summary, to summarize
consequently	then
finally	therefore
	thus

EXERCISE G20 Use Exercise G20 to practice your skills in using connecting words.

EXERCISE G20 *Choosing connecting words*

Choose the letter of the connecting word that best completes the sentence.

Walls that are smooth and flat enable sound to bounce back as an echo. _____, rooms enclosed by such walls tend to be noisy.

(A) Consequently
(B) Nevertheless
(C) In any case
(D) In contrast

You should choose *A* because a noisy room would be a consequence of walls that enable sound to make an echo.

1. Whiskers are very sensitive, _____ animals can use them to avoid obstacles in the dark.

   (A) so
   (B) regardless of this
   (C) besides
   (D) granted that

2. Soil fertility is largely a consequence of the action of earthworms. _____, they have played an important part in world history.

   (A) Likewise
   (B) Because of this
   (C) For example
   (D) In contrast

3. In 1927, critics gave bad reviews to Buster Keaton's film *The General*, which is now regarded as both a classic _____ the best work of a cinematic genius.

   (A) and
   (B) furthermore
   (C) nevertheless
   (D) beyond

4. _____ Emily Dickinson wrote some of the most haunting lines of American poetry, only seven of her poems were published during her lifetime.

   (A) But
   (B) When
   (C) Before
   (D) Although

5. America was probably not discovered by Columbus _____ by the Vikings.

   (A) but
   (B) neither
   (C) however
   (D) in addition

6. We see around us an amazing diversity of life forms. _____ this, it is possible to detect some sort of order in the natural world.

   (A) In the event of
   (B) In contrast to
   (C) Providing
   (D) Despite

7. During a heart attack, the blood flow to the heart is blocked and _____, cells of the heart muscle die from the lack of oxygen.

   (A) overall
   (B) incidentally
   (C) consequently
   (D) anyway

8. Neither Anne Bonny nor Mary Read chose to live conventional female lifestyles, _____ became pirates instead.

   (A) in both cases
   (B) although
   (C) at least
   (D) but

9. Every air molecule has weight. _____, just as a heavy object propelled upward falls back toward the ground, molecules of air return towards the planet's surface.

   (A) As
   (B) So
   (C) After all
   (D) Presently

10. Security threads, watermarks, tiny hidden print, _____ other hard-to-copy features are incorporated into paper money.

   (A) and
   (B) so that
   (C) that is
   (D) namely

GRAMMAR REVIEW: NOUNS

Count and noncount nouns

Nouns can be count or noncount. *Count nouns* refer to people or things that can be counted. You can put a number before this kind of noun. If the noun refers to one person or thing, it needs to be in the singular form. If the noun refers to more than one person or thing, it needs to be in the plural form:

one desk   three desks   one book   50 books

Noncount nouns refer to general things such as qualities, substances, or topics. Noncount nouns cannot be counted and have only a singular form:

food   air   money   intelligence

Some noncount nouns can become count nouns when they are used to indicate types:

the wines of California
the fruits of the Northwest

Quantifiers

Quantifiers are words that indicate an amount or a quantity of a noun. Some quantifiers are used with both plural count nouns and noncount nouns:

all	any	lots of	most	some
a lot of	enough	more	plenty of	

I have **enough** money to buy the watch. (noncount)
I have **enough** sandwiches for everyone. (count)

Some quantifiers are used only with noncount nouns:

a little much

There's **a little** milk.
There's not **much** sugar.

Some quantifiers are used only with plural count nouns:

both many a few several

I took **both** apples.
We saw **several** movies.

Some quantifiers are used only with singular count nouns:

another each every

Joe wanted **another** piece of pie.
Every child in the contest received a ribbon.

Singular and plural nouns

Most count nouns have a singular form and a plural form. The plural form for most nouns has an *-s* or *-es* ending. However, there are other singular and plural patterns.

Some nouns form their plurals with a vowel change or an ending change:

Singular	Plural
foot	feet
goose	geese
tooth	teeth
mouse	mice
louse	lice
man	men
woman	women

Some nouns form their plurals by changing a consonant before adding *-s* or *-es*:

Singular	Plural
wolf	wolves
leaf	leaves
wife	wives
knife	knives

Some nouns form their plurals by adding an ending:

Singular	Plural
child	children
ox	oxen

Some nouns have the same plural and singular form. These nouns frequently refer to animals or fish. However, there are exceptions:

bison	fish	series	offspring
deer	salmon	species	spacecraft
sheep	trout	corps	

One **fish** is on the plate.
Two **fish** are in the pan.

When a noun is used as an adjective, it takes a singular form:

We are leaving for two **weeks**. (noun)
We are going on a two-**week** vacation. (adjective)

Collective nouns refer to an entire group. When a collective noun indicates a period of time, a sum of money, or a measurement, it takes a singular verb:

Two weeks is enough time to finish the contract.
Ten dollars is all I have.
Seven pounds is an average weight for a newborn.

Some nouns end in *-s* but are actually singular and take singular verbs. These include academic subjects (mathematics, politics, physics, economics, civics, statistics) and diseases (measles, mumps, rabies):

Physics is Professor Brown's specialty.
Measles is usually contracted during childhood.

EXERCISE G21

Use exercise G21 to practice your skills in using correct noun forms.

EXERCISE G21 *Checking noun forms*

In each sentence, one of the underlined nouns is incorrect. Circle the incorrect noun and write the correct form in the blank.

> The art of calligraphy has been passed from one generation to another generations over the centuries.
>
> *generation*
>
> You should write *generation* because the word *another* is used only with singular nouns.

1. A goal of the Young Politicians of America is to provide young citizen with the opportunity to participate in government.

   ____

2. Many highly paid executives owe their success to motivations rather than to brilliance.

   ____

3. The most renowned of America's metalworker, Samuel Yellin, designed the ironwork for the New York Federal Reserve Bank building.

   ____

4. The research project looked at the importance of childrens as consumers of fashion.

   ____

5. Curious animals by nature, calf learn about their environment by first sniffing objects and then licking them.

   ____

6. Although small-claims courts use very simplified procedures, a person unfamiliar with law may need some advices with a complicated case.

   ____

GRAMMAR REVIEW: ARTICLES

Articles can be indefinite or definite. The indefinite article *a* is used before a consonant sound, and the indefinite article *an* is used before a vowel sound.

Some words that begin with the letter *u* have an initial consonant sound and some have an initial vowel sound:

a university *but* an umbrella

The letter *h* is sometimes not pronounced:

a horse *but* an ~~h~~our

The indefinite article

Use the indefinite article *a/an* in the cases listed below:

Before singular count nouns when the noun is mentioned for the first time:

I see **a** house.

When the singular form is used to make a general statement about all people or things of that type:

A concert pianist spends many hours practicing. (All concert pianists spend many hours practicing.)

In expressions of price, speed, and ratio:

60 miles **an** hour four times **a** day

A and *an* are not used before plural nouns or before noncount nouns:

Flowers were growing along the riverbank.
I wanted advice.

The definite article

Use the definite article *the* in the cases listed below:

Before a noun that has already been mentioned, or when it is clear in the situation which thing or person is referred to:

I saw a man. **The** man was wearing a hat.
The books on the shelf are first editions.
I went to **the** bank. (a particular bank)

Before a singular noun that refers to a species or group:

The tiger lives in Asia. (Tigers, as a species, live in Asia.)

Before adjectives used as nouns:

The children collected money to donate to a charity for **the** poor.
(*the poor* = poor people)

When there is only one of something:

The sun shone down on **the** Earth.
This is **the** best horse in **the** race.

The definite article with proper nouns

The definite article *the* is usually used with canals, deserts, forests, oceans, rivers, seas, and plural islands, lakes, and mountains:

the Suez Canal	the Black Forest
the Hawaiian Islands	the Atlantic Ocean

The is not usually used with planets and singular islands, lakes, mountains, and parks:

Mars	Central Park	Lake Michigan
Venus	Paradise Island	Mount Rushmore

The is usually used when the name of a country or state includes the word *of*, the type of government, or a plural form:

the Republic of Ireland
the United Kingdom
the Philippines

The is not usually used with the names of countries and states, continents, or cities:

Japan	Africa	Chicago
Brazil	Asia	Mexico City
Germany	Europe	Hong Kong

Choosing the correct article

The expression *a number of* means *several* or *many* and takes a plural verb. The expression *the number of* refers to the group and takes a singular verb:

A large number of tourists *get* lost because of that sign.
The number of lost tourists *has* increased recently.

The following nouns have different meanings depending on whether or not they are used with an article:

prison	school	college	university	church
jail	bed	home	court	sea

Look at how the meaning of *bed* changes:

No article	Jack went to bed. (= Jack went to sleep. *Bed* refers to the general idea of sleep.)
With the	Jack went to the bed. (= Jack walked over to a particular bed. *The bed* is referred to as a specific object. He may or may not have lain down and gone to sleep.)
With a	Jack bought a bed. (= Jack purchased an object called a bed.)

Articles are not used with possessive adjectives (*my, your,* etc.); possessive pronouns (*mine, yours,* etc.); or demonstratives (*this, that, these,* and *those*):

This is my coat. Where's yours?
That watch is broken.

Note that in the following question, the demonstrative pronoun *this* is not used as part of the noun phrase *the* book:

Is this the book you wanted?

This is the subject of the sentence. *The book* is the complement of the sentence. They are beside each other because of the subject/auxiliary inversion in the question form. They are not used together as a single phrase.

Noncount nouns are used without an article to refer to something in general. However, sometimes an article is used to show a specific meaning:

People all over the world want peace. (= peace in general)
The peace was broken by a group of passing children. (*The peace* refers to peace at a specific time and place.)

The imparting of knowledge was the job of the elders in the community. (= knowledge in general)
A knowledge of computers is useful in many occupations. (= a specific type of knowledge)

EXERCISE G22 Use Exercise G22 to practice your skills in article usage.

EXERCISE G22 *Checking article usage*

If the underlined article is used incorrectly, write the correct article in the blank.

> A island in the Pacific Ocean was used for the experiment. *An*
> You should write *An* in the blank because *island* begins with a vowel sound.

1. Countless tourists throng to the Greek islands. _____
2. The tomato originated in Central America. _____
3. The steam engine was developed in an eighteenth century. _____
4. The Russia has a very diverse culture. _____
5. A university education is a requirement for many highly paid positions. _____
6. Bacteria exist everywhere in the nature. _____

GRAMMAR REVIEW: WORD ORDER

The order of the subject and verb in an English sentence can be changed for various reasons. In a statement, the subject is followed by the verb. In a question, an auxiliary verb or the verb *be* comes before the subject:

S AUX V She has seen the Grand Canyon.	S V The boxes are on the table.
AUX S V Have you seen the Grand Canyon?	V S Where are the boxes?

An auxiliary verb is used in a question except when the main verb is *be*. An auxiliary verb can be understood or used in a statement, for emphasis and for negatives:

Do you live in a small town? (*Do* is the auxiliary verb.)
I live in a small town. (*Do* is understood.)
I do live in a small town. (*Do* can be used in statements for emphasis.)
I don't live in a large town. (*Do* is used with *not* in negative statements.)

Word order can also be changed to avoid repetition:

Jane works at Spencer Motors, and Bill works at Spencer Motors.
Jane works at Spencer Motors and **so does Bill**.

Jane isn't working on Saturday, and Bill isn't working on Saturday.
Jane isn't working on Saturday and **neither is Bill**.

Word order is also changed when a statement begins with a prepositional phrase of location:

S V
Austin, Texas, lies at the edge of the Hill Country.

V S
At the edge of the Hill Country **lies Austin, Texas**.

Word order is changed when the conditional *if* has been omitted:

If I had gone to the post office, I would have bought stamps.
Had I gone to the post office, I would have bought stamps.

The negative words and phrases below are followed by a change in word order when they begin a sentence or an independent clause:

hardly ever
neither
never
nor
no sooner . . . than
not often
not once
not only . . . as well
not only . . . but also
not until
nowhere

only (when followed by an adverbial)
only by
only in this way
only then
on no account
rarely
scarcely
scarcely . . . when
seldom
so
under no circumstances

S V
Mary **not only** works at the post office, **but** she **also** works at the grocery store.

AUX S V
Not only does Mary work at the post office, **but** she **also** works at the grocery store.

S V
Max **never** bought another motorcycle again.

AUX S V
Never again did Max buy another motorcycle.

S AUX V
Mark won't like that bread, and he won't like that cheese.

AUX S V
Mark won't like that bread **nor** will he like that cheese.

EXERCISE G23 Use Exercise G23 to practice your skills in identifying word order.

EXERCISE G23 *Locating inversions*

Underline and label the subject, auxiliary verb, and verb that have been inverted in each sentence. Not all sentences contain an auxiliary verb.

> *AUX* *S* *V*
> Only once every 76 years does Halley's Comet appear in the sky.

1. Had Napoleon succeeded in his dream of conquering Europe, the map of the continent would look very different today.
2. Only under unusual circumstances are federal officials impeached.
3. Coffee contains caffeine and so does tea.
4. Not until a person has had a medical checkup should he or she start an exercise program.
5. Only when an institute is given funding will it be able to undertake research programs.
6. The potato is not indigenous to Europe and neither is the tomato.
7. Should a medical crisis occur, call the emergency services.
8. On Easter Island remain the mysterious giant stone heads carved by a forgotten civilization.

GRAMMAR REVIEW: COMPARISONS

Forming comparatives and superlatives

One-syllable adjectives and adverbs form their comparative and superlative forms by adding *-er* and *-est* to the base:

Base	Comparative	Superlative
small	smaller	smallest
fast	faster	fastest

This ring is **smaller** than that ring.
It is **the smallest** one in the box.

Note: The superlative structure includes *the*. The comparative structure includes *the* only when the comparative takes a noun position (for example, "I like **the smaller** of the two.").

Two-syllable adjectives and adverbs ending in *-er, -y,* or *-ly* add *-er* and *-est* to the base form:

Base	Comparative	Superlative
clever	cleverer	cleverest
happy	happier	happiest
early	earlier	earliest

Some two-syllable adjectives and adverbs and all those with three or more syllables use *more* and *most* with the base form:

Base	**Comparative**	**Superlative**
joyful	more joyful	most joyful
intelligent	more intelligent	most intelligent
happily	more happily	most happily

Irregular comparatives and superlatives are as follows:

Base	**Comparative**	**Superlative**
good (adj)	better	best
well (adv)	better	best
bad (adj)	worse	worst
badly (adv)	worse	worst
little (adj & adv)	less	least
many (adj)	more	most
much (adj & adv)	more	most
far (adj & adv)	farther	farthest
	further	furthest
late (adv)	later	last, latest
old (adj)	older	oldest
	elder	eldest

The comparative form *less* and the superlative form *least* are used with adjectives and adverbs to indicate that something does not have as much of a particular quality as what it is being compared to:

I have become **less** anxious about the project [than I was before].
This is the **least** populated island of the archipelago.

Using comparatives and superlatives

Comparatives and superlatives can be used to modify a noun:

A **harder** exam would discourage the students.
The **taller** boy won the wrestling match.
The **earliest** time I can come is ten o'clock.

Comparatives and superlatives can be used after a verb:

We need to be **more** understanding.
The black horse is the **fastest**.

Some structures using comparatives take the word *than*. (*Note:* The words *the* and *than* are not used together in a comparative structure.):

Before nouns	Jackie is **more active than** her brother.
Before phrases	Last year the test results were **better than** in previous years.
Before clauses	He is **taller than** I thought he was.

The superlative is used in the following structures:

With prepositions	The first step is **the most** important of all. He has **the worst** temper in the world.
With clauses	That meal was **the best** I've had for a long time. That is **the most convincing** movie I've ever seen.

Using expressions of equality or inequality

Expressions of equality or inequality can be made using the base form of the adjective or adverb with *as . . . as, not as . . . as,* or *not so . . . as*:

Jim is **as clever as** Nancy, but he doesn't work **as hard as** she does.
I am just **as good** a typist **as** Bobby is.

Using parallel comparison

When a two-clause sentence begins with a comparative, the second clause also begins with a comparative:

The more encouragement Edna got, **the harder** she tried to succeed.

EXERCISE G24 Use Exercise G24 to practice your skills in using comparatives.

EXERCISE G24 *Checking comparatives*

In the blank, write the correct form for any phrase that is used incorrectly.

Both the épée and foil are descendants of the dueling sword, but the épée is heavier of the two fencing weapons.

the heavier

Today as many as ten thousand crocodiles thrive in the warm waters of Lake Nasser.

____

You should write *the heavier* in the first blank because two swords are being compared. The word *heavier* is used as a noun in this case and, therefore, needs the word *the.* The second sentence is correct.

1. More often than not, a honking goose frightens off strangers best than a barking dog.

   ____

2. As adaptable as wolves were, they were not able to survive human encroachment into the Rocky Mountains as well as coyotes.

   ____

3. Australia is the flatter and drier of all the continents.

   ____

4. Although the drought was as not severe as the previous one, its effect was more damaging.

   ____

5. The calmer of the two horses was more suitable for amateur riders.

   ____

6. The lower the temperature and longer the cooking time used for baking a potato, the crunchier and tough the skin will be.

   ____

7. The further west the Native Americans were driven, the harder they fought to secure their lands.

 ____

8. The *George W. Wells*, a six-masted schooner, was a largest sailing ship lost on the East Coast.

 ____

9. Turkey's the largest city, Istanbul, played a central role in history as Constantinople, the capital of the Byzantine Empire.

 ____

10. The world's longest-running sports competition began at Olympia in 776 BCE.

 ____

GRAMMAR REVIEW: PREPOSITIONAL PHRASES

Prepositional phrases consist of a preposition and an object. The object is a noun or pronoun:

PREP OBJ
into the house

PREP OBJ
above it

The noun can have modifiers:

PREP OBJ
into the old, broken-down house

Prepositional phrases that are used as adverbs can take various positions:

The city park is just **around the corner**.
Just **around the corner** is the city park.

"Around the corner" answers the question "Where is the city park?" and, therefore, is used like an adverb.

Prepositional phrases that are used as adjectives follow the noun they describe:

NOUN PREP PHRASE
I walked into the house with the sagging porch.

"With the sagging porch" describes the house and, therefore, is used like an adjective.

A list of commonly used prepositions follows:

about	behind	in	through
above	below	in spite of	throughout
across	beneath	into	till
after	beside	like/unlike	to
against	between	near	toward
along	beyond	of	under
among	by	off	until
around	despite	on	up
as	down	out	upon
at	during	out of	with
because of	for	over	within
before	from	since	without

Some of these words can have other functions in a sentence. To check whether a prepositional phrase is being used, look for a preposition and an object:

PREP OBJ
Because of the time, we had to leave.

CLAUSE MARKER CLAUSE
Because it was late, we had to leave.

PREP OBJ
We wrote the correction above the error.

ADV
Study the sentences above.

PREP OBJ
We climbed up the spiral staircase.

PHRASAL VERB
We had to get up early.

(Note: A phrasal verb is a verb + one or two other words that give the verb a different meaning. *Get* means "obtain," whereas *get up* means "arise.")

Some prepositions have several meanings:

I hung the picture **on** the wall. (upon)
I bought a book **on** philosophy. (about)
I called her **on** the phone. (using)
I worked **on** the research committee. (with)

EXERCISE G25 Use Exercise G25 to practice your skills in using prepositions.

EXERCISE G25 *Identifying correct phrases*

Choose the letter of the phrase that correctly completes the sentence.

1. _________ of his rule, Ataturk introduced significant changes to the Turkish people's way of life.

   (A) As the years
   (B) Through the years

2. The Mississippi region is _________ astonishingly diverse people.

   (A) full of
   (B) entirely filled

3. Doctors anticipate _________ will bring a revolution in surgical techniques.

   (A) that the twenty-first century
   (B) from the twenty-first century

4. _________ their complex structures, trilobites are ideal for studying small evolutionary changes.

   (A) Because
   (B) Because of

5. No animal sheds tears when in trouble or pain _________ the large, gentle marine mammal called the dugong.

   (A) except that
   (B) except for

6. In Europe, the tradition _________ persisted well into the fourteenth and fifteenth centuries.

   (A) spring fertility celebrations was
   (B) of spring fertility celebrations

7. The degradation of plant and animal populations underscores the need _________ toward the ecosphere.

   (A) for a new attitude
   (B) being a new attitude

8. A prehistoric cairn is a pile of stones raised as a landmark or memorial and is usually erected _________.

   (A) over a burial site
   (B) that was a burial site

PART 2

BUILDING SKILLS

Reading

The Reading section of the TOEFL® iBT test measures your ability to understand written academic English. You will be asked to read three to five passages and answer 12–14 comprehension questions about each passage. All the information needed to answer the questions can be found within the passage. It is not necessary for you to have any prior knowledge about the topic in order to answer the questions.

Most questions in the Reading section of the TOEFL test are worth one point. The last question in each set is worth more than one point. If a question is worth more than one point, this will be stated in the directions to the question.

The Reading section is divided into 2–3 separately timed parts. The tool bar on the computer screen will allow you to see the total number of questions within each part and the number of the item you are answering. There will also be a clock that shows the number of minutes and seconds you have left in each part. You can hide the clock at any time by clicking on the **Hide Time** icon.

When reading a passage, you may see a word or phrase underlined in blue. If you click on the underlined word or phrase, a definition or explanation will appear.

After reading an entire passage, answer the questions that follow. When you want to go on to the next question, click on **Next**. You can also click on **Back** to go back to the previous question. Try to answer all the questions in order. However, within each part you can choose to skip a question and go back to it later. Click on **Review** to see which questions within the Reading part you are in you have already answered. You can go back to questions that you want to reconsider or that you have skipped.

Strategies to Use for Building Reading Fluency

1. Read extensively.
The more you read, the better reader you will become. Read on a variety of topics in order to build your vocabulary. The larger your vocabulary, the less time you will need to spend trying to understand unfamiliar words and the more time you will have to understand the material presented in the text.

2. Read challenging material.
Read material that challenges you. If you always read things that are easy for you, you will not develop your ability to read more difficult material.

3. Read about topics commonly found on the TOEFL test.
The reading passages on the test concern subjects taught in colleges and universities: science, technology, the social sciences, and the humanities. Choose reading material that will give you experience reading about these subjects and help you become familiar with the concepts and vocabulary commonly used in these fields.

4. Read actively.
Think about what you are reading. Ask yourself what the text is about. Ask yourself how the material is organized and how the ideas presented are supported.

5. Increase your formal and academic vocabulary.
Increase your vocabulary by reading extensively and practicing the strategies taught in Vocabulary, pp. 63–69.

Strategies to Use for the Reading Section of the TOEFL iBT Test

1. Read the entire passage first.
The reading passages are too long to fit on one computer screen. Use the scroll bar to move the passage up and down the screen. You must scroll through the entire passage before you can go on to the questions.

The main topic is usually stated at the beginning of the passage. Understanding the main topic and looking for the ideas that support that topic will help you answer questions concerning the organization of the passage. Don't spend time trying to understand every detail. You can return to the passage to search for specific details when you come to those questions.

2. Use context clues to understand the passage.
Even native speakers do not always understand the meaning of all the words used or the implications made in the passages. Instead, they use other words in the passage (context clues) to determine the meaning of unfamiliar words, the organization of the passage, and the supporting details of the text.

3. Read the passage even if you are familiar with the topic.
Sometimes you will come across a passage about a topic you are already familiar with. Read the passage anyway. Never try to answer the questions without reading the passage first. It might contain new information concerning the topic or concepts that are different from your ideas about the topic.

4. Read the question and the information carefully.
The Reading section contains different question types. Read each question carefully and pay attention to any special instructions. Study the four basic question types that you will encounter and the examples of each type on pp. 140–143.

5. Try to answer all the questions following a passage before going on to the next one.
Although the test allows you to return to any question you have already seen, it is best to focus your attention on one passage and its set of questions at a time. Jumping around to questions in different passages requires rereading and refocusing your attention – something that you should try to avoid.

6. Use your time wisely.

The Reading section has a time limit of 60–100 minutes, depending on how many passages appear on your particular test. Pacing yourself in order to make good progress is essential. Check the clock on the screen when you start the Reading section to know how much time you have. The following suggestions will help you use your time wisely:

- Be familiar with the question types and test directions so that you don't have to spend time trying to understand what to do. If you are well prepared for the test, you will be able to click on the **Dismiss Directions** icon the moment the directions appear, giving yourself more time to focus on the question items themselves.
- Pay attention to the number of questions displayed on the computer screen and the amount of time remaining on the clock. Pace yourself according to the number of questions and the time you have left.
- Be familiar with scrolling techniques. Be sure to scroll down to read the entire passage before you go on to the questions. The passage will be available to you if you need to refer to it once you have started answering the questions. Use the **View Text** icon if you need to see the entire passage.
- Be familiar with the use of the **Next, Back,** and **Review** icons to move back and forth among the questions.
- Some questions are more difficult than others, but it is important that you answer them all – even if it means guessing. Rather than spending a lot of time on an answer that you are not sure of, quickly eliminate the answer choices you know are wrong, then decide which answer is best and move on. If you have time at the end of the section, you can go back to questions you were unsure of.

BASIC READING QUESTION TYPES

There are four basic question formats in the TOEFL iBT Reading section. Familiarizing yourself with these formats and becoming skilled at how to answer them will help you navigate more quickly on the day of the test.

1. Multiple choice with one correct answer This question type consists of a question and four answer choices. They include basic comprehension questions, choosing a synonym for a highlighted word in the passage, and choosing the correct paraphrasing for a sentence highlighted in the passage. These items appear as follows:

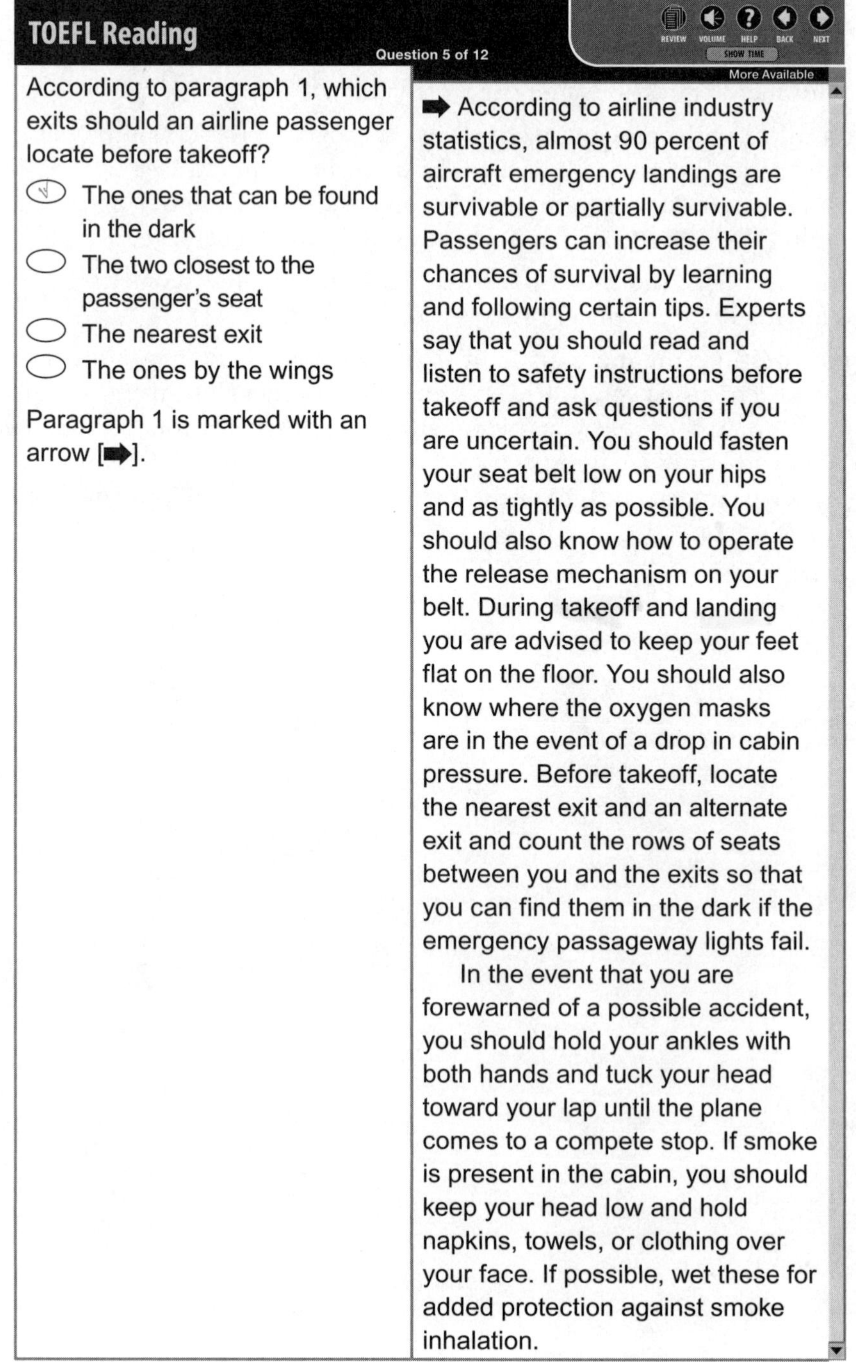

TOEFL Reading
Question 5 of 12
REVIEW VOLUME HELP BACK NEXT
SHOW TIME
More Available
According to paragraph 1, which exits should an airline passenger locate before takeoff?
The ones that can be found in the dark
The two closest to the passenger's seat
The nearest exit
The ones by the wings
Paragraph 1 is marked with an arrow [➡].
➡ According to airline industry statistics, almost 90 percent of aircraft emergency landings are survivable or partially survivable. Passengers can increase their chances of survival by learning and following certain tips. Experts say that you should read and listen to safety instructions before takeoff and ask questions if you are uncertain. You should fasten your seat belt low on your hips and as tightly as possible. You should also know how to operate the release mechanism on your belt. During takeoff and landing you are advised to keep your feet flat on the floor. You should also know where the oxygen masks are in the event of a drop in cabin pressure. Before takeoff, locate the nearest exit and an alternate exit and count the rows of seats between you and the exits so that you can find them in the dark if the emergency passageway lights fail.
In the event that you are forewarned of a possible accident, you should hold your ankles with both hands and tuck your head toward your lap until the plane comes to a compete stop. If smoke is present in the cabin, you should keep your head low and hold napkins, towels, or clothing over your face. If possible, wet these for added protection against smoke inhalation.

2. Insert a sentence This question type consists of a sentence and four places marked in the text. You are asked to choose where the sentence best fits into the passage. These items appear as follows:

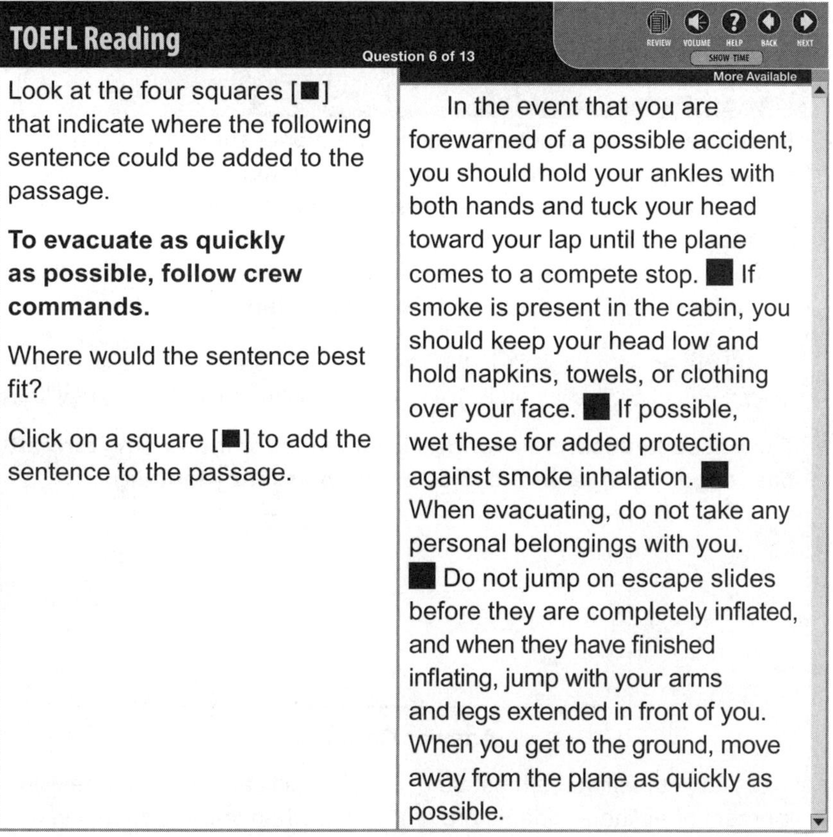

TOEFL Reading
Question 6 of 13
REVIEW VOLUME HELP BACK NEXT
SHOW TIME
More Available
Look at the four squares [■] that indicate where the following sentence could be added to the passage.
To evacuate as quickly as possible, follow crew commands.
Where would the sentence best fit?
Click on a square [■] to add the sentence to the passage.
In the event that you are forewarned of a possible accident, you should hold your ankles with both hands and tuck your head toward your lap until the plane comes to a compete stop. ■ If smoke is present in the cabin, you should keep your head low and hold napkins, towels, or clothing over your face. ■ If possible, wet these for added protection against smoke inhalation. ■ When evacuating, do not take any personal belongings with you. ■ Do not jump on escape slides before they are completely inflated, and when they have finished inflating, jump with your arms and legs extended in front of you. When you get to the ground, move away from the plane as quickly as possible.

3. Summary This question type contains six answer choices. You are asked to select three of the choices and drag and drop your three choices next to bullets. This question type is worth more than one point. These items appear as follows:

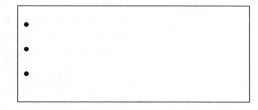

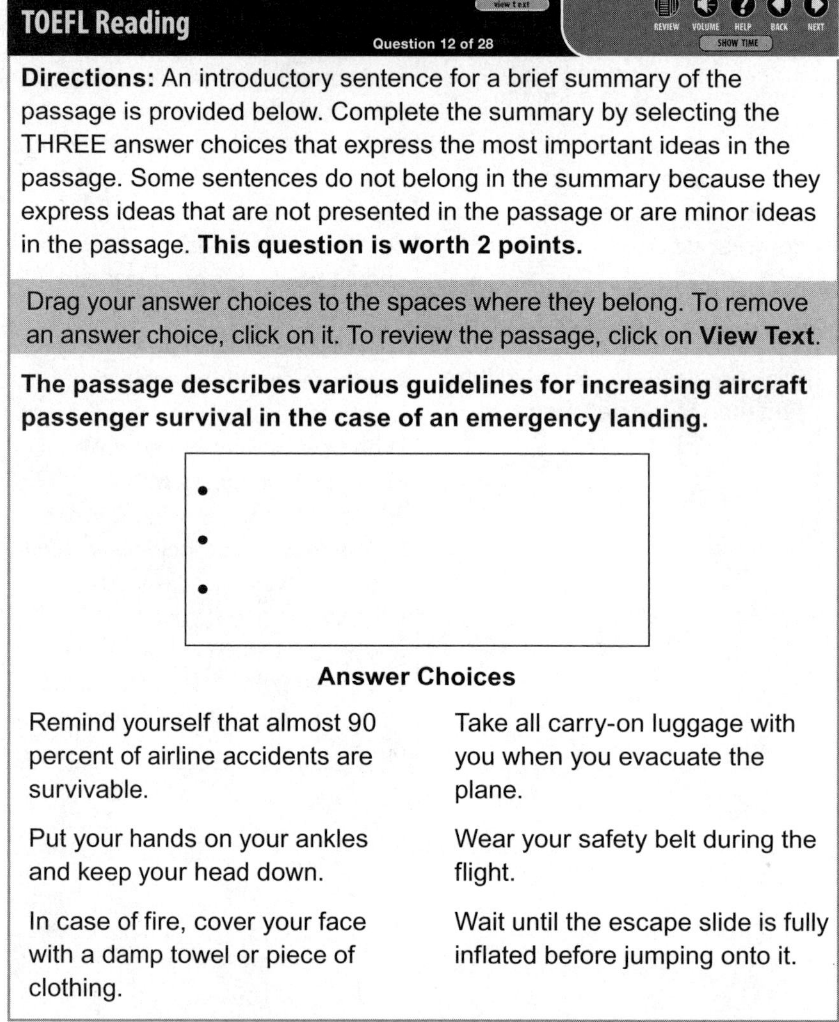

TOEFL Reading
View Text
Question 12 of 28
REVIEW
VOLUME
HELP
BACK
NEXT
SHOW TIME
Directions: An introductory sentence for a brief summary of the passage is provided below. Complete the summary by selecting the THREE answer choices that express the most important ideas in the passage. Some sentences do not belong in the summary because they express ideas that are not presented in the passage or are minor ideas in the passage. **This question is worth 2 points.**
Drag your answer choices to the spaces where they belong. To remove an answer choice, click on it. To review the passage, click on **View Text**.
The passage describes various guidelines for increasing aircraft passenger survival in the case of an emergency landing.
Answer Choices
Remind yourself that almost 90 percent of airline accidents are survivable.
Take all carry-on luggage with you when you evacuate the plane.
Put your hands on your ankles and keep your head down.
Wear your safety belt during the flight.
In case of fire, cover your face with a damp towel or piece of clothing.
Wait until the escape slide is fully inflated before jumping onto it.

4. Category chart This question type consists of five to seven answer choices and two categories into which you are asked to drag and drop the choices. You may not use all of the answer choices in answering the question. This question type is worth more than one point. These items appear as follows:

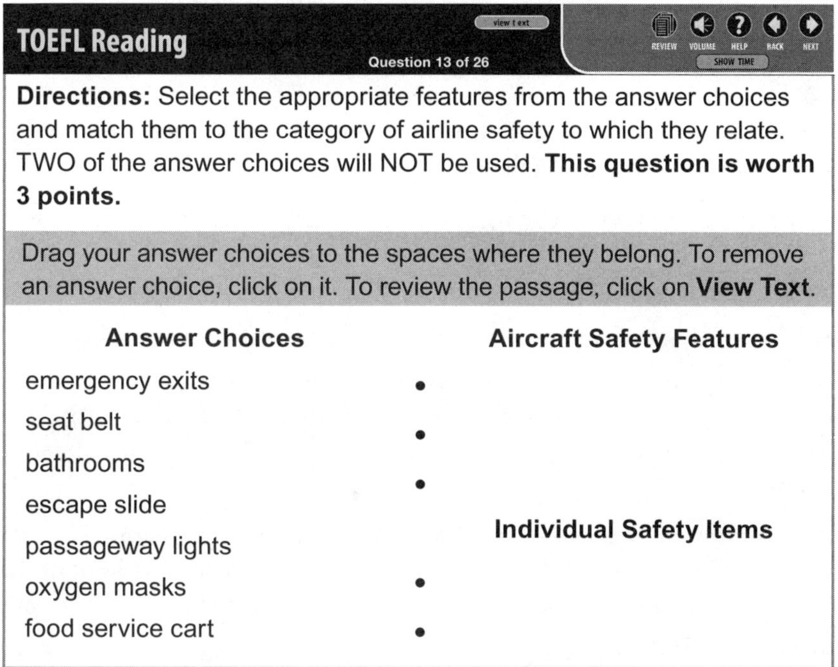

TOEFL Reading
view text
Question 13 of 26
REVIEW VOLUME HELP BACK NEXT
SHOW TIME
Directions: Select the appropriate features from the answer choices and match them to the category of airline safety to which they relate. TWO of the answer choices will NOT be used. This question is worth 3 points.
Drag your answer choices to the spaces where they belong. To remove an answer choice, click on it. To review the passage, click on View Text.
Answer Choices
emergency exits
seat belt
bathrooms
escape slide
passageway lights
oxygen masks
food service cart
Aircraft Safety Features
Individual Safety Items

PRACTICE WITH UNDERSTANDING MEANING FROM CONTEXT

The Reading section of the TOEFL test includes multiple-choice vocabulary questions that test your understanding of certain words in the reading passages. You will be given a word that is highlighted in the passage and four different words from which to choose the one that is closest in meaning to the highlighted word.

Determining meaning from context

It may be possible to determine the meaning of the highlighted word from the context. For example, consider this sentence:

Timothy scowled when he saw the dent in his new car.

We can guess that Timothy was upset when he noticed a dent in his new car. Although we can't know the exact meaning of *scowl* from the context, we can guess that it is a way of showing displeasure. Since most people show that they are upset by their facial expression or body language, we might guess that a scowl is a physical display of displeasure.

It is not always possible to get a clue to a meaning of a word from the context of the immediate sentence. For example, consider this sentence:

> Timothy scowled when he saw Aunt Lauren.

Unless we know how Timothy feels about Aunt Lauren, we cannot guess the meaning of *scowled* in this sentence. However, other sentences in the passage might indicate his opinion of Aunt Lauren, and these could give a clue to the meaning.

> Timothy scowled when he saw Aunt Lauren. Whenever she came to visit, pleasant family conversations turned into angry family feuds.

We can now guess that Timothy might be upset about Aunt Lauren's visit because of the way she affects family conversations. His displeasure might be indicated by his facial expression or body posture.

Sometimes a word is defined by another word or phrase in the passage.

> A scowl came over Timothy's face when he saw Aunt Lauren. Whenever she came to visit, pleasant family conversations turned into angry family feuds. His look of displeasure deepened when he noticed that she was carrying an overnight bag.

We can guess from this passage that a scowl is a facial expression. The situation indicates that it is probably a disagreeable look. The phrase "his look of displeasure" refers to *scowl* and thus gives us the meaning that a scowl is a facial expression showing displeasure.

Identifying meaning from a given definition

Vocabulary can be defined in a passage in the ways outlined below.

1. the verb *be*

   An object following the verb *be* is frequently used to define the subject.

   > A salmon **is** a fish.

   The meaning of *salmon* is identified by the word *fish.*

2. appositives

   A noun or noun group that follows another noun and is set off by commas is called an *appositive.* It defines the noun it follows.

   > Mercury, **the silver-colored metal used in thermometers**, is usually in a liquid form.

   The meaning of *mercury* is identified by its appositive: "the silver-colored metal used in thermometers."

   By adding the words *which is/are* or *who is/are,* you can test if a noun is an appositive. If the sentence is still grammatical, the phrase is an appositive.

   > Mercury, **which is** the silver-colored metal used in thermometers, is usually in a liquid form.

3. punctuation

   Punctuation marks are sometimes used to set off a word that defines another word. Some punctuation marks you may see used in this way are:

comma ,	brackets [ ]
dash –	single quotation marks ' '
parentheses ( )	double quotation marks " "

Mercury – the silver-colored metal used in thermometers – is usually in a liquid form.

The meaning of *mercury* is identified by the words between the dashes, "the silver-colored metal used in thermometers."

4. the word *or*

A word or phrase is sometimes defined by a synonym following the word *or*.

The husky, **or** sled dog, of the North is a hardy breed.

The meaning of the word *husky* is identified by the phrase *sled dog* following the word *or*.

5. examples

A word or phrase is sometimes defined by examples. These terms often introduce examples:

as	for example	such as
like	for instance	

Percussion instruments, **such as** drums, cymbals, and tambourines, were the preferred instruments in the study.

The meaning of *percussion instruments* is identified by three examples: drums, cymbals, and tambourines.

Sometimes the word or words used in the example can be defined by the word that is exemplified.

Everything we know about early humans **such as** Neanderthals is based on fossilized remains.

The meaning of *Neanderthals* is identified by the phrase "early humans," of which Neanderthal is one example.

6. adjective clauses

Adjective clauses sometimes define words. (See Grammar Review: Noun, Adjective, and Adverb Clauses, p. 89.) They are introduced by these words:

that	where	who
when	which	whom

Airships, **which** are cigar-shaped steerable balloons, can be used for many purposes, such as filming, advertising, and entertainment.

The meaning of *airships* is identified by the adjective clause "which are cigar-shaped steerable balloons."

7. referents

Referents are words that refer back to or forward to other words in the sentence or paragraph. (See Grammar Review: Referents, p. 113.)

The solar-powered batteries in the ERS-1 are expected to function for at least two years, during which time **this satellite** will be able to gather more information than any previous satellite.

The meaning of *ERS-1* is identified by its referent, *this satellite*.

8. contrasts

   Sometimes the meaning of a word can be understood because it is in contrast to another word in the sentence. Some words that indicate a contrast are:

but	in contrast	or
despite	in spite of	unlike
however	instead	whereas

   The brief scenes in the movie focus on the boy's point of view, **whereas** the longer scenes depict the father's side.

   Brief scenes are understood to be short scenes because they are in contrast to the *longer* scenes.

9. other words in the sentence

   Other words in a sentence can sometimes give a general meaning of a word but not always a specific definition.

   In order to sip the nectar with its long tongue, the bee must dive into the flower and in so doing becomes dusted with the fine pollen grains from the anthers.

   We can guess that *nectar* is the substance that bees collect from a flower because the bee must "sip . . . with its long tongue" and "dive into the flower." We can guess that *anther* is a part of the flower because the bee gets "dusted with the fine pollen grains from the anthers" when it dives into the flower.

Improving your ability to understand words in context and increasing your vocabulary in general will help you succeed in the Reading section of the TOEFL test.

Exercises R1–R3

Use Reading Exercises R1–R3 to practice understanding meaning from context.

EXERCISE R1 *Understanding words in context*

This exercise consists of two types of questions. Examples of these two types, including directions, are shown in the boxes below.

> Read the sentence and write the definition of the underlined word.
>
> A cutlass is a short, curved sword.
>
> *a short, curved sword*
>
> You should write *a short, curved sword* as the meaning of *cutlass* because the definition is included in the sentence. The definition follows the verb *be*.

Read the paragraph, and choose the letter of the word or phrase that completes the sentence that follows it.

In law, a nuisance is an act that has no legal justification and that interferes with the safety or comfort of other people. Public nuisances, those that are injurious to the community, may be prosecuted as crimes.

A public nuisance is

(A) a protective law
(B) an injurious act
(C) a legal justification
(D) a safety precaution

You should choose *B* because a *public nuisance* is an act that interferes with the safety of others; that is, an injurious act.

Using *be* to understand meanings

1. Hypoxia is an illness caused by a deficiency of oxygen in the tissues of the body.

   ____

2. A porcupine is a large climbing rodent that is covered with sharp spines for defense.

   ____

3. The atom is the smallest part of a chemical element that can exist and still have the properties of the element.

   ____

4. The Celtic religion centered on the worship of a pantheon of nature deities. Their religious ceremonies included animal sacrifices and various forms of magic. Druids were the priests who led the people in this highly ritualistic worship.

   Druids are

   (A) deities
   (B) ceremonies
   (C) sacrifices
   (D) priests

5. Waste that has been made useful is said to have been recycled. Empty bottles can be returned and used again. Other things that can be recycled are paper, plastic, and metals. Besides the aesthetic value of recycling, there are many environmental reasons to do so.

   Recycled material is

   (A) strewn garbage
   (B) common waste materials
   (C) paper, glass, and coffee
   (D) reused waste

6. Both the Rocky Mountains in North America and the Swiss Alps in Europe have high peaks that challenge the most skilled of mountain climbers. As these climbers ascend the steep, rocky crevices, they may come across edelweiss.

Although edelweiss is the Swiss national flower, it is also found in the Rocky Mountains. It grows wild near areas with year-round snow and can be recognized by its small, white, star-shaped blossoms.

Edelweiss is a

(A) crevice
(B) flower
(C) star
(D) peak

Using appositives to understand meanings

7. Pacemakers, small electrical devices that stimulate the heart muscle, have saved many lives.

____

8. Many residents of Hawaii used to believe that a volcano's flarings were tirades of their goddess, Pele.

____

9. Studying supernovas, the catastrophic explosions of dying stars, may give answers to questions of modern cosmology.

____

10. Seventeenth-century attempts to preserve anatomical specimens brought about modern techniques of embalming, the preservation of the body tissue after death by artificial chemical means. The most common agent used today is formaldehyde, which is infused to replace body fluids.

    Embalming is

    (A) death by a chemical means
    (B) the preservation of body tissue
    (C) a common agent related to formaldehyde
    (D) the replacement of body fluids

11. The grasslands of the world are inhabited by the magnificent and impressive ungulates, the long-legged hoofed mammals, such as bison. The greatest varieties of ungulates are found on the African savanna, where the herds of gazelles and wildebeests in mass movement are a spectacular sight.

    Ungulates are

    (A) grasslands
    (B) herds
    (C) African animals
    (D) hoofed mammals

12. Samuel Morse spent twelve years perfecting his own version of André Ampère's idea for an electric telegraph. However, this inventor is best known for the Morse code, a system of telegraphic signals composed of dots and dashes. The dot represents a very brief depression of the telegraph key. The dash represents a depression three times as long as the dot. Different combinations of dots and dashes are used to code the alphabet, numerals, and some punctuation.

    Morse code is a system of telegraphic

    (A) signals
    (B) keys
    (C) dots
    (D) depression

Using punctuation to understand meanings

13. Long barrows – Stone Age burial mounds made of earth or rubble – are widely distributed throughout northern Europe.

____

14. If you are ectomorphic, "the slender type," you are likely to be good at such sports as track, tennis, and basketball.

____

15. The occlusal (biting) surfaces of the back teeth tend to be the most frequent sites for dental cavities.

____

16. At the age of 19, Galileo discovered isochronism – the principle in which each oscillation of a pendulum takes the same time despite changes in amplitude.

    Isochronism is

    (A) a principle
    (B) an oscillation
    (C) a pendulum
    (D) an amplitude

17. A composer indicates to a musician how a musical passage is to be played through the use of dynamic markings. The symbol for soft is *p*, whereas the one for loud is *f*. The intensity – loudness or softness – depends on the extent or amplitude of the vibrations made by the particular instrument being played.

    Intensity is

    (A) dynamic markings
    (B) the symbol for soft and loud
    (C) the extent of the vibrations
    (D) loudness or softness

18. Oral history, the use of the tape recorder to capture memories of the past in private interviews, has become increasingly popular among professional historians. Studs Terkel is the best known of America's historians to use this method for recording historical events. He has interviewed people about their experiences during important events such as the Great Depression and World War II.

    Oral history is

    (A) private interviews
    (B) the recording of people's memories
    (C) experiences during important events
    (D) the history of tape recording

Using *or* to understand meanings

19. Altitude, or the height above sea level, is a factor that determines climate.

____

20. Osteoblasts, or cells responsible for the formation of new bone, tend to be concentrated on bone surfaces.

____

READING

21. In seagoing vessels, bulkheads, or internal walls, form watertight compartments and strengthen the overall structure.

____

22. According to many psychologists, phobias, or irrational fears, represent or are symbolic of repressed anxiety. They are usually persistent, illogical, and intense. The most useful treatment has been behavior-modification therapy.

A phobia is a

Ⓐ psychologist
Ⓑ fear
Ⓒ symbol
Ⓓ treatment

23. Honeybees live in colonies of many thousand members. A typical colony has a queen that lays eggs; fertile males, or drones; and sexually undeveloped females called workers. The workers care for the queen and larvae, gather nectar, make and store honey, and protect the hive.

A drone is

Ⓐ an egg
Ⓑ a male bee
Ⓒ an undeveloped female
Ⓓ a worker

24. The nervous system of an insect is not a simple electrical circuit. When a signal gets to one end of a nerve cell, the cell sprays various molecules out for the next cell to pick up. The central nervous system of grasshoppers, fruit flies, and other insects includes both the brain and a chain of simpler segmental ganglia, or groups of nerve cells.

Ganglia are

Ⓐ nervous systems
Ⓑ electrical circuits
Ⓒ groups of nerve cells
Ⓓ the molecules the cells send out

Using examples to understand meanings

25. Large fish such as groupers and moray eels recognize the wrasse as a friend that will help them.

____

26. Creatures such as the camel and the penguin are so highly specialized that they can only live in certain areas of the world.

____

27. The sand absorbs enough moisture to support drought-resistant plants such as mesquite, as well as several species of grasses.

____

28. Much can be done to halt the process of desertification. For example, an asphalt-like petroleum can be sprayed onto sand dunes, and seeds of trees and shrubs can then be planted. The oil stabilizes the sand and retains moisture, allowing vegetation to become established where the desert had previously taken over.

Desertification is the

(A) spraying of oil onto sand dunes
(B) planting of trees and shrubs
(C) vegetation becoming established
(D) desert taking over a fertile area

29. Of all the electronic devices that engineers have produced, the computer has had the greatest impact on society. At the heart of every computer, there are microchips. Microchips consist of large collections of tiny devices like the diode and transistor, connected on a single piece ("chip") of silicon.

Diodes and transistors are

(A) collections of computers
(B) microelectronic devices
(C) silicon pieces
(D) computer engineers

30. How complicated the preparations for a camping trip are depends on the duration of the trip as well as the isolation of the area in which the camper intends to be. If a camper intends to stay at one of the many commercial campsites, most needs are provided for. However, for outdoor enthusiasts who want to get far from civilization, choosing camping paraphernalia such as tents, sleeping bags, cooking implements, and other supplies should be done with care.

Paraphernalia is

(A) equipment
(B) food supplies
(C) sleeping bags
(D) campsites

Using adjective clauses to understand meanings

31. Recent tests show that silver sulfadiazine, which is a compound used in the treatment of burns, can cure the most serious types of African sleeping sickness.

____

32. Melody, which is the succession of sounds, takes on new interest when fit into a rhythmic pattern.

____

33. The *O* at the beginning of many Irish names comes from the Gaelic word *ua*, which means "descended from."

____

34. The Pueblo Indians are those who dwell in pueblos, a name derived from the Spanish word for *village*. The pueblo is usually built against the face of a cliff and generally consists of connected houses rising in a series of receding terraces. The roof of one house is the yard or patio of the next house. The kiva, where Pueblo Indians hold their secret ceremonies, is entered by an opening in the roof.

A kiva is a

(A) patio
(B) ceremonial room
(C) series of terraces
(D) Pueblo Indian village

35. The coyote resembles a medium-sized dog with a pointed face, thick fur, and a black-tipped, bushy tail. Although its main diet consists of rabbits and other rodents, it is considered dangerous to livestock. Consequently, thousands of coyotes are killed yearly. In recent years, nonlethal techniques, those that do not kill coyotes, have been developed to protect sheep and other livestock while allowing the coyote to remain in the wild.

    Nonlethal techniques are those that

    (A) are dangerous to livestock
    (B) injure thousands of coyotes yearly
    (C) allow livestock to live in the wild
    (D) are not deadly to wild animals

36. The phenomenon of a mirage, which is an atmospheric optical illusion in which an observer sees a nonexistent body of water, can be explained by two facts. First, light rays are bent in passing between media of differing densities. Second, the boundary between two such media acts as a mirror for rays of light coming in at certain angles.

    A mirage is

    (A) an illusion
    (B) a body of water
    (C) a medium acting as a mirror
    (D) the boundary between two media

Using referents to understand meanings

37. An agricultural concern is the growing number of <u>boll weevils</u>. An infestation of these insects is capable of destroying a cotton crop overnight.

    ____

38. The analysis of carbon and nitrogen isotopes can be used to identify the skeletal remains of <u>carnivores</u>. Because they are higher up the food chain, these meat-eating animals have larger proportions of heavy isotopes in their bone remains.

    ____

39. The perfection of the <u>chronometer</u> by John Harrison was a lifesaving development for sailors. This marine timekeeping device allowed accurate computation of longitude during long sea voyages.

    ____

40. Important officials visiting President Theodore Roosevelt were surprised by his menagerie of pets. No previous president had filled the White House with such a variety of animals.

    A menagerie is a varied group of

    (A) officials
    (B) presidents
    (C) animals
    (D) staff members

41. At least 50 different weed species fight off competitors by emitting toxins from their roots, leaves, or seeds. These poisons do their work in a variety of ways, such as inhibiting germination of seeds and destroying photosynthesis abilities.

Toxins are

Ⓐ roots
Ⓑ leaves
Ⓒ seeds
Ⓓ poisons

42. The English longbowmen did not draw their bows but bent them by leaning on them with one arm and the upper part of their body. This method utilized the strength of the body instead of just the arm and gave the archers endurance to use the longbow for extended periods.

A longbowman is

Ⓐ an archer
Ⓑ a bowing technique
Ⓒ a method for utilizing the strength of the body
Ⓓ a way to increase endurance for longer use of the longbow

Using contrasts to understand meanings

43. The bite of a garter snake, unlike that of the deadly cobra, is benign.

____

44. The bluebonnet, the Texas state flower, thrives in dry, poor soil but struggles in overly wet conditions.

____

45. In contrast to some fluids like water, which has relatively low resistance to motion, honey is highly viscous.

____

46. A unified field theory is one in which two forces, seemingly very different from each other, are shown to be basically identical. According to such a theory, unification will take place at various stages as the energy and temperature increase.

Identical is

Ⓐ different
Ⓑ unified
Ⓒ equal
Ⓓ level

47. The campanile is chiefly a medieval form of Italian architecture. Built in connection with a church or town hall, it served as a belfry, watchtower, and sometimes a civil monument. Unlike other bell towers that are attached to buildings, the campanile generally stands as a detached unit.

A campanile is a

Ⓐ church
Ⓑ town hall
Ⓒ tower
Ⓓ unit

48. While the methods used at other learning institutions are based on the theory that children need a teacher, the Montessori method is based on the theory that a child will learn naturally if placed in an environment rich in learning materials. These

materials are suited to children's abilities and interests, and learning takes place as the child plays. Children following this method are autodidactic, and only when a child needs help does the teacher step in.

Autodidactic is

Ⓐ playful
Ⓑ self-taught
Ⓒ able to learn
Ⓓ dependent on teachers

Using other words in the sentence to understand meanings

49. The bright purple gentian grows wild in Colorado and blooms in late summer.

____

50. While blowing air into the leather bag, a bagpipe player produces melodies by fingering the chanter.

____

51. Unfortunately, the modified potato plant's hairs kill useful insects, but this problem can be alleviated by controlling the amount of hair.

____

52. The much larger hull of the multidecked round ship allowed it to carry more supplies, more men, more guns, and more sails, all of which were necessary for long voyages of commerce and discovery.

A hull is a

Ⓐ storage place
Ⓑ deck
Ⓒ kind of sail
Ⓓ type of commerce

53. In the third century BCE, Ctesibius, the Greek engineer and theorist, first exercised his inventive talents by making an adjustable mirror and then creating ingenious toys that could move under their own power.

Inventive is

Ⓐ regional
Ⓑ creative
Ⓒ flexible
Ⓓ effective

54. Vitamin D is called the sunshine vitamin because it is absorbed through bare skin. The body uses it to form strong bones, and therefore, it is essential for growing children. People who are not exposed to the sun can become deficient in vitamin D and may develop the bone disease rickets.

Deficient is

Ⓐ overexposed
Ⓑ infected
Ⓒ lacking
Ⓓ improved

EXERCISE R2 *Choosing the best synonym*

Read each passage. Choose the letter of the word or phrase that best completes each of the sentences that follow it.

The horse has played a little-known but very important role in the field of medicine. Horses were injected with toxins of diseases until their blood built up immunities. Then a serum was made from their blood. Serums to fight both diphtheria and tetanus were developed in this way.

The word "serum" is closest in meaning to

(A) ointment
(B) antitoxin
(C) blood
(D) acid

According to the passage, horses were given toxins to which they became immune. The blood was made into serums, which acted as antitoxins against the toxins of diseases. Therefore, you should choose *B*.

READING

Questions 1–6

The fork, which did not become a standardized item in Europe until the eighteenth century, was almost unheard of in America. With the absence of forks, it can be assumed that colonists used a spoon instead. The knife was probably held in the right hand, generally the preferred hand for manipulating utensils. The spoon would have been held in the left hand with the concave part of the bowl facing downward. In this position, the diner would be more adept at securing a piece of meat against a plate while the cutting took place. Once the meat was cut, the down-turned spoon would not have been suitable for picking up the morsel. Probably the diner would have put the knife down and shifted the spoon to the right hand. This action would bring the spoon into the correct position for scooping up the bite of food.

This practice of shifting utensils back and forth between hands continued when the fork made its way to America and replaced the spoon as the tool to secure the food being cut. The fork kept the food against the plate more adequately, and its curving tines served the same function as the bowl of the spoon. The custom of shifting the fork from the left hand to the right was no longer necessary, but people continued to use the style that they were used to. This American style of handling eating utensils persists to this day.

1. The word "utensils" is closest in meaning to

(A) gadgets
(B) cutlery
(C) hammers
(D) weapons

2. The word "adept" is closest in meaning to

(A) cultivated
(B) agreeable
(C) cumbersome
(D) proficient

3. The word "morsel" is closest in meaning to

Ⓐ piece
Ⓑ meat
Ⓒ food
Ⓓ spoon

4. The phrase "scooping up" is closest in meaning to

Ⓐ packing up
Ⓑ hoisting up
Ⓒ messing up
Ⓓ picking up

5. The word "tines" is closest in meaning to

Ⓐ handles
Ⓑ blades
Ⓒ prongs
Ⓓ bowls

6. The word "persists" is closest in meaning to

Ⓐ continues
Ⓑ operates
Ⓒ traces
Ⓓ impresses

Questions 7–12

When Jessye Norman's parents were knocking on the wall of their young daughter's room as a signal for her to stop singing and to go to sleep, little did they dream that this small child who seemed to have been born singing would grow up to be an internationally renowned opera singer.

It is not surprising that Jessye loved to sing. Music was an integral part of her family's lifestyle. Although Jessye remembers her mother singing spirituals, it was her grandmother who was always singing. Every hour of her day and every mood was highlighted with a song that fit the occasion. As Jessye was growing up, her piano-playing mother and trumpet- and trombone-playing brothers accompanied her when the family was called upon to provide special music for church services, parent-teacher meetings, and ribbon-cutting ceremonies.

During her childhood, Jessye knew only three operatic songs: one that she learned from a recording and two others – the only opera scores she could find at the local music store. Although singing was in her blood, it was not until she attended Howard University that Jessye Norman took her first voice lesson with Carolyn Grant, who recognized her talent and knew how to channel it. It was almost immediately after leaving the university in 1968, on her first visit to Europe, that Jessye won the singing prize in the International Music Competition of German Radio. The following year, she was invited to go to Berlin to perform at the Deutsche Opera. Since that time, Jessye Norman has become a world superstar whose singular voice reaches audiences all over the world.

7. The word "renowned" is closest in meaning to

Ⓐ infamous
Ⓑ celebrated
Ⓒ notorious
Ⓓ precocious

8. The word "integral" is closest in meaning to
   (A) demanding
   (B) persistent
   (C) essential
   (D) intuitive

9. The word "highlighted" is closest in meaning to
   (A) emphasized
   (B) contradicted
   (C) conveyed
   (D) belittled

10. The word "scores" is closest in meaning to
   (A) points
   (B) experts
   (C) voice lessons
   (D) sheet music

11. The word "channel" is closest in meaning to
   (A) station
   (B) irrigate
   (C) exploit
   (D) direct

12. The word "singular" is closest in meaning to
   (A) flattering
   (B) exceptional
   (C) fluctuating
   (D) different

Questions 13–18

Many laws that were passed in the various states of the United States over the years are now out of date or seem ludicrous. For example, the laws in one state make it illegal for women to expose their ankles and for men to go without their guns. Obviously, these laws are broken daily. With current trends in fashion, every woman who walks down the street or goes to a beach or public swimming pool is committing a crime. While it was once considered of utmost importance that a man be armed and ready for action on the frontier, it is hardly necessary for a man to tote guns to work today. However, a man without a gun is also technically breaking the law.

On the other hand, other laws aren't ever likely to be broken. For example, another law makes it illegal to tether one's horse to the fence surrounding the capitol building. It is hard to imagine anyone riding a horse into the city and leaving it tied outside of the capitol building today. One would have to go to great lengths in order to break this law.

These outdated laws remain on the record because the time needed for state legislatures to debate the issues and make changes in the existing laws would keep the members from attending to more important current and relevant issues. It would be hard to calculate the cost to the taxpayers for these laws to be purged or updated. Consequently, it is likely that these laws will remain on the books.

13. The word "ludicrous" is closest in meaning to

Ⓐ insipid
Ⓑ demeaning
Ⓒ ridiculous
Ⓓ incomprehensible

14. The word "expose" is closest in meaning to

Ⓐ sprain
Ⓑ conceal
Ⓒ decorate
Ⓓ display

15. The word "tether" is closest in meaning to

Ⓐ gallop
Ⓑ fasten
Ⓒ saddle
Ⓓ conduct

16. The word "debate" is closest in meaning to

Ⓐ challenge
Ⓑ contemplate
Ⓒ discuss
Ⓓ overturn

17. The word "relevant" is closest in meaning to

Ⓐ pertinent
Ⓑ fashionable
Ⓒ extraneous
Ⓓ inadequate

18. The word "purged" is closest in meaning to

Ⓐ eliminated
Ⓑ restored
Ⓒ remedied
Ⓓ amended

EXERCISE R3 *Understanding the author's meaning*

Read each passage. Choose the letter of the word or phrase that best completes the sentence that follows it.

> Although originally formed to prevent illegal trade in whiskey, the Royal Canadian Mounted Police, or "Mounties" as they are informally called, now enforce all federal laws throughout Canada. Their diverse duties also include participating in peacekeeping efforts and supplying expertise in areas like forensics to Canadian and international police forces. About 1,000 members of the force are assigned exclusively to the task of controlling the spread of illicit drugs.
>
> In stating that "1,000 members of the force are assigned exclusively to the task of controlling the spread of illicit drugs," the author means that these members
>
> (A) deal only with work involving drug control
> (B) are excluded from the task force assigned to drug control
> (C) work with those who are assigned to the task of drug control
> (D) are assigned all law enforcement tasks excluding that of drug control
>
> You would choose *A* because the word *exclusively* means *without exception.* The members' only task is that of controlling the spread of illicit drugs.

1. Astronomers have recently gained new knowledge of the behavior of galaxies. It has been discovered that spiral galaxies sometimes collide with each other. The huge forces created in such a cosmic event can tug long trails of stars and create new ones from compressed gases. After repeated collisions, galaxies may eventually merge, forming a single elliptical shape. Our own galaxy, the Milky Way, is on a collision course with the nearby Andromeda Galaxy. Hundreds of millions of years from now, these two star systems may combine to form one giant configuration.

   In stating that "the Milky Way is on a collision course," the author means that

   (A) the Milky Way is going to crash into our own galaxy
   (B) the Milky Way is heading toward the Andromeda Galaxy
   (C) the Milky Way is the result of an impact that created one giant configuration
   (D) the Milky Way will crash into two star systems in hundreds of millions of years

2. As long ago as the thirteenth century, Roger Bacon, the celebrated philosopher and Franciscan friar, postulated that humankind could fly with the aid of a large ball constructed of thin copper filled with air. Throughout the centuries, other scientific dreamers hypothesized the construction of a variety of flying devices. Leonardo da Vinci, in particular, studied aspects of flight and made sketches for flying machines. It was not until 1783 that the first people, Pilâtre de Rozier and the Marquis d'Arlandes, successfully took off from the ground, in a balloon designed by the Montgolfier brothers.

   In stating that "Roger Bacon . . . postulated that humankind could fly," the author means that Roger Bacon

   (A) witnessed human flight
   (B) wanted to show how humans could fly
   (C) knew why it was important that humans fly
   (D) thought that human flight was possible

3. Christmas Island, discovered by Captain James Cook on Christmas Eve in 1777, was once populated by a wide variety of bird species. In recent years, at least 18 species of birds – a total of 17 million birds – have been observed to leave or to perish on the island. It is suspected that the cause of the disappearance may be related to a cyclical weather phenomenon in the Pacific that alters winds, salinity, and ocean currents. These variously repeating conditions have resulted in higher water temperatures, which may have caused the fish and squid that the birds live on to die.

   In stating that "the cause of the disappearance may be related to a cyclical weather phenomenon," the author means that the cause is related to

   (A) hurricanes and cyclones
   (B) recurring climatic conditions
   (C) a succession of environmental patterns
   (D) a combination of wind, salt, and ocean currents

4. The historic centers of the American sister cities Savannah, Georgia, and Charleston, South Carolina, have fortunately been saved from demolition or neglect and now attract tourists eager to view the gracious old houses. Of particular interest for the visitor is the exquisite decorative ironwork found throughout the older parts of both cities, especially on porch and stair railings and banisters. Both wrought and cast iron became popular there in the early 1800s, since fire was a constant threat and iron would not burn. Pig iron, which was used as ballast in ships coming from Europe to pick up cargoes of cotton, was bought cheaply, and a local industry producing beautiful ironwork developed.

   In stating that "the historic centers of the American sister cities . . . have fortunately been saved from demolition," the author means that the city centers have

   (A) been kept intact
   (B) remained neglected
   (C) been elegantly restored
   (D) saved the tourist industry

Reading Mini-test 1

Check your progress in understanding meaning from context (Exercises R1–R3) by completing the following Mini-test. This Mini-test uses question types used in the Reading section of the TOEFL iBT test.

Select the correct answer.

Questions 1–4

The incorporation of broken-down scrap tires into asphalt to produce a blend suitable for the construction of road surfaces is becoming widespread. The resulting material, asphalt-rubber, has several advantages over customary road-building materials. It can be applied in a reduced thickness, and this means that less material has to be mined and transported to the road site. Furthermore, roads constructed with this material require less maintenance than more conventional roads. Another benefit is the abatement of traffic noise, a serious issue in urban areas. Perhaps most important, the reduction and possible eventual elimination of waste tires with all their attendant environmental problems may one day become a reality.

1. The word "scrap" is closest in meaning to

Ⓐ waste
Ⓑ outdated
Ⓒ rough
Ⓓ broken

2. The word "customary" is closest in meaning to

Ⓐ special
Ⓑ unusual
Ⓒ regular
Ⓓ suitable

3. In stating "Another benefit is the abatement of traffic noise," the author means that the traffic noise has

Ⓐ subsided
Ⓑ become beneficial
Ⓒ become a serious issue
Ⓓ benefited from thc construction

4. The word "elimination" is closest in meaning to

Ⓐ revision
Ⓑ fulfillment
Ⓒ reduction
Ⓓ eradication

Questions 5–8

Emily Dickinson published only a handful of poems during her lifetime, and she was so secretive about her writing that even her own family was not aware of her literary activities. Emily never married, and after the age of 30 she became increasingly reclusive, rarely venturing out of her family home in Amherst, Massachusetts. She did, however, take a keen interest in contemporary culture and science and was a lively and prolific correspondent.

Her poetry was also abundant, and it was much concerned with the themes of religious conflict, nature, love, and death. Technically her poems show innovative use of rhyme and rhythm and exhibit intense emotion clearly and concisely expressed. After her death in 1886, her sister, Lavinia, discovered her entire unpublished output, over 1,700 poems in all, concealed in drawers. Four years after Emily's death, a selection of these was published, and since then her reputation has grown immensely. Her poetry is now acclaimed throughout the world.

5. The word "reclusive" is closest in meaning to

Ⓐ solitary
Ⓑ distinct
Ⓒ hostile
Ⓓ lonely

6. In stating that Emily Dickinson was a "prolific correspondent," the author means that
   - (A) her letters were profound
   - (B) her letters were entertaining
   - (C) she held many serious discussions
   - (D) she communicated a lot through letters

7. The word "intense" is closest in meaning to
   - (A) focused
   - (B) inhibited
   - (C) weird
   - (D) strong

8. The word "concisely" is closest in meaning to
   - (A) accurately
   - (B) cryptically
   - (C) movingly
   - (D) succinctly

Questions 9–12

In the last couple of decades, marine researchers have observed that epidemic diseases are attacking a variety of sea creatures. Some of them are affecting rare species that are already at risk of extinction. For example, in the 1980s a mysterious epidemic struck a species of sea urchin in the Caribbean, wiping out over 90 percent of the population. Later in the same decade, harbor seals in the Baltic and North Seas succumbed to an unidentified affliction. The green sea turtle has expired in large numbers as a result of developing tumors, known as fibropapillomas, which eventually cover the creature and prevent it from seeing or eating.

Coral reefs and the species that inhabit them have also witnessed an explosion of new diseases. Most of these reported diseases are infections that have appeared recently or are increasing in incidence or geographic range. Some scientists infer that human activity is responsible for spreading these afflictions. Perhaps industrial pollution is weakening the immune systems of marine populations and making them more susceptible to pathogens.

9. The word "affliction" is closest in meaning to
   - (A) situation
   - (B) toxin
   - (C) disease
   - (D) seizure

10. In stating "The green sea turtle has expired in large numbers," the author means that the sea turtles have
    - (A) died from an illness
    - (B) declined in numbers
    - (C) quit coming to the Caribbean
    - (D) become extinct in the Baltic and North Seas

11. The word "incidence" is closest in meaning to

   (A) rate of occurrence
   (B) degree of circumstance
   (C) degree of severity
   (D) rate of exposure

12. The word "susceptible" is closest in meaning to

   (A) attractive
   (B) heedful
   (C) perilous
   (D) vulnerable

Questions 13–16

Psychologists have found that privately made resolutions are rarely followed, whereas a public commitment to achieve some goal, such as losing weight or giving up smoking, is likely to be much more effective. This is because the approval of others for reaching one's target is valued. In contrast, disapproval for failure can lead to feelings of shame.

Advertising agencies have designed studies bearing out the truth of this observation. In their research, a group of strangers was bombarded with information about the qualities of a particular product. They were then asked to either announce out loud or write down privately whether they intended to buy the product. It was later discovered that those who publicly declared their intention to buy were considerably more likely to do so than those who affirmed their intentions in private.

In another study, an experimenter claiming to represent a local utility company interviewed homeowners, telling them he was investigating ways in which energy consumption could be reduced. Half the subjects, randomly selected, were told that if they agreed to conserve energy, their names would be mentioned in an article published in the local newspaper; the remaining half were told their names would not be used. All those interviewed agreed to cooperate and signed a form either giving consent for their names to be used or stating that their names would not be used. Later in the year, the amount of gas consumed in each house was recorded. The owners who had agreed to their names being published had used significantly less gas than those who remained anonymous.

13. The word "resolutions" is closest in meaning to

   (A) declarations
   (B) explanations
   (C) speculations
   (D) persuasions

14. The word "bombarded" is closest in meaning to

   (A) bombed
   (B) attacked
   (C) saturated
   (D) hampered

15. In stating "an experimenter claiming to represent a local utility company interviewed homeowners," the author means that the experimenter who interviewed the homeowners was

   Ⓐ committing fraud
   Ⓑ working for a state utility company
   Ⓒ hiding his identity from the people in the study
   Ⓓ representing a claimant in a law case against the utility company

16. The word "consent" is closest in meaning to

   Ⓐ permission
   Ⓑ submission
   Ⓒ justification
   Ⓓ consideration

PRACTICE WITH UNDERSTANDING THE CONNECTION OF IDEAS

Recognizing and understanding how sentences and ideas are linked throughout a passage will help your comprehension of the passage. Your ability to follow the flow and organization of a passage depends upon your ability to understand how the major points, facts, and details are arranged in support of the main idea. The skills you will need in order to make these connections are outlined below.

Understanding referents

Instead of repeating the same words over and over, writers use pronouns and short phrases to refer to these words. These pronouns and short phrases are called *referents.* They may refer back to a previously used word, phrase, or idea. They can also be used to anticipate a word, phrase, or idea that follows. Read the following example:

> Instead of picking the children up on his way to the supermarket, Tom waited until he was on his way home to get them.

In this sentence, *them* refers to *the children* and *he* refers to *Tom. Them* and *he* are referents.

Improving your understanding of referents will help you to follow the flow of ideas in reading passages, to answer specific referent questions, and to answer many other questions on the TOEFL test.

(For more information on and practice with referents, see Grammar Review: Referents, p. 113; Practice with Understanding Connections, p. 257; Practice with Cohesion, p. 317; and Practice with Cohesion, p. 379.)

Understanding transitional expressions

Recognizing and understanding transitional expressions will help you follow the flow and organization of ideas in the reading passages on the test. (For more information on and practice with transition words and phrases, see Grammar Review: Connecting Ideas, p. 116; Practice with Understanding Connections, p. 257; Practice with Cohesion, p. 317; and Practice with Cohesion, p. 379.)

Becoming familiar with the following list of transition words and phrases will help you follow the flow of ideas in a passage. Recognizing these words will help you recognize the organization and purpose of a passage more clearly and quickly.

Words that:	
qualify	but, however, although, yet, except for
emphasize	surely, certainly, indeed, above all, most importantly
illustrate	for example, next, for instance, thus, such, such as
contrast	unlike, in contrast, whereas, on the other hand, instead
concede	although, yet, nevertheless, of course, after all
conclude	finally, in conclusion, at last, in summary, to sum up
add	in addition, also, moreover, then, first, second (etc.)
compare	similarly, like, in the same way, both, equally important
explain	now, in addition, furthermore, in fact, in this case, at this point
state a consequence	therefore, as a result, consequently, accordingly, otherwise

Understanding the organization of ideas

One of the question types that you will encounter on the TOEFL test requires you to insert a sentence in the correct place in a passage. Referents, connecting words, and surrounding words can help you identify where the sentence fits best. The sentence can be one of the following three types:

1. A general sentence that introduces the topic A well-written passage has a main idea, called the *topic*. The topic is what the passage is about. The topic of the passage is usually stated in the first sentence, although other positions are also possible. The sentence that states the topic is called the *topic sentence*.

If the sentence to be inserted is the topic sentence, it will introduce the general topic of the passage and it will contain words that relate to words in the first sentence of the passage. Read the passage below and the sentence to be inserted.

> **A** The Korean Warrior kite is usually constructed of four or five spars tied together in the center. **B** The spars form a sturdy frame for a rectangular cover whose center is pierced by a circular hole several inches in diameter. **C** The surface of the cover is often decorated with stripes and designs reminiscent of the sun. **D** This kite is especially suited for flying in strong winds.
>
> **Kite design varies around the world.**

This sentence describes a general topic and would precede the sentence introducing the specific topic – the design of the Korean Warrior kite. The sentence would logically be the first sentence in the passage and would be inserted at *A*.

2. A sentence that gives details of a supporting idea within the passage If the sentence to be inserted gives details of a supporting idea, it will probably contain transitions or connecting words. Additionally, it will often contain a word or phrase that refers to the supporting idea. Read the passage below and the sentence to be inserted.

Cheese is made from the curd of milk. **A** Although there are literally thousands of varieties, which differ according to the method of preparation and quality of milk, they can be divided into three main classes. **B** Soft cheeses are those with rinds and very soft, creamy centers. Of these, Brie and Camembert are perhaps the most famous. **C** Blue-veined cheeses have been injected with a penicillin mold, which creates the characteristic blue veins. **D** Pressed cheeses are those placed in a mold and firmly pressed. There are uncooked pressed cheeses, such as Cheddar, and cooked pressed cheeses, such as Gruyère.

Roquefort, for example, is a well-known blue-veined cheese from France.

This passage is about the three main classes of cheese. Roquefort is "a well-known blue-veined cheese," the second class of cheese that is discussed. The connecting words *for example,* along with the phrase "blue-veined cheese," link this sentence to the sentence that explains blue-veined cheeses. The sentence would logically be inserted at *D*.

3. A sentence that ends the paragraph A sentence that is meant to be inserted at the end of a paragraph will either be a detail of the final supporting idea of the passage or will summarize the ideas in the passage. Referents and/or transitions and connecting words will refer to the previous sentence. Read the passage below and the sentence to be inserted.

A In areas of extreme conditions, people have found functional ways to use limited resources. **B** A case in point is the desert dwellers who, for thousands of years, have sheltered themselves in extremely functional buildings. **C** These buildings are constructed of one of the most readily available, dependable, and inexpensive materials we know of on earth: mud, the ideal insulator. **D**

This material absorbs heat during the day and slowly releases it at night.

The phrase "this material" refers back to "mud, the ideal insulator." The rest of the sentence describes mud's ideal insulating properties. The sentence would logically be inserted at *D*.

Improving your ability to recognize and use all the clues given through referents, transitions/connectors, and surrounding words will help you identify where a given sentence should be inserted in the passage items on the TOEFL test.

Exercises R4–R8

Exercises R4–R8 Use Exercises R4–R8 to build your skills in understanding the connection of ideas in reading passages.

EXERCISE R4 *Locating referents within sentences*

Read the sentence. Find the referent for each underlined word or words, and write it in the space.

> Under the ice, bubbles gather against the ice roof until they overflow and escape through the tide cracks.
>
> they *bubbles* ____________
>
> You should write *bubbles* because *they* (plural) agrees with *bubbles*, and bubbles can overflow and escape.

1. Arctic people must not only defend themselves from the environment and wild animals, but they must also protect these natural resources.

   themselves ____________

   they ____________

   these natural resources ____________

2. Amnesty International consists of over 900 groups of individuals who work for the release of political prisoners incarcerated for their beliefs.

   who ____________

   their ____________

3. In 1863, when a Hungarian count recognized the potential of Californian soil and sun for growing wine grapes, he planted the first European variety there near the town of Sonoma.

   when ____________

   he ____________

   the first European variety ____________

   there ____________

4. The first complete American dictionary of the English language was compiled in 1828 by the lawyer and lexicographer Noah Webster, who was particularly eager to show at this time that the English spoken in America was distinct from that spoken in Britain.

   the lawyer and lexicographer ____________

   who ____________

   at this time ____________

   that ____________

EXERCISE R5 *Locating referents within a passage*

Read the passage. Choose the letter of the word or phrase that best completes the sentence that follows it.

Differences in the way men and women process language is of special interest to brain researchers. It has been known that aphasia – a kind of speech disorder – is more common in men than in women when the left side of the brain is damaged in an accident or after a stroke. However, women are more likely than men to suffer aphasia when the front part of the brain is damaged. This clearly indicates that the brains of men and women are organized differently in the way they process speech.

The word "they" in the passage refers to

(A) men
(B) women
(C) brains
(D) researchers

You should choose *C* because *they* (plural) agrees with *brains,* and brains can process speech.

1. One of the most potentially explosive international problems is that of mass tourism. Of the more than six billion people in the world, an increasing number of them are determined to travel. Annually a vast number of travel-hungry tourists traipse around the globe, and thousands of perfect beaches, quaint villages, historic cities, and regions of exquisite natural beauty have become victims of developers' building schemes. Attempts to accommodate these people have led to the destruction of the very attractions that they have come to enjoy and have made daily living almost impossible for the local residents.

   The phrase "these people" in the passage refers to

   (A) people in the world
   (B) tourists
   (C) developers
   (D) residents

2. Traditionally, America's fast-food companies have hired teenagers. While teenagers provide cheap labor, they are sometimes unreliable. Consequently, fast-food companies often use another source of cheap labor – the elderly. Older people are less likely to skip a day of work or quit without giving notice, but because they have not been brought up with computers, they view the high-tech fast-food counter with terror. Training centers have opened in order to teach "mature workers" how to operate computerized cash registers, timed deep-fat fryers, and automatic drink-dispenser software. These students are put into classrooms with their peers and, since mental arithmetic is a thing of the past, are taught how to use a calculator.

   The phrase "These students" in the passage refers to

   (A) teenagers
   (B) fast-food employers
   (C) the elderly
   (D) peers

3. The Bettmann Archive is a picture library that was founded in the 1930s by German immigrant Otto Bettmann. He arrived in New York City with two suitcases of photographs and opened a picture library, which he built into the biggest commercial operation of its kind in the world. Among the millions of photographs the archive contains are some of the most memorable images of the twentieth century: Marilyn Monroe standing by a street grate ventilating her skirt, Einstein sticking out his tongue, and the Hindenburg exploding into flames. According to Bettmann, the archive's success was due to his unique filing system which he designed to suit journalistic needs. For example, the Mona Lisa was not filed under "Paintings" or "Leonardo da Vinci"; it was filed under "Smiling."

   The word "some" in the passage refers to

   Ⓐ suitcases of photographs
   Ⓑ picture libraries
   Ⓒ commercial operations
   Ⓓ archive photographs

EXERCISE R6 *Locating multiple referents within a passage*

Read the passage. Then draw a line from each highlighted word to its referent.

People often assume that athletes are healthier and more attuned to their overall well-being than nonathletes. However, two researchers recently conducted a survey of college students. They reported that athletes are more likely than those who aren't into sports to engage in behaviors that put their health at risk.

1. Scientists used to believe that animals scream to startle predators into loosening their grip or to warn their kin. However, now some researchers have concluded that the piercing, far-reaching cries of animals may have another function. Recent studies indicate that these screams may have evolved to attract other predators, which will give the prey a chance to escape during the ensuing struggle between predators.

2. When cartoonists take on the task of drawing real people, they do so by making a caricature. These kinds of cartoon drawings are frequently used to satirize well-known people. Most famous people have several particular characteristics that distinguish them, such as facial features, body posture, or gestures, which are familiar to the general public. Cartoonists can cleverly exaggerate them to the point of ridiculousness.

3. Satellites routinely relay pictures of desert areas. From these pictures, it can be determined where locusts are likely to breed. With information on the locusts' breeding areas, agriculture officials can use pesticides to kill these insects before they become a menace. If not eradicated, a single swarm can devour 80,000 tons of corn a day – sustenance for half a million people for one year.

EXERCISE R7 *Understanding transition words*

Complete the sentences by choosing the letter of the phrase or clause that would most likely follow the underlined transition words.

> Although potatoes are richer in food value than any other vegetable, they are not always a wise choice for a garden crop because they need a considerable amount of space to grow. <u>Consequently</u>,
>
> (A) they are the most common vegetable in a garden
> (B) people don't eat potatoes very much
> (C) they can be more economically grown on farms
> (D) farmers overcharge for their potatoes
>
> You should choose *C* because *consequently* introduces a consequence of a previously stated fact. If potatoes are not a wise choice for a garden because of the amount of space they need, they could be grown on a farm more economically, since a farm has more space than a garden.

1. Glass was precious to Egyptians, who used it interchangeably with gemstones, <u>but</u>
   (A) it is over 4,000 years old
   (B) its novelty as an artist's material prevents its being taken seriously
   (C) today it has come out of factories and into the workshops
   (D) today it is so commonplace that it is seldom given a second thought

2. Glimpses into the prenatal world via ultrasound imaging occasionally show behavior <u>such as</u>
   (A) the development of the central nervous system
   (B) the sex of the baby-to-be
   (C) a fetus sucking its thumb
   (D) structures as small as the pupil of an eye of a second-trimester fetus

3. <u>Although</u> the animals and plants that live in the world's various deserts come from different ancestral stocks,
   (A) they have solved their problems of survival differently
   (B) none of them have adapted to the jungles
   (C) they are from different deserts
   (D) they resemble one another to a surprising degree

4. Children dress up in witches' hats or ghost costumes to play pranks when celebrating the fun October holiday of Halloween. <u>In contrast</u>,
   (A) Thanksgiving is a traditional holiday
   (B) Thanksgiving is always celebrated on the fourth Thursday of November
   (C) families dress more formally and set elegant tables for the more serious occasion of Thanksgiving
   (D) children enjoy Thanksgiving

5. Everything from chairs and fishing poles to rope and paper can be made from bamboo. <u>Equally important</u>,
   (A) this giant grass grows in warm climates
   (B) fresh spring bamboo shoots take longer to cook than winter ones
   (C) a variety of foods can be made from this giant grass
   (D) preserved bamboo shoots can be used in soups instead of fresh ones

6. Earth satellites transmit telephone and television signals, relay information about weather patterns, and enable scientists to study the atmosphere. This information has helped people communicate ideas and expand their knowledge. In conclusion,
   - (A) satellites have enriched the lives of humankind
   - (B) satellites are expensive to send into space and sometimes are difficult to maintain
   - (C) a dish antenna can pick up 300 TV channels from satellites
   - (D) satellites are placed in an orbital region around Earth called the geostationary belt

7. In the 1940s, when today's astronauts hadn't even been born, comic-strip detective Dick Tracy fought crime in an atomic-powered space vehicle. In addition to that,
   - (A) many of today's astronauts have used a kind of atomic-powered space vehicle
   - (B) he used lasers to process gold and a two-way wrist TV for communication
   - (C) "Dick Tracy" was a very popular comic strip in the United States
   - (D) astronauts used lasers to process gold and communicated on long-distance flights using two-way wrist TVs

8. According to dental researchers, a vaccine that could significantly reduce the number of microorganisms thought to cause cavities will soon be ready for human trials. Consequently,
   - (A) cavity prevention programs may soon be eliminated
   - (B) immunization of test animals will no longer be necessary
   - (C) children will be able to consume more sugary foods and drinks
   - (D) long-term protection against tooth decay could soon be available on the market

9. Medical researchers have recently developed a nonsurgical method of treating heart disease that, in some cases,
   - (A) is just as effective as coronary bypass surgery but is much less expensive and disabling
   - (B) can replace a clogged artery by the transplantation of a vein or artery from another part of the body
   - (C) continues to be underused because coronary bypass operations are lucrative for hospitals and surgeons
   - (D) requires opening up the chest and operating under local anesthesia

10. Neurons, which cannot divide, are the basic cells of the brain. Glial cells, which can increase in number, provide support and nourishment to the neurons. It was hypothesized that if Einstein's brain had been more active, more glial cells would be found there. Indeed,
   - (A) scientists found that the physicist's brain contained more glial cells per neuron than the brains of eleven normal males
   - (B) scientists' previous work had shown that animals put in environments that stimulate mental activity develop more glial cells per neuron
   - (C) scientists examined sections of the upper front and lower rear of both hemispheres because these areas are involved in "higher" thinking
   - (D) scientists found that even though there was evidence he had greater intellectual processing, it cannot be determined whether Einstein was born with this or developed it later

READING

EXERCISE R8 *Inserting sentences*

For each passage, choose the letter of the square where the **bold** sentence would best fit.

For more than 2,000 years, nomads of Central Asia and the Far East have lived in portable, circular dwellings called *yurts*. A These structures are highly durable and use resources very efficiently. B They typically have a low profile and circular shape. C This allows the wind to slip around and over them so they can withstand very high winds. The basic shape is formed from wooden poles crisscrossed to form a circular lattice frame in which a wooden door is set. D The outside covering is made of fabric that is supplemented with animal skins during cold weather.

Roof poles are made from wooden beams that are tied at the lower end to the lattice and are secured to a central roof ring.

The sentence to be added gives details on how the basic shape is made. It would follow the sentence describing the basic shape and precede the sentence that describes the covering of the basic shape. The sentence would logically be inserted at *D*.

1. A Pragmatism is essentially an American school of thought that has had few supporters elsewhere. B One of the first pragmatists, William James, wrote that it was impossible to discover the real world outside our senses and therefore we must concern ourselves primarily with human experience. C Because the world would be a worse place without a belief in human responsibility, morals, and free will, it was necessary, he considered, to believe in these concepts. D Another pragmatist, John Dewey, held that since truth is an instrument for solving problems, it must change as the problems it confronts change.

   Pragmatists believe that the test of any belief should be its practical consequences and that the truth of a proposition should be judged on how well it corresponds with experimental results.

2. In the early years of the twentieth century, the American art scene was dominated by painters who had established their reputations in the previous century. A At this time, there was a general intolerance both by critics and by the public of any deviation from the kind of work championed by academic institutions. B Acceptable art generally employed detailed realistic technique and focused on subject matter of historical or mythological scenes or sentimental landscapes. C In 1908 a group of artists organized an exhibition in a New York gallery that constituted a revolt against these current orthodoxies. D Their unconventional work often depicted the seamy side of urban life in settings such as backyards, saloons, dance halls, and theaters. Surprisingly, the show was a success, and for a time these artists enjoyed widespread popularity.

   The artists, who came to be called "the Eight" and were later dubbed the "Ashcan School," used vigorous brush strokes and dramatic lighting.

3. Seeds are dispersed to new sites by various means. Many, such as dandelion or thistle seeds, have fine tufts that allow them to be scattered by the action of the wind. A Some seeds such as the coconut can float and are dispersed by currents around the islands of the Pacific Ocean. Other seeds have evolved ways of getting around through the activities of an intermediary animal. B This can happen in a number of different ways. For example, animals may devour the fruit containing seeds. C Sometimes a seed needs to be buried before it can germinate. This might

happen when a hoarding animal such as a squirrel fails to return for its hidden meal. D Some seeds have sticky or spiky surfaces, often called burrs, which may catch on the coat of a passing animal and later drop off at a considerable distance from their origin.

In fact, a seed may require passage through the gut of the bird or animal before it can germinate.

4. The technique of using wind power to grind grain between stones to produce flour is ancient and was widely practiced. Exactly where the first windmill was constructed is unknown, although certainly the Persians ground corn more than 2,000 years ago. A Tradition has it that the knowledge spread to the Middle East and from there to Northern Europe during the Middle Ages. B The power of the wind replaced animal power in several regions of Europe where millwrights became highly skilled craftsmen and rapidly developed the technology. C In England the device became a ubiquitous feature of the landscape, and by 1400 there were 10,000 windmills concentrated in the southeast part of the country, each capable of grinding 10,000 bushels of grain a week. Starting in the nineteenth century the mill started to decline in importance with the advent of steam power. D By the mid–twentieth century few working mills remained in use, but in recent years efforts have been made to restore and maintain these romantic souvenirs of a bygone age.

The Dutch in particular made considerable improvements and used windmills to pump water as well as to produce flour.

Reading Mini-test 2

Check your progress in understanding connections (Exercises R4–R8) by completing the following Mini-test. This Mini-test uses question types used in the Reading section of the TOEFL iBT test.

Select the correct answer.

Questions 1–3

In the twentieth century, architects in large cities designed structures in a way that reduced noise and yet made living as comfortable as possible. A They used such techniques as making walls hollow and filling this wall space with materials that absorb noise. Thick carpets and heavy curtains were used to cover floors and windows. Air conditioners and furnaces were designed to filter air through soundproofing materials. B However, after much time and effort had been spent in making buildings less noisy, it was discovered that people also reacted adversely to the lack of sound. C Now architects are designing structures that reduce undesirable noise but retain the kind of noise that people seem to need. D

1. The word "They" in the passage refers to

Ⓐ cities
Ⓑ structures
Ⓒ architects
Ⓓ techniques

2. According to the passage, making walls hollow and filling this wall space with materials that absorb noise results in
   - (A) filtered air
   - (B) a lack of sound
   - (C) an adverse reaction to noise
   - (D) a reduction in undesirable noise

3. The following sentence can be added to the passage:

   A silent home can cause feelings of anxiety and isolation.

   Look at the four squares [■] that indicate where the sentence could be added. Where would the sentence best fit? Choose the letter of the square [■] that shows where the sentence should be added.

Questions 4–6

> The gambrel roof design has an enduring appeal to many builders and homeowners. Originally a feature of Dutch colonial architectural style, the gambrel is a straight double-sloped roof joined at a central ridge. [A] The main distinguishing feature is that each roof side is broken into two planes, with the lower slope inclined at a steeper pitch than the upper. Sometimes the angle of the gambrel roof becomes shallower again at the eaves and projects over the wall of the house, giving a bell-shaped appearance in cross section. [B] The main advantage of the gambrel roof is that it creates a spacious interior on the upper floor of the house. [C] This makes it a perfect choice for a growing family. [D]

4. The phrase "a feature" in the passage refers to
   - (A) the gambrel roof design
   - (B) the straight sloping roof
   - (C) the roof design in Holland
   - (D) the roof joined at a central ridge

5. The gambrel roof design of the Dutch colonial architectural style is appealing to homeowners because
   - (A) it has a bell-shaped appearance
   - (B) it creates a spacious upper floor
   - (C) the shape is traditional
   - (D) the angle becomes shallower at the eaves

6. The following sentence can be added to the passage:

   This spaciousness also makes the gambrel roof highly suitable for barn construction, since the upper floor can be used as a hayloft.

   Look at the four squares [■] that indicate where the sentence could be added. Where would the sentence best fit? Choose the letter of the square [■] that shows where the sentence should be added.

Questions 7–9

Diamond value is based on four characteristics: carat, color, clarity, and cut. The size of a diamond is measured by carat weight. There are 100 points in a carat and 142 carats in an ounce. Each point above 1 carat is more valuable than each one below 1 carat. In other words, a stone that weighs more than 1 carat is more valuable per point than a stone that is smaller than 1 carat.

The scale used for rating color begins with D, which means the gem is absolutely colorless and, therefore, the most valuable. E and F are almost colorless. All three are good for investment purposes. A stone rated between G and J is good for jewelry. Beyond J the stones take on a slightly yellowish color, which gets deeper as the grade declines.

The clarity of a stone is determined by its lack of carbon spots, inner flaws, and surface blemishes. While most of these are invisible to the unaided eye, they do affect the diamond's brilliance. For jewelry, a diamond rated VVS1 (very, very slight imperfections) is as close to flawless as one will find. After that the scale goes to VVS2, VS1, VS2, SI1, SI2, I1, I2, and so on.

➡ The final characteristic is cut. [A] When shaped – whether round, oval, emerald, marquise, pear, or heart – the diamond should be faceted so that light is directed into the depths of the prism and then reflected outward again. [B] A well-cut diamond will separate the light into different colors when the light is reflected. [C] Only stones of similar shape should have their reflective qualities compared, as some shapes are more reflective than others. The round shape is the most reflective. [D]

7. The word "one" in the passage refers to
   - (A) a diamond
   - (B) an ounce
   - (C) each point
   - (D) 1 carat

8. Even though they affect a diamond's brilliance, slight carbon spots, inner flaws, and surface blemishes
   - (A) lack imperfections
   - (B) are rated VVS1
   - (C) cannot be seen with the naked eye
   - (D) can make a diamond more valuable

9. The following sentence can be added to paragraph 4:

   In contrast, a nearly flawless diamond that is not professionally cut will not acquire its full reflective potential, and thus, its value may be diminished.

   Paragraph 4 is marked with an arrow [➡]. Look at the four squares [■] that indicate where the sentence could be added. Where would the sentence best fit? Choose the letter of the square [■] that shows where the sentence should be added.

Questions 10–12

People who suffer from excessive drowsiness during the daytime may be victims of a condition known as "narcolepsy." Although most people may feel sleepy while watching TV or after eating a meal, narcoleptics may fall asleep at unusual or embarrassing times. They may doze while eating, talking, taking a shower, or even driving a car.

Victims can be affected in one of two ways. Most narcoleptics have several sleeping periods during each day with alert periods in between, but a minority feel drowsy almost all the time and are alert for only brief intervals. Many people with this condition also suffer from cataplexy – a form of muscular paralysis that can range from a mild weakness at the knees to complete immobility affecting the entire body. This condition lasts from a few seconds to several minutes and is often set off by intense emotions.

➡ No reliable data exist showing how many people have narcolepsy. ■A Unfortunately, there is also little knowledge about the causes of this illness. ■B Researchers suggest that the problem may stem from the immune system's reacting abnormally to the brain's chemical processes. ■C Further studies have shown a link between narcolepsy and a number of genes, although it is quite possible for an individual to have these genes and not develop the disease. ■D There are also cases of twins where one member has narcolepsy but the other does not. Thus, an explanation based on genetics alone is not adequate.

There is currently no cure for narcolepsy, so sufferers of this condition can only have their symptoms treated through a combination of counseling and drugs. The available drugs can help control the worst of the symptoms, but their administration has unwanted side effects such as increased blood pressure and heart rate and, sometimes, even increased sleepiness. It is clear that improved medications need to be developed.

10. Unlike most people who may feel drowsy after a meal or while watching TV, narcoleptics
    - (A) doze off at odd times
    - (B) sleep most of the time
    - (C) suffer in one of two ways
    - (D) have no trouble falling asleep

11. The word "their" in the passage refers to
    - (A) sufferers
    - (B) symptoms
    - (C) drugs
    - (D) side effects

12. The following sentence can be added to paragraph 3:

    Some estimates put the number as high as 300,000 in the United States alone.

    Paragraph 3 is marked with an arrow [➡]. Look at the four squares [■] that indicate where the sentence could be added. Where would the sentence best fit? Choose the letter of the square [■] that shows where the sentence should be added.

Questions 13–15

On December 4, 1872, the brigantine *Mary Celeste,* carrying 1,700 barrels of crude alcohol en route from New York to Genoa, was found abandoned and drifting in the Atlantic Ocean between the Azores and Portugal. The crew of the *Dei Gratia,* the cargo ship that found the *Mary Celeste,* inspected her carefully and then sailed her to Gibraltar to collect the large salvage reward. Their report given at the inquiry suggests that the captain, his wife, his young daughter, and the seven-man crew had deserted the ship in a great hurry. The captain's bed was unmade, something unheard of in a well-run ship, which the *Mary Celeste* was known to be. The oilskin boots and pipes belonging to the crew had also been left, although the chronometer, sextant, and lifeboat were missing. The cargo was intact, although some barrels had leaked and two of the hatches were not in place.

Several theories have been propounded to explain why those aboard left a perfectly seaworthy vessel to risk their lives on an open boat. It has been suggested that they were the victims of alien abduction or sea-monster attacks. Such outlandish notions are hardly credible. The idea that the ship was a victim of piracy can also be discounted, since the cargo and other valuables were untouched. Likewise, mutiny does not seem plausible, since the captain and first officer were known to be fair and experienced, the voyage was relatively short, and mutineers would probably have taken over the ship, not forsaken it.

➡ A possible explanation is that some event made the captain fear for the safety of the ship. **A** In fact, recently studied seismic records indicate that a violent earthquake, whose epicenter was on the seafloor in the region where the *Mary Celeste* was sailing, occurred some days before the ship's discovery. **B** If the ship had been subjected to intense shocks caused by the quake, all aboard may have hastily abandoned ship to avoid what they imagined might be its imminent destruction from an explosion of the combustible cargo. **C** A severed rope found dangling from the side of the *Mary Celeste* suggests that the evacuees trailed behind in the lifeboat, attached to the ship, waiting for the crisis to pass. **D** Great waves may then have snapped the rope and capsized the smaller boat, whose occupants would have disappeared without a trace.

13. The word "Their" in the passage refers to
    - (A) the captain's family
    - (B) the crew of the *Dei Gratia*
    - (C) the crew of the *Mary Celeste*
    - (D) all those aboard the ships sailing between the Azores and Portugal

14. The phrase "Such outlandish notions" in the passage refers to
    - (A) risking their lives in an open boat
    - (B) alien abduction or sea-monster attacks
    - (C) piracy
    - (D) mutiny

15. The following sentence can be added to paragraph 3:

    The need to circulate air to prevent such a blast could explain why the crew left two hatches open.

    Paragraph 3 is marked with an arrow [➡]. Look at the four squares [■] that indicate where the sentence could be added. Where would the sentence best fit? Choose the letter of the square [■] that shows where the sentence should be added.

PRACTICE WITH UNDERSTANDING DETAILS AND RECOGNIZING PARAPHRASES

Understanding details

Some of the questions in the Reading section of the TOEFL test will require you to understand details within a reading passage. Several details may be mentioned within a passage. To answer these questions successfully, you must be able to recognize them.

Detail questions are frequently introduced in the following ways:

According to the passage, . . .
The author states that . . .

The remaining part of the question will tell you what to look for, as shown in the example below:

According to the astronomers, **the blue arcs are**

Ⓐ a visual phenomenon
Ⓑ actually imaginary
Ⓒ invisible to the human eye
Ⓓ bending massive galaxies

The details in the answer choices may use words and phrases that are different from (but have similar meaning to) those in the reading passage. Here is the part of the passage that contains the answer to the example:

The discoverers of these arcs think they are actually optical illusions created by light that has been bent by the immense gravitational pull of a massive galaxy.

In order to answer the question, you will have to recognize that the discoverers of the arcs must be astronomers, and the pronoun *they* refers to *these arcs*. The word *optical* is related to *visual* and an illusion could be a phenomenon. Therefore, you should choose *A*.

Recognizing paraphrases

Improving your ability to recognize details from a passage that are stated in a different way in the questions and answer choices will help you succeed on the TOEFL test.

Identifying restated information from a passage

Some test questions will require you to choose a sentence that has the same meaning as a highlighted sentence in the reading passage. The answer choices use words similar to those in the highlighted statement, but the incorrect choices do not have the same meaning. Incorrect choices can also leave out pertinent details in the highlighted sentence. Read the excerpt below. An example of this type of multiple-choice question follows.

The discoverers of these arcs think they are actually optical illusions created by light that has been bent by the immense gravitational pull of a massive galaxy. The arcs are probably formed when the light from a distant galaxy is bent by the gravitational pull of another, less distant, intervening galaxy. Even though such light-bending galaxies contain billions of stars, they do not contain enough visible ones that alone could exert the pull needed to create a blue arc. It has been theorized that there must be huge amounts of invisible or "dark" matter within these galaxies.

Which of the sentences below best expresses the essential information in the highlighted sentence? Incorrect answer choices change the meaning in important ways or leave out essential information.

Ⓐ Billions of stars are contained in the galaxies, which alone could exert the pull needed to create a blue arc.
Ⓑ Those galaxies that cause light to bend into a blue arc do not have enough visible stars to exert such a pull.
Ⓒ The light-bending galaxies contain billions of visible and invisible stars that exert enough pull to cause a blue arc.
Ⓓ Since the light-bending galaxies don't contain enough visible stars to exert the pull needed to create a blue arc, dark matter is considered a possibility.

In choice A, the information is contrary to that in the highlighted statement. The visible stars are not enough to excrt the pull that creates a blue arc. In choice C, the information has introduced "invisible stars." Choice D has introduced "dark matter." The passage may contain information about invisible stars and dark matter. However, this information is not mentioned in the highlighted sentence and is therefore incorrect as a restatement. Therefore, you should choose *B* as the correct restatement of the highlighted sentence.

Identifying information not stated in a passage

Some questions will ask you to identify information that has *not* been stated explicitly in the reading passage. These multiple-choice questions are frequently introduced in the following ways:

All of the following are mentioned in the passage . . . EXCEPT
All of the following are mentioned in paragraph . . . EXCEPT

The remaining part of the question will tell you what to look for. To answer these questions successfully, you will need to read all of the answer choices and determine whether the details described in each one can be found in the passage.

The details in the answer choices may use words and phrases that are different from (but have similar meaning to) those in the reading passage. Read the excerpt about arcs again. An example of this type of question follows on the next page.

The discoverers of these arcs think they are actually optical illusions created by light that has been bent by the immense gravitational pull of a massive galaxy. The arcs are probably formed when the light from a distant galaxy is bent by the gravitational pull of another, less distant, intervening galaxy. Even though such light-bending galaxies contain billions of stars, they do not contain enough visible ones that alone could exert the pull needed to create a blue arc. It has been theorized that there must be huge amounts of invisible or "dark" matter within these galaxies.

All of the following are mentioned in the paragraph **as factors in the blue arc phenomenon** EXCEPT

Ⓐ the light being bent by the gravitational pull of galaxies
Ⓑ the light coming from a distant galaxy and bent by a closer one
Ⓒ the amount of gravity needed being explained by dark matter theory
Ⓓ the light-bending dark matter existing in such distant intervening galaxies

Choice *A* is found in the passage in the phrase "light that has been bent by the immense gravitational pull of a massive galaxy." Choice *B* is found in the words "the light from a distant galaxy is bent by the gravitational pull of another, less distant, intervening galaxy." Choice *C* is found in the phrase "theorized that there must be huge amounts of invisible or 'dark' matter within these galaxies," which refers to the fact that there are not enough visible stars to exert the needed pull. There is no information in the passage concerning the galaxies where dark matter exists. Therefore, you should choose *D*.

Exercises R9–R14

Use Exercises R9–R14 to build your skills in understanding details and recognizing paraphrases in reading passages.

EXERCISE R9 *Finding facts*

Read each passage and the statements that follow. Write *T* in the space if the statement is true according to the information in the passage. Write *F* in the space if the statement is false or if the information is not given in the passage.

Micromygale diblemma is a spider that inhabits the coastal, forested regions of Panama. It has only two eyes whereas most spiders have six or eight. Unlike most spiders, it does not have lungs but instead absorbs oxygen through its skin. Just three one-hundredths of an inch long, the size of the head of a pin, *M. diblemma* is one of the world's smallest spiders.

A. __T__ The coastal, forested regions of Panama are where one of the world's smallest spiders lives.
B. __F__ While most spiders have six or eight eyes and absorb oxygen through the skin, *Micromygale diblemma* has only two eyes and lungs.
C. __F__ The world's smallest spider is the size of the head of a pin.

Statement A is true. According to the passage, the spider that inhabits the coastal, forested regions of Panama is one of the world's smallest spiders. Statement B is false. Most spiders have six or eight eyes and have lungs. *Micromygale diblemma* has two eyes, but does not have lungs. It takes in oxygen through its skin. Statement C is false because there is no information about the world's smallest spider. We only know that *one* of the world's smallest spiders is about the size of the head of a pin.

1. The plan to join Britain to the European continent by boring a tunnel under the English Channel between Dover, England, and Calais, France, was originally proposed in the second half of the nineteenth century. The bill authorizing the work was rejected in 1883. The plan was again proposed in 1930 by many enthusiastic supporters. The tunnel was to be the longest ever made and an engineering wonder. However, the estimated cost, the military risks, and the doubt as to the feasibility of construction led to the rejection of the proposal in June 1930. Finally, in the 1980s, the proposal was accepted and tunneling began. The great engineering feat was completed in 1994, and for the first time passengers could travel underwater between England and the European mainland.

A. _____ The plan to unite Britain with the European continent was proposed three times.
B. _____ The plan to unite Britain with the continent was rejected three times.
C. _____ It was believed by some that the tunnel posed a security threat.
D. _____ Some people did not believe that the tunnel was a viable idea in the 1930s.
E. _____ The plan was rejected in 1883 because the people were bored.
F. _____ The construction of the tunnel led to the rejection of the proposal in 1930.
G. _____ The tunnel made in 1930 was the longest ever constructed.
H. _____ The predicted expense of the proposed tunnel was prohibitive in 1930.

2. The 50-million-year-old fossils of an ancient whale found in the Himalayan foothills of Pakistan give strong evidence that modern whales are descended from a four-legged, land-dwelling animal. The fossils consist of part of the skull, some teeth, and the well-preserved middle ear of an animal that was 6 to 8 feet long, weighed about 350 pounds, had a wolf-like snout, and had two foot-long jaws with sharp, triangular teeth. It is the middle ear that suggests that the ancient whale lived on land. Analysis indicated that the animal had eardrums, which would not have worked in water and which modern whales have only in vestigial form. Furthermore, the right and left ear bones were not isolated from each other. The separation of these bones in marine whales enables them to detect the direction of underwater sounds.

A. _____ The 50-million-year-old fossils found in Pakistan are most likely from a four-legged, land-dwelling animal.
B. _____ The fossils are 6 to 8 feet long and about 350 pounds in weight.
C. _____ The whale's skull, teeth, and middle ear are evidence that the Himalayan foothills were once under water.
D. _____ Because eardrums do not function under water, the ancient whale probably lived on land.
E. _____ Whales with eardrums would not be able to hear well in the water.
F. _____ A marine whale can recognize the source of a sound because the middle ear is in a vestigial form.
G. _____ When the right and left ear bones are isolated from each other, a whale can detect the direction of underwater sounds.
H. _____ Whales with isolated right and left ear bones live in the sea.

3. The potato, which is nutritious and popular, is an important food source for millions of people. It is so important that destruction of the potato crop by pests has resulted in famines. Plant researchers, studying the hundreds of varieties of potatoes, have uncovered a wild hairy variety of potato from Bolivia that emits a strong glue from the end of its hairs. This glue traps and kills insects. A new hairy potato was developed when researchers successfully crossed the common potato with the hairy potato. This new hybrid potato not only reduces aphid populations by 40 to 60 percent, but also emits a substance that checks the population of the Colorado potato beetle, one of the most destructive potato pests. Unfortunately, the hairs also trap beneficial insects. Plant researchers are currently trying to alleviate this problem by limiting the density of hairs.

A. _____ The potato, an important food for millions of people, is nutritious and popular.
B. _____ There are hundreds of varieties of potatoes that are hairy.
C. _____ Plant researchers are studying a potato from Bolivia that gives off a scent from the end of its hairs.
D. _____ Insects get trapped in the sticky hairs and die.
E. _____ The hairy potato was crossed with the common potato to develop a new hairy potato.
F. _____ All insect populations have been reduced by 40 to 60 percent by the wild hairy potato.
G. _____ The Colorado potato beetle is one of the pests affected by the substance the hairy potato emits.
H. _____ The hybrid potato harms insects that help potatoes.

4. A Stradivarius violin is unmatched in tonal quality and responds more quickly and easily to the touch than any other violin. Unfortunately, the secrets for making such a superb instrument were lost in 1737 with the death of Antonio Stradivari, the master craftsman who built them. Many attempts have been made to reproduce an instrument of such quality, but all have failed. It is believed that the secret lies in the wood that was used and the distinctive varnish, which ranges from orange to a deep reddish-brown color. Only around 650 Stradivarius violins are believed to be in existence today, and the average price for such a rare instrument is well into the hundreds of thousands of dollars. Even a "cheap" Stradivarius costs around a quarter of a million dollars. It is not surprising that Stradivarius violins are sought after by great violinists and musical-instrument collectors alike.

A. _____ A Stradivarius violin cannot match the tonal quality of any other violin.
B. _____ The main qualities of the Stradivarius are tone and response.
C. _____ Antonio Stradivari was the man who crafted the violins.
D. _____ Stradivari's notes on making such a superb instrument were preserved.
E. _____ People believe that the quality comes from the type of wood and the color of the varnish that was used.
F. _____ The varnish color ranges between an orange and a deep reddish-brown.
G. _____ The 650 Stradivarius violins in existence cost a quarter of a million dollars in total.
H. _____ Both musicians and instrument collectors would like to own a Stradivarius.

5. The most traditional American food may well be cornmeal. Cornmeal, as we know it today, began as a Native American staple. The Native Americans grew corn of six different varieties: black, red, white, yellow, blue, and multicolored. They ground the corn kernels into cornmeal and mixed it with salt and water. Then they baked it. This recipe was introduced to the early colonists, who experimented with it and developed their own uses for cornmeal. Succotash (a meat stew with cornmeal added) and mush (leftover cornmeal porridge cooled, cut, and fried) are two meals invented by early colonists. Today, visitors can travel to the South and enjoy spoon bread, a smooth puddinglike dish, or to New England for johnnycakes, a kind of flat pancake. But probably the most common recipes using cornmeal nationwide are cornbread, cornmeal muffins, and the "hush puppy" – a round ball of cornmeal batter that is fried in oil.

A. _____ The multicolored corn was made up of six different colors.
B. _____ Cornmeal was ground into kernels that were baked.
C. _____ The Native Americans shared their recipe of baked cornmeal with the early settlers.
D. _____ The colonists did not like the meal of the Native Americans and thus developed their own meals.
E. _____ Succotash and mush are two meals the colonists shared with the Native Americans.
F. _____ Succotash is a meal that is made from meat and cornmeal.
G. _____ Mush is fried leftovers from a cornmeal dish.
H. _____ Common forms of cornmeal are restricted to certain regions in America.

EXERCISE R10 *Understanding exceptions*

Read each passage. Choose the letter of the word or phrase that best completes the sentence that follows it.

Today's readers look for knowledge and information from more than just an encyclopedia. Knowledge, information, data, and images race around the world with ever-increasing speed and availability. With a quick press of a key on the computer keyboard, data from some of the great libraries in the world can be called onto a screen for immediate perusal.

The author mentions all of the following means of accessing information EXCEPT

Ⓐ encyclopedias
Ⓑ television
Ⓒ computers
Ⓓ libraries

The author's mention of a screen is in reference to a computer screen and not to a television screen. The only means of accessing information not mentioned is television. Therefore, you should choose *B*.

1. Whereas the scene of colonial North America was one of complex cultural negotiations and explosive interactions among Native Americans, Africans, and Europeans, history books have portrayed the settlement of North America as a unilateral push of Europeans into a virgin land. Although primary documentation – government reports, travel accounts, trade journals, all written from a European perspective – is filled with observations concerning Native American customs and beliefs, history books are more interested in outlining important battles.

Ethnohistorians, the scholars who blend anthropology's insights with historical research to produce a cultural understanding of the past, have been making advances in understanding the Native American perspective on European colonialization.

The author mentions all of the following as sources of primary documentation EXCEPT

Ⓐ government reports
Ⓑ travel accounts
Ⓒ trade journals
Ⓓ history books

2. Although Winslow Homer (1836–1910) is best known for his realistic watercolors of powerfully dramatic seascapes, he first won acclaim in the art world as an illustrator for the reportage of the American Civil War. This led to his illustrating texts of prose and poetry. His more than 160 drawings reached print as lithographs, wood engravings, and photomechanical cuts. Despite the skill and serious intent he invested in them, Homer's book illustrations made little impact during his lifetime. Even today, most of his illustrations are not discussed in the literature covering his work, and nearly all of them have been excluded from even the most comprehensive exhibitions of Homer's art.

The author mentions all of the following as types of work Winslow Homer did EXCEPT

Ⓐ photography
Ⓑ lithographs
Ⓒ watercolors
Ⓓ illustrations

3. Almost all sports and outdoor leisure activities carry real risks. Swimmers drown, mountaineers fall, skiers are swept away by avalanches, and boxers are killed by blows to the head. A person's skill or experience is no guarantee against disaster. In fact, the better an athlete is, the greater the temptation to break records or succeed in doing something that has never been done before. Danger, which tests nerves, courage, and skill, is an essential element that adds thrill and enjoyment to a sport. Although those who organize sports formulate their rules in a way to minimize the risk of injury and to ensure that medical assistance is readily available, no amount of caution can alter basic facts: even the best-trained horse may panic; motorcycles give little protection in a crash; and a hard-driven golf ball can go astray.

According to the passage, all of the following are risks in sports EXCEPT

Ⓐ falls
Ⓑ storms
Ⓒ accidents
Ⓓ avalanches

4. Perhaps one of the most hazardous ways of making a living from the sea was diving for pearls. Only the most daring would risk their lives in this profession. The technique of pearl diving was simple. Divers attached themselves to ropes that were used to keep them in contact with an assistant on board the ship. Attached to a different rope were large weights that helped to speed the divers' descent and, hence, conserve their breath for searching the seabed. Also needed were nose clips, heavy gloves that provided protection for their hands against the sharp edges of the oyster shells, and a net in which they collected the oysters. These nets were slung around

the divers' necks so as not to impede the movement of their hands. When the divers signaled their intention to surface, the assistant hauled them and their load of oysters up. The oysters were then opened, and any pearls found were sifted through sieves and graded according to size and quality. Once a widely practiced profession, pearl diving has largely disappeared with the development of the cultured pearl.

The author mentions all of the following as the pearl divers' underwater activities EXCEPT

(A) the contact with an assistant on board
(B) the attachment of a heavy weight to make them descend faster
(C) the collection of oysters
(D) the opening of the oyster

5. Margaret Mitchell wrote only one novel, *Gone with the Wind*. It was published in 1936 and proved to be such a huge success that Mitchell's life was irrevocably altered. She lost all her privacy and lamented this fact constantly until her death in 1949. The novel, which has been translated into 28 languages and has sold more copies than any other book except for the Bible, won the Pulitzer Prize in 1937. Two years later, the movie produced by David O. Selznick had its premiere in Atlanta. This movie holds the record of having been viewed more times than any other movie produced. Throughout her life, Mitchell denied that her main characters, Scarlett and Rhett, or any of her other characters, were biographical in any way. She did have access to family correspondence dating from the 1850s to the 1880s, the time of the American Civil War. It seems natural that a woman with Margaret Mitchell's vivid imagination and historical awareness, and in possession of a collection of family correspondence that documents such a volatile era as that of a civil war, could weave a story that still enthralls.

The author of the passage gives all the relevant dates about Mitchell EXCEPT the date of

(A) the family letters
(B) her birth
(C) the first showing of the movie
(D) the first printing of the novel

EXERCISE R11 *Determining whether statements are the same or different*

Write *S* in the space if the two sentences have the same meaning. Write *D* if they have different meanings.

_D_ A collection of fascinating tales called *The Arabian Nights* was introduced to Europe by the French scholar Antoine Galland.

The French scholar Antoine Galland introduced to Europe a collection of fascinating tales that he named *The Arabian Nights*.

You should write *D* because the sentences do not mean the same thing. The first sentence means that the scholar introduced the tales, whereas the second sentence means that the scholar both introduced and named the tales.

1. _____ Scree, which abounds in the Rocky Mountains, has its origins in the ice ages.

The Rocky Mountains have a lot of scree, the formation of which dates back to the ice ages.

2. _____ Many reef organisms avoid dead-end caves, which lack the steady currents necessary for bringing a continuous food supply.

   Dead-end caves don't have currents that bring in food supplies, so many reef organisms don't go there.

3. _____ Two theaters in Stratford-upon-Avon and two in London are the ones regularly used by the Royal Shakespeare Company.

   The Royal Shakespeare Company regularly uses four theaters – two in Stratford-upon-Avon and two in London.

4. _____ Police reconstruct scenes because people seem to recall things best when they are in the same physical situation.

   When people are in the same physical situation, they seem to remember better scenes than the ones police have reconstructed.

5. _____ Despite the cold Alaskan temperatures, which freeze perspiration and breath in men's beards, cabin fever forces inhabitants to challenge the elements.

   Alaskan inhabitants suffer from cabin fever, which causes perspiration and breath to freeze in men's beards.

6. _____ Leather, when improperly handled and exposed to changeable temperatures, cracks easily.

   Leather cracks easily when it is handled incorrectly and is exposed to variable temperatures.

7. _____ Despite the increasing pollution of their shorelines over the past decade, oceans have become cleaner in the vast open-sea areas.

   During the last ten years, pollution has been increasing along the coasts of the oceans and spreading to the once clean open-sea areas.

8. _____ The Hitler diaries, the greatest known publishing fraud in history, were written by a man who copied material from Hitler's speeches and medical reports.

   By copying material from Hitler's speeches and medical reports, a man wrote the Hitler diaries, known as the greatest publishing fraud in history.

EXERCISE R12 *Locating restated information*

Read each passage and the restatement that follows it. Underline the words or phrases in the passage that give the information that is restated.

> The damp British climate may be infuriating to humans, but it is ideal for plants. The Gulf Stream flows across the Atlantic to warm the west coast of these islands, which occupy the same latitudes as Newfoundland. Moisture-laden Atlantic winds bring almost constant rain and mist.
>
> The perfect weather conditions for plants to flourish are found in the wet British Isles.
>
> You should underline *British climate* (weather conditions in the British Isles), *ideal for plants* (perfect for plants), and *constant rain and mist* (wet) because these are ideas from the passage that are restated.

1. Europa, one of Jupiter's moons, is the only place in the solar system – outside of Earth – where enormous quantities of water are known to exist. Although this water is in ice form, there is a possibility that there is only a crust of ice with a liquid ocean underneath. Because of powerful thermal pulses caused by the tidal forces of Jupiter and the other moons, Europa may be the best place in the solar system for finding life forms.

   Europa's vast oceans are unequaled in the solar system, with one exception.

2. Using sophisticated instrumentation, lightning experts have learned that lightning travels at one-third the speed of light. A lightning bolt is five times hotter than the surface of the sun and can have ten times more power than the output of a large power company. A single discharge can actually contain twenty or more successive strokes, occurring too fast for the eye to separate. Some seem to stretch for 500 miles when observed from outer space.

   It is possible that a lightning bolt, which seems very large, is really a series of bolts.

3. Once porpoises reach speeds of 12 miles per hour, they frequently leap out of the water to escape the pull of surface drag. At that point, leaping out of the water actually requires less energy than swimming. These leaps are most efficient at speeds of 40 miles per hour and greater.

   Porpoises conserve energy by traveling through the air, which creates less drag than water.

4. In the earliest stages of a star's formation – a process that takes some 10,000 years – the star is surrounded by an extremely dense layer of gas and dust. This matter eventually condenses and heats up to 1 million degrees and hotter, triggering a thermonuclear explosion. During the flare-up, strong winds blowing off the surface of the star disperse the surrounding dust and expose the newborn star to observers on Earth.

   People can see the birth of a star because of the strong winds that scatter the dust particles.

5. Perhaps the greatest navigators in history were the Vikings. Without compasses or other modern instruments, they explored Iceland, Greenland, and even crossed the Atlantic Ocean to the shores of North America. To find their way, they stayed close to shorelines or used the position of the sun to plot the latitude.

   The Vikings were expert sailors.

6. Since the first dolphin was trained by the United States Navy in 1965 to help divers in their underwater home, *Sealab II*, many other dolphins have been drafted into the Navy. Originally, dolphins were used as messengers or to answer calls for help. Today, dolphins do such dangerous and necessary work as locating explosives hidden in the sea and helping ships navigate safely in war zones.

   An important task for a dolphin is to find mines.

7. Saint Bernard dogs are large, shaggy animals. They were bred by Augustinian monks, who trained them to search for travelers lost in snowstorms or avalanches in the Alps. For hundreds of years, Saint Bernards served this purpose. But nowadays journeys across the Alps are on well-maintained road and tunnel systems, and the dogs are no longer needed.

   Saint Bernards aided travelers for centuries.

8. Every year in Japan, the competitions for the longest human-powered flights are held. Out on Lake Biwa, participants attempt to break records by flying their own inventions over the water without propeller or jet assistance. The would-be human birds glide until their craft meets its inevitable crash landing. A flotilla of small boats lines the flight path waiting to rescue the pilot. In the first Japanese event, a world record of 88.53 meters was established. Since then, new records have been set almost every year. These days, flights of several kilometers are regularly achieved.

   Participants fly in craft they have designed themselves.

EXERCISE R13 *Choosing the restatement of highlighted sentences*

Which of the sentences below best expresses the essential information in the highlighted sentence? Incorrect choices change the meaning in important ways or leave out essential information.

The bulk of Kafka's writings was not published until after his early death from tuberculosis.

Ⓐ It was not until after Kafka's early death from tuberculosis that the bulk of his writings was published.
Ⓑ After the bulk of his writings was published, Kafka died an early death from tuberculosis.
Ⓒ After Kafka had written the bulk of his published writings, he met with an early death from tuberculosis.
Ⓓ An early death from tuberculosis kept Kafka from publishing the bulk of his writings.

You should choose *A* because this is the only sentence that contains the same information as the first sentence: First Kafka died, and then most of his writings were published.

1. Fainting is caused by a sudden drop in the normal blood supply to the brain.

   Ⓐ The brain reacts to a drop in the normal blood supply by fainting.
   Ⓑ Fainting occurs when the brain suddenly loses its normal blood supply.
   Ⓒ Fainting happens when the brain drops its normal blood supply.
   Ⓓ The brain faints when the normal blood supply drops.

2. Gorillas, which are vegetarians, have been observed to demonstrate gentle behavior toward small creatures in the wild.

   (A) Vegetarians have been observed to demonstrate gentle behavior toward gorillas and small creatures in the wild.
   (B) Only vegetarian gorillas have been observed as demonstrating gentle behavior toward small creatures in the wild.
   (C) Small creatures in the wild have been observed as behaving gently and demonstratively when near gorillas.
   (D) It has been observed in the wild that gorillas, by nature vegetarians, treat small animals gently.

3. In fighting forest fires, the initial attack crews dig a fire line, which varies in width depending on the strength and nature of the fire.

   (A) Initial attack crews dig a forest fire to vary the fire line's width.
   (B) Initial attack crews depend on the strength and nature of the fire to vary the fire line.
   (C) The width of the fire line, which the initial attack crews dig, varies according to the strength and nature of the fire.
   (D) In digging a fire line, the initial attack crews depend on fighting forest fires.

4. Medical quackery, which promises cures for all existing and even nonexisting diseases, has a powerful appeal even to the well educated.

   (A) Well-educated people in medicine promise to find powerful cures for diseases.
   (B) Even well-educated people are attracted to fake cures for diseases that may or may not exist.
   (C) Medical quackery promises the well educated a cure for diseases.
   (D) The medical profession has appealed to the well educated for funding to find cures for diseases.

5. A silver compound has been found to kill the parasitic protozoa that are carried by the dreaded tsetse fly and that cause sleeping sickness.

   (A) The dreaded tsetse fly causes sleeping sickness and kills the parasitic protozoa used for finding silver compounds.
   (B) It has been found that the silver compound that is carried by the dreaded tsetse fly and causes sleeping sickness kills the parasitic protozoa.
   (C) Sleeping sickness, which is caused by the dreaded tsetse fly, has been found to kill the parasitic protozoa in silver compounds.
   (D) Parasitic protozoa that cause sleeping sickness and are carried by the dreaded tsetse fly can be killed with a silver compound.

6. While working as a postmaster at the University of Mississippi, William Faulkner submitted thirty-seven stories to magazines, six of which were accepted.

   (A) Of the thirty-seven stories that Faulkner submitted while working at the University of Mississippi as a postmaster, six were published in magazines.
   (B) Faulkner wrote six out of thirty-seven stories after accepting a job as postmaster at the University of Mississippi.
   (C) Faulkner published thirty-seven stories in magazines, six of which were accepted by the University of Mississippi.
   (D) The six accepted stories by Faulkner were about his job as a postmaster at the University of Mississippi.

7. The continental drift theory proposes that the Earth's crustal plates are driven by a global system of convection currents in the hot magma below that behave like giant conveyor belts.
   (A) Theoretically, the Earth's crustal plates behave like giant conveyor belts, driving the convection currents across the hot magma, which causes the continents to drift.
   (B) A global system of convection currents in the underlying hot magma acts as giant conveyor belts to drive the Earth's crustal plates.
   (C) The continental drift theory suggests that global plates cover hot magma, which acts as a giant conveyor belt for convection currents.
   (D) The continental drift theory is proposed by the Earth's crustal plates, which drive a global system of convection currents in the hot magma below, behaving like giant conveyor belts.

8. Medical authorities have been reluctant to support the findings of some nutritionists that vitamin C given in large doses can prevent the common cold.
   (A) Medical authorities support nutritionists' views about the value of vitamin C in preventing the common cold.
   (B) Nutritionists have found that medical authorities are not in favor of using vitamin C to prevent the common cold.
   (C) Some nutritionists have found that large doses of vitamin C can prevent the common cold, but this has not been completely accepted by medical authorities.
   (D) According to nutritionists and some medical authorities, the common cold can be prevented by giving large doses of vitamin C.

9. Female cowbirds, which cannot sing, are nonetheless able to teach songs to their young by responding to specific chirps and ignoring others.
   (A) Even though female cowbirds cannot sing, they teach their chicks to do so by responding to specific chirps and ignoring others.
   (B) Female cowbirds can neither sing nor teach songs to their babies by responding to certain chirps more than to others.
   (C) Female cowbirds, which cannot sing, have other birds teach their young to sing.
   (D) Female cowbirds, which cannot sing, unsuccessfully attempt to teach their young to sing by responding to other bird songs.

10. The conflict between those who wish to conserve a large area of unaltered and unimproved spaces and those who want the abolition of the last remnants of wilderness in the interest of industrial profit will not be resolved in the near future.
   (A) The people who desire to conserve a large area of untouched natural land and those who want to use all land for industrialization are in a conflict that will not have an immediate resolution.
   (B) The conflict over whether a large area of unaltered and unimproved space should be given over for industrial development and profit is of interest to those resolved to abolish the last remnants of wilderness.
   (C) Lawyers are profiting from the unresolved conflict between the people who wish to save the last remnants of wilderness and those who want to alter and improve the space for industry.
   (D) There is an unresolved conflict caused by people who wish to abolish industry and turn the spaces back into a natural wilderness state.

EXERCISE R14 *Choosing the restatement of highlighted sentences in paragraphs*

Read each passage. Then choose the letter of the sentence that best expresses the essential information in the highlighted sentence. Incorrect choices change the meaning in important ways or leave out essential information.

Between the late 1920s and 1950s, the Osborne Calendar Company produced a series of calendars featuring trains of the Pennsylvania Railroad. Up to 300,000 of these, featuring large, colorful scenes of trains at work, were published each year to hang in depots and shippers' offices along the lines of the famous railroad company. The scenes, mostly painted by one artist, Grif Teller, are now valuable collectibles.

(A) The scenes of trains, for the most part painted by Grif Teller, are collectibles.
(B) The Osborne Calendar series of train scenes are collector's items.
(C) Grif Teller has a valuable collection of the Osborne Calendar scenes of trains at work.
(D) Grif Teller's paintings of depots and shippers' offices are valued by collectors.

You should choose *A* because the scenes of trains are the valuable collectibles.

1. Tree rings have long been used to determine the ages of trees and to gauge past climatic conditions. New evidence adds considerable weight to the theory that tree rings also record earthquakes. The rings reflect the effects of earthquakes, such as tilting, the disruption of root systems, and breakage, as well as shifts in environments. Older trees and petrified trees may give information about earthquakes that took place hundreds and even thousands of years ago.

   (A) The effects of earthquakes on trees can be seen in tree rings.
   (B) Earthquakes cause a lot of damage to trees in the environment.
   (C) The effects of earthquakes are tilting, disruption of root systems, breakage, and shifts in environments.
   (D) Tilting, disruption of root systems, breakage, and shifts in environments are examples of how an earthquake affects trees.

2. Yuzen dyeing is a Japanese art that produces a lavish, multicolored type of kimono design that dates from the seventeenth century. First, a pattern is sketched on a kimono of plain, undyed silk. The garment is then taken apart and the design carefully painted onto the fabric with a paste that prevents the fabric from absorbing dye. Next, dyes are brushed over the silk, their colors penetrating only the untreated areas. After the paste is rinsed out, the strips of silk are again sewed into the kimono. Elaborate embroidery often completes the decoration.

   (A) The paste keeps the unstitched garment together while the fabric is absorbing the colors.
   (B) The dye is prevented from being absorbed into the fabric pieces by the paste that covers the design.
   (C) The design is painted onto the pieces of garment with a paste that keeps the dye from destroying the design.
   (D) The design is painted onto the fabric in places where the paste does not prevent the paint being absorbed by the garment.

READING

3. The beaver's comical-looking flat tail, which is three-quarters of an inch thick, six or seven inches wide, and perhaps a foot long, is unique in the animal world. In the water, it serves as a rudder for swimming, and on land it props the beaver upright while the animal is cutting trees. It also serves as a radiator through which the heavily insulated beaver passes off excess body heat. The beaver uses its broad tail for an early warning system by slapping it against the water's surface, making a resounding whack that can be heard half a mile away.

   (A) The beaver's tail is like a big fan that disperses heat.
   (B) The beaver gets rid of extra body heat through its tail.
   (C) The beaver's body heat radiates through its heavily insulated body.
   (D) The beaver has a heavy coat and, therefore, needs a radiator to reduce its body heat.

4. If pearls are protected properly, they can last for centuries. One reason a pearl loses its luster or cracks is that the mineral constituent of the pearl can be dissolved by weak acids. There are several kinds of acids that pearls may come in contact with. Human perspiration contains one such acid. Much of the cotton that pearls are wrapped in when not in use is treated with an acid. Another kind of acid that damages pearls is found in many modern cosmetics. The chemicals in commercial brands of makeup seep into the string canal and may penetrate into the layers of a pearl and cause deterioration. The best protection to give pearls to ensure their long life is having them cleaned and restrung at prescribed intervals.

   (A) The penetration through the pearl of the string canal causes damage to the layers.
   (B) The deterioration of the pearl is usually caused by string canal seepage and penetration.
   (C) The infiltration of cosmetics into the pearl may cause it to disintegrate.
   (D) A pearl's deterioration can be prevented through cosmetic usage.

Reading Mini-test 3

Check your progress in understanding details and recognizing restatements (Exercises R9–R14) by completing the following Mini-test. This Mini-test uses question types used in the Reading section of the TOEFL iBT test.

Select the correct answer.

Questions 1–5

Every year about two million people visit Mount Rushmore, where the faces of four U.S. presidents were carved in granite by the sculptor Gutzon Borglum and his son. The creation of the Mount Rushmore monument took 14 years – from 1927 to 1941 – and nearly a million dollars. These were times when money was difficult to come by, and many people were jobless. To help him with this sculpture, Borglum hired laid-off workers from the closed-down mines in the Black Hills area of South Dakota. He taught these men to dynamite, drill, carve, and finish the granite as they were hanging in midair in his specially devised chairs, which had many safety features.

Borglum used dynamite to remove 90 percent of the 450,000 tons of rock from the mountain quickly and relatively inexpensively. His workmen became so skilled that without causing damage, they could blast to within four inches of the finished surface and grade the contours of the facial features. Borglum was proud of the fact that no workers were killed or seriously injured during the years of blasting and carving the granite. Considering the workers regularly used dynamite and heavy equipment, this was a remarkable feat.

During the carving, many changes in the original design had to be made to keep the carved heads free of large fissures that were uncovered. However, not all the cracks could be avoided, so Borglum concocted a mixture of granite dust, white lead, and linseed oil to fill them.

Every winter, water from melting snow gets into the fissures and expands as it freezes, making the fissures bigger. Consequently, every autumn maintenance work is done to refill the cracks. To preserve this national monument for future generations, the repairers swing out in space over a 500-foot drop and fix the monument with the same mixture that Borglum used.

1. The author of the passage indicates that the men Borglum hired were
   - (A) trained sculptors
   - (B) laid-off stone carvers
   - (C) Black Hills volunteers
   - (D) unemployed miners

2. According to the passage, what achievement did Borglum pride himself on?
   - (A) The four presidential faces in granite that he had sculpted
   - (B) The removal of 90 percent of the 450,000 tons of rock quickly and at a relatively low cost
   - (C) His safety record of no deaths or serious injuries during the years of work with heavy equipment and dynamite
   - (D) His skillful training of the labor force that enabled blasts of dynamite to be within inches of the contour lines of the faces

3. Which of the sentences below best expresses the essential information in the highlighted sentence in the passage? Incorrect choices change the meaning in important ways or leave out essential information.

   (A) Since cracks could not be avoided, Borglum tried various materials to cover them.
   (B) In order to fill the unavoidable cracks, Borglum invented a mixture for filling them.
   (C) A mixture was uncovered by Borglum during the changes in design needed to avoid cracks.
   (D) Because cracks could not be avoided, Borglum bought a mixture of granite dust, white lead, and linseed oil.

4. According to the passage, today Mount Rushmore needs to be

   (A) protected from air pollution
   (B) polished for tourists
   (C) restored during the winter
   (D) repaired periodically

5. The passage discusses all of the following aspects of the creation of the Mount Rushmore carvings EXCEPT

   (A) where the people who worked on Mount Rushmore came from
   (B) why Borglum carved the heads of four U.S. presidents
   (C) how Borglum dealt with fissures that could not be avoided
   (D) when repairs to this national monument are made

Questions 6–10

Teotihuacán is the largest and most impressive urban archaeological site of ancient America, covering an area of roughly 20 square kilometers. The city was at one time thought to be the religious center of the Toltecs but is now believed to be a creation of an earlier civilization about whose origins little is known. The earliest artifacts from Teotihuacán date from over 2,000 years ago, but the period of greatest expansion dates from 200 CE to 500 CE. At its peak the city is estimated to have had a population of up to 200,000 inhabitants, with residential areas extending throughout the built-up area. Judging by regionally dispersed finds of the image of the rain god Tlaloc, of "thin orange wear" pottery, and of the characteristic architectural forms, the influence of Teotihuacán was widespread. It is not clear what caused the city's decline and eventual abandonment, but the evidence points to overpopulation, a depletion of resources, and the possible sacking by adversaries.

The primary axis of the city was the Avenue of the Dead, which extends for 2.5 kilometers through the center of the urban area, starting in the north at the Moon Plaza and continuing beyond the Great Compound complexes to the south. The avenue divided Teotihuacán into two sections with apartment compounds arranged on either side, often symmetrically, suggesting a highly planned layout from the earliest phases of construction.

The vast Pyramid of the Sun, located in the middle of the central zone, is the tallest and most dominant structure of Teotihuacán, with a height of 65 meters and a base covering approximately 10 acres. At one time the edifice was surmounted by a temple. A cave located underneath the pyramid and possibly used for ritual activities hints at its religious importance. The Pyramids of the Moon and Feathered Serpent are other notable ceremonial sites nearby.

A particular feature of the architecture of many of the pyramidal platforms at this site is the series of sloping apron walls, known as *taluds,* interspersed with vertical panels – *tableros* – producing a step-like appearance. Originally all such structures would have been covered with a layer of stucco and then painted, often with pictures of animals and mythological creatures.

6. According to the passage, the dispersed finds from Teotihuacán indicate that
   - (A) the city is over 2,000 years old
   - (B) the city had an estimated population of as many as 200,000 inhabitants
   - (C) the residential areas extended throughout the urbanized area
   - (D) the city greatly influenced the surrounding areas

7. According to the passage, which of the following statements about the decline of Teotihuacán is known to be true?
   - (A) The people migrated to another city.
   - (B) The population of the city starved.
   - (C) The city was invaded by neighbors.
   - (D) The cause of the decline is uncertain.

8. According to the passage, the symmetrical layout around the Avenue of the Dead
   - (A) divided the city into two sections, one of which had apartment compounds for the living
   - (B) started at the Moon Plaza, continued past the Great Compound complexes, and extended as far as the center of the urban area
   - (C) included a primary axis of the city
   - (D) indicated that the city layout was planned before building began

9. Which of the sentences below best expresses the essential information in the highlighted sentence in the passage? Incorrect choices change the meaning in important ways or leave out essential information.
   - (A) A feature of the pyramidal architecture is the many platforms that make up the steps.
   - (B) The sloping walls of the pyramid have occasional vertical panels, which gives the appearance of steps.
   - (C) The architectural features known as *taluds* and *tableros* are a particular feature of the many pyramidal platforms.
   - (D) A series of sloping walls combined with vertical panels produces the appearance of steps that form the pyramidal platforms.

10. All of the following are mentioned as having been found in the Teotihuacán area EXCEPT
    - (A) market streets
    - (B) religious artifacts
    - (C) ceremonial structures
    - (D) residential districts

Questions 11–15

In the eleventh century, people noticed that if a small hole were put in one wall of a darkened room, then light coming through the aperture would make a picture of the scene outside on the opposite wall of the room. A room like this was called a camera obscura. Artists later used a box to create a camera obscura, with a lens in its opening to make the picture clearer. But it was not possible to preserve the image that was produced in the box.

In 1727, Johann Heinrich Schulze mixed chalk, silver, and nitric acid in a bottle. He found that when the mixture was subjected to light, it became darker. In 1826, Joseph Nicéphore Niépce put some paper dipped in a light-sensitive chemical into his camera obscura, which he left exposed in a window. The result was probably the first permanent photographic image. The image Niépce made was a negative, a picture in which all the white parts are black and all the black parts are white. Later, Louis Daguerre found a way to reverse the black and white parts to make positive prints. But when he looked at the pictures in the light, the chemicals continued to react and the pictures went dark. In 1837, he found a way to fix the image. These images are known as daguerreotypes.

Many developments of photographic equipment were made in the nineteenth century. Glass plates coated with light-sensitive chemicals were used to produce clear, sharp, positive prints on paper. In the 1870s, George Eastman proposed using rolls of paper film, coated with chemicals, to replace glass plates. Then, in 1888, Eastman began manufacturing the Kodak® camera, the first "modern" lightweight camera that people could carry and use.

During the twentieth century, many technological improvements were made. One of the most important was color film. Color film is made from layers of chemicals that are sensitive to red, green, and blue light, from which all other colors can be made. Despite the fact that the space age has witnessed the creation of an array of technological marvels, until recently even the ability to take photographs of distant galaxies from above the Earth's atmosphere via orbiting satellites was grounded in the basic principles of photography that Niépce used when he took his first fuzzy negative pictures.

11. The first camera obscura can be described as nothing more than
    - (A) a darkened room in which an image was projected onto a wall
    - (B) a preserved image of a darkened room projected in a box
    - (C) a box with a lens, which projected an image onto a wall in a dark room
    - (D) a hole in a wall into which a lens could be inserted to project an image

12. According to the passage, what problem did Daguerre encounter?
    - (A) His pictures were all negative images.
    - (B) He could not find a way to make positive images.
    - (C) His positive images would darken.
    - (D) He could not reverse the fixed image.

13. According to the passage, George Eastman built a camera that
    - (A) used chemically coated glass plates
    - (B) produced light-sensitive prints
    - (C) used chemicals to produce clear, sharp, and positive prints
    - (D) was portable

14. Which of the sentences below best expresses the essential information in the highlighted sentence in the passage? Incorrect choices change the meaning in important ways or leave out essential information.
    - (A) The layers of chemicals that make up color film are sensitive to all colors that can be made.
    - (B) Color film uses chemicals that are sensitive to red, green, and blue light.
    - (C) Red, green, and blue light are the essential colors from which all colors can be chemically made.
    - (D) The layers of chemicals on color film are sensitive to red, green, and blue light that, combined, can make all colors.
15. All of the following people are mentioned as working with photographic images EXCEPT
    - (A) Johann Heinrich Schulze
    - (B) Joseph Nicéphore Niépce
    - (C) Louis Daguerre
    - (D) George Eastman

Questions 16–20

Generations of American schoolchildren have been taught the story of how the Great Fire of Chicago in October 1871 was started by Daisy, a cow belonging to one Mrs. O'Leary. The cow, stabled in a barn behind Mrs. O'Leary's house, supposedly kicked over a kerosene lamp, which set fire to hay and other combustible materials stored there. The blaze quickly spread, and fanned by a strong southwest wind and aided by intensely dry conditions, the conflagration engulfed and entirely destroyed more than three square miles of built-up area. Almost 100,000 people were left homeless, and about 300 lost their lives. Property damage was estimated at 200 million dollars, an immense sum in those days.

Soon after the fire, the O'Leary-cow story became an almost unchallenged truth and, over the years, took on the status of a modern-day myth – a staple ingredient in the fabric of American folklore. However, there are good reasons to believe that neither Mrs. O'Leary nor Daisy was culpable. First, a police reporter later claimed to have invented the whole story. Of course, this is not a conclusive refutation, but his reasoning was valid and his alternative suggestions credible. Furthermore, the testimony of one of the main witnesses, a neighbor called "Peg Leg" Sullivan, is now thought to be questionable. Some claim he invented the story to avoid censure, since he himself was not above suspicion and there were inconsistencies in his account. Other accusers have focused the blame on a variety of targets – some local boys smoking in the barn, a different neighbor, an unnamed terrorist organization, spontaneous combustion, and, most recently, an asteroid. The asteroid theory gains credence from the fact that on the same night as the Chicago fire, neighboring states suffered more than a dozen major fires. One fire destroyed the entire town of Peshtigo, Wisconsin, with the loss of more than 1,200 lives.

Whatever the real origin of the fire, the truth is that it was inevitable, given the near-drought conditions of the time and the fact that much of the city consisted of densely packed wooden shacks served by an undermanned fire department. It seems that Mrs. O'Leary and her cow were perhaps no more than convenient and vulnerable scapegoats on which a devastated populace could center its frustrations.

16. What myth has been told to generations of American schoolchildren?

    (A) That many people lost their lives and many were left homeless
    (B) That the Great Fire of Chicago was started by a cow kicking over a lamp
    (C) How much the property damage caused by the Great Fire of Chicago cost
    (D) How fast the Great Fire of Chicago spread and how much of the Chicago area was destroyed

17. What did "Peg Leg" Sullivan do?

    (A) He set the barn on fire while smoking.
    (B) He accused some local boys.
    (C) He gave a suspicious account.
    (D) He came up with some believable alternatives.

18. Which of the sentences below best expresses the essential information in the highlighted sentence in the passage? Incorrect choices change the meaning in important ways or leave out essential information.

    (A) The number of fires in the surrounding states on the same night as the Chicago fire supports the asteroid theory.
    (B) There were a number of fires throughout the city of Chicago, and this supports the asteroid theory.
    (C) The numerous fires on the same night as the Chicago fire means that asteroids were to blame.
    (D) Asteroids may have caused the unusually high number of fires in Chicago on the same night.

19. All of the following are mentioned as possible reasons that the fire was so devastating EXCEPT

    (A) the lack of rain
    (B) fire-prone building materials
    (C) too few firefighters
    (D) a riotous populace

20. According to the passage, Mrs. O'Leary's cow

    (A) is a myth
    (B) is folklore
    (C) was a scapegoat
    (D) did not exist

PRACTICE WITH MAKING INFERENCES AND DRAWING CONCLUSIONS

Some details in a passage are not stated explicitly, but they can be inferred from other details that are stated. On the TOEFL test, you will be required to make inferences from the passages that you read. Sometimes you must use the information given to you in a passage to draw conclusions about the topic.

This section will build your skills in making inferences and drawing conclusions from details that are stated or implied in a reading passage. Read the following statement:

> Dr. Smitten and two other psychologists chose 25 children for their study: 5 from Campbell, 10 from other multiracial schools in Miami, and the rest from multiracial schools in other cities in Florida.

The details stated explicitly are:

- Dr. Smitten and two other psychologists chose 25 children for a study.
- Five children were from Campbell.
- Ten children were from other schools in Miami.
- The rest were from schools in other Florida cities.

The answers to the following questions were not stated in the sentence but can be understood or inferred.

1. What kind of doctor is Dr. Smitten?

   You understand that Dr. Smitten is a psychologist because it can be inferred from the phrase "and two other psychologists."

2. How many psychologists were doing the study?

   You understand that three psychologists were doing the study because it can be inferred from the phrase "Dr. Smitten and two other psychologists."

3. What and where is Campbell?

   You understand that Campbell is a multiracial school in Miami because it can be inferred from the phrase "other multiracial schools in Miami."

4. What and where is Miami?

   You understand that Miami is a city in Florida because it can be inferred from the phrase "other cities in Florida."

5. How many children from other cities in Florida were chosen for the study?

   You understand that 10 children came from other cities because it can be inferred from the phrase "chose 25 children: 5 from . . . , 10 from . . . , and the rest from . . . other cities in Florida."

Some details are neither stated nor implied. Therefore, you cannot answer the following questions:

- When did the study take place?
- Why was the study done?
- What were the results of the study?

You can answer the question below by drawing a logical conclusion from details implied in the passage.

> What was the study probably about?

You should draw the conclusion or understand that the study was probably about some aspect of children in multiracial school environments because it can be inferred from the phrases "multiracial schools in Miami" and "multiracial schools in other cities" that a multiracial environment was an important factor in choosing children from those particular schools.

Exercises R15–R21

Use Exercises R15–R21 to build your skills in making inferences and drawing conclusions in reading passages.

EXERCISE R15 *Identifying inferences*

Choose the letter of those inferences that can be made from the information given in the statement. More than one inference may be possible.

The lesser North American poets are more popular with children than major poets because they are direct and clear.

(A) Children may have difficulty understanding major poets.
(B) Minor poets write poetry for children.
(C) There are fewer poets writing for children than writing for adults.
(D) Indirect and hidden meanings are used in the poetry of major poets.

You should choose *A* because it can be inferred that the poetry of major poets is difficult for children because, unlike that of lesser poets, it is not direct and clear. You should not choose *B* because it cannot be inferred that either minor or major poets write for children or *C* because *lesser* means *minor poets*, not *fewer poets*. You should also choose *D* because it can be inferred that if children like the lesser poets because they write more directly and clearly, the major poets use indirect ways of expressing ideas.

1. Three of the published reports came from official investigations, but the other two came from private individuals.
   (A) Private individuals cannot submit reports for publication.
   (B) Only the three official reports were considered for publication.
   (C) Five reports were published.
   (D) Official investigations were made on private individuals.

2. The Institute of Anthropology plans to computerize archaeological data to help restore the Native American villages in Chaco Canyon.
   (A) The Chaco Canyon Native American villages were destroyed by European people.
   (B) The Institute of Anthropology collects information about Native American villages that are in ruins.
   (C) The Native Americans in Chaco Canyon have computers to help them store data.
   (D) Computers can be helpful in restoring archaeological plans.

3. Some scientists believe that the African bees that have devastated the Latin American beekeeping industry will become gentler as they interbreed with the previously introduced European varieties.

   (A) European bees will not be advantageous to the Latin American beekeeping industry.
   (B) African bees are ferocious and destructive.
   (C) The Latin American beekeeping industry will become gentler as African bees and European bees interbreed.
   (D) African bees, as well as European bees, live in Latin America.

4. No partner helps the male pheasant-tailed jacana protect and nurture his chicks in their floating nest.

   (A) The female pheasant-tailed jacana does not take care of her babies.
   (B) The pheasant-tailed jacana is an aquatic bird.
   (C) The male pheasant-tailed jacana doesn't help to protect and nurture its partner.
   (D) The male pheasant-tailed jacana does not mate.

5. Elephants are slowly becoming trapped in isolated forest enclaves completely surrounded by land cleared for agriculture.

   (A) Hunters are trapping elephants in isolated forest enclaves to get their ivory tusks.
   (B) People are destroying the elephants' habitat to make farms.
   (C) Elephants would have to cross over farmland to migrate to different forest areas.
   (D) People are trapping elephants to use them for clearing land for agriculture.

6. To safeguard sunken ships from adventurers or thieves, ship salvagers keep the wrecks under constant surveillance by electronic and other means.

   (A) Thieves sink ships to steal the cargo.
   (B) Sunken ships contain things that are valuable.
   (C) Ship salvagers are usually caught before they steal anything because of safeguards.
   (D) There are various ways to guard sunken ships from pilferers.

7. A species of weed known as the gopher plant has earned a new name – the gasoline plant – because it yields a milky latex containing hydrocarbons that can be refined into substitutes for crude oil and gasoline.

   (A) Some weeds have been renamed "gasoline plants" because their latex can be made into a gasoline substitute.
   (B) Gasoline refined from the gasoline plant will soon replace the need for gasoline from other sources.
   (C) Substitutes for crude oil and gasoline can come from hydrocarbons.
   (D) Milk contains hydrocarbons necessary for crude oil and gasoline substitutes.

8. Not yet profitably synthesized, morphine, a drug unsurpassed for controlling pain, is still being scraped from opium poppy heads as it was at least 5,000 years ago.

   (A) Morphine, a drug from the poppy plant, is no longer profitable to cultivate.
   (B) Cocaine is not as effective as morphine for stopping pain.
   (C) Morphine has been used for pain control for at least 5,000 years.
   (D) It is possible to make artificial morphine economically.

EXERCISE R16 *Locating sources for inferred information*

Read the passage and the statement about inferences that follows it. Underline the part or parts of the passage from which the inference can be made.

> Is it true that crime doesn't pay? Although it is impossible to report every dollar that was generated in the U.S. economy by Watergate, figures pointed at what could be termed a first-class growth industry. Fees, royalties, fines, bills, and other miscellaneous payments added up into the millions of dollars moving around in the U.S. economy.
>
> It can be inferred from this passage that Watergate is the name for a crime that took place in the United States.
>
> You should underline *crime* and *dollar that was generated in the U.S. economy by Watergate* because it can be inferred that Watergate was a crime or else it wouldn't have been cited in the discussion of whether or not crime pays. The passage goes on to discuss how crime has paid by generating money in the U.S. economy.

1. Unlike other toads, the male golden toad is nearly voiceless. It attracts its mate through its unmistakable orange color. When the clouds are thick in the rain forest, usually in April and May, the male toads appear like flashing neon signals, which is as effective as croaking in luring females during the mating season.

   It can be inferred from this passage that most toads attract their mates by making sounds.

2. The great temple of Borobudur is a stepped pyramid of unmortared andesite and basalt volcanic stone, with a perimeter of 403 feet and standing 105 feet high. This holy place lay abandoned and forgotten for more than 800 years after a devastating earthquake and an eruption of one of the four surrounding volcanoes caused its population to flee in 1006. Besides earthquakes and volcanoes, torrential rains, encroaching tropical vegetation, and time have all taken their toll.

   It can be inferred from this passage that the temple of Borobudur is in ruins.

3. Some multiple sclerosis victims are experimenting with deadly snake venom to ease the pain and tiredness caused by their disease. First, the poison is milked from cobra, krait, and viper snakes. One part of it is then mixed to 4,000 parts of a saline solution. Although medical authorities are skeptical of the treatment, those using it claim that the venom has startling healing qualities.

   It can be inferred from this passage that snake venom for the treatment of multiple sclerosis has not yet been approved by doctors.

4. The cassowary, one of the world's largest and least known birds, grows to a height of 6 feet and a weight of 120 pounds. Its powerful legs, which it uses for defense, are fearful weapons because the inner toe of each foot is equipped with a sharp claw, four inches long. The cassowary has glossy black plumage, which hangs coarse and brushlike because it lacks the barbules that are needed to lock feathers into a flat vane. The naked neck is of iridescent blue on the sides and pink on the back. Its head is crowned by a leathery helmet that protects it when it is charging through the jungle.

   It can be inferred from this passage that the cassowary probably doesn't fly.

5. Prior to 1870, little stone decoration was done on New York buildings, except for churches and public buildings. With the arrival of artisans among the groups of European immigrants, architectural carving began to flourish. Architects would buy sculptures already done or show sketches of what they wanted carved. Away from the master carver, who had dictated what was to be carved, the artisans created eclectic and uninhibited sculptures, which became integrated into a purely American style.

   It can be inferred from this passage that in Europe, artisans did not carve what they wanted to carve.

6. The Society for Creative Anachronism is a nonprofit club that joins together people who enjoy reenacting life as it was lived before the 1700s. Members of both sexes not only learn the art of sword fighting in mock combat but learn a wide range of authentic medieval skills as well. These include such skills as armor making, equestrian arts, games, jewelry making, astrology, and magic. Since the first tournament held in 1966, in which a dozen fighters took part, the society has increased by thousands of members.

   It can be inferred from this passage that female members of the Society for Creative Anachronism fight in battles.

7. Computer-driven cameras, lights, and servomotors, as well as lasers and tiny lens assemblies, are just a few of the complex instruments that have brought to today's television viewers effective scientific informational films. Two crucial problems in such films are finding arresting visuals and creating special effects to illustrate complex scientific concepts. Computer-generated motion pictures allow the viewer to see the meaning of data and complex relationships instantly and are a new aid to human understanding of almost limitless power.

   It can be inferred from this passage that computers used in the film industry have enabled people to understand science better.

8. Fish rubbings and nature printing have been developing as art forms in North America over the past several decades, although the techniques may date as far back as the time of early cave dwellers. To make a fish print, one should choose a very fresh fish with large rough scales and a flat body. Other needed materials are several brushes, including a fine brush for painting the eyes on the print, a thick waterbased ink, newspaper, modeling clay for supporting the fins, straight pins, and cloth or absorbent paper such as newsprint. Handmade paper is best, but it is more expensive and not recommended for beginners. The fish should be washed, dried, and laid out on the newspaper. A thin layer of ink should be brushed on in both directions. The paper is then placed over the fish and pressed carefully with the fingers, avoiding wrinkles or movement of the paper.

   It can be inferred from this passage that it takes practice to become proficient in using this technique.

9. Characteristics of tropical rain forests are high and steady levels of heat and moisture, as well as a wide variety of organisms. It is believed that two-thirds of all species live in the tropics, and half of those live in the tropical rain forests. Nowhere else, except perhaps in tropical coral reefs, is nature so great in its diversity of organisms and complex in its biological interaction.

   It can be inferred from this passage that tropical coral reefs contain a wide variety of organisms.

10. Even though historians think that ice-skating has been a sport for the last 2,000 years, it is within the last five decades that skating has gained recognition as a form of art. Champion athletes combine new heights of athleticism with the elegance of dance in what is now called figure skating. Ice-skaters performing daring jumps in flamboyant costumes have brought ballet to the ice rink. Ice-skating is now seen as an exciting and innovative sport that has won millions of new admirers.

    It can be inferred from this passage that ice-skaters are both athletes and artists.

EXERCISE R17 *Checking if an inference is correct*

Read each sentence and answer *Yes* or *No* to the question that follows.

> Volunteers for organizations such as Save the Children make an extremely important personal contribution toward improving the daily lives of millions of children throughout the world.
>
> Can it be inferred that Save the Children volunteers contribute a lot of money to aid children?
>
> <u>No</u>
>
> You should write *No* in the space because a "personal contribution" does not necessarily mean a monetary contribution. Volunteers may contribute time or a special personal skill that they have in order to aid children.

1. Each day, more and more communities discover that they have been living near dumps or on top of ground that has been contaminated by toxic chemicals.

   Can it be inferred that communities aren't always told when and where toxic wastes are being disposed?

   ____

2. E. B. White's death, at 86, was cause for sadness in millions of homes.

   Can it be inferred that E. B. White was famous?

   ____

3. There is evidence that a global firestorm raged about the time the dinosaurs disappeared.

   Can it be inferred that dinosaurs became extinct because of a global firestorm?

   ____

4. Of the twelve sulfite-associated deaths, one was caused by wine, one by beer, and one by hashed brown potatoes; the rest were linked to fresh fruits or vegetables.

   Can it be inferred that nine people died from sulfite-contaminated fresh foods?

   ____

5. Quinolone, a recently discovered antibiotic, inhibits an enzyme that controls the way bacterial DNA unravels and rewinds when microbes reproduce.

   Can it be inferred that quinolone will eventually replace all other antibiotics?

   ____

6. For people whose nerves have been damaged by illness or injuries, actions such as walking or grasping an object may be impossible.

   Can it be inferred that the nervous system is important for muscle control?

   ____

EXERCISE R18 *Identifying inferences in paragraphs*

Read the passage and the statements that follow it. Write *I* in the space if the statement is an inference. Write *R* if the statement is a restatement. Leave the space blank if the statement is neither an inference nor a restatement.

> Francis Gary Powers survived when his high-flying reconnaissance aircraft was shot down over the Soviet Union in 1960. He was convicted of espionage after a trial in Moscow. Later, Powers was returned to the United States in exchange for Soviet spy Rudolf Abel. Powers was killed in a helicopter crash in California in 1977.
>
> A. __R__ Powers was found guilty of spying in the Soviet Union.
> B. __I__ Rudolf Abel was imprisoned by the United States for spying.
> C. _____ Powers was killed during a reconnaissance mission.
>
> You should write *R* for *A* because to be "convicted of espionage" means the same as to be "found guilty of spying." You should write *I* for *B* because Rudolf Abel must have been imprisoned by the United States if the Americans exchanged him for Powers. You should leave *C* blank because no information is given on why Powers was flying in the helicopter. It might have been for work or for pleasure.

1. The MacArthur Prizes, or "genius awards," are large grants of money given to individuals who show outstanding talents in their fields. According to a foundation spokesperson, this money frees these people from financial worries and allows them the time to devote themselves to creative thinking. The recipients of MacArthur Prizes are people who have already achieved considerable success. It may be asked whether they attained success despite the fact that they had to worry about money or because of it.

   A. _____ Someone who is not already known in his or her field will probably not be a recipient of a MacArthur Prize.
   B. _____ Some people may become successful because they are worried about money.
   C. _____ Some individuals receive large sums of money to think.

2. The CDC (Centers for Disease Control) is responsible for the research done in solving or attempting to solve medical mysteries. Teams of epidemiologists crisscross the country investigating outbreaks of disease. They ask questions, look for clues, and track down pieces of puzzles in a relentless pursuit to find answers that will bring about breakthroughs in the prevention or cure of serious diseases. The CDC rushes in to study epidemics because it is possible to quickly determine patterns and common links among the victims.

   A. _____ The CDC is not always successful in its research of diseases.
   B. _____ Epidemiologists travel across the nation to do their research.
   C. _____ Because there are more victims when an epidemic strikes, more data can be collected to find answers to medical questions.

3. Astronomers have long believed that frozen gases and water account for up to 80 percent of a comet's mass. While observing Comet Bowell, astronomers were able to measure the amount of light this comet absorbed and reflected. On the basis of these observations, they determined that comets do indeed contain frozen water.

   A. _____ Astronomers have proved the theory that comets contain frozen water.
   B. _____ The ice content of other comets can be ascertained by measuring how much light they absorb and reflect.
   C. _____ The name of the observed comet is Bowell.

4. Although most honeybees die in the field while gathering pollen, some bees die in the hives and must be removed in order to prevent the spread of disease and to keep the nest from filling up with corpses. These corpses emit a chemical that signals death. While some bees ignore the corpses, others poke at them, lick them, or inspect them. Usually within an hour, the bees that are in charge of removing dead bees grasp the corpses in their mandibles, pull them through the hive toward the entrance, then fly away and drop them as far as 400 feet from the hive.

   A. _____ Dead bees cannot be left in the hive because they may make the other bees sick.
   B. _____ The honeybees know there is a dead bee in the hive because of the death chemical that is emitted.
   C. _____ In less than one hour, the dead bees have usually been removed from the hive.

5. The northern elephant seal, a 2,000-pound mammal, is making a dramatic comeback after being hunted to near extinction in the late nineteenth century. The seals that once thrived off the coast of California now receive protection from both the Mexican and United States governments. A contributing factor to their survival is the reduced demand for seal oil due to the ready availability of petroleum products.

   A. _____ Products that were once made from seal oil are now made from petroleum.
   B. _____ Petroleum is easier to obtain now than seal oil is.
   C. _____ Northern elephant seals are now numerous.

6. Diverse in culture and language, the tenacious men and women who inhabit the world's harshest environment, the land above the Arctic Circle, probably descended from hunting societies pushed north from Central Asia by population pressure about 10,000 years ago. "Scarcity" is the word that best describes the Arctic ecosystem, where life-giving solar energy is in short supply. In the winter, the sun disappears for weeks or months depending on the latitude. Even during the months of prolonged sunlight, the slanted rays cannot thaw the frozen subsurface soil. But more than the severe cold, the lack of resources for food, clothing, and shelter defines the lifestyles that the Arctic peoples lead.

   A. _____ Scarcity of food, clothing, and shelter influences Arctic living conditions more than the harsh climate does.
   B. _____ Anthropologists are not completely certain about the ancestry of the Arctic peoples.
   C. _____ The further north one is, the less sunshine there is.

7. Half of all the astronauts on space flights are afflicted with debilitating space sickness, an ailment akin to car sickness and marked by nausea and vomiting. It is believed that zero gravity and its effect on the inner ear and the flow of body fluids are the cause. Scientists are attempting to find a way to predict who is susceptible to the illness because it interferes with the important work that must be done efficiently during space missions.

   A. _____ Scientists cannot tell whether an astronaut who suffers from car sickness will suffer from space sickness.
   B. _____ Space sickness makes it difficult for afflicted astronauts to do their work.
   C. _____ Space sickness and car sickness are related illnesses.

8. The white shark, which has acquired a reputation for mindless ferocity unequaled among terrestrial or aquatic predators, belongs to the family known as the mackerel shark. Nothing about this terrifying fish is predictable: not its behavior, range, or diet. Despite this fearsome reputation, evidence from the remains of victims of shark attacks suggests that the white shark does not eat people.

   A. _____ A white shark is a kind of mackerel shark.
   B. _____ The white shark has gained a terrifying reputation because it attacks people.
   C. _____ The white shark attacks its victims for reasons other than hunger.

9. Because they seem to be taking a measure with each looping stride, some caterpillars are called geometrids, or earth measurers. From this comes their common name, inchworms. This caterpillar grasps a twig with its back legs, extends itself forward, then draws its back end up to its front legs and repeats the sequence.

   A. _____ The geometrid moves by stretching forward, then moving its back to its front, then repeating this process.
   B. _____ Not all caterpillars are inchworms.
   C. _____ All inchworms are earth measurers.

10. The Merlin is propelled by six compact engines, each encased in a separate duct. With no exposed blades, the craft is much safer to maneuver on the ground than either a helicopter or small plane. The Merlin takes off and hovers by blasting a column of air straight down and moves forward by directing some of that air backward with movable vanes behind each engine.

   A. _____ The Merlin is a kind of aircraft.
   B. _____ Exposed blades make some aircraft unsafe.
   C. _____ Production of the Merlin has not yet begun.

EXERCISE R19 *Making inferences*

Read the passage and the question that follows it. Then choose the letter of the best answer based on the information given.

In the third and fourth centuries, the Germanic tribes of central Europe joined forces and plundered the crumbling Roman Empire. But they in turn became the victims of the Norse invasions of the eighth century. The Norsemen raided villages in every region. They killed the men, abducted the women and children, and then departed in their fast-sailing ships, leaving nothing but a few smoldering ruins.

What does the author mean by the statement "they in turn became the victims"?

- (A) The Germanic tribes turned on the Norse invaders in the eighth century.
- (B) The Germanic tribes and the Norse invaders took turns in attacking the Roman Empire.
- (C) The Germanic tribes received the same treatment from the Norsemen that they had given the Roman Empire.
- (D) The Roman Empire was first plundered by the Germanic tribes in the third and fourth centuries and then by the Norsemen in the eighth century.

You should choose *C* because the author is pointing out how the invaders later became the victims of another group of invaders.

1. Erosion of America's farmland by wind and water has been a problem since settlers first put the prairies and grasslands under the plow in the nineteenth century. By the 1930s, more than 282 million acres of farmland were damaged by erosion. After decades of conservation efforts, soil erosion has accelerated due to new demands placed on the land by heavy crop production. In the years ahead, soil erosion and the pollution problems it causes are likely to replace petroleum scarcity as the nation's most critical natural resource problem.

   Why does the author mention "petroleum scarcity"?

   - (A) To show that petroleum scarcity will become the most critical natural resource problem
   - (B) To prove that petroleum is causing heavy soil erosion and pollution problems
   - (C) To indicate that soil erosion has caused humans to place new demands on heavy crop production
   - (D) To emphasize the fact that soil erosion will become the most critical problem the nation faces

2. Contamination of the sea caused by oil spills is a critical problem as wind and wave action can carry oil spills a great distance across the sea. However, there are ways in which oil spills in the sea can be dealt with. For example, straw, which can absorb up to four times its weight in oil, can be thrown on the spill and then be burned. Oil can be broken up and sunk by sand, talcum powder, or chalk. Under experimentation, some chemicals have been shown to disperse the spill into droplets, which microbes can then destroy.

   Why does the author mention that straw "can absorb up to four times its weight in oil"?

   - (A) To emphasize the versatility of straw
   - (B) To show why straw is useful in cleaning oil spills
   - (C) To compare the weight of straw to that of oil spills
   - (D) To give background on the properties of straw

3. The quality of the graphics output on a computer printer is measured in dpi (dots per inch). Simply by changing the density of dots that make up each part of an image, the printer can produce graphics that look almost photographic. To understand how this works, consider how a black-and-white photograph shows the shades that, in real life, are colors. Each color is a different shade of gray. For graphics to be produced on the computer printer, a piece of software called a printer driver decides upon a dot pattern that will represent each color shade. These different patterns or textures each create an individual effect that your eye translates into gray shades. The closer you look at the image, however, the less lifelike it looks.

Why does the author mention " a black-and-white photograph "?

Ⓐ To explain how a printer makes graphics
Ⓑ To compare the clarity of computer graphics to photographs
Ⓒ To emphasize the difference between colored graphics and black-and-white graphics
Ⓓ To convince the reader that dpi is preferable to photography

4. Endesha Ida Mae Holland became a playwright by a mere twist of fate. While studying at the University of Minnesota, Ms. Holland was consumed by activities other than academics. She helped start student groups dedicated to racial progress and black unity. Off campus, she formed an organization to get former prisoners back on their feet. So diverted, it took her nearly 15 years to earn her bachelor's degree. When she found herself four credit hours short of a degree, she enrolled in an acting course, which she thought would be easy because of her experience on speaking tours. But by transposing two numbers, Ms. Holland accidentally signed up for an advanced playwriting seminar. An author was born.

What does the author mean by stating " Endesha Ida Mae Holland became a playwright by a mere twist of fate "?

Ⓐ It took nearly 15 years to complete her bachelor's degree.
Ⓑ An author was born.
Ⓒ She didn't intend to take the playwriting seminar.
Ⓓ She had experience because of her speaking tours.

EXERCISE R20 *Drawing conclusions*

Read the statement and the question that follows it. Then choose the letter of the best answer based on the information given.

Few school curriculums include a unit on how to deal with bereavement and grief, and yet all people at some point in their lives suffer from loss through death and parting.

What topic would probably NOT be included in a unit on bereavement?

Ⓐ How to write a letter of condolence
Ⓑ What emotional stages are passed through in the healing process
Ⓒ How to give support to a grieving friend
Ⓓ What the leading causes of death are

Bereavement is the state of experiencing the death of a relative or friend. Since the leading causes of death are not relevant to the particular death that a person may have to deal with, you should choose *D*.

1. Studies show that bike races in Mexico City, where the air is 20 percent less dense than at sea level, tend to be 3 to 5 percent faster than at lower altitudes.

   In which area would a bike race probably be the slowest?

   (A) Along the coast
   (B) On an indoor track
   (C) On a high plateau
   (D) Near the snow line of a volcano

2. Owners of famous and valuable paintings have recently been commissioning talented artists to paint copies of these art treasures to exhibit in their homes.

   What is the most likely reason an owner of a valuable painting might want to exhibit a copy instead of the original?

   (A) Because they need to trick the experts
   (B) Because they hope to foil would-be thieves
   (C) Because they want to encourage talented artists
   (D) Because they enjoy buying fake paintings

3. The Academy of Dog Training supplies law enforcement agencies with German shepherds that are trained to recognize the smell of marijuana and other drugs.

   In which of the following places would these German shepherds most likely be used?

   (A) At scenes of violent crimes
   (B) Where burglaries have taken place
   (C) At public swimming pools
   (D) At customs checks between borders

4. Schools based upon the philosophy of Rudolph Steiner are all coeducational, practice mixed-ability teaching, and discourage competition among children.

   Which of the following activities would probably NOT be seen in a Steiner school?

   (A) A class period devoted to the teaching of mathematics
   (B) A game involving both boys and girls
   (C) A poetry-writing contest
   (D) A classroom of children reading at different levels

5. The microbiologist exposed bacteria to increasingly higher levels of cyanide until he had a type of bacteria that could destroy the cyanide that had been dumped into rivers by chemical plants.

   In what way could these bacteria be useful?

   (A) For saving the water life from toxic wastes
   (B) For poisoning undesirable fish
   (C) For cleaning swimming pools
   (D) For increasing the cyanide in the chemical plants

EXERCISE R21 *Reviewing inferences*

Read each passage and the items that follow it. Then choose the letter of the best answer for each.

Questions 1–4

The Malabar Pied-Hornbill usually nests in the fruit trees that bear its food. First, the female enters a hole in the tree and sheds her feathers. Then, she and her mate seal the hollow with mud and dung, leaving a crack through which he feeds her. When the chicks hatch and her plumage returns, she breaks out, resealing the nest to guard the young, which emerge later.

1. The Malabar Pied-Hornbill is probably a
   (A) chicken
   (B) seal
   (C) bird
   (D) bear

2. What can be said about the Malabar Pied-Hornbill's nest?
   (A) It is padded with feathers.
   (B) It is so warm that the female Malabar Pied-Hornbill loses its plumage.
   (C) The female Malabar Pied-Hornbill breaks it up after losing her plumage.
   (D) Its cracks are covered by the feathers which the female Malabar Pied-Hornbill plucks off herself.

3. Which of the following statements can be inferred?
   (A) The male is afraid of other males and, therefore, forces his mate into the nest and seals it.
   (B) The female is so involved in building her nest that she doesn't realize she's locked herself inside it.
   (C) The female purposely imprisons herself to lay her eggs.
   (D) The female has to keep the male from hurting the babies, so she encloses herself in the nest.

4. The male Malabar Pied-Hornbill probably
   (A) feeds the eggs through a crack in the nest
   (B) doesn't help the female until she has enclosed herself in the nest
   (C) uses his plumage to guard the recently hatched chicks
   (D) doesn't hatch the eggs by keeping them warm with his own body

Questions 5–7

The Mississippi River and its tributaries form the world's fourth-longest river system. Two Canadian provinces and all or parts of 31 states in the United States have rivers that drain into the Mississippi. As the Mississippi River flows down to join the sea, it deposits sand, silt, and clay, building the delta seaward across Louisiana's shallow continental shelf. The delta marsh and its bays, lakes, and sounds provide shelter and nutrients for North America's most fertile marine nursery.

5. It can be inferred from the passage that
   (A) Canada has only two drainage areas in its provinces
   (B) there are 31 states in the United States
   (C) the 31 states mentioned have no other river systems to carry silt, sand, and clay
   (D) some of the silt deposited in the Louisiana delta is from Canada

6. It is probably true that
   (A) the delta system formed by the Mississippi River is very important for marine life
   (B) nurseries have been set up in the delta so that children can take part in aquatic sports in the bays, lakes, and sounds
   (C) the delta marshland is an excellent area for medical people to study diseases caused by mosquitoes and other insects
   (D) the United States government has established nurseries to provide shelter and food for migrating birds

7. It can be inferred from the passage that
   (A) the delta is being destroyed by the Mississippi River depositing sand, silt, and clay
   (B) the geographic features of the delta are always changing
   (C) the sea movement is building a delta on the continental shelf at the mouth of the Mississippi
   (D) the river, delta, and sea all play an important role in building Louisiana's continental shelf

Questions 8–10

An ultralight airplane is very different from a conventional airplane. It looks like a lawn chair with wings, weighs no more than 254 pounds, flies up to 60 miles an hour, and carries about 5 gallons of fuel. Most ultralights are sold as kits and take about 40 hours to assemble. Flying an ultralight is so easy that a pilot with no experience can fly one. Accidents are rarely fatal or even serious because the ultralight lands so slowly and gently and carries so little fuel. Some models now have parachutes attached, while others have parachute packs which pilots can wear.

8. Ultralights are powered by
   (A) an engine
   (B) human energy
   (C) remote control
   (D) solar energy

9. It is probably true that
   (A) an ultralight can be purchased at the airport
   (B) people can put their own ultralights together
   (C) people who fly ultralights have no experience
   (D) ultralight builders need to have training in aviation

10. It can be inferred from the passage that
    (A) accident statistics are inaccurate because ultralights are not registered at airports
    (B) fatal accidents are frequent because of the lack of experienced pilots
    (C) ultralight pilots can walk away from most of the accidents they are in
    (D) because of the frequency of fatal accidents, laws requiring parachutes have been enacted

Reading Mini-test 4

Check your progress with making inferences and drawing conclusions (Exercises R15–R21) by completing the following Mini-test. This Mini-test uses question types used in the Reading section of the TOEFL iBT test.

Select the correct answer.

Questions 1–4

Jacob Epstein's sculptures were the focus of much controversy during the sculptor's lifetime. Epstein was born in the United States of Russian-Jewish immigrants in 1880. He moved to Paris in his youth and later to England, where he eventually settled and obtained British citizenship in 1907. His first major public commission, on a building in London, offended public taste because of the expressive distortion and nudity of the figures. In 1937, the Rhodesian government, which at that time owned the building, actually mutilated the sculptures to make them conform to public notions of decency. Many other of Epstein's monumental carvings received equally adverse criticism.

While the general public denounced his work, many artists and critics praised it. They admired in particular the diversity of his work and noted the influence on it of primitive and ancient sculptural motifs from Africa and the Pacific. Today, Epstein's work has received the recognition it deserves, and Epstein is considered one of the major sculptors of the twentieth century.

1. The author's attitude toward Epstein's work is
   (A) critical
   (B) derisive
   (C) amusing
   (D) admiring

2. Which of the following was most probably an important influence on Epstein's work?
   (A) public tastes
   (B) African carvings
   (C) Russian painting
   (D) the Rhodesian government

3. Today, a newly erected Epstein sculpture would probably
   (A) be mutilated
   (B) conform to public opinions
   (C) be well received
   (D) be expressive

4. What does the author mean by the statement "Many other of Epstein's monumental carvings received equally adverse criticism"?
   - (A) Many of Epstein's monuments were defaced.
   - (B) People have taken equal offense to other critical works of art.
   - (C) Epstein's monuments were usually denounced for their nudity.
   - (D) Other sculptures of Epstein's elicited negative comments.

Questions 5–9

History books record that the first moving picture with sound was *The Jazz Singer* in 1927. But sound films, or "talkies," did not suddenly appear after years of silent screenings. From the earliest public performances in 1896, films were accompanied by music and sound effects. These were produced by a single pianist, a small band, or a full-scale orchestra; larger movie theaters could buy sound-effects machines.

Research into sound that was reproduced at exactly the same time as the pictures – called "synchronized sound" – began soon after the very first movies were shown. With synchronized sound, characters on the movie screen could sing and speak. As early as 1896, the newly invented gramophone, which played a large disc carrying music and dialogue, was used as a sound system. The biggest disadvantage was that the sound and pictures could become unsynchronized if, for example, the gramophone needle jumped or if the speed of the projector changed. This system was only effective for a single song or dialogue sequence.

A later development was the "sound-on-film" system. Here, sounds were recorded as a series of marks on celluloid read by optical sensors. These signals would be placed on the film alongside the images, guaranteeing synchronization. Short feature films were produced in this way as early as 1922. This system eventually brought us "talking pictures."

5. Why does the author mention "a single pianist, a small band, or a full-scale orchestra"?
   - (A) To show how badly paid musicians were
   - (B) To explain how sound that accompanied early films was made
   - (C) To emphasize the role sound effects played in *The Jazz Singer*
   - (D) To refute history books that claim the first movie with sound was made in 1927

6. It can be inferred that
   - (A) most movie theaters had a pianist
   - (B) sound-effects machines were common
   - (C) orchestras couldn't synchronize sound with the pictures
   - (D) gramophones were developed about the same time as moving pictures

7. Why could gramophones be considered ineffective?
   - (A) They were subject to variations in speed.
   - (B) They were too large for most movie theaters.
   - (C) They couldn't always match the speed of the projector.
   - (D) They were newly invented.

8. It can be understood that the synchronization system
   - (A) could be placed alongside the images
   - (B) developed at the same time as sound for movies
   - (C) was an important development for talking pictures
   - (D) was a guarantee that short feature films could be produced

9. It can be inferred that short feature films produced as early as 1922
   - (A) preceded talking pictures
   - (B) put musicians out of work
   - (C) were recorded by optical sensors
   - (D) were only effective for dialogue sequences

Questions 10–13

Experiments have shown that in selecting personnel for a job, interviewing is at best a hindrance and may even cause harm. These studies have disclosed that the judgments of interviewers differ markedly and bear little or no relationship to the adequacy of job applicants. Of the many reasons why this should be the case, three in particular stand out. The first reason is related to an error of judgment known as the halo effect. If a person has one noticeable good trait, their other characteristics will be judged as better than they really are. Thus, an individual who dresses smartly and shows self-confidence is likely to be judged capable of doing a job well regardless of his or her real ability. The horns effect is essentially the same error, but focuses on one particular bad trait. Here the individual will be judged as incapable of doing a good job.

Interviewers are also prejudiced by an effect called the primacy effect. This error occurs when interpretation of later information is distorted by earlier connected information. Hence, in an interview situation, the interviewer spends most of the interview trying to confirm the impression given by the candidate in the first few moments. Studies have repeatedly demonstrated that such an impression is unrelated to the aptitude of the applicant.

The phenomenon known as the contrast effect also skews the judgment of interviewers. A suitable candidate may be underestimated because he or she contrasts with a previous one who appears exceptionally intelligent. Likewise, an average candidate who is preceded by one who gives a weak showing may be judged as more suitable than he or she really is.

Since interviews as a form of personnel selection have been shown to be inadequate, other selection procedures have been devised that more accurately predict candidate suitability. Of the various tests devised, the predictor that appears to do this most successfully is cognitive ability as measured by a variety of verbal and spatial tests.

10. What does the author mean by the phrase "essentially the same error"?
    - (A) The effect of the error is the same.
    - (B) The error is based on the same kind of misjudgment.
    - (C) The effect focuses only on negative traits.
    - (D) The individual is considered less capable of the job.

11. Which of the following applicants would probably be hired for the job based on an interview in which the typical interview errors are made?
    - (A) A well-dressed, confident person following someone who appears very intelligent
    - (B) An unconfident, well-dressed person following someone who is well-dressed and confident
    - (C) A well-dressed, confident person following someone who has apparent flaws
    - (D) A confident person following a well-dressed, confident person

12. Which of the following statements would the author most likely agree with concerning the actions of an interviewer looking for the best applicant for a job?
    - (A) The interviewer should spend time trying to confirm a first impression.
    - (B) The interviewer should be confident and well-dressed.
    - (C) The interviewer should be aware that this process is a hindrance to finding the right person.
    - (D) The interviewer should look for other ways to choose the best applicant.

13. The paragraphs following the passage most likely discuss which of the following?
    - (A) Other reasons for misjudgments about applicants
    - (B) More information on the kinds of judgmental effects
    - (C) More information on tests measuring cognitive ability
    - (D) Other selection procedures included in interviewing

PRACTICE WITH SUMMARIES AND CHARTS

Your ability to understand how a reading passage is organized and to grasp the relationships between details and main ideas will be tested in the Reading section of the TOEFL test. In the last item for each reading passage, you will be required to extract information from the entire passage and arrange the given text options into a summary or a category chart. Your ability to recognize and understand compare-and-contrast, cause-and-effect, and agree-and-disagree relationships, as well as steps in a process, will help you to succeed on these questions.

Summary questions

These questions require you to understand the main ideas that together form a summary of the passage. You will be given the first sentence in a summary and a list of other sentences. You will then be asked to choose which of the other sentences complete the summary by clicking on your choices and dragging them into a box. It is not necessary for you to put them in the correct order. The number of choices will be apparent by the number of spaces in the box.

Incorrect answer choices can be sentences that are details from the passage but are not critical to the understanding of the passage or to the formation of a summary. Incorrect choices can also be sentences that contain ideas that were not explicitly stated or information that is not mentioned within the passage.

Category chart questions

These questions require you to organize important material from the passage into a chart. You will be given a two-column chart with answer choices on the left and category headings on the right. You will then be asked to sort the answer choices under the appropriate headings by clicking on the choices and dragging them from the left column to the right. You will not always use all of the answer choices.

Incorrect answer choices may include information that is not mentioned in the text. Incorrect choices can also be incorrect generalizations or conclusions.

Exercises R22–R24 Use Exercises R22–R24 to build your skills in recognizing the relationships between details and main ideas in reading passages.

EXERCISE R22 *Understanding summaries*

Read each passage and the statements that follow it. Write *S* in the blank if the sentence summarizes the passage. Write *D* if the sentence expresses a detail in the passage. If the sentence expresses ideas not found in the passage, write *N*.

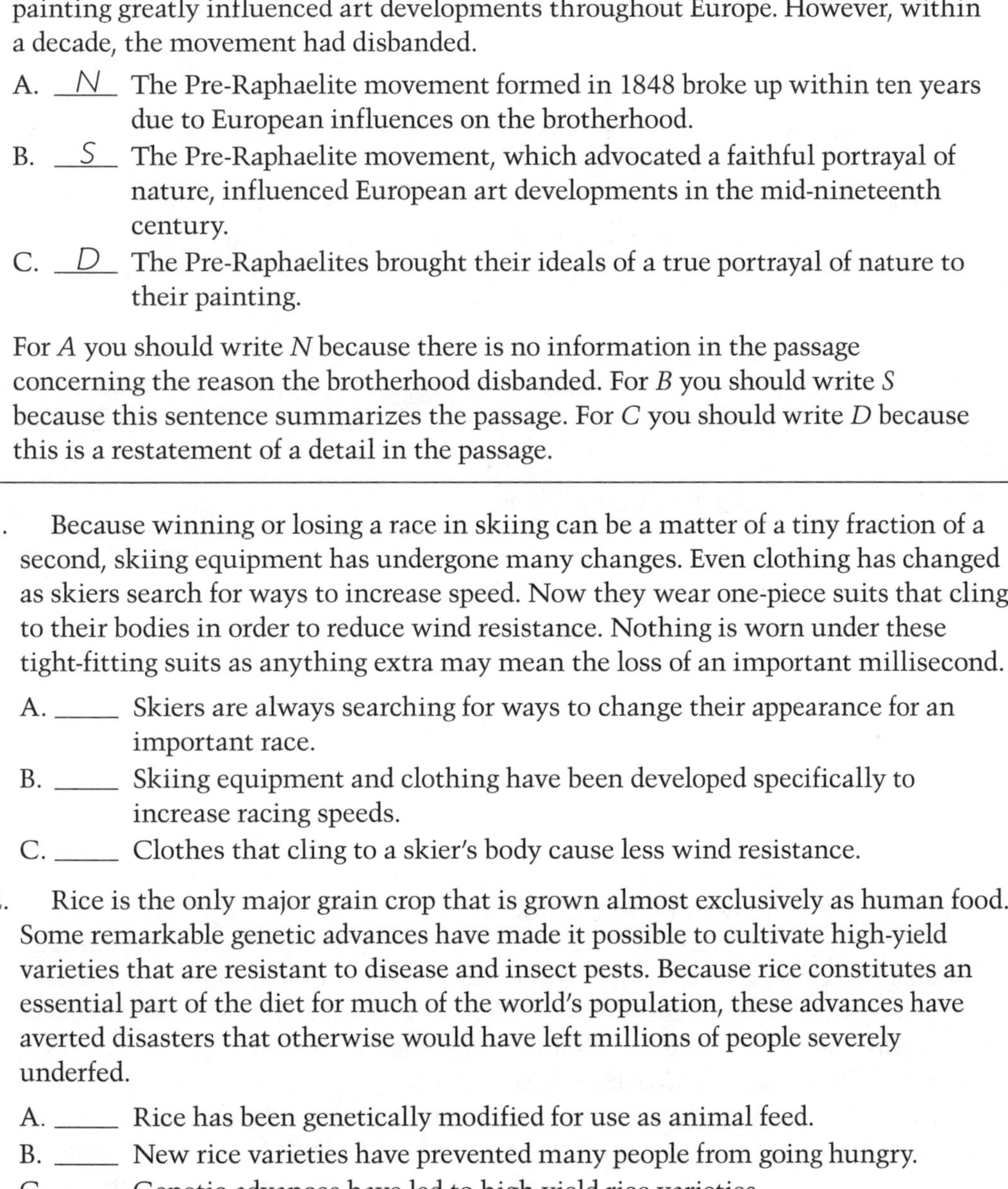

The Pre-Raphaelite brotherhood was a school of artists formed in about 1848. The Pre-Raphaelites' ideal was absolute fidelity to nature. For a time, this school of painting greatly influenced art developments throughout Europe. However, within a decade, the movement had disbanded.

A. __N__ The Pre-Raphaelite movement formed in 1848 broke up within ten years due to European influences on the brotherhood.

B. __S__ The Pre-Raphaelite movement, which advocated a faithful portrayal of nature, influenced European art developments in the mid-nineteenth century.

C. __D__ The Pre-Raphaelites brought their ideals of a true portrayal of nature to their painting.

For *A* you should write *N* because there is no information in the passage concerning the reason the brotherhood disbanded. For *B* you should write *S* because this sentence summarizes the passage. For *C* you should write *D* because this is a restatement of a detail in the passage.

1. Because winning or losing a race in skiing can be a matter of a tiny fraction of a second, skiing equipment has undergone many changes. Even clothing has changed as skiers search for ways to increase speed. Now they wear one-piece suits that cling to their bodies in order to reduce wind resistance. Nothing is worn under these tight-fitting suits as anything extra may mean the loss of an important millisecond.

   A. _____ Skiers are always searching for ways to change their appearance for an important race.

   B. _____ Skiing equipment and clothing have been developed specifically to increase racing speeds.

   C. _____ Clothes that cling to a skier's body cause less wind resistance.

2. Rice is the only major grain crop that is grown almost exclusively as human food. Some remarkable genetic advances have made it possible to cultivate high-yield varieties that are resistant to disease and insect pests. Because rice constitutes an essential part of the diet for much of the world's population, these advances have averted disasters that otherwise would have left millions of people severely underfed.

   A. _____ Rice has been genetically modified for use as animal feed.

   B. _____ New rice varieties have prevented many people from going hungry.

   C. _____ Genetic advances have led to high-yield rice varieties.

3. Addiction to cigarette smoking is basically an addiction to nicotine. Those who are attempting to overcome their addiction have found the most common cures ineffective. Switching to low-nicotine cigarettes simply causes problem smokers to smoke more. Cigarettes without any of this chemical substance are usually rejected because they don't satisfy smokers' needs. One aid, which some quitters have found effective, is a chewing gum containing nicotine, which allows them to stop without the unpleasant withdrawal symptoms. A similar kind of treatment provides a measured nicotine dose through an inhaler.

A. _____ Smokers have tried to overcome their addiction to cigarettes using various methods.
B. _____ Nicotine is the chemical substance that all cigarettes contain.
C. _____ Methods that provide those trying to quit smoking with a way to get nicotine without smoking a cigarette have been effective in some cases.

4. Two-thirds of China's vast territory is either mountainous or covered by desert. Every spring, windstorms come raging out of the mountains and cross the great deserts, gathering dust. A dense cloud of dust forms that is hundreds of miles wide. It is blown thousands of miles, traveling from the North Pacific to the Gulf of Alaska and from there moving south and then east. As the prevailing winds lose their velocity, dust particles fall from the cloud. It is believed that as much as 10 percent of the soil in Hawaii comprises dust particles collected from China's deserts and dispersed in the journey across the Pacific.

A. _____ As the winds abate, dust particles drop from the clouds.
B. _____ The raging windstorms are increasing the great deserts in China.
C. _____ The winds coming out of China scatter dust particles across the Pacific.

EXERCISE R23 *Identifying summary ideas*

Each of the passages below is followed by an introductory sentence that begins a brief summary of the passage. Choose the letters of the three statements that express the most important ideas in the passage. Incorrect choices express minor details or are not presented in the passage.

In 1836, crews building a canal from Washington, D.C., to the Ohio River found a major obstacle in their path: a long, steep crest of mountains known as Paw Paw Ridge. Various options for surmounting this hurdle were proposed. One idea, to build directly over the sheer cliffs, proved impractical. Another option was to create a series of aqueducts to skirt around the difficult terrain. This idea was rejected because of the anticipated time and expense.

The company's project engineer, Lee Montgomery, finally decided to tunnel through the ridge, a distance of about one kilometer. This was expected to take only two years. Perhaps this was optimistic on his part, given that power drills and dynamite had not yet been invented. Montgomery had invested much of his own money in the project and was keen to see the deadlines met. However, the construction crews found that the ridge was composed of soft shale, which frequently caved in and hampered progress. Other problems followed. Cholera, aided by the unsanitary living conditions, swept through the shantytowns, claiming many lives. At one point the laborers could not be paid.

The major obstacle for the completion of the Paw Paw Canal was the Paw Paw Ridge.

Ⓐ The Paw Paw Canal is named after the mountain ridge that had to be traversed.
Ⓑ Several ideas for overcoming the Paw Paw Ridge Canal were considered.
Ⓒ It was decided that a one-kilometer tunnel was the best way to overcome the barrier.
Ⓓ Power drills and dynamite were not available during the time that the canal was being built.
Ⓔ The project was beset with financial setbacks, disease, and unexpected terrain characteristics.
Ⓕ Unpaid laborers held protests that led to the loss of lives.

You should choose *B* because the first paragraph states and discusses ideas that were considered for overcoming the obstacle, *C* because it concerns the decision on how the ridge was to be dealt with, and *E* because these were obstacles encountered during the tunneling. *A* might be inferred but is not stated as fact. *D* is a detail. The laborers were unpaid at one point, but there is no mention of their possible response as stated in *F*.

1. A recent survey found that nine out of ten drivers admit to having felt intense anger toward other drivers at some time. "Road rage" seems to be on the rise, and several explanations for this have been presented. First, there are more cars today competing for road space. People also are far more subject to time constraints. A person who must meet a time deadline, but is caught in a tangle of traffic, may feel increasingly frustrated. Soon this stress may result in an outburst of road rage ranging anywhere from pounding on the car horn to getting out of the car and attacking another driver.

Of the three major responses to stress which have evolved – fight, flight, or freeze – only one is available to the driver who is suddenly caught behind a dawdler in the fast lane. The car itself prohibits the driver from fleeing the situation or freezing in one place. The only stress response left is fight.

Another explanation may be that people are not as courteous as they used to be. A person who is worried about getting to work on time, having a report ready for the afternoon mail, and running into the boss while coming into the office late may forget how to be polite. Other drivers become the enemy and the car, a weapon.

Road rage has become a serious problem that is on the rise.

Ⓐ These days the roads are very congested.
Ⓑ Stress caused by the frustration of dealing with the traffic is a major reason for people to succumb to road rage.
Ⓒ The major responses to stress are fight, flight, or freeze.
Ⓓ The fight response is the only recourse for the driver who cannot flee nor freeze because of the situation the car puts him or her in.
Ⓔ The car is now a weapon and all other drivers are the enemy.
Ⓕ The stresses of modern-day living may cause people to forget courtesy and give in to road rage.

2. For a fossil to be found, a complicated series of steps must occur in sequence. The first is that the animal (or plant) must be buried quickly. Animals that die on the plains or in the mountains are soon found by scavengers, such as hyenas or ceratosaurs, and rapidly reduced to bone chips. Most animals that are fossilized are caught in a flash flood, or die in or near a river and are buried in a sand bar, or are caught in a sandstorm. If the current in the river is fairly strong, even those few animals that die in the water are soon torn apart and their bones scattered over acres of river bottom. It is estimated that perhaps one animal in a thousand is fossilized, likely a generous estimate.

The second condition necessary for an animal to be fossilized is that it must be buried in a depositional area: that is, more and more layers of mud or gravel must be laid down over it. If the area is subject to erosion – and nearly all land surfaces are – the fossil will soon be washed out and destroyed.

The third step is that this depositional area must at some time become an erosional area, so that wind and water wear it down and uncover the buried remains.

The fourth step necessary for the recovery of a fossil is that when the fossil is uncovered, someone knowledgeable has to walk along that ridge, or study the face of that cliff, and locate the fossil and recover it. The time frame for this recovery varies, but it is necessarily short. The fossil is protected, but also invisible, until it is exposed. As soon as it is exposed, wind and water attack it, and they can destroy it quickly. The best fossils are found when someone spots an exposed bone that turns out to be part of a buried skeleton and is therefore still well preserved. But many fine fossils have been washed away because no one happened to see them when they were first exposed, or the people who saw them didn't realize what they were seeing.

The conditions that have to be met in order for a fossil to be found are relatively rare.

- (A) Animals that die are quickly eaten by scavengers and reduced to bone chips within a short period of time.
- (B) For an animal or a plant to become fossilized, it must be buried before other animals or the elements destroy the body.
- (C) A fossilized animal must first be covered by layers of soil for a length of time and then be uncovered by erosional forces.
- (D) A fossil must be protected from the elements for as long as it is buried.
- (E) The best fossils are those that have not been washed away and scattered before they are found.
- (F) An exposed fossil needs to be found and recognized by someone for what it is before it is destroyed by the elements.

3. One of the major hazards for deep-sea divers is decompression sickness (DCS), more commonly known as "the bends." This sometimes fatal condition is caused by gas bubbles forming in the bloodstream if the diver ascends too rapidly. These bubbles travel in the blood and may become lodged anyplace in the body. Most commonly, they get trapped in joints, particularly the spine. The resulting pain causes the diver to bend over, hence the name of the condition.

The reason gas bubbles form has to do with the saturation and desaturation of body tissues with various gases. At increasingly great depths, the diver breathes air at higher pressures. This results in an increased quantity of air being dissolved in the bloodstream. Different body tissues are saturated with different gases from the air at different rates. When the diver rises to the surface, oxygen is used by the body tissues, carbon dioxide is released quickly, and nitrogen remains. The nitrogen needs to be released gradually from the bloodstream and body tissues. If nitrogen is subjected to a too rapid pressure reduction, it forms bubbles. Not only do these bubbles collect in joints, but they also become trapped in capillaries. This prevents blood and oxygen from supplying necessary nutrients to body tissues, which consequently begin to die.

Saturation and desaturation are affected by various factors such as the depth, length of time, and amount of exertion under water. There are other factors that must be taken into account when determining a safe ascent rate. These include the diver's sex and body build, the number of dives undertaken within the previous 12 hours, the time spent at the dive location before the dive, and the composition of the respiration gas.

Diving tables set guidelines based on statistical probabilities of getting the bends. However, someone who stays within the suggested limits can still get DCS. Since even a mild case can leave a diver permanently disabled, it is imperative that divers recognize the symptoms. Unfortunately, such symptoms can be similar to those of the flu or a strained muscle, something that occurs frequently when divers are handling heavy equipment, using improperly fitted gear, or engaging in unaccustomed activity. Because even professionals can have difficulty diagnosing DCS, the most reliable test is to recompress the patient and see whether the symptoms abate.

Decompression sickness (DCS) is a sometimes fatal condition that affects deep-sea divers.

- (A) DCS is the formation of gas bubbles in the bloodstream caused by the different saturation and desaturation rates of gases under pressure.
- (B) Most people are more familiar with the term "the bends," referring to the way a diver bends over in pain.
- (C) Body tissues die when nitrogen prevents blood and oxygen from bringing important nutrients.
- (D) Saturation and desaturation rates of gases are affected by factors that divers need to take into consideration.
- (E) DCS can be misdiagnosed as the flu.
- (F) The best way to diagnose DCS is to put the patient through recompression.

4. One of the most basic laws of economics is that nothing of value is free. Sometimes this is dubbed "tanstaafl." The word *tanstaafl* is formed from the initials of the statement: "There ain't no such thing as a free lunch." What this means is that everything that has value must be paid for in currency, labor, or by some other means.

Not only do people have to pay for everything that has value, but governments do as well. Governments have a lot of expenditures – public buildings, roads, military, etc. – and to get the necessary money, they tax their citizens. Nobody likes to pay taxes, and history has shown that when taxes get too high, people eventually revolt and overthrow the offending government. To avoid raising taxes, a government must find another way to deal with the problem of getting money to meet its expenses.

A case in point is the government of the Roman Empire. The Roman government taxed its citizens in order to pay for the expenses of running such a vast empire. It became apparent that if it raised taxes further, it risked provoking unrest. So it came up with the idea of clipping the denarius, a coin made of 94 percent silver. When the tax collectors brought in people's taxes paid in silver coins, the Roman treasury clipped, or shaved the edges off, the coins. The clippings were minted into new coins. For a time, this gave the government the money necessary for its budget.

But it did not take the Roman people long to realize that some of their coins were missing silver. Therefore, they either refused to accept the clipped coins or charged more coins for their goods or services.

In later centuries a system called reeding came into practice. A reeded coin has grooves along its edge making it easy to see whether or not clipping has taken place. But since the Roman government still needed money and clipping no longer served its purpose, the Roman treasury started melting down coins and reminting them with a mixture of base metal, such as copper. However, each time a coin was melted down and reminted with a base-metal mixture, the content of precious metal became less and that of base metal, more. When the Roman people realized that their money was being debased, they responded by hoarding coins. Whenever they got a good coin, one with a high percentage of silver in it, they kept it. They spent only bad coins, those with a low percentage of silver. This behavior is explained by Gresham's Law, which states: Bad money drives good money out of circulation. When debasement happens, money loses its value and prices inevitably rise.

The Roman government tried various ways of dealing with the economic problem of running their Empire.

Ⓐ The Roman officials understood the concept of *tanstaafl* – that nothing of value is free.

Ⓑ Like Roman people, the Roman government had expenses, which in the case of the Empire included building cities, maintaining roads, and keeping an army.

Ⓒ The Roman Treasury met expenditures by taxing citizens until further tax increases would have caused discontent.

Ⓓ The Roman currency was the denarius, which was composed of 94 percent silver.

Ⓔ By clipping silver from an old coin, the Treasury was able to mint new coins until the people became wise and the coins had to be reeded.

Ⓕ A further need for money caused the Roman Treasury to start the practice of minting coins that were debased.

EXERCISE R24 *Organizing information into charts*

In the following exercise, each passage is followed by a list of answer choices and two categories. Follow the specific instructions underneath each passage about how to match the answer choices to the correct categories. Not all of the answer choices will be used.

Early Greek columns were built in two main styles, or orders – the Doric and the Ionic – named after Greek dialects. Of these two orders, the Ionic is the more slender – but is most notably different in the decoration of the capital, the part that rests on top of the column. While the capital of the Doric column is plain and unadorned, that of the Ionic is characterized by two pairs of prominent spiral scrolls, one pair on each side of the capital, which may have been inspired by curling leaves of foliage. Between the scrolls other ornamentation, such as an egg and dart pattern, were often carved for added embellishment.

Select the appropriate phrases from the answer choices and match them to the style of column to which they relate. TWO of the answer choices will NOT be used.

Answer Choices	Ionic
A. Larger in comparison	• D
B. Styles of Greek dialects	• F
C. An unembellished capital	**Doric**
D. A capital adorned with spiral scrolls	• A
E. A split column	• C
F. Added decoration between scrolls	

You should write *D* and *F* in the Ionic column because it is described as having spiral scrolls on the capital and added embellishment between them. You should write *A* and *C* in the Doric column because the Doric column is described as larger and its capital is described as unadorned. Since *B* concerns the origin of the names for the two types of columns and *E* concerns information not stated in the passage, they are not appropriate for either category.

1. Initially, underground homes are more expensive to build than conventional houses. In order to avoid a home resembling a dark, dank basement, much care and expense must be put into designing a home with well-placed windows and skylights that ensure brightness and fresh air. Conventional homes have much more straightforward designs. Also, expensive and sophisticated waterproofing techniques need to be used to keep moisture out of an underground home. However, in the long term, underground homes save the owner a great deal of money in heating and air-conditioning costs. Underground houses require much less energy than conventional homes because the soil temperature is relatively stable and the concrete walls can store the sun's heat and radiate it into the rooms at night.

Select the appropriate phrases from the answer choices and match them to the type of home to which they relate. ONE of the answer choices will NOT be used.

Answer Choices	Underground Homes
A. Expensive to build	• ____
B. Higher energy costs	• ____
C. Unstable soil temperatures	**Conventional Homes**
D. Waterproofing to avoid dampness	• ____
E. Easier to design	• ____

2. The earliest form of dueling was the clash of mounted knights armed with lances in medieval tournaments. These duels were often purely sporting affairs in which special nonlethal lances were used. They provided entertainment for the spectators and kept the knights in good condition for battle. Later, in Elizabethan days, duels no longer took place on horseback, and the lance was exchanged for a sword and dagger. The sword was held in the right hand and used for attacking, while the dagger was held in the left hand and used for defense. Dueling with swords was not a sport but used as a means to decide a point of honor. This form of dueling later became obsolete with the invention of pistols, which brought about a whole new set of rules and etiquette unique to that form of dueling.

Select the appropriate phrases from the answer choices and match them to the period of dueling to which they relate. ONE of the answer choices will NOT be used.

Answer Choices		
A. Unique set of rules	•	**Early Forms of Dueling** ____
B. Clashes in battle	•	____
C. Defense of one's honor		**Later Forms of Dueling**
D. Entertaining spectacles	•	____
E. Use of horses	•	____

3. Playing marbles was supposedly popular in ancient Egypt, and it has yet to lose its popularity. There are several different games played with marbles, but the main object of all marble games is to hit a target with a marble. "Shooting the marble" is accomplished by flicking a marble that is balanced on the index finger with a quick movement of the thumb. The best-known marble game is called "ringtaw." In this game, the players draw a circle on the ground. From a prearranged distance, they take turns shooting one of their marbles at other marbles placed in the circle. The object is to knock as many marbles out of the circle as possible. In another game, "fortification," the marbles are placed in the center of a series of concentric circles marked on the ground. The players must knock marbles out of the center circle and into the adjacent circle. A marble is considered out when a player has knocked it through all the circles. A third popular game uses holes instead of circles. In fact, this game is called "holes." Here, the players shoot their marbles into shallow holes dug in the ground.

Select the appropriate phrases from the answer choices and match them to the type of game to which they relate. ONE of the answer choices will NOT be used.

Answer Choices		
A. Marbles knocked out of the circle completely	•	**Ringtaw** ____
B. Marbles flicked into holes	•	____
C. Circles within circles drawn on ground		**Fortification**
D. One circle drawn on ground	•	____
E. Marbles knocked through one circle at a time	•	____

4. Sun City, South Africa; Disney World; and Sentosa Island are examples of the artificial, all-purpose holiday resort. These "tourism ghettoes," as they are referred to by seasoned travelers, isolate tourists from the real world and provide instead a sanitized package of pleasures. However much they are ridiculed and avoided by those looking for a cultural experience or seeking to study local fauna, they have proved their worth to those who are environmentally concerned with the welfare of the planet. Sun City, for example, was built on what had been useless scrubland, but now provides a haven for endangered or elusive wildlife. Unlike some traditional vacation spots, such as beach resorts that have destroyed the beauty of the area and have put heavy burdens on the infrastructure of coastal villages not designed for a large influx of people, these all-purpose resorts were carefully planned to

accommodate large numbers of tourists. Incorporated in this planning is concern for the environment and for the local inhabitants. An artificial resort can gather into one compact area the best that the host country has to offer. Artificial lakes can attract birds that would not normally be seen. Trees can be planted to provide homes for animals and insects. Even species that have been wiped out in the wild could be reintroduced.

Select the appropriate phrases from the answer choices and match them to the type of resort to which they relate. ONE of the answer choices will NOT be used.

Answer Choices	Artificial Resort
A. Accommodates large numbers of people	• ____
B. Is responsible for wiping out some species	• ____
C. Has damaged natural beauty	**Traditional Resort**
D. Provides sanctuary for wildlife	• ____
E. Puts burdens on local infrastructures	• ____

5. A few investigators, known as cryptozoologists, are dedicated to researching mysterious, unclassified beasts that orthodox scientists refuse to believe exist. One of the most celebrated mysteries being investigated by cryptozoologists is "Bigfoot," a large hairy humanoid creature that many people claim to have seen in parts of North America. In 1967, a film of what was purported to be Bigfoot was actually taken by an amateur photographer. Of course, this footage is almost certainly a hoax. Nevertheless, many people remain convinced of Bigfoot's existence.

Another humanoid creature, the Yeti or "abominable snowman" of the Himalayas, may be the most fascinating undiscovered creature. Many climbers and Sherpas claim to have seen the Yeti or its footprints, and local inhabitants of the mountains are convinced of its existence. As in the case of Bigfoot, some film footage that is alleged to be of this creature exists.

While cryptozoologists keep an open mind about their object of study, they are quick to point to cases in which the skeptics were proved mistaken. Those interested in water life can name as an example the giant squid, which was dismissed as the product of an overactive imagination until a specimen was washed up on a beach in 1873. The coelacanth, a large-bodied, hollow-spined fish and predecessor of the amphibians, was considered extinct until one was caught by a fisherman off the coast of South Africa in 1938. The Loch Ness Monster, however, has not been found and continues to provoke disagreements among researchers. In this case some authorities argue that while some kind of creature may really have been seen, it is probably a type of whale that penetrates the loch when the river feeding the loch floods.

Besides humanlike creatures and sea animals, cryptozoologists are also interested in land animals. The pygmy hippopotamus, for example – once claimed to be extinct – was eventually found to exist in East Africa. However, the Congo dinosaur and the Queensland tiger have not been found. These and other intriguing creatures will no doubt be the objects of much speculation as well as pursuit for years to come.

Select the appropriate phrases from the answer choices and match them to the type of creature to which they relate. TWO of the answer choices will NOT be used.

Answer Choices

A. The hairy humanoid creature in North America called Bigfoot
B. The Yeti, known as the abominable snowman, of the Himalayas
C. The footage of North America
D. The specimen of a giant squid
E. The large-bodied, hollow-spined coelacanth
F. The Loch Ness Monster
G. The land animals that cryptozoologists are interested in
H. The East African pygmy hippopotamus
I. The Congo dinosaur and the Queensland tiger

Creatures Found to Exist

- ____
- ____
- ____

Creatures That Perhaps Don't Exist

- ____
- ____
- ____
- ____

6. Research investigating what happens when people sleep has shown that they typically journey through five distinct levels or stages of sleep. Each level corresponds to changes in body temperature, respiration and body movements, and electroencephalograph (EEG) patterns. EEG patterns refer to the patterns of electrical activity in the brain as measured by a device called an electroencephalograph.

The first stage is a period of quiet sleep during which muscle tension decreases and the brain produces irregular, rapid waves. If woken at this time, a sleeper may jerk suddenly and deny having been asleep. In the second stage, breathing and the heart rate slow down and brain waves become larger. In the third and fourth stages, bodily functions decrease more and brain waves become even larger.

The deepest sleep occurs in the fourth stage and is very difficult to awaken from. This is considered a regenerative period, when the body repairs itself. In fact, during illness people may fall immediately into a deep sleep because infection-fighting antibodies are produced in greater numbers in this stage. After a period of time in Stage 4, a sleeper ascends back through each of the stages. He or she then enters a new stage that is sometimes known as Stage 5, even though it is, in a sense, higher than Stage 1.

The fifth stage is reached, judging by brain activity, when a person appears to be sleeping lightly as in Stage 1 but is very hard to rouse. Because of this, the stage is sometimes called "paradoxical sleep." During this stage, people exhibit what are known as rapid eye movements (REMs), and frequently their toes and facial muscles twitch, whereas the large muscles seem paralyzed. It is believed that during this stage most dreaming occurs. If something happens to awaken someone during this stage, the sleeper frequently recalls vivid dreams.

During the course of an eight-hour period, most people seem to pass through five or six cycles of sleep. In the earlier cycles, sleepers typically descend down to Stage 4. However, after several complete cycles earlier in the night, they do not reenter the deeper stages, but fluctuate between REM and Stage 2. As the end of the sleep period approaches, body temperature begins to rise and the breathing and heart rate normalize.

Select the appropriate sentences from the answer choices and match them to the stages of sleep to which they relate. TWO of the answer choices will NOT be used.

Answer Choices

A. The muscles relax and the brain waves become uneven.
B. The EEG patterns indicate the different brain activities.
C. The phase for dreaming is considered to take place.
D. Denial of having been asleep if disturbed is a common reaction.
E. A person feels paralyzed despite having twitching muscles.
F. Rapid eye movement is observed.
G. There is a slowing down of both breathing and body movements.
H. To all appearances the person is sleeping lightly, but is difficult to arouse.
I. The person is sleeping the most profoundly.

One of the First Four Stages

- _____
- _____
- _____
- _____

Final Stage

- _____
- _____
- _____

READING

Reading Mini-test 5

Check your progress in understanding summaries and charts (Exercises R22–R24) by completing the following Mini-test. This Mini-test uses question types used in the Reading section of the TOEFL iBT test.

Read each passage, then answer the question that follows.

One of the foremost American entertainers of the first part of the twentieth century was a part-Cherokee Native American named Will Rogers (1879–1935). Rogers was born in territory that would later become the state of Oklahoma and spent much of his youth riding horses and mastering the use of the lariat. These skills were refined into an entertainment act based on fancy rope tricks interspersed with humorous anecdotes and witty remarks. Traveling widely as a vaudeville entertainer, by 1915 Rogers had become a star act with the Ziegfeld Follies, a famous stage show. In 1918 his stage skills led to a new career as a movie actor both in silent films and later in the "talkies."

In the early 1920s, Rogers embarked on another profession, this time as a journalist writing weekly newspaper columns that reached millions of people worldwide. Beginning in 1930 he also broadcast regular radio addresses. What distinguished his journalistic approach was his firsthand experience of ordinary people and places and a wry sense of humor, often debunking establishment figures and institutions. This poking fun at the serious side of life, combined with an optimistic homespun philosophy, gave him immense popular appeal. He became a national and international celebrity and acquired the unofficial status of a goodwill ambassador during his travels in Europe. He also had a strong philanthropic streak and devoted money and time to charitable causes.

Rogers also had a keen interest in flying. He often wrote about the development of aviation and made friends with trailblazing flyers such as Charles Lindbergh. Another pioneering aviator, Wiley Post, invited Rogers to join him in testing the viability of a commercial route between the United States and Asia. Tragically, both Rogers and Post were killed when their plane crashed in northern Alaska. Rogers's death was felt deeply throughout the United States, and the public displays of mourning were heartfelt and widespread. The epitaph by his tomb is taken from one of his numerous quotable remarks and reminds us of the essential dignity of the man. It reads, "Never Met A Man I Didn't Like."

1. An introductory sentence for a brief summary of the passage is provided below. Complete the summary by selecting the THREE answer choices that express the most important ideas in the passage. Some sentences do not belong in the summary because they express ideas that are not presented in the passage or are minor ideas in the passage.

   Will Rogers was a much loved, charismatic figure from the first part of the twentieth century.

   (A) The state of Oklahoma had been part of the Cherokee Native American nation to which Rogers belonged.

   (B) Rogers's interests as a youth gave him the skills to succeed in the entertainment world.

   (C) The Ziegfeld Follies was a famous stage show that Rogers participated in.

   (D) A sense of humor and an optimistic philosophy were characteristics that brought Rogers worldwide distinction as a journalist and goodwill ambassador.

   (E) Rogers's death in an airplane crash brought about widespread mourning for the highly esteemed celebrity.

   (F) Written on Rogers's tombstone is "Never Met A Man I Didn't Like," one of his remarks that highlights his dignity.

The importance of background music in a film cannot be overstated. It is instrumental in creating the mood the moviemaker wants to evoke. During the infancy of cinema, the importance of music was understood, but the relationship between music and the screen action was not fully appreciated. Thus, early musical material consisted of anything available, often bearing little relation to the emotional impact of the movie. Since techniques for movies to include sound had not yet been developed, music was provided by a single musician, a small band, or a full orchestra. These musicians played what they wanted, and a pianist good at improvisation was highly regarded.

As the commercial potential of the cinema became apparent, producers realized the advantage of each film having its own music. In 1908, Camille Saint-Saëns composed music specifically for a French film. However, this idea was before its time and was not embraced by the movie industry. Perhaps cinema musicians weren't ready to learn new pieces for each movie that came along, or perhaps the costs were prohibitive.

By 1913, special catalogs of music for specific dramatic purposes were available. Thus, musicians had at their disposal music that could be used for any scene from any movie. Much of this music consisted of works by famous composers and predated the advent of motion pictures. For example, Mendelssohn's wedding march was a typical catalog piece for wedding scenes and had been written before the appearance of motion pictures.

In 1922 a system that guaranteed synchronization of sound with image was developed, thus making music an essential part of filmmaking. At first, background music was used only if there was an orchestra or performer on screen because it was believed people would be bewildered about the origin of the sound.

A 1930s Western called *Cimarron* was the first film to experiment with background music without a visible means of production. The composer for this sound track was Max Steiner, a pioneer of film scoring. Steiner also composed the film score for *Symphony of Six Million* in 1932, the first film to have music underlying dialogue. The simple, somewhat naïve music of early film scores quickly developed into the sophisticated musical experience that moviegoers encounter today.

2. An introductory sentence for a brief summary of the passage is provided below. Complete the summary by selecting the THREE answer choices that express the most important ideas in the passage. Some sentences do not belong in the summary because they express ideas that are not presented in the passage or are minor ideas in the passage.

The way music is made to create mood in movies has undergone many changes throughout the history of cinema.

Ⓐ Live musicians, who in earlier times had been improvising or playing what they wanted, were later given collections of pieces to play to set the mood.

Ⓑ Camille Saint-Saëns was ahead of his time when he wrote music for a specific French film in 1908.

Ⓒ Synchronization of sound and image made a practical reality of the previously failed idea that each film should have its own music.

Ⓓ *Cimarron* and *Symphony of Six Million,* both movies from the 1930s, were breakthroughs in the music industry.

Ⓔ Music evolved to underlie dialogues and to be heard in the background by an invisible means of production.

Ⓕ In the infancy of cinema, people were naïve but since then have become sophisticated moviegoers.

Water scarcity is fast becoming one of the major limiting factors in world crop production. In many areas, poor agricultural practices have led to increasing desertification and the loss of formerly arable lands. Consequently, those plant species that are well adapted to survival in dry climates are being looked at for an answer to the development of more efficient crops to grow on marginally arable lands.

Plants use several mechanisms to ensure their survival in desert environments. Some involve purely mechanical and physical adaptations, such as the shape of the plant's surface, smaller leaf size, and extensive root systems. Xerophytes and phraetophytes are two kinds of plants that survive in the desert environment through adaptations of their physical structure. Xerophytes, which include cactuses, an adaptation from the rose family, are effective desert plants because they have spines instead of leaves. These spines protect the plant from animals, shade it from the sun, and help it collect moisture. Another adaptation is their shallow but extensive root systems. The roots radiate out from the plant and quickly absorb large quantities of water when it rains.

The mesquite tree is a type of phraetophyte. These plants have tiny leaves that close their pores during the day to avoid water loss and open them at night when they can absorb moisture. All phraetophytes have developed extremely long root systems that draw water from the water table deep underground. Some phraetophytes have developed a double-root system – the typical long and deep root system to collect ground water and a shallow one like the xerophytes to collect surface water.

Some desert plant adaptations are related to chemical mechanisms. For instance, some phraetophytes depend on their unpleasant smell and taste for protection, while many xerophytes have internal gums and mucilages that give them water-retaining properties. Another chemical mechanism is that of the epiticular wax layer. This wax layer acts as an impervious cover to protect the plant. It prevents excessive loss of internal moisture. It also protects the plant from external aggression, which can come from inorganic agents such as gases, or organic agents, which include bacteria and plant pests.

Researchers have proposed that synthetic waxes with similar protective abilities could be prepared based on knowledge of desert plants. If successfully developed, such a compound could be used to greatly increase a plant's ability to maintain health in such adverse situations as inadequate water supply, limited fertilizer availability, attack by pests, and poor storage after harvesting.

3. Select the appropriate survival tactics from the answer choices and match them to the type of plant to which they relate. TWO of the answer choices will NOT be used.

Answer Choices

A. Epiticular wax coating causes difficulties for storage after harvesting.
B. Internal chemical mechanisms allow water to be held.
C. Small leaves open to collect water and close to retain it.
D. Spines were adapted from leaves.
E. The smell and taste of the plant is unpleasant for predators.
F. The long roots spread out close to the surface of the ground.
G. The roots descend deep into the ground.
H. The cactus is an adaptation of the rose to desert environments.
I. Two sets of root systems collect ground and surface water.

Xerophytes

- ____
- ____
- ____

Phraetophytes

- ____
- ____
- ____
- ____

[illegible]ding Section Practice Test

When you have taken the Diagnostic Test and completed the exercises recommended in the Answer Key for any Reading questions you marked incorrectly, you can test your skills by taking this Reading Section Practice Test. You can take this test either in this book or on the CD-ROM that accompanies this book. The Reading Section Practice Test in the book is identical to the Reading section of Test 2 on the CD-ROM.

During the Reading Section of the actual TOEFL test, you may go back and check your work or change your answers before your time limit is up. Maintain the same test conditions now that would be experienced during the real test.

READING SECTION

Directions

In this section, you will read three passages and answer reading comprehension questions about each passage. Most questions are worth one point, but the last question in each set is worth more than one point. The directions indicate how many points you may receive.

You have 60 minutes to read all of the passages and answer the questions. Some passages include a word or phrase followed by an asterisk (*). Go to the bottom of the page to see a definition or an explanation of these words or phrases.

Questions 1–13

Cellular Slime Molds

Cellular slime molds are extraordinary life forms that exhibit features of both [illegible] and protozoa, although often classed for convenience with fungi. At one time they w[illegible]egarded as organisms of ambiguous taxonomic status, but more recent analysis of DN[illegible]uences has shown that slime molds should be regarded as inhabiting their own separ[illegible]ngdom. Their uniqueness lies in their unusual life cycle, which alternates between a f[illegible]ng stage in which the organism is essentially unicellular and a reproductive stage in whi[illegible]the organism adopts a multicellular structure. At the first stage they are free-living, separ[illegible] amoebae, usually inhabiting the forest floor and ingesting bacteria found in rotting wood, dung, or damp soil. But their food supplies are relatively easily exhausted since the cells' movements are restricted and their food requirements rather large.

When the cells become starved of nutrition, the organism initiates a new genetic program that permits the cells to eventually find a new, food-rich environment. At this point, the single-celled amoebae combine together to form what will eventually become a multicellular creature. The mechanism by which the individual members become a single entity is essentially chemical in nature. At first, a few of the amoebae start to produce periodic chemical pulses that are detected, amplified, and relayed to the surrounding members, which then move toward the pulse origin. In time, these cells form many streams of cells, which then come together to form a single hemispherical mass. This mass sticks together through the secretion of adhesion molecules.

The mass now develops a tip, which elongates into a finger-like structure of about 1 or 2 millimeters in length. This structure eventually falls over to form a miniature slug, moving as a single entity orienting itself toward light. During this period the cells within the mass differentiate into two distinct kinds of cell. Some become prestalk cells, which later form into a vertical stalk, and others form prespore cells, which become the spore head.

As the organism migrates, it leaves behind a track of slime rather like a garden slug. Once a favorable location has been found with a fresh source of bacteria to feed on, the migration stops and the colony metamorphoses into a fungus-like organism in a process known as "culmination." The front cells turn into a stalk, and the back cells climb up the stalk and form a spherical-shaped head, known as the sorocarp. This final fruiting body is about 2 millimeters in height. The head develops into spores, which are dispersed into the environment and form the next generation of amoebae cells. Then the life cycle is repeated. Usually the stalk disappears once the spores have been released.

The process by which the originally identical cells of the slime mold become transformed into multicellular structures composed of two different cell types – spore and stalk – is of great interest to developmental biologists since it is analogous* to an important process found in higher organisms in which organs with highly specialized functions are formed from unspecialized stem cells. Early experiments showed which parts of the slime mold organism contributed to the eventual stalk and which parts to the head. Scientists stained the front part of a slug with a red dye and attached it to the back part of a different slug. The hybrid creature developed as normal. The experimenters then noted that the stalk of the fruiting body was stained red and that the spore head was unstained. Clearly, the anterior part of the organism culminated in the stalk and the posterior part in the spore head. Nowadays, experiments using DNA technology and fluorescent proteins or enzymes to label the prespore and prestalk cells have been undertaken. This more molecular approach gives more precise results than using staining dyes but has essentially backed up the results of the earlier dye studies.

***analogous:** similar

1. According to paragraph 1, how the slime mold should be classified used to be

   Ⓐ unknown
   Ⓑ uncertain
   Ⓒ controversial
   Ⓓ unfamiliar

Paragraph 1 is marked with an arrow [➡].

➡ Cellular slime molds are extraordinary life forms that exhibit features of both fungi and protozoa, although often classed for convenience with fungi. At one time they were regarded as organisms of ambiguous taxonomic status, but more recent analysis of DNA sequences has shown that slime molds should be regarded as inhabiting their own separate kingdom. Their uniqueness lies in their unusual life cycle, which alternates between a feeding stage in which the organism is essentially unicellular and a reproductive stage in which the organism adopts a multicellular structure. At the first stage they are free-living, separate amoebae, usually inhabiting the forest floor and ingesting bacteria found in rotting wood, dung, or damp soil. But their food supplies are relatively easily exhausted since the cells' movements are restricted and their food requirements rather large.

2. The word "ingesting" in the passage is closest in meaning to

   Ⓐ chewing
   Ⓑ catching
   Ⓒ absorbing
   Ⓓ consuming

Cellular slime molds are extraordinary life forms that exhibit features of both fungi and protozoa, although often classed for convenience with fungi. At one time they were regarded as organisms of ambiguous taxonomic status, but more recent analysis of DNA sequences has shown that slime molds should be regarded as inhabiting their own separate kingdom. Their uniqueness lies in their unusual life cycle, which alternates between a feeding stage in which the organism is essentially unicellular and a reproductive stage in which the organism adopts a multicellular structure. At the first stage they are free-living, separate amoebae, usually inhabiting the forest floor and ingesting bacteria found in rotting wood, dung, or damp soil. But their food supplies are relatively easily exhausted since the cells' movements are restricted and their food requirements rather large.

3. According to the passage, what is unusual about the slime molds' life cycle?

   Ⓐ They inhabit their own kingdom.
   Ⓑ They are organisms whose classification is ambiguous.
   Ⓒ They alternate between unicellular and multicellular structures.
   Ⓓ They are free-living organisms.

[Refer to the full passage.]

4. According to the passage, what is the primary reason the cells need to combine into a single larger creature? (A) To move to find a new food source (B) To slow the rate of ingesting food (C) To become separate creatures (D) To create their own kingdom	[Refer to the full passage.]

5. Look at the four squares [■] that indicate where the following sentence could be added to the passage. **Starvation is reached when the population of cells is high in relation to the abundance of the food source.** Where would the sentence best fit? Choose the letter of the square that shows where the sentence should be added.	When the cells become starved of nutrition, the organism initiates a new genetic program that permits the cells to eventually find a new, food-rich environment. **A** At this point, the single-celled amoebae combine together to form what will eventually become a multicellular creature. **B** The mechanism by which the individual members become a single entity is essentially chemical in nature. **C** At first, a few of the amoebae start to produce periodic chemical pulses that are detected, amplified, and relayed to the surrounding members, which then move toward the pulse origin. **D** In time, these cells form many streams of cells, which then come together to form a single hemispherical mass. This mass sticks together through the secretion of adhesion molecules.

6. The word "entity" in the passage is closest in meaning to (A) division (B) species (C) piece (D) unit	When the cells become starved of nutrition, the organism initiates a new genetic program that permits the cells to eventually find a new, food-rich environment. At this point, the single-celled amoebae combine together to form what will eventually become a multicellular creature. The mechanism by which the individual members become a single entity is essentially chemical in nature. At first, a few of the amoebae start to produce periodic chemical pulses that are detected, amplified, and relayed to the surrounding members, which then move toward the pulse origin. In time, these cells form many streams of cells, which then come together to form a single hemispherical mass. This mass sticks together through the secretion of adhesion molecules.

7. The word "others" in the passage refers to (A) cells (B) stalks (C) spores (D) kinds	The mass now develops a tip, which elongates into a finger-like structure of about 1 or 2 millimeters in length. This structure eventually falls over to form a miniature slug, moving as a single entity orienting itself toward light. During this period the cells within the mass differentiate into two distinct kinds of cell. Some become prestalk cells, which later form into a vertical stalk, and others form prespore cells, which become the spore head.

8. All of the following are mentioned in paragraph 4 as being parts of the multicellular slug EXCEPT

   (A) the head
   (B) the stalk
   (C) legs
   (D) spores

Paragraph 4 is marked with an arrow [➡].

➡ As the organism migrates, it leaves behind a track of slime rather like a garden slug. Once a favorable location has been found with a fresh source of bacteria to feed on, the migration stops and the colony metamorphoses into a fungus-like organism in a process known as "culmination." The front cells turn into a stalk, and the back cells climb up the stalk and form a spherical-shaped head, known as the sorocarp. This final fruiting body is about 2 millimeters in height. The head develops into spores, which are dispersed into the environment and form the next generation of amoebae cells. Then the life cycle is repeated. Usually the stalk disappears once the spores have been released.

9. In paragraph 4, why does the author refer to the fungus-like organism as a fruiting body?

   (A) Because it has become one entity
   (B) Because it is 2 millimeters in height
   (C) Because it now has a stalk and head
   (D) Because it has reached its reproductive stage

Paragraph 4 is marked with an arrow [➡].

➡ As the organism migrates, it leaves behind a track of slime rather like a garden slug. Once a favorable location has been found with a fresh source of bacteria to feed on, the migration stops and the colony metamorphoses into a fungus-like organism in a process known as "culmination." The front cells turn into a stalk, and the back cells climb up the stalk and form a spherical-shaped head, known as the sorocarp. This final fruiting body is about 2 millimeters in height. The head develops into spores, which are dispersed into the environment and form the next generation of amoebae cells. Then the life cycle is repeated. Usually the stalk disappears once the spores have been released.

10. Which of the sentences below best expresses the essential information in the highlighted sentence? Incorrect choices change the meaning in important ways or leave out essential information.

   (A) The next generation of amoebae cells disperses into the environment by attaching themselves to spores on the head.
   (B) After the spores that form the head are scattered around the area, they develop into a new generation of amoebae cells.
   (C) The spores develop into amoebae cells and then become spread around the head of the slug.
   (D) The spores spread throughout an area and develop into a new generation of amoebae cells.

As the organism migrates, it leaves behind a track of slime rather like a garden slug. Once a favorable location has been found with a fresh source of bacteria to feed on, the migration stops and the colony metamorphoses into a fungus-like organism in a process known as "culmination." The front cells turn into a stalk, and the back cells climb up the stalk and form a spherical-shaped head, known as the sorocarp. This final fruiting body is about 2 millimeters in height. The head develops into spores, which are dispersed into the environment and form the next generation of amoebae cells. Then the life cycle is repeated. Usually the stalk disappears once the spores have been released.

READING

11. It can be inferred that developmental biologists are especially interested in the slime mold because (A) the change in degree of specialization in its cells helps them to understand cell development in more complex organisms (B) it is convenient to perform experiments on a creature that is composed of two different cell types (C) scientists could form hybrid organisms in their experiments using the same process that slime mold uses to transform itself (D) it is easy to find specimens on which to perform experiments	[Refer to the full passage.]

12. According to the passage, the recent DNA studies (A) give similar results to the dye studies (B) contradict the dye studies (C) are less exact than the dye studies (D) have introduced confusion about the dye study results	[Refer to the full passage.]

13. **Directions:** Select the appropriate phrases from the answer choices and match them to the stage of slime mold life cycle to which they relate. TWO of the answer choices will NOT be used. **This question is worth 4 points.**

Write the letters of the answer choices in the spaces where they belong.
Refer to the full passage.

Answer Choices

(A) Alteration between feeding and reproduction

(B) Bacteria-consuming amoebae inhabiting the forest floor

(C) Culmination of dyed cells in stalk and head

(D) Development of sorocarp

(E) Dispersal of spores

(F) Mass formed through the secretion of adhesion molecules

(G) Migration oriented to fresh source of food

(H) Production of chemical pulses causing members to merge

(I) Transformation of cells into stalk and head

Unspecialized Cells

•
•
•
•

Specialized Cells

•
•
•

READING

Questions 14–26

The Coriolis Force

In the early part of the twentieth century, the Norwegian scientist and polar explorer Fridtjof Nansen noted that icebergs did not follow the path of the wind as common sense had assumed. Instead they tended to move to the right side of the direction in which the wind blew. A student of Nansen's, V. W. Ekman, showed that the rotation of the Earth leading to an inertial force known as the Coriolis force was responsible for this phenomenon. He further demonstrated that in the Northern Hemisphere the deflection was toward the right of the prevailing wind, and in the Southern Hemisphere the deflection was toward the left. The icebergs observed by Nansen were moved by ocean currents that also moved at an angle to the prevailing wind.

The Coriolis force itself is caused by the fact that the Earth rotates on its axis once per day, and hence all points on the planet have the same rotational velocity; that is, they take one whole day to complete a rotational circle. However, since a complete rotation around the Earth is shorter the further one is away from the equator, different points on the Earth travel at different speeds depending on degree of latitude. For example, a point on the equator travels the whole distance around the sphere (about 40,000 kilometers), whereas a point near the poles will travel a much shorter distance. Therefore, we can say that the linear speed of a point depends on its latitude above or below the equator. Thus the actual linear speed of a point on the surface is faster the nearer that point is to the equator.

Now if an untethered object (or current) is moving northward away from the equator in the Northern Hemisphere, it will also maintain the initial speed imparted to it by the eastward rotation of the Earth. That eastward deflection is faster at the equator than at more northerly (or southerly) latitudes, and thus, when the object reaches a more northerly point, it will be traveling faster in an eastward direction than the surrounding ground or water. The moving object will appear to be forced away from its path by some mysterious phenomenon. In reality the ground is simply moving at a different speed from the original speed at the object's (or current's) home position. The resulting direction of movement will therefore be at an angle of about 45 degrees to the original direction, so an object traveling north will move to the right in the Northern Hemisphere and to the left in the Southern Hemisphere with respect to the rotating Earth. An object traveling south will be deflected to the left in the Northern Hemisphere and to the right in the Southern Hemisphere.

As the surface water in the ocean is moved by the wind, it tends to veer* off at an angle of 45 degrees to the right or left. This movement exerts a drag on the water immediately below it, and the Coriolis force causes this layer to move and also to deflect to the right or left. This layer in turn drags the layer below, which in turn is deflected. At successively deeper layers, the water is deflected in relation to the layer above until at a depth of around 150 meters, the water is moving in a direction opposite to the surface water. At successively greater depths, the frictional forces between layers reduce the energy of the flow, causing water to move more slowly the deeper the layer. The resulting deflections produce a spiral pattern known as the Ekman spiral. The net movement of water is roughly at 90 degrees from the wind direction and is known as Ekman transport.

This phenomenon is an important factor in the movement of water in the oceans. Among other things, it creates zones of upwelling by forcing surface waters apart and other zones of downwelling by forcing surface waters together. For example, wind blowing parallel to the shore may create a net movement of water at 90 degrees away from the shore. Nutrient-rich deeper ocean water will upwell to take the place of the displaced water and thus profoundly influence the marine ecosystem.

***veer:** to suddenly change direction

14. The phrase "path of the wind" in the passage is closest in meaning to (A) wind strength (B) wind variation (C) wind direction (D) wind phenomenon	In the early part of the twentieth century, the Norwegian scientist and polar explorer Fridtjof Nansen noted that icebergs did not follow the path of the wind as common sense had assumed. Instead they tended to move to the right side of the direction in which the wind blew. A student of Nansen's, V. W. Ekman, showed that the rotation of the Earth leading to an inertial force known as the Coriolis force was responsible for this phenomenon. He further demonstrated that in the Northern Hemisphere the deflection was toward the right of the prevailing wind, and in the Southern Hemisphere the deflection was toward the left. The icebergs observed by Nansen were moved by ocean currents that also moved at an angle to the prevailing wind.

15. The phrase "this phenomenon" in the passage refers to (A) the movement of icebergs (B) the rotation of the Earth (C) the direction of the wind (D) the inertial Coriolis force	In the early part of the twentieth century, the Norwegian scientist and polar explorer Fridtjof Nansen noted that icebergs did not follow the path of the wind as common sense had assumed. Instead they tended to move to the right side of the direction in which the wind blew. A student of Nansen's, V. W. Ekman, showed that the rotation of the Earth leading to an inertial force known as the Coriolis force was responsible for this phenomenon. He further demonstrated that in the Northern Hemisphere the deflection was toward the right of the prevailing wind, and in the Southern Hemisphere the deflection was toward the left. The icebergs observed by Nansen were moved by ocean currents that also moved at an angle to the prevailing wind.

16. The word "rotates" in the passage is closest in meaning to (A) spins (B) travels (C) twirls (D) swivels	The Coriolis force itself is caused by the fact that the Earth rotates on its axis once per day, and hence all points on the planet have the same rotational velocity; that is, they take one whole day to complete a rotational circle. However, since a complete rotation around the Earth is shorter the further one is away from the equator, different points on the Earth travel at different speeds depending on degree of latitude. For example, a point on the equator travels the whole distance around the sphere (about 40,000 kilometers), whereas a point near the poles will travel a much shorter distance. Therefore, we can say that the linear speed of a point depends on its latitude above or below the equator. Thus the actual linear speed of a point on the surface is faster the nearer that point is to the equator.

17. We can infer that rotational velocity is (A) the same as speed in kph (B) different at different latitudes (C) the same at different latitudes (D) dependent on latitude	[Refer to the full passage.]

READING

18. In paragraph 2, the author explains the differences in linear speed by
    (A) arguing that an object moving north moves faster
    (B) describing the linear velocity of the Earth
    (C) identifying the eastward deflection of a current
    (D) relating speed to the distance of a point from the equator

Paragraph 2 is marked with an arrow [➡].

➡ The Coriolis force itself is caused by the fact that the Earth rotates on its axis once per day, and hence all points on the planet have the same rotational velocity; that is, they take one whole day to complete a rotational circle. However, since a complete rotation around the Earth is shorter the further one is away from the equator, different points on the Earth travel at different speeds depending on degree of latitude. For example, a point on the equator travels the whole distance around the sphere (about 40,000 kilometers), whereas a point near the poles will travel a much shorter distance. Therefore, we can say that the linear speed of a point depends on its latitude above or below the equator. Thus the actual linear speed of a point on the surface is faster the nearer that point is to the equator.

19. According to the passage, a point near the equator in the Northern Hemisphere travels
    (A) at the same speed as any other point
    (B) faster than a point at a higher latitude
    (C) slower than a point in the Southern Hemisphere
    (D) at different speeds in different seasons

[Refer to the full passage.]

20. Look at the four squares [■] that indicate where the following sentence could be added to the passage.

And conversely, if the object is traveling southward toward the equator, it will be moving more slowly than the surrounding land or water.

Where would the sentence best fit?

Choose the letter of the square that shows where the sentence should be added.

Now if an untethered object (or current) is moving northward away from the equator in the Northern Hemisphere, it will also maintain the initial speed imparted to it by the eastward rotation of the Earth. [A] That eastward deflection is faster at the equator than at more northerly (or southerly) latitudes, and thus, when the object reaches a more northerly point, it will be traveling faster in an eastward direction than the surrounding ground or water. [B] The moving object will appear to be forced away from its path by some mysterious phenomenon. In reality the ground is simply moving at a different speed from the original speed at the object's (or current's) home position. [C] The resulting direction of movement will therefore be at an angle of about 45 degrees to the original direction, so an object traveling north will move to the right in the Northern Hemisphere and to the left in the Southern Hemisphere with respect to the rotating Earth. [D] An object traveling south will be deflected to the left in the Northern Hemisphere and to the right in the Southern Hemisphere.

21. According to paragraph 4, where does water move in a direction contrary to surface layers of water?

    (A) Directly below the surface
    (B) At 90 degrees to the surface
    (C) At all depths below the surface
    (D) At 150 meters below the surface

Paragraph 4 is marked with an arrow [➡].

➡ As the surface water in the ocean is moved by the wind, it tends to veer off at an angle of 45 degrees to the right or left. This movement exerts a drag on the water immediately below it, and the Coriolis force causes this layer to move and also to deflect to the right or left. This layer in turn drags the layer below, which in turn is deflected. At successively deeper layers, the water is deflected in relation to the layer above until at a depth of around 150 meters, the water is moving in a direction opposite to the surface water. At successively greater depths, the frictional forces between layers reduce the energy of the flow, causing water to move more slowly the deeper the layer. The resulting deflections produce a spiral pattern known as the Ekman spiral. The net movement of water is roughly at 90 degrees from the wind direction and is known as Ekman transport.

22. In paragraph 4, why does the author explain that the wind tends to deflect the water to the right or left?

    (A) To explain the concept of upwelling
    (B) To demonstrate the effect of the Coriolis force
    (C) To point out causes of rotational velocity
    (D) To introduce the movement of ocean currents

Paragraph 4 is marked with an arrow [➡].

➡ As the surface water in the ocean is moved by the wind, it tends to veer off at an angle of 45 degrees to the right or left. This movement exerts a drag on the water immediately below it, and the Coriolis force causes this layer to move and also to deflect to the right or left. This layer in turn drags the layer below, which in turn is deflected. At successively deeper layers, the water is deflected in relation to the layer above until at a depth of around 150 meters, the water is moving in a direction opposite to the surface water. At successively greater depths, the frictional forces between layers reduce the energy of the flow, causing water to move more slowly the deeper the layer. The resulting deflections produce a spiral pattern known as the Ekman spiral. The net movement of water is roughly at 90 degrees from the wind direction and is known as Ekman transport.

23. The word "deflected" in the passage is closest in meaning to

    (A) turned
    (B) pushed
    (C) shoved
    (D) urged

As the surface water in the ocean is moved by the wind, it tends to veer off at an angle of 45 degrees to the right or left. This movement exerts a drag on the water immediately below it, and the Coriolis force causes this layer to move and also to deflect to the right or left. This layer in turn drags the layer below, which in turn is deflected. At successively deeper layers, the water is deflected in relation to the layer above until at a depth of around 150 meters, the water is moving in a direction opposite to the surface water. At successively greater depths, the frictional forces between layers reduce the energy of the flow, causing water to move more slowly the deeper the layer. The resulting deflections produce a spiral pattern known as the Ekman spiral. The net movement of water is roughly at 90 degrees from the wind direction and is known as Ekman transport.

24. Based on the information in paragraphs 1 and 4, which of the following best explains the term "Coriolis force"? (A) The force that creates currents (B) The force that moves icebergs (C) The force that opposes wind movement (D) The force that deflects ocean water	[Refer to the full passage.]

25. According to the passage, the Ekman spiral may affect (A) the distribution of ocean life forms (B) the direction of the wind (C) the speed of ocean currents (D) the frictional forces of water layers	[Refer to the full passage.]

26. **Directions:** An introductory sentence for a brief summary of the passage is provided below. Complete the summary by selecting the THREE answer choices that express the most important ideas in the passage. Some sentences do not belong in the summary because they express ideas that are not presented in the passage or are minor ideas in the passage. **This question is worth 2 points.**

Write the letters of the answer choices in the spaces where they belong.
Refer to the full passage.

Different linear speeds at different latitudes on the Earth cause the prevailing winds in the Earth's Northern and Southern Hemispheres to deflect water movements, thus creating Ekman spirals.

-
-
-

Answer Choices

(A) Due to the Coriolis force, icebergs move at a right angle to the prevailing wind.

(B) Because of the Earth's rotation, objects moving away from or toward the equator travel at different speeds in relation to fixed points at different latitudes.

(C) In order to reach the correct destination, an airplane pilot must adjust direction to compensate for the Coriolis force.

(D) Because of deflection and differences in linear speed, ocean currents move at an angle to the wind.

(E) Water at successively lower levels is deflected at an angle to the layer immediately above it, and this creates a spiral.

(F) Due to upwelling of water, marine life is rich in areas where Ekman spirals operate.

Questions 27–39

The Battle of Gettysburg

In June 1863, a Confederate army under the command of General Lee encountered a Union army commanded by General Meade near the town of Gettysburg, Pennsylvania. The ensuing battle, which lasted three days, is considered the most important single engagement of the American Civil War in that it effectually ended the Confederates' last major invasion of the North. Once the Southern Confederate army's offensive strategy was destroyed at Gettysburg, the Southern states were forced to fight a defensive war in which their weaker manufacturing capacity and transportation infrastructure led ultimately to defeat.

General Lee had ordered his Confederate army to invade the northern state of Pennsylvania in the hope of enticing the Union army into a vulnerable position. The strategy was also aimed at increasing the war weariness of the North and ultimately at leading Abraham Lincoln's government into concluding a peace deal and recognizing the independence of the Confederate South.

On the morning of July 1, the battle opened with Confederate troops attacking a Union cavalry division to the west of Gettysburg at McPherson Ridge. The Union forces were outnumbered but managed to hold their positions initially. Reinforcements came to both sides, but eventually the Union forces were overpowered and were driven back to the south of Gettysburg. Thousands of their soldiers were captured in this retreat. During the night the bulk of the Union army arrived and the troops labored to create strong defensive positions along Cemetery Ridge, a long rise of land running southward from outside the town, and on two hills just to the north and east of this crest. When it was fully assembled, the whole Union army formed a defensive arc resembling a fishhook. The Confederate forces, about one mile distant, faced the Union positions from the west and north in a larger concave arc.

Throughout July 2 Lee's forces attacked both Union flanks, leaving thousands of dead on both sides. To the south the Confederates overran the Union's advance lines, but they failed to dislodge the Union forces from their main positions. A strategically important hill on the Union army's left flank known as Little Round Top was stormed by the Confederates, but Meade's forces fought a skillful defensive battle and the attacks were unsuccessful. There was a devastating number of casualties on both sides.

On the third day of battle, General Lee decided to concentrate his attack on the center of the Union forces ranged along Cemetery Ridge. He reasoned, against the advice of others in his senior staff, that since the Union forces had reinforced both their flanks, their central defensive positions would be weaker and easier to overrun. As a prelude to the attack, the Confederate artillery bombarded the ridge for two hours, but inflicted less damage than they had expected, due to poor visibility. When the bombardment ceased, a Confederate infantry force of about 13,000 men charged courageously across the open land toward the Union lines on Cemetery Ridge about a mile away. This attack, now known as Pickett's Charge after the general whose division led it, failed in its objective to break the Union line.

With the failure of Pickett's Charge, the battle was essentially over and Lee's retreat began the following day. His exhausted army staggered toward safer territory in the South, leaving behind a scene of terrible devastation. Both sides had suffered excessive losses of men, but the Union had succeeded in preventing the Confederates from invading the North. So Gettysburg proved to be a decisive turning point in the Civil War and was celebrated as the biggest Union victory of the war.

27. The word "engagement" in the passage is closest in meaning to (A) agreement (B) meeting (C) battle (D) defeat	In June 1863, a Confederate army under the command of General Lee encountered a Union army commanded by General Meade near the town of Gettysburg, Pennsylvania. The ensuing battle, which lasted three days, is considered the most important single engagement of the American Civil War in that it effectually ended the Confederates' last major invasion of the North. Once the Southern Confederate army's offensive strategy was destroyed at Gettysburg, the Southern states were forced to fight a defensive war in which their weaker manufacturing capacity and transportation infrastructure led ultimately to defeat.

28. In paragraph 1, the author suggests that the Confederates lost the Civil War largely because their (A) leaders were ineffective (B) industrial capacity was weaker (C) soldiers were unprofessional (D) strategy was poorly planned Paragraph 1 is marked with an arrow [➡].	➡ In June 1863, a Confederate army under the command of General Lee encountered a Union army commanded by General Meade near the town of Gettysburg, Pennsylvania. The ensuing battle, which lasted three days, is considered the most important single engagement of the American Civil War in that it effectually ended the Confederates' last major invasion of the North. Once the Southern Confederate army's offensive strategy was destroyed at Gettysburg, the Southern states were forced to fight a defensive war in which their weaker manufacturing capacity and transportation infrastructure led ultimately to defeat.

29. Which of the sentences below best expresses the essential information in the highlighted sentence in the passage? Incorrect choices change the meaning in important ways or leave out essential information. (A) General Lee tried to lure his soldiers into invading the North in order to defeat the Union army. (B) The Union army was in danger of an invasion by General Lee's army due to its location in Pennsylvania. (C) In the hope of luring the Union army into an exposed situation, General Lee's forces marched into Pennsylvania. (D) The state of Pennsylvania was a suitable location for drawing out the Union army into a dangerous situation.	General Lee had ordered his Confederate army to invade the northern state of Pennsylvania in the hope of enticing the Union army into a vulnerable position. The strategy was also aimed at increasing the war weariness of the North and ultimately at leading Abraham Lincoln's government into concluding a peace deal and recognizing the independence of the Confederate South.

30. What can be inferred from paragraph 2 about the North's attitude about the war?

(A) It was angry at the loss of freedoms.
(B) It was keen on continuing the war.
(C) It was keen on independence.
(D) It was tired of waging war.

Paragraph 2 is marked with an arrow (➡).

➡ General Lee had ordered his Confederate army to invade the northern state of Pennsylvania in the hope of enticing the Union army into a vulnerable position. The strategy was also aimed at increasing the war weariness of the North and ultimately at leading Abraham Lincoln's government into concluding a peace deal and recognizing the independence of the Confederate South.

31. We can infer from the passage that, at Gettysburg, the Union army largely played which kind of strategy?

(A) An offensive strategy
(B) A strategy of hit and run
(C) A defensive strategy
(D) A strategy of wait and see

[Refer to the full passage.]

32. The phrase "this crest" in the passage refers to

(A) the Confederate forces
(B) Cemetery Ridge
(C) Union army reinforcements
(D) the town of Gettysburg

On the morning of July 1, the battle opened with Confederate troops attacking a Union cavalry division to the west of Gettysburg at McPherson Ridge. The Union forces were outnumbered but managed to hold their positions initially. Reinforcements came to both sides, but eventually the Union forces were overpowered and were driven back to the south of Gettysburg. Thousands of their soldiers were captured in this retreat. During the night the bulk of the Union army arrived and the troops labored to create strong defensive positions along Cemetery Ridge, a long rise of land running southward from outside the town, and on two hills just to the north and east of this crest. When it was fully assembled, the whole Union army formed a defensive arc resembling a fishhook. The Confederate forces, about one mile distant, faced the Union positions from the west and north in a larger concave arc.

33. Why does the author say the positions of the Union army resembled a fishhook?

(A) To give the reader a mental picture of the troops' positions
(B) To explain the appearance of the sharp pointed hooks used as weapons
(C) To suggest that taking a fishhook formation is a good tactic in war
(D) To imply that the ridge had a curved shape like that of a fishhook

[Refer to the full passage.]

34. The word "devastating" in the passage is closest in meaning to Ⓐ important Ⓑ desperate Ⓒ decisive Ⓓ ruinous	Throughout July 2 Lee's forces attacked both Union flanks, leaving thousands of dead on both sides. To the south the Confederates overran the Union's advance lines, but they failed to dislodge the Union forces from their main positions. A strategically important hill on the Union army's left flank known as Little Round Top was stormed by the Confederates, but Meade's forces fought a skillful defensive battle and the attacks were unsuccessful. There was a devastating number of casualties on both sides.

35. All of the following are implied in paragraph 5 as contributing to the failure of Pickett's Charge EXCEPT Ⓐ General Lee's refusal to listen to his generals' opinion Ⓑ the Confederate artillery's failure to cause much damage Ⓒ the Union's center being stronger than anticipated Ⓓ the Confederate infantry not performing at full strength Paragraph 5 is marked with an arrow (➡).	➡ On the third day of battle, General Lee decided to concentrate his attack on the center of the Union forces ranged along Cemetery Ridge. He reasoned, against the advice of others in his senior staff, that since the Union forces had reinforced both their flanks, their central defensive positions would be weaker and easier to overrun. As a prelude to the attack, the Confederate artillery bombarded the ridge for two hours, but inflicted less damage than they had expected, due to poor visibility. When the bombardment ceased, a Confederate infantry force of about 13,000 men charged courageously across the open land toward the Union lines on Cemetery Ridge about a mile away. This attack, now known as Pickett's Charge after the general whose division led it, failed in its objective to break the Union line.

36. Look at the four squares [■] that indicate where the following sentence could be added to the passage. **They were subjected to heavy artillery and rifle fire and sustained a huge number of casualties.** Where would the sentence best fit? Choose the letter of the square that shows where the sentence should be added.	On the third day of battle, General Lee decided to concentrate his attack on the center of the Union forces ranged along Cemetery Ridge. [A] He reasoned, against the advice of others in his senior staff, that since the Union forces had reinforced both their flanks, their central defensive positions would be weaker and easier to overrun. [B] As a prelude to the attack, the Confederate artillery bombarded the ridge for two hours, but inflicted less damage than they had expected, due to poor visibility. [C] When the bombardment ceased, a Confederate infantry force of about 13,000 men charged courageously across the open land toward the Union lines on Cemetery Ridge about a mile away. [D] This attack, now known as Pickett's Charge after the general whose division led it, failed in its objective to break the Union line.

37. According to the passage, the battle of Gettysburg ended with (A) Lee signing a document of surrender (B) the Southern territories becoming much safer (C) Lee's army devastating the countryside in their retreat (D) a high death toll for both the Union and the Confederates	[Refer to the full passage.]

38. According to the passage, why was the battle of Gettysburg so decisive? (A) The Confederates lost so many troops. (B) It created war weariness on both sides. (C) The Confederates failed to capture Northern territory. (D) The Union troops gained confidence.	[Refer to the full passage.]

39. **Directions:** An introductory sentence for a brief summary of the passage is provided below. Complete the summary by selecting the THREE answer choices that express the most important ideas in the passage. Some sentences do not belong in the summary because they express ideas that are not presented in the passage or are minor ideas in the passage. **This question is worth 2 points.**

Write the letters of the answer choices in the spaces where they belong.
Refer to the full passage.

The battle of Gettysburg was the battle that turned the tide of the American Civil War.

-
-
-

Answer Choices

(A) The Confederate army's strategy was aimed at getting the North to seek a peace deal.

(B) The fighting was heavy from the beginning, and after two indecisive but bloody days, the main battle lines were drawn with reinforcements coming to both sides.

(C) The initial fighting was heavy, but at the end of the first two days General Meade's army seemed to be in a superior position.

(D) The Union army successfully overran most of General Meade's positions on the Confederates' left flank.

(E) A large-scale and devastating infantry advance by troops of the Confederate army failed to dislodge the Union army from their positions.

(F) The invading Confederate army retreated, leaving the North in a stronger position militarily and strategically.

Listening

The Listening section of the TOEFL® iBT test measures your ability to understand spoken English. You will see photographs of students and professors speaking and hear parts of conversations and academic lectures lasting from three to five minutes. Some of the lectures include classroom discussions. Each listening passage is followed by five or six questions. Each listening passage begins with a spoken statement that sets the context. For example, you will hear, "Listen to part of a conversation between a student and an advisor."

When listening, you must concentrate carefully and focus all your attention on the passage. Taking notes is permitted and recommended. All the information necessary to answer the questions can be found within the passage. You do not need any prior knowledge about the topic of the passage in order to answer the questions. Some questions begin by replaying a short excerpt from the listening passage, but most questions require you to remember what you heard.

You must choose the correct answer to each question from the choices on the computer screen by either clicking on the best choice of four possible answers or by following the special directions that appear in a box on the screen. After you choose your answer, click on the **Next** icon. You are then given the opportunity to check your answer. When you are ready, click on the **OK** icon. You must confirm your answer by clicking **OK** in order to continue.

Strategies to Use for Building Listening Skills

1. Listen to spoken English as much as possible.
The more you practice listening, the better listener you will become. There are many ways in which you can practice your listening skills. If you don't have the opportunity to listen to native English speakers in person, you can hear English spoken in movies, on TV, on the radio, or on the Internet. Try to understand unfamiliar words in context. Write down any words you don't understand so you can look them up in a dictionary later.

2. Listen to natural speech.
Most of what you hear in movies, documentaries, and TV or radio news reports is scripted speech. This means that what you are listening to has been planned and written down so that it can be read aloud. Although these sources provide good listening practice, they do not contain many of the natural speech features that will be heard in TOEFL listening passages. By listening to unscripted interviews, discussions, or debates, you can improve your ability to understand natural speech.

3. Listen to different accents.
Speakers from different English-speaking countries may be featured in the Listening section of the TOEFL iBT test. To become familiar with different accents and speech patterns, watch movies and TV shows and listen to radio programs from various English-speaking areas of the world.

4. Listen to authentic academic lectures.
Try to attend lectures given in English and take notes. If you have access to the Internet, the Web sites of some universities and research institutions provide free lectures and discussions that you can listen to as many times as you want. These lectures and discussions are useful for several reasons:

- You can improve your ability to listen to longer discourse.
- You have a choice of lectures and discussions on different topics.
- You have the opportunity to hear different accents and speech patterns.

5. Listen for stance.
When you listen to lectures and conversations in English, practice listening for clues that will help you understand the speaker's purpose, attitude, and degree of certainty. Look at the examples below:

(man) *I can't get this printer to feed the paper through.*

(woman) *Don't look at me. I'm hopeless at these things.*

In this conversation, we can infer that the man is seeking help to solve his problem, even though he doesn't directly ask for help. The woman's response indicates that she doesn't know how to help him, even though she doesn't say it directly.

(woman) *The exciting thing about this artist's innovative creativity is how the exhibition is bringing in such a wide range of people.*

The woman has not said that she likes the artist's work, but we can understand that she does because she has used the word *exciting* and the phrase *innovative creativity* when she refers to it.

(man) *As far as I know, no one has come up with a viable solution to this problem.*

In this statement, we can understand that the speaker himself does not know of anyone with a solution, but he is letting his listeners know that there might be someone who has one.

Strategies to Use for the Listening Section of the TOEFL iBT Test

Strategies for listening to the conversations or lectures

1. Take notes.
Taking notes will help you concentrate on and remember what's being said. You can use your notes to help you answer the questions. Try to write what you hear in a rough outline form that organizes the main ideas and details of the conversation or lecture.

2. Identify the main idea and the important details that support it.
The main idea is usually found at the beginning of the listening passage. Details may be found throughout the passage. The language in the conversations is often informal and concerns topics common to the everyday lives of young adults studying at a university. The language in the lectures and classroom discussions is more formal and usually concerns an academic topic. It is not necessary to have previous knowledge of a topic in order to answer the questions about a passage. All the information needed to answer each question is stated or implied within the passage.

3. Understand the purpose of the visual material.

There are three types of visual material that will appear on the screen in the Listening section of the TOEFL test. Each type has a different purpose, as described below.

Photographs of the speakers These pictures are provided to give you a general idea of who the speakers are and the context of the discussions, but they do not provide any information that will help you answer the questions. Focus your attention on what is being said – not on the photographs of the people.

Blackboards These visuals show a word or words that the professor refers to during the lecture or discussion. They are provided to help you with an unfamiliar term or concept the professor is discussing and appear only while the professor is referring to it.

Illustrations or graphs These visuals support the content of the discussion or lecture, and they appear only while the professor is referring to them. The illustrations or graphs may be a key to understanding the information the professor is presenting. Focus your attention on how the visual relates to what is being said.

4. Pay attention to stance.

Listen for clues to help you understand the speaker's stance. *Stance* refers to the speaker's purpose, attitude, or degree of certainty. Being aware of these features will help you answer some of the questions on the test.

Questions about stance often begin by repeating a short section of the passage. This repeated section gives the context for the question that follows. Read this conversation and the example of this question type that follows it:

(woman) *Have you really decided to change your major?*

(man) *Well, yeah, the engineering department will accept most of the work that I did toward my physics degree, so I switched to engineering just last week.*

(woman) *But won't the change set you back, I mean . . . uh . . . as far as graduating is concerned?*

(man) *A bit, maybe, but it looks like I will be able to catch up with most of the engineering courses by next year, so it really won't set me back too much, not that much. Besides, I think that I'll be happier in engineering.*

Listen again to part of the conversation. Then answer the question.

(man) *Well, yeah, the engineering department will accept most of the work that I did toward my physics degree, so I switched to engineering just last week.*

(woman) *But won't the change set you back, I mean . . . uh . . . as far as graduating is concerned?*

Why does the woman say this: *But won't the change set you back?*

In this question, the first repeated part sets the context – the man's change of major. The second part contains the information that the question relates to. In this case, the underlying meaning of the woman's question is that she is concerned that the man's change of major will mean that he will "set back," or delay, his graduation date.

Strategies for choosing answers

1. Be familiar with the types of questions on the test.
Many items consist of a question and multiple-choice answers. Other items have special instructions. You may be instructed to choose two answers. You may be instructed to click on the appropriate space in a chart. If you do not follow the instructions, you will get an "error" message telling you what you need to do. Not paying close attention to the instructions for each item or set of items can cause you to lose valuable time.

2. Listen to and read the question carefully.
Make sure you understand what is being asked before you read the answer choices.

3. Read the answer choices carefully.
All correct and incorrect answers include details mentioned in the conversation or lecture. An incorrect answer may contain information that is true but that does not answer the question. Sometimes an incorrect answer contains information that has been stated in a way that changes its meaning, and therefore does not answer the question.

4. Pay attention to time.
The total number of questions in the Listening section and the number of the item you are answering are displayed on the computer screen. There is also a clock on the screen showing the number of minutes and seconds you have left. You have a total of 20 minutes to answer the questions in the Listening section. The clock stops while you are listening to the passages and resumes when you start answering. Pace yourself according to the time and the number of questions you have left. Answer each question and proceed to the next one as quickly as possible.

5. Check your answer before moving on to the next question.
In the Listening section, you cannot go back and change an answer after you have confirmed it. You will be asked to confirm your answer before you can go on to the next question. This gives you an opportunity to make sure you have chosen the answer you want. If you decide you have made a mistake after you have clicked on the **Next** icon, you can change your answer before you click on the **OK** icon. After you have confirmed an answer by clicking **OK**, you may not go back and change it.

6. Answer every question.
You must answer every question in the Listening section. If you do not know an answer, eliminate the answer choices you know are wrong. Then quickly decide which answer you think is best by taking a guess from the remaining choices. If you try to skip a question, you will get an "error" message and lose valuable time.

BASIC LISTENING QUESTION TYPES

There are three basic question types in the TOEFL iBT Listening section. Familiarizing yourself with these question types and becoming skilled at how to answer them will help you navigate more quickly on the day of the test.

1. Multiple choice with one correct answer This question type, also found in the Reading section, consists of a question and four answer choices.

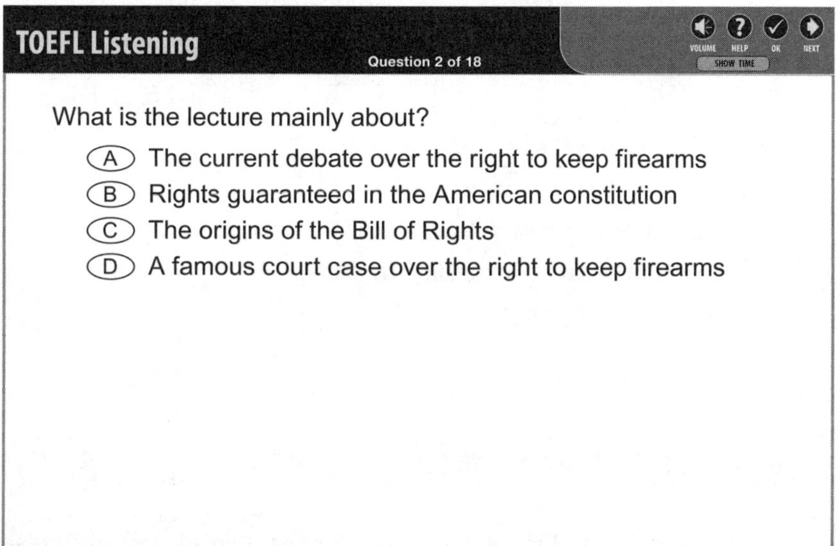

TOEFL Listening
Question 2 of 18
VOLUME HELP OK NEXT
SHOW TIME
What is the lecture mainly about?
A The current debate over the right to keep firearms
B Rights guaranteed in the American constitution
C The origins of the Bill of Rights
D A famous court case over the right to keep firearms

2. Multiple choice with two or more correct answers This question type consists of a question and two or more answers out of four or more answer choices. These items appear as follows:

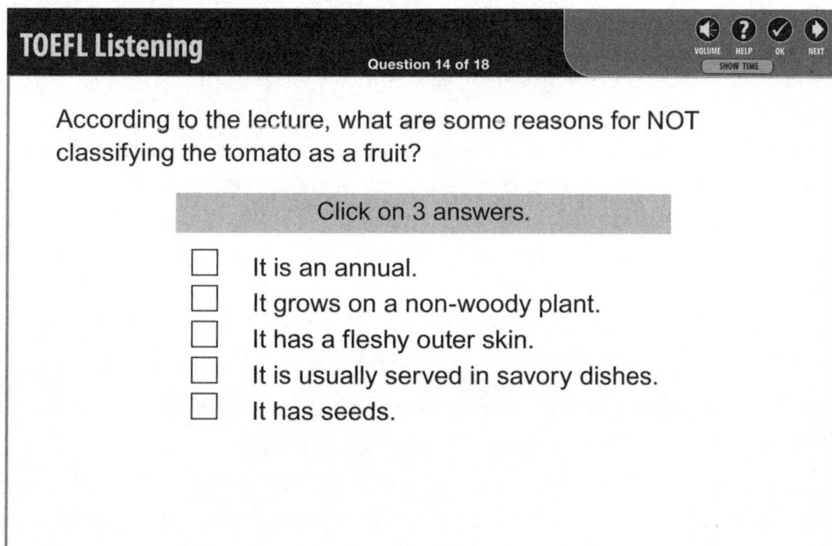

TOEFL Listening
Question 14 of 18
VOLUME HELP OK NEXT
SHOW TIME
According to the lecture, what are some reasons for NOT classifying the tomato as a fruit?
Click on 3 answers.
It is an annual.
It grows on a non-woody plant.
It has a fleshy outer skin.
It is usually served in savory dishes.
It has seeds.

3. Chart This question type requires test takers to complete a chart. These items appear as follows:

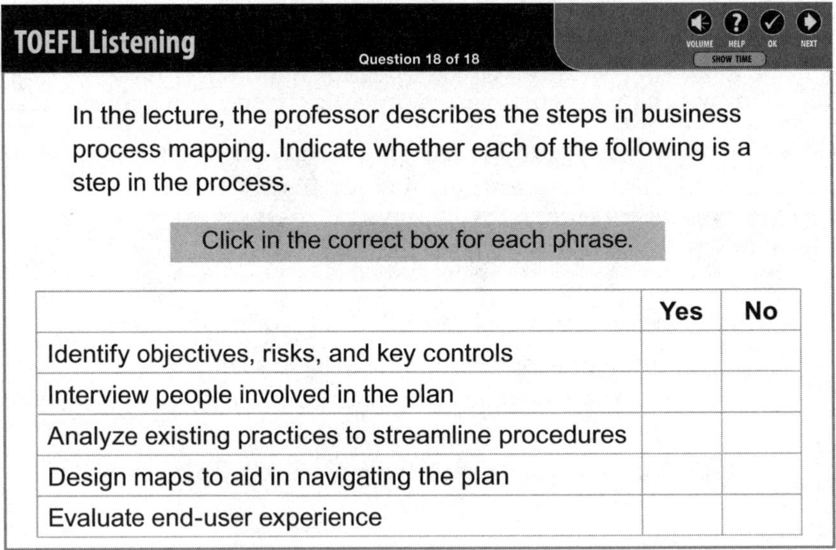

In the lecture, the professor describes the steps in business process mapping. Indicate whether each of the following is a step in the process.

Click in the correct box for each phrase.

	Yes	No
Identify objectives, risks, and key controls		
Interview people involved in the plan		
Analyze existing practices to streamline procedures		
Design maps to aid in navigating the plan		
Evaluate end-user experience		

PRACTICE WITH UNDERSTANDING NATURAL SPEECH

The passages you hear in the Listening section of the TOEFL test are presented in natural speech. In natural speech, speakers interrupt themselves and make mistakes, then correct themselves. They hesitate in the middle of a phrase or use a filler such as *um* or *uh* while they think. They may stutter, repeat phrases, or restart what they were saying by either repeating the same words or using different words.

Read this scripted speech sample that has had all the elements of natural speech taken out.

> *The answer to the question of which flying bird is the largest in the world depends on whether birds are measured by weight, wingspan, or wing area. The South African bustard is the heaviest. The average male weighs about 40 pounds. The bird with the longest wingspan is the albatross. The longest measured was 3.4 meters, but there are sure to be others with a span of 3.6 meters. The bird with the largest wings is the South American vulture, commonly called the condor.*

Compare the script above with the one below that includes the features of natural speech.

> *The answer to the question – your question – of what, which flying bird is the largest in the world depends on – well, you need to think about whether you are talking about birds' weight, wingspan or uh, wing area. You c-can see how the biggest bird is different, right, based on what you're measuring. OK? So the South Amer . . . uh, South African, the South African bustard is the heaviest. Um . . . the average male weighs about . . . lemme think . . . um . . . about 40 pounds. And . . . uh . . . the bird with the longest wingspan,*

the albatross, the albatross is the bird that when measured from, you know, the tip of a wing to the tip of the other, is the longest wingspan. The longest measured was 3.4 meters, but there are sure to be others . . . others, say, with a span of approaching 4 meters. Now, the bird with the largest wings – that means area – is, is the South American vulture, commonly called . . . you would know it as the condor.

The speaker in the sample above uses many features of natural speech:

- He interrupts himself: *the question – your question – of*
- He restarts the sentence: *which flying bird is the largest in the world depends on – well, you need to think about whether you are talking about birds' weight, wingspan or uh, wing area.*
- He stutters: *You c-can see*
- He corrects himself: *So the South Amer . . . uh, South African, the South African bustard*
- He hesitates and uses fillers: *weighs about . . . lemme think . . . um . . . about 40 pounds*
- He repeats phrases: *the albatross, the albatross is the bird*

There are no question items on the test that relate specifically to these speech patterns. However, as a listener, you must be able to understand the content of what you hear in spite of these natural speech features.

LISTENING

Exercises L1–L3

Use Listening Exercises L1–L3 to develop your skills in listening to natural speech.

EXERCISE L1 *Writing what the speaker means*

Listen to the natural speech sample. Write what the speaker means.

You hear:

Decay . . . umm, radioactive decay . . . all right . . . is uh . . . the element is breaking down . . . and mmmm losing particles.

You write:

Radioactive decay is when the element breaks down and loses particles.

The speaker is explaining what the term *radioactive decay* means.

START ▶

1. ______________________________

____

____

2. ______________________________

____

____

3. ______________________________

____

____

4. ______________________________

____

____

STOP ■

EXERCISE L2 *Answering questions about content*

Listen to the natural speech sample. Answer the question that follows.

> You hear:
>
> *Of . . . umm . . . two kinds . . . sliding and static . . . of friction. Two kinds of friction.*
>
> You read and hear:
>
> What are the two kinds of friction mentioned?
>
> You write:
>
> *sliding and static*

START ▶

1. Where does food storage occur?

____

____

____

2. Why does the professor believe teachers have not succeeded in teaching critical-thinking skills?

____

____

____

3. What is the professor pointing out?

____

____

____

4. Under what conditions does the speaker think it is acceptable to borrow money?

____

____

____

STOP ■

EXERCISE L3 *Identifying the meaning of filler phrases and reductions*

Listen to the natural speech sample. Choose the answer that identifies what the speaker means.

> You hear:
> (woman) *D'you know someone who can help me with Spanish?*
> (man) *You betcha.*
>
> You read and hear:
> What does the man mean by "You betcha"?
> The man is
>
> (A) telling the woman that he knows a Spanish speaker
> (B) suggesting that the woman find someone herself
>
> You should choose *A* because *you betcha* is a reduced form of "you bet your life" and indicates an affirmative answer to the woman's question.

START ▶

1. What does the woman mean by "let's say that"?
   The woman is
   (A) suggesting that they say what needs to be communicated
   (B) indicating that she is giving the man an example
2. What does the woman mean by "lemme see"?
   The woman
   (A) wants the man to show her his ID
   (B) is looking for the man's records
3. What does the woman mean by "come on now"?
   The woman is
   (A) showing her disbelief that the man doesn't remember
   (B) inviting the man to join her at the math lecture
4. What does the man mean by "see"?
   The man is indicating that
   (A) he is going to give an explanation
   (B) the woman should look at the blood samples

STOP ■

PRACTICE WITH UNDERSTANDING CONNECTIONS

Speakers connect their ideas by using referents and transitional expressions. When listening to the lectures and conversations on the TOEFL test, it is important that you follow the speaker's signals and understand referents.

Understanding referents

Instead of repeating information, speakers often use pronouns and short phrases that may refer back to a previously mentioned word or phrase or anticipate a word or phrase that will be mentioned. These pronouns and short phrases are called *referents*. Referents are like links in a chain that connect information.

Look at the conversation below. Notice how the conversation is linked through the use of referents.

(man) *Twenty people are coming to our graduation party, so we'd better get some plastic cups.*

(woman) *There are a dozen in each package. We could buy two of them.*

(man) *Hmmm. That would be only four extra cups. Do you think we might need more than that?*

When the woman says there are "a dozen," she is referring to cups. When she suggests buying "two of them," she is referring to the packages, not the cups. When the man is concerned that they might need "more than that," he is referring to more than four extra cups.

Look at this example of how referents link the information in a passage:

> The Aztecs of Mexico were probably the first people to domesticate the turkey. After Hernán Cortés conquered Mexico in 1521, he returned to Spain with specimens of this large bird. Its popularity spread throughout Europe. Later, domestic turkeys returned to the Western Hemisphere when the Pilgrims brought them from England.

"The first people" refers to "the Aztecs of Mexico." "He" refers to "Hernán Cortés." "The turkey" is linked throughout the passage by the words and phrases "this large bird," "its popularity," "domestic turkeys," and "them."

Look at how the above example may have sounded in a lecture.

Probably, but we can't know for sure, uh, the Aztecs of Mexico were the first Indi- . . . uh, people, the first people to domesticate the turkey. Hernán Cortés, uh, after Hernán Cortés conquered Mexico, that is, um, the A-Aztecs of Mexico, in 1521, he took specimens of this bird back to Spain, along with other New World items, of course. Now once in Spain, its popularity spread through different countries in Europe, like to England . . . England was one of those countries. Then later, when the Pilgrims left England, they brought with them domestic turkeys. So in this way, the turkeys then returned to the Western Hemisphere . . . via, uh, via the Pilgrims.

Understanding transitional expressions

To connect ideas, speakers use transition words and phrases that give signals to their listeners. These signals smooth the flow of ideas by showing the relationship of one idea to the next. Good listeners use them to understand the relationships between the ideas in a conversation or lecture. Good speakers use them to lead their audience smoothly through their ideas.

Read the following passage. It does not have any transition words to help the listener understand how the ideas are related.

The bioluminescent flashlight fish does not actually light up. It has a saclike organ under each eye that contains luminous bacteria. The bacteria glow constantly. The fish can control the light by eye movements. The flashlight fish uses its lights to search for food in the dark depths. The fish finds food. It blinks rapidly to signal its mates. An intruder threatens. The fish can startle it by shining its light. It can flash its light and abruptly change directions. Its predators are confused, and the flashlight fish makes its escape. Bioluminescence has many advantages for the flashlight fish.

Now read the same passage with transition words, which are underlined.

The bioluminescent flashlight fish does not actually light up. Instead, it has a saclike organ under each eye that contains luminous bacteria. Although the bacteria glow constantly, the fish can control the light by eye movements. The flashlight fish uses its lights to search for food in the dark depths. Once the fish finds food, it blinks rapidly to signal its mates. If an intruder threatens, the fish can startle it by shining its light. It can also flash its light and then abruptly change directions. As a result, its predators are confused, and the flashlight fish makes its escape. In short, bioluminescence has many advantages for the flashlight fish.

The connecting words and phrases above help lead the listener by signaling contrasts (*instead, although*), sequences (*once, then*), conditions (*if*), additions (*also*), results (*as a result*), and a summary (*in short*).

(For more information and practice, see Practice with Understanding the Connection of Ideas, p. 164; and Exercises R4–R8 and Reading Mini-test 2, pp. 167–177.)

LISTENING

Exercises L4–L8

Use Listening Exercises L4–L8 to develop your skills in understanding connections.

EXERCISE L4 *Identifying referents*

The referents in each sentence are underlined. If the reference word or phrase refers back to information already given in the sentence, draw a backwards arrow (<—) and write the information that it refers to to the left of the arrow. If the reference word or phrase anticipates information, draw a forward arrow (—>) and write the information that it refers to to the right of the arrow.

While tide pools can survive natural assaults, they are defenseless against humans.

tide pools <— they

The pronoun referent *they* refers back to *tide pools.*

Because of their vitality and pervasiveness, Greek myths and legends should be studied for a full appreciation of European culture.

their —> *Greek myths and legends*

The possessive adjective *their* anticipates *Greek myths and legends.*

1. People once thought the word *abracadabra* had mystical powers, so they wore this word inscribed on amulets as a good-luck charm.

   ______ they ______

   ______ this word ______

2. For the subject matter of her novels, Willa Cather used the frontier life of the Nebraska prairie of her youth.

subject matter

her

her

3. During a drying time of six to eight weeks, the nutmeg shrinks away from its hard seed coat until the kernels rattle in their shell when shaken.

a drying time

its

their

4. To pass his time away in jail, Charles duc d'Orléans smuggled out rhyming love letters to his wife, and this may have been the beginning of the custom of sending Valentine cards to loved ones.

his

his

this

EXERCISE L5 *Identifying referents in conversation*

Listen to part of a conversation. Then write the word or phrase that each referent refers to. After you have completed all the items, listen again and check your answers.

(For additional practice, see Exercises G17, p. 112, and G19, p. 115; Exercises R4–R8 and Reading Mini-test 2, pp. 167–177; Exercise S11, p. 321; and Exercise W4, p. 382.)

You hear:

(man) *I've never been to Scandinavia, so I've decided I'm gonna spend the summer there.*

(woman) *That'll be expensive, won't it?*

(man) *Hmmm, not really. My grandfather is from a small Swedish town near the Norwegian border. He has a sis . . . H-His sister still lives there. In Sweden.*

(woman) *Will you stay with her?*

(man) *For some of the time. The expensive part will be my stay in Denmark. I don't know anyone there.*

A. there *Scandinavia*

B. That *spending the summer in Scandinavia*

C. He *the man's grandfather*

D. His *the man's grandfather*

E. there *in a small Swedish town*

F. her *the grandfather's sister*

G. the time *the summer in Scandinavia*

H. there *Denmark*

START ▶

1. A. the one who wrote *Uncle Tom's Cabin* ______
   B. he ______
   C. her ______
   D. her ______
   E. the little lady who started the Civil War ______
2. A. when ______
   B. he ______
   C. it ______
   D. the idea ______
   E. that ______
3. A. one thing ______
   B. its ______
   C. something ______
   D. they ______
   E. they ______
4. A. it ______
   B. These ______
   C. one ______
   D. that ______

STOP ■

EXERCISE L6 *Identifying referents in a lecture*

Listen to part of a lecture. Write the word or phrase that each referent refers to. After you have completed all the items, listen again and check your answers.

You hear:

A mushroom recently found in New Jersey is more than three times as old as any previously discovered. As you know, mushrooms are rather fragile, so fragile that they are seldom preserved for long. So we don't have many specimens. However, this particular mushroom . . . that was found, . . . uh . . . 90 million years ago this mushroom was surrounded by tree resin, which then solidified into amber. Bark fibers and leaves were found in other pieces of amber in close vicinity of the mushroom. This sugg . . . suggests that the mushroom was growing on the rotting remains of a cedar tree. The New Jersey mushroom – tiny, only a few millimeters across – the New Jersey mushroom looks very similar to those belonging to the group of fungi, uh, those that make up "fairy rings" . . . you know . . . those kind of circles of mushrooms that you sometimes see on lawns.

A. any *previously discovered mushrooms*
B. specimens *preserved mushrooms*
C. this particular mushroom *the mushroom found in New Jersey*
D. This suggests *bark fibers and leaves in pieces of amber found close by*
E. those kind of circles of mushrooms *fairy rings*

START ▶

1. A. this happening ____________________
   B. these people ____________________
   C. these problems ____________________
   D. their ideas ____________________
2. A. the dream ____________________
   B. this climb ____________________
   C. these are granted ____________________
   D. a few groups ____________________
3. A. He did this ____________________
   B. a particular problem ____________________
   C. such divisions ____________________
   D. which are divisible ____________________

STOP ■

EXERCISE L7 🎧 *Following signals*

Listen to part of a lecture. Underline the transition word or phrase that the speaker uses to indicate the relationship of one idea to the next. Then in your own words, write the information that the speaker is emphasizing with the signal (transition word) used. There may be more than one signal in an item.

> You read and hear:
>
> The dramatic changes during an insect's life cycle through metamorphosis are of utmost importance. This is what prevents competition for resources within the species itself.
>
> You write:
>
> *metamorphosis prevents a species from competing with itself*
>
> You should underline the phrase *utmost importance* because this is the speaker's signal for the listener to pay particular attention to what is important. The speaker is highlighting the importance of metamorphosis as the phenomenon that prevents a species from competing with itself, so you should write this in the space.

START ▶

1. Land reform can involve large estates being parceled out in smaller plots. In contrast, it can also involve small landholdings being consolidated into larger estates.

   ____

2. Using word connotations that have powerful associations for your reader or listener has the effect of making your facts or opinions appear more attractive or less attractive. Consequently, writers and speakers use connotations to persuade their audience.

   ____

3. Sea defenses are built to prevent beaches from being washed away. However, these defenses may be the cause of land erosion further along the coastline.

   ____

4. After the beginning draft of a paper is finished, first put away the paper and do something else and then go back to it later with a clear mind.

___

5. The decomposition in organic matter is important for the release and circulation of minerals into the environment. In particular, detritus feeders, like shrimp in the sea and earthworms on land, have a role in the breakdown of dead material.

___

STOP ■

EXERCISE L8 🎧 *Using signals for understanding conversations and lectures*

Read the question, then listen to the conversation or lecture. Use the signals to help you answer the questions.

> You read:
>
> The speaker talks about the making of cloisonné in different time periods. What is contrasted in the making of cloisonné?
>
> You hear:
>
> *Cloisonné is a kind of fine pottery made from a particular kind of clay and fired in a kiln. It has . . . cloisonné has an enameled surface decorated with elaborate designs, the, uh, outlines are formed by small bands of metal. The, uh, Byzantines excelled in making this kind of pottery up until the 15th century. However, in the last hundred years, Japan and China have been the leaders in the . . . in the production of cloisonné.*
>
> You write:
>
> the Byzantines making cloisonné in the 15th century, and Japan and China being the producers during the last century
>
> The connecting word *however* signals that a contrast is being made. The Byzantines' production of cloisonné until the 15th century is contrasted with production in Japan and China in the last century.

START ▶

1. The professor tells the students that features of dinosaur tracks provide information. What are the features, and what information does each provide?

___

___

___

___

2. The professor talks about reactions of trees against pest attacks. What are the results of pest attacks?

___

___

___

___

3. The students review information about three kinds of tail fins. What are the kinds of fins, and what details are given about them?

   ____

   ____

   ____

   ____

4. The student gives an extended example as an explanation for concepts in physics. What is the example, and what concepts does it explain?

   ____

   ____

   ____

   ____

STOP ■

PRACTICE WITH IDENTIFYING TOPICS

Identifying the topic of a conversation or lecture immediately will help you anticipate the information you will hear and the details you will need to remember in order to answer the questions.

The topic is what the conversation or lecture is mainly about. It is usually found at the beginning of the listening passage. Look at the following example:

> *Arthritis is one of the oldest complaints that has tormented not only humans but animals as well. Even dinosaurs suffered from it millions of years ago. The earliest known example of one with arthritis is the platycarpus. So it is natural that you will also see arthritis in the animals that are brought into pet clinics. Today we will be comparing slides of the bone structure of healthy animals and arthritic animals to help you diagnose arthritis in the future.*

The topic of arthritis is stated at the beginning of this lecture. Although the speaker discusses different aspects of the topic, arthritis remains the main topic of the lecture.

Sometimes a broad topic is narrowed down to a specific topic. Other times, it appears that the speaker or speakers are going to discuss one topic, but then the topic is changed. Read the following example:

(woman) *Before we start today, I would like to remind you that the video conference will be shown in the Franklin auditorium . . . uh, the debates between the candidates for the coming election.*

(man) *Excuse me. Uh, will we be able to ask the speakers questions and uh, or take part in any of the deb- . . . uh, the discussions?*

(woman) *No, we won't. Some of the larger state universities will be able to take part, but we only have the facilities to listen . . . unfortunately.*

(man) *Is the university doing anything toward improving our facilities?*

(woman) *Well, yes, in fact, they are. They are budgeting a large sum of money, so, uh, in order to build a conference center, here on this, the main, campus. This center is supposed to include all the facilities needed.*

(man) *When will that be? I mean, is there a proposed date for these facilities to be ready?*

(woman) *Uh-huh, but I'm afraid they will probably be, uh, the center will be open after you have graduated. You know, because the building will take at least a year to complete and it's still only in the planning stage.*

Although the first speaker introduces the first topic of the discussion – a video conference of debates between candidates for an election – the topic changes to the facilities for video conferencing at the speakers' university. The remainder of the conversation concerns the university's plans for improving its facilities.

Exercises L9–L12

Use Listening Exercises L9–12 to develop your skills in identifying topics.

EXERCISE L9 *Predicting the topic*

Listen to the statement. Predict the topic to be discussed, and write your prediction in the space.

> You hear:
>
> *The molecular structure of synthetic vitamins is the same as that of natural vitamins.*
>
> You write:
>
> *vitamins*
>
> The lecture will probably continue with more information about vitamins.

START ▶

1. ______________________
2. ______________________
3. ______________________
4. ______________________
5. ______________________

STOP ■

EXERCISE L10 *Identifying the topic from the first statement*

Listen to the first statement of a conversation or lecture. Choose the answer that states the topic.

> You hear:
>
> *Of all nonprofessional architects, Michelangelo was the most adventurous.*
>
> (A) professional architects
> (B) adventurous architects
> (C) Michelangelo's architecture
> (D) Michelangelo's adventures
>
> You should choose *C* because the speaker will probably continue the talk by explaining in what ways Michelangelo's architecture was adventurous.

START ▶

1. (A) uses of acupuncture in the West
   (B) China in recent years
   (C) the practice of acupuncture
   (D) ancient cures for arthritis

2. (A) fabric
   (B) muscles
   (C) millimeters
   (D) lengths

3. (A) communications technology
   (B) challenges in communications
   (C) educational satellites
   (D) educational possibilities

4. (A) the Spanish literature seminars
   (B) the Spanish courses offered
   (C) the history of Spain
   (D) the Golden Age of Spanish literature

5. (A) the signs and symptoms of influenza
   (B) the signs and symptoms of the common cold
   (C) similarities between the common cold and influenza
   (D) highly contagious diseases

6. (A) the lack of human protein in diets
   (B) causes of malnutrition in the world
   (C) serious world problems
   (D) deficiency of animal protein in the human diet

STOP ■

EXERCISE L11 🎧 *Determining if the topic is stated in the first sentence*

Listen to the conversation or talk. Write *Yes* in the blank if the topic can be identified in the first sentence. Write *No* if it is not stated immediately.

You hear:

When a disaster such as an earthquake or a flood strikes, time is often a critical factor in providing needed shelter for people who are suddenly homeless and exposed to the elements. Ideally, the erection of a shelter should take a short time. The emergency use of tents has been the conventional answer to these situations. However, in many cases, those left homeless are in need of shelter for an extensive period of time. The temporary and insufficient nature of tent housing does not meet these longer-term requirements.

You write:

Yes

The talk is mainly about shelters for people left suddenly homeless. This is mentioned in the first sentence of the talk, and the speaker does not change to a different topic.

You hear:

By nine o'clock in the morning, the streets were lined with people. Somewhere in the distance a band was heard playing a marching song. Shopkeepers were locking their doors and joining the crowds. Everyone was craning their necks to see how long it would be before the first float in the parade reached them.

You write:

No

The talk is mainly a description of the start of a parade. The topic is not stated until the end of the passage.

START ▶

1. ________
2. ________
3. ________
4. ________
5. ________

STOP ■

EXERCISE L12 *Identifying a change in topic*

Listen to the passage. Write the topic in the space.

You hear:

Hygiene was almost unheard of in Europe during the Middle Ages. Consequently, millions of people died during various epidemics that raged throughout Europe. The worst outbreak of plague, called the Black Death, struck between the years 1347 and 1351. The populations of thousands of villages were wiped out. In fact, it is thought that about one-third of all the people in Europe perished during the Black Death.

You write:

the Black Death

Although the speaker begins by discussing hygiene, the talk is mainly about the epidemic of plague called the Black Death.

START ▶

1. ______________________
2. ______________________
3. ______________________
4. ______________________

STOP ■

Listening Mini-test 1

Check your progress in understanding natural speech, following the flow of information through referents and connecting words, and identifying the topic of a conversation or talk (Exercises L1–L12) by completing the following Mini-test. This Mini-test uses a format similar to the format used in the Listening section of the TOEFL iBT test.

Listen to the passage. Then answer the questions by choosing the letter of the best answer choice.

Now get ready to listen.

START ▶

Questions 1–3

Listen to part of a discussion between two friends.

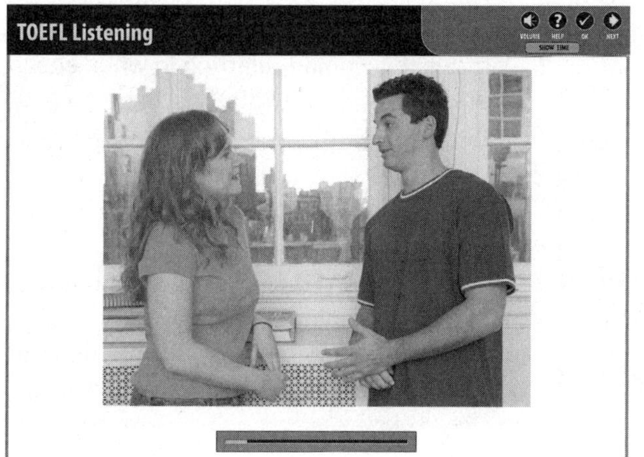

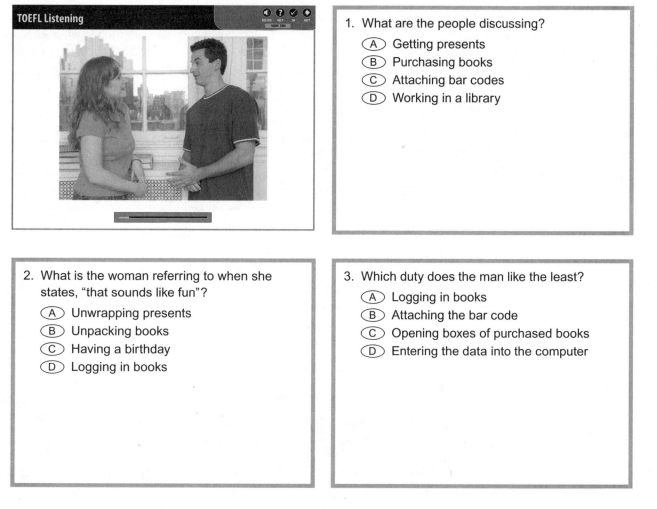

1. What are the people discussing?
   (A) Getting presents
   (B) Purchasing books
   (C) Attaching bar codes
   (D) Working in a library

2. What is the woman referring to when she states, "that sounds like fun"?
   (A) Unwrapping presents
   (B) Unpacking books
   (C) Having a birthday
   (D) Logging in books

3. Which duty does the man like the least?
   (A) Logging in books
   (B) Attaching the bar code
   (C) Opening boxes of purchased books
   (D) Entering the data into the computer

Questions 4–6

Listen to part of a lecture from a history class.

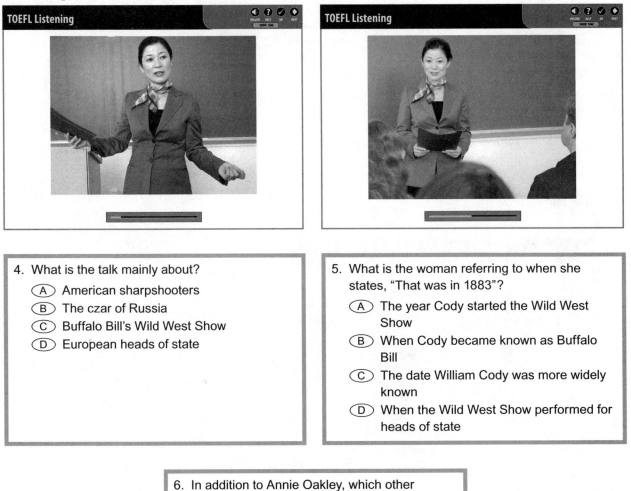

4. What is the talk mainly about?
   (A) American sharpshooters
   (B) The czar of Russia
   (C) Buffalo Bill's Wild West Show
   (D) European heads of state

5. What is the woman referring to when she states, "That was in 1883"?
   (A) The year Cody started the Wild West Show
   (B) When Cody became known as Buffalo Bill
   (C) The date William Cody was more widely known
   (D) When the Wild West Show performed for heads of state

6. In addition to Annie Oakley, which other famous person traveled with Buffalo Bill?
   (A) William Cody
   (B) Queen Victoria
   (C) Chief Sitting Bull
   (D) Czar Alexander the II

Questions 7–9

Listen to part of a lecture from a music class.

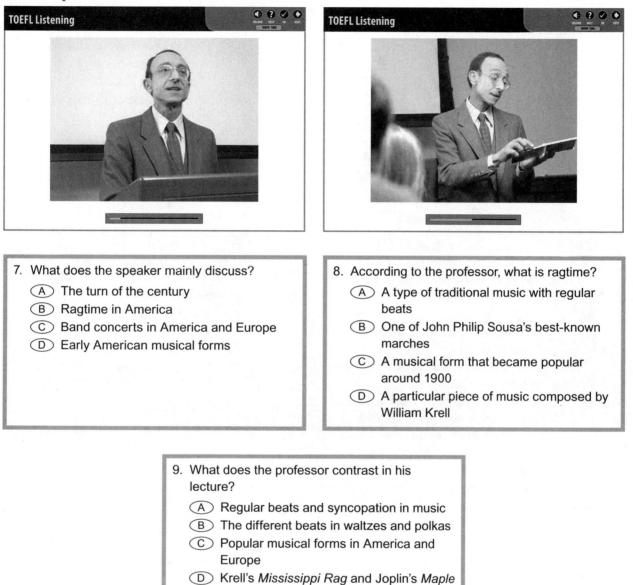

7. What does the speaker mainly discuss?
   - (A) The turn of the century
   - (B) Ragtime in America
   - (C) Band concerts in America and Europe
   - (D) Early American musical forms

8. According to the professor, what is ragtime?
   - (A) A type of traditional music with regular beats
   - (B) One of John Philip Sousa's best-known marches
   - (C) A musical form that became popular around 1900
   - (D) A particular piece of music composed by William Krell

9. What does the professor contrast in his lecture?
   - (A) Regular beats and syncopation in music
   - (B) The different beats in waltzes and polkas
   - (C) Popular musical forms in America and Europe
   - (D) Krell's *Mississippi Rag* and Joplin's *Maple Leaf Rag*

Questions 10–12

Listen to a conversation between two students.

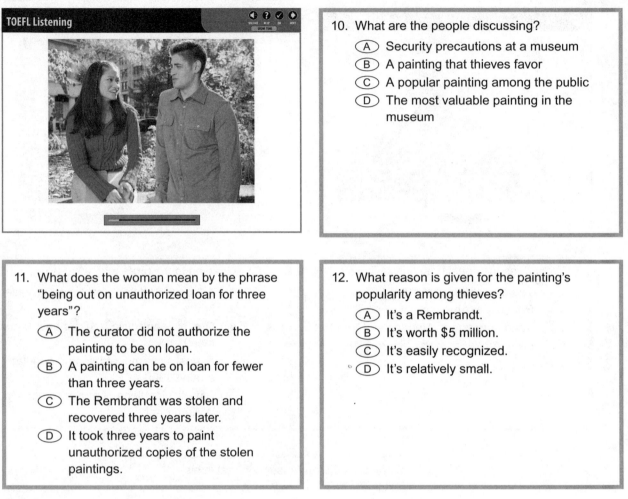

10. What are the people discussing?
    - (A) Security precautions at a museum
    - (B) A painting that thieves favor
    - (C) A popular painting among the public
    - (D) The most valuable painting in the museum

11. What does the woman mean by the phrase "being out on unauthorized loan for three years"?
    - (A) The curator did not authorize the painting to be on loan.
    - (B) A painting can be on loan for fewer than three years.
    - (C) The Rembrandt was stolen and recovered three years later.
    - (D) It took three years to paint unauthorized copies of the stolen paintings.

12. What reason is given for the painting's popularity among thieves?
    - (A) It's a Rembrandt.
    - (B) It's worth $5 million.
    - (C) It's easily recognized.
    - (D) It's relatively small.

STOP ■

PRACTICE WITH DETAILS

On the TOEFL test you may be asked about the details in a conversation or lecture. There are different types of questions that deal with details. These question types are described below.

Restatements

Sometimes the correct answer choice restates the detail using different words. Sometimes an incorrect answer choice will use the same words, but a change in word order has changed their meaning. Look at the example on the next page.

You hear:

(man) *What did you do over the summer, Donna?*

(woman) *Mostly I helped my father in his clothing store.*

(man) *I can't imagine you selling clothes.*

(woman) *I didn't. Remember, I'm studying accounting. I helped him with the bookkeeping. Also, I put price tags on the new clothes and designed the window displays.*

You read and hear:

What did Donna do over the summer?

(A) She helped her father do the accounting.
(B) She sold clothes in her father's store.
(C) She displayed prices in the windows.
(D) She designed new clothes.

You should choose *A* because Donna helped her father with the bookkeeping. This means the same as helping him do the accounting. Donna told the man that she didn't sell clothes. She designed window displays, not clothes, and she put prices on new clothes, not prices in the window.

Two correct answers

Some detail questions require two answers. These items have boxes instead of ovals in front of the answer choices on the screen.

You hear:

(man) *Why hasn't Frank come yet? He told me he'd be here first thing in the morning.*

(woman) *I'm sorry. Didn't I tell you he called and said he couldn't make it until this afternoon?*

(man) *No, you didn't. What time did he say he'd be here?*

(woman) *About four o'clock.*

(man) *Four o'clock! That means we'll be working on this report until midnight.*

You read and hear:

What did Frank tell the woman about getting together to work on the report? Choose 2 answers.

[A] He'd be there first thing in the morning.
[B] He couldn't make it first thing in the morning.
[C] He would come in the afternoon.
[D] He could stay from four o'clock until midnight.

You should choose *B* and *C* because Frank told the woman he couldn't make it in the morning but would be there in the afternoon.

Linking content

Sometimes you will hear a series of related bits of information, such as the steps in a process. The question will ask you to identify which sentences or phrases are part of the series described.

You hear:

Tomatoes are usually picked green. They are washed and sorted according to size and quality, and then they are packaged and sent to supermarkets. During transportation the tomatoes ripen to the bright red color we are accustomed to seeing on the shelves.

You read and hear:

The professor briefly describes a process. Indicate whether each of the following is a step in the process.

	Yes	No
A. The tomatoes are picked before they are ripe.	✓	
B. The tomatoes are cleaned and divided by size.	✓	
C. The tomatoes are transported to the grocery stores in boxes.	✓	
D. The tomatoes ripen when they are on the shelves.		✓

You should check *Yes* for *A, B,* and *C,* and *No* for *D.*

Matching

Some questions ask you to match descriptive terms or phrases with whatever was described.

You hear:

The fork, knife, and spoon are the most common eating utensils. These instruments all have handles, which are basically the same. They differ from each other in their use and the shape that use has dictated. The knife has a sharp blade for cutting and is not normally used for transferring food from the plate to one's mouth. The fork has three to four prongs, which are used to secure food that needs to be cut. It is also used to take more solid kinds of foods to the mouth. The spoon has a bowl shape in order for its user to consume liquid or semi-liquid food.

You read and hear:

Based on the professor's description, indicate the basic differences between the given utensils.

	Forks	Knives	Spoons
A. cutting blade		✓	
B. prongs	✓		
C. bowl shape			✓

You should check *Knives* for *A, Forks* for *B,* and *Spoons* for *C.*

Exercises L13–L17

Use Listening Exercises L13–L17 to develop your skills in understanding details. (For further information and practice, see Practice with Understanding Details and Recognizing Paraphrases, pp. 178–180; and Exercises R9–R14 and Reading Mini-test 3, pp. 180–198.)

EXERCISE L13 *Understanding restatements*

You will hear a statement. Choose the answer that gives the same information as the spoken statement.

> You hear:
> *Minute as atoms are, they consist of still tinier particles.*
> (A) Atoms are made up of even smaller particles.
> (B) Small particles consist of minute atoms.
>
> You should choose *A* because it gives the same information in different words.

START ▶

1. (A) In Homer's time, the people used many old words from the Kárpathos dialect.
   (B) The people in Kárpathos use many words that were used in Homer's time.
2. (A) In 1783, a Frenchman made the first manned flight in a hot-air balloon.
   (B) In 1783, a Frenchman made a twenty-five-minute flight in the first hot-air balloon.
3. (A) The Aztec word for "beautiful bird" is "quetzal," which means "tail feather."
   (B) The Aztec word for "tail feather" is the name given to one of the world's most beautiful birds – the quetzal.
4. (A) After an all-night march, 22 men stormed onto the Luding Bridge, thus cutting off the escape route of Mao Tse-tung's forces.
   (B) After an all-night march, 22 men captured the Luding Bridge to secure an escape route for Mao Tse-tung's forces.
5. (A) Centers were established to relieve those people stricken by the drought.
   (B) The drought-stricken areas set up many relief centers.
6. (A) The human past has been revolutionized by our concept of recently discovered fossils.
   (B) Our concept of the human past has been revolutionized by recently discovered fossils.
7. (A) In March 1783, explorers had not been able to locate the island that was vividly described in the captain's log.
   (B) In the captain's log, dated March 1783, is the vivid description of an island that explorers have been unable to locate.
8. (A) That numerous dead fish, dolphins, and whales have been spotted off the East Coast was reported by the authorities.
   (B) The authorities have spotted and reported numerous dolphins, whales, and dead fish off the East Coast.

STOP ■

EXERCISE L14 *Finding two answers*

Listen to the conversation or talk. Answer the question by selecting the TWO best answers.

You hear:

The black bear may seem friendly, but it is a dangerous animal that can maim or kill easily. If a bear is disturbed during the hibernation period, it is easily angered, and it is very hazardous to come between a mother and her cubs at any time. Because of the risk, it is never advisable to go closer than one hundred meters to a bear in the wild.

You read and hear:

When is the black bear most dangerous? Choose 2 answers.

- [A] When it maims someone
- [B] When it is separated from its cubs
- [C] When it is closer than one hundred meters
- [D] When it is awakened from its sleep

You should choose *B* and *D*.

START ▶

1. What can be said about fish rubbings? Choose 2 answers.
   - [A] The art was practiced in various cultures.
   - [B] The prints were slimy.
   - [C] It is an ancient art.
   - [D] It is a dying art.
2. What is true about Mughal Emperor Jahangir? Choose 2 answers.
   - [A] He was from Baghdad.
   - [B] He did not follow minting traditions.
   - [C] He issued coins in the caliph's name.
   - [D] He encouraged many art forms to flourish.
3. How is a metallurgical microscope different from an optical microscope? Choose 2 answers.
   - [A] It can measure three-dimensional objects.
   - [B] It allows for examination of unwieldy samples.
   - [C] It is more delicate.
   - [D] It has inadequate illuminating systems.
4. What is true about communication disorders? Choose 2 answers.
   - [A] A problem with speech or hearing mechanisms is often caused by communication disorders.
   - [B] Communication disorders can result from emotional or psychological problems.
   - [C] Speech pathologists can help people with communication disorders improve their ability to communicate.
   - [D] Communication disorders frequently result from the normal functioning of the brain.

STOP ■

EXERCISE L15 Getting all the facts

Listen to a passage. Then choose ALL the answers that contain information asked for in the question.

You hear:

Pioneers wanting to reach the West Coast of North America arrived by riverboat at Missouri River towns in the early spring. They hoped to cross the plains during the summer, when the prairie grass would provide food for their animals. They needed to cross the plains quickly because it was essential to get through the Rocky Mountains and arrive in California before the winter snows closed the mountain passes. Those who didn't make it through were stranded in the mountains without sufficient provisions for the entire winter.

You read and hear:

What details about the pioneer movement across North America does the passage include?

Ⓐ The way pioneers reached Missouri River towns
Ⓑ The time of year that pioneers traveled across the continent
Ⓒ The importance of sufficient provisions
Ⓓ The consequences of not passing through the Rocky Mountains before winter

You should choose *A*, *B*, and *D* because the passage states that *A* the pioneers reached the Missouri River towns by riverboat, *B* they hoped to cross the plains during the summer, and *D* the pioneers faced getting stranded by snow if they were late in getting through the mountain passes.

START ▶

1. What details about Victoria C. Woodhull's life does the lecture include?

   Ⓐ The U.S. president she ran against
   Ⓑ Examples of the radical movements she was involved in
   Ⓒ The name of the journal she established
   Ⓓ The role she adopted after losing the election

2. What details are included in the diving teacher's instructions to the students?

   Ⓐ The depth at which the reef is found
   Ⓑ The safety precautions she expects the students to follow
   Ⓒ The way to signal for help in case of an emergency
   Ⓓ The names of the corals she wants the students to identify

3. What details about the "hundredth-monkey" study does the professor give?

   Ⓐ The area where the study took place
   Ⓑ The people who conducted the study
   Ⓒ The way the study was conducted
   Ⓓ The type of publication in which the study was printed

4. What details about puppetry does the presentation include?

   Ⓐ The puppets' cultural importance
   Ⓑ The forms that traditional puppets have
   Ⓒ The ways that puppets are made to move
   Ⓓ The audiences' response to puppet shows

STOP ■

LISTENING

EXERCISE L16 Recognizing information

Listen to the discussion or lecture. Check (✓) the *Yes* column if the statement is true according to the details you heard. Check the *No* column if the statement is false according to the details you heard.

You hear:

The debt of lawn tennis to its French origins is illustrated in the unusual scoring system. This system probably stems from the habit of betting on individual points by the players or supporters. A game was worth one denier, *at that time a unit of French currency, so the points were worth the most convenient divisions of a denier. These were 15, 30, and 45* sous. *In time, the latter became 40.*

Deuce, *when both players have reached 40 in a game, is a corruption of the French* à deux, *meaning* both. *This may refer to both players having the same score – or to the fact that a player will need to take both of the next two points to win. The term (as dewce) was first known in England in 1598.*

The word love, *which means* zero, *may well come from the French word* l'oeuf, *meaning* egg. *The explanation for the use of the word* l'oeuf *is said to be the similarity of the shape of an egg to a zero. Modern player slang for a 6–0, 6–0 result is "egg and egg."*

You read and hear:

In the lecture, the professor explains how the vocabulary in lawn tennis is related to the French language. Indicate whether each of the following illustrates this relationship.

	Yes	No
A. The point system in tennis is based on the divisions of an old French monetary unit.	✓	
B. The word referring to two players needing two points is French for "both."	✓	
C. The word for zero is the French word for "love."		✓
D. The French word for "egg" refers to a score of 0.	✓	

You should check the *Yes* column for sentences *A, B,* and *D*. In *A*, the point system relates to the money divisions that were used for betting purposes. In *B*, the word *deuce,* which refers to when players have the same score and need two points to win, is a corruption of the French expression *à deux,* which means both. In *D*, an egg has a similar shape to a zero and the word that is used to mean zero in tennis is pronounced like the French word for *egg.* You should check the *No* column for sentence *C* because the word *love* is from the French *l'oeuf,* meaning *egg.*

START ▶

1. In the lecture, the speaker describes the steps in pigeon training. Indicate whether each of the following is a step in the process.

	Yes	No
A. Giving the young pigeon short practice flights		
B. Getting the bird to respond to its owner's call		
C. Removing the tag when the bird enters the cote		
D. Increasing the bird's stamina through extending the flight distance		
E. Releasing the bird with other birds from a central meeting place		

2. In the lecture, the professor describes events that undermined the gains the suffragettes had made in women's rights. Indicate whether each of the following is an event that hampered the movement.

	Yes	No
A. The Equal Rights Amendment passed in 1923		
B. The job crises during the Great Depression		
C. The passing of the married-persons clause law		
D. The campaign toward maintaining family morale		
E. The breaking away from traditional roles		

3. In the lecture, the professor describes a relationship between ants and aphids. Indicate whether each of the following is a benefit that aphids get from ants.

	Yes	No
A. Metabolizing of sap		
B. Production of honeydew		
C. Building of shelters		
D. Protection from predators		
E. Transportation to fresh leaves		

STOP ■

EXERCISE L17 *Organizing information*

Listen to the passage. Then match the words or phrases with the topics.

You hear:

The cavalry is the part of an army consisting of troops that serve on horseback. In Greek and Roman times, it was comprised of members of noble families and this distinction continued up to the Middle Ages. However, after the invention of gunpowder, this branch of the military service underwent great changes. With the development of heavy artillery and air forces, the cavalry has been displaced by armored regiments. Other than cavalry regiments that still retain a mounted squadron for ceremonial duties, this service has almost entirely disappeared.

You read and hear:

Indicate the era to which each of the details belongs.

	Cavalry regiments	Armored regiments
A. Troops from noble families	✓	
B. Heavy artillery		✓
C. Air force		✓
D. Mounted ceremonial duties	✓	

You should check the boxes under *Cavalry regiments* for *A* and *D*. The cavalry troops were members of noble families. The cavalry regiment still has a squadron on horseback, but they are only used for ceremonies. You should check the boxes under *Armored regiments* for *B* and *C* because the heavy artillery and the air force are the regiments that displaced the cavalry.

START ▶

1. The speaker talks about the shapes of snowflakes. Match each type below with the conditions under which it develops.

	Stars	Prisms	Plates
A. Extremely cold and dry			
B. Very cold and moderately humid			
C. Cold and humid			

2. The speaker talks about folk cures and what they were used for. Match the folk treatment to the properties it supposedly has.

	Antiviral	Antibacterial
A. Wormwood		
B. Powdered sugar		
C. Catfish slime		

3. The class discussion is about the development of refrigeration. Match each description with the corresponding form of refrigeration.

	Icehouse	Icebox	Refrigerator
A. Use of electricity			
B. Community use			
C. Home delivery			

4. The professor talks about cave formations. Match each cave formation with the corresponding water condition.

	Drops of water	Flow of water
A. Soda straws		
B. Stalactites		
C. Stalagmites		
D. Draperies		
E. Flowstones		

STOP ■

LISTENING

Listening Mini-test 2

Check your progress in understanding details in a conversation or lecture (Exercises L13–L17) by completing the following Mini-test. This Mini-test uses a format similar to the format used in the Listening section of the TOEFL iBT test.

Listen to the passage. Then answer the questions by choosing the letter of the best answer choice or by following the directions given.

Now get ready to listen.

START ▶

Questions 1–4

Listen to part of a discussion in an environmental science class.

1. In the discussion, the professor briefly explains the process that breaks down the ozone layer. Indicate whether each of the sentences is a step in the process of ozone depletion.

	Yes	No
(A) Artificial chemicals called CFCs are released into the atmosphere during the production of goods.		
(B) For economic reasons, CFCs continue to be used in some parts of the world.		
(C) Oxygen combines with CFCs, causing the depletion of the ozone layer.		
(D) The use of products containing CFCs allows CFCs to enter the atmosphere.		
(E) Ultraviolet light is able to reach the Earth's surface and damage DNA.		

2. Why is the professor cautious in her prediction of the future?
   (A) She is not certain everyone will comply with the international agreements.
   (B) She doesn't think the CFCs will disperse without some assistance.
   (C) She doesn't believe the ozone layer can recover from the environmental abuse.
   (D) She doesn't know if alternatives to CFCs are acceptable.

3. According to the professor, how do CFCs get into the atmosphere?
   (A) They are a chemical reaction caused by ultraviolet rays.
   (B) They migrate from the stratosphere.
   (C) They are in the DNA of humans and plants.
   (D) They are released through some products and processes.

4. According to the discussion, which of the following are contaminants?

   Choose 2 answers.

   [A] Dry-cleaning components
   [B] Nitrogen fertilizers
   [C] Oxygen atoms
   [D] Ultraviolet light

Questions 5–8

Listen to part of a lecture in a psychology class.

5. In the lecture, the professor describes three types of mind control. Match each behavior with the associated mind-control technique.

	Subception	Hypnosis	Brainwashing
(A) accepting implanted ideas after losing sense of reality			
(B) buying ice cream after an unconscious intrusion			
(C) carrying out a command at a given signal			

6. According to the professor, what is true of subliminal perception?
   (A) It is used on unsuspecting people with great frequency.
   (B) It is based on the fact that people are aware of a lot more than they realize.
   (C) It could be used to make people do something they would consider unethical.
   (D) It has been given special attention because of the uses it could be put to.

7. What else is true of subliminal perception?
   (A) People forget what they were told after the experience.
   (B) People are unaware that their minds are being influenced.
   (C) People do silly things when given a signal.
   (D) People may behave in a way that previously they would have considered unacceptable.

8. Which of the following did the professor NOT mention when speaking about brainwashing?
   (A) Drugging
   (B) Starvation
   (C) Intimidation
   (D) Sleep deprivation

Questions 9–12

Listen to part of a lecture on biotechnology.

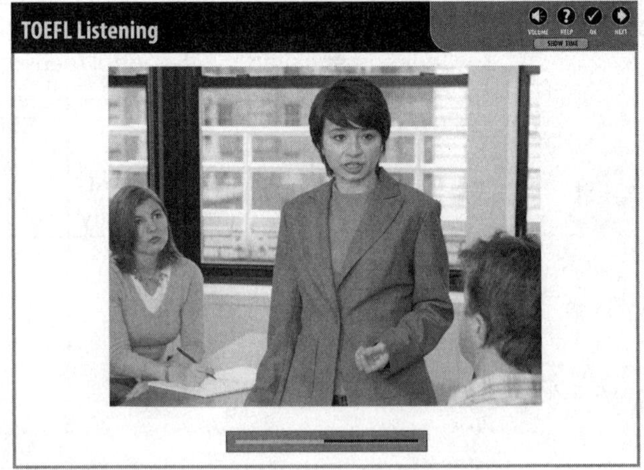

9. In the lecture, the professor explains the field of study called biomimetics. Indicate whether each of the following is an example of biomimetic application.

	Yes	No
(A) Flying machines that emulate birds		
(B) Fastening devices that have hooks for grasping fabric		
(C) Skeletons that soften to change shape		
(D) Antler bone that is extraordinarily tough		
(E) Substances that copy photosynthesis to create energy		

10. According to the professor, what inspires architects and engineers?

(A) Natural forms
(B) Inventive ideas
(C) Freedom to create
(D) Biological problems

11. When talking about smart structures, what is the professor doing?

(A) Comparing the intelligence of structures with that of nature
(B) Stressing the similarity of the structures to fashion
(C) Referring to the self-directed nature of some processes
(D) Satirizing the processes in the natural world

12. What are some of the areas that researchers are investigating?

Choose 2 answers.

[A] The high resistance of wood to impacts
[B] The stimulus provided for inventive minds
[C] The structure of antler bone for its toughness
[D] The impact of biomimetic research in the twenty-first century

Questions 13–16

Listen to part of a discussion in a criminology class.

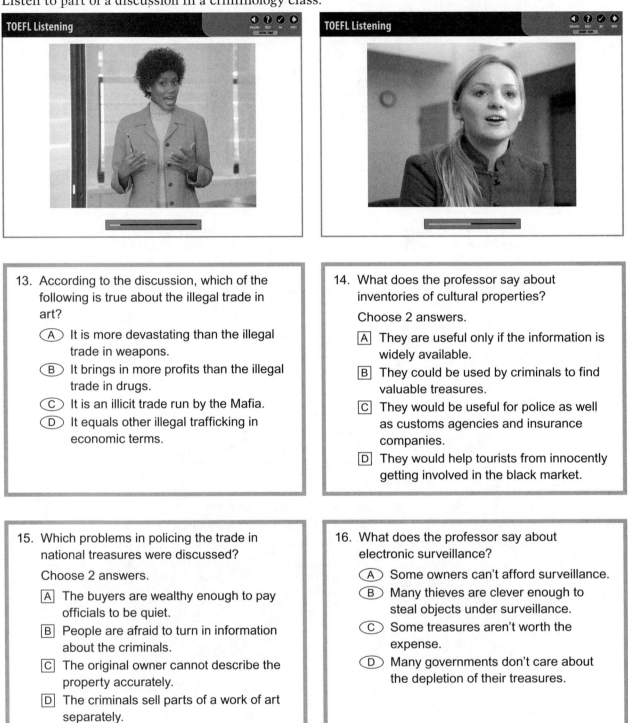

13. According to the discussion, which of the following is true about the illegal trade in art?
    - (A) It is more devastating than the illegal trade in weapons.
    - (B) It brings in more profits than the illegal trade in drugs.
    - (C) It is an illicit trade run by the Mafia.
    - (D) It equals other illegal trafficking in economic terms.

14. What does the professor say about inventories of cultural properties?

    Choose 2 answers.
    - [A] They are useful only if the information is widely available.
    - [B] They could be used by criminals to find valuable treasures.
    - [C] They would be useful for police as well as customs agencies and insurance companies.
    - [D] They would help tourists from innocently getting involved in the black market.

15. Which problems in policing the trade in national treasures were discussed?

    Choose 2 answers.
    - [A] The buyers are wealthy enough to pay officials to be quiet.
    - [B] People are afraid to turn in information about the criminals.
    - [C] The original owner cannot describe the property accurately.
    - [D] The criminals sell parts of a work of art separately.

16. What does the professor say about electronic surveillance?
    - (A) Some owners can't afford surveillance.
    - (B) Many thieves are clever enough to steal objects under surveillance.
    - (C) Some treasures aren't worth the expense.
    - (D) Many governments don't care about the depletion of their treasures.

STOP ■

PRACTICE WITH MAKING INFERENCES AND DRAWING CONCLUSIONS

Some things are not stated directly in a conversation or lecture. You have to understand the meaning through other clues within the passage.

Making inferences

Some questions require you to make inferences. These questions may be stated in the following ways:

- What does the woman imply about . . . ?
- Why does the professor mention . . . ?
- What can be said about . . . ?

Sometimes you will listen again to part of the lecture in order to answer the question.

You hear:

(professor) *When the person at bat hits the baseball, the ball and bat accelerate in opposite directions. The ball bounces back with a rebound energy equal to that of the bat. Uh, does my use of the term* bounce *in this case sound wrong to you? We say something bounces when it hits a stationary object. But, is it correct to say* bounces *when one moving object hits another moving object?*

You read and hear:

What does the professor imply when she says this: 

You hear:

Uh, does my use of the term bounce *in this case sound wrong to you?*

(A) She's concerned that the students may not understand baseball.
(B) She has made a mistake in her description and is correcting herself.
(C) She wants to focus the students' attention on a particular feature.
(D) She's concerned the students will confuse *bounce* and *rebound energy.*

You should choose *C*. The professor has used the term *bounce* in a way that she thinks the students may think is incorrect. She wants the students to think about the way she has used the word.

Sometimes part of the lecture is repeated before the question is asked. The question contains part of the repeated lecture.

You read and hear:

Listen again to part of the lecture. Then answer the question.

You hear:

(professor) *Uh, does my use of the term* bounce *in this case sound wrong to you? We say something bounces when it hits a stationary object. But is it correct to say* bounces *when one moving object hits another moving object?*

You read and hear:

Why does the professor say this: 

LISTENING

You hear:

But is it correct to say bounces *when one moving object hits another moving object?*

Ⓐ To indicate to the students that she has made a mistake in her description
Ⓑ To make the students think about what happens when two moving objects meet
Ⓒ To indicate that she is going to focus the discussion on bouncing objects
Ⓓ To correct the students' misunderstanding of rebound energy and bouncing

You should choose *B*. The professor has explained a concept in physics and is trying to get the students to think about whether the same thing happens when a moving object hits a stationary one as when a moving object hits another moving object.

Drawing conclusions

Some questions require you to draw a conclusion. Through details that are expressed or through general knowledge, you need to come to a conclusion.

You hear:

(professor) *OK. Now I would like to have you get into groups of three or four. I'm going to pass out an assignment sheet, and I would like you to decide in your group how you are going to approach the problems set in the handout. I think the handout is self-explanatory, but if you have questions, I'd like you to work out a solution of your own.*

You read and hear:

What can be inferred about the professor?

Ⓐ He wants the students to make group decisions without his help.
Ⓑ He does not expect the students to understand his explanations.
Ⓒ He wants the students to come to the solution he thinks is correct.
Ⓓ He is not concerned with helping students learn how to approach problems.

You should choose *A*. The professor has stated that the handout is self-explanatory, and he indicates that he is not willing to answer questions about the handout. He wants the group to work out their own solutions. You can conclude that he wants the students to work as a group to reach a solution without his help.

Exercises L18–L23

Use Exercises L18–L23 to develop your skills in understanding meanings that are not explicitly stated in conversations, discussions, and lectures.

EXERCISE L18 *Understanding inferences*

Listen to the following spoken passages. Answer *Yes* or *No* to the statement that follows each passage.

You hear:

(professor) *In a recent survey on smell, men and women were asked to smell samples of scents and to identify them. It was established that women in general have a more acute sense of smell than men, unless they are pregnant when, contrary to popular belief, a temporary loss of smell occurs.*

(narrator) *Both pregnant and nonpregnant women probably took part in the survey.*

You write:

Yes

You should write *Yes* in the space because women in both conditions must have taken part in the survey in order for the researchers to discover that nonpregnant women have a more acute sense of smell than men and that pregnant women have a less acute sense of smell than men.

START ▶

1. _________ 3. _________

2. _________ 4. _________

STOP ■

EXERCISE L19 *Drawing conclusions*

Listen to the passage. Choose the best answer based on the information given.

You hear:

"Moonshiner" was the name given to a person who made illegal alcohol. Many people preferred the taste of whiskey made in the old-fashioned way from recipes and techniques dating back to America's earliest Scotch-Irish pioneers.

You read and hear:

What might have been the reason that the makers of illegal alcohol were called "moonshiners"?

(A) Because there was no electricity, the early pioneers had to read their recipes by moonlight.

(B) Alcoholics probably like to see the shining moon.

(C) The people involved probably made it and sold it at night.

(D) The best whiskey is probably made during a full moon.

You should choose *C*. Since the makers of illegal alcohol were breaking the law, they probably worked at night, when there was less chance of being caught. They would have had to work by moonlight because lamplight could have been seen by the authorities.

START ▶

1. For what field might the new knowledge about polio be most useful?
   - (A) Statistics
   - (B) Medicine
   - (C) Education
   - (D) History
2. What will the man probably do as a result of this conversation?
   - (A) Take the course next semester
   - (B) Speak to the Spanish teacher
   - (C) Sign up for Spanish
   - (D) Take Italian
3. Why might Jean Muir have given so much attention to her staff?
   - (A) So her business could continue after her death
   - (B) So her collection could not be plagiarized
   - (C) So her collections could be sold quickly
   - (D) So her staff could take over the training
4. To what group of university students might this talk have been given?
   - (A) Political science majors
   - (B) Education majors
   - (C) English majors
   - (D) Art majors

STOP ■

EXERCISE L20 *Inferring reasons*

Listen to the passage. Then answer the question.

> You hear:
>
> (man) *Snow is a fantastic insulator. Ask the Inuits. However, the extraordinary efficiency of snow as an insulator makes it difficult to find a person buried in an avalanche.*
>
> (narrator) *Why does the speaker mention the Inuits?*
>
> You write:
>
> *Because the Inuit people would be authorities on snow.*
>
> The Inuit people live in a snowy climate. Therefore, they would know a lot about the properties of snow.

START ▶

1. ______________________________
2. ______________________________
3. ______________________________
4. ______________________________

STOP ■

EXERCISE L21 *Identifying attitudes*

Listen to the conversation. Choose the answer choices that identify the speakers' attitudes.

> You hear:
>
> (man) *Darn! I think I'm catching a cold – just when I need to be well to give my presentation. I've been sneezing all morning.*
>
> (woman) *Oh, you're not coming down with anything . . . unless you have other symptoms. You've probably just breathed in some irritant.*
>
> The man is
>
> (A) annoyed
> (B) angry
>
> The woman is
>
> (C) doubtful
> (D) irritated
>
> You should choose *A* because the speaker is annoyed about the possibility of being ill when he has to give a presentation. You should choose *C* because the woman gives her reasons for doubting that the man is getting ill.

START ▶

1. The woman is

   (A) critical
   (B) offended

   The man is

   (C) forgiving
   (D) defensive

2. The woman is

   (A) sympathetic
   (B) excited

   The man is

   (C) worried
   (D) uninterested

3. The woman is

   (A) overworked
   (B) enthusiastic

   The man is

   (C) welcoming
   (D) annoyed

4. The man is

   (A) upset
   (B) surprised

   The woman is

   (C) helpful
   (D) sarcastic

STOP ■

EXERCISE L22 *Identifying the speaker's purpose*

Listen to the passage. You will then hear part of the passage repeated. Choose the answer that identifies the speaker's purpose.

> You hear:
>
> (professor) *Well, today I had hoped to show you some computer slides but, uh, this morning when I popped into the lab to set up the equipment, I discovered that, uh, the projector needs a bulb replacement. Needless to say, we didn't have a spare. So, today you get to see my drawing skills, or, uh, shall I say lack . . . my lack of drawing skills instead of nice computer illustrations. So, please bear with me.*
>
> You read and hear:
>
> Why does the professor say this: 
>
> You hear:
>
> *So, please bear with me.*
>
> (A) To joke with the class
> (B) To ask the class for their patience
> (C) To make excuses for the situation
> (D) To encourage the students to make sketches
>
> You should choose *B* because the professor cannot show the computer illustrations and therefore has to draw the illustrations. He would like the students to be understanding about this situation.

START ▶

1. Why does the professor say this:
   (A) To find out if the students can think critically
   (B) To locate the competitive students in the class
   (C) To encourage students to oppose the premise of the question
   (D) To get the students to consider the question more deeply
2. Why does the professor say this:
   (A) To define a word that might be unfamiliar
   (B) To explain the effects of acidic by-products
   (C) To contrast two different dietary habits
   (D) To illustrate the dangers of eating carbohydrates
3. Why does the professor say this:
   (A) To direct the students in how to do well in exams
   (B) To explain why the students' answers to his question are wrong
   (C) To convince students not to be upset if they fail a test
   (D) To direct the students to consider another interpretation
4. Why does the professor say this:
   (A) To explain why she will be attending the workshop
   (B) To show her acquaintance with professional climbers
   (C) To give her approval of the rock-climbing workshop leaders
   (D) To convince students that they should pay as soon as possible

STOP ■

EXERCISE L23 🎧 *Identifying the speaker's meaning*

Listen to the conversation or lecture. Then choose the answer that identifies what the speaker means.

You hear:

(man) *Dr. Johnson, would you . . . uh . . . I need your signature on, this per- permission form so that I can get into Chemistry 205 . . . because, because my grade for the prerequisite course was low.*

(woman) *Well, Bill, a low grade indicates that you don't understand essential concepts. Are you up to taking the course?*

(man) *I think so. My brother . . . uh . . . kind of tutored me over the summer. We went back over all the material. I-I think I have a good grasp of it . . . now.*

You read and hear:

Listen again to part of the lecture. Then answer the question.

You hear:

Well, Bill, a low grade indicates that you don't understand essential concepts. Are you up to taking the course?

You read and hear:

What does the professor mean when she says this: 

You hear:

Are you up to taking the course?

Ⓐ She is refusing to sign the permission form for the man to register for chemistry.
Ⓑ She is concerned the man doesn't have the background knowledge to do well.
Ⓒ She doesn't have confidence in the brother's teaching abilities.
Ⓓ She wants the man to go back over the prerequisite course materials.

You should choose *B* because the woman does not want to sign the form for the man if he doesn't have the knowledge from the prerequisite course in order to do well in the following course.

START ▶

1. What does the professor mean when he says this: 🎧

Ⓐ He wants the student to stop wasting his time and her time and money.
Ⓑ He is annoyed with students who consistently miss getting their work done on time.
Ⓒ He is worried the missed deadline is a symptom of the student not being able to keep up.
Ⓓ He is certain that the woman is too far behind to catch up and should drop the course.

2. What is the man doing when he says this: 🎧

Ⓐ He is showing the woman his excitement on getting the information.
Ⓑ He is telling the woman that he thinks she is teasing him.
Ⓒ He is letting the woman know that he considers what she said to be untrue.
Ⓓ He is asking for confirmation about his understanding of what the woman said.

LISTENING

3. What does the professor mean when she says this:
   (A) The students will see an obvious relationship immediately.
   (B) The statistics will be really interesting for the students.
   (C) The students will have difficulty interpreting the statistics.
   (D) The students will be able to see the projection of the transparency better than what is written on the board.

4. What can be inferred about the students?
   (A) They disagree with the professor's statement about political strife.
   (B) They have opposing views about the validity of the Declaration of Independence.
   (C) They do not agree on the premise that the pursuit of happiness is a good thing.
   (D) They believe that development, progress, and materialism meet the political goal.

STOP ■

Listening Mini-test 3

Check your progress in making inferences and drawing conclusions (Exercises L18–L23) by completing the following Mini-test. This Mini-test uses a format similar to the format used in the Listening section of the TOEFL iBT test.

Listen to the passage. Then answer the questions by choosing the letter of the best answer choice.

Now get ready to listen.

START ▶

Questions 1–5

Listen to an architecture professor talk about hazards in the home.

1. Listen again to part of the lecture. Then answer the question.
   Why does the professor say this:
   (A) To correct a mistake she made
   (B) To apologize for the use of asbestos
   (C) To explain why asbestos is dangerous
   (D) To present another disease caused by asbestos

2. Listen again to part of the lecture. Then answer the question.
   Why does the professor say this:
   (A) She is trying to shock the students.
   (B) She is emphasizing the seriousness of the situation.
   (C) She is impressing the students with her artistic abilities.
   (D) She is introducing a cure for the diseases caused by synthetic materials.

3. Why does the speaker mention fires?
   (A) To illustrate how unsafe wooden houses are
   (B) To show other ways in which synthetic materials are dangerous
   (C) To let people know about the toxic fumes when using natural alternatives
   (D) To demonstrate what happens when cadmium is added to paint

4. What would be an example of a natural building material?
   (A) Stone walls
   (B) Aluminum door frames
   (C) Linoleum flooring
   (D) Plywood paneling

5. What might the listeners do as a result of this lecture?
   (A) Tear down their houses
   (B) Buy older homes
   (C) Build new houses
   (D) Modify their homes

LISTENING

Questions 6–9

Listen to a discussion between a professor and his students.

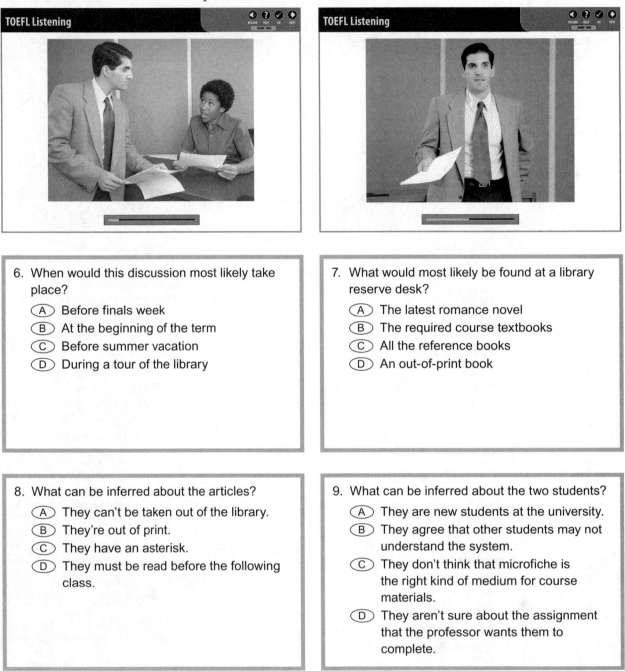

6. When would this discussion most likely take place?
   (A) Before finals week
   (B) At the beginning of the term
   (C) Before summer vacation
   (D) During a tour of the library

7. What would most likely be found at a library reserve desk?
   (A) The latest romance novel
   (B) The required course textbooks
   (C) All the reference books
   (D) An out-of-print book

8. What can be inferred about the articles?
   (A) They can't be taken out of the library.
   (B) They're out of print.
   (C) They have an asterisk.
   (D) They must be read before the following class.

9. What can be inferred about the two students?
   (A) They are new students at the university.
   (B) They agree that other students may not understand the system.
   (C) They don't think that microfiche is the right kind of medium for course materials.
   (D) They aren't sure about the assignment that the professor wants them to complete.

Questions 10–14

Listen to a talk given by a guest inventor.

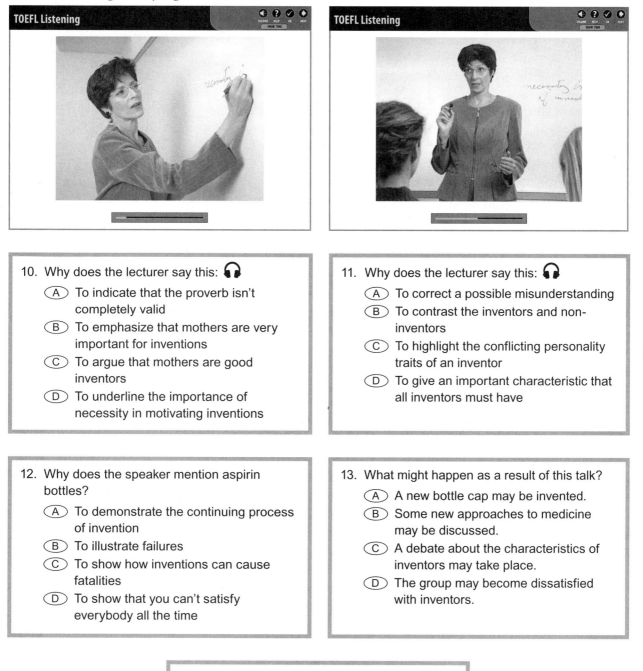

10. Why does the lecturer say this: 
    - (A) To indicate that the proverb isn't completely valid
    - (B) To emphasize that mothers are very important for inventions
    - (C) To argue that mothers are good inventors
    - (D) To underline the importance of necessity in motivating inventions

11. Why does the lecturer say this: 
    - (A) To correct a possible misunderstanding
    - (B) To contrast the inventors and non-inventors
    - (C) To highlight the conflicting personality traits of an inventor
    - (D) To give an important characteristic that all inventors must have

12. Why does the speaker mention aspirin bottles?
    - (A) To demonstrate the continuing process of invention
    - (B) To illustrate failures
    - (C) To show how inventions can cause fatalities
    - (D) To show that you can't satisfy everybody all the time

13. What might happen as a result of this talk?
    - (A) A new bottle cap may be invented.
    - (B) Some new approaches to medicine may be discussed.
    - (C) A debate about the characteristics of inventors may take place.
    - (D) The group may become dissatisfied with inventors.

14. How does the speaker close the talk?
    - (A) By opening the floor to questions
    - (B) By suggesting a break
    - (C) By giving some hints
    - (D) By involving the audience

LISTENING

Questions 15–18

Listen to a discussion in a cultural anthropology course.

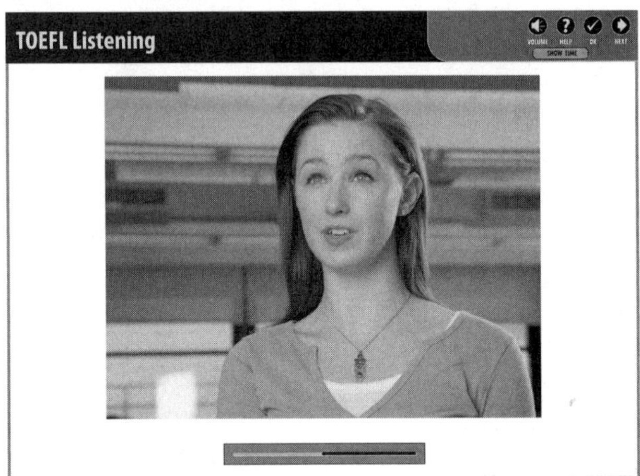

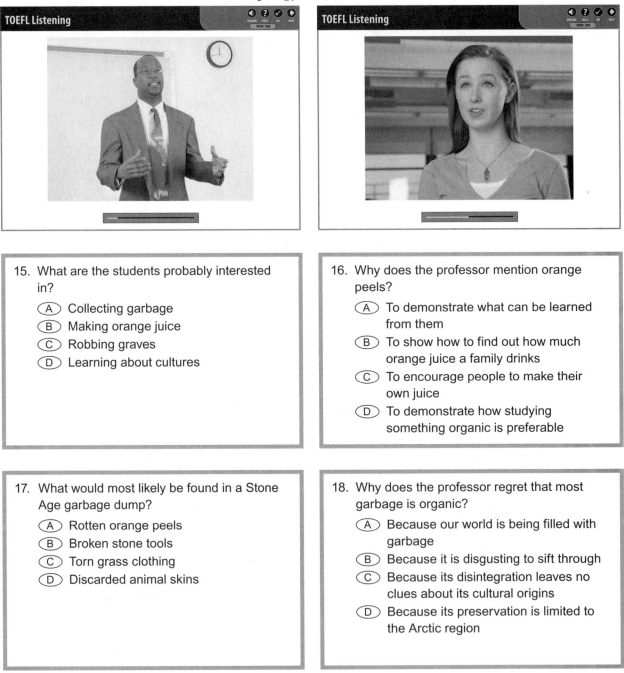

15. What are the students probably interested in?
    - (A) Collecting garbage
    - (B) Making orange juice
    - (C) Robbing graves
    - (D) Learning about cultures

16. Why does the professor mention orange peels?
    - (A) To demonstrate what can be learned from them
    - (B) To show how to find out how much orange juice a family drinks
    - (C) To encourage people to make their own juice
    - (D) To demonstrate how studying something organic is preferable

17. What would most likely be found in a Stone Age garbage dump?
    - (A) Rotten orange peels
    - (B) Broken stone tools
    - (C) Torn grass clothing
    - (D) Discarded animal skins

18. Why does the professor regret that most garbage is organic?
    - (A) Because our world is being filled with garbage
    - (B) Because it is disgusting to sift through
    - (C) Because its disintegration leaves no clues about its cultural origins
    - (D) Because its preservation is limited to the Arctic region

STOP ■

Listening Section Practice Test

When you have taken the Diagnostic Test and completed the exercises recommended in the Answer Key for any Listening questions you marked incorrectly, you can test your skills by taking this Listening Section Practice Test. You can take this test either in this book or on the CD-ROM that accompanies this book. The Listening Section Practice Test in the book is identical to the Listening section of Test 2 on the CD-ROM.

During the Listening Section of the actual TOEFL test, you may not go back to check your work or change your answers. Maintain the same test conditions now that would be experienced during the real test.

LISTENING SECTION

Directions

This section measures your ability to understand conversations and lectures in English. You will hear each conversation or lecture only one time. After each conversation or lecture, you will answer some questions about it.

The questions typically ask about the main idea and supporting details. Some questions ask about a speaker's purpose or attitude. Answer the questions based on what is stated or implied by the speakers.

You may take notes while you listen. You may use your notes to help you answer the questions. Your notes will not be scored.

In some questions, you will see this icon: 🎧. This means that you will hear, but not see, part of the question.

Some questions have special directions. These directions appear in a gray box.

Most questions are worth one point. A question worth more than one point will have special instructions indicating how many points you can receive.

You will have 20 minutes to answer the questions in this section.

Now get ready to listen. You may take notes.

START ▶

Questions 1–7

Listen to part of a lecture in a psychology class.

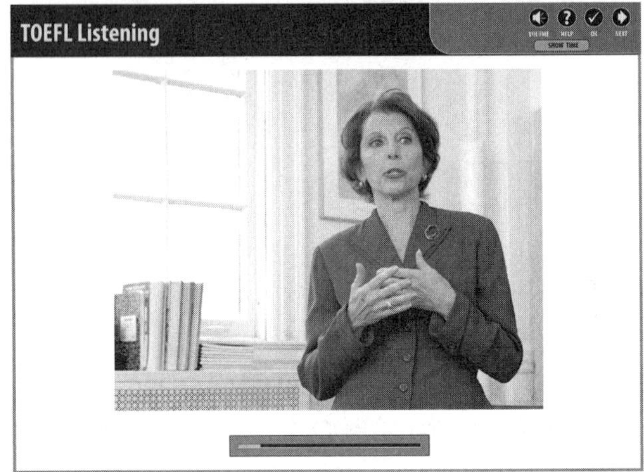

Now get ready to answer the questions. You may use your notes to help you answer.

1. What is the lecture mainly about?
   - (A) An analysis of genetically caused mental disorders
   - (B) A description of some common anxiety disorders
   - (C) An evaluation of the causes of some anxiety disorders
   - (D) A method of comparing different mental disorders

2. Why does the professor say that many people feel anxious when they visit a dentist?
   - (A) To emphasize the problems faced by social phobics
   - (B) To indicate that it is rational to have an anxiety attack in some situations
   - (C) To show that it is irrational to be anxious in many situations
   - (D) To give an example of a common anxiety trigger for most people

3. What does the professor say about specific phobias?
   - (A) Their object is usually safe.
   - (B) Their object is often dangerous.
   - (C) They become worse with age.
   - (D) They usually start in childhood.

4. Listen again to part of the lecture. Then answer the question.
   Why does the professor say this: 🎧
   - (A) To check that the students understand the joke
   - (B) To express disapproval of the students' behavior
   - (C) To emphasize her belief that this is truly bizarre
   - (D) To imply that this phobia seems funny to most people

5. Social phobia might include which of the following fears?
   - (A) Fear of heights
   - (B) Fear of enclosed spaces
   - (C) Fear of eating in front of others
   - (D) Fear of encountering dangerous animals

6. What does the professor imply when she says this: 🎧
   - (A) The term may not be familiar to the students.
   - (B) The term is not relevant to the lecture.
   - (C) The students should already know the term.
   - (D) The students should know the term from their textbooks.

7. What does the professor imply about treatment of phobias?
   - (A) Treatment rarely succeeds.
   - (B) Treatment is not usually necessary.
   - (C) Treatment is long and difficult.
   - (D) Treatment takes various forms.

Questions 8–12

Listen to a conversation between a student and a professor.

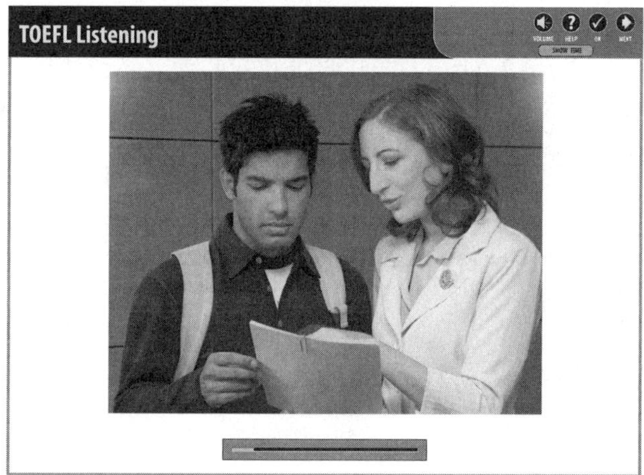

Now get ready to answer the questions. You may use your notes to help you answer.

8. Why does the student go to see his professor?
   - (A) To give the professor a questionnaire
   - (B) To find out why the professor asked to see him
   - (C) To ask the professor how to write a good questionnaire
   - (D) To let the professor know the results of the questionnaire

9. Why does the professor talk about fruit and vegetables?
   - (A) To illustrate a point
   - (B) To encourage a healthy diet
   - (C) To highlight people's preferences
   - (D) To give an example of a good statement

10. According to the professor, what should the student avoid in writing his questionnaire?

    Choose 2 answers.

   - [A] Thinking about the statements critically
   - [B] Helping the subjects answer the questions
   - [C] Alienating his subjects with statements that may be offensive
   - [D] Including statements for which he knows the probable response

11. Listen again to part of the conversation. Then answer the question.
    Why does the professor say this:
   - (A) To indicate that she needs to get some exercise
   - (B) To encourage the student to run through the statements
   - (C) To explain why she needs to answer the questionnaire
   - (D) To indicate that she can't remember the exact difficulties

12. What can be inferred about the questionnaire?
   - (A) It is a class assignment.
   - (B) It will be passed out to classmates.
   - (C) It has annoyed the women subjects.
   - (D) It is part of a larger research project.

Questions 13–17

Listen to part of a discussion in a geology class.

Now get ready to answer the questions. You may use your notes to help you answer.

13. What is the discussion mainly about?
    - (A) The lack of moisture in the tundra
    - (B) The severe climate of the tundra
    - (C) The characteristics of tundra plants
    - (D) The availability of tundra soil

14. Why does the professor not want to discuss Alpine tundra?
    - (A) The topic is outside the course objectives.
    - (B) The topic warrants a lesson to itself.
    - (C) The topic might confuse students at this stage.
    - (D) The topic had been discussed previously.

15. According to the professor, what features are typical of tundra regions?

    Choose 2 answers.

    - [A] The landscape is relatively flat.
    - [B] The summers tend to be hot and humid.
    - [C] The trees adapt to the lack of rain.
    - [D] The melted snow stays on the surface.

16. According to the professor, why do tundra plants often cluster together in depressions?
    - (A) To help themselves gain adequate amounts of water
    - (B) To compensate for the lack of nutrients in the ground
    - (C) To protect themselves against the cold winds
    - (D) To provide shade against the prolonged summer sun

LISTENING

17. In the discussion, various facts about plants in the tundra are mentioned. Indicate whether each of the following describes tundra vegetation.

Check the correct box for each statement.

	Yes	No
(A) Plant roots are adapted to penetrate the frozen ground.		
(B) Plants are protected from the cold by a snow covering.		
(C) Plant growth is dependent on heavy rainfall.		
(D) Trees tend to be protected by the forest.		
(E) Plant growth is rapid in the summer.		

Questions 18–24

Listen to part of a lecture in a cultural studies class.

Now get ready to answer the questions. You may use your notes to help you answer.

18. What is the lecture mainly about?
    - (A) The importance of Isadora Duncan to modern dance
    - (B) The failure of nineteenth-century dance conventions
    - (C) The innovations in ballet dancing in the twentieth century
    - (D) Isadora Duncan's use of costume in modern dance

19. What does the professor imply about other artists of Duncan's time?
    - (A) Most were very conventional.
    - (B) Many were looking for different forms of movement.
    - (C) Many were looking for new ways to express themselves.
    - (D) Most were content to make only a few new contributions.

20. Which of the following may have been an influence on Duncan's art?

    (A) Audience participation
    (B) Folk dancing
    (C) Modern ballet dance
    (D) Other artists

21. Which of the following does the professor consider a contribution of Duncan's?

    (A) Ritualized step movements
    (B) Performance in the open air
    (C) Copying of theatrical impulses
    (D) Classical music in performances

22. In the lecture, the professor describes some of the main contributions made by Isadora Duncan to modern dance. Indicate whether each of the following is a contribution made by this dancer.

Check the correct box for each statement.

	Yes	**No**
(A) Tight-fitting shoes are worn.		
(B) Loose-fitting gowns are worn.		
(C) Mainly the arms are used for expression.		
(D) A variety of popular music forms accompany the dancing.		
(E) Emotional expression is important.		

23. What is the professor's attitude toward Isadora Duncan's innovations?

    (A) He is ironic.
    (B) He is critical.
    (C) He is appreciative.
    (D) He is unconcerned.

24. What does the professor imply about Duncan's current status?

    (A) It may not always be fully appreciated.
    (B) It often excites critical scorn.
    (C) It has stimulated anger and grief.
    (D) It is less esteemed than previously.

Questions 25–30

Listen to part of a lecture in an astronomy class.

Now get ready to answer the questions. You may use your notes to help you answer.

25. What is the main topic of the lecture?
    - (A) How the solar system formed
    - (B) Competing theories about the formation of rocks
    - (C) The stratification of the Earth's interior
    - (D) How gravity helped heat the Earth

26. Why does the professor say this: 
    - (A) She rejects most of the traditional views of planetary formation.
    - (B) She hopes the students will review the traditional theory.
    - (C) She thinks new theories offer a better explanation of planetary formation.
    - (D) She believes that scientific theories are open to challenge.

27. What does the professor imply about the formation of the Earth?
    - (A) It is familiar to some of the students.
    - (B) A lot of background reading is necessary.
    - (C) The theory has explanatory gaps.
    - (D) A later course will deal with it in detail.

28. According to the professor, how was rock distributed before differentiation?
    - (A) In various layers
    - (B) Randomly
    - (C) With the heaviest near the surface
    - (D) Heavy material was stratified

29. According to the professor, which is probably the main reason for the heating of the Earth?
    - (A) Pressure due to the force of gravity
    - (B) Solar radiation
    - (C) The impact of objects from space
    - (D) Radioactive decay

30. What two points are true according to the lecture?

    Choose 2 answers.

    - [A] The core of the planet has the densest material.
    - [B] Differentiation occurred when the planetary sphere formed.
    - [C] The atmosphere was formed during the process of differentiation.
    - [D] The heating of the Earth produced a random distribution of material.

Questions 31–35

Listen to part of a conversation between a student and an advisor at the University Learning Center.

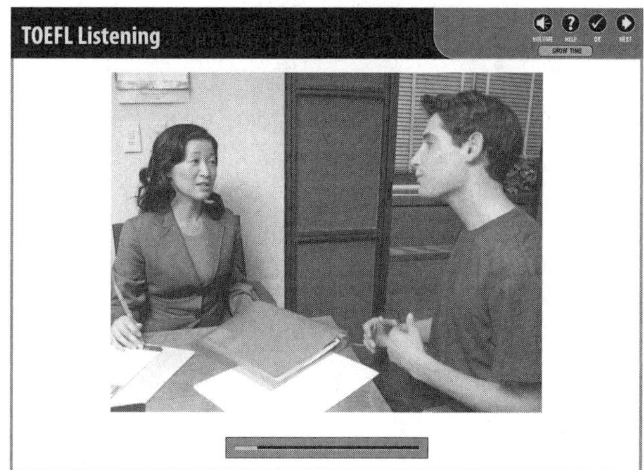

Now get ready to answer the questions. You may use your notes to help you answer.

31. What does the student need from the advisor?
    - (A) Advice on how to apply for funding for graduate research
    - (B) Help in finding universities that offer marine biology degrees
    - (C) Application forms for the graduate program in marine biology
    - (D) Information on meeting the requirements to apply to graduate school

32. Where will the student and the advisor look for the information the student needs on university degree programs?
    - (A) On the Internet
    - (B) In the biology department
    - (C) In reference books
    - (D) In marine biology articles

LISTENING

33. What can be inferred about applying to graduate school?
   - (A) There is an application fee.
   - (B) There are too many to apply to.
   - (C) There are no research opportunities.
   - (D) There are no restrictions on applicants.

34. Listen again to part of the conversation. Then answer the question.
   Why does the advisor say this:
   - (A) To help the student narrow his search
   - (B) To advise the student of the competition
   - (C) To find out about the student's hobbies
   - (D) To suggest some articles to read in his field

35. Why does the advisor suggest that the student read some of the published articles about intertidal zones?
   - (A) To get more information about the marine environment
   - (B) To locate the universities where people do marine research
   - (C) To find professors who might be helpful in his field of interest
   - (D) To make decisions about going on for a doctorate in marine biology

STOP ■

Speaking

The Speaking section of the TOEFL® iBT test measures your ability to communicate orally. There are six speaking tasks on the test. They are divided into two types: independent speaking tasks and integrated speaking tasks.

Independent tasks

The independent speaking tasks measure your ability to speak about topics that are familiar to you. There are two independent speaking tasks: a personal preference task and a personal choice task. For each one, you will hear the speaking task and see it on the screen. You will then have 15 seconds to prepare your response and 45 seconds to speak.

The personal preference task asks you to state and support a personal choice from a particular category, such as activities you enjoy, events, or important people and places. The personal choice task asks you to make and support a choice between two contrasting behaviors or actions.

Integrated tasks

The integrated speaking tasks measure your ability to combine information from several sources in a spoken response. You do not need any prior knowledge of the topic in order to do these tasks. There are four integrated tasks: two reading/listening/speaking tasks and two listening/speaking tasks.

Reading/listening/speaking tasks

The integrated reading/listening/speaking tasks are divided into two categories: a campus situation topic and an academic topic. For each, you will have 45 seconds to read a short passage. You will then hear a related passage. You may take notes. You will have 30 seconds to prepare your response and 60 seconds to speak.

The campus situation task requires you to read a passage that addresses a campus-related issue. You will then listen to a conversation between two people who discuss the issue. You will be asked to use the information from the reading and the conversation to summarize the speakers' opinions about the issue within the context of the reading passage.

The academic task requires you to read a passage that discusses an academic topic in a general way. You will then listen to a classroom lecture that provides examples and specific information that expand upon the reading passage. You will be asked to combine and convey important information from the two sources.

Listening/speaking tasks

The integrated listening/speaking tasks are divided into two categories: a campus situation topic that presents a problem and possible solutions, and an academic course topic that you will be asked to summarize and explain. For each, you will listen to a passage. You may take notes. You will then have 20 seconds to prepare your response and 60 seconds to speak.

The campus situation task requires you to listen to a conversation about a student-related problem and two possible solutions. You will be asked to use the information from the conversation to show that you understand the problem and to give your opinion about how to solve it.

The academic task requires you to listen to a classroom lecture on an academic subject. You will be asked to summarize the lecture and explain how the details and examples relate to the topic.

Your responses for all six speaking tasks are scored based on how successfully you meet the demands of the task, the overall intelligibility of your speech, the accuracy and variety of the structures you use, your vocabulary, and your organization of ideas.

Strategies to Use for Building Speaking Fluency

1. Practice speaking in English.
All speaking practice will help you build fluency in speaking. If you do not know someone who is a native English speaker, practice speaking English with nonnative English speakers. It is even useful to practice speaking aloud to yourself when you are alone.

2. Follow a deliberate practice regime.
Fluency refers to speaking with accuracy and natural speed. There are several language features to concentrate on for building language fluency:

- pronunciation
- intonation
- grammatical correctness
- correct use of vocabulary
- use of a variety of vocabulary
- coherence

You can isolate these features and practice them daily. (See Grammar: Assessing Your Skills, p. 74, and Vocabulary, p. 63.)

3. Avoid translating.
Translating from your own language into English prevents you from speaking fluently and naturally. To overcome dependency on translating, practice simple phrases in English until you can use them with the same fluency as you can use your own language. Then build up from those phrases to more complex sentences.

4. Become comfortable with using native English speakers' pausing techniques.
When native English speakers are thinking or are searching for a better way to say something, they use fillers such as *uh* or *um*. If you use these pausing techniques, you will sound more natural.

5. Try to relax when speaking.
Remember that native English speakers make mistakes, too. They repeat phrases, correct themselves, and hesitate. Don't let your errors in speaking undermine your confidence.

6. Use natural speed and rhythm.
Listen to native English speakers and try to use the same speed and rhythms that they use. To practice imitating native English speakers, use the listening scripts in this book to mark the pauses, stresses, and intonation patterns that you hear in the audio program. Then practice the passages on your own.

7. Train yourself in fluency.
A good method for developing fluency is following a speaker on an audio recording. Start the recording. Wait a few seconds and then start repeating what the speaker says. If you have difficulty, listen and repeat the particular words or phrases that are causing you trouble. Then go back to the beginning of the recording and start again as often as necessary. Continue this practice until you can follow the speaker fluently. Any of the listening passages in this text could be used to practice this method.

PRACTICE WITH PRONUNCIATION

English has certain pronunciation features that you need to become aware of and imitate in order to produce speech that sounds like that of a native speaker. The closer you are to achieving this goal, the higher your score will be on the Speaking section of the TOEFL test. Speech features that you need to be familiar with are described below.

Individual sounds and groups of sounds

Your listeners will understand your responses better if you pronounce the individual sounds and groups of sounds correctly. These sounds are vowels, combinations of vowels, consonants, and consonant clusters. For example:

vowels: a, e, i
vowel combinations: oi, ay
consonants: p, t, k
consonant clusters: str, scr

Since letters in English do not always represent the same spoken sounds, it is useful to learn a phonetic alphabet. The International Phonetic Alphabet (IPA) is the most common one. (See Pronunciation, p. 69.) However, your dictionary may use a different phonetic alphabet to represent sounds. Identify which English sounds you have difficulty making and work on reproducing them as accurately as possible.

Stress patterns

Even if you put all the correct sounds together, you may not be understood unless you use the correct stress patterns. Stress refers to the emphasis you place on certain words in a sentence or on a syllable within a word. A stressed word or syllable is louder, longer, and higher pitched than unstressed words or syllables.

Every word in English has a stress pattern. Using the wrong stress pattern can cause misunderstandings. In some cases, the stress pattern of a word can determine its part of speech. Look at the following noun-verb pairs of words. They are alike except for the stress pattern. The nouns are stressed on the first syllable and the verbs are stressed on the second. The stressed syllables are shown in bold.

Contest (noun): a competition
Con**test** (verb): argue against

Record (noun): written documentation
Re**cord** (verb): make an audio recording

Adding suffixes often changes the stress pattern of a word. Look at the following forms of the word *authority.*

Noun	**Verb**	**Adjective**	**Adverb**
au**thor**ity	**au**thorize	au**thor**itative	authori**ta**tively

Longer words can have a primary stress as well as a secondary stress. Look at the following words. The primary stress is in **bold** and the secondary stress is in *italics.*

con*ta*mi**na**tion
re*ci*pro**ca**tion

The stress pattern of a sentence indicates the main focus of the sentence. A change in the stress pattern of a sentence can change its meaning. Compare these examples:

Sue bought the red dress. (It was Sue – not Ellen – who bought the red dress.)
Sue **bought** the red dress. (Sue bought the dress – she did not borrow it.)
Sue bought the **red** dress. (Sue did not buy the blue dress.)
Sue bought the red **dress**. (Sue did not buy a red skirt.)

Stressing the wrong word in a sentence may cause confusion about the meaning you want to express.

Rhythm patterns

Rhythm refers to the timing patterns of a language. Rhythm patterns in English are based on stress. Stressed words or the stressed parts of words occur at regular intervals of time and are given an equal amount of speech time. Unstressed words or parts of words fit in between these intervals. Below are two ways to determine if a word should be stressed in a sentence or not.

1. Content words (nouns, verbs, adjectives, and adverbs) are stressed or have a stressed syllable, whereas function words (helping verbs, prepositions, articles, etc.) are usually not stressed. Look at the following sentence:

   Tom walked into the **room** and **o**pened the **win**dow.

   The words *Tom, walked,* and *room* are one-syllable content words, and each one is stressed. The words *opened* and *window* are also content words with a stressed syllable. The words *into, and,* and *the* are function words. They are not stressed.

   The stressed words and stressed syllables in the example above are all given the same amount of speech time and the unstressed words and syllables are spoken faster, softer, lower pitched, and with relaxed vowel sounds.

   Look at the sentences on the next page. The first sentence has 10 syllables with 5 stresses. The second sentence has 15 syllables and 5 stresses. Even though the second sentence has more syllables, both sentences, as spoken by a native English speaker, would take the same amount of time.

Tom walked into the **room** and **closed** the **door**.
Marilyn **walked** into the **of**fice and **o**pened the **win**dow.

2. To maintain a steady rhythm pattern, speakers often use contractions and relaxed vowels. They reduce words by dropping the final vowels or consonants. They link the end of a word with the beginning of the following word. Look at the following pairs of sentences:

The complete sentence	**How the sentence may sound**
Is he going to join us?	Izzi gonna joi nus?
And I would like to stay for a while.	An I'd like ta stay fera while.
Do you want to go with him?	D'ya wanna go wi thim?

Intonation patterns

Intonation patterns involve changes in pitch. They are different from the pitch changes in stressed syllables because they frequently cover longer units of speech, such as clauses or a complete sentence. Sometimes the pitch change occurs within a single word.

A range of information can be understood through intonation patterns. A falling pitch at the end of a sentence signals that the speaker has completed a statement or an idea. Falling pitch is also used at the end of a wh-question. A rise at the end of a sentence signals that the speaker is asking a yes-no question.

The statement intonation pattern:	The question intonation patterns:
I'm invited to Linda's party. ↘	Where will it be held? ↘
	I'm invited to Linda's party? ↗

A rise at the end of a phrase or clause indicates that the speaker has more to say. A drop indicates that the speaker is finished.

I went to the market ↗, I bought a dozen eggs ↗, and then I came home ↘.

Intonation patterns can signal the speaker's attitude. They can also signal the speaker's emotions. Speakers show their certainty, enthusiasm, anger, excitement, etc., through subtle shifts in intonation.

SPEAKING

Exercises S1–S6

Use Exercises S1–S6 to develop your pronunciation skills.

EXERCISE S1 *Concentrating on individual consonant sounds*

Each of the following sentences focuses on an English consonant sound found in different positions within words. Listen to and repeat each sentence. Concentrate on the sounds represented by the letters in bold.

START ▶

1. /p/ **P**eter called us u**p** and invited us for su**pp**er.
2. /b/ The ro**bb**ers escaped in a stolen ca**b** and drove to their hideout, **b**ut they were eventually caught.

3. /t/ The children went on a scavenger hunt, and the victorious team was given a prize.
4. /d/ The dog followed the caddy around the golf course.
5. /k/ Schools can do more to encourage students to take on the responsibilities of learning.
6. /g/ The big logging companies are gone from the region.
7. /f/ If the fish stocks are depleted, it will be the fishermen who suffer.
8. /v/ The very first editions of the manuscripts are available for everyone to see.
9. /θ/ They are rethinking the rule of thumb that requires people to stay on the path.
10. /ð/ The mother decided to bathe her baby.
11. /s/ A lesson in building a house made of sod was offered at the outdoor museum.
12. /z/ The zoologists use tranquilizers when tagging the deer that enter the park.
13. /m/ Careful land management has saved the rim area from overgrazing.
14. /n/ The judges named the winner as soon as the race was over.
15. /ŋ/ Singing a favorite song is a good way to cheer oneself up.
16. /l/ The land grant allows for full use of resources.
17. /r/ Cooperative games help children to realize their potential in a nonthreatening situation.
18. /w/ The people in the tower witnessed how fast the fire was spreading.
19. /h/ The children's hospital has perhaps the best doctors to deal with the problem.
20. /j/ A layer of yellowish sandstone marks the division between the two geological periods.
21. /ʃ/ Since the idea in a demolition derby is to demolish the car, drivers should continue until this has been achieved.
22. /ʒ/ The genre of art called the collage is a pleasure to work in.
23. /tʃ/ By chance, a farmer uncovered the rich burial site that had survived in nature for several centuries.
24. /dʒ/ According to Jim, changing over to the computerized system led to a surge in interest.

STOP ■

EXERCISE S2 *Concentrating on consonant clusters*

The following passage focuses on consonant clusters. Listen to the passage. Then read it aloud. Then listen to the passage again while reading aloud at the same time. Pause and repeat phrases that are difficult for you.

START ▶

Snowflakes swirled around the makeshift huts as the **drifts**, shifted by the howling winds, mounted up against the walls. The **drafty** huts **creaked** and **groaned** in response. Then door hinges **squeaked** as abominable snowmen **stepped** across the **thresholds** into the sparsely furnished rooms. Marge **strained** her vocal cords as she **screamed** in an attempt to bring help. Her bloodcurdling **screams** woke her from the terrible dream.

STOP ■

EXERCISE S3 🎧 *Focusing on stress patterns*

Read the following passage. Underline the words or syllables that you expect will be stressed. Then listen to the passage and check your predictions. You may want to listen to the complete passage first and then listen again, pausing the recording at short intervals.

START ▶

Theaters of the Elizabethan period were open-air constructions in which poorer members of the audience, "the groundlings," stood in a space called "the pit" around three sides of a projecting rectangular platform that formed the main stage. Most of the perimeter of the building comprised covered, tiered galleries, and it is here that the wealthier members of the audience sat. A roof supported on two pillars projected from the back wall and covered part of the stage. The main stage was hollow and could be accessed from below through trapdoors set in the floor. The main stage also had a door on either side at the back, which gave access to the dressing rooms. Between these doors was a small recess, usually curtained off, that could be used for extra stage space. Above this recess was a balcony sometimes used by musicians or, when necessary, by actors in a performance.

STOP ■

For further practice, listen to the passage again and try to reproduce the speech patterns.

EXERCISE S4 🎧 *Focusing on linking words*

Read the passage as you listen to it. Mark the passage to show where the speaker links words in the speech. You may need to listen to the passage several times.

START ▶

It is simply not feasible for every university library in the nation to contain all the books, journals, and resource materials that university students and faculty need for their research. So what have libraries done to meet the needs of their users? Well, several things, in fact. While some money is used for the yearly purchasing of hardbound books and current journals that are recommended by professors, other funds are used to obtain materials that have been put on microfilm and microfiche. These techniques have proved extremely useful for adding informative materials to a library's collection at a low cost and without taking up much space. Another way libraries have increased access has been to invest in computers. Computers are linked to collections in other libraries. Professors and students can perform a computer search to find a library that has the material they need. The material can then be ordered and checked out through the interlibrary loan system, which costs the user a nominal shipping fee.

STOP ■

For further practice, listen to the passage again and try to reproduce the speech patterns.

EXERCISE S5 🎧 *Focusing on intonation*

Read the passage as you listen to it. Mark the passage to show the overall intonation patterns.

START ▶

(man) *Professor Cline?*

(woman) *Yes?*

(man) *I'm Robert Daley. The work-study office sent me.*

(woman) *Oh, I've been waiting for them to send someone. Did you say your name was Robert?*

(man) *Yes.*

(woman) *What's your major, Robert?*

(man) *Zoology.*

(woman) *Good. You have some science background then. Let me show you what we're doing in our lab.*

(man) *Will I be working in the biology lab?*

(woman) *Yes. We're studying the speed of reproduction of paramecia. Uh, paramecia are the most complex single-celled organisms.*

(man) *Oh, that sounds interesting.*

(woman) *Well, what we need you to do is probably not so interesting.*

(man) *And what is that?*

(woman) *We'll need you to come in every day at the same time and count the paramecia.*

(man) *Count paramecia?*

(woman) *Yes. It's very important to keep an accurate count and fill the numbers in on a form. I'll show you where the forms are and explain how to complete it later. After you have completed the form, you need to give it to Nancy. She's the woman that you met in the lab office. She'll feed your numbers into the computer for our statistical analysis. Right now, though, I want to introduce you to the other members of our team so that we can arrange a convenient time for you to come in.*

STOP ■

For further practice, listen to the passage again and try to reproduce the speech patterns.

EXERCISE S6 🎧 *Putting it all together*

Read the passage as you listen to it. Repeat as many times as necessary. Underline the stressed words or syllables, indicate the linked words, and mark the intonation patterns. After you have marked the passage, listen to it again and use your markings to reproduce the individual sounds and the overall speech patterns.

START ▶

Treasured since ancient times, saffron is obtained from the autumn-flowering *Crocus sativus*. It is the dried flower stigmas – the three slender threads in the center of each flower – that are the source of saffron. This "king of spices" is one of the world's most prized and expensive foodstuffs. The finest variety is grown in La Mancha in the central plateau of Spain. Spain is by far the biggest producer. It contributes 70 percent of the world's output, with India and Iran the only other producers of note. The cultivation of saffron in Spain goes back to the Moorish invasion of the eighth century, when the crocuses were first introduced from the Middle East. Not only is Spain the largest producer of saffron, but it is also the largest consumer. Up to one-third of the crop is bought in Spain, and the remainder is exported. The biggest buyers are Middle Eastern countries, followed by the United States, Italy, and France.

STOP ■

PRACTICE WITH COHESION

Cohesion refers to how well the ideas in your spoken response fit together. You will sound more fluent and get a higher score on the speaking tasks if your responses are cohesive. You can achieve cohesion by using the techniques described in this section.

Organizing ideas

Your listeners will understand your talk better if you organize what you say in a logical sequence or linear pattern. This means that you tell the listeners what you are going to talk about and then go through the points you want to make. The most common pattern of organization is outlined below:

Introductory statement
  Point 1
  Point 2
  Point 3
Concluding statement

An example of this pattern is shown below:

Breeding butterflies has many advantages for the collector.

1. way of obtaining specimens
2. spares can be released into the wild
3. helps survival because butterflies have been protected from natural predators

The experience is a learning experience for the collector and a benefit to the species.

Using transitional expressions

Connecting ideas by using transition words and phrases tells your listeners the relationship of one idea to the next. You can signal to your listener that you are going to put events in a sequence, add information, or make a comparison. You can signal that you want to emphasize or clarify a point. Using transition words and phrases helps your listener follow the flow of your ideas. Read the following example without transitional expressions:

In my physics class, we did lots of experiments that helped clarify scientific principles. I understood those principles better by doing those experiments.

These sentences would flow better if the speaker used transitional expressions as in the following example:

In my physics class, we did lots of experiments that helped clarify scientific principles. ***As a result****, I understood those principles better.*

See Grammar Review: Connecting Ideas, p. 116, for more information and a list of transition words and phrases.

Defining unknown terms

In order to help your listeners understand, you may need to define a term that you use in your response. Read the following example:

My hobby is telemark skiing.

If the speaker does not define the term and listeners do not know what telemark skiing is, they might not understand the rest of the passage. Sometimes listeners can guess the meaning through the context of the passage, but sometimes they cannot. Here is the definition this speaker gave of telemark skiing:

That means skiing using telemark skis.

Even though the speaker defined telemark skiing, listeners still may not understand what it means because the speaker defined the term with the same word. To effectively define a word, use a three-part definition:

1. State the word or phrase to be defined.
2. Give the category that the word or phrase fits into.
3. Tell how the word is different from other words that fit the same category.

Read this example of an effective definition:

Telemark is a type of alpine skiing in which the boots are connected to the skis only at the toes, so traditional skiing techniques have to be modified.

Using parallel structures

Your listener can understand the flow of your ideas better if you use parallel structures when you speak. Read the following incorrect example:

My teacher gave interesting assignments and motivating the students.

The listener may be confused because the speaker has mixed different grammatical structures. Does the speaker mean *My teacher gave* ***interesting*** *and* ***motivating*** *assignments to the students*?

In this sentence, *interesting* and *motivating* are parallel adjectives. Or does the speaker mean *My teacher* ***gave*** *interesting assignments and* ***motivated*** *the students*?

In this sentence, *gave* and *motivated* are parallel verbs. See Grammar Review: Parallel Structures, p. 115, for more information on parallel structures.

Rephrasing or replacing key words

When a speaker keeps repeating a word or phrase, listeners can get confused. Read the following example:

> *My teacher wrote the assignment on the chalkboard. The assignment was on the chalkboard until the teacher erased the assignment after we had all done the assignment.*

This speaker's ideas would be clearer if the repeated words were replaced with other expressions or with pronouns. Look at the way this example can be improved:

> *My teacher wrote the assignment on the chalkboard. She erased the board after we had all completed the task.*

The word *assignment* has been replaced with *task;* the word *teacher* with *she;* and the word *chalkboard* with *board.* See Grammar Review: Referents, p. 113, for more information on referents.

Using consistent tense, person, and number

Your listener can get confused if you are not consistent. Look at the following example:

> *My teacher brought five paper bags to school one day. He put us into groups and gave each group a bag. You have to take the objects out of the bags in turn and then a person has to tell a story involving the object from the bag.*

The listener may get confused by the change from the past tense to the present tense, and the change from *us* to *you* and then to *a person.* The listener might also be confused by the change from the plural form *objects* and *bags* to the singular forms *object* and *bag.*

The listener could follow this speaker's ideas better if the speaker were consistent. Look at the way this example can be improved:

> *One day my teacher put us into five different groups. He gave each group a bag and told us to take turns pulling out an object and telling the other members of the group a story involving that object.*

Exercises S7–S13

Use Exercises S7–S13 to develop your skills in being cohesive.

EXERCISE S7 *Connecting ideas using transitional expressions*

Join the following ideas using transitional expressions. Record your answers, and then evaluate your responses. An example is shown below.

> You read:
> We had to hand in our essays on time. They wouldn't be marked.
>
> You say:
> *We had to hand in our essays on time. Otherwise, they wouldn't be marked.*

1. I admired my high school history teacher for several reasons. He could explain historical events as if he were telling a story.

2. I enjoyed doing quiet activities like playing chess. My brother preferred more physical activities like football.
3. Our teacher would walk around the classroom looking at our work. We were busy on our individual projects.
4. The rain poured down for several days. The river banks in my city overflowed.
5. I took as many science courses as I could. I studied biology, chemistry, biochemistry, and physics.
6. The rain forest provides us with many products. The forests are being cleared for crops.

EXERCISE S8 *Defining words and phrases*

Practice defining words by giving a three-part definition to the following words. Record your answers, and then evaluate your responses. You may need to use a dictionary to help you with your definitions.

> You read:
> angling
>
> You say:
> *Angling is a type of recreational fishing that is done with a hook and line that are usually attached to a pole.*

1. childhood
2. avalanche
3. fiction
4. loan
5. accountant
6. whales

EXERCISE S9 *Connecting ideas by using parallel structures*

Join the following ideas using parallel structures. Record your answers, and then evaluate your responses.

> You read:
> To learn how to snowboard requires a lot of practice. The learner has to be patient.
>
> You say:
> *Learning how to snowboard takes practice and patience.*
> or
> *To learn how to snowboard not only takes a lot of practice but also a lot of patience.*

> You read:
> You have to be fit. Sometimes you have to travel a lot to get to the snowboarding areas. The equipment is expensive.
>
> You say:
> *To be a snowboarder, you have to be fit, travel long distances, and buy expensive equipment.*

1. Wind energy is an alternative form of energy. So is solar energy.
2. To get accepted into some universities, you have to send copies of your high school diploma. The university might want letters of recommendation from a teacher who knows your work. Also, you frequently have to write an essay stating why you want to study there.
3. Students tend to get out of shape because they spend a lot of time studying. Frequently they eat a lot of junk food, too.
4. Rivers are polluted by factories dumping their waste products into the water. People also throw their garbage into the river.

EXERCISE S10 *Connecting ideas by rephrasing key words*

Read the following sentences. Replace words or rephrase the sentence to avoid repeating key words. Record your answers, and then evaluate your responses.

> You read:
> I learned how to play the guitar first and then the piano. I practiced on both the guitar and piano for several hours every day.
>
> You say:
> *First I learned how to play the guitar and then the piano. I practiced both instruments for several hours every day.*

1. Since I frequently can't find the definition of words I need in a dictionary, I've had to buy a specialized dictionary. I also need to use an encyclopedia that gives more detailed information. Using my dictionaries and encyclopedia, I can collect information for my course papers.
2. My grandfather taught me woodcarving when I was young. When I need to relax, I go out into my yard and practice my woodcarving.
3. Many people enjoy reading fantasy stories about imaginary worlds and extraordinary events. Fantasy is also common in popular movies.
4. A pitfall trap can be used to get a sample of small ground-living creatures. To make a pitfall trap, a glass jar is put into the ground with its rim at ground level. The trapped creatures can then be counted and identified.

EXERCISE S11 *Connecting ideas by using pronouns*

Read the sentences on the next page. Use pronouns to replace repeated words. Record your answers, and then evaluate your responses.

You read:

I learned how to play the guitar first and then the piano. I practiced on both the guitar and piano for several hours every day.

You say:

First I learned how to play the guitar and then the piano. I practiced them both for several hours every day.

1. I prefer to spend my leisure time with different friends. Since my friends have diverse interests, one friend or the other is always involving me in different activities.
2. Many children are sent to school at an early age to get a head start in a formal education. That is unfortunate because children learn very important lessons about life through play.
3. The woman believes that the new plan to reserve study rooms will affect students adversely. Because of the plan, students won't be able to reserve the rooms ahead of time, and it is possible that a room will not be available when the room is needed.
4. The computer program contains activities for dyslexic children. The children work through the activities to help improve reading abilities.

EXERCISE S12 *Finding inconsistencies*

Underline the sections where you see inconsistencies in tense, person, or number.

Inconsistency in tense

On our campus, the dormitories are close to the classrooms. Since the students lived in the dorms, they didn't need a car. They could go to the campus police and get a parking sticker if they want to bring a car.

You should underline *lived, didn't need,* and *could* because these past tense verbs are inconsistent with the present tense verbs. The first sentence explains the situation in the present tense. In the second and third sentences, the verbs shift in tense.

Inconsistency in person

We can learn how to ride a motorcycle very quickly. This is especially true if you have experience riding a bicycle. In that case, a person already understands how to balance on a two-wheeled vehicle.

You should underline *We, you,* and *a person*. This passage is confusing because the speaker changes from the first-person plural *we* to the impersonal *you* and then to an indefinite person.

Inconsistency in number

We had to read three stories a week and write a brief summary of it in our notebooks. When our notebooks were full of stories, we chose our favorite one and told them to the class.

You should underline *three, it, one,* and *them*. This passage is confusing because of the shift from *three* to *it* and from *one* to *them*.

1. Cooking is fun when you are planning a nice meal for visitors. You can make a starter, main course, a salad, and a dessert. Then, when your guest arrives, you can surprise him with how well you have cooked it. Guests will appreciate all the work one does to make tasty meals.
2. It is very important for a teacher to be patient because their students don't always understand what they are expected to do. Sometimes one has to guess what the teacher means. It is very upsetting if you guess wrong and then they get angry when it isn't your fault.
3. A movie is never as good as the novel they are based on. Sometimes the novel has two or three subplots. Since all these subplots can't be addressed in a two-hour movie, the main plot is frequently changed. But without the subplot, they don't make sense. In the end, the movie tells a completely different story than that of the novels.
4. The professor talked about the rise and fall of empires. He notes that the conquerors spread through the valleys, the most fertile and accessible parts of a country. However, the people who live in the less accessible areas, like the tropical forests or the high mountain regions, are frequently not affected by the conquerors and continued to maintain languages and traditions throughout the many invasions that will take place over the centuries.

EXERCISE S13 *Practicing consistency*

Look at the inconsistent items in the example boxes in Exercise S12 and study how they have been corrected in the example boxes below. Practice consistency by correcting the items you underlined in Exercise S12. Record your answers, and then evaluate your responses.

SPEAKING

Inconsistency in tense

You read:

On our campus, the dormitories are close to the classrooms. Since the students lived in the dorms, they didn't need a car. They can go to the campus police and get a parking sticker if they wanted to bring a car.

You could change this to the present tense:

On our campus, the dormitories are close to the classrooms, so students who live in the dorms ***don't need*** *a car. If they* ***want*** *to bring a car to campus, they* ***can go*** *to the campus police and* ***get*** *a parking sticker.*

Or you could change it to the past tense:

On our campus, the dormitories ***were*** *close to the classrooms. Students who* ***lived*** *in the dorms* ***didn't need*** *a car. They* ***could have gone*** *to the campus police for a parking sticker if they* ***had wanted*** *to bring a car.*

Inconsistency in person

You read:

We can learn how to ride a motorcycle very quickly, especially if you have experience riding bicycles. In that case, a person already understands how to balance on a two-wheeled vehicle.

You could change this to the impersonal *you*:

You *can learn how to ride a motorcycle very quickly if* ***you*** *have experience riding bicycles. If* ***you*** *can ride a bike,* ***you*** *already know how to balance on a two-wheeled vehicle.*

Or you could change it to the indefinite plural:

People *who have experience riding bicycles know how to balance on a two-wheeled vehicle, and therefore* ***they*** *can learn how to ride a motorcycle very quickly.*

Inconsistency in number

You read:

We had to read three stories a week and write a brief summary of it in our notebooks. When our notebooks were full of stories, we chose our favorite one and told them to the class.

You could improve this by saying:

We had to read ***three*** *stories a week and write a brief summary of our* ***favorite one****. When our notebooks were full, we each chose our favorite story and told* ***it*** *to the class.*

Or you could use the plural form throughout:

We had to read ***three*** *stories a week and write brief summaries of* ***them*** *in our notebooks. When our notebooks were full, we chose our favorite stories and told* ***them*** *to the class.*

INDEPENDENT SPEAKING TASKS

In the independent speaking portion of the TOEFL iBT test, you will give two short speeches on topics that are familiar to you. For the personal preference task, you will choose and support a preference from a particular category. For the personal choice task, you will make and support a choice between two contrasting options.

An effective speech begins with an introductory statement that tells the listener what the speech is about. The body of the speech is made up of explanations and details. A concluding statement completes the speech.

Strategies to Use for the Personal Preference Task

1. Listen carefully to the task and think about what you must do in your response.

Ask yourself these questions:

- What is the topic of the task?
- What am I being asked to do?

Then make a mental list of the answers to these questions. For example, look at the following task:

> Name a skill you have learned and explain why it is important to you. Include details and examples to support your explanation.

For this task, you would make a mental list like the following:

The topic is about a skill I have learned. I need to:
- Name the skill
- Define the skill if the listener might not know what it is
- Explain its importance
- Include details and examples

2. Quickly decide on a topic.
It is easy to run out of preparation time while trying to decide what topic within the given category you will discuss. Quickly choose a topic and start thinking about the examples and details you can include for that particular topic. Remember, examiners are not interested in what the topic is but in how well you can express yourself.

3. Restate the task to include the topic that you are going to speak about.
For the task in Strategy 1 above, you might choose to focus on the skill of touch-typing. Your restatement could be:

> *I have learned how to touch-type, and this has been very important during my studies.*

4. Work through your mental list of requirements.
For the task in Strategy 1 above, your list might be:
- Name the skill. You have already named the skill in your restatement of the task statement.
- Define the skill. Ask yourself if you need to define your topic. Will the listener know about the topic you have chosen?
- Explain the importance to you of the topic you have chosen.
- Include details and examples from your own experience.

5. Know your goal.
When studying, record your speech and make a transcript, writing it exactly as you said it. Then make improvements to it: correct mistakes, eliminate long hesitations, and replace words or rephrase sentences to avoid repetition. Practice reading the corrected version aloud, and time yourself. Read it again while timing yourself, and stop reading at 45 seconds. How far did you get?

You will find that 45 seconds is only enough time for you to restate the task with your topic and to give one or two examples and one or two details. Eliminate unnecessary examples and details from your transcript and read it again with a timer. Once you have eliminated enough to be able to read your response aloud in about 35–40 seconds, and the topic does not suffer from a lack of examples or detail, you know your goal. The remaining 5–10 seconds are for the natural hesitations and corrections a speaker generally makes when talking.

6. Get ready for the next item.
It is easy to get anxious if you run out of time and have not finished what you intended to say, or if you finish what you want to say and there is still time left. Take a deep breath to help you relax and get ready for the next part of the test.

PRACTICE WITH THE PERSONAL PREFERENCE TASK

Preparing to give a timed response

The exercises that follow this section prepare you step by step for giving a timed response to the personal preference task in the speaking portion of the TOEFL test.

In the personal preference task, you have 15 seconds to choose your topic from a given category and plan how you are going to introduce the topic, present the ideas, and conclude the speech. Then you have 45 seconds to give your speech.

Study the task and the steps outlined in the example below. As you prepare for this portion of the test, you will practice these steps to build your skills and lessen the time it takes you to give a complete response.

Task

Name a skill you have learned and explain why it is important to you. Include details and examples to support your explanation.

Step 1 Ask yourself what the topic is and what you are being asked to do.

The topic is about a skill I have learned. I need to:

- Name the skill
- Define the skill if the listener might not know what it is
- Explain its importance
- Include details and examples

Step 2 Choose your topic and quickly think of a few details and examples.

Topic:	touch-typing
Details and examples:	work faster, fewer mistakes, typing more quickly and accurately on TOEFL test

Step 3 Work through your list of requirements. Record your speech.

- Name the skill.

  I have learned how to touch-type, and this has been very important during my studies.

- Define the skill. Ask yourself if you need to define your topic. Will the listener know about the topic you've chosen?

  Touch-typing is a technique that uses the sense of touch instead of sight to find the keys.

- Explain the importance to you of the topic you've chosen.

  The main importance of being able to touch-type is that it helps me to work faster and more efficiently when using a keyboard.

- Include details and examples.

  Since a computer has a keyboard that . . . that requires the user to type, and since computers are useful tools to, uh, tools to know how to use, being able to type quickly is good, uh, advantageous. If I need to search for information on the Web, I can quickly type the keywords into the . . . into the, uh, the search engine. Being able to search for materials quickly helps me to get the information I need to do my research papers or . . . to get background information that I need. That I need for my studies. When I need to turn in my papers, uh, assignments in a typed format, I can do . . . I can get the work done quickly. Because I know where the keys on the keyboard are, I do not have to go back and correct a lot of mistakes. Mistakes that might have been made otherwise. And now, while I'm preparing for the TOEFL test, I know that my typing skills will be valuable because I will be able to concentrate on what I want to say. I can concentrate on what, uh, what I want to say instead of getting anxious about finding the keyboard characters. I also feel confident about being able to complete the task. Complete it in the given time considering the speed I can type.

The following is an outline of the details and examples in the previous speech.

Detail 1: Use of the computer keyboard
- Example – speeds up information searches
- Example – helps in gathering information for papers

Detail 2: Typing assignments quickly and accurately
- Example – don't have to correct mistakes

Detail 3: Taking the TOEFL test
- Example – can concentrate on task
- Example – can complete task in the time given

Step 4 Make a transcript of your speech, as shown above.

Step 5 Make corrections to your speech, eliminating mistakes, long hesitations, self-corrections, or repetitions.

I have learned how to touch-type, and this has been very important during my studies. Touch-typing is a technique that uses the sense of touch instead of sight to find the keys. The main importance of being able to touch-type is that it helps me to work faster and more efficiently when using a keyboard. Since a computer has a keyboard that requires the user to type and since computers are useful tools to know how to use, being able to type quickly is advantageous. If I need to search for information on the Web, I can quickly type the keywords into the search engine. Being able to search for materials quickly helps me to get the information I need to do my research papers or to get background information that I need for my studies.

When I need to turn in my assignments in a typed format, I can get the work done quickly. Because I know where the keys on the keyboard are, I do not have to go back and correct a lot of mistakes that might have been made otherwise. And now, while I am preparing for the TOEFL test, I know that my typing skills will be valuable because I will be able to concentrate on what I want to say instead of getting anxious about finding the keyboard characters. I also feel confident about being able to complete the task in the given time considering the speed at which I can type.

Step 6 Follow these steps to set a realistic goal to attain while preparing for the TOEFL test.

a. Time yourself as you read the corrected transcript above at your normal speaking speed. How many seconds did it take you to read the speech? _____
b. Time yourself as you read the speech aloud again. This time, stop when 45 seconds have passed. How far did you get? Line _____

c. How many of the examples do you think the person who gave this speech would be able to discuss in 45 seconds? Remember, the speaker would have made natural hesitations and speaking mistakes. Eliminate unnecessary examples and details.

Exercises S14–S18

Use Exercises S14–S18 to develop your skills in choosing your topic for the personal preference task, planning your speech, and presenting it.

EXERCISE S14 *Choosing a topic for the personal preference task*

Read the following categories and quickly decide on a topic within each category that you could speak about comfortably. Do not take more than five seconds to decide.

hobbies	*stamp collecting*

1. sports ____________
2. animals ____________
3. food ____________
4. courses ____________
5. teachers ____________

EXERCISE S15 *Restating the task and defining your choice*

Read the following tasks. Quickly decide on a topic for each. Record your restatement of the task to include the topic of your speech. Add a definition if you think your listeners might not understand.

> You read and hear:
>
> Name a hobby you have and explain why it is important to you. Include details and examples to support your explanation.
>
> You say:
>
> *I like to work on cryptic crossword puzzles because the clues are a challenge. Cryptic crossword puzzles are crosswords that have special clues instead of just straightforward synonyms like most crossword puzzles.*

START ▶

1. Name a teacher who has influenced you and explain why that teacher was important. Include details and examples to support your explanation.
2. Describe a class you have taken and explain why that class was important to you. Include details and examples to support your explanation.

STOP ■

EXERCISE S16 *Sequencing ideas for personal experiences*

Take 10 seconds to consider the details and examples you want to discuss about the topics you chose in Exercise S15. Think about how those details and examples should be ordered. You will not have time to write them down. Record those points in your speech. An example is shown below. It is based on the example in Exercise S15.

Your topic:
Cryptic crossword puzzles

You think:
Clues that challenge me
Anagrams
Homophones
Double meanings
Symbols

You say:
When I am working on a puzzle, I get very involved in breaking the code. For example, the clue may have a word like crazy *or* fractured, *which could mean that a neighboring word is an anagram of the word I'm looking for. The word* say *might mean the answer has the same pronunciation as a word with a different meaning and spelling, like* horse *and* hoarse. *Sometimes the clue contains two different meanings for the answer. There are also symbols that might be used. For instance, the word* five *might mean that I need to use the letter* v *because of the Roman numeral for* five.

SPEAKING

EXERCISE S17 *Making a concluding statement*

To complete your speech, you can conclude by tying in your introductory statement with the details and examples you have included. Take a few seconds to think of a concluding statement. Record a concluding statement for the tasks you started in Exercise S15 and continued in Exercise S16.

I find great satisfaction in breaking the codes in cryptic puzzles. But it is really great for me if I manage to complete an entire puzzle.

EXERCISE S18 *Putting it all together*

Practice planning speeches using the tasks that have already been presented, but choose different topics to speak about. Record your speeches. Don't worry about the time limit at first. Gradually work up to completing the task within the time limit.

START ▶

1. Name a skill you have learned and explain why it is important to you. Include details and examples to support your explanation.
2. Name a hobby you have and explain why it is important to you. Include details and examples to support your explanation.
3. Name a person who has influenced you and explain why that influence was important. Include details and examples to support your explanation.

4. Describe a class you have taken and explain why that class was important to you. Include details and examples to support your explanation.

STOP ■

PRACTICE WITH ANALYZING YOUR RESPONSES

Keep the following list of questions in mind as you analyze your responses to the independent speaking tasks:

1. Is the pronunciation in the speech easy to understand?
2. Does the intonation in the speech sound natural?
3. Does the speech show control of a variety of grammatical structures?
4. Has the word choice been effective?
5. Is the speech coherent?
6. Do the details and examples support the chosen topic?
7. Has the speech been completed within the allotted time?

Exercise S19 Use Exercise S19 to practice analyzing and scoring your responses to independent speaking tasks.

EXERCISE S19 *Analyzing and scoring your responses*

Listen to your recorded responses from Exercise S18. Check the list above to see whether you have met the requirements of the independent speaking tasks. Give each response a score and state why you decided on that score.

- A score of 4 is for a response that meets all the requirements.
- A score of 3 indicates that the speech was appropriate but was weak in some of the areas mentioned in the list.
- A score of 2 indicates some difficulties in clarity of speaking, a limited range of grammar and vocabulary, or a lack of organization of ideas.
- A score of 1 indicates a lack of clarity in speech, a very limited range of vocabulary, and a lack of ideas to support the topic.
- A score of 0 is given when no attempt has been made, or when the attempt does not address the task.

1. Score _____ Reasons ______________________________
2. Score _____ Reasons ______________________________
3. Score _____ Reasons ______________________________
4. Score _____ Reasons ______________________________

Strategies to Use for the Personal Choice Task

1. Listen carefully to the question and think about what you must do in your response.
Ask yourself these questions:
- What are the two situations or actions presented?
- Which one do I prefer and why?

Then make a mental list of the answers to these questions. For example, look at the following task:

> Some students prefer to do group projects. Other students prefer to do individual projects. Which kind of projects do you think produce more learning and why?

For this task, you would make a mental list like the following:

The question concerns group projects versus individual projects. I need to:
- State my choice
- Defend my choice with reasons, details, and examples

2. Quickly make your choice.
It is easy to run out of time while trying to decide which position you are going to take, especially if you can see the advantages of both options you have been given. Quickly choose one of the two, and start thinking about examples and details you can use in order to defend the preference you have chosen. Remember, examiners are not interested in the position you choose but in how well you can express yourself in defending it.

3. Restate the question to include the topic and your preference.
The task in Strategy 1 above is about the effectiveness of two different ways of working. If you chose to focus on the benefits of working on projects individually rather than in groups, you might say:

> *While many students prefer to work as a group on projects, I think that individual projects benefit more students.*

4. Work through your list of requirements.
For the task in Strategy 1 above, your list might be:
- State your position – this is your restatement of the task topic.
- Defend your choice with reasons, details, and examples from your own experience.

5. Know your goal.
When studying, record your speech and make a transcript, writing it exactly as you said it. Then make improvements to it, correct mistakes, eliminate long hesitations, and replace words or rephrase sentences to avoid repetition. Practice reading the corrected version aloud, and time yourself. Read it again while timing yourself, and stop reading at 45 seconds. How far did you get?

You will find that 45 seconds is only enough time for you to restate the task with your choice and to give one or two reasons and one or two details for your choice. Eliminate unnecessary reasons and details from your transcript and read it again with a timer. Once you have eliminated enough to be able to read your response aloud in about 35 – 40 seconds, and the topic does not suffer from a lack of reasons or detail, you know your goal. The remaining 5 – 10 seconds are for the natural hesitations and corrections a speaker generally makes when talking.

6. Get ready for the next item.
It is easy to get anxious if you run out of time and have not finished what you intended to say, or if you finish what you want to say and there is still time left. Take a deep breath to help you relax and to get ready for the next part of the test.

PRACTICE WITH THE PERSONAL CHOICE TASK

Preparing to give a timed response

The exercises that follow this section prepare you step by step for giving a timed response to the personal choice task in the speaking portion of the TOEFL test. In the personal choice task, you have 15 seconds to choose between two given alternatives and to plan how you are going to introduce the topic, present the ideas, and conclude the speech. Then you have 45 seconds to give your speech.

Study the task and the steps outlined in the example below. As you prepare for this portion of the test, you will practice these steps to build your skills and lessen the time it takes you to give a complete response.

Task

Some students prefer to do group projects. Other students prefer to do individual projects. Which kind of projects do you think produce more learning and why?

Step 1 Ask yourself what the topic is and what you are being asked to do.

The question concerns group projects versus individual projects. I need to:

- State my choice
- Defend my choice with reasons, details, and examples

Step 2 Make your choice and quickly think of a few reasons and details.

Topic:	individual projects
Reasons, details, and examples:	full responsibility for project, learn more, scheduling easier

Step 3 Work through your list of requirements. Record your speech.

- State your choice.

  While many students prefer to work as a group on projects, I think that individual projects benefit more students.

- Defend your choice with reasons, details, and examples from your own experience.

  I consider individual projects to be better for learning for several reasons. One is, it is too easy for one or more of the group members to not be, uh, to be inactive and allow the better . . . the more capable member or members to do the work. When people are working on a . . . an individual project they cannot leave it to the more capable members to complete, but take, or . . . must take the responsibility of doing the work themselves. Their inactivity has roots in not knowing how to proceed and that those members who know, uh . . . with the know-how can act like private tutors. However, it is more often that the ones who understand the project the best just, just take over the work.

  By doing an individual project, the person not only learns how to tackle the work, but also learns the content of the project. Um, next is, uh, it is almost impossible to schedule a meeting time that works, that is suitable for everyone. This is not a problem when the students are working on individual projects. Third, teacher feedback on an individual project is good for . . . beneficial to . . . the individual. Feedback on a group project may be irrelevant for some of the individuals involved in a group project. And then, uh, finally, a student working on his own learns more in his own time, and the given feedback is relevant.

The following is an outline of the reasons and examples in the above speech.

Reason 1: Can't be an inactive group member
  Defense – must learn how to plan the project
  Defense – learns the material of the project

Reason 2: Scheduling meeting times
  Defense – no time is convenient for all
  Defense – scheduling is not an issue for the individual

Reason 3: Getting feedback
  Defense – feedback is relevant to the individual

Step 4 Make a transcript of your speech, as shown above.

Step 5 Make corrections to your speech, eliminating mistakes, long hesitations, self-corrections, or repetitions.

While many students prefer to work as a group on projects, I think that individual projects benefit more students. I consider individual projects to be better for learning for several reasons. First, it is too easy for one or more of the group members to be inactive and allow the more capable member or members to do the work. When people are working on an individual project, they cannot leave it to the more capable members to complete, but must take the responsibility of doing the work themselves. It could be argued that their inactivity has roots in their not knowing how to proceed and that those members with more know-how can act like private tutors. However, it is more often the case that the ones who understand the project the best just take over the work. By doing an individual project, the individual not only learns how to tackle the project work, but also learns the content of the project. Second, it is almost impossible to schedule a meeting time that is suitable for everyone. This is not a problem when the students are working on individual projects. Third, teacher feedback on an individual project is beneficial to the individual. Feedback on a group project may be irrelevant for some of the individuals involved in a group project. In conclusion, a student working on his or her own learns more in his or her own time and the given feedback is relevant to that particular person's development.

Step 6 Follow these steps to set a realistic goal to attain while preparing for the TOEFL test.

a. Time yourself as you read the corrected transcript above at your normal speaking speed. How many seconds did it take you to read the speech? _____
b. Time yourself as you read the speech aloud again. This time, stop when 45 seconds have passed. How far did you get in the speech? Line _____
c. How many of the examples do you think the person who gave this speech would be able to discuss in 45 seconds? Remember, the speaker would have made natural hesitations and speaking mistakes. Eliminate unnecessary examples and details.

Other ways to organize your speech

The pattern shown above for organizing your ideas is a simple, straightforward way to plan your response to the personal choice task. However, you might want to compare or contrast the two choices. There are two basic patterns that you can use to compare the two choices and indicate your preference. If you choose to compare and contrast, it is important to choose only one of them. If you mix the two patterns, you will confuse your listeners.

All of one, then all of the other	**Point by point**
Topic statement	Topic statement
Option 1	Positive points
Positive points	Option 1
Negative points	Option 2
Option 2	Negative points
Positive points	Option 1
Negative points	Option 2
Concluding statement	Concluding statement

Exercises S20–S25

Use Exercises S20–S25 to develop your skills in making your choice, planning your speech, and presenting it.

EXERCISE S20 *Making a personal choice*

Look at the following choices and quickly decide which choice you could most easily defend. Do not take more than five seconds to decide.

cats or dogs as pets *dogs*

1. movies on TV or movies at the theater ____________
2. traditional food or exotic food ____________
3. outdoor sports or indoor sports ____________
4. city life or country life ____________
5. the sciences or the arts ____________

EXERCISE S21 🎧 *Restating the task and stating your position*

Read the following task. Quickly choose your preference. Record your restatement of the task to include the topic of your speech.

> You read and hear:
>
> Some people believe that students should immediately go on to college after completing high school. Others believe that students should take a year or more off between high school and college. Which approach do you think is better for students interested in getting a college degree? Include details and examples in your explanation.
>
> You say:
>
> *While many people believe students should go straight on to college after graduating from high school, I think that individuals benefit from time away from studying.*

START ▶

Some students would like to have a long vacation during the academic year. Other students would like to have several shorter vacations during the academic year. What is your preference and why? Include details and examples in your explanation.

STOP ■

EXERCISE S22 *Sequencing ideas for personal choices*

Take 10 seconds to think about the points you want to discuss for the preference you stated in Exercise S21. Think about how those points should be ordered. You will not have time to write them down. Record the points in a speech format. An example is shown below. It is based on the example in Exercise S21.

> You think:
>
> Benefits from waiting
> - Student burnout
> - Can think about what student wants to study
> - Can get a job
> - Money for studies
> - Learn responsibilities
> - Can travel
> - Gain experiences
> - Learn self-reliance
>
> You say:
>
> *First, many students are burned out after intense studying to pass the exams that will get them into college. After a break, they will be able to concentrate better. Second, many students are not really sure about what they want to study. They might have a better idea of their true goals as well as be more mature in approaching those goals after a year or so away from academic work. Finally, students can learn how to be responsible and gain self-reliance from either holding down a job or traveling. Both a job and traveling will also provide experiences that students can use to support their studies.*

EXERCISE S23 *Making a concluding statement*

To complete your speech, you can conclude by tying your introductory statement in with the points you have made. Take a few seconds to think of a concluding statement. Record a concluding statement for the task you started in Exercise S21 and continued in Exercise S22.

> *In conclusion, students can benefit from a break from studying if they use the time in a profitable way.*

EXERCISE S24 🎧 *Putting it all together*

Practice planning speeches using the tasks that have already been presented, but make a different choice or provide different supporting ideas. Record your speeches. Don't worry about the time limit at first. Gradually work up to completing the task within the time limit.

START ▶

1. Some students prefer to do group projects. Other students prefer to do individual projects. Which kind of projects do you think produce more learning and why?
2. Some people believe that students should immediately go on to college after completing high school. Others believe that students should take a year off between high school completion and starting college. Which approach do you think is better for students interested in getting a college degree? Include details and examples in your explanation.
3. Some students would like to have a long vacation during the academic year. Other students would like to have several shorter vacations during the academic year. What is your preference and why? Include details and examples in your explanation.

STOP ■

EXERCISE S25 *Analyzing and scoring your responses*

Listen to your taped responses from Exercise S24. Check the list in Practice with Analyzing Your Responses on p. 330 to see whether you have met the requirements of the independent speaking tasks. Give each response a score and state why you decided on that score.

- A score of 4 is for a response that meets all the requirements.
- A score of 3 indicates that the speech was appropriate but was weak in some of the areas mentioned in the list.
- A score of 2 indicates some difficulties in clarity of speaking, a limited range of grammar and vocabulary, or a lack of organization of ideas.
- A score of 1 indicates a lack of clarity in speech, a very limited range of vocabulary, and a lack of ideas to support the preference.
- A score of 0 is given when no attempt has been made or when the attempt does not address the task.

1. Score _____ Reasons ____
2. Score _____ Reasons ____
3. Score _____ Reasons ____

PRACTICING THE INDEPENDENT SPEAKING TASKS

Now that you have studied the process for responding to the independent tasks, review the steps below and practice more speaking tasks. Respond to the tasks in Exercise S26 below. Record your responses, analyze them, and score them.

1. Listen carefully to the task.
2. Decide what you must do in your response. Ask yourself these questions:
   - What personal preference or personal choice must I address?
   - What must I do to meet the requirements of the task?
3. Quickly decide on your topic.
4. Take 15 seconds to plan your introductory statement, the ideas you will present, and the concluding statement.
5. Give your speech.

EXERCISE S26 Use Exercise S26 to practice responding to independent speaking tasks.

EXERCISE S26 *Practice responding to independent speaking tasks*

Practice responding to the following independent speaking tasks. Try to prepare your response in 15 seconds and give your speech in 45 seconds. Record your speech and give it a score, using the list of questions in Practice with Analyzing Your Responses on p. 330 as a guide.

START ▶

Personal preference tasks

1. Name an academic subject that you like and explain why it attracts you. Include details and examples to support your explanation.
2. Describe a personal possession that is special to you and explain why it is important. Include details and examples to support your explanation.
3. Describe a feature of your city that you consider interesting and explain why you think it is interesting. Include details and examples to support your explanation.

Personal choice tasks

4. Some people prefer television programs that present serious issues. Other people prefer those that are for entertainment only. Which kind of program do you consider the most important for people to watch and why?
5. Some people prefer to focus their energy to excel in one activity. Other people prefer to participate in many different activities. Which method do you think is better for the development of a person's intellect and why?
6. Some people believe that children should begin their formal education at an early age (three to five years old). Other people believe that children should begin their formal education later (six to seven years old). Which age do you think is best for a child to begin a formal education and why?

STOP ■

For further practice, use the above tasks but choose a different topic or preference to support.

INTEGRATED SPEAKING TASKS

In the integrated speaking portion of the TOEFL iBT test, you will give a short speech based on a subject presented in a passage or passages. For the reading/listening/speaking tasks, you will read a short passage on a given topic, then listen to a speaker (or speakers) talk about the same topic. You will then see and hear a question. You will be asked to respond to the question by synthesizing and summarizing the information you have read and heard.

For the listening/speaking tasks, you will listen to a conversation or part of a lecture. You will then see and hear a question. You will be asked to respond to the question by summarizing the information you have heard. In some cases, you will be asked to summarize and then give your opinion about the information you heard.

An effective response begins with a statement that introduces the focus of the task. The body of the speech is made up of information that addresses the task using information from the passage or passages. A concluding statement completes the speech.

THE INTEGRATED READING/LISTENING/SPEAKING TASKS

Strategies to Use for the Integrated Reading/Listening/Speaking Tasks

1. Read the question carefully and make sure you understand the requirements of the task.

You will be asked to complete two integrated reading/listening/speaking tasks, one about a campus situation and the other about an academic subject. The campus situation task starts with a short reading passage that presents a campus-related problem. The listening passage that follows is a conversation that relates to or comments on the issue in the reading. You will be asked to show your understanding of the issue or problem by briefly summarizing the opinions presented in the listening passage based on the information given in the reading passage.

The academic task presents a concept, process, or idea in a short reading passage. The listening passage that follows is a short lecture that illustrates the concept or process with more specific examples and information. You will be asked to show your understanding of the topic by combining information from both passages and describing how the specific examples illustrate the broader concept or process.

2. Read the passage carefully and take notes.
The reading passage sets the context for the conversation or lecture. The main ideas stated in the reading will be needed to synthesize information from the conversation or lecture. You will have to use information from the reading passage in your response.

You will have 45 seconds to read the passage. You will not see the passage again. Take notes while you read so that you can remember the important points of the reading when you begin to speak.

3. Listen carefully to the conversation or lecture and take notes.
You will hear the listening passage only once. Take notes while you listen so that you can remember the important points and how they relate to the reading passage.

4. Read and listen carefully to the question. Consider the task and what it is asking you to do.
You will have 30 seconds to plan a response that addresses the task. A response that is not connected to the task will get a low score.

Ask yourself these questions:

- What is the topic I need to address?
- What am I being asked to do?
- How can I introduce my speech?

5. Look over your notes and plan your response.
You will have 30 seconds to plan your response. Compare your notes from the two passages and decide on the relevant information. You will not have time to write a response, and a written response would not show your natural speaking abilities. However, you will want to use your notes in order to refer to points made in the reading and listening passages.

6. Be familiar with the time limit.
Practice with a timer to get a sense of how much you can say in 60 seconds. On test day, pay attention to the timer on the screen to see how much time is left to make your points.

7. Get ready for the next item.
It is easy to get anxious if you run out of time and have not finished what you intended to say, or if you finish what you want to say and there is still time left. Take a deep breath to help you relax and get ready for the next part of the test.

Preparing to give a timed response

Study the steps and the example task on the pages that follow. You can use these steps to prepare for the reading/listening/speaking tasks. *Note:* The example task in this section does not contain a full-length reading or listening passage.

Step 1 Read the passage carefully and take notes.

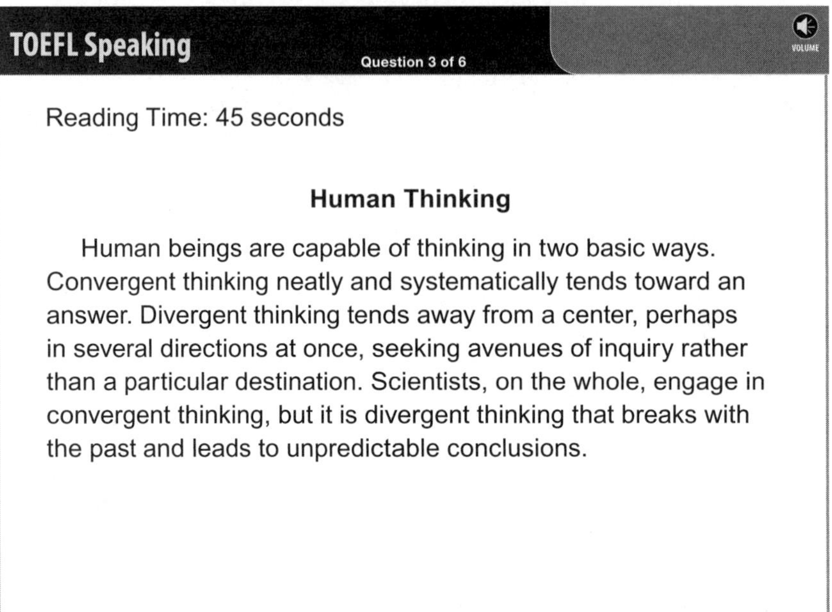

TOEFL Speaking
Question 3 of 6
VOLUME
Reading Time: 45 seconds
Human Thinking
Human beings are capable of thinking in two basic ways. Convergent thinking neatly and systematically tends toward an answer. Divergent thinking tends away from a center, perhaps in several directions at once, seeking avenues of inquiry rather than a particular destination. Scientists, on the whole, engage in convergent thinking, but it is divergent thinking that breaks with the past and leads to unpredictable conclusions.

Reading notes

Convergent thinking – neat, tends toward answer, scientists' thinking
Divergent thinking – several directions, unpredictable results

Step 2 Listen carefully to the conversation or lecture and take notes.

On your screen you will see a photograph of the speaker or speakers with a timer bar to indicate time elapsed. The photograph is to show the context only.

The idea of convergent and divergent thinking stems from the discovery that the hemispheres of the brain are specialized. The left side is more systematic and the right more creative. Obviously, since we have at our

disposal both hemispheres, we are all capable of both convergent and divergent thinking. However, supposedly we each have our favorite side, the one we use when we are not forced by circumstances to think using the other side. However, it is quite likely that when we encounter a problem we go back and forth between hemispheres, engaging in both convergent thinking on the left side and divergent thinking on the right side. Even though people favor one way or the other, there are exercises that supposedly increase one's ability to use both sides effectively.

Note: You will not see a transcript of the listening passage on the day of the test.

Listening notes

The brain hemispheres – specialized
Left side – systematic, convergent
Right side – creative, divergent
People favor one side but can use both in problem solving
Exercises to increase abilities

Step 3 Read and listen carefully to the question. Consider the task and what it is asking you to do.

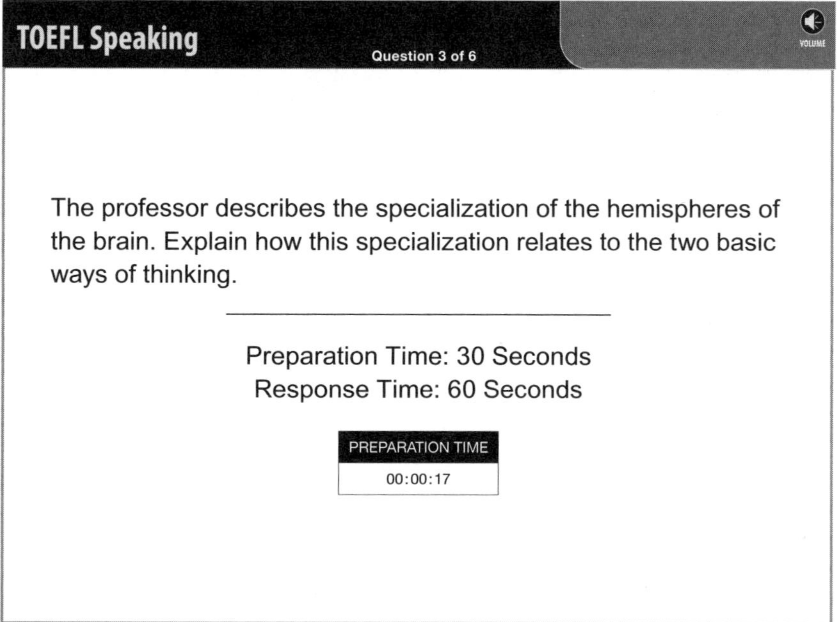

TOEFL Speaking
Question 3 of 6
VOLUME
The professor describes the specialization of the hemispheres of the brain. Explain how this specialization relates to the two basic ways of thinking.
Preparation Time: 30 Seconds
Response Time: 60 Seconds
PREPARATION TIME
00:00:17

Step 4 Ask yourself what the topic is and what you are being asked to do.

The topic concerns specialization of the brain hemispheres. I need to:

- Introduce the topic
- Explain the relationship between ways of thinking and brain specialization
- Finish with a concluding statement

Step 5 Look over your notes and plan your response.

Reading notes	**Listening notes**
Convergent thinking – neat, tends toward answer, scientists' thinking *Divergent thinking – several directions, unpredictable results*	*The brain hemispheres – specialized* *Left side – systematic, convergent* *Right side – creative, divergent* *People favor one side but can use both in problem solving* *Exercises to increase abilities*

Step 6 Record your speech. Be familiar with the time limit.

You will have 60 seconds to give your speech. Study the following example response. *Note:* The example below does not contain a full-length response, and the natural speech features (hesitations, corrections, etc.) have been taken out for easier analysis.

The two kinds of thinking discussed are convergent and divergent thinking. These kinds of thinking are related to how the hemispheres of the brain are specialized. One side of the brain – the left side – is more systematic, and this is where convergent thinking occurs. The other side of the brain is more creative, and this is where divergent thinking occurs. The professor indicates that people probably use both sides of the brain when thinking about a problem, but that if they aren't trying to solve a problem, they think with their favorite side. People can do exercises that improve their ability to use both sides of their brains well.

Step 7 Learn to give a response within the time limit.

Follow steps 4–6 on pp. 333–334 to help you learn to give a good response within the specified time frame.

The following analysis of the above example response can also help you set an attainable goal for yourself while preparing for the integrated reading/listening/speaking tasks.

Introductory statements The response begins with a restatement of the task – the two kinds of thinking – and indicates that the speaker is going to talk about how this relates to the specialization of the brain hemispheres.

Ideas and details in the body of the speech

- left hemisphere is used for systematic thinking or convergent thinking
- right hemisphere is used for creative thinking or divergent thinking
- people can use both sides of the brain for problem solving
- people favor one side

Conclusion The response is completed with the point that exercises improve a person's ability to use both kinds of thinking.

PRACTICE WITH THE CAMPUS SITUATION TASK

In the campus situation task, you will have 30 seconds to plan how you are going to introduce the topic, present the ideas, and conclude the speech. Then you will have 60 seconds to give your speech.

First, a narrator will introduce the context or setting. This is followed by a reading passage that discusses a problem or issue related to campus life. Then you will listen to a conversation in which two people give opinions about that problem or issue. After the conversation, the narrator will state the speaking task.

Exercises S27–S31

Use Exercises S27–S31 to practice the steps for responding to a question that relates to a reading and a conversation. *Note:* The skill-building exercises are not full length.

EXERCISE S27 *Identifying important points in a reading passage*

Read the passage, and write the important points on the lines below.

START ▶

An announcement about a change in one of the University of the Rockies courses is posted on the classroom door. You have 45 seconds to read the announcement. Begin reading now.

STOP ■

Reading Time: 45 seconds

Due to a sudden emergency, Professor Blake's Course 101 – Survey of American Literature – class will not be held this semester. Registered students are encouraged to join Course 104 – Literature of Minority Groups – held in Room 345 at the same time. Arrangements for your attendance have already been made. If you do not want to attend this course, go to the Registrar's Office to complete the drop/add procedure.

____

____

____

EXERCISE S28 *Identifying important points in a conversation*

Listen to the conversation that relates to the reading in Exercise S27. Write down the important points. Keep track of each speaker's opinion.

START ▶

Now listen to two students as they discuss the announcement.

Man's points:	Woman's points:
______________	______________
______________	______________
______________	______________
______________	______________
______________	______________

STOP ■

SPEAKING

EXERCISE S29 🎧 *Analyzing the task that relates to the conversation*

Listen to the task that relates to the reading in Exercise S27 and the conversation in Exercise S28. Think about what you will need to do in your response. Although you will not have time to write notes for your response on the day of the test, you may want to practice writing them in this exercise.

START ▶

The woman expresses her opinion about the course replacement. State her opinion and explain the reasons she gives for that opinion.

STOP ■

I need to:

1. state the topic ____________________
2. state the woman's opinion ____________________
3. state her reasons for the opinion ____________________

____

EXERCISE S30 *Planning your speech*

Think through the following steps. Take as much time as you need to prepare in this exercise. As you work through other exercises, try to gradually shorten your preparation time to 30 seconds.

1. Plan your introduction using the information from the reading in Exercise S27, the speaker's opinion in Exercise S28, and the task requirements in Exercise S29.
2. Use the notes you took in Exercises S27 and S28 to help you plan your response to the task.
3. Plan a concluding statement to complete the task.

EXERCISE S31 *Recording your speech*

Give the speech you planned in Exercise S30. Record your speech so you can analyze and evaluate it.

PRACTICE WITH THE ACADEMIC TASK

In the academic task, you will have 30 seconds to plan how you are going to introduce the topic, present the ideas, and conclude the speech. Then you will have 60 seconds to give your speech.

A narrator will introduce the context of the reading passage. The reading passage presents information on an academic topic. Then you will listen to part of a lecture that relates to the reading topic. After the lecture, the narrator will state the speaking task.

Exercises S32–S36

Use Exercises S32–S36 to practice the steps for responding to a question that relates to a reading and a lecture: *Note:* The skill-building exercises are not full length.

EXERCISE S32 *Identifying important points in a reading passage*

Read the passage and write down the important points on the lines below.

START ▶

Now read a passage about an incident leading up to the American War of Independence. You have 45 seconds to read the passage. Begin reading now.

STOP ■

Reading Time: 45 seconds

The Boston Tea Party of 1773 was not a tea party at all, but the first major act of defiance on the part of the American colonists against their British rulers. The British Parliament under King George III had imposed taxes on the colonies. A party of prominent citizens disguised themselves as Native Americans and secretly boarded ships that were laden with tea. They then threw the entire cargo of tea overboard. This incident was a prelude to the American War of Independence.

____

____

____

____

____

____

EXERCISE S33 *Identifying important points in a lecture*

Listen to a lecture that relates to the reading in Exercise S32. Write down the important points.

START ▶

Now listen to part of a lecture on the background to the American War of Independence.

____

____

____

____

____

____

STOP ■

EXERCISE S34 🎧 *Analyzing the task that relates to the lecture*

Listen to the task. Think about what you will need to do in your response. Although you won't have time to write your analysis in the test, you may want to practice writing it in this exercise.

START ▶

The professor gives the background information about the incident that was the prelude to the American War of Independence. Explain how the events were related to the colonists' behavior.

STOP ■

I need to:

1. state the topic ______________________________
2. state the events ______________________________
3. state the relationship ______________________________

____

EXERCISE S35 *Planning your speech*

Think through the following steps. Take as much time as you need in this exercise. As you work through other exercises, try to gradually shorten your preparation time to 30 seconds.

1. Plan your introduction using the information in the reading in Exercise S32, the lecture in Exercise S33, and the task requirements in Exercise S34.
2. Use the notes you took in Exercises S32 and S33 to help you plan your response to the task.
3. Plan a concluding statement.

EXERCISE S36 *Recording your speech*

Give the speech you planned in Exercise S35. Record your speech so you can analyze and evaluate it.

PRACTICE WITH ANALYZING YOUR RESPONSES

Keep the following list of questions in mind as you analyze your responses to the reading/listening/speaking tasks:

1. Is the pronunciation in the speech easy to understand?
2. Does the intonation in the speech sound natural?
3. Does the speech show control of a variety of grammatical structures?
4. Has the word choice been effective?
5. Is the speech coherent?
6. Are the ideas from the reading and listening passages well organized?
7. Have the main ideas been presented?
8. Have the appropriate supporting details been used?
9. Does the response paraphrase the ideas and details accurately?
10. Has the speech been completed within the allotted time?

Exercise S37 Use Exercise S37 to develop your skills in analyzing your responses to the reading/listening/speaking tasks.

EXERCISE S37 *Analyzing and scoring your responses*

Listen to your taped responses from Exercise S31 and Exercise S36. Check the list in Practice with Analyzing Your Responses, p. 346, to see whether you have met the requirements of the reading/listening/speaking tasks. Give each response a score and state why you decided on that score.

- A score of 4 is for a response that meets all the requirements.
- A score of 3 indicates that the speech was appropriate but was weak in some of the areas mentioned in the list.
- A score of 2 shows some difficulties in clarity of speaking. Inaccurate information may have been presented, or essential information from the reading or listening may be missing.
- A score of 1 is for a speech that meets only a few of the requirements.
- A score of 0 is given when no attempt has been made or the attempt does not address the task.

1. Score _____ Reasons ____

2. Score _____ Reasons ____

PRACTICING THE INTEGRATED READING/LISTENING/ SPEAKING TASKS

Now that you have studied the approach for responding to the integrated reading/listening/speaking tasks, review the six steps outlined in Preparing to Give a Timed Response, pp. 339 – 342, and practice more speaking tasks. Respond to the tasks in Exercise S38. Record your responses and score them.

Exercise S38 Use Exercise S38 to develop your skills in responding to the reading/listening/speaking tasks.

EXERCISE S38 *Responding to the integrated reading/listening/speaking tasks*

Give yourself 45 seconds to read each passage. Then you will hear a conversation or lecture. Try to prepare your response in 30 seconds and give your speech in 60 seconds. Record your speech and give it a score according to the checklist in Practice with Analyzing Your Responses on p. 346 and the guidelines in Exercise S37 above. The screens in the first item appear as they will on the actual test.

START ▶

1. The University of the Rockies is planning to tear down a building on campus. Read the announcement about the demolition of the building. You have 45 seconds to read the announcement. Begin reading now.

PAUSE II (for 45 seconds)

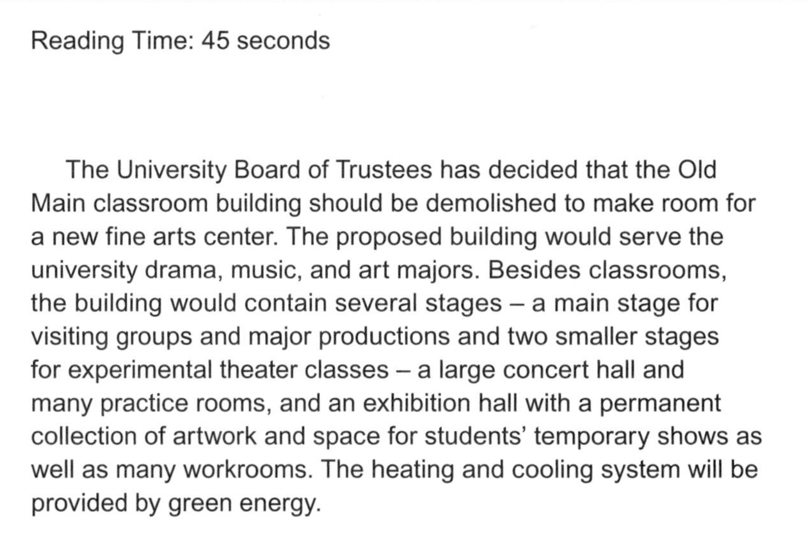

Now listen to two students as they discuss the announcement.

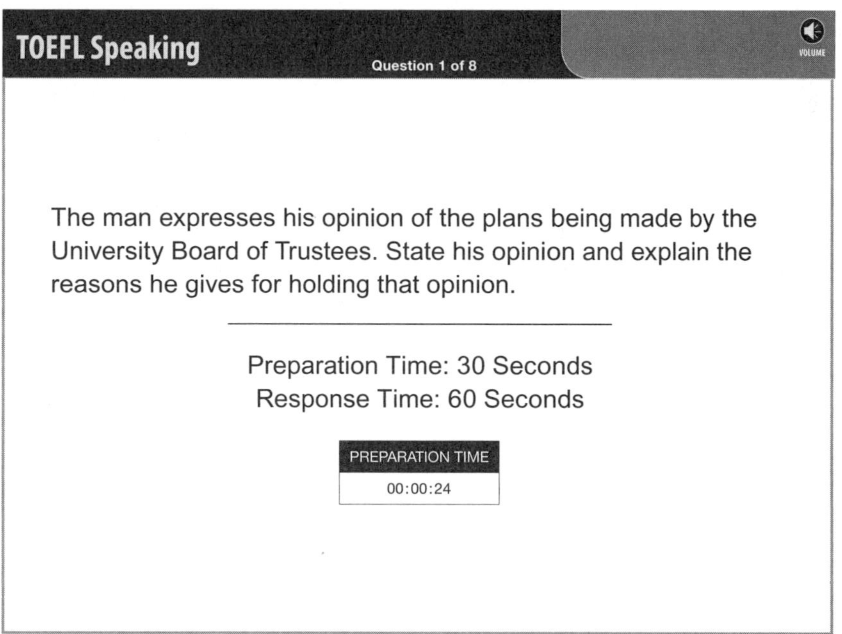

TOEFL Speaking
Question 1 of 8
VOLUME
The man expresses his opinion of the plans being made by the University Board of Trustees. State his opinion and explain the reasons he gives for holding that opinion.
Preparation Time: 30 Seconds
Response Time: 60 Seconds
PREPARATION TIME
00:00:24

2. The Medical Faculty has announced that a guest speaker will be giving a talk. Read the announcement about the talk. You have 45 seconds to read the announcement. Begin reading now.

   Reading Time: 45 seconds

   As part of the "Endeavor Toward Health" workshop sponsored by the Medical Faculty, Dr. James Filbert from the Monterey Health Organization will be presenting a lecture titled "Living with Restless Leg Syndrome" at 2:00 p.m. in the campus auditorium. This illness is frequently misdiagnosed because of the difficulties its sufferers have describing their pain. The fact that it tends to be found within families indicates an underlying genetic cause. Dr. Filbert will be discussing the symptoms of Restless Leg Syndrome and ways to alleviate the pain. The public is invited to attend.

   Now listen to two students as they discuss the announcement.

The woman explains her interest in listening to the guest lecturer. State her interest and explain the problems surrounding the syndrome.

3. The University of the Rockies is planning to make a change in the number of required courses in physical education. Read the president's quote, taken from his interview with a reporter from the student newspaper. Begin reading now.

   Reading Time: 45 seconds

   "The reality is that physical education courses are not considered to be essential by students themselves, who resent having so many required courses when they want to concentrate on their major subject. This requirement almost seems like a continuation of high school requirements. We believe that students should take responsibility for their own physical condition. Money saved from reducing the number of physical education courses offered will be useful in updating our science and computer labs, as well as going toward more acquisitions for the library."

   Now listen to two students as they discuss the quote.

   The woman expresses her opinion of what the president was quoted to have said to the reporter. State her opinion and explain the reasons she gives for holding that opinion.

4. The Maintenance Department has announced that the main classroom building will be undergoing some changes. Read the announcement about the renovation. You have 45 seconds to read the announcement. Begin reading now.

Reading Time: 45 seconds

During the summer session, classes will be held in the geology complex while the main classroom building is being renovated. When the renovation is completed, each room will be equipped with state-of-the-art equipment, such as computers that will allow teachers to project their lecture notes and supporting data onto a screen. Some of the classrooms will be turned into multimedia labs. Although the building has already been made accessible for the disabled, further improvements will be made to provide even better access to all classrooms. Motion sensors will be installed that turn lights on and off to conserve energy.

Now listen to two students as they discuss the announcement.

The woman expresses her opinion of the announcement made by the University's Maintenance Department. State her opinion and explain the reasons she gives for holding that opinion.

5. Now read the passage about marine organisms known as phytoplankton. You will have 45 seconds to read the passage. Begin reading now.

   Reading Time: 45 seconds

   Inhabiting the photic zone, that upper layer of water where sunlight penetrates the world's oceans, phytoplankton provide the basis of almost all marine life. Found in greater abundance near land masses where there is a concentration of nutrients in the water, these single-celled plants enrich the food chain. Sunlight provides them with the energy needed for photosynthesis, turning the phosphates and nitrates in the water and carbon dioxide from the atmosphere into the molecules that they live on. The by-product of photosynthesis is oxygen. It is estimated that 75 percent of the world's oxygen is produced by phytoplankton. Phytoplankton usually go unnoticed until physical conditions cause some species to bloom, a phenomenon known as the red tide.

   Now listen to part of a lecture on ocean plants in a marine biology class.

   The professor describes an experiment done on phytoplankton. Explain how the implications of this experiment relate to phytoplankton.

6. Now read the passage about road management. You will have 45 seconds to read the passage. Begin reading now.

Reading Time: 45 seconds

Road signs and markings are a ubiquitous feature of towns and cities around the world. The purpose of this system is to ensure the safety of both drivers and pedestrians by separating them and by controlling traffic speed and flow. Drivers are obligated to restrict their speed, follow directions, and park and stop only in designated areas. Pedestrians are further protected by raised sidewalks from which motor traffic is restricted. At road intersections motor vehicle movement is strictly managed by traffic lights and road markings. The requirement of road users to obey road markings, signs, and signals is backed up by legal sanctions leveled against those who ignore the traffic rules.

Now listen to part of a lecture in a civil engineering class.

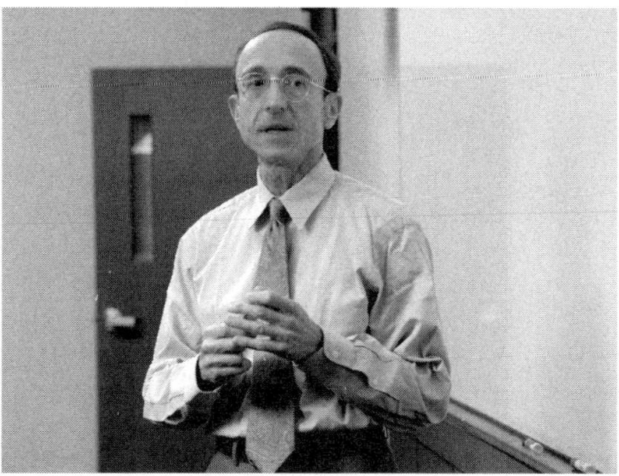

The professor describes an experimental system of road management. Explain how this experiment is related to road users' behavior.

7. Now read the passage about cultural perceptions of time. You will have 45 seconds to read the passage. Begin reading now.

   Reading Time: 45 seconds

   Time can be regarded as neither a biological nor a physical absolute but as a cultural invention. Different cultures have differing perceptions about the passage of time. At opposing ends of the spectrum are the "monochronic," or linear, cultures and the "polychronic," or simultaneous, cultures. In monochronic societies, schedules and routines are primary. Monochronic societies tend to be more efficient and impartial. However, they may be blind to the humanity of their members. In polychronic societies, people take precedence over schedules. People are rarely alone, even at home, and are usually dealing with several people at once. Time and schedules are not priorities.

   Now listen to part of a lecture in a cultural studies class.

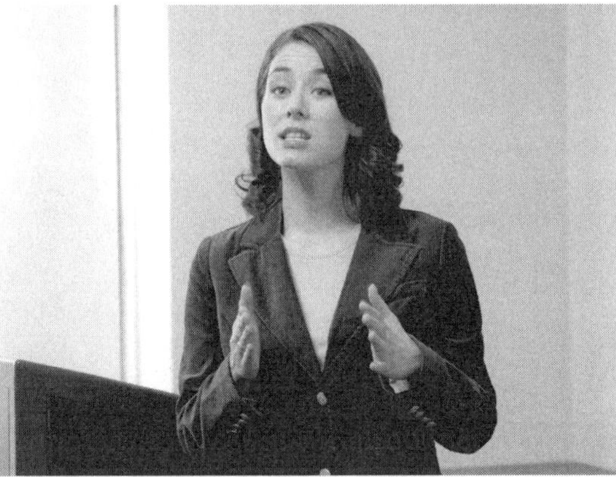

   The professor describes the behavior of monochronic and polychronic people. Explain how their behavior is related to their suitability in the workplace.

8. Now read the passage about weathering. You have 45 seconds to read the passage. Begin reading now.

   Reading Time: 45 seconds

   The weathering of rocks refers to a breakdown due to the exposure to atmospheric elements. Weathering is different from erosion in that in weathering, there is no movement of material. Weathering processes are generally classified into three groups: mechanical, chemical, and biological. Mechanical processes such as the freeze-thaw cycle of water can shatter rocks. A chemical process occurs when rain causes a chemical reaction with the minerals in the rock. Biological processes refer to processes that are caused by organisms. An analysis of a rock and the way it has weathered can provide the geologist with information about the processes that were or are taking place in any given area.

   Now listen to part of a lecture on weathering in a geology class.

   The professor describes climatic conditions. Explain how these conditions relate to different weathering processes.

STOP ■

THE INTEGRATED LISTENING/SPEAKING TASKS

Strategies to Use for the Integrated Listening/Speaking Tasks

1. Read the question carefully and make sure you understand the requirements of the task.
You will be asked to complete two integrated listening/speaking tasks, one about a campus situation and the other about an academic subject. The campus situation task presents a student-related problem and possible solutions. You will be asked to show your understanding of the problem by summarizing it and to give your opinion about how it should be solved.

SPEAKING

The academic task presents a term or a concept within an academic lecture. Examples and details within the lecture illustrate the topic. You will be asked to show your understanding of the topic by summarizing the lecture and describing how the examples relate to the topic discussed.

2. Listen carefully to the conversation or lecture and take notes.
The conversation or lecture passages are longer than those in the integrated reading/listening/speaking task. The conversation is between two students, between a student and an employee of the university, or between a student and a faculty member. The lecture is about an academic topic. Take notes as you listen so that you can remember the important points.

3. Read and listen carefully to the question. Consider the task and what it is asking you to do.
You will have 20 seconds to plan a response that addresses the task. A response that is not connected to the task will get a low score.

Ask yourself these questions:
- What is the topic I need to address?
- What am I being asked to do?
- How can I introduce my speech?

4. Look over your notes and plan your response.
You will have 20 seconds to plan your response. You will not have time to write a response, and a written response would not show your natural speaking abilities. However, you will want to follow your notes in order to refer to the points made in the listening passage.

5. Be familiar with the time limit.
Practice with a timer to get a sense of how much you can say in 60 seconds. On test day, pay attention to the timer on the screen to see how much time is left to make your points.

6. Get ready for the next item.
It is easy to get anxious if you have run out of time and not finished what you intended to say, or if you have finished what you want to say and there is still time left. Take a deep breath to help you relax and to get ready for the next part of the test.

Preparing to give a timed response

Study the steps and the example below. You can use these steps to prepare for the listening/speaking tasks. *Note:* The example task in this section does not contain a full-length listening passage.

Step 1 Listen carefully to the conversation or lecture and take notes.

On your screen you will see a photograph of the speaker or speakers with a timer bar to indicate time elapsed. The photograph is to show the context only.

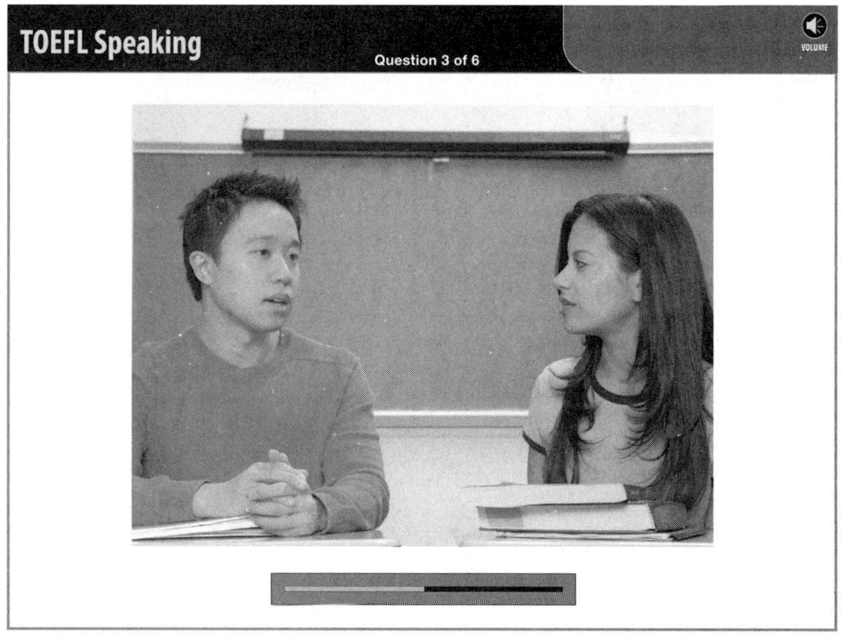

(man) *When are you giving your presentation?*

(woman) *I'm on for next week.*

(man) *Next week? You must have been late signing up.*

(woman) *No, actually I signed up to give it early. I wanted to get it out of the way so that I could sit back and enjoy the other presentations without the thought lurking in my mind that I still had to face giving one.*

(man) *That's a thought, but I would feel pressed for time. I'd like to get a feel for how the presentations are going and what kind of feedback the professor gives. You know, get a feel for what he's looking for.*

(woman) *Yeah, but at the beginning of the term, you have more time to work on it. You know what I mean?*

(man) *Not really. I mean, you have two weeks to prepare, and I have two months.*

(woman) *That's what you think. You'll probably put off preparing until a week before you have to give your presentation, so the amount of time we have is the same. Besides, later in the semester, you have all the work in your other courses, whereas at the beginning of the semester, the workload tends to be lighter. I mean, the big papers and projects are usually due closer to the end of the semester.*

Note: You will not see a transcript of the listening passage on the day of the test.

Listening notes

Man: more time is better; feedback from professor
Woman: early presentation better; more time at beginning of term

Step 2 Read and listen carefully to the question. Consider the task and what it is asking you to do.

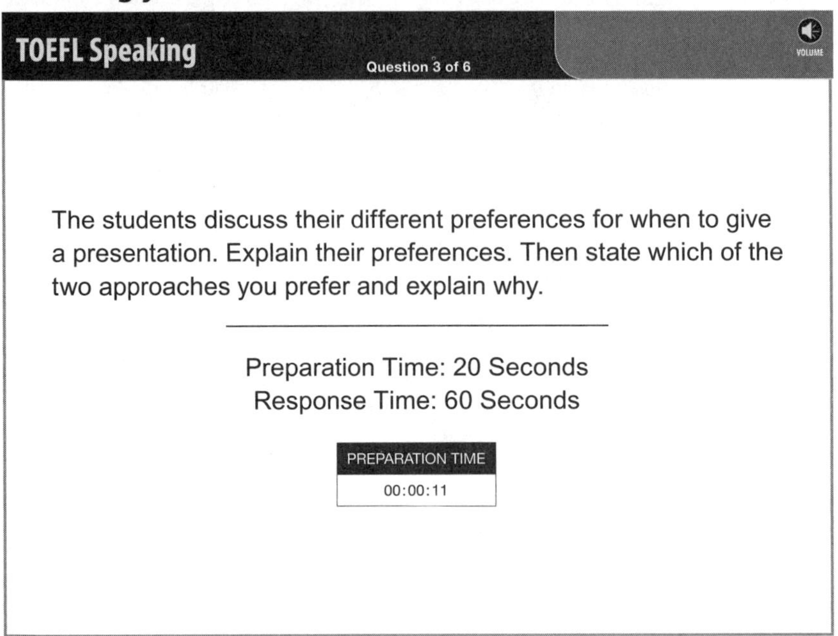
TOEFL Speaking
Question 3 of 6
VOLUME
The students discuss their different preferences for when to give a presentation. Explain their preferences. Then state which of the two approaches you prefer and explain why.
Preparation Time: 20 Seconds
Response Time: 60 Seconds
PREPARATION TIME
00:00:11

Step 3 Ask yourself what the topic is and what you are being asked to do.

The topic concerns the best time during a semester to give a presentation. I need to:

- Introduce the topic
- Explain the two students' preferences
- State my own preference
- Finish with a concluding statement

Step 4 Look over your notes and plan your response.

Man	**Woman**
prefers presentation later because: *1. prepare based on professor's comments to others* *2. have more time*	*prefers presentation early because:* *1. can do work early and then relax through the rest of semester* *2. less work from other courses*

Step 5 Record your speech. Be familiar with the time limit.

You will have 60 seconds to give your speech. Study the following example response. *Note:* The example below does not contain a full-length response, and the natural speech features (hesitations, corrections, etc.) have been taken out for easier analysis.

The students are discussing the problem of the best time of the semester to give a presentation. The woman prefers to do hers early in the semester and the man later. Like the man, I would prefer to give my presentation later in the semester, but not too close to the end. I think the professor's feedback to other students would determine how I organize my presentation and that my presentation would be better because of that knowledge. I would also feel more comfortable giving a presentation after I get to know my classmates better. Furthermore, it would be good to see what kind of questions my classmates ask so that I can prepare to answer them. I agree with the woman that there might be conflicts between the amount of time to prepare the presentation and the amount of time that must be spent on other coursework. However, if I am careful about budgeting my time, I can complete the task without worrying about those conflicts. The woman is correct in that it will be difficult to relax when I listen to the other presentations until I no longer have my presentation to think about. After considering the woman's points, I would still follow the man's solution of waiting and learning.

Step 6 Learn to give a response within the time limit.

Follow steps 4–6 on pp. 333 – 334 to help you learn to give a good response within the specified time frame. The following analysis of the above example response can also help you to set an attainable goal for yourself while preparing for the TOEFL test.

Introductory statement The response begins with a restatement of the preferences being discussed by the two students – the best time during the semester to givc a presentation.

Ideas and details in the body of the speech:

- Woman prefers early
- Man prefers later
- Speaker agrees with man
- Speakers present reasons for preference
- Includes the opinions of the two people in the listening passage
- Adds more reasons in the explanation for why he/she prefers one solution over the other solution

Conclusion The response is completed with a restatement of the speaker's preference for the man's solution.

PRACTICE WITH THE CAMPUS SITUATION TASK

In the campus situation task, you will have 20 seconds to plan your response and 60 seconds to speak.

A narrator will set the context for the campus situation conversation. The language in the conversation may be informal and will concern issues that face many university students. After you hear a discussion between two people, the narrator will state the speaking task. You will need to use the points made in the discussion to complete the task.

Exercises S39–S42

Use Exercises S39–S42 to practice the steps for developing a speech that relates to information from a conversation. *Note:* The skill-building exercises are not full length.

EXERCISE S39 🎧 *Identifying important points in a conversation*

Listen to the conversation and write the important points. Keep track of each speaker's opinion.

START ▶

Now listen to a conversation between two students.

Man's points:	Woman's points:
______________________	______________________
______________________	______________________
______________________	______________________
______________________	______________________
______________________	______________________

STOP ■

EXERCISE S40 🎧 *Analyzing the task that relates to the conversation*

Listen to the task you must respond to. Think about what you will need to do in your response. Although you won't have time to write notes for your response on the day of the test, you may want to practice writing them in this exercise.

START ▶

The students are discussing the possible choices in a decision they must make. State their problem. Then explain which decision you prefer and why.

STOP ■

I will need to:

1. state the topic ______________________
2. state the problem ______________________
3. explain and support my preference ______________________

   ____

   ____

EXERCISE S41 *Planning your speech*

Think through the following steps. Take as much time as you need in this exercise. As you work through other exercises, try to gradually shorten your preparation time to 20 seconds.

1. Plan your introduction using the information in the conversation in Exercise S39 and the task requirements in Exercise S40.
2. Use the notes you took in Exercise S39 to help you plan your response to the task.
3. Plan a concluding statement to complete the task.

EXERCISE S42 *Recording your speech*

Give the speech you planned in Exercise S41. Record your speech so you can analyze and evaluate it.

PRACTICE WITH THE ACADEMIC TASK

In the academic task, you will have 20 seconds to plan your response and 60 seconds to speak.

A narrator will set the context for the academic lecture. The language in the lecture is formal and usually concerns an academic topic. The topic is usually stated at the beginning of the lecture. After you hear the lecture, the narrator will state the speaking task. You will need to use the points made in the lecture to complete the task.

Exercises S43–S46 Use Exercises S43–S46 to practice the steps for developing a speech that relates to information from a lecture. *Note:* The skill-building exercises are not full length.

EXERCISE S43 *Identifying important points in a lecture*

Listen to the lecture and write down the important points.

START ▶

Now listen to part of a lecture in a cultural geography class.

____

____

____

____

____

____

STOP ■

EXERCISE S44 *Analyzing the task that relates to the lecture*

Listen to the task you must respond to. Think about what you will need to do in your response. Although you won't have time to write notes for your response on the day of the test, you may want to practice writing them in this exercise.

START ▶

Using points and examples from the lecture, explain how the population age distribution is contributing to financial problems for governments.

STOP ■

I need to:

1. state the topic ______________________________
2. explain the points ______________________________
3. discuss the financial problem ______________________________

____

____

EXERCISE S45 *Planning your speech*

Think through the following steps. Take as much time as you need in this exercise. As you work through other exercises, try to gradually shorten your preparation time to 20 seconds.

1. Plan your introduction using the information in the lecture in Exercise S43 and the task requirements in Exercise S44.
2. Use the notes you took in Exercise S43 to help you plan your response to the task.
3. Plan a concluding statement to complete the task.

EXERCISE S46 *Recording your speech*

Give the speech you planned in Exercise S45. Record your speech so you can analyze and evaluate it.

PRACTICE WITH ANALYZING YOUR RESPONSES

Keep the following list of questions in mind as you analyze your responses to the listening/speaking tasks.

1. Is the pronunciation in the speech easy to understand?
2. Does the intonation in the speech sound natural?
3. Does the speech show control of a variety of grammatical structures?
4. Has the word choice been effective?
5. Is the speech coherent?
6. Are the ideas from the listening passage well organized?
7. Have the main ideas been presented?
8. Have the appropriate supporting details been used?
9. Does the response paraphrase the ideas and details accurately?
10. Has the speech been completed within the allotted time?

Exercise S47 Use Exercise S47 to develop your skills in analyzing your responses to the listening/speaking tasks.

EXERCISE S47 *Analyzing and scoring your responses*

Listen to your taped responses from Exercise S42 and Exercise S46. Check the list above to see that you have met the requirements of the listening/speaking tasks. Give your response a score, and state why you decided on that score.

- A score of 4 is for a response that meets all the requirements.
- A score of 3 indicates that the speech was appropriate but was weak in some of the areas mentioned in the list.
- A score of 2 shows some difficulties in clarity of speaking. Inaccurate information may have been presented, or essential information from the listening passage may be missing.
- A score of 1 is for a speech that meets only a few of the requirements.
- A score of 0 is given when no attempt has been made or the attempt does not address the task.

1. Score _____ Reasons ____

2. Score _____ Reasons ____

PRACTICING THE INTEGRATED LISTENING/SPEAKING TASKS

Now that you have studied the approach for responding to the integrated listening/speaking tasks, review the five steps outlined in Preparing to Give a Timed Response, pp. 356 – 359, and practice more speaking tasks. Respond to the tasks in Exercise S48. Record your responses and score them.

Exercise S48 Use Exercise S48 to develop your skills in responding to the listening/speaking tasks.

EXERCISE S48 *Responding to the integrated listening/speaking tasks*

You will hear a conversation or lecture. Try to prepare your response in 20 seconds and give your speech in 60 seconds. Record your speech and give it a score according to the list in Practice with Analyzing Your Responses on p. 362 and the guidelines in Exercise S47 above. The screens in the first item appear as they will on the actual test.

START ▶

1. Listen to a conversation between two students.

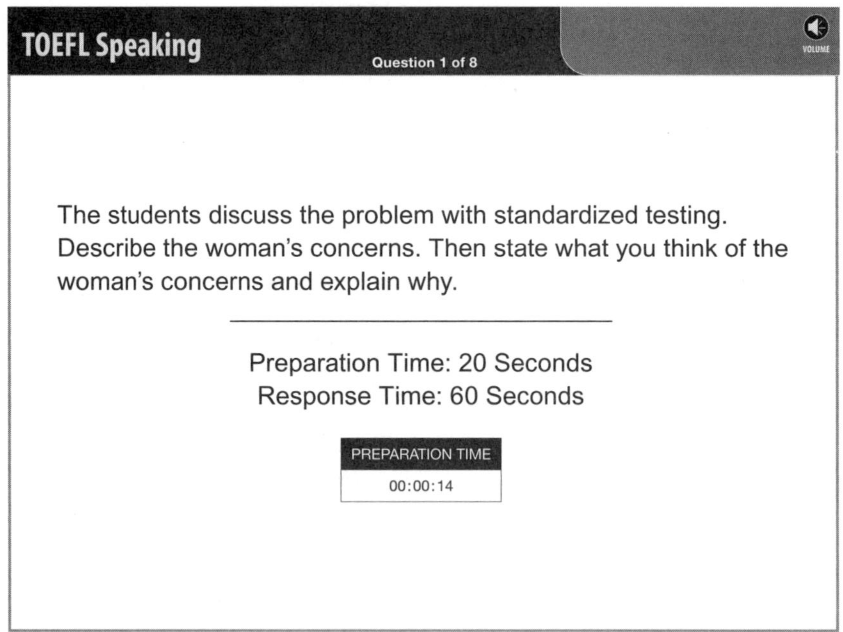

TOEFL Speaking
Question 1 of 8
VOLUME
The students discuss the problem with standardized testing. Describe the woman's concerns. Then state what you think of the woman's concerns and explain why.
Preparation Time: 20 Seconds
Response Time: 60 Seconds
PREPARATION TIME
00:00:14

2. Listen to a conversation between two students.

The students discuss two possible solutions to the woman's problem. Describe the problem. Then state which of the two solutions you prefer and explain why.

3. Listen to a conversation between two students.

The students are discussing two possible places to meet to finalize their presentation plans. Describe their problem. Then state which of the two solutions you prefer and explain why.

4. Listen to a conversation between two students.

The man expresses his opinion about the changes in the physical education requirements for students. State his opinion, and explain the reasons he gives for that opinion.

5. Listen to part of a lecture in an agriculture class.

Using points and examples from the lecture, explain how goats are related to the spread of desertification.

6. Listen to part of a lecture in a criminal law class.

Using specific information from the lecture, explain the professor's concern about changing the justice system and what needs to be done before reforms are made.

7. Listen to part of a lecture in an ecology class.

Using points and examples from the lecture, explain how the use of intermediate technology is important for rural societies.

8. Listen to part of a lecture in a world history class.

Using points and examples from the lecture, explain how maritime nations affected the spice trade in Europe.

STOP ■

Speaking Section Practice Test

When you have taken the Diagnostic Test and completed the exercises recommended in the Answer Key for any Speaking questions you marked incorrectly, you can test your skills by taking this Speaking Section Practice Test. You can take this test either in this book or on the CD-ROM that accompanies this book. The Speaking Section Practice Test in the book is identical to the Speaking section of Test 2 on the CD-ROM.

During the Speaking Section of the actual TOEFL test, you may not go back and check your work or change your answers. Maintain the same test conditions now that would be experienced during the real test.

SPEAKING SECTION

Directions

In this section of the test, you will be able to demonstrate your ability to speak about a variety of topics. You will answer six questions by recording your response. Answer each of the questions as completely as possible.

In questions 1 and 2, you will first hear a statement or question about familiar topics. You will then speak about these topics. Your response will be scored on your ability to speak clearly and coherently about the topics.

In questions 3 and 4, you will first read a short text. You will then listen to a talk on the same topic.

You will be asked a question about what you have read and heard. You will need to combine appropriate information from the text and the talk to provide a complete answer to the question. Your response will be scored on your ability to speak clearly and coherently and on your ability to accurately convey information about what you read and heard.

In questions 5 and 6, you will listen to part of a conversation or a lecture. You will be asked a question about what you heard. Your response will be scored on your ability to speak clearly and coherently and on your ability to accurately convey information about what you heard.

You may take notes while you read and while you listen to the conversations and lectures. You may use your notes to help prepare your response.

Listen carefully to the directions for each question. For each question you will be given a short time to prepare your response. When the preparation time is up, you will be told to begin your response.

START ▶

1. Please listen carefully.

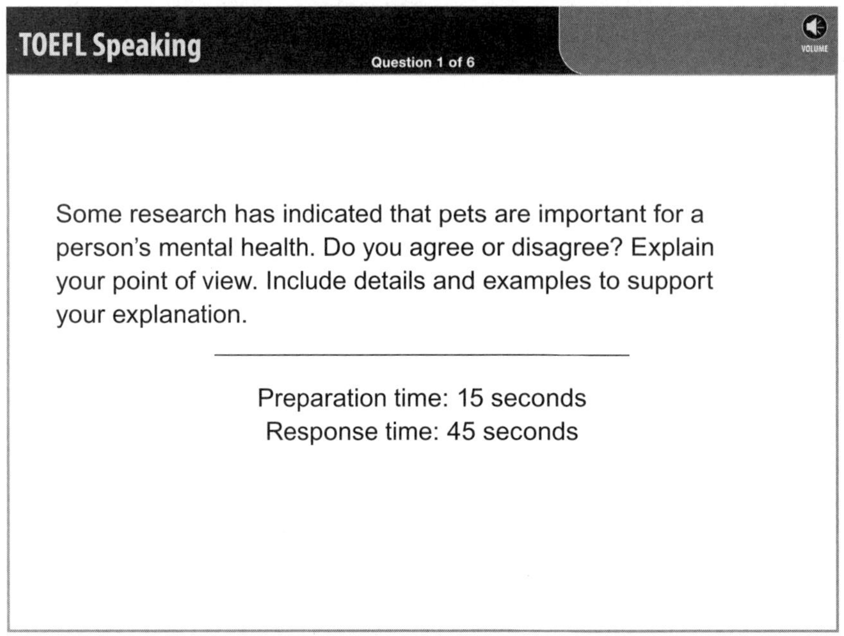
TOEFL Speaking
Question 1 of 6
VOLUME
Some research has indicated that pets are important for a person's mental health. Do you agree or disagree? Explain your point of view. Include details and examples to support your explanation.
Preparation time: 15 seconds
Response time: 45 seconds

You may begin to prepare your response after the beep.

Please begin speaking after the beep.

STOP ■

START ▶

2. Please listen carefully.

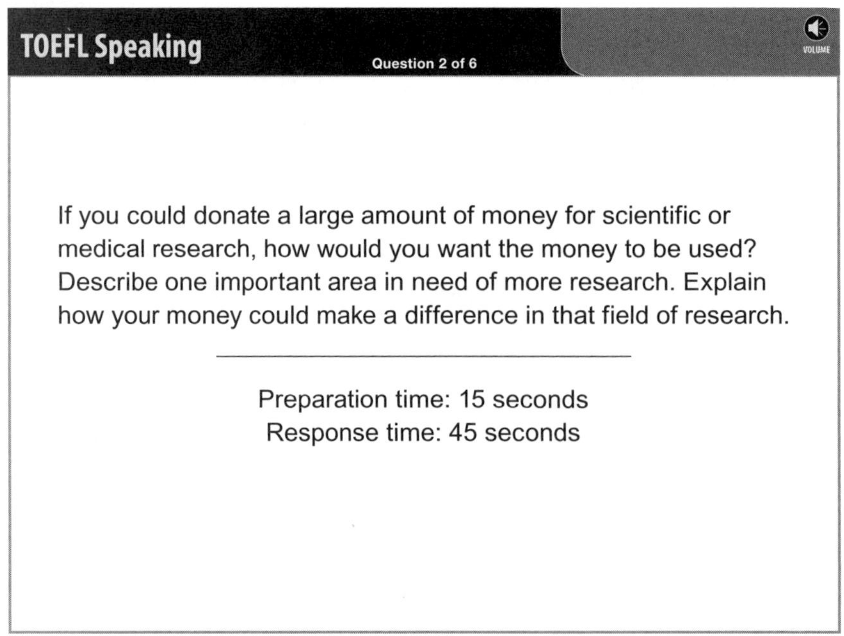
TOEFL Speaking
Question 2 of 6
VOLUME
If you could donate a large amount of money for scientific or medical research, how would you want the money to be used? Describe one important area in need of more research. Explain how your money could make a difference in that field of research.
Preparation time: 15 seconds
Response time: 45 seconds

You may begin to prepare your response after the beep.

Please begin speaking after the beep.

STOP ■

START ▶

3. Please listen carefully.

The student newspaper has published an article about different services offered on campus. Read the description of the Legal Aid Project. You will have 45 seconds to read the description. Begin reading now.

PAUSE II (for 45 seconds)

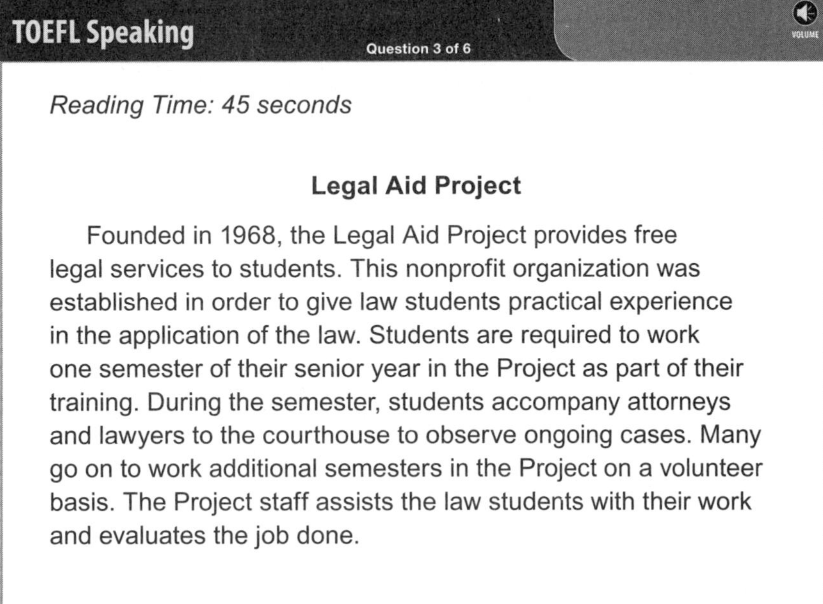

TOEFL Speaking

Question 3 of 6

VOLUME

Reading Time: 45 seconds

Legal Aid Project

Founded in 1968, the Legal Aid Project provides free legal services to students. This nonprofit organization was established in order to give law students practical experience in the application of the law. Students are required to work one semester of their senior year in the Project as part of their training. During the semester, students accompany attorneys and lawyers to the courthouse to observe ongoing cases. Many go on to work additional semesters in the Project on a volunteer basis. The Project staff assists the law students with their work and evaluates the job done.

Now listen to two students as they discuss the Legal Aid Project.

Now get ready to answer the question.

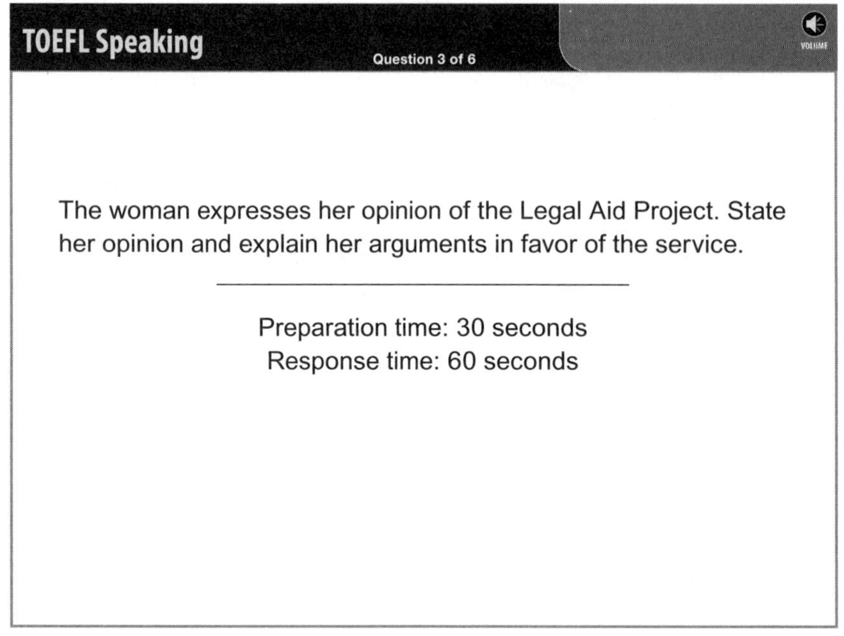

TOEFL Speaking
Question 3 of 6
VOLUME
The woman expresses her opinion of the Legal Aid Project. State her opinion and explain her arguments in favor of the service.
Preparation time: 30 seconds
Response time: 60 seconds

You may begin to prepare your response after the beep.

Please begin speaking after the beep.

STOP ■

START ▶

4. Please listen carefully.

Read the passage about the transportation of agricultural goods. You have 45 seconds to read the passage. Begin reading now.

PAUSE II (for 45 seconds)

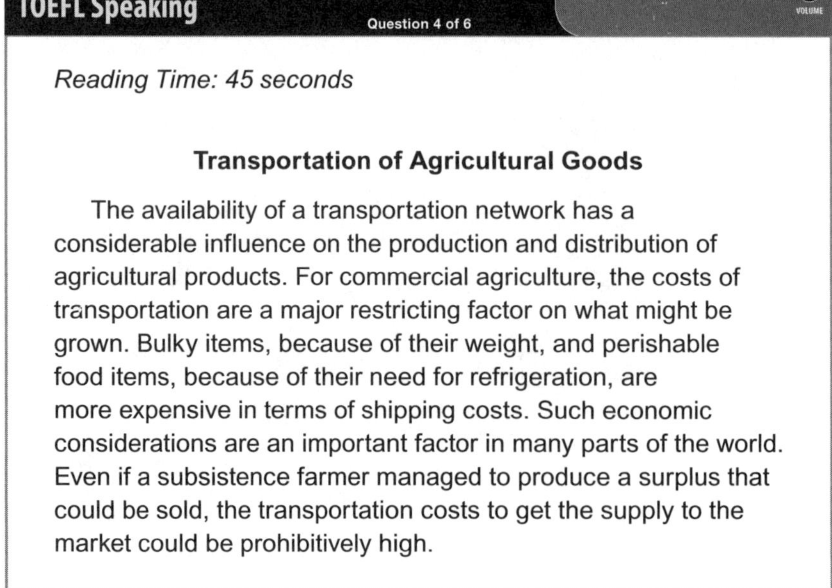

Now listen to part of a lecture on this topic in a cultural geography class.

Now get ready to answer the question.

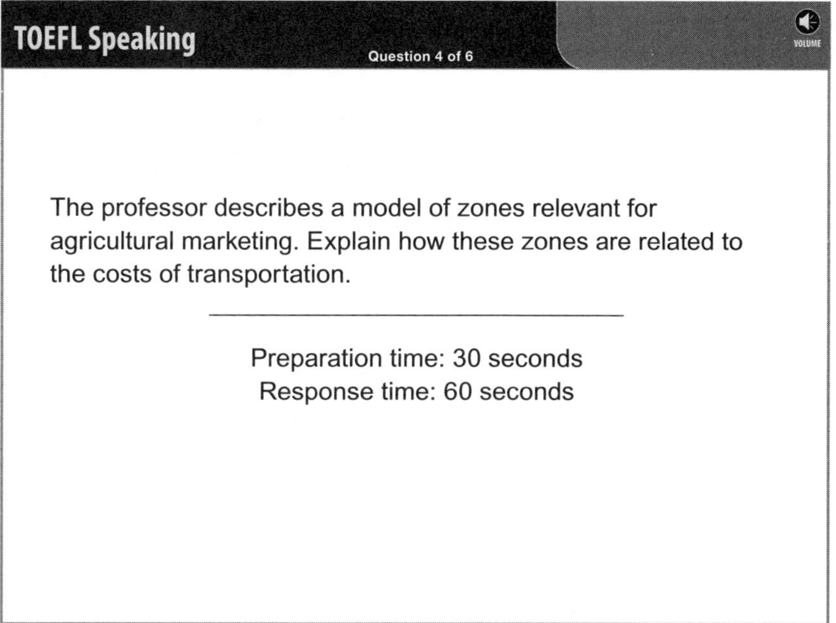

TOEFL Speaking
Question 4 of 6
VOLUME
The professor describes a model of zones relevant for agricultural marketing. Explain how these zones are related to the costs of transportation.
Preparation time: 30 seconds
Response time: 60 seconds

You may begin to prepare your response after the beep.

Please begin speaking after the beep.

STOP ■

START ▶

5. Please listen carefully.

Listen to a conversation between two students.

TOEFL Speaking
Question 5 of 6
VOLUME

Now get ready to answer the question.

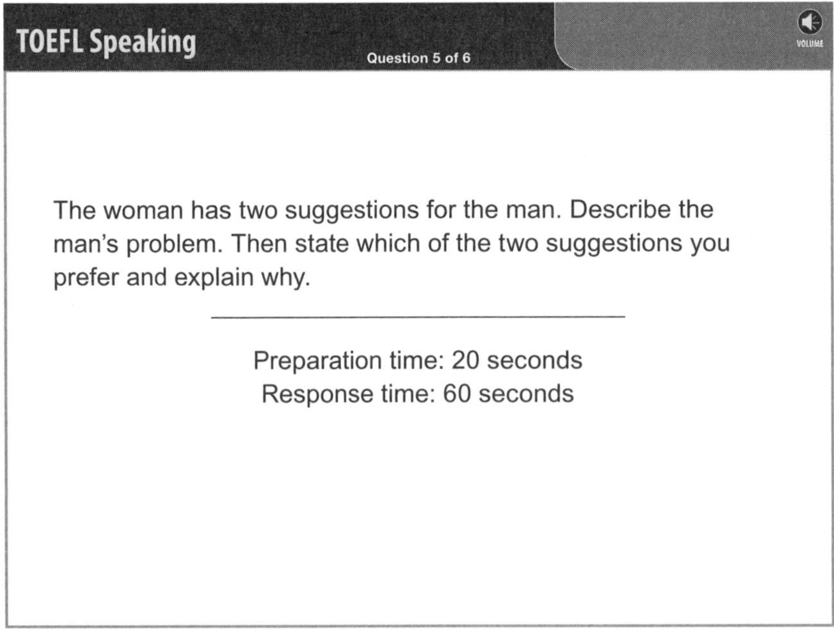
TOEFL Speaking
Question 5 of 6
VOLUME
The woman has two suggestions for the man. Describe the man's problem. Then state which of the two suggestions you prefer and explain why.
Preparation time: 20 seconds
Response time: 60 seconds

You may begin to prepare your response after the beep.

Please begin speaking after the beep.

STOP ■

START ▶

6. Please listen carefully.

Listen to part of a lecture in a music education class.

TOEFL Speaking
Question 6 of 6
VOLUME

Now get ready to answer the question.

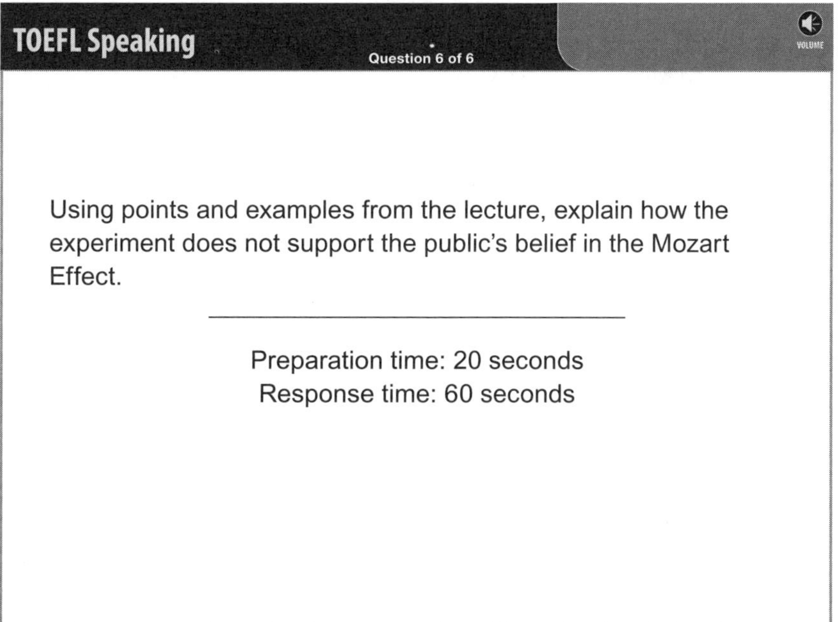
TOEFL Speaking
Question 6 of 6
VOLUME
Using points and examples from the lecture, explain how the experiment does not support the public's belief in the Mozart Effect.
Preparation time: 20 seconds
Response time: 60 seconds

You may begin to prepare your response after the beep.

Please begin speaking after the beep.

STOP ■

Writing

The Writing section of the TOEFL® iBT test measures your ability to write standard academic English. Students in an English-speaking academic environment are required to write essays and papers for several different purposes. Some writing assignments require students to express their opinion or comment upon an issue or topic based on their personal knowledge and experience. Other writing assignments, for example, essays on class exams, require students to demonstrate that they have understood material in a comprehensive way. Students are also asked to write term papers, which expand on a topic learned about in class or synthesize information from class lectures and outside reading.

Independent writing refers to essays that express and support the student's point of view on a particular topic. *Integrated writing* refers to essays that combine what students have learned from assigned reading as well as class lectures. Integrated writing assignments require students to be able to organize and synthesize information from different sources, including their own notes; summarize and paraphrase information from these sources; and make comparisons or draw conclusions about the information from these sources.

There are two writing tasks on the TOEFL test: one independent and one integrated.

The independent task measures your ability to compose an essay. You will have 30 minutes to write an essay of at least 300 words in response to an assigned question. To answer the question, you must either state, explain, and support an opinion or state, explain, and support a preference.

There is no right or wrong answer to the question. Your response is scored on your organization, development of ideas, and accuracy of language in addressing all parts of the question.

The integrated task measures your ability to synthesize information from a reading passage and a listening passage. You will have three minutes to read a passage of 230–300 words. The reading passage is then hidden while you listen to a two-minute excerpt from a lecture that is related to the reading. You may take notes during both. Then you have 20 minutes to write a 150- to 225-word response to a question. The reading passage reappears during this time so that you may refer to it while you are writing.

To answer the integrated task, you must identify the relevant ideas and relationships from the passages and organize that information in a coherent manner.

Your response is scored on your organization, your discussion of the key ideas and supporting details, and your accuracy of language in addressing all parts of the question.

Strategies to Use for Building Writing Fluency

1. Practice writing in English on a computer keyboard.
You will be required to use a computer to type your essays on the TOEFL test. Practice typing on a keyboard using English characters. Do as many of the writing exercises in the Writing section of this book as you can directly on a computer.

2. Practice writing essays.
Set aside regularly scheduled times to practice writing essays. Use the topics in this book or topics of your own to develop your writing fluency. Start writing down your ideas as soon as you have read the topic. Use the strategies suggested in Strategies to Use for the Independent Writing Task, p. 387, both for writing practice essays and for the actual test.

3. Practice organizing information in written form.
Use passages from the Reading and the Listening sections of this book to practice taking notes on main ideas and organizing those ideas in your writing. Strategies to Use for Building Listening Skills on p. 249 lists good sources for listening material. For more information on note taking, see Note Taking, Paraphrasing, and Summarizing, p. 52.

4. Practice paraphrasing and summarizing information in written form.
Use your notes to paraphrase key statements and to summarize passages you have read or heard. For more information on paraphrasing and summarizing, see Paraphrasing, p. 54, and Summarizing, p. 54.

5. Read and listen to the kinds of material you will encounter on the test.
Select material on topics in the fields of science, technology, the social sciences, and the humanities to practice taking notes on main ideas. Organize those main ideas in your writing.

6. Increase your skills in using a variety of sentence structures and vocabulary.
A good written response includes a variety of structures and vocabulary. See Grammar: Assessing Your Skills, p. 74, to familiarize yourself with writing compound and complex sentences, and Vocabulary, p. 63, to build your vocabulary for writing.

7. Pay attention to time.
Check the amount of time it takes you to respond to the essay-writing tasks. At first, don't worry if the amount of time it takes you is longer than the time allotted on the test. With more practice, you can decrease your time. In this way, you can build up your writing fluency so that you can complete the writing tasks within the time allotted on the TOEFL test.

PRACTICE WITH COHESION

Cohesion refers to how well your writing flows. Your responses on the TOEFL test will receive a higher score if your paragraphs are cohesive. You can achieve this by practicing the techniques listed below.

- Organizing ideas in a logical sequence
- Connecting ideas with transitional expressions
- Defining uncommon terms
- Using parallel structures
- Rephrasing or replacing key words
- Being consistent in your use of tense, person, and number

See Practice with Cohesion, p. 317, for complete explanations of these techniques.

Exercises W1–W4

Use Exercises W1–W4 to develop your skills in writing cohesively.

EXERCISE W1 *Connecting ideas using transitional expressions*

Complete the paragraphs by choosing the transition word or phrase that best joins the two parts of the sentence. (For more information on transition words, see Grammar Review: Connecting Ideas, p. 116.)

Traffic has become very troublesome in the downtown areas of many large cities. ________, town planning authorities have pedestrianized many important shopping districts.

(A) Furthermore
(B) In contrast
(C) Consequently
(D) Secondly

You would choose *C*. The word *consequently* indicates a result of a situation. The pedestrianizing of shopping districts is a result of the troublesome traffic.

Questions 1–7

___1___ the exhaust from cars contributes to greenhouse gases, I think that students should not use cars powered by gasoline. ___2___ city buses usually pass by the university, many universities have a special shuttle bus that is provided for student transportation. ___3___, many students can get to class by either city buses or university buses. ___4___ option is for students to ride to class on bicycles. Not only is this good exercise, ___5___ it is also easier to find a space to leave a bicycle than to find a parking space for a car on a crowded university campus. ___6___, students who live close to campus can enjoy a leisurely walk to their classes. ___7___, it seems that students don't want to give up using their cars.

1. (A) So that
   (B) Earlier
   (C) Because
   (D) Although

2. (A) Even though
   (B) Granted that
   (C) Since
   (D) Meanwhile

3. (A) Therefore
   (B) Initially
   (C) Simultaneously
   (D) Alternatively

4. (A) To illustrate an
   (B) Another
   (C) The resulting
   (D) To summarize an

5. (A) nevertheless
   (B) particularly
   (C) and
   (D) but

6. (A) Whereas
   (B) Finally
   (C) Still
   (D) Hence

7. (A) Unfortunately
   (B) As a result
   (C) For instance
   (D) Specifically

Questions 8–12

___8___ most women in Germany during her time, Caroline Herschel was not allowed to learn anything other than useful household skills such as knitting. ___9___, all this changed for her in 1772, ___10___ her astronomer brother, William, took her to live with him in England. ___11___ he taught her mathematics, she began to help him keep a record of his discoveries. The two would often stay up until dawn, gazing upward. ___12___, they built their own telescopes, which were even bigger and better than those at the Royal Observatory in Greenwich.

8. (A) Since
   (B) Before
   (C) Yet
   (D) Like

9. (A) Consequently
   (B) However
   (C) Specifically
   (D) Thus

10. (A) when
    (B) thereafter
    (C) if
    (D) subsequently

11. (A) To illustrate
    (B) For example
    (C) Besides
    (D) After

12. (A) Particularly
    (B) Eventually
    (C) Therefore
    (D) In summary

EXERCISE W2 *Defining words and phrases*

Practice defining words by giving a three-part definition of the following words. For more information and practice, see Defining Unknown Terms, p. 318, and Exercise S8, p. 320.

> human migration
> *Human migration is the movement of people who are relocating in order to find a more satisfactory living environment.*

1. passive smoking

   ____

2. subsistence farming

   ____

3. expectorant

   ____

4. nonfiction

   ____

5. trowel

   ____

EXERCISE W3 *Connecting ideas using parallel structures*

Rewrite the incorrect part of each sentence to create a parallel structure. For information on parallel structures, see Grammar Review: Parallel Structures and Exercise G19, p. 115. For more practice, see Using Parallel Structures, p. 318, and Exercise S9, p. 320.

> Labels should include the information that allows shoppers to compare the ingredients and weighing of the food they are buying.
> *the ingredients and weight of the food*

1. The questionnaire indicated that many students wanted to study in the library rather than home.

   ____

2. From this experience, I learned not only to read the instructions more carefully, but also pay attention to safety features.

   ____

3. My mathematics teacher required us to work on a set of problems individually, compare our answers with a classmate, and then working together on those answers that did not agree.

   ____

4. Bryce Canyon is 56 square miles of towering pinnacles, and with eroded forms that are grotesque.

   ____

WRITING

5. Today sheepdogs are seen both in their traditional role as working animals and they are pets.

   ____

6. Julius Caesar did not conquer Britain but instead stayed a few weeks, took some hostages, and he returned to Gaul.

   ____

EXERCISE W4 *Adding cohesion*

Read the following paragraphs. Rewrite the paragraphs by rephrasing key words and using pronouns and demonstratives to add cohesion. For more information and practice, see Exercises S10 and S11, p. 321.

> I have always wanted to see Old Faithful Geyser in Yellowstone National Park. Besides the Old Faithful Geyser, vast wilderness areas can be found in Yellowstone National Park. Interesting wildlife inhabits the vast wilderness areas. The interesting wildlife found in Yellowstone National Park includes bison, moose, elk, and bears.
>
> *I have always wanted to see Old Faithful Geyser in Yellowstone National Park. Besides this geyser, vast wilderness areas can be found there. Interesting wildlife inhabits these areas. Wild animals found in the park include bison, moose, elk, and bears.*

1. Adults tend to cherish soft values. Soft values are family, health, and career satisfaction, to name a few. Soft values are hard to put a monetary value on. In contrast, children take for granted soft values that apply to their lives. Children put more importance on material objects, such as a favorite toy. Material objects become less important to children as they become more interested in best friends.

   ____

   ____

   ____

   ____

   ____

   ____

2. The boundary that separates the Earth's crust from the upper mantle is commonly called the Moho. The Moho is like an exaggerated mirror image of the surface profile. So the highest mountain ranges result in the deepest thickness of crust. Beneath the highest mountain ranges, the thickness of the crust can attain 50 miles. Beneath the oceans, the thickness of the crust is about 3 miles, whereas beneath the continents the thickness of the crust averages about 20 miles. The reason for the Moho profile is that the material that makes up the upper mantle is denser than the crust and therefore, the crust floats rather like an iceberg floats in

the sea. You can get an idea of how the material floats like icebergs by thinking of different-sized ice cubes in a glass of water. The biggest ice cube in the water extends to the highest point and also to the greatest depth.

____

____

____

____

____

____

PRACTICE WITH WRITING CONCISELY

Being concise means writing in a way that expresses your essential ideas without extra words that do not add anything important. You can achieve this by practicing the techniques listed below.

Avoiding "empty" words and phrases

Empty words and phrases don't add important or relevant information. Many empty phrases can be deleted entirely. Look at the following example:

Inconcise When all things are considered, young adults of today live more satisfying lives than those of their parents, in my opinion.

Concise Young adults of today live more satisfying lives than those of their parents.

Other empty phrases can be replaced with more concise constructions. Look at the following example:

Inconcise Due to the fact that our grandparents were under an obligation to help their parents, they did not have the options that young people have at this point in time.

Concise Because our grandparents were obligated to help their parents, they did not have the options that young people have now.

Avoiding repetition

Although sometimes it is necessary to repeat a phrase, useless repetition weakens your writing. Not only should you try to avoid repeating words and phrases, avoid repetition of meaning as well.

Sometimes a word or phrase carries meaning that is already supplied by other words in the sentence and is therefore unnecessary. Look at the following example:

Inconcise The farm my grandfather grew up on was large in size.

Concise The farm my grandfather grew up on was large.

More concise My grandfather grew up on a large farm.

Sometimes a phrase can be replaced with a single word that carries the same meaning. Use a single word to make your writing more concise. Look at the following example:

Inconcise My grandfather has said over and over again that he had to work on his parents' farm.

Concise My grandfather has said repeatedly that he had to work on his parents' farm.

Choosing the best grammatical structures

Choosing the right grammatical structure can make your sentences stronger and more concise. Although it is important to have variety in sentence structure, think about the best structure to use. Some guidelines for choosing the best structure are outlined below.

1. The subject and verb of a sentence should reflect what is most important in the sentence. In the first sentence below, the subject is *situation* and the verb is *was*. However, the important idea in the sentence is the grandfather's not being able to study. In the second sentence, the focus is on the most important idea, and the sentence is more concise.

   Inconcise The situation that resulted in my grandfather's not being able to study engineering was that his father needed help on the farm.

   Concise My grandfather couldn't study engineering because his father needed help on the farm.

2. Postponing the subject with structures like *there is* and *it is* can be effective to emphasize a point. But frequently they are just extra words that weaken your sentences. The important idea in the sentences below is the grandfather's hard work.

   Inconcise There were 25 cows on the farm that my grandfather had to milk every day. It was hard work for my grandfather.

   Concise My grandfather worked hard. He had to milk 25 cows on the farm every day.

   More concise My grandfather worked hard milking 25 cows daily.

3. Complex sentences can often be made more concise by reducing clauses to phrases and phrases to single words.

   Inconcise Dairy cows were raised on the farm, which was located 100 kilometers from the nearest university and was in an area that was remote.

   Concise The dairy farm was located in a remote area, 100 kilometers from the nearest university.

4. Use the passive voice only when the object, not the subject, is the focus. The passive voice is indirect, and in this structure the actor (subject) loses its importance. The passive voice also requires more words than the active voice because it needs a helping verb and the prepositional phrase that names the actor.

   Inconcise In the fall, not only did the cows have to be milked, but also the hay was mowed and stacked by my grandfather's family.

   Concise In the fall, my grandfather's family not only milked the cows but also mowed and stacked the hay.

5. Some verbs need extra words to convey meaning. A verb like this can often be replaced by one that carries the complete meaning by itself. In the first sentence below, the words *stand around doing nothing* can be replaced by one verb that means the same thing, as shown in the second sentence.

   Inconcise My grandfather didn't have time to stand around doing nothing with his school friends.

   Concise My grandfather didn't have time to loiter with his school friends.

6. Information in two or more sentences can often be combined into one sentence.

   Inconcise Profits from the farm were not large. Sometimes they were too small to meet the expenses of running a farm. They were not sufficient to pay for a university degree.

   Concise Profits from the farm were sometimes too small to meet operational expenses, let alone pay for a university degree.

Exercises W5–W6

Use Exercises W5–W6 to develop your skills in writing concise sentences.

EXERCISE W5 *Making sentences concise*

The following sentences are not concise. Rewrite them in a more concise way.

As far as I'm concerned, teenagers adopting more or less extreme forms of behavior that affront the adult population is a result of a necessity to become independent.

Teenagers gain independence by adopting extreme forms of behavior that affront adults.

1. The first and the foremost thing to do if a person is not breathing and if the heart is not beating is to start resuscitation.

   ____

2. If a child must inhale the smoke from her mother's cigarettes for 12 years, it is likely to cause her harm during such a long period of time.

   ____

3. I try to make my first e-mail as clear as possible so that it will give the reader the impression that my e-mail is important for me and that I have put some thought into it.

   ____

4. As learning, so is research also a fundamentally collaborative effort in which people cooperate together.

   ____

5. In my opinion, for humankind the car has been a success, but for nature it has not been a success.

   ____

6. In my country, the birthrates are falling lower than ever before. As a result, we could face a severe lack of employees in the workforce when the baby boomers reach retirement age. Also, the employees will not be able to support such a large number of people who are retired.

 ____

7. My friend was getting some exercise by running along the side of the river when a pack of dogs was suddenly in front of him on the path.

 ____

8. My best hobby is the collection of stamps for which I have stamps from all over the world and from countries, like Rhodesia, that no longer have the same name.

 ____

EXERCISE W6 *Making paragraphs concise*

Many of the sentences in the following paragraphs are not concise. On your own paper, rewrite the paragraphs in a more concise way.

> In my opinion, it is critical to be informed about what is happening all over the world. There are lots of problems like famines, and we cannot help those people if we do not know that a famine is happening. Only by knowing what is happening in the world can we respond to lots of problems that are critical in the world.
>
> *We should be informed about world events such as famines so that we can help those people in need. Only by being informed can we respond to crises.*

1. It has occurred to me that one of the most important subjects that we study in school is mathematics. Although it is true that it is important to know how to read, if we do not know how to do simple arithmetic when we do some everyday kind of activity like go to the grocery store, we will not be able to keep track of our finances. It is necessary for us to understand things such as interest rates on bank accounts and loans for houses or cars in order to keep track of our personal accounts without going bankrupt. Many people are poor not because they do not earn enough money, but because they don't understand the mathematics behind finances.

   Besides the importance that mathematics has in our financial lives, it is also important in many other parts of our lives. There is the need that we have to measure and calculate numbers when we cook, for example. In the kitchen, we have to know about mathematical functions like fractions or multiplication. Sometimes we cut amounts in half because fewer people are being cooked for or we have to double or triple amounts if a lot of people are coming over to visit us for a special occasion. Not being able to figure out the sums for cooking a cake could have the final result of a terrible-tasting disaster.

2. The electric streetcar was popular among the people in cities in the United States after 1880 when an engineer invented a cable that could run from wire overhead to a streetcar's electric engine. Because there was this overhead wire, it wasn't necessary to have a dangerous electric rail running along the street at ground level, and this was a very important feature of the streetcar in those cities that used them.

   During the next 20 or 30 years or so, from 1880 onwards, the electric streetcar was very popular with passengers in big cities all over the USA. It was not polluting, and it was very efficient, carrying large numbers of passengers without costing very much money for the passengers. It was also profitable for the companies. However, early in the next century, automobile manufacturers and other business interests made an effort to get rid of all the streetcars in the streets of big cities and replace them with buses and cars. Eventually the situation was that all the streetcars disappeared, and cars completely took over all the city streets.

INDEPENDENT WRITING TASK

The independent writing task of the TOEFL iBT test requires you to write an essay that explains and supports your opinion on an issue or on a solution to a problem. You will be asked to develop reasons for your opinion and give specific details and examples in support of your position.

Strategies to Use for the Independent Writing Task

1. Be familiar with the organization of an effective essay.
An effective essay begins with an introductory paragraph that includes a thesis statement. The thesis statement tells the reader what the essay is about. The body of the essay is made up of paragraphs that support the introduction. A concluding paragraph completes the essay.

2. Study the question carefully.
Be sure you understand what the task requires. Consider a few ways to address the question. Quickly organize your thoughts and write down your ideas.

3. Organize your ideas.
Organize your ideas into a logical progression by using a mind map (see Practice with Preparing to Write, p. 390) or a traditional outline. Check your ideas to make sure they cover the requirements of the task. Then start typing your essay.

4. Write cohesively and concisely.
While you are organizing your ideas, keep in mind the techniques for making your essay cohesive (see Practice with Cohesion, p. 317). While you are writing the essay, keep in mind the techniques for making your sentences cohesive and concise (see Practice with Writing Concisely, p. 383).

5. Budget your time so that you will be able to complete and correct your essay.
You have only 30 minutes to write your essay. Use your time efficiently while you read and think about the question, organize your ideas in a simple form, write the essay, and make minor revisions.

6. Use sentence structures and vocabulary you know to be correct.
Use sentence structures and vocabulary that you know how to use well. A well-written essay includes a variety of structures and vocabulary.

7. Check your grammar.
When you are writing, look out for the kinds of grammar errors that you know you commonly make. Check your grammar when you review your essay.

8. Don't lose time worrying about whether the evaluator will agree with your opinions and the support you have used.
Your essay is evaluated on how well you present your opinion, not on whether the evaluator agrees with you. Be sure you have supported your opinion well and have responded to all parts of the task.

LOOKING AT THE ORGANIZATION OF AN ESSAY

Example essay question and response

Read the question below and the example essay that follows.

Question

Some people believe that mothers should not work. Others argue against this. Consider the problems that a working mother faces. Do you believe mothers should work?

Introductory paragraph

Nowadays it is very common for mothers to work outside the home. Whether a woman should stay at home or join the workforce is debated by many people. Some argue that the family, especially small children, may be neglected. However, many women need to work because of economic reasons or want to work to maintain a career. I believe that every mother has the right to work, and the decision should be one that a woman makes on her own. But first she should carefully consider the many problems that she might encounter.

Developmental paragraph 1

The major problems a working mother faces concern her children. She must either find a reliable person who will be loving toward the children or a good day-care center that the children can attend. If a child gets sick, the mother must make special arrangements for the child to be cared for at home, or she must stay home from work herself. While at work, the mother may worry about her children. She may wonder if they are safe, if they are learning the values she wants them to have, and if her absence is hurting them emotionally. She may also regret not being able to take them to after-school activities or participate in family activities with them.

Developmental paragraph 2

Even though a mother is frequently forced into working for economic reasons, she soon discovers that there are added expenses. The biggest expense is child care. Another expense is transportation, which includes not only going to work but also getting her children to school or day care. This may include purchasing and maintaining a car. Yet another expense is clothing, such as a uniform or business suits, to maintain a professional appearance.

Conclusion After a mother takes into account all of the above problems and perhaps other problems unique to her situation, she must decide if a job outside the home is worth it. I believe that even though she faces major obstacles, these obstacles are not insurmountable. Many mothers do work and manage a family very successfully. In conclusion, it is a woman's right to make this choice, and only the woman herself should decide this matter.

Analysis of the example essay

Study the following analysis of the example essay you just read.

Introductory paragraph
Notice that the essay has an introductory paragraph that states the general topic: working mothers. It addresses the question directly and shows both sides of the argument. It states the author's opinion that every mother has the right to work and that the decision to work should be a mother's choice. It then tells the reader that the essay will focus on a specific idea or the *controlling idea*: the problems that a woman must first consider before making this decision. The sentence containing the controlling idea of an essay is called the *thesis statement*. The thesis statement is usually the last sentence of the introductory paragraph.

Developmental paragraph 1
The next paragraph in this essay is the first *supporting* or *developmental paragraph*. It supports and develops the controlling idea of "problems" that was identified in the introduction. The topic sentence (the first sentence) of this paragraph introduces the idea of problems concerning children. All the other sentences in this paragraph describe either a problem concerning children or a detail explaining a problem concerning children.

Developmental paragraph 2
The next paragraph, or second developmental paragraph, in this essay also supports the controlling idea – problems – that was identified in the introduction. The topic sentence of this paragraph introduces the idea of problems of added expenses. The remaining sentences in this paragraph describe either an added expense or a detail explaining the added expense.

Conclusion
The last paragraph in this essay is the conclusion. The conclusion restates the topic of working mothers. Again, the controlling idea of problems that face a working mother is repeated. Also, the opinion that it should be a woman's choice is restated. All of these restatements use words that are different from those used in the first paragraph. The last statement is the concluding statement. It completes the essay.

PRACTICE WITH PREPARING TO WRITE

Before you write your essay, you need to analyze the task and organize your ideas.

Analyzing the task

Start by reading the question carefully and analyzing exactly what it is asking you to do. An example follows.

Question Modern technology has brought about changes in the roles of men and women. Discuss some of these changes. Do you think these changes have been beneficial?

This question is about changes in gender roles caused by technology. It asks the writer to:

- Discuss some of these changes
- Give an opinion about these changes

Organizing your ideas

Making a mind map will help you generate ideas and organize them. In your analysis of the question, identify the topic or idea that you need to discuss in your essay. Write the main idea you need to discuss in a circle in the middle of your paper. Write down any related ideas that come into your head. Use circles, arrows, or lines to link your ideas. Afterwards you can go through your ideas and pick the ones you want to write about. You will have to do this quickly when you do the TOEFL independent writing task. A model of a mind map appears below.

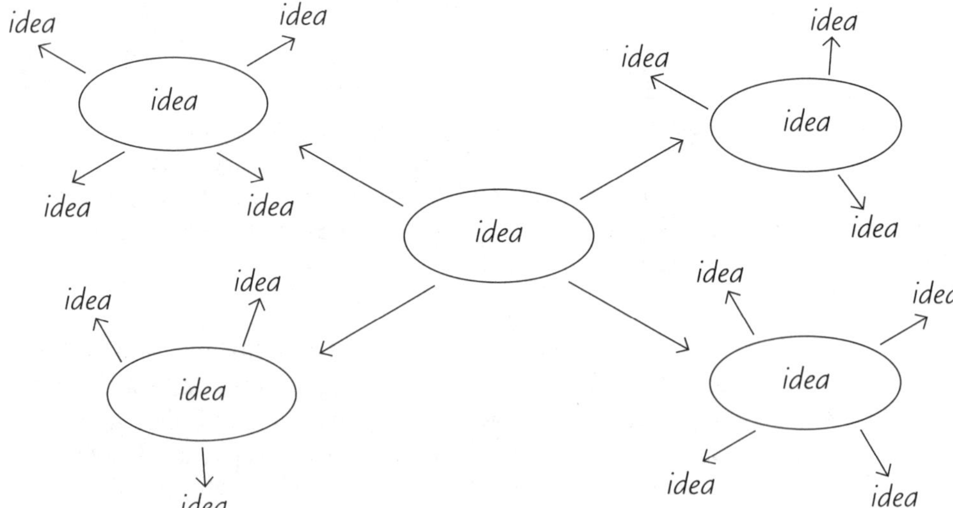

Exercises W7–W9 Use Exercises W7–W9 to practice the preparation skills for the independent writing task.

EXERCISE W7 *Identifying topics and tasks*

Read the question. Write the topic (what the essay should be about) and the task you are being asked to do.

> In your opinion, what is the most important characteristic a successful student must have? Describe the characteristic and give reasons for your opinion.
>
> Topic: *the most important characteristic for student success*
>
> Task: *describe characteristic and give reasons for its importance*

1. Do you agree or disagree with the following statement?

   Smoking should be banned in all public places.

   Use reasons and specific examples to support your opinion.

   Topic: ______________________________

   Task: ______________________________

2. Compare the advantages of marrying at a young age to marrying at an older age. State and support your preference.

   Topic: ______________________________

   Task: ______________________________

3. Do you agree or disagree with the following statement?

   A university education is necessary for success in today's world.

   Use reasons and specific examples to support your opinion.

   Topic: ______________________________

   Task: ______________________________

EXERCISE W8 *Making a mind map*

Choose one of the questions in Exercise W7. What do you need to focus on according to the question you chose? Put that idea in the middle of your page and make a mind map of ideas. Do not worry about whether some ideas are important or not. You are trying to generate as many ideas as possible.

An example of a mind map appears in the example box on the next page. It is based on the question in the example box in Exercise W7.

In your opinion, what is the most important characteristic a successful student must have? Describe the characteristic and give reasons for your opinion.

You could decide that *diligence* is the most important characteristic for a student to have. Ask yourself, "What are the reasons that diligence is essential?" and then start your mind map.

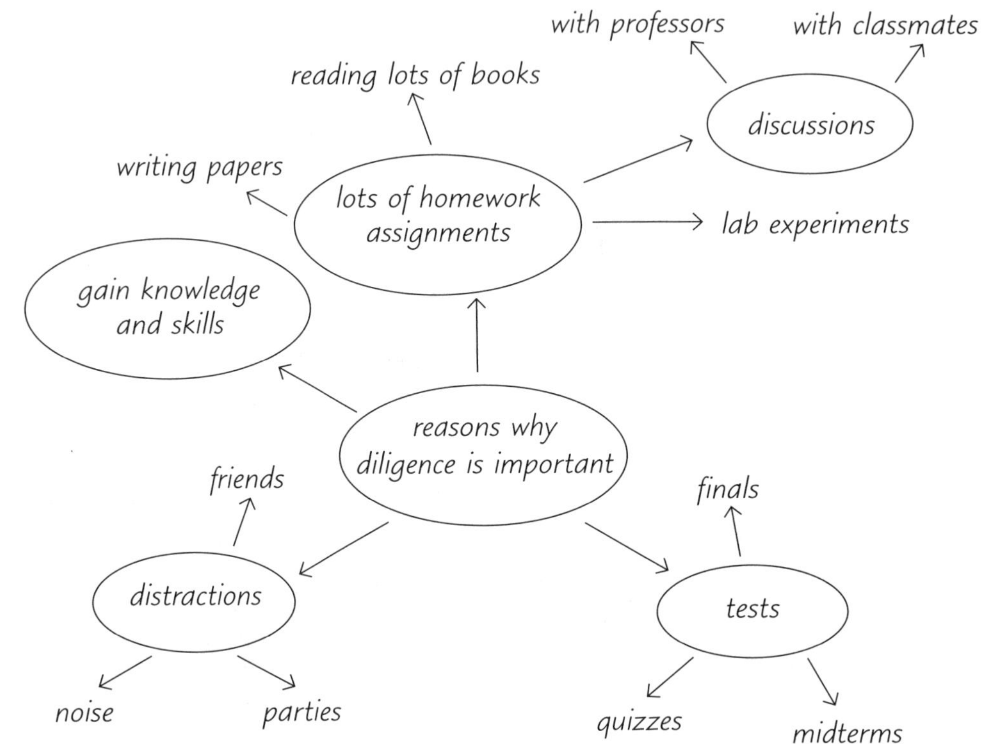

This mind map shows that the writer has decided on the characteristic *diligence* and has mapped the reasons that diligence is an important characteristic for success.

EXERCISE W9 *Checking the ideas on your mind map*

Review the mind map that you drew in Exercise W8. Decide which of the ideas that you wrote support the point you want to address in your essay. Cross out ideas that are not important or relevant.

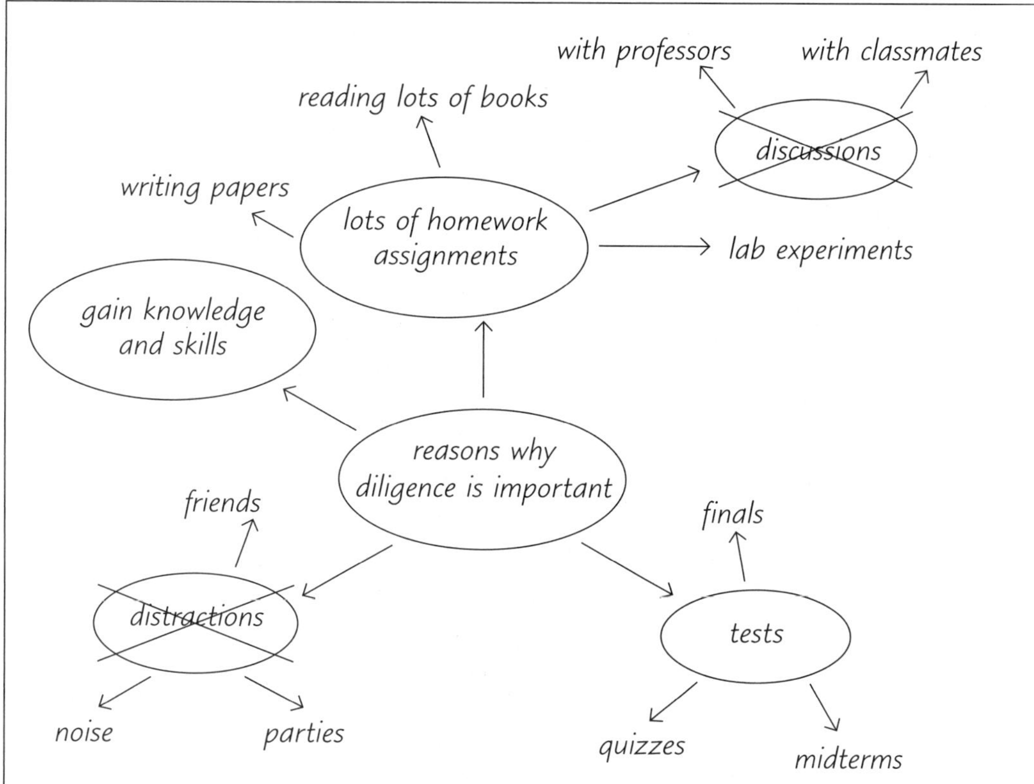

This writer wants to focus on reasons why diligence is an important characteristic. *Distractions* does not qualify as a reason why diligence is important and has been crossed out. *Discussions* are not homework, and those ideas have also been crossed out.

PRACTICE WITH INTRODUCTIONS

An effective essay begins with an introduction so that the reader knows what the essay is about. Guidelines for writing good introductions are presented below.

Writing Introductions

To write an introduction for the independent writing task, follow these steps:

1. In the first sentence, introduce the general topic.
2. In the next sentence, narrow the topic down to focus more on the question.
3. Restate the question in your own words, in statement form.
4. Write a concluding sentence that indicates the controlling idea of the essay. This is the thesis statement.

Read the question below and the example introduction that follows.

Question Living in an apartment instead of a university dormitory has advantages and disadvantages. Discuss some of the advantages and disadvantages of apartment living. Then state and defend your preference.

Introduction

When a person decides to enter a university away from home, he or she must also consider living accommodations. Although most universities offer student dormitories, students frequently opt to live in an apartment. While there are many advantages to apartment living, there are also disadvantages. Before a student decides to live in an apartment, all of the aspects of that kind of living accommodation should be reviewed.

1. The first sentence introduces the general topic of university living accommodations.

   When a person decides to enter a university away from home, he or she must also consider living accommodations.

2. The second sentence narrows the topic down to apartment living.

   Although most universities offer student dormitories, students frequently opt to live in an apartment.

3. The third sentence restates the specific question.

   While there are many advantages to apartment living, there are also disadvantages.

4. The fourth sentence is the thesis statement. It gives the controlling idea of the essay.

   Before a student decides to live in an apartment, all of the aspects of that kind of living accommodation should be reviewed.

Tips for writing introductions

When writing an introduction for the independent writing task, remember the following things:

Keep it simple A good introduction strengthens your essay. However, it is better to use your time writing the supporting paragraphs than spending too much time on the introductory paragraph.

Be sure it addresses the question fully Your thesis statement introduces the topic of the essay. It includes a controlling idea that focuses your essay. You may want to use one of the following phrases, or ones similar to these, to focus your essay:

the reasons for
the causes of
the effects of
the steps for
the procedure for
the advantages/disadvantages of

the ways/methods of
the different parts/kinds/types of
the characteristics/traits/qualities of
the problems of
the precautions for
the changes to

Your developmental paragraphs support your thesis statement. If you support a thesis statement that does not answer the question, you may not get credit for your essay.

Exercises W10–W14 Use Exercises W10–W14 to practice writing introductions.

EXERCISE W10 *Writing introductory statements*

On the lines below, write an introductory statement that states the general topic for the question you chose in Exercise W8.

> In your opinion, what is the most important characteristic a successful student must have? Describe the characteristic and give reasons for your opinion.
>
> *In order to be successful, a student must have certain characteristics.*
>
> The general topic that you are asked to discuss is characteristics of successful students. That general topic is stated in the first sentence.

EXERCISE W11 *Narrowing the topic*

Reread the statement of the general topic that you wrote in Exercise W10. Narrow the topic by focusing on the main point of the question. On the lines below, write a statement that focuses on the specific point you will be discussing.

> The general topic was introduced in the statement:
> In order to be successful, a student must have certain characteristics.
>
> You write a statement that focuses on a specific point:
> *Perhaps the most important characteristic is diligence.*

EXERCISE W12 *Writing your thesis statement*

Look at the statement with the general topic that you wrote in Exercise W10 and how you narrowed the topic to focus on the main point of the question in Exercise W11. On the lines below, write a thesis statement that:

1. Will guide the essay toward answering the question
2. Can be supported by the ideas you generated in your mind map

The introductory sentences from the example boxes in Exercises W10 and W11 are:

In order to be successful, a student must have certain characteristics. Perhaps the most important characteristic is diligence.

Now you could write:

Being diligent is essential for many reasons.

This thesis statement tells the readers that the essay will discuss the reasons why being diligent is essential to a student's success. *Reasons* is the controlling idea that focuses this essay.

____

____

EXERCISE W13 *Improving your introductory paragraph*

Reread the introductory statements in the example box in Exercise W12. What needs to be added to make a complete introductory paragraph?

To make a complete introductory paragraph, you could add:

- A definition

  In order to be successful, a student must have certain characteristics. Perhaps the most important characteristic is diligence. **A person who is diligent works hard in a very careful and steady way.** Being diligent is essential **for success** for many reasons.

- Another sentence that narrows the topic

  In order to be successful, a student must have certain characteristics. **These characteristics include such qualities as motivation and intelligence. However,** perhaps the most important characteristic **of all** is diligence. A person who is diligent works hard in a very careful and steady way. Being diligent is **an** essential **characteristic** for many reasons.

Reread the introductory statements you wrote in Exercises W10–W12. Ask yourself the following questions:

1. Have I introduced the general topic of the question I have been asked to answer?
2. Have I narrowed the general topic to a specific topic?
3. Would a definition or further explanation improve my introduction?
4. Have I included a thesis statement that tells my reader exactly what I am going to discuss?

Rewrite your introductory statements in paragraph form, adding any improvements or additional information you think is needed.

____

____

____

____

____

____

____

____

EXERCISE W14 *Writing introductory paragraphs*

On your own paper, use the steps in Exercises W8–W13 to write introductory paragraphs for the other questions you analyzed in Exercise W7. Make a mind map for each question and write each introductory paragraph on a different sheet of paper. You will have an opportunity to complete these essays after working through Practice with Organizing and Writing Developmental Paragraphs, below, and Practice with Conclusions, p. 404.

Example introductory paragraphs for the three questions from Exercise W7 are on pp. 568 – 569.

PRACTICE WITH ORGANIZING AND WRITING DEVELOPMENTAL PARAGRAPHS

The body of your essay should contain at least two developmental paragraphs. Each developmental paragraph should have a topic sentence that supports and develops the controlling idea presented in the thesis statement of your essay. The ideas in each paragraph should support the topic sentence of that paragraph.

Writing developmental paragraphs

To write effective developmental paragraphs, follow these steps:

1. Use your mind map. Your mind map will help you focus on the ideas that support the thesis statement in your introduction.
2. Write a topic sentence for each paragraph you plan to write. Each topic sentence should relate to your thesis statement and introduce what the paragraph will be about.

   If you find that the topics you want to discuss do not support the thesis statement you have written, revise your thesis statement or reconsider your topic sentences.
3. Write ideas that support your topic sentences. The topic sentence for each paragraph tells the reader what the paragraph will be about. The ideas stated in the rest of the paragraph should all relate to the topic sentence.

   Read the following example paragraph:

   > Hobbies are important for many reasons. First, a hobby can be educational. For example, if the hobby is stamp collecting, the person can learn about the countries of the world and even some of their history. Second, engaging in a hobby can lead to meeting other people with the same interests. A person can also meet other people by going to parties. Third, a person's free time is being used in a positive way. The person has no time to be bored or get into mischief while engaged in the hobby. Finally, some hobbies can lead to a future job. A person who enjoys a hobby-related job is more satisfied with life.

WRITING

The topic sentence tells the reader that the paragraph is about hobbies. The controlling idea is reasons they are important. All of the sentences that follow should be about reasons for the importance of hobbies. However, the sentence, "A person can also meet other people by going to parties," does *not* refer to the reasons hobbies are important. This sentence weakens the paragraph and should be deleted.

4. Add details. To write a more fully developed paragraph, you need to add details to your supporting ideas. Your details can be facts, examples, personal experiences, or descriptions.

Read the example paragraph below. The topic is the Smithsonian Institution, and the controlling idea is reasons for a visit. The supporting ideas and details are labeled.

Topic sentence	The Smithsonian Institution is worth visiting for a number of reasons.
Supporting idea 1	The Smithsonian Institution comprises various museums that offer something for everyone.
Details – facts	These museums include the National Museum of History and Technology, the National Aeronautics and Space Museum, the National Collection of Fine Arts, the National Museum of Natural History, and several others.
Supporting idea 2	A person can do more than just look at the exhibits.
Details – examples	For example, in the insect zoo at the National Museum of Natural History, anyone who so desires can handle some of the exhibits.
Supporting idea 3	The museums provide unforgettable experiences.
Details – personal experience	In climbing through the Skylab exhibit at the National Aeronautics and Space Museum, I was able to imagine what it would be like to be an astronaut in space.
Supporting idea 4	Movies shown at regular intervals aid in building an appreciation of our world.
Details – description	In the National Aeronautics and Space Museum, there is a theater that has a large screen. When the movie is shown, it gives the viewer the feeling that he or she is in the movie itself, either floating above the Earth in a hot-air balloon or hang gliding over cliffs.

Exercises W15–W23

Use Exercises W15–W23 to develop your skills in writing developmental paragraphs.

EXERCISE W15 *Writing topic sentences for your developmental paragraphs*

In Exercise W9, you crossed out all of the ideas in your mind map that did not support the main point you chose to cover in your essay. On the lines below, write a topic sentence for each of the developmental paragraphs that you have decided to focus on after refining your mind map in Exercise W9. It is not necessary to have more than two or three paragraphs to support your thesis statement.

I. *One reason a student must work hard is the number of assignments that must be completed.*

According to the example above, the topic for the developmental paragraph is: one reason to work hard. The controlling idea is the number of assignments.

II. *Another reason for a student to be diligent is that there are many tests to prepare for.*

According to the example above, the topic for this developmental paragraph is: another reason to be diligent. The controlling idea is that there are many tests to prepare for.

I. ______________________________

____

II. ______________________________

____

III. ______________________________

____

IV. ______________________________

____

EXERCISE W16 *Checking topic sentences for your developmental paragraphs*

Reread the topic sentences on student diligence in the example box in Exercise W15. Answer the following questions:

1. Is the number of assignments to be completed a reason for a student to be diligent?
2. Is the number of tests to be taken a reason for a student to be diligent?

Compare the topic sentences you wrote in Exercise W15 with the thesis statement you wrote for your introductory paragraph in Exercise W12. Answer the following questions:

3. What are the topics presented in your topic sentences?
4. What are the controlling ideas in your topic sentences?
5. Do your topic sentences support your thesis statement?

Rewrite any topic sentences that do not support your thesis statement.

EXERCISE W17 *Writing supporting ideas*

Use your topic sentences from Exercises W15 and W16 to create an outline. Write your supporting ideas in the order you want to present them. Check to make sure that all the ideas support the topic sentence that you wrote. You may have fewer or more ideas than the number of spaces given below.

I. *One reason a student must work hard is the number of assignments that must be completed.*
   A. *reading lots of assignments*
   B. *writing papers*
   C. *doing lab experiments*

II. *Another reason for a student to be diligent is that there are many tests to prepare for.*
   A. *weekly quizzes*
   B. *midterm exams*
   C. *final exams*

I. ______________________________

____

   A. ______________________________
   B. ______________________________
   C. ______________________________
   D. ______________________________

II. ______________________________

____

   A. ______________________________
   B. ______________________________
   C. ______________________________
   D. ______________________________

III. ______________________________

____

   A. ______________________________
   B. ______________________________
   C. ______________________________
   D. ______________________________

IV. ______________________________

____

   A. ______________________________
   B. ______________________________
   C. ______________________________
   D. ______________________________

EXERCISE W18 *Practice in adding details*

Write one sentence that adds a detail to each of the following ideas. Use facts, examples, personal experiences, or descriptions.

1. The capital city of my country is _______________________.

____

2. My favorite pastime is reading.

____

3. It is important for me to score well on the TOEFL test.

____

4. A long vacation at the beach is a nice way to relax.

____

5. Habits such as smoking are hard to break.

____

6. Many bad traffic accidents could be prevented.

____

7. Modern architecture has its critics as well as its admirers.

____

8. The suburban shopping mall has taken away a lot of business from city centers.

____

EXERCISE W19 *Adding details to paragraphs*

Many paragraphs can be made better by adding details. Look at the example box below. Asking and answering the kinds of questions shown in the box will help you strengthen your paragraphs.

On your own paper, rewrite the "weak" paragraphs shown on the next page using the questions as a guide for adding details.

Although seat belts have been shown to save lives, people give a number of reasons for not using them. First, many people think they are a nuisance. Second, many people are lazy. Third, some people don't believe they will have an accident. Finally, some people are afraid the seat belt will trap them in their car. All of these reasons seem inadequate since statistics show that wearing seat belts saves lives and prevents serious injuries.

The paragraph can be improved by adding details to answer the following questions:

- Why don't people like seat belts?
- In what way are people lazy?
- Why do people think they won't have an accident?
- Under what circumstances might people get trapped?

Now read the paragraph with added details. Notice how adding answers to these questions has improved it.

Although seat belts have been shown to save lives, people give a number of reasons for not using them. First, many people think they are a nuisance. **They say the belt is uncomfortable and inhibits freedom of movement.** Second, many people are lazy. **For them, it is too much trouble to put on and adjust a seat belt, especially if they are only going a short distance.** Third, some people don't believe they will have an accident **because they are careful and experienced drivers. They think they will be able to respond quickly to avoid a crash.** Finally, some people are afraid the seat belt will trap them in their car. **They feel that if they have an accident, they might not be able to get out of a car that is burning, or they might be unconscious and another person won't be able to get them out.** All of these reasons seem inadequate since statistics show that wearing seat belts saves lives and prevents serious injuries.

1. When you plant a tree, you are helping your environment in many ways. Your tree will provide a home and food for other creatures. It will hold the soil in place. It will provide shade in the summer. You can watch it grow and someday show your children, or even grandchildren, the tree you planted.
   - What kind of home would the tree provide?
   - What kind of food would the tree provide?
   - What kind of creatures might use the tree?
   - Why is holding the soil in place important?
   - Why is shade important?
2. Airplanes and helicopters can be used to save people's lives. Helicopters can be used for rescuing people in trouble. Planes can transport food and supplies when disasters strike. Both types of aircraft can transport people to hospitals in emergencies. Helicopters and airplanes can be used to provide medical services to people who live in remote areas.
   - In what situations do people need rescuing by helicopters?
   - What kinds of disasters might happen?
   - What kinds of emergencies may require people to be transported to hospitals?
   - How can helicopters and airplanes be used to provide medical services for people in remote areas?
3. Studying in another country is advantageous in many ways. A student is exposed to a new culture. Sometimes he or she can learn a new language. Students can often have learning experiences not available in their own countries. A student may get the opportunity to study at a university where a leading expert in his or her field may be teaching.
   - How can exposure to a new culture be an advantage?
   - How can learning a new language be an advantage?
   - What kinds of experiences might a student have?
   - What are the benefits of studying under a leading expert?

EXERCISE W20 *Further practice in adding details to paragraphs*

The following paragraphs are weak. They could be improved by adding details. On your own paper, write questions about details that could be added. Then rewrite the paragraphs, making them stronger by inserting the answers to your questions.

1. Even though airplanes are fast and comfortable, I prefer to travel by car. When traveling by car, I can look at the scenery. Also, I can stop along the road. Sometimes I meet interesting people from the area I am traveling through. I can carry as much luggage as I want, and I don't worry about missing flights.

2. Wild animals should not be kept in captivity for many reasons. First, animals are often kept in poor and inhumane conditions. In addition, many suffer poor health from lack of exercise and exhibit frustration and stress through their neurotic behavior. Also, some animals will not breed in captivity. Those animals that mate often do so with a close relative. In conclusion, money spent in the upkeep of zoos would be better spent in protecting natural habitats.

3. Good teachers should have the following qualities. First, they must know the material that they are teaching very well. Second, they should be able to explain their knowledge. Third, they must be patient and understanding. Last, they must be able to make the subject matter interesting to the students.

EXERCISE W21 *Adding details to your developmental paragraphs*

On your own paper, write detail questions about the supporting ideas you wrote in your outline in Exercise W17.

I. One reason a student must work hard is the number of assignments that must be completed.
   A. reading lots of assignments
   B. writing papers
   C. doing lab experiments

- *What kinds of reading assignments are there?*
- *How will these readings be different from reading for fun?*
- *What kinds of papers might have to be written?*
- *How long will the papers have to be?*
- *What kind of lab work needs to be done?*

EXERCISE W22 *Completing your developmental paragraphs*

On your own paper, use the supporting ideas you wrote in your outline in Exercise W17 and the detail questions that you wrote in Exercise W21 to write your developmental paragraphs.

WRITING

> One reason a student must work hard is the number of homework assignments that must be completed. Most of the homework will be reading assignments. Besides the reading assignments in the textbook, a student may have to get journals or articles from the library or online to supplement the readings in the book. Because this kind of reading is academic, a lot of critical thinking is involved, and the student must work hard to understand it. In addition, there may be papers to write. These might include summaries of the readings or reports on research done in the library or online. Furthermore, there might be lab assignments. A language lab might require the student to listen as well as to read and write. A science lab might require the student to do experiments that will require writing a lab report.

EXERCISE W23 *Writing developmental paragraphs*

For more practice, write developmental paragraphs for the introductions that you wrote in Exercise W14, p. 397. You can refer to the original questions in Exercise W7, p. 391.

Model developmental paragraphs for the three questions from Exercise W7 are on pp. 569 – 570.

PRACTICE WITH CONCLUSIONS

So far, you have practiced writing the introduction (which restates the question and states the controlling idea) and writing the body (which discusses the question). An effective essay also includes a concluding paragraph. A concluding paragraph summarizes your ideas. It is important to have a conclusion. Without one, it may be difficult for the reader to know whether you have completed your essay or simply run out of time.

To write an effective concluding paragraph, follow these steps:

1. Restate the thesis statement in different words.
2. Restate the topic sentences from the developmental paragraphs.
3. State your opinion or preference, make a prediction, or give a solution.
4. Conclude with a statement that sums up the essay.

When writing a conclusion for the independent writing task, remember the following things:

Keep it simple A good conclusion strengthens your essay. However, it is better to use your time writing the developmental paragraphs than to spend too much time on the concluding paragraph.

Be sure it completes the essay Your concluding statement tells your reader that you are finished. Be careful not to include new ideas in your conclusion, which could make your reader think you are moving on to another topic.

Exercises W24–W28

Use Exercises W24–W28 to develop your skills in writing concluding paragraphs.

EXERCISE W24 *Restating the thesis statement*

On the lines below, rewrite the thesis statement you wrote in Exercise W12, p. 395, using different words.

The original thesis statement was:
Being diligent is an essential characteristic for many reasons.

The restated thesis statement could be:
In conclusion, students have good reasons for being diligent.

____

____

EXERCISE W25 *Restating the topic sentences of the developmental paragraphs*

On the lines below, rephrase the topic sentences you wrote for your developmental paragraphs in Exercises W15 and W16, p. 399.

The original topic sentences were:
One reason a student must work hard is the number of assignments that must be completed.
Another reason for a student to be diligent is that there are many tests to prepare for.

These topic sentences could be restated as follows:
Students must complete a large number of homework assignments and study for many exams.

____

____

____

EXERCISE W26 *Writing a concluding statement*

On the lines on the next page, rewrite the sentences you wrote in the two exercises above, and add a concluding statement. Your concluding statements should restate the general topic expressed in the introductory statement that you wrote in Exercise W10 and the specific topic that you wrote in Exercise W11.

The general topic and specific topic of the essay was:
In order to be successful, a student must have certain characteristics.
Perhaps the most important characteristic is diligence.

The concluding statement could be:
It is very important that a student develop the characteristic of diligence if he or she wishes to succeed at studying.

WRITING

EXERCISE W27 *Improving your concluding paragraph*

Look at the concluding paragraph you wrote in Exercise W26. Ask yourself the questions below and rewrite your paragraph accordingly.

1. Have I restated the thesis statement from my introductory paragraph?
2. Have I restated the topic sentences from my developmental paragraphs?
3. Have I concluded by repeating the topic of the essay?
4. Can I improve my conclusion by using pronoun references, rephrasing key words, and using connecting words?

The concluding paragraph for the example essay about the importance of diligence is:

> Students have good reasons for being diligent. Students must complete a large number of homework assignments and study for many exams. It is very important that a student develop the characteristic of diligence if he or she wishes to succeed at studying.

This paragraph could be improved by using pronoun references and connecting words and by changing words and phrases to avoid repetition:

> **In conclusion,** students have good reasons for being diligent. **They** must complete a large number of homework assignments and study for many exams. **Thus,** it is of **utmost importance** that students develop **this** characteristic if they wish to succeed **in their studies**.

EXERCISE W28 *Practicing the steps for writing essays*

For more practice, write concluding paragraphs for the introductions and the developmental paragraphs that you wrote in Exercises W14 and W23. You can refer to the original questions in Exercise W7, p. 391.

Model concluding paragraphs for the three questions in Exercise W7 are on pp. 570.

PRACTICE WITH ANALYZING ESSAYS

The list below covers the most important features of a well-written essay. You will not have time to rewrite your essay during the test. Therefore, keep this list in mind as you make an outline or mind map and write your essay.

1. Is there an introductory paragraph?
2. Does the introductory paragraph restate the question?
3. Does the introductory paragraph narrow the general topic to a specific topic?
4. Does the introductory paragraph have a thesis statement (a controlling idea)?
5. Does each paragraph have a clear topic sentence?
6. Do the topic sentences of the paragraphs support the thesis statement?
7. Do the ideas in each paragraph support its topic sentence?
8. Are the details (examples, facts, descriptions, personal experiences) clear?

9. Is there a concluding paragraph?
10. Does the concluding paragraph convey that the essay is complete?
11. Does the essay answer all parts of the question?
12. Is the essay cohesive?
13. Are the sentences concise?
14. Have the grammar and spelling been corrected?

Exercises W29–W31

Use Exercises W29–W31 to develop your skills in analyzing and scoring essays.

EXERCISE W29 *Analyzing essays*

Practice analyzing essays by reading the following student-written essays and answering each of the 14 questions in the list above.

Question A

Both large cars and small cars have their advantages and disadvantages. Write about some of these advantages and disadvantages. State which type of car you prefer and why.

Student-written essay A

Both large and small cars have their advantages and disadvantages.

First, large cars have many advantages. For example, many people can be carried inside the car. Also, large cars are stronger in bad accidents, and they are very good for big families. About the disadvantages. Large cars cannot get through small streets, and they use a lot of gas to start and run.

Second, small cars also have advantages and disadvantages. About the advantages. You can drive the small car any place. Small car uses less gas and many people call them economical. The last advantage is that the small car is good for the small family like a father, mother, and one child. About the disadvantages of small cars. The small car is not strong if someone has a bad accident. Moreover, small cars cannot go very fast because of their size.

For all this I like small cars.

Question B

In your opinion, what is one of the major problems in the world today? Discuss some reasons for its existence. Give some possible solutions.

Student-written essay B

Every day on the radio, on TV, and in the newspapers, we hear, see, or read about many problems in the world. Because of this we must think about these problems. We must also try to find a solution for them. Our lives depend on this. For example, there are pollution problems.

Air pollution is the first kind. It mostly comes from fumes released from cars, airplanes, and trains. Also, factories dump waste anywhere, even in the city where many people are living. Public safety does not concern the factory owners, who must know that people don't want to live in pollution that is dangerous for their health. Nobody in this world wants to breathe dirty air.

The second pollution problem is sea pollution. Many people earn their living from fishing in the sea, and the fish they catch feed many people. Their lives depend on the fish. But the sea has become so polluted from oil spills and factory wastes that the fish are dying. This pollution is not only killing the fish, but is also affecting those people who depend on the sea for food.

Seldom do you find a place nowadays that is not polluted. This problem is growing more difficult every day. We must find a good solution that makes the world a better place to live. A good way to keep these dangerous fumes away from the people must be found. Also, programs about pollution should be shown on TV. When people understand the bad effect of pollution on the human body, maybe they will stop doing those things that make the air or the sea polluted. Also, we should plant trees, which are very useful for the land. In conclusion, I hope we can find a solution for every kind of pollution in the world.

For further practice, rewrite the preceding essays and improve them.

EXERCISE W30 *Scoring essays*

Read the following six student essays. Use the list in Practice with Analyzing Essays, pp. 406 – 407, to see whether they meet the requirements of a good essay. Give each essay a score.

- A score of 5 is for an essay that indicates strong writing abilities.
- A score of 4 indicates average writing abilities.
- A score of 3 indicates minimal writing abilities.
- Scores of 2, 1, or 0 indicate a lack of writing abilities.

When you are finished, compare the score you gave the essays with the score given in the Answer Key. Read the analysis of the essays to understand the given score.

Question

Some people claim that reading novels is a waste of time. They say that reading nonfiction works is more beneficial. Do you agree? Support your opinion.

Student essays

1. Score _____

The main point is whether it is better to read fiction or nonfiction. The questions about this depends on the people who read. I am going to talk about both people.

The people who read the novels like to emphasize with the characters in the book. They can feel what to be another people. They can do things like traveling to the moon in their imagines during the read.

On the other hand, the people who read the nonfiction novels like to learn about facts. For these people, it solves problems and make them happy.

As you can see, I have discussed both novels and nonfiction works. Because of the above mentioned things both novels and nonfiction work is very important in our living.

2. Score _____

Some people claim that reading nonfiction works is beneficial whereas reading novels is a waste of time. Those who think this way do not realize the importance of the novel. The fictional world affects mankind in several ways.

When people read a novel, they are entering into a new world. Frequently, the story takes place in a real part of the world at a particular time in history. The reader then learns about this place and time. Also, the reader learns new words or about something unfamiliar. For example, someone who lives in the mountains might learn ship terms and how to sail a schooner.

Reading also stimulates the imagination. In our complex society, we need people who can find ways of solving problems. People who have been reading a lot of fiction have developed good imaginations. They can use their imaginations creatively to solve problems in ways that other people could never dream of.

Sometimes novels can change world events. For example, Harriet Beecher Stowe's antislavery novel may have helped end slavery in the United States. Sometimes novels can help us see things in a different way. *Animal Farm* may have influenced many readers about communism.

In conclusion, reading novels is not a waste of time. It provides readers with many satisfying hours that teaches them about life, stretches their imaginations, and focuses their minds on today's problems. Reading novels is and should always be an important activity for the people in the world.

3. Score _____

I think that reading novels is not a waste of time. In many years ago, people can't read. Therefore, grandfathers told their little boy about the stories. That is how knowledge about things that happen. For example, Helen of Troy. In these days, our grandfather don't tell stories. Most people in the life know how to read. We read the stories that in before times grandfathers say them. We can read about many adventures. People who don't want to read novels are not having a big adventure.

4. Score _____

I agree with the people who claim that reading novels is a waste of time. It is silly to spend the time reading about things that never can happen or that are not real such as science fiction is. But nonfiction works are beneficial.

There are many demands on our living these days. We must know about a lot of math and science. We must know more about computers and computer technology. Also, it is important to learn about other people and cultures. These are real things that we learn about them from nonfiction books.

People used to read novels for entertainment. We do not need to read fiction any more because of the television set. Now when people need to relax themselves, they can watch TV or go to the movies.

In conclusion, we need to read nonfiction works to improve our mental. Novels are no longer needed because things that are not real, we can see on TV. Therefore, reading nonfiction books is the more beneficial.

5. Score _____

Nowadays people read nonfiction works is better. Because it gave technology. Also, gave too much information the many things in the world. People need know too much nowadays can have a good life.

6. Score _____

Nonfiction works refer to those books that are informative. Novels are books that tell a story. Sometimes the story is completely made up. Sometimes it has real facts inside it. Reading either kind of book is beneficial.

Nonfiction works are not a waste of time. They are beneficial because they teach us things about our world. The things they teach us may be interesting information such as the history of our city. Sometimes the information is necessary for our lives such as a book on first-aid techniques.

Novels are not a waste of time either. They are beneficial because they help us enjoy our lives. We can do things vicariously with the people in the book that we would never experience in real life. Sometimes true events in history are more interesting because of the viewpoint of the fictional character in the story.

Since learning about life is necessary and since both kinds of books help us understand our world better, we should read both kinds of books. Therefore, the people who claim that reading novels is a waste of time are wrong about that. But they are right that reading nonfiction books is beneficial.

EXERCISE W31 *Scoring your own essays*

Look at the completed essays you wrote for the questions in Exercise W7. Use the list in Practice with Analyzing Essays, pp. 406 – 407, to score your essays.

PRACTICE WITH RESPONDING TO THE INDEPENDENT WRITING TASK

Now that you have studied all the parts of an essay, analyzed problems in other students' work, and written some of your own responses, review the steps to follow for the independent writing task.

Step 1 Read the question carefully and analyze the task.

Ask yourself questions. (What is the question about? What is it asking me to do?) Underline and number the key parts of the question.

Question Violent TV programs have been blamed for causing crime rates to rise in many countries. But many people do not agree that violence is related to TV viewing. Discuss the possible reasons for both opinions. (1) Give your opinion (2) as to whether or not violent programs should be taken off the air.

The question is about TV violence. It asks me to:

1. Discuss reasons for both opinions
   - Opinion that TV violence is bad
   - Opinion that TV violence is acceptable
2. Give my own opinion

Step 2 Make a mind map or a traditional outline.

In eight minutes or less, write down your ideas and group them into related ideas, using a mind map or a traditional outline. Two outlines are provided below as examples. Your mind map or outline does not need to be as orderly or complete as these.

Example of a detailed outline

I. Introduction
   A. state general topic
   B. restate question
   C. give thesis statement – reasons for both sides

II. Body
  A. crime related to violent TV programs
    1. children imitate what they see
      a. learn unacceptable values
      b. copy behavior
    2. heroes are frequently violent
    3. gives ideas for crimes
  B. crime not related to violent TV programs
    1. crime related to social pressures
      a. unemployment
      b. homelessness
    2. aggressive feelings vicariously released
    3. parental guidance more influential
    4. frequently bad consequences of violence shown

III. Conclusion
  A. my opinion
    1. shouldn't be censored
      a. people enjoy it
      b. change station
      c. turn off
    2. censorship questions
      a. who decides?
      b. what else may they censor?
    3. concluding statement

Example of a brief outline

T.S. (thesis statement): reasons to support both

  A. why crime related to TV
    imitate
    violent heroes
    gives ideas
  B. why crime not related to TV
    social pressures – joblessness, homelessness
    rids aggression
    parental influence
    bad consequences

Conclude with opinion
  no censor – enjoyment, change, or turn off
  censor – who decides what

C.S. (concluding statement): need evidence

Step 3 Study your mind map or outline and decide on a thesis statement.

According to the preceding outlines, the thesis statement will introduce the essay with reasons for both sides of the question.

Step 4 Make sure the topic sentences support the thesis statement.

Topic sentence A indicates that the paragraph will discuss one side of the question: reasons why crime is related to TV. This sentence supports the thesis statement. Topic sentence B indicates that the paragraph will discuss the other side of the question: reasons why crime is not related to TV. This sentence also supports the thesis statement.

If your topic sentences do not support the thesis statement, you can do one of two things:

1. Rewrite the topic sentences.
2. Rewrite the thesis statement.

Step 5 Make sure that all supporting ideas relate to the topic.

According to the preceding outlines, the topic sentence of the first developmental paragraph will discuss reasons why crime is related to TV. The supporting ideas – children imitate what is seen, heroes are frequently violent, and it gives ideas for crimes – support the argument that TV and crime are related.

The topic sentence of the second developmental paragraph will discuss reasons why crime is not related to TV. The supporting ideas – social pressures, rids aggression, parental influence, and bad consequences – support the argument that TV and crime are not related.

Step 6 Add more details if necessary.

Step 7 Put ideas in a logical order if necessary.

Step 8 Write the introduction.

Keep in mind the list in Practice with Analyzing Essays, pp. 406 – 407. You will not have time to rewrite your essay during the test, so be certain your introduction is clear.

> The crime rate in many countries is rising at an alarming rate. Some people have the idea that violent TV programs are the real cause of crime. However, many others disagree that TV violence can be blamed for this rise. Both sides of the question of whether TV may or may not be to blame can be supported by good reasons.

Step 9 Write the body of the essay.

Keep in mind the list on pp. 406 – 407. You will not have time to rewrite your essay, so be certain the paragraphs support the thesis statement.

> Those who believe that violent TV programs cause crime give many reasons. First, many viewers are children who have not formed a strong understanding of right and wrong. They imitate what they see. If a person on TV gets what he or she wants by stealing it, a child may copy this behavior. Thus, the child has learned unacceptable values. Second, many heroes in today's programs achieve their goals by violent means. Unfortunately, viewers might use similar means to achieve their objectives. Finally, people get ideas about how to commit crimes from watching TV.
>
> Other people argue that violent programs have no relation to the rise in crime rates. First, they claim that social factors, such as unemployment and homelessness, are to blame. Second, some argue that watching violence on TV is an acceptable way to reduce aggressive feelings. In other words, people may become less aggressive through viewing criminal and violent scenes. Third, even though children learn by imitation, their parents are the most influential models. Finally, the villains on TV are usually punished for their crimes.

Step 10 Write the conclusion.

Keep in mind the list on pp. 406 – 407. You will not have time to rewrite your essay, so be certain your conclusion completes the essay.

> Whether or not violent programs are a factor in the rising crime rate, I am against their removal for the following reasons. First, some people enjoy them, and those who don't can change channels or turn off their TVs. Second, I disagree with other people deciding what I should watch. If violent programs can be censored, perhaps other programs that may be important for our well-being will also be censored. In conclusion, even though I am not fond of violent programs, I am against their removal from TV until conclusive evidence proves that viewing violence creates violence.

Step 11 Read over the essay.

Make any minor corrections in spelling and grammar that will make your essay clearer. You will not have time to make major changes.

Exercise W32 Use Exercise W32 to practice your skills in writing essays.

EXERCISE W32 *Writing essays*

Plan your test preparation schedule to include writing essays at regular intervals. Follow the steps above to answer the following essay questions. Try to complete a 250- to 300-word essay and check it within 30 minutes. This is the amount of time you will be given to complete the independent writing task on the TOEFL test.

Type your essays on a computer. The computer screens for the independent writing task appear as shown in the first item below.

1.

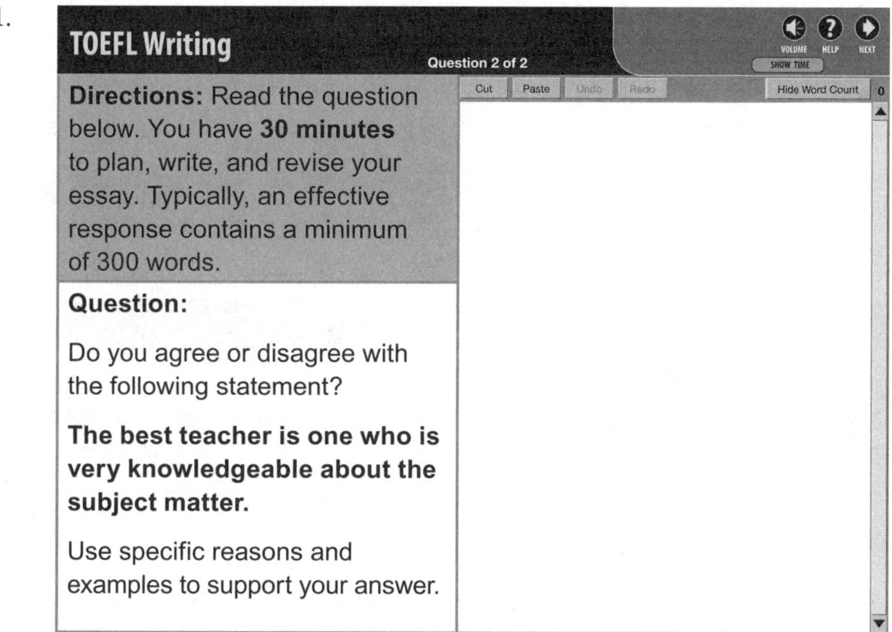

TOEFL Writing
Question 2 of 2
VOLUME HELP NEXT
SHOW TIME
Cut Paste Undo Redo
Hide Word Count 0
Directions: Read the question below. You have 30 minutes to plan, write, and revise your essay. Typically, an effective response contains a minimum of 300 words.
Question:
Do you agree or disagree with the following statement?
The best teacher is one who is very knowledgeable about the subject matter.
Use specific reasons and examples to support your answer.

2. Compare and contrast the advantages of city living and country living. Defend your preference.
3. Think critically about the following statement.
   A universal language should replace all languages.
   Discuss the advantages and disadvantages of a universal language.
4. Do you agree or disagree with the following statement?
   Students learn better when they are not threatened with possible failure.
   Use reasons and specific examples to support your opinion.
5. Do you agree or disagree with the following statement?
   The private car has brought more harm than benefits to the planet.
   Use reasons and specific examples to support your opinion.
6. Many people believe that parents are too permissive with their children nowadays. Do you agree that this is a problem? Defend your answer.
7. Do you agree or disagree with the following statement?
   The best things in life are free.
   Use reasons and specific examples to support your opinion.
8. Drug abuse has become a major social problem in many parts of the world. Discuss the consequences of drug abuse and ways to deal with the problem.
9. Billions of dollars go into space exploration projects every year. Some people feel that this money should be used to solve problems on Earth. Discuss reasons supporting both opinions. State and support your opinion.
10. Compare and contrast the advantages of choosing a stable career over an adventurous lifestyle. Use reasons and specific examples to support your opinion.

INTEGRATED WRITING TASK

The integrated writing task of the TOEFL iBT test requires you to relate information from a reading passage and a listening passage. The listening passage may give a different perspective on the information presented in the reading passage, or it may provide further support. You will be asked to integrate the two passages in your response. Your response should be about 150–225 words in length.

Strategies to Use for the Integrated Writing Task

1. Be familiar with the organization of an effective response.
An effective response begins with an introductory paragraph that presents the topic and the controlling idea of the essay. The body of the response should integrate the reading and listening passages. The conclusion completes the response.

2. Be familiar with the task.
You will be asked to summarize the points in the listening passage and explain how those points support or provide a different perspective on the points made in the reading passage.

3. Organize your notes.
You may take notes while you read the passage. Write down the main points in your own words. If there is a word or phrase unique to the passage that you might want to use, put it in quotation marks. Organize the notes you take from the reading passage in such a way that you can add the notes you take from the listening. For example, fold your paper in half lengthwise, and write your notes about the reading passage on the left side of the fold. Then, during the lecture, write notes on the right side of the fold. Put related ideas from the lecture near the corresponding ideas from the reading passage. You will be able to return to the reading passage after you have heard the lecture. However, you will hear the lecture only once.

4. Write cohesively and concisely.
While you are organizing the main points from the passages, keep in mind the techniques for making your response cohesive (see Practice with Cohesion, p. 317). While you are writing your response, keep in mind the techniques for making your sentences both cohesive and concise (see Practice with Writing Concisely, p. 383). Be careful not to introduce ideas that are not in the passages.

5. Budget your time so that you will be able to complete and correct your response.
You have only 20 minutes to write your response. Use your time efficiently while you organize your ideas, write your response, and make minor corrections. Practice using your time efficiently while doing the exercises in this section.

6. Use sentence structures and vocabulary you know to be correct.
Use sentence structures and vocabulary that you know how to use well. A well-written response includes a variety of structures and vocabulary.

7. Check your grammar.
When you are writing, look out for the kinds of grammar errors that you know you commonly make. Check your grammar when you review your essay.

LOOKING AT THE ORGANIZATION OF AN EFFECTIVE RESPONSE

Example question and response

Read the reading and listening passages below and the question that follows. Then study the example response. Note: the passages below are not full, test-length reading and listening passages. However, the example response meets the required length.

Reading passage

Peptic ulcer disease is a condition in which open sores develop on the inside lining of the stomach and intestine. The main symptoms of this common affliction are pain in the abdominal region and occasionally weight loss, nausea, and the vomiting of blood. The general belief has been that peptic ulcers are caused by lifestyle choices including diet and stress. Natural acids, which help food digestion, and pepsin, an enzyme in the stomach that also helps with digestion, were thought to damage the protective layer of the gastrointestinal tract as a result of psychological stresses and the overindulgence of certain foods, alcohol, and tobacco. Treatment with medications that inhibit acid production was found to significantly relieve the symptoms of the disease.

Listening passage

I'm going to bring you up to date with the research here. Many doctors now think that most peptic ulcers are not really a result of stress at all. Rather, it is believed that bacteria known as Helicobacter pylori *are responsible. What happens is that these bacteria get into the stomach and injure the protective mucous layer. At this point, the stomach acid can worsen the damage since it can penetrate the injured area.*

Now, what proof do we have that ulcers are caused by these bacteria? Well, remember that peptic ulcers used to be treated fairly successfully with drugs that reduced stomach acid production. Well, what usually happened was that in the majority of patients, the symptoms reappeared within a year or two. So clearly the underlying causes were still untreated. This older treatment didn't get to the root of the problem.

More recently, we have found that antibacterial medications directed at bacteria, uh, the Helicobacter pylori *bacteria, have had remarkable success. After treatment, symptoms don't recur. And so, antibiotics are now the treatment of choice in dealing with this condition. Having said that, however, please note that there are still some researchers who think that stress could be one factor in peptic ulcer disease. Nevertheless, the success of antibiotic treatment has been an important breakthrough in this field.*

Question Summarize the points made in the lecture you just heard, explaining how they cast doubt on the points made in the reading.

Example response

The belief that stress and bad food choices allowed stomach acids and an enzyme to damage the digestive tract, eventually resulting in an ulcer, has come under question because the treatment for the problem seemed to work only temporarily.

The fact that ulcer treatment led to only short-term improvements made researchers think that only symptoms were being treated rather than the underlying cause. An antibiotic that fights a particular bacteria has proved successful for long-term treatment of ulcers. It is now believed that bacteria do the initial damage to the tissue lining and that stomach acid and the pepsin enzyme worsen the damage rather than being the primary cause.

The finding that this bacterium may be the cause of ulcers could be the breakthrough for a cure instead of just a treatment of symptoms. Nevertheless, even though antibacterial medicine has proved effective, some researchers of peptic ulcer disease believe that stressful lifestyles are still a factor in the problem.

Analysis of the example response

Study the following analysis of the example response you just read.

Introductory statement

The response begins by introducing the topic, the cause of ulcers, and the controlling idea that the original belief about the cause of ulcers is under question.

Summary of ideas
The main points from the listening passage that are summarized in the response are:

1. The original belief as to the cause of ulcers is under question. Temporary relief casts doubt on the reading as this points to the symptoms being treated instead of a cure being found.
2. The effectiveness of antibiotics in ulcer treatment points to the underlying cause being a bacterium. This casts doubt on the effectiveness of acid-suppressing medicines in the treatment of ulcers.
3. The damage to the tissue lining by stomach acids and enzymes is possible because of the damage caused by the bacteria. This casts doubt on the primary cause being lifestyle choices.

Conclusion
The concluding paragraph begins with a mention of the importance of the antibiotic treatment. The fact that stress is still thought by some people to be a factor ties the listening to the reading and completes the response.

PRACTICE WITH PARAPHRASES AND SUMMARIES

To write an effective response for the integrated writing task on the TOEFL iBT test, it is necessary to extract information from both the reading and the listening passages. To use this information in your response, you will need to be able to paraphrase and summarize ideas.

A *summary* is your condensed version of the ideas presented in a reading passage or a lecture. A *paraphrase* is an idea that you have restated in your own words. When you paraphrase or summarize, it is important to:

- Keep the same meaning as the original. Be careful not to change the meaning.
- Include only the author's information. Be careful not to add new information.

For a more complete explanation of paraphrasing and summarizing, see Note Taking, Paraphrasing, and Summarizing, pp. 52–62.

Exercises W33–W36

Use Exercises W33–W36 to practice your skills in paraphrasing and summarizing.

EXERCISE W33 *Paraphrasing sentences*

Rewrite the sentences on the next page in your own words.

Not until Edward Jenner developed the first anti-smallpox serum in 1796 was there protection against this terrible disease.

Defense against smallpox was achieved in the late eighteenth century with Edward Jenner's anti-smallpox serum.

Notice how the paraphrase differs from the original passage grammatically and in the words used. However, a different term cannot be substituted for the name of the disease or for the name of the man who developed the serum.

1. The Mediterranean monk seal is distinguished from the more familiar gray seal by its size.

____

____

2. Estimates from scientists suggest that only one percent of the world's extinct animals and plants have been identified.

____

____

3. Early sailors, navigating sometimes in uncharted seas, faced many hazards in reaching their destination.

____

____

4. This report from the United Nations suggests that water will be at the heart of many future international disputes.

____

____

5. Square-rigged ships, which can attain high speeds only when traveling with the trade winds, are no longer commercially viable.

____

____

6. A fine tomb, erected in the sixteenth century, marks the grave of the poet Geoffrey Chaucer.

____

____

7. There are up to 600 butterfly species worldwide known collectively as "swallowtails."

____

____

8. Even though city parks often serve as places of public entertainment and festivals, they can also be places where people can find peace and solitude.

____

____

9. Drying food by means of solar energy is an ancient process applied wherever crops and climatic conditions make it possible.

____

____

10. The Victorian constructions of Haight-Ashbury are among the few architectural survivors of the San Francisco earthquake of 1906.

____

____

EXERCISE W34 *Checking paraphrases*

Compare the following sentences and the paraphrase of those sentences. If the paraphrase does not mean the same as the original sentences, rewrite it so that it conveys the same meaning.

Original: People who have made significant contributions to humanity are granted a financial award from a legacy left by the Swedish scientist Alfred B. Nobel.

Paraphrase: Alfred B. Nobel from Sweden awarded important people money to help others.

The Swedish scientist Alfred B. Nobel left money to be awarded to people who have done something important to help humankind.

There are several mistakes in the paraphrase of the statement. Nobel left money when he died – he does not personally give out these awards. The award is not given to important people, but to people who make important contributions to society. People are awarded the money for what they have done; they are not given the prize money to help other people.

Original: Some Paleolithic artifacts are given special names indicating the location of their discovery.

Paraphrase: Paleolithic artifact names sometimes refer to the place they were discovered.

The paraphrase above contains correct information, so it does not need to be rewritten.

1. *Original:* The Seeing Eye Puppy-Raising Program places future guide dogs with volunteers who start preparing the puppies for the job ahead.

   Paraphrase: Volunteers prepare Seeing Eye dogs for the future needs of the blind by raising puppies for the program.

   ____

   ____

2. *Original:* The black moths surviving in industrial areas have become genetically more tolerant of pollution.

   Paraphrase: The black moth has survived industrialization by genetically adapting to pollution.

   ____

   ____

3. *Original:* Windmills have made a comeback in Denmark, where centuries ago the people of this windswept country used wind power to pump water and grind grain.

   Paraphrase: In Denmark, a windy country, the people have returned to using windmills to pump water and grind grain.

   ____

   ____

4. *Original:* In order to develop to its full potential, a baby needs to be physically able to respond to the environment.

   Paraphrase: Full physical potential is needed in order for a baby to be able to respond to the environment.

   ____

   ____

5. *Original:* Crazy Horse's vision of a painted rider galloping through a storm was seen as a sign that he would become a great warrior leading his people into battle.

   Paraphrase: Crazy Horse's people believed that his dream of a warrior riding through a storm was an indication of his impending leadership in battle.

   ____

   ____

EXERCISE W35 *Writing summaries of listening passages*

Listen to the following passages. Pause the recording after each one. Write a one-sentence summary of the passage you hear.

> You hear:
>
> *Since the dawn of civilization, the bow and arrow have been used to secure food, protect people from enemies, and provide competitive games of skill. Although archery is no longer a necessary skill for survival, it is becoming increasingly popular as a sport. Today's bows are much easier to handle than those of the past were, but the basic form has not changed.*
>
> You could write:
>
> *While shooting with bow and arrow is no longer needed for survival, recreational archery is gaining popularity.*
>
> The essential information of the paragraph is that people still practice archery. The list of reasons for practicing it in the past and the change in bows for easier handling are details that can be excluded from the summary.

START ▶

1. ____

   ____

2. ____

   ____

3. ____

   ____

STOP ■

EXERCISE W36 *Revising summaries of listening passages*

Listen to the following lecture segments. Pause the recording after each one and read the summary of the lecture segment you just heard. The summary gives incorrect information. Rewrite the summary to give correct information.

You hear:

Scientists have reported that positive thinkers seem to live healthier lives. Even though this theory has not yet been proved, there is no doubt that positive thinkers live happier lives. They look at life with an attitude of hope that influences their environment in a way that creates positive results.

You read:

Positive results leading to healthier lives influence positive thinkers according to a theory proposed by scientists.

You could write:

According to a theory on positive thinking, the well-being of a person can be influenced by how he or she regards life.

START ▶

1. The main advantage of herding animals instead of killing them is that they can be bred selectively to produce more milk or more meat.

2. Fun-seekers maintain their thinking abilities into their old age because they have played general knowledge games.

3. The *kiva* was a circular walled area with a hole that held the entrance to the underworld for the Anasazi people of the American Southwest.

STOP ■

PRACTICE WITH INTEGRATING PASSAGES

The integrated writing task requires that you explain how the points made in the listening passage support or provide a different perspective on the points made in the reading passage. The passages you read and hear will contain numerous ideas. In order to explain how these ideas compare, you will need to paraphrase and summarize them.

Exercises W37–W40

Use Exercises W37–W40 to practice combining information from your paraphrases of the reading passages and your summaries of the listening passages.

EXERCISE W37 *Paraphrasing main ideas in reading passages*

Read the following passages. On your own paper, paraphrase the main ideas.

1. Shortly after eight o'clock on Sunday evening, October 30, 1938, many Americans became anxious or panic-stricken after listening to a realistic live one-hour radio play depicting a fictitious Martian landing at a farm in the tiny hamlet of Grovers Mill, New Jersey. Those living in the immediate vicinity of the bogus invasion appeared to have been most frightened, although the broadcast could be heard in all regions of the continental United States and no one particular location was immune. The play included references to real places, buildings, highways, and streets. The broadcast also contained prestigious speakers, convincing sound effects, and realistic special bulletins.

   The drama was produced by a 23-year-old theatrical prodigy named George Orson Welles, who was accompanied by a small group of actors and musicians in a New York City studio. The actual broadcast script was loosely based on the 1898 book *The War of the Worlds* by acclaimed science-fiction writer H. G. Wells. In the original Wells novel, the Martians had landed in nineteenth century England. More than sixty years after the 1938 event, it remains arguably the most widely known delusion in United States – and perhaps world – history, and many radio stations around the world continue to broadcast the original play each Halloween.

   Not only does the Martian panic demonstrate the enormous influence of the mass media on contemporary society, but in recent years an ironic twist has developed. There is a growing consensus among sociologists that the extent of the panic was greatly exaggerated. The irony here is that for many years the public may have been misled by the media to believe that the panic was far more extensive and intense than it apparently was. However, regardless of the extent of the panic, there is little doubt that many Americans were genuinely frightened and some did try to flee the Martian gas raids and heat rays.

2. The construction of the Brooklyn Bridge spanning the East River in New York City was one of the great engineering triumphs of the nineteenth century. The project, approved in 1866, met with its first setback with the death of its designer and chief engineer, John Roebling. His son, Washington Roebling, took over the work of supervising the project.

   Because work had to be performed below water level, enormous watertight chambers were developed. The bottom of each chamber was open and rested on the riverbed. Tubes extending above the water level allowed compressed air to be pumped in to prevent the entry of water and to provide air for the workers excavating the soil on the bottom. The extracted debris was removed through other vertical shafts. With the soil removal, the chambers sank into the riverbed until they rested securely on underlying rock. On their upper sides, the granite towers from which the bridge was suspended were built to the height of 270 feet above water level.

   To support the weight of the roadway, four immense spun-wire cables, 16 inches in diameter, were fed out from cast-iron blocks mounted on the tops of the towers. From the cables, steel rope suspenders reached down to the roadway itself, and steel stays leading directly from the towers to the deck gave extra support.

   Many novel problems were faced during construction. One was caused by the compressed air pumped into the chambers. Workers ascending too rapidly through the chambers suffered from the disease *the bends,* caused by nitrogen bubbles forming in the blood. Roebling himself became disabled by the bends and spent the remainder of the building period supervising from his apartment overlooking the river. Roebling's wife took over the management and eventually became an expert on bridge construction.

Despite numerous accidents, engineering difficulties, and some financial scandals, in 1883 the bridge was opened to public traffic, a testament to the determination, skill, and daring of those who envisioned and built it.

EXERCISE W38 *Summarizing listening passages*

Listen to the following lecture excerpts. On your own paper, summarize the important ideas. After you have summarized those ideas, write a topic sentence that gives the main idea of the complete listening passage.

START ▶

1. Topic sentence: ______________________________
2. Topic sentence: ______________________________

STOP ■

EXERCISE W39 *Linking ideas in reading and listening passages*

On your own paper, take notes on the following reading and listening passages to find the conflicting or supporting information. Paraphrase and summarize in your notes.

1. The use of fluoride in preventative dentistry has been a great breakthrough in improving the dental health of large populations. Small amounts of soluble fluoride ions are present in all water sources, including oceans, and also to some extent in food and beverages, although quantities vary considerably from region to region.

   The importance of fluoride for tooth development has been well documented in the scientific literature. Studies of data from as far back as the 1930s showed that children living in areas of naturally occurring fluoridated water had superior dental health to children living in areas where the water was relatively deficient in this element. In fluoride-deficient regions this element can be added to the water supply in minute quantities.

   When this is done, the benefits in improved dental health in the population exposed to fluoride-supplemented water are similar to those obtained by exposure to fluoride occurring naturally. In either case, researchers have observed the preventative effects working through various mechanisms, chief among which are that fluoride reduces the solubility of tooth enamel and also reduces the ability of plaque organisms to produce enamel-attacking acids. During the formation of teeth in the young, fluoride joins with the enamel surface and makes it harder and hence more resistant to decay.

   According to research, fluoride can even help repair cavities by rebuilding the enamel layer of teeth. Topical application by way of fluoride toothpaste or drops is also helpful in older adults since it can help prevent decay and sensitivity in the roots of teeth.

START ▶

(narrator) *Now listen to part of a lecture on the topic you just read about.*

STOP ■

WRITING

2. The belief that animals can sense an earthquake before it occurs has been held since at least the ancient Greeks. Countries such as China and Japan, which suffer frequently from the devastation brought about by seismic disturbances, have a long history of attempting to use animals to predict earthquakes.

Apparently animals of all kinds act in peculiar ways just prior to an earthquake. Many animals have more sensitive auditory capacities than humans, and perhaps because of this, react to ultrasound originating from fracturing rock. Some researchers have also pointed out that some animals can pick up variations in the earth's magnetic field occurring near the epicenters of seismic events. Examples of unusual animal behavior include dogs barking for hours and wild animals appearing confused or losing their natural fear of people. Some people claim that even fish, reptiles, and insects engage in abnormal behavior at this time. Catfish, for example, are reputed to jump out of the water onto the land, and snakes have been seen leaving the nests where they were hibernating. Such strange behavior occurs from just moments before to a couple of weeks in advance of the quake.

A famous example of the successful use of animal behavior to predict a quake occurred in China in 1975 when the authorities ordered the evacuation of the city of Haicheng, just a few days before a 7.3 magnitude quake, thus saving the lives of thousands of people.

START ▶

(narrator) *Now listen to part of a lecture on the topic you just read about.*

STOP ■

EXERCISE W40 *Writing responses*

Use the notes that you took from the reading passage and listening passage in Exercise W39 to write responses to the following questions on your own paper.

1. Summarize the points made in the lecture you heard on fluoride, explaining how the points cast doubt on the points made in the reading.
2. Summarize the points made in the lecture you heard on earthquakes, explaining how the points cast doubt on the points made in the reading.

PRACTICE WITH ANALYZING RESPONSES

The list below covers the important features of a well-written response to an integrated writing task. You will not have time to rewrite your response during the test. Therefore, keep this list in mind as you organize the information and write your response.

1. Is there a topic sentence that introduces the main idea of the listening passage?
2. Have all the key points been presented?
3. Is the response well organized?
4. Is the information presented accurately?
5. Is the information presented in your own words?
6. Is all the information found in the passages?
7. Is the response cohesive?
8. Are the sentences written concisely?
9. Is the response completed with a concluding statement?
10. Have grammar and spelling errors been corrected?

Exercises W41–W43

Use Exercises W41–W43 to develop your skills in analyzing and scoring integrated writing responses.

EXERCISE W41 *Analyzing responses*

Practice analyzing responses by reading the following student-written answers to item 1 in Exercise W40. Use the questions on the previous page as a guide.

1. People are questioning the addition of fluoride to water since studies have shown that it may lead to potential health hazards.

   Fluoride exists in different quantities in our water supplies. Early studies showed that it was important for the development and health of teeth. According to these studies fluoride improved the enamel of developing teeth so that teeth were stronger, acid resistant, and helped the body rebuild damaged enamel.

   Without people giving their consent, fluoride was added to the water in some areas where the amounts were low. However, new studies do not show a difference between the development of healthy teeth in areas of low and high amounts of fluoride in the water. The extra fluoride in the water may actually harm the environment. Also, it has been shown to accumulate in people's bodies and cause side effects.

   People should not allow themselves to be guinea pigs in a fluoride experiment, and fluoride supplements should not be added to water or toothpaste.

2. Fluoride should not be added to water like the dentists said that it should in the 1930s studies. It has been found that the teeth of children in areas where there is little fluoride in the water are no different than those of children in areas where there is a lot of fluoride in the water. So the results of the early studies are wrong.

   Not only does fluoride not do all the things that it supposedly does, like reduce the solubility of tooth enamel and stop plaque organisms from making acids that break down enamel, but it also causes problems in the water supply, like is a poisonous waste in water. It can also cause side effects in animals, but I don't think animals should be used in testing experiments and neither should people. People should be able to say if they want to have fluoride in their water.

   In conclusion, our governments should not allow fluoride to be added to our water supply cause it is bad for us.

EXERCISE W42 *Scoring responses*

Read the following six student responses to item 2 in Exercise W40 and give them a score.

- A score of 5 is for a response that indicates strong writing abilities.
- A score of 4 indicates average writing abilities.
- A score of 3 indicates minimal writing abilities.
- Scores of 2, 1, or 0 indicate a lack of writing abilities.

When you are finished, compare the score you gave each response with the score given in the Answer Key. Read the analysis of the responses to understand the given score.

1. Score _____

   Animals seem to be able to predict that an earthquake is coming and therefore, can be used as a way to warn people to evacuate a city like Haicheng in China. However, according to the lecture, it was not animals that warned the people of a coming earthquake. The authorities order the city to be evacuated because there were small earthquakes before the big one.

Sometimes animals do behavior that isn't normal, like fish leaping out of the water and dogs barking all the time. Because animals have better hearing than people, they can hear the movement of the earth before the people. That is why the dogs keep barking. However, according to the lecture, animals don't act any differently. People just notice a behavior that they didn't noticed before because an earthquake didn't forced them to notice the strange behavior.

2. Score _____

People believe that animals and things like fish and snakes know when an earthquake is going to happen. They do weird things like jump out of the water and if people pay attention to the weird things they do, they would know that an earthquake starting.

The lecture say that it is not true that animals can to know that an earthquake happens. People focussing on their pets because of the earthquake remember different things that did not really happen. Stories of animals who run away is the people making up things because they have been upset by the catastrophe.

The Chinese City of Haicheng had a 7.3 magnitude quake in 1975 but nobody died because the authorities predict the big quake and told everyone to leave the city.

3. Score _____

The notion that animals could be used as an early warning signal to alert people of impending earthquakes is not supported by the proven evidence.

Many people believe that because creatures seem to know when an earthquake is going to occur and act strangely or go missing, they can be used as indications that there is danger. Because the animals have senses that are more acute than those of people, they can detect minor movements in the earth or changes in the earth's magnetic field. However, the evidence that people give is their personal interpretation of an event after the fact.

Supposedly, pets run away when they sense a pending earthquake. However, a California scientist researched reports of missing pets and did not find any correlation between the number of animals reported to have gone missing immediately before an earthquake and those reported missing during times when there is no seismic activity. People tend to remember events more vividly when suffering trauma caused by something like an earthquake and therefore, may remember their dogs acting differently. However, the dog may have acted that way before, but the pet owner did not notice because an earthquake had not yet occur to fix that behavior in their minds.

Even the evidence of the thousands of people being saved by animals in the Chinese earthquake has proved false because some shock waves occurred before the earthquake and this gave the people real warning of an impending disaster.

4. Score _____

There is earthquakes animal tell big. Go away and be saved.

5. Score _____

It has been believed since before the Greek civilization that animals can predict earthquakes. People report that animals act in strange ways and frequently evacuate an area before the earthquake occurs. They are able to do this because they have senses that are better than humans. According to many people, paying attention to these animal behaviors could be an important way to predict earthquakes and save the lives of thousands of people.

However, according to the lecture, it is not true that animals are a reliable way to predict earthquakes. It is true that animals have better senses, but that doesn't mean they can actually predict earthquakes. The evidence that they can do this is based on people remembering something vividly because something bad happened. But what they remember is probably something that occurs normally that they had never paid attention to before.

A scientist in California did a study to see if there is a correlation between dogs running away from home and there occurring an earthquake. He did not find that dogs ran away any more often before an earthquake than at other times during the three year study.

Even the famous story of animals saving thousands of people in China in 1975 was disputed in the lecture. Apparently, some tiny earthquakes occurred first and this alerted the authorities to evacuate the city.

6. Score _____

The people believe that animals can tell an earthquake since the ancient Greeks. Animals have ears that can hear the earth move because of ultrasound. Even they know near epicenters. And animals predict an earthquake in China and saving the lives of thousands of people. So animals are good for people.

EXERCISE W43 *Scoring your own responses*

Look at the completed integrated writing responses that you wrote for Exercise W40. Use the list in Practice with Analyzing Responses, p. 424, to score your responses.

PRACTICE WITH RESPONDING TO THE INTEGRATED WRITING TASK

Now that you have studied the ways to approach the integrated writing task, analyzed problems in other students' responses, and written some of your own responses, review the steps to follow for writing the integrated writing task response.

Step 1 Read the passage carefully.

Reading passage

The remote Easter Island has been inhabited from about the fourth century CE. Much academic debate has centered on accounting for the origins of the people who migrated there and created its huge stone statues, which are the island's most well-known cultural artifacts. The Norwegian explorer Thor Heyerdahl believed that the initial colonization came from South America, several thousand kilometers to the east. He based his claims on several factors including the similarities in prehistoric cultural remains between parts of the continent and the island. In order to help prove his theory, Heyerdahl and his crew sailed a simple balsa wood raft from the Peruvian coast and reached the Polynesian archipelago using only the prevailing winds. His successful navigation bolstered the theory of the South American origins of the Easter Islanders.

Step 2 Make a list of the important points.

- Debate on who originally inhabited Easter Island in the fourth century CE
- Thor Heyerdahl noted cultural remains were similar to South America's.
- Thor Heyerdahl sailed from Peru across the Pacific Ocean in simple raft using prevailing winds. This showed it was possible for prehistoric people to make similar voyages.

Step 3 Listen to the lecture and take notes as you listen or immediately afterward.

Listening passage

OK. You're all familiar, I'm sure, with Heyerdahl's famous wind-powered voyage. His trip seemed to clinch the argument for the theory of the South American origins of the Easter Island people. However, nowadays most anthropologists tend to argue that the migration to the island came from Polynesia – uh, in other words, from the west.

So why did people abandon the idea that the migrants came from South America? Well, the evidence is partly linguistic. In other words, linguists have found clear similarities in certain linguistic features of Polynesia and Easter Island. Also, researchers have found similarities in the oral traditions – the stories and myths – and also of the material culture – the human artifacts – remaining. The two places share all of these things to a certain extent.

Finally, measurements of skull shapes, what is known as craniometric measurements, show that Easter Island skull measurements have more in common with populations in Polynesia than from uhh, skulls found in say Peru or other parts of South America. So for all these reasons, nowadays we tend to accept that the settlers of Easter Island came across the Pacific Ocean from the west, not the east.

Step 4 Listen to the task and write down the main points of the lecture.

- Linguistic features like those of Polynesia
- Stories and myths like Polynesians
- Skull shapes like Polynesians

Step 5 Listen to the task and make a mind map or outline to organize your response.

I. Evidence from reading that points to South American origins
 A. Cultural remains
 B. Prevailing winds for sailing to the island

II. Evidence from lecture that points to Polynesian origins
 A. Language
 B. Legends
 C. Artifacts
 D. Skull shape

Step 6 Write a topic sentence that expresses the gist of the lecture.

Thor Heyerdahl's theory that the Easter Islanders emigrated from South America in rafts using the prevailing winds has been shown to be unlikely.

Step 7 Write the response combining the essential information from the reading and lecture.

Keep in mind the list of questions in Practice with Analyzing Responses, p. 424. You will not have time to rewrite your complete response on the test, so check your sentences for clarity and correct information as you write.

One argument against Heyerdahl's theory is based on linguistic evidence. The language spoken by the descendants of these people has more Polynesian language features than features of South American languages. Stories and myths handed down through the generations also show more in common with those of Polynesian cultures.

Although Heyerdahl claimed a similarity to South Americans' ancient cultural remains, the human artifacts that remain have closer links to Polynesia. But perhaps the main argument against Heyerdahl's theory is that the measurements of skull remains of the Easter Islanders are similar to the Polynesian people and not so similar to measurements of South American people.

Step 8 Write a concluding statement that completes the response.

Heyerdahl's famous trip of several thousand kilometers across the open ocean in a raft gave compelling evidence toward his theory, but the opposing evidence seems more conclusive.

Step 9 Read over your response to make any final improvements.

EXERCISE W44 *Practice responding to the integrated writing task*

Plan your test preparation schedule to include writing integrated responses at regular intervals. Use the steps above to do the following integrated writing tasks. You have three minutes to read and take notes from the reading passage. Then you hear a related lecture. You may take notes. Try to write a 150- to 225-word response to the question in 20 minutes. This is the amount of time you will be given to complete the integrated writing task on the TOEFL test.

Type your response on a computer. The computer screens for the integrated writing task appear as shown in the first item below.

1.

TOEFL Writing Question 1 of 2 VOLUME HELP NEXT SHOW TIME

Investigations made at laboratories in the various parts of the world indicate that apes are capable of understanding language and using linguistic responses at the level of young children. Just because these animals do not have the physical apparatus for producing the speech, we should not assume that they cannot understand and learn language. According to researchers who have worked closely with apes, when these animals are given other means to communicate, they do indeed show sophisticated communicative abilities. These researchers provide evidence of gorillas using signs to show humor, to insult, to threaten, to produce metaphorical language, and to engage in fantasy play.

Koko, a lowland gorilla, seems to have understood a poem written about her. Tests of Koko's auditory comprehension showed that she was able to distinguish between words such as "funny," "money," and "bunny." Similar claims have been made for Michael, a male companion of Koko's, who also learned to discriminate between many sounds.

Washoe, an adult chimpanzee raised as if she were a deaf child, was able to translate words she heard into American Sign Language. Another study consisted of teaching a chimpanzee named Kanzi how to communicate using a keyboard of symbols. This study compared the series of stages that a human child goes through with those of Kanzi. Kanzi moved through these stages in much the same way as children, up to a particular stage of development, and in fact, did better than a young child on a test that measured only the ability to comprehend given requests.

START ▶

(narrator) *Now listen to part of a lecture on the topic you just read about.*

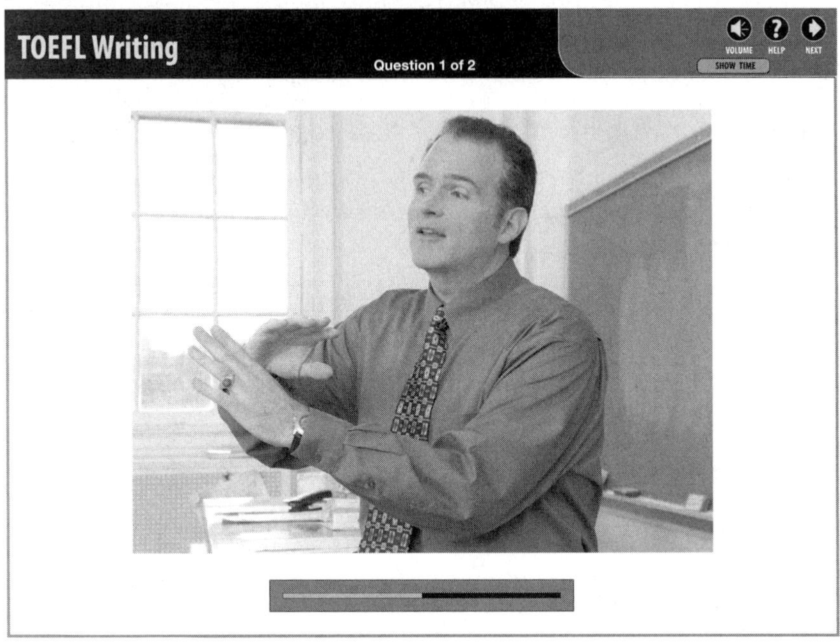
TOEFL Writing
Question 1 of 2
VOLUME HELP NEXT
SHOW TIME

STOP ■

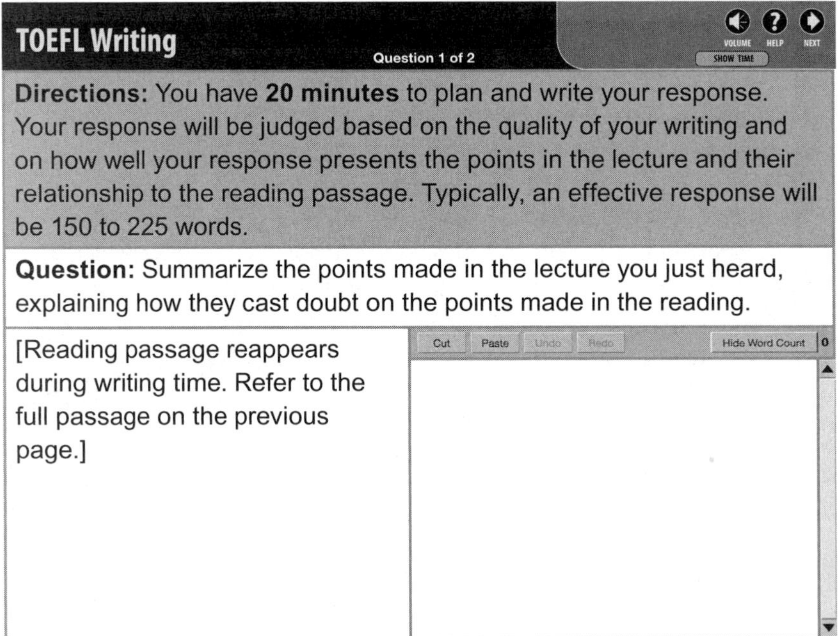
TOEFL Writing
Question 1 of 2
VOLUME HELP NEXT
SHOW TIME
Directions: You have **20 minutes** to plan and write your response. Your response will be judged based on the quality of your writing and on how well your response presents the points in the lecture and their relationship to the reading passage. Typically, an effective response will be 150 to 225 words.
Question: Summarize the points made in the lecture you just heard, explaining how they cast doubt on the points made in the reading.
[Reading passage reappears during writing time. Refer to the full passage on the previous page.]
Cut
Paste
Undo
Redo
Hide Word Count
0

2. Salmon, a fish prized for both food and sport, has a complex life cycle. After spending several years in the ocean, adult salmon travel back to the freshwater streams where they were originally spawned, to lay their eggs. The females bury the eggs under the sand at the bottom of the streams. When the fish are large enough, two years after hatching, the young salmon, called *smolts*, drift into rivers from smaller streams. The smolts use the strong flow from the melting snows to get to the Pacific Ocean, where they travel until they return to start the cycle again.

The damming of river systems in the northwestern region of the United States has had devastating effects on salmon. Not only are dams an obstacle for salmon navigating upstream, but they are also an impediment for the smolts traveling to the sea. The current itself has become very slow, not just because of the construction of numerous dams but also because companies intentionally operate the dams to slow the current. They store the water from the melting snow until the winter, when more electric power is needed. As fewer smolts reach the oceans and fewer adults return, salmon fail to produce a sufficiently numerous new generation. This could eventually lead to the extinction of the fish.

Attempts are being made to get the young salmon downriver more quickly. One such attempt has consisted of transporting the smolts by barge. Another suggestion, proposed by environmentalists, is to increase the rate of water flow. Also under consideration is the reduction of the water level in the reservoirs for a period in the spring when the smolts are migrating downstream. This would also increase the flow rate temporarily, without requiring massive amounts of water, and thus enable the young salmon to move downstream faster.

START ▶

(narrator) *Now listen to part of a lecture on the topic you just read about.*

STOP ■

Question

Summarize the points made in the lecture you just heard, explaining how they support the points made in the reading.

3. The insecticidal properties of DDT, a white crystalline compound, were discovered in 1942. During World War II this pesticide was used to control the spread of typhus and malaria. Then in the postwar era it began to be used extensively as an agricultural insecticide. Its success in eradicating malaria and controlling other insect-borne diseases dangerous both to humans and crops led it to be labeled a "miracle" pesticide.

   Its usage increased and peaked in the early 1960s. In that decade, however, studies began to show that this method of pest control had serious environmental consequences. Perhaps most damaging for the reputation of DDT was the wide popularity of Rachel Carson's book *Silent Spring,* which exposed the dangers of continued use of this pesticide on bird and animal species and ultimately on human beings. Carson's influential exposé of the harmful effects of DDT showed that several species of birds were experiencing population declines as a result of ingesting this chemical in their customary diet. Research showed that birds of prey such as the bald eagle and peregrine falcon, which are high on the food chain, accumulated excessive amounts of the pesticide in their bodies, and this caused them to lay eggs with thin shells, which would break before hatching. Research also showed that the human population was at risk from increased levels of liver and breast cancer caused by exposure to DDT. Furthermore, environmentalists pointed out that the toxicity of this substance is not easily degraded and can remain in the environment and food chain for prolonged periods. Due to these reasons, and also to the fact that DDT seemed to be losing its effectiveness on the insect populations it was designed to control, many countries banned the use of this product during the early 1970s.

START ▶

(narrator) *Now listen to part of a lecture on the topic you just read about.*

STOP ■

Question

Summarize the points made in the lecture you just heard, explaining how they cast doubt on the points made in the reading.

Main points from the reading passages and listening passages for Exercise W44 are on p. 575.

Writing Section Practice Test

When you have taken the Diagnostic Test and completed the exercises recommended in the Answer Key for any Writing questions you marked incorrectly, you can test your skills by taking this Writing Section Practice Test. You can take this test either in this book or on the CD-ROM that accompanies this book. The Writing Section Practice Test in the book is identical to the Writing section of Test 2 on the CD-ROM.

During the Writing Section of the actual TOEFL test, you may not go back and check your work or change your response after you finish each writing task. Maintain the same test conditions now that would be experienced during the real test.

WRITING SECTION

Directions

This section measures your ability to use writing to communicate in an academic environment. There will be two writing tasks.

For the first writing task, you will read a passage and listen to a lecture, and then answer a question based on what you have read and heard. For the second writing task, you will answer a question based on your own knowledge and experience.

Now read the directions for the first writing task.

Writing Based on Reading and Listening

Directions

For this task, you will have three minutes to read a passage about an academic topic. You may take notes on the passage while you read. Then you will listen to a lecture about the same topic. While you listen, you may also take notes.

Then you will have 20 minutes to write a response to a question that asks you about the relationship between the lecture you heard and the reading passage. Try to answer the question as completely as possible using information from the reading passage and the lecture. The question does **not** ask you to express your personal opinion. You can refer to the reading passage again when it is time for you to write. You may use your notes to help you answer the question.

Typically, an effective response will be 150 to 225 words long. Your response will be judged on the quality of your writing and on the completeness and accuracy of the content. If you finish your response before time is up, go on to the second writing task.

On the day of the test, you will be required to type your response into a computer. Therefore, if you are taking this test in the book, practice typing your response on a computer.

INTEGRATED TASK

Directions: You have three minutes to read and take notes from the reading passage. Next, listen to the related lecture and take notes. Then write your response.

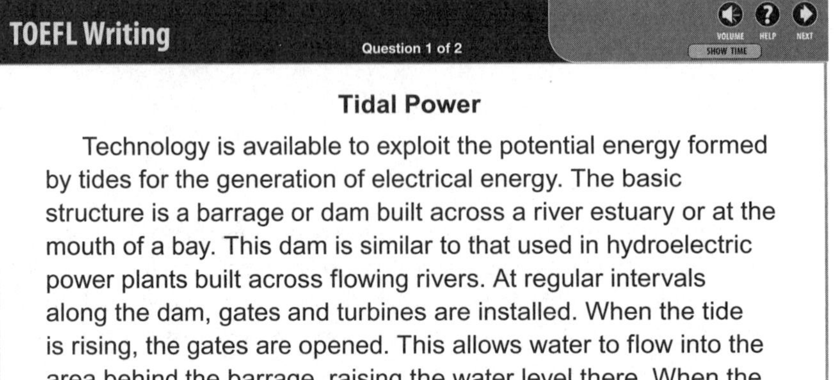

Tidal Power

Technology is available to exploit the potential energy formed by tides for the generation of electrical energy. The basic structure is a barrage or dam built across a river estuary or at the mouth of a bay. This dam is similar to that used in hydroelectric power plants built across flowing rivers. At regular intervals along the dam, gates and turbines are installed. When the tide is rising, the gates are opened. This allows water to flow into the area behind the barrage, raising the water level there. When the water has reached its highest level, the gates are closed. Then the tide drops on the seaward side, and this trapped water is several meters above the sea level. The gates are then opened, allowing the water to discharge out. The force of the flow turns the turbines and generates electricity. It is also possible to use tidal energy when the water flows in the other direction – through the gates into the estuary from the sea.

In this way, four periods of energy production are possible every day, since coastal regions experience two high and two low tides in just over 24 hours. In order for practical amounts of electricity to be generated, the difference between high and low tides must be at least five meters. Tidal power is renewable, non-polluting, and contributes no greenhouse gases to the atmosphere. This kind of system can provide a useful energy supplement to other sources in an era of diminishing fossil fuel reserves.

START ▶

Now listen to part of a lecture on the topic you just read about.

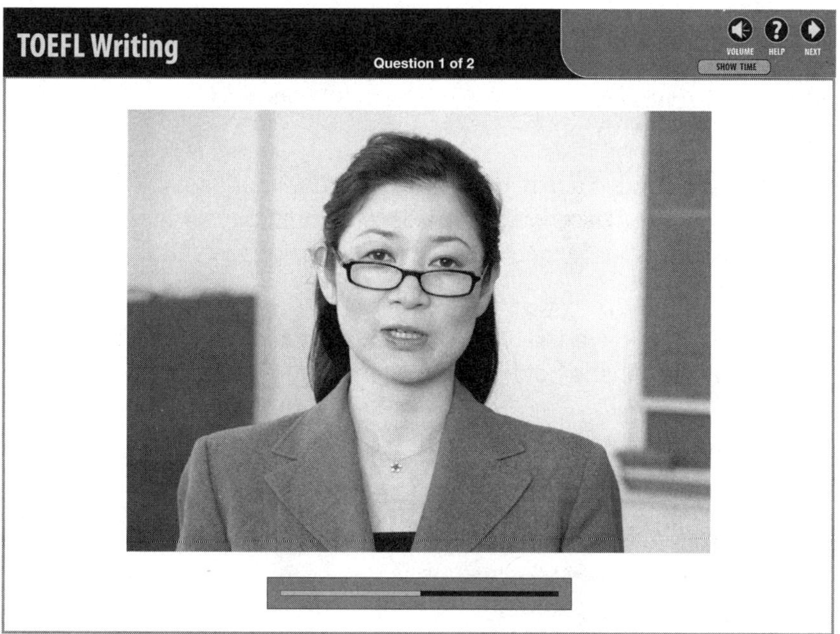

TOEFL Writing
Question 1 of 2
VOLUME
HELP
NEXT
SHOW TIME

STOP ■

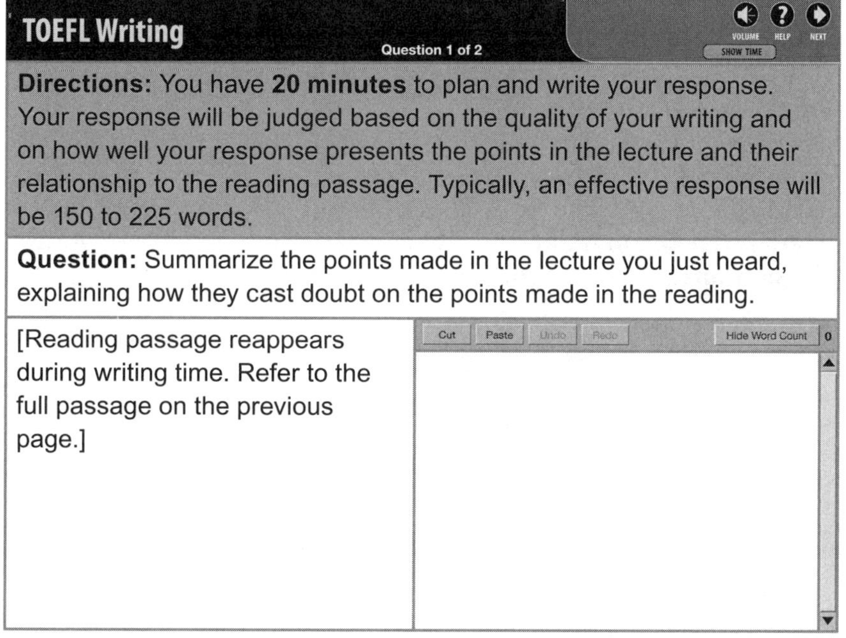

TOEFL Writing
Question 1 of 2
VOLUME
HELP
NEXT
SHOW TIME
Directions: You have **20 minutes** to plan and write your response. Your response will be judged based on the quality of your writing and on how well your response presents the points in the lecture and their relationship to the reading passage. Typically, an effective response will be 150 to 225 words.
Question: Summarize the points made in the lecture you just heard, explaining how they cast doubt on the points made in the reading.
[Reading passage reappears during writing time. Refer to the full passage on the previous page.]
Cut
Paste
Undo
Redo
Hide Word Count
0

WRITING

Writing Based on Knowledge and Experience

Directions

For this task, you will write an essay in response to a question that asks you to state, explain, and support your opinion on an issue. You will have 30 minutes to plan, write, and revise your essay.

Typically, an effective essay will contain a minimum of 300 words. Your essay will be judged on the quality of your writing. This includes the development of your ideas, the organization of your essay, and the quality and accuracy of the language you use to express your ideas.

On the day of the test, you will be required to type your response into a computer. Therefore, if you are taking this test in the book, practice typing your response on a computer.

INDEPENDENT WRITING TASK

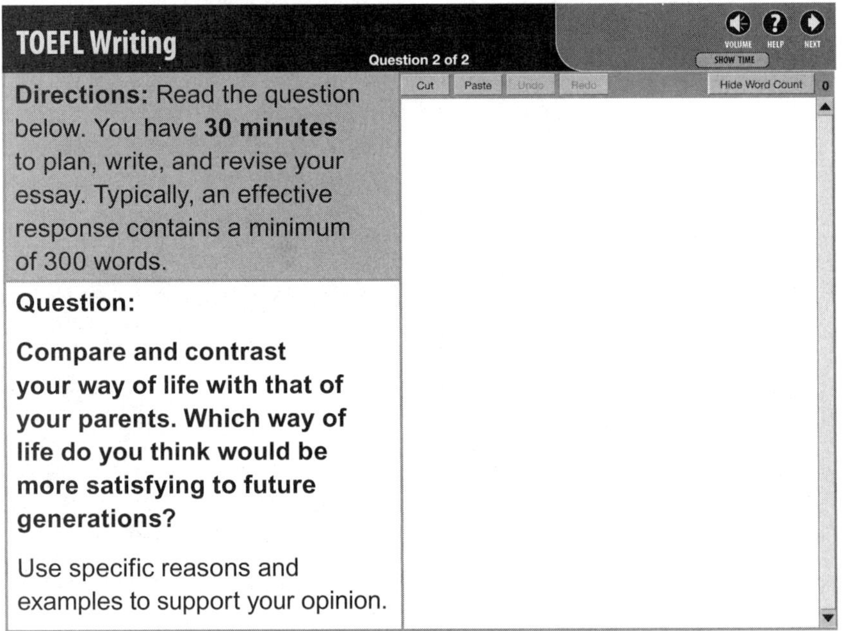
TOEFL Writing
Question 2 of 2
VOLUME HELP NEXT
SHOW TIME
Cut Paste Undo Redo
Hide Word Count 0
Directions: Read the question below. You have **30 minutes** to plan, write, and revise your essay. Typically, an effective response contains a minimum of 300 words.
Question:
Compare and contrast your way of life with that of your parents. Which way of life do you think would be more satisfying to future generations?
Use specific reasons and examples to support your opinion.

PRACTICE TESTS

Practice Test 1

READING SECTION

Directions

In this section, you will read three passages and answer reading comprehension questions about each passage. Most questions are worth one point, but the last question in each set is worth more than one point. The directions indicate how many points you may receive.

You have 60 minutes to read all of the passages and answer the questions. Some passages include a word or phrase followed by an asterisk (*). Go to the bottom of the page to see a definition or an explanation of these words or phrases.

Questions 1–12

Panspermia

The idea that life did not originate on Earth, but was carried here either deliberately or by natural processes, has its roots at least as far back as the ancient Greeks. This idea, often referred to as *panspermia*, took on a scientific form in the work of various nineteenth-century authors. It later gained widespread popular appeal through the work of the Swedish chemist Svante Arrhenius, who argued that spores of life could survive in space and travel between star systems through the pressure of solar radiation.

The panspermia hypothesis eventually fell out of favor for a variety of reasons. Skeptics pointed out that microorganisms could not possibly survive the damage caused by ultraviolet radiation and cosmic rays while being propelled out of a solar system away from a star. Indeed, it was unclear how biological material could escape from a planet by natural processes in the first place. If unprotected, the molecules of life would quickly be destroyed by radiation near the ejecting planet. Furthermore, it was not clear how microorganisms, having made a journey across the huge distances of interstellar space, could have safely descended to the surface of the Earth or any other planet. Arrhenius himself argued that organisms caught inside meteorites would be subjected to incandescent* temperatures while entering the atmosphere of a terrestrial body. Such heat would destroy any life-forms lucky enough to have survived to this point.

Despite the seeming implausibility* of the panspermia hypothesis, some theorists have resurrected the notion in recent decades since laboratory research has shown that many of the objections to the hypothesis can be overcome. Scientists have shown that microorganisms protected from radiation by grains of material could be ejected from a solar system if the repulsive force (p) of the ejecting star is greater than the attractive force (g) of the star's gravity. Such ejecting stars cannot be too luminous since brighter stars emit too much ultraviolet radiation for the survival of bacteria. Organisms can only enter new solar systems whose stars' p/g ratio is low, thus allowing the gravity to pull the microbes into the planetary orbits. According to some researchers, material ejected from a planetary system could also eventually become part of an interstellar molecular cloud, which eventually produces a new planetary system as well as a large number of comets. Comets can retain microorganisms protected by other material and water, and impact onto new planets, which by then would have cooled sufficiently for the life in the grains to take hold.

Further supporting evidence about the likelihood of survival of bacteria traveling through space and entering a planetary atmosphere has been gained from studies of a meteorite of Martian origin found in Antarctica in 1984. Whether or not the meteorite contains fossils of Martian bacteria (and many researchers now seem to reject this possibility), microscopic studies of its internal structure have shown that the interior was not heated to more than 40 degrees Celsius since before leaving the Martian surface. In other words, neither the original impact that must have ejected the rock away from the Martian surface nor the heat generated by its entry into the Earth's atmosphere did, in fact, melt or vaporize the internal portions of the meteorite. So it is quite possible that any life-form that had undergone such a trip would survive. As for the long journey itself, experiments aboard a European Space Agency mission have shown that bacterial spores can survive in deep space for at least five years. This is sufficient time for viable interplanetary travel, although not, of course, for interstellar travel.

Today, the panspermia hypothesis is being regarded with less skepticism than formerly. Although the orthodox view is still that life evolved on Earth (and possibly other planets in the universe) without extraterrestrial input, more and more research is pointing to the feasibility of some form of interstellar "seeding." Wickramasinghe and Hoyle, who championed the hypothesis of the interstellar transmission of life during the 1970s, argued persuasively that prebiotic chemicals have been shown to exist by remote sensing data of Comet Halley. Furthermore, they point out that evidence for viable microorganisms existing in comets could be attained in the near future if unmanned space missions could capture and return to Earth with cometary material.

***incandescent:** producing a bright light after being heated to a high temperature
***implausibility:** the condition of being difficult to believe

1. Early supporters of the panspermia hypothesis
   (A) rejected the main elements of the hypothesis
   (B) argued that some primitive life has been detected on a comet
   (C) pointed out that space missions will find life elsewhere
   (D) suggested that the "seeds" of life may have been deliberately planted

[Refer to the full passage.]

2. The word "propelled" in the passage is closest in meaning to
   (A) rejected
   (B) plunged
   (C) heaved
   (D) thrust

The panspermia hypothesis eventually fell out of favor for a variety of reasons. Skeptics pointed out that microorganisms could not possibly survive the damage caused by ultraviolet radiation and cosmic rays while being propelled out of a solar system away from a star. Indeed, it was unclear how biological material could escape from a planet by natural processes in the first place. If unprotected, the molecules of life would quickly be destroyed by radiation near the ejecting planet. Furthermore, it was not clear how microorganisms, having made a journey across the huge distances of interstellar space, could have safely descended to the surface of the Earth or any other planet. Arrhenius himself argued that organisms caught inside meteorites would be subjected to incandescent temperatures while entering the atmosphere of a terrestrial body. Such heat would destroy any life-forms lucky enough to have survived to this point.

3. According to the passage, the panspermia hypothesis fell out of favor for all of the following reasons EXCEPT Ⓐ the potential damage caused by ultraviolet radiation Ⓑ the unlikelihood of natural processes leading to the ejection of biological material Ⓒ the probability that heat would destroy incoming life-forms Ⓓ the knowledge that life can't exist elsewhere in the universe	[Refer to the full passage.]

4. The word "resurrected" in the passage is closest in meaning to Ⓐ destroyed Ⓑ reintroduced Ⓒ initiated Ⓓ succeeded	Despite the seeming implausibility of the panspermia hypothesis, some theorists have resurrected the notion in recent decades since laboratory research has shown that many of the objections to the hypothesis can be overcome. Scientists have shown that microorganisms protected from radiation by grains of material could be ejected from a solar system if the repulsive force (p) of the ejecting star is greater than the attractive force (g) of the star's gravity. Such ejecting stars cannot be too luminous since brighter stars emit too much ultraviolet radiation for the survival of bacteria. Organisms can only enter new solar systems whose stars' p/g ratio is low, thus allowing the gravity to pull the microbes into the planetary orbits. According to some researchers, material ejected from a planetary system could also eventually become part of an interstellar molecular cloud, which eventually produces a new planetary system as well as a large number of comets. Comets can retain microorganisms protected by other material and water, and impact onto new planets, which by then would have cooled sufficiently for the life in the grains to take hold.

5. The word "retain" in the passage is closest in meaning to (A) prevent (B) erode (C) avert (D) keep	Despite the seeming implausibility of the panspermia hypothesis, some theorists have resurrected the notion in recent decades since laboratory research has shown that many of the objections to the hypothesis can be overcome. Scientists have shown that microorganisms protected from radiation by grains of material could be ejected from a solar system if the repulsive force (p) of the ejecting star is greater than the attractive force (g) of the star's gravity. Such ejecting stars cannot be too luminous since brighter stars emit too much ultraviolet radiation for the survival of bacteria. Organisms can only enter new solar systems whose stars' p/g ratio is low, thus allowing the gravity to pull the microbes into the planetary orbits. According to some researchers, material ejected from a planetary system could also eventually become part of an interstellar molecular cloud, which eventually produces a new planetary system as well as a large number of comets. Comets can retain microorganisms protected by other material and water, and impact onto new planets, which by then would have cooled sufficiently for the life in the grains to take hold.

6. According to the passage, the panspermia hypothesis is (A) of historical interest only (B) being taken seriously again (C) not really good science (D) probably true	[Refer to the full passage.]

7. The word "its" in the passage refers to Ⓐ the Martian Ⓑ the bacteria Ⓒ the meteorite Ⓓ the interior	Further supporting evidence about the likelihood of survival of bacteria traveling through space and entering a planetary atmosphere has been gained from studies of a meteorite of Martian origin found in Antarctica in 1984. Whether or not the meteorite contains fossils of Martian bacteria (and many researchers now seem to reject this possibility), microscopic studies of its internal structure have shown that the interior was not heated to more than 40 degrees Celsius since before leaving the Martian surface. In other words, neither the original impact that must have ejected the rock away from the Martian surface nor the heat generated by its entry into the Earth's atmosphere did, in fact, melt or vaporize the internal portions of the meteorite. So it is quite possible that any life-form that had undergone such a trip would survive. As for the long journey itself, experiments aboard a European Space Agency mission have shown that bacterial spores can survive in deep space for at least five years. This is sufficient time for viable interplanetary travel, although not, of course, for interstellar travel.

8. The phrase "such a trip" in the passage refers to Ⓐ a journey from Mars to Earth Ⓑ the descent through Earth's atmosphere Ⓒ a trip from another solar system Ⓓ interstellar traveling	Further supporting evidence about the likelihood of survival of bacteria traveling through space and entering a planetary atmosphere has been gained from studies of a meteorite of Martian origin found in Antarctica in 1984. Whether or not the meteorite contains fossils of Martian bacteria (and many researchers now seem to reject this possibility), microscopic studies of its internal structure have shown that the interior was not heated to more than 40 degrees Celsius since before leaving the Martian surface. In other words, neither the original impact that must have ejected the rock away from the Martian surface nor the heat generated by its entry into the Earth's atmosphere did, in fact, melt or vaporize the internal portions of the meteorite. So it is quite possible that any life-form that had undergone such a trip would survive. As for the long journey itself, experiments aboard a European Space Agency mission have shown that bacterial spores can survive in deep space for at least five years. This is sufficient time for viable interplanetary travel, although not, of course, for interstellar travel.

9. According to the passage, the meteorite found in Antarctica

(A) does not contain bacteria fossils
(B) might contain bacteria fossils
(C) has fossils originating on Earth
(D) could not originate from Mars

[Refer to the full passage.]

10. Which of the sentences below best expresses the essential information in the highlighted sentence in the passage? Incorrect choices change the meaning in important ways or leave out essential information.

(A) Nowadays, the panspermia hypothesis has been more or less rejected.
(B) Currently, the panspermia hypothesis is looked on with more astonishment than previously.
(C) These days, the panspermia hypothesis is judged more plausible than before.
(D) The modern scientific establishment now generally accepts the validity of the panspermia hypothesis.

Today, the panspermia hypothesis is being regarded with less skepticism than formerly. Although the orthodox view is still that life evolved on Earth (and possibly other planets in the universe) without extraterrestrial input, more and more research is pointing to the feasibility of some form of interstellar "seeding." Wickramasinghe and Hoyle, who championed the hypothesis of the interstellar transmission of life during the 1970s, argued persuasively that prebiotic chemicals have been shown to exist by remote sensing data of Comet Halley. Furthermore, they point out that evidence for viable microorganisms existing in comets could be attained in the near future if unmanned space missions could capture and return to Earth with cometary material.

11. Look at the four squares [■] that indicate where the following sentence could be added to the passage.

However, even if organisms were somehow shielded inside fine grains of carbon they would be too heavy to be ejected from a planetary system by the pressure of radiation.

Where would the sentence best fit?

Choose the letter of the square that shows where the sentence should be added.

The panspermia hypothesis eventually fell out of favor for a variety of reasons. [A] Skeptics pointed out that microorganisms could not possibly survive the damage caused by ultraviolet radiation and cosmic rays while being propelled out of a solar system away from a star. Indeed, it was unclear how biological material could escape from a planet by natural processes in the first place. [B] If unprotected, the molecules of life would quickly be destroyed by radiation near the ejecting planet. [C] Furthermore, it was not clear how microorganisms, having made a journey across the huge distances of interstellar space, could have safely descended to the surface of the Earth or any other planet. [D] Arrhenius himself argued that organisms caught inside meteorites would be subjected to incandescent* temperatures while entering the atmosphere of a terrestrial body. Such heat would destroy any life-forms lucky enough to have survived to this point.

12. **Directions:** Select the appropriate phrases from the answer choices and match them to the category to which they relate. THREE of the answer choices will NOT be used. **This question is worth 4 points.**

Write the letters of the answer choices in the spaces where they belong. Refer to the full passage.

Answer Choices

(A) Prebiotic chemicals exist in comets.

(B) Bright stars emit a lot of ultraviolet radiation.

(C) Distances in interstellar space are huge.

(D) Comets are made up of water and other materials.

(E) Interstellar space has ultraviolet radiation and cosmic rays.

(F) Meteorites are subjected to burning temperatures when entering Earth's atmosphere.

(G) Meteorites from Mars have been found on Earth in areas of Antarctica where the cold temperatures protected life-forms.

(H) The meteorite found in Antarctica contained frozen fossils.

(I) Bacterial spores have been shown capable of surviving for several years in space.

(J) Stars with a repulsive force greater than their attractive force are able to eject material.

Arguments Against Panspermia Hypothesis

-
-
-

Support for Panspermia Hypothesis

-
-
-
-

Questions 13–25

Ocean Energy Systems

In recent years, the oceans have been seen as a potential source of energy. Oceans are huge reservoirs of renewable energy, which have yet to be properly harnessed*. Some estimates say that during the second decade of this century, ocean energy sources will generate more than 1,000 megawatts of electricity, which is enough to power a million homes in the industrialized world. Several technologies have been developed for exploiting these resources in a practical way, among which ocean thermal energy conversion (OTEC) is one of the most promising. Experimental OTEC plants have been constructed using different operating principles, although as yet no large-scale commercially viable plant has been launched.

The basic operation behind this system uses the heat energy stored in the oceans as a source of power. The plant exploits the difference in water temperature between the warm surface waters heated by the sun and the colder waters found at ocean depths. A minimum temperature difference of 20 degrees Celsius between surface and depth is required for efficient operation, and this situation is typically found only in tropical and subtropical regions of the world. There are two basic kinds of OTEC system: the open cycle system and the closed cycle system. In the open cycle system, the warm surface water is converted into steam in a partial vacuum and this steam drives a turbine connected to an electrical generator. In a closed cycle system, the warm surface water is used to boil a fluid, such as ammonia, which has a low boiling point. In both systems cold water pumped up from the ocean depths condenses the vapor. In the open system, the steam is condensed back into a liquid by cold water pumped from deep-ocean water and then discharged. In the closed system, the condensed ammonia is used to repeat the cycle continuously. Various hybrid systems using characteristics of both open and closed cycle plants have also been designed.

The OTEC system is potentially an important source of clean, renewable energy, which could significantly reduce our reliance on fossil fuels and nuclear fission. Unlike other forms of renewable energy, such as those provided directly by the sun and wind, OTEC plants can generate power 24 hours per day, 365 days per year. Furthermore, the design of this technology avoids any significant release of carbon dioxide into the atmosphere. OTEC can offer other important benefits apart from power production. Aquaculture is one important spinoff. It may also be economically feasible to extract minerals from the pumped seawater. Freshwater for drinking and irrigation is another by-product, and this will be an important advantage in regions where freshwater is limited.

Some drawbacks to this form of power generation have been noted. Perhaps the biggest drawback at present is the high capital cost of initial construction due mainly to the expense of the large pipeline used to pump water from 1,000 meters below the surface. Furthermore, the conversion of thermal to electrical energy in the OTEC system works at very low efficiency, which means that these plants will have to use a lot of water to generate practical amounts for the power grid. For this reason, the net power output is reduced, since a significant portion of the output must be used to pump water. There are also potential ecological drawbacks, since the water discharges will change the water temperature and disturb some marine habitats. This impact could, however, be minimized if the water is discharged at greater depths.

The main obstacle created by high initial expenses will have to be met before OTEC competes with conventional alternatives, and until such time, OTEC will remain restricted to experimental plants. When technology permits lower start-up costs, this technology will make an important contribution to world energy requirements.

***harnessed:** controlled for use

13. The word "viable" in the passage is closest in meaning to

(A) clever
(B) feasible
(C) optimistic
(D) convenient

In recent years, the oceans have been seen as a potential source of energy. Oceans are huge reservoirs of renewable energy, which have yet to be properly harnessed. Some estimates say that during the second decade of this century, ocean energy sources will generate more than 1,000 megawatts of electricity, which is enough to power a million homes in the industrialized world. Several technologies have been developed for exploiting these resources in a practical way, among which ocean thermal energy conversion (OTEC) is one of the most promising. Experimental OTEC plants have been constructed using different operating principles, although as yet no large-scale commercially viable plant has been launched.

14. It can be inferred from the passage that

(A) renewable energy can be put into reservoirs
(B) the experimental plants are ready to be launched
(C) the oceans could be used in the future to generate electricity
(D) 1,000 megawatts of electricity is the amount needed in the average home

[Refer to the full passage.]

15. According to the passage, what can be inferred about the factor that allows the ocean to be used as an energy source?

(A) The oceans are so large that they can produce a lot of energy.
(B) In polar climates, the sun does not sufficiently heat the deeper water for practical energy use.
(C) The oceans can store vast amounts of heat energy to be used to run basic electricity plants.
(D) The plants are typically found in the tropical and subtropical regions of the world because of the warm weather.

[Refer to the full passage.]

16. According to the passage, in what way are the basic kinds of OTEC systems similar?

   (A) They turn surface water into steam.
   (B) They use cold water to cause condensation.
   (C) They discharge unused water into the ocean.
   (D) They convert water in a vacuum.

[Refer to the full passage.]

17. The phrase "other forms" in the passage refers to energy produced through

   (A) fossil fuels and nuclear fission
   (B) chemical reactions
   (C) OTEC systems
   (D) sun and wind

The OTEC system is potentially an important source of clean, renewable energy, which could significantly reduce our reliance on fossil fuels and nuclear fission. Unlike **other forms** of renewable energy, such as those provided directly by the sun and wind, OTEC plants can generate power 24 hours per day, 365 days per year. Furthermore, the design of this technology avoids any significant release of carbon dioxide into the atmosphere. OTEC can offer other important benefits apart from power production. Aquaculture is one important spinoff. It may also be economically feasible to extract minerals from the pumped seawater. Freshwater for drinking and irrigation is another by-product, and this will be an important advantage in regions where freshwater is limited.

18. In paragraph 3, what can be inferred about the different sources of energy?

   (A) We rely too much on fossil fuels and nuclear fission.
   (B) Renewable energy releases a lot of carbon dioxide into the atmosphere.
   (C) Energy from OTEC is provided directly by the sun and wind.
   (D) Energy forms other than OTEC do not have important benefits.

Paragraph 3 is marked with an arrow [➡].

➡ The OTEC system is potentially an important source of clean, renewable energy, which could significantly reduce our reliance on fossil fuels and nuclear fission. Unlike other forms of renewable energy, such as those provided directly by the sun and wind, OTEC plants can generate power 24 hours per day, 365 days per year. Furthermore, the design of this technology avoids any significant release of carbon dioxide into the atmosphere. OTEC can offer other important benefits apart from power production. Aquaculture is one important spinoff. It may also be economically feasible to extract minerals from the pumped seawater. Freshwater for drinking and irrigation is another by-product, and this will be an important advantage in regions where freshwater is limited.

19. In paragraph 3, why does the author write about aquaculture and mineral extractions? (A) To give examples of possible developments related to OTEC (B) To demonstrate what other activities can be done in the ocean (C) To point out OTEC's advantages in regions of limited resources (D) To show how the environment can be improved by using clean, renewable energy Paragraph 3 is marked with an arrow [➡].	➡ The OTEC system is potentially an important source of clean, renewable energy, which could significantly reduce our reliance on fossil fuels and nuclear fission. Unlike other forms of renewable energy, such as those provided directly by the sun and wind, OTEC plants can generate power 24 hours per day, 365 days per year. Furthermore, the design of this technology avoids any significant release of carbon dioxide into the atmosphere. OTEC can offer other important benefits apart from power production. Aquaculture is one important spinoff. It may also be economically feasible to extract minerals from the pumped seawater. Freshwater for drinking and irrigation is another by-product, and this will be an important advantage in regions where freshwater is limited.

20. According to the passage, all of the following are problems with the OTEC system as a power-generating system EXCEPT (A) the costs of constructing the power system (B) the damage caused to fishing grounds (C) the effect of discharged water on the environment (D) the amount of water needed to produce a useful amount of electricity	[Refer to the full passage.]

21. The word "conventional" in the passage is closest in meaning to (A) conservative (B) traditional (C) tentative (D) natural	The main obstacle created by high initial expenses will have to be met before OTEC competes with conventional alternatives, and until such time, OTEC will remain restricted to experimental plants. When technology permits lower start-up costs, this technology will make an important contribution to world energy requirements.

22. Which of the sentences below best expresses the essential information in the highlighted sentence in the passage? Incorrect choices change the meaning in important ways or leave out essential information.

(A) Water outflow temperatures could upset local marine life.

(B) Water discharges will disturb the ecology of the oceans.

(C) The OTEC system has a tendency to upset marine environments.

(D) Outflows of water will affect the ocean temperature at great depths.

Some drawbacks to this form of power generation have been noted. Perhaps the biggest drawback at present is the high capital cost of initial construction due mainly to the expense of the large pipeline used to pump water from 1,000 meters below the surface. Furthermore, the conversion of thermal to electrical energy in the OTEC system works at very low efficiency, which means that these plants will have to use a lot of water to generate practical amounts for the power grid. For this reason, the net power output is reduced, since a significant portion of the output must be used to pump water. There are also potential ecological drawbacks, since the water discharges will change the water temperature and disturb some marine habitats. This impact could, however, be minimized if the water is discharged at greater depths.

23. Which of the following statements most accurately reflects the author's opinion about OTEC technology?

(A) OTEC will eventually supply most of the world's energy needs.

(B) The disadvantages of OTEC energy outweigh its advantages.

(C) OTEC technology has a useful role to play in total energy production.

(D) Only very large OTEC plants can be made efficient.

[Refer to the full passage.]

24. Look at the four squares [■] that indicate where the following sentence could be added to the passage.

The nutrient-rich cold water is an excellent medium for growing phytoplankton, which provide support for various commercially exploitable fish and shellfish.

Where would the sentence best fit?

Choose the letter of the square that shows where the sentence should be added.

The OTEC system is potentially an important source of clean, renewable energy, which could significantly reduce our reliance on fossil fuels and nuclear fission. **A** Unlike other forms of renewable energy, such as those provided directly by the sun and wind, OTEC plants can generate power 24 hours per day, 365 days per year. Furthermore, the design of this technology avoids any significant release of carbon dioxide into the atmosphere. OTEC can offer other important benefits apart from power production. **B** Aquaculture is one important spinoff. **C** It may also be economically feasible to extract minerals from the pumped seawater. **D** Freshwater for drinking and irrigation is another by-product, and this will be an important advantage in regions where freshwater is limited.

25. **Directions:** An introductory sentence for a brief summary of the passage is provided below. Complete the summary by circling the THREE answer choices that express the most important ideas in the passage. Some sentences do not belong in the summary because they express ideas that are not presented in the passage or are minor ideas in the passage. **This question is worth 2 points.**

Write the letters of the answer choices in the spaces where they belong.
Refer to the full passage.

The OTEC system of power generation is a promising source of energy.

-
-
-

Answer Choices

(A) OTEC systems use ocean temperature differences at different climates to create a significant amount of energy.

(B) OTEC systems can produce clean, renewable energy without harmful environmental effects.

(C) The OTEC system's pump would require a significant amount of energy of the total output.

(D) OTEC plants can produce more than enough electricity to supply over a million energy users.

(E) The OTEC system can generate power nonstop, unlike other renewable resources like sun and wind energy.

(F) The OTEC system has the added benefit of providing nutritious cold water suitable for fish production.

Questions 26–39

Neolithic Agriculture Development

In the Neolithic period, starting around 10,000 years ago, perhaps the most important economic revolution in human history occurred – the commencement of agriculture and the domestication of animals for human consumption. From this point in time, people could start to rely on a more consistent and much increased food supply. As a corollary of this, considerably larger populations could be supported and people could settle in one place without the need to migrate in search of food supplies. Equally important, the surpluses of crops and animals meant that not all the population needed to dedicate their time and energy to farming; some could now learn specialized skills such as crafts or trade. The building of permanent settlements where skills could be developed brought about the conditions necessary for the first growth of towns. But several thousand years elapsed between the beginnings of agriculture and the rise of what we call civilization about 6,000 years ago.

Recent evidence seems to indicate that while the Neolithic revolution first took place in the Middle East – in the valleys of the Tigris-Euphrates and of the Nile – it occurred independently in other areas of the world. The origins of the revolution are not known in great detail, but it is known that the wild grasses that were the ancestors of wheat and barley grew natively in the Eastern Mediterranean area. It may be that Mesolithic (Middle Stone Age) foragers* simply supplemented their diet by reaping these wild grasses, and later came to understand the advantage of returning some of the grain to the soil as seed. Whatever the case, we know that at an early date people living in the Eastern Mediterranean region, who lived by hunting, fishing, and gathering, began to make sickles, with stone teeth set in bone handles. Such tools were certainly used for reaping some grass crop, whether cultivated or wild.

Around this time, other communities in the Middle East cultivated plants from which they learned how to obtain flour. Evidence shows that they ground down the grain with a simple type of mill, consisting of a large saddle-shaped stone on which a smaller stone was rubbed up and down. The livestock they bred – cattle, sheep, pigs, and goats – was exploited for their meat, skins, and milk.

Both in Egypt and Mesopotamia, the periodic floods of great rivers such as the Nile and the Tigris-Euphrates not only supplied water to the fields but also brought down fresh soil in the form of fertile muddy sediments. This sediment was deposited on flood plains around such rivers, thus annually restoring the fruitfulness of the land. This regular flooding and sediment deposit allowed these early farmers to continue cultivating the same fields repeatedly for generations without exhausting the fertility of the soil, and crop surpluses were, therefore, available to allow an increase in population and a growth in trade and skills development. The area available for cultivation was expanded when people learned to draw off the river water into man-made irrigation canals and ditches, watering and fertilizing larger and larger areas of land.

The practice of artificial irrigation affected the soil in various ways, but not always for the good. Since the channels were often shallow, there was frequently a great loss of water through evaporation in a hot climate. This could lead to a marked increase in soil salinity, since the salts held in solution or suspension were deposited as the water evaporated, and too much salinity could eventually damage the soil. But overall the effect of the irrigation system was to create an artificial environment – and to some extent an artificial climate – with a range of conditions that favored both human experiment and agricultural development. Beyond this, settled agriculture led to the development of property rights and hence to a legal framework and mechanisms to enforce laws. This in turn led to a more extensive and hierarchical government organization and hence to the development of large, stable communities.

***foragers:** people who go searching for food

26. The word "corollary" in the passage is closest in meaning to

Ⓐ basis
Ⓑ result
Ⓒ source
Ⓓ purpose

In the Neolithic period, starting around 10,000 years ago, perhaps the most important economic revolution in human history occurred – the commencement of agriculture and the domestication of animals for human consumption. From this point in time, people could start to rely on a more consistent and much increased food supply. As a corollary of this, considerably larger populations could be supported and people could settle in one place without the need to migrate in search of food supplies. Equally important, the surpluses of crops and animals meant that not all the population needed to dedicate their time and energy to farming; some could now learn specialized skills such as crafts or trade. The building of permanent settlements where skills could be developed brought about the conditions necessary for the first growth of towns. But several thousand years elapsed between the beginnings of agriculture and the rise of what we call civilization about 6,000 years ago.

27. According to paragraph 1, what condition allowed people to learn specialized skills?

Ⓐ The ability to migrate
Ⓑ The growth of population
Ⓒ The surplus of farm products
Ⓓ The spread of settlements

Paragraph 1 is marked with an arrow [➡].

➡ In the Neolithic period, starting around 10,000 years ago, perhaps the most important economic revolution in human history occurred – the commencement of agriculture and the domestication of animals for human consumption. From this point in time, people could start to rely on a more consistent and much increased food supply. As a corollary of this, considerably larger populations could be supported and people could settle in one place without the need to migrate in search of food supplies. Equally important, the surpluses of crops and animals meant that not all the population needed to dedicate their time and energy to farming; some could now learn specialized skills such as crafts or trade. The building of permanent settlements where skills could be developed brought about the conditions necessary for the first growth of towns. But several thousand years elapsed between the beginnings of agriculture and the rise of what we call civilization about 6,000 years ago.

28. According to paragraph 1, why did people migrate before the Neolithic revolution? (A) To search for better climates (B) To improve trading skills (C) To avoid enemies (D) To find food Paragraph 1 is marked with an arrow [➡].	➡ In the Neolithic period, starting around 10,000 years ago, perhaps the most important economic revolution in human history occurred – the commencement of agriculture and the domestication of animals for human consumption. From this point in time, people could start to rely on a more consistent and much increased food supply. As a corollary of this, considerably larger populations could be supported and people could settle in one place without the need to migrate in search of food supplies. Equally important, the surpluses of crops and animals meant that not all the population needed to dedicate their time and energy to farming; some could now learn specialized skills such as crafts or trade. The building of permanent settlements where skills could be developed brought about the conditions necessary for the first growth of towns. But several thousand years elapsed between the beginnings of agriculture and the rise of what we call civilization about 6,000 years ago.

29. Which of the sentences below best expresses the essential information in the highlighted sentence in the passage? Incorrect choices change the meaning in important ways or leave out essential information. (A) The conditions for the growth of the first towns were established in permanent settlements where skills developed. (B) The first towns and the skills that were developed were also found in the earliest permanent settlements. (C) Skills were developed and early permanent settlements were established before towns could be built. (D) The conditions necessary for permanent settlements and the practice of skills were found in the first towns.	In the Neolithic period, starting around 10,000 years ago, perhaps the most important economic revolution in human history occurred – the commencement of agriculture and the domestication of animals for human consumption. From this point in time, people could start to rely on a more consistent and much increased food supply. As a corollary of this, considerably larger populations could be supported and people could settle in one place without the need to migrate in search of food supplies. Equally important, the surpluses of crops and animals meant that not all the population needed to dedicate their time and energy to farming; some could now learn specialized skills such as crafts or trade. The building of permanent settlements where skills could be developed brought about the conditions necessary for the first growth of towns. But several thousand years elapsed between the beginnings of agriculture and the rise of what we call civilization about 6,000 years ago.

30. The word "independently" in the passage is closest in meaning to

(A) separately
(B) collectively
(C) individually
(D) originally

Recent evidence seems to indicate that while the Neolithic revolution first took place in the Middle East – in the valleys of the Tigris-Euphrates and of the Nile – it occurred independently in other areas of the world. The origins of the revolution are not known in great detail, but it is known that the wild grasses that were the ancestors of wheat and barley grew natively in the Eastern Mediterranean area. It may be that Mesolithic (Middle Stone Age) foragers simply supplemented their diet by reaping these wild grasses, and later came to understand the advantage of returning some of the grain to the soil as seed. Whatever the case, we know that at an early date people living in the Eastern Mediterranean region, who lived by hunting, fishing, and gathering, began to make sickles, with stone teeth set in bone handles. Such tools were certainly used for reaping some grass crop, whether cultivated or wild.

31. According to paragraph 2, sickles found in the eastern Mediterranean are evidence that

(A) the makers of these sickles were skilled craftsmen
(B) wild grasses were eaten before domesticated grasses
(C) the sickles were useful for fishing and hunting
(D) grasses were cut down for food consumption

Paragraph 2 is marked with an arrow [➡].

➡ Recent evidence seems to indicate that while the Neolithic revolution first took place in the Middle East – in the valleys of the Tigris-Euphrates and of the Nile – it occurred independently in other areas of the world. The origins of the revolution are not known in great detail, but it is known that the wild grasses that were the ancestors of wheat and barley grew natively in the Eastern Mediterranean area. It may be that Mesolithic (Middle Stone Age) foragers simply supplemented their diet by reaping these wild grasses, and later came to understand the advantage of returning some of the grain to the soil as seed. Whatever the case, we know that at an early date people living in the Eastern Mediterranean region, who lived by hunting, fishing, and gathering, began to make sickles, with stone teeth set in bone handles. Such tools were certainly used for reaping some grass crop, whether cultivated or wild.

32. The word "fertile" in the passage is closest in meaning to

(A) forceful
(B) productive
(C) creative
(D) shallow

Both in Egypt and Mesopotamia, the periodic floods of great rivers such as the Nile and the Tigris-Euphrates not only supplied water to the fields but also brought down fresh soil in the form of fertile muddy sediments. This sediment was deposited on flood plains around such rivers, thus annually restoring the fruitfulness of the land. This regular flooding and sediment deposit allowed these early farmers to continue cultivating the same fields repeatedly for generations without exhausting the fertility of the soil, and crop surpluses were, therefore, available to allow an increase in population and a growth in trade and skills development. The area available for cultivation was expanded when people learned to draw off the river water into man-made irrigation canals and ditches, watering and fertilizing larger and larger areas of land.

33. According to paragraph 4, why was it easy for people to grow food near large rivers?

(A) Flooding eroded the soil.
(B) The soil was continuously enriched.
(C) Surplus crops were regular.
(D) The population was large enough.

Paragraph 4 is marked with an arrow [➡].

➡ Both in Egypt and Mesopotamia, the periodic floods of great rivers such as the Nile and the Tigris-Euphrates not only supplied water to the fields but also brought down fresh soil in the form of fertile muddy sediments. This sediment was deposited on flood plains around such rivers, thus annually restoring the fruitfulness of the land. This regular flooding and sediment deposit allowed these early farmers to continue cultivating the same fields repeatedly for generations without exhausting the fertility of the soil, and crop surpluses were, therefore, available to allow an increase in population and a growth in trade and skills development. The area available for cultivation was expanded when people learned to draw off the river water into man-made irrigation canals and ditches, watering and fertilizing larger and larger areas of land.

34. According to paragraph 4, why did early Neolithic people build irrigation ditches?

(A) To increase the growing areas
(B) To enlarge the fertilized areas
(C) To produce crop surpluses
(D) To water the early canals

Paragraph 4 is marked with an arrow [➡].

➡ Both in Egypt and Mesopotamia, the periodic floods of great rivers such as the Nile and the Tigris-Euphrates not only supplied water to the fields but also brought down fresh soil in the form of fertile muddy sediments. This sediment was deposited on flood plains around such rivers, thus annually restoring the fruitfulness of the land. This regular flooding and sediment deposit allowed these early farmers to continue cultivating the same fields repeatedly for generations without exhausting the fertility of the soil, and crop surpluses were, therefore, available to allow an increase in population and a growth in trade and skills development. The area available for cultivation was expanded when people learned to draw off the river water into man-made irrigation canals and ditches, watering and fertilizing larger and larger areas of land.

35. The word "This" in the passage refers to

(A) irrigation
(B) hot climate
(C) evaporation
(D) loss of water

The practice of artificial irrigation affected the soil in various ways, but not always for the good. Since the channels were often shallow, there was frequently a great loss of water through evaporation in a hot climate. This could lead to a marked increase in soil salinity, since the salts held in solution or suspension were deposited as the water evaporated, and too much salinity could eventually damage the soil. But overall the effect of the irrigation system was to create an artificial environment – and to some extent an artificial climate – with a range of conditions that favored both human experiment and agricultural development. Beyond this, settled agriculture led to the development of property rights and hence to a legal framework and mechanisms to enforce laws. This in turn led to a more extensive and hierarchical government organization and hence to the development of large, stable communities.

36. According to paragraph 5, what negative effect did the building of irrigation ditches create?

(A) Too much salt in the soil
(B) A worsening climate
(C) Destruction of settlements
(D) Too much experimentation

Paragraph 5 is marked with an arrow [➡].

➡ The practice of artificial irrigation affected the soil in various ways, but not always for the good. Since the channels were often shallow, there was frequently a great loss of water through evaporation in a hot climate. This could lead to a marked increase in soil salinity, since the salts held in solution or suspension were deposited as the water evaporated, and too much salinity could eventually damage the soil. But overall the effect of the irrigation system was to create an artificial environment – and to some extent an artificial climate – with a range of conditions that favored both human experiment and agricultural development. Beyond this, settled agriculture led to the development of property rights and hence to a legal framework and mechanisms to enforce laws. This in turn led to a more extensive and hierarchical government organization and hence to the development of large, stable communities.

37. What can be inferred from paragraph 5 about the development of an organized government?

(A) Stable communities function best with a hierarchical government.
(B) Human experiment is most often practiced if government enforces laws.
(C) An organized government is necessary to extend artificial irrigation.
(D) The need to enforce property laws required government organization.

Paragraph 5 is marked with an arrow [➡].

➡ The practice of artificial irrigation affected the soil in various ways, but not always for the good. Since the channels were often shallow, there was frequently a great loss of water through evaporation in a hot climate. This could lead to a marked increase in soil salinity, since the salts held in solution or suspension were deposited as the water evaporated, and too much salinity could eventually damage the soil. But overall the effect of the irrigation system was to create an artificial environment – and to some extent an artificial climate – with a range of conditions that favored both human experiment and agricultural development. Beyond this, settled agriculture led to the development of property rights and hence to a legal framework and mechanisms to enforce laws. This in turn led to a more extensive and hierarchical government organization and hence to the development of large, stable communities.

38. Look at the four squares [■] that indicate where the following sentence could be added to the passage.

In much of the Middle East region, the earth was mainly watered not by rain but by natural irrigation.

Where would the sentence best fit?

Choose the letter of the square that shows where the sentence should be added.

A Both in Egypt and Mesopotamia, the periodic floods of great rivers such as the Nile and the Tigris-Euphrates not only supplied water to the fields but also brought down fresh soil in the form of fertile muddy sediments. **B** This sediment was deposited on flood plains around such rivers, thus annually restoring the fruitfulness of the land. **C** This regular flooding and sediment deposit allowed these early farmers to continue cultivating the same fields repeatedly for generations without exhausting the fertility of the soil, and crop surpluses were, therefore, available to allow an increase in population and a growth in trade and skills development. **D** The area available for cultivation was expanded when people learned to draw off the river water into man-made irrigation canals and ditches, watering and fertilizing larger and larger areas of land.

39. **Directions:** An introductory sentence of a brief summary of the passage is provided below. Complete the summary by selecting the THREE answer choices that express the most important ideas in the passage. Some sentences do not belong in the summary because they express ideas that are not presented in the passage or are minor ideas in the passage. **This question is worth 2 points.**

Write the letters of the answer choices in the spaces where they belong.
Refer to the full passage.

During the Neolithic period, people started to domesticate animals, grow crops, and build permanent settlements, leading eventually to the beginnings of civilization.

-
-
-

Answer Choices

(A) It is likely that early hunters ate wild grasses and later understood how to cultivate, reap, and grind grain.

(B) The floodwaters of rivers in the Middle East enriched the soil, which led to food surpluses and an enlarged population.

(C) At one time, people in the Eastern Mediterranean region lived by hunting animals, catching fish, and gathering edible plants.

(D) We know that early people learned how to cultivate grasses since they developed a simple type of grinding mill.

(E) The large increase in the number of irrigation canals led to the worsening of the soil condition due to deposits of salt.

(F) Artificial irrigation increased the arable area, and despite some negative effects, overall this development led to improvement in life and eventually to an organized government system.

LISTENING SECTION

Directions

This section measures your ability to understand conversations and lectures in English. You will hear each conversation or lecture only one time. After each conversation or lecture, you will answer some questions about it.

The questions typically ask about the main idea and supporting details. Some questions ask about a speaker's purpose or attitude. Answer the questions based on what is stated or implied by the speakers.

You may take notes while you listen. You may use your notes to help you answer the questions. Your notes will not be scored.

In some questions, you will see this icon: 🎧. This means that you will hear, but not see, part of the question.

Some questions have special directions. These directions appear in a gray box.

Most questions are worth one point. A question worth more than one point will have special instructions indicating how many points you can receive.

You will have 20 minutes to answer the questions in this section.

Now get ready to listen. You may take notes.

START ▶

Questions 1–6

Listen to part of a lecture in a business studies class.

Now get ready to answer the questions. You may use your notes to help you answer.

1. What is the lecture mainly about?
   - (A) A method for evaluating outcomes
   - (B) A technique for avoiding controversy
   - (C) A comparison of beneficial inputs
   - (D) A formula for sidestepping failure

2. In the lecture, the professor describes some costs and benefits of investing in new machinery. Indicate whether each of the following is a cost or a benefit for a company planning on making an investment decision.

Check the correct box for each statement.

	Cost	Benefit
(A) The new machine has lower energy consumption than the old one.		
(B) The insurance payments are higher for the new machine.		
(C) The new machine produces higher-quality products.		
(D) Additional floor space is required for the new machine.		
(E) The new machine has more safety features than the old one.		

PRACTICE TEST 1

3. Why does the professor mention the introduction of machinery?
   (A) To underline the importance of monetary units
   (B) To help explain how costs and benefits are worked out
   (C) To show that many machines are too expensive
   (D) To emphasize the financial side of business decisions

4. Why does the professor say this: 
   (A) She thinks some costs are difficult to see.
   (B) She does not think the analysis is complicated.
   (C) She wants students to understand the loss of money.
   (D) She does not think all benefits are really benefits.

5. Listen again to part of the lecture. Then answer the question.
   Why does the professor say this: 
   (A) To verify how tricky it is to apply CBA to a transportation business
   (B) To introduce impressive software for building roads
   (C) To show how to calculate the building of a new road
   (D) To give an example of an analysis done in the public domain

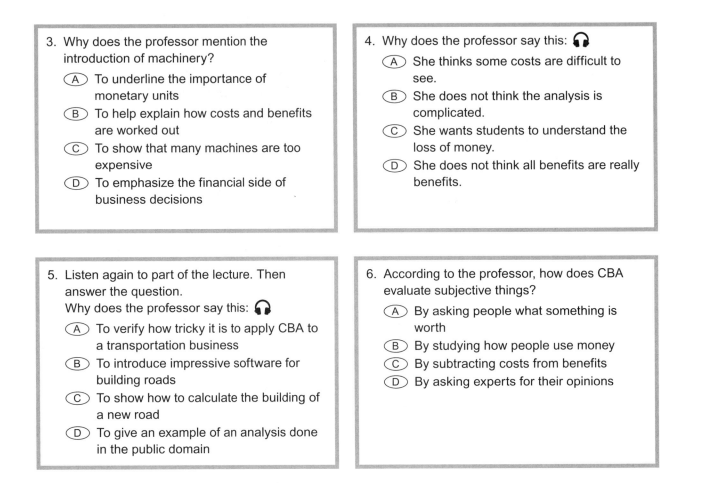

6. According to the professor, how does CBA evaluate subjective things?
   (A) By asking people what something is worth
   (B) By studying how people use money
   (C) By subtracting costs from benefits
   (D) By asking experts for their opinions

Questions 7–11

Listen to a conversation between a student and a professor.

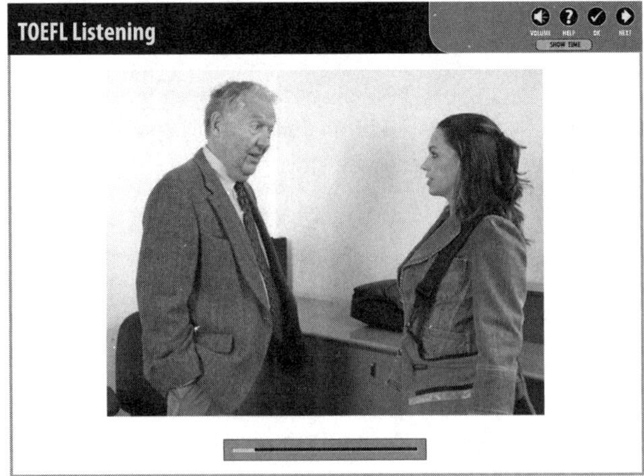

Now get ready to answer the questions. You may use your notes to help you answer.

7. Why does the student go to see her professor?
   - (A) To pick up her research paper
   - (B) To get advice on citing sources
   - (C) To get feedback on her research paper
   - (D) To discuss the nutritional value of chocolate

8. Listen again to part of the conversation. Then answer the question.
   Why does the professor say this:
   - (A) To show how experts are biased
   - (B) To explain why the Web site is bad
   - (C) To encourage the student to visit the professor
   - (D) To indicate that she needs to pay attention to other details

9. Why does Dr. Johnson criticize the student's use of a university Web site?
   - (A) The research was put together by students.
   - (B) The professor was not an expert in the field.
   - (C) The Web site wasn't from a prestigious university.
   - (D) The Web site did not have the *.edu* domain in its address.

10. Listen again to part of the conversation. Then answer the question.
    Why does the professor say this: 
    - (A) To encourage the student to investigate the claims further
    - (B) To indicate that the research on chocolate was well funded
    - (C) To encourage the student to be closed-minded about the study
    - (D) To explain that the research suggests salt should be added to chocolate

11. What does the professor say about the research sponsored by a company?
    - (A) It is biased.
    - (B) It is not well funded.
    - (C) It should be repeatable.
    - (D) It should be thrown out.

Questions 12–17

Listen to part of a lecture in an architecture class.

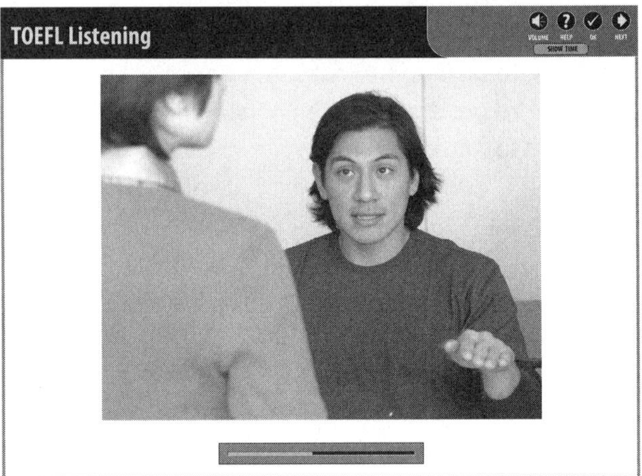

Now get ready to answer the questions. You may use your notes to help you answer.

12. What is the lecture mainly about?

(A) The first skyscrapers in America
(B) The influence of the English Arts and Crafts movement
(C) The Prairie School of Architecture
(D) Oriental motifs in American architecture

13. What can be said about the nature of Prairie School architecture?

Choose 2 answers.

[A] It tried to harmonize with nature.
[B] It was mostly expressed in large public buildings.
[C] It was mainly concerned with domestic living spaces.
[D] It was Midwestern American in nature with no foreign influences.

14. Listen again to part of the lecture. Then answer the question.
Why does the professor say this: 

(A) To introduce a new discussion topic for the lecture
(B) To suggest that the name of the school is slightly inappropriate
(C) To find out whether the students have understood the concept of prairie
(D) To express disagreement with the stated aims of the Prairie School architects

15. According to the professor, how did the Prairie School architects make living space more compatible with human needs?

Choose 2 answers.

[A] Through the use of vertical windows
[B] By abolishing closed interior corners
[C] Through the use of elaborate ornamentation
[D] By decreasing the number of separate rooms

16. What does the professor say about the use of ornamentation by Prairie School architects?
    - (A) They liked colorful designs and a variety of decorations.
    - (B) They tended to use ornamentation only if it complemented a design.
    - (C) The only ornamentation they used was based on Japanese models.
    - (D) The only decoration they permitted was in furniture design.

17. Why does the professor mention traditional Japanese houses?
    - (A) To contrast Japanese architectural design with the Prairie School design
    - (B) To show the relationship between Japanese use of space and overall ornamentation
    - (C) To give an example of how turned-up roof edges don't blend in with the horizontal lines of the flat prairies
    - (D) To show how the influence of Oriental themes was expressed in the Prairie School designs

Questions 18–23

Listen to part of a lecture in a psychology class.

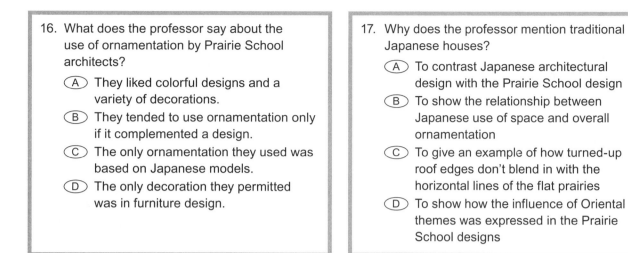

Now get ready to answer the questions. You may use your notes to help you answer.

18. What aspect of a meme's behavior does the professor mainly discuss?
    - (A) Its genetic structure
    - (B) Its ability to disappear
    - (C) Its physical appearance
    - (D) Its tendency to be copied

19. Why does the professor say this: 
    - (A) To find out if students already know the main points
    - (B) To suggest that some of the information is controversial
    - (C) To hint that most of the discussion is wrong
    - (D) To explain why gene theory is considered out of date

20. What does the professor say about memes?
    - (A) They will eventually disappear.
    - (B) They cause us to mutate.
    - (C) They are passed on to other people.
    - (D) They are usually harmful.

21. Listen again to part of the lecture. Then answer the question.
    Why does the professor say this: 🎧
    - (A) To make a joke about what could be considered as a meme
    - (B) To indicate that important ideas could be transferred by memes
    - (C) To show how memes can be used for the preparation of food
    - (D) To show a contrast between the idea of constructing bridges and making fires

22. What does the professor imply about the importance of memes in our minds?
    - (A) Memes are related to our thoughts.
    - (B) Memes are controlled by our brains.
    - (C) Memes and emotions are identical.
    - (D) Memes are necessary for our emotions.

23. Which of the following is NOT true about memes?
    - (A) Memes can be found in our genes.
    - (B) Memes can be passed on to other people.
    - (C) Memes can represent true or false ideas.
    - (D) Memes can die out.

Questions 24–29

Listen to part of a lecture in an anthropology class.

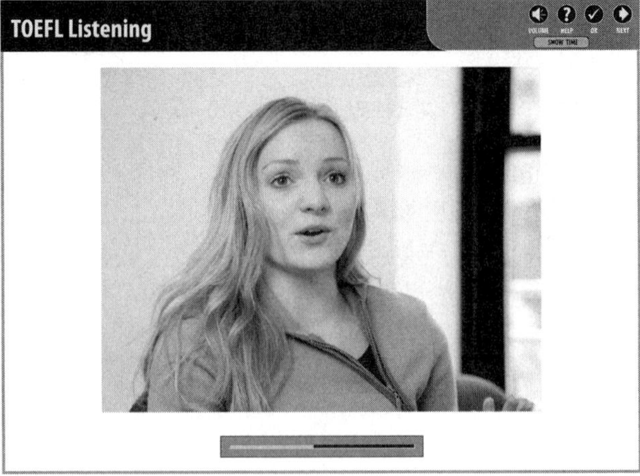

Now get ready to answer the questions. You may use your notes to help you answer.

24. What is the main topic of the lecture?
    - (A) Reasons for the disappearance of the Anasazi culture
    - (B) Reasons for the fighting between different cultures
    - (C) Reasons for environmental degradation
    - (D) Reasons for the development of the Anasazi culture

25. What does the professor imply about the term *Anasazi*?
    - (A) It should not be used.
    - (B) There are better alternatives.
    - (C) It is not a well-known name.
    - (D) It is no longer acceptable to some people.

26. According to the professor, why did the Anasazi start making pottery?
    - (A) They wanted to trade with other cultures.
    - (B) They wanted to develop artistic skills.
    - (C) Pottery is better for keeping food.
    - (D) Their baskets were ineffective.

27. Why does the professor say this:
    - (A) She was trying to recall where in the lecture she was.
    - (B) She was unsure which culture she was describing.
    - (C) She realized that the students were not listening carefully.
    - (D) She forgot to tell the students about road-building techniques.

28. Based on the information in the discussion, indicate whether each of the following is accepted by most scientists.

Check the correct box for each statement.

	Yes	No
(A) They left their villages because of the spread of diseases.		
(B) They left their villages because of invaders.		
(C) They left their villages because of lack of resources.		

29. What does the professor imply about the Anasazi's use of their environment?
    - (A) They were aware of the damage they were causing.
    - (B) They did not protect their environment well.
    - (C) They tried to manage their resources properly.
    - (D) They were sophisticated in their use of resources.

Questions 30–34

Listen to part of a conversation between two students.

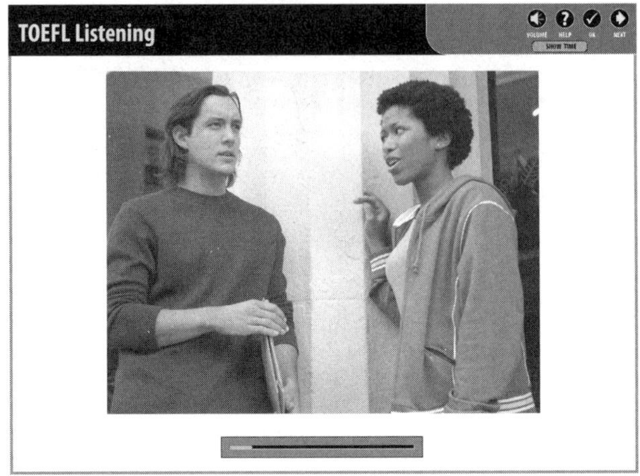

Now get ready to answer the questions. You may use your notes to help you answer.

30. What are the students mainly discussing?
    - (A) The importance of being presumed innocent
    - (B) Court procedure in criminal cases
    - (C) The definitions of some legal terms
    - (D) Legal rights of defendants

31. Why does the woman say this: 🎧
    - (A) To invite the man to accompany her
    - (B) To let the man know she doesn't have much time
    - (C) To ask the man if he would like to meet her roommate
    - (D) To check that the man has finished his test review

32. According to the conversation, which of the following statements are correct?

    Choose 2 answers.

    - [A] The defendant tries to show that he or she is not guilty.
    - [B] The prosecutor usually works for the government.
    - [C] The plaintiff is often convicted.
    - [D] The burden of proof rests with the jury.

33. What can be inferred about the value of circumstantial evidence for prosecutors?
    - (A) It is useful but never sufficient for gaining a conviction.
    - (B) All court cases require it.
    - (C) Prosecutors often use it to gain a conviction.
    - (D) Without direct evidence, it is unreliable.

34. According to the conversation, what do most people think about circumstantial evidence?
    - (A) It is better than direct evidence for gaining a conviction.
    - (B) It is not very useful for gaining a conviction.
    - (C) It cannot be used in criminal court cases.
    - (D) It is very persuasive in court cases.

STOP ■

SPEAKING SECTION

Directions

In this section of the test, you will be able to demonstrate your ability to speak about a variety of topics. You will answer six questions by recording your response. Answer each of the questions as completely as possible.

In questions 1 and 2, you will first hear a statement or question about familiar topics. You will then speak about these topics. Your response will be scored on your ability to speak clearly and coherently about the topics.

In questions 3 and 4, you will first read a short text. You will then listen to a talk on the same topic.

You will be asked a question about what you have read and heard. You will need to combine appropriate information from the text and the talk to provide a complete answer to the question. Your response will be scored on your ability to speak clearly and coherently and on your ability to accurately convey information about what you read and heard.

In questions 5 and 6, you will listen to part of a conversation or a lecture. You will be asked a question about what you heard. Your response will be scored on your ability to speak clearly and coherently and on your ability to accurately convey information about what you heard.

You may take notes while you read and while you listen to the conversations and lectures. You may use your notes to help prepare your response.

Listen carefully to the directions for each question. For each question you will be given a short time to prepare your response. When the preparation time is up, you will be told to begin your response.

START ▶

1. Please listen carefully.

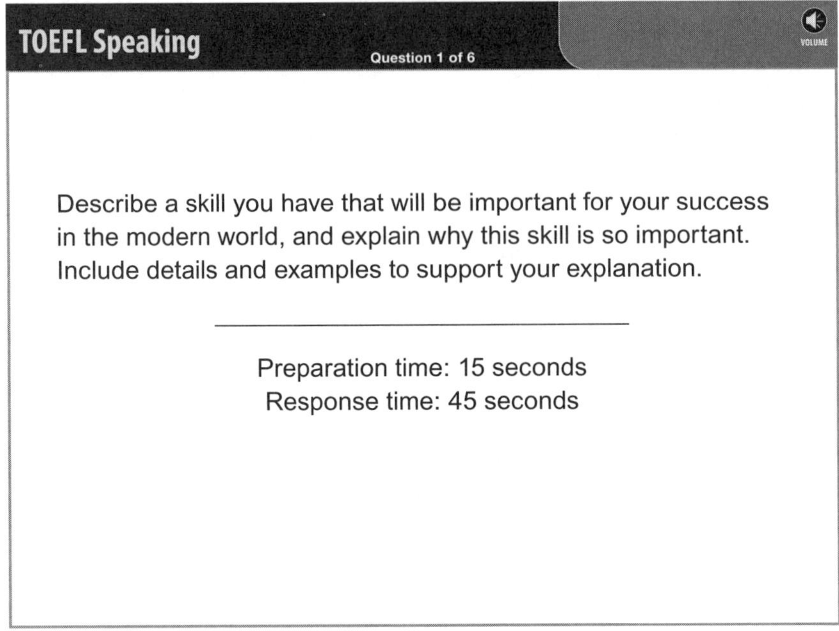
TOEFL Speaking
Question 1 of 6
VOLUME
Describe a skill you have that will be important for your success in the modern world, and explain why this skill is so important. Include details and examples to support your explanation.
Preparation time: 15 seconds
Response time: 45 seconds

You may begin to prepare your response after the beep.

Please begin speaking after the beep.

STOP ■

START ▶

2. Please listen carefully.

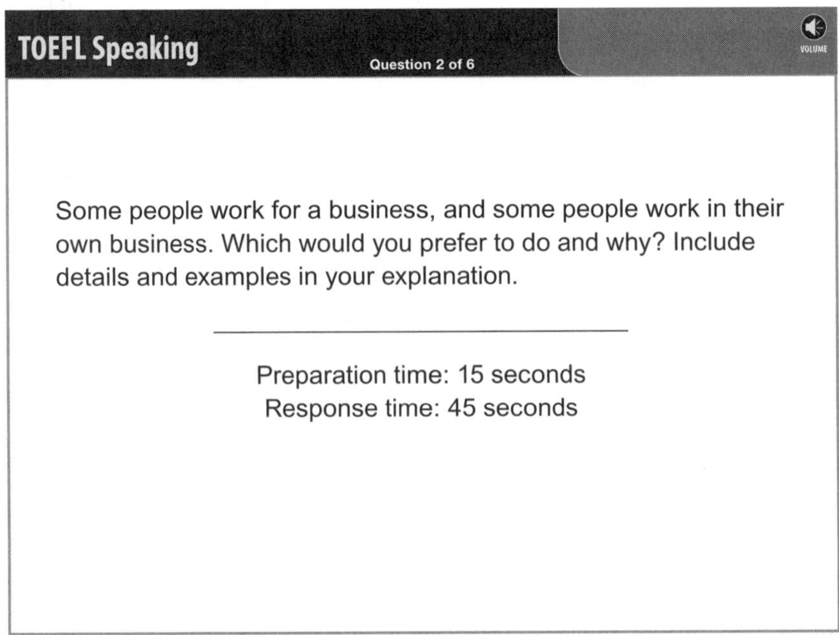
TOEFL Speaking
Question 2 of 6
VOLUME
Some people work for a business, and some people work in their own business. Which would you prefer to do and why? Include details and examples in your explanation.
Preparation time: 15 seconds
Response time: 45 seconds

You may begin to prepare your response after the beep.

Please begin speaking after the beep.

STOP ■

START ▶

3. Please listen carefully.

The University of the Rockies Financial Aid Office has posted information about work-study grants. You will have 45 seconds to read the announcement. Begin reading now.

PAUSE II (for 45 seconds)

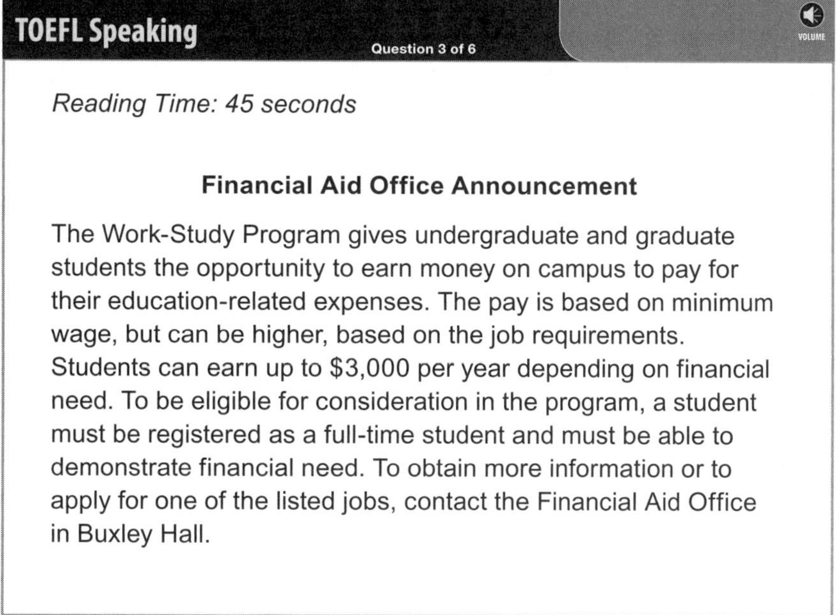

Now listen to two students as they discuss the announcement.

Now get ready to answer the question.

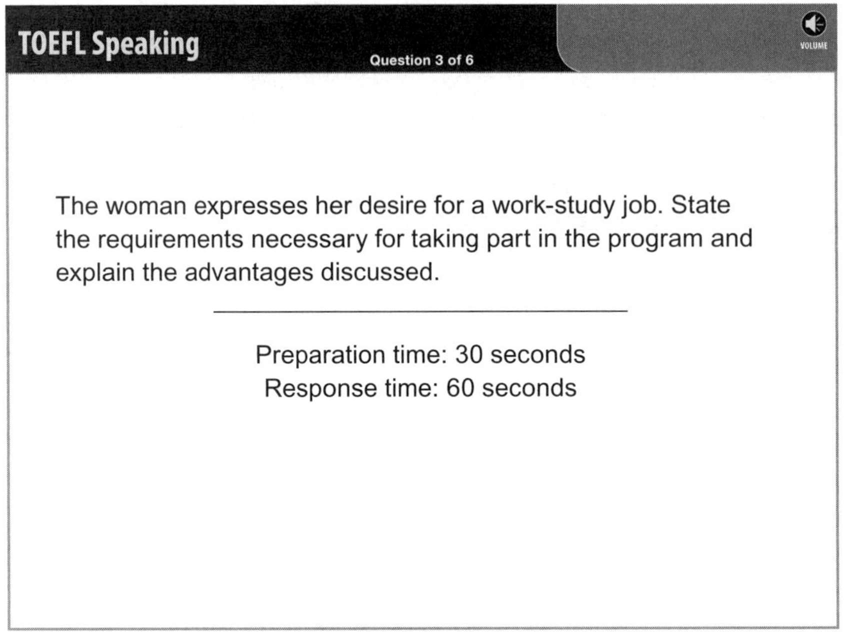

TOEFL Speaking
Question 3 of 6
VOLUME
The woman expresses her desire for a work-study job. State the requirements necessary for taking part in the program and explain the advantages discussed.
Preparation time: 30 seconds
Response time: 60 seconds

You may begin to prepare your response after the beep.

Please begin speaking after the beep.

STOP ■

START ▶

4. Please listen carefully.

Read the passage about symbiotic relationships. You have 45 seconds to read the passage. Begin reading now.

PAUSE II (for 45 seconds)

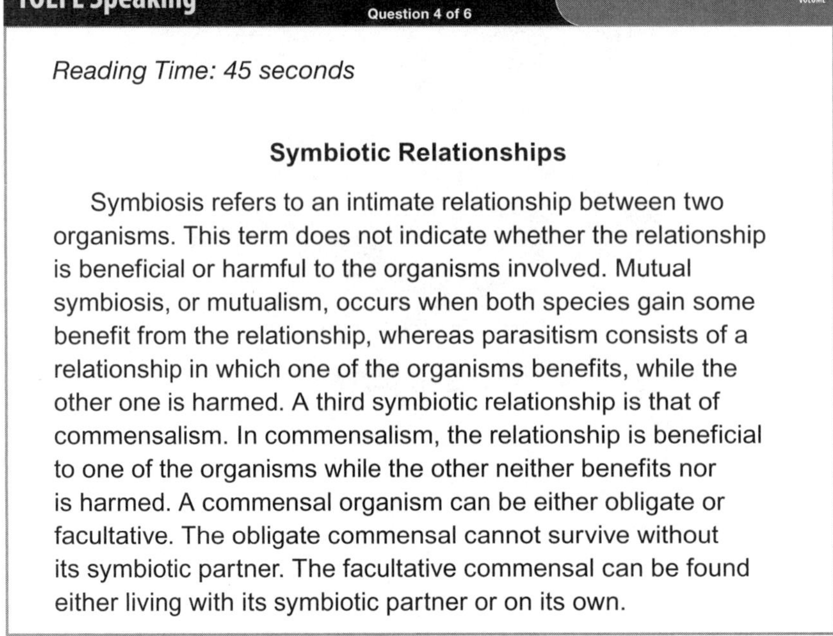

TOEFL Speaking
Question 4 of 6
VOLUME
Reading Time: 45 seconds
Symbiotic Relationships
Symbiosis refers to an intimate relationship between two organisms. This term does not indicate whether the relationship is beneficial or harmful to the organisms involved. Mutual symbiosis, or mutualism, occurs when both species gain some benefit from the relationship, whereas parasitism consists of a relationship in which one of the organisms benefits, while the other one is harmed. A third symbiotic relationship is that of commensalism. In commensalism, the relationship is beneficial to one of the organisms while the other neither benefits nor is harmed. A commensal organism can be either obligate or facultative. The obligate commensal cannot survive without its symbiotic partner. The facultative commensal can be found either living with its symbiotic partner or on its own.

Now listen to part of a lecture on this topic in a biology class.

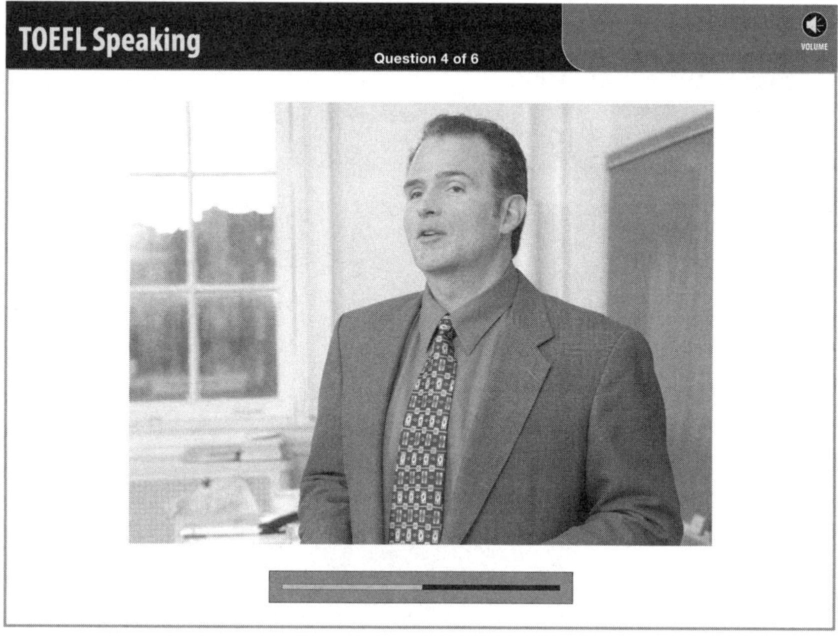

Now get ready to answer the question.

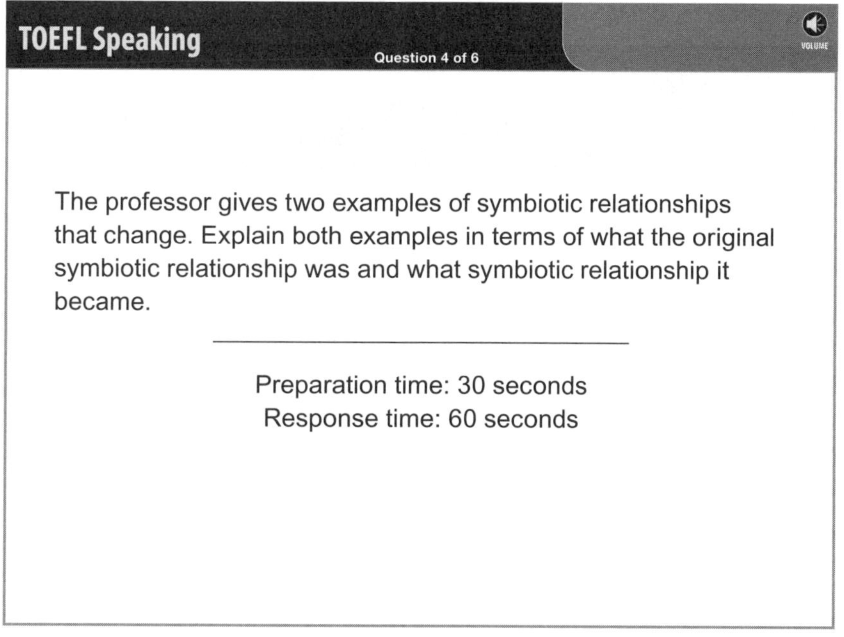

TOEFL Speaking
Question 4 of 6
VOLUME
The professor gives two examples of symbiotic relationships that change. Explain both examples in terms of what the original symbiotic relationship was and what symbiotic relationship it became.
Preparation time: 30 seconds
Response time: 60 seconds

You may begin to prepare your response after the beep.

Please begin speaking after the beep.

STOP ■

START ▶

5. Please listen carefully.

Listen to a conversation between two students.

TOEFL Speaking
Question 5 of 6
VOLUME

Now get ready to answer the question.

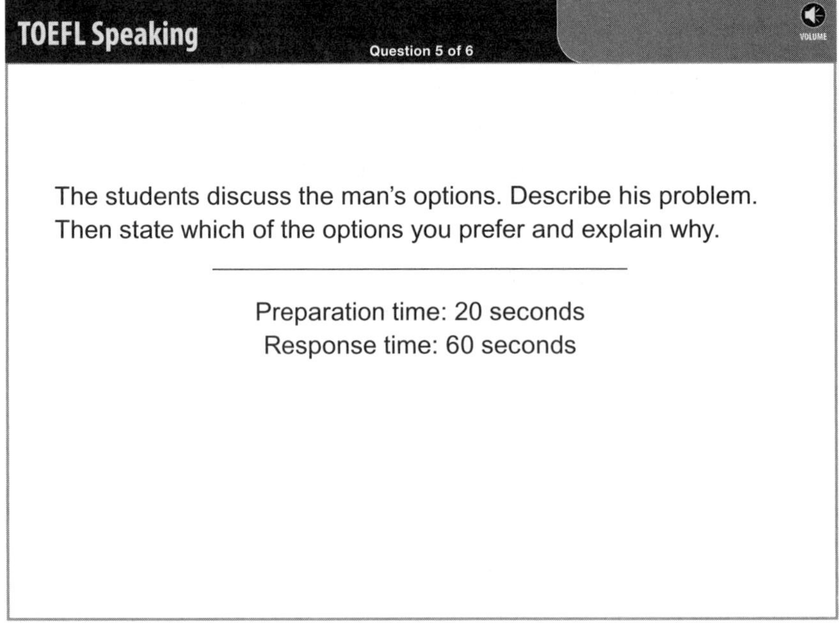
TOEFL Speaking
Question 5 of 6
VOLUME
The students discuss the man's options. Describe his problem. Then state which of the options you prefer and explain why.
Preparation time: 20 seconds
Response time: 60 seconds

You may begin to prepare your response after the beep.

Please begin speaking after the beep.

STOP ■

START ▶

6. Please listen carefully.

Listen to part of a lecture in a cultural studies class.

TOEFL Speaking
Question 6 of 6
VOLUME

Now get ready to answer the question.

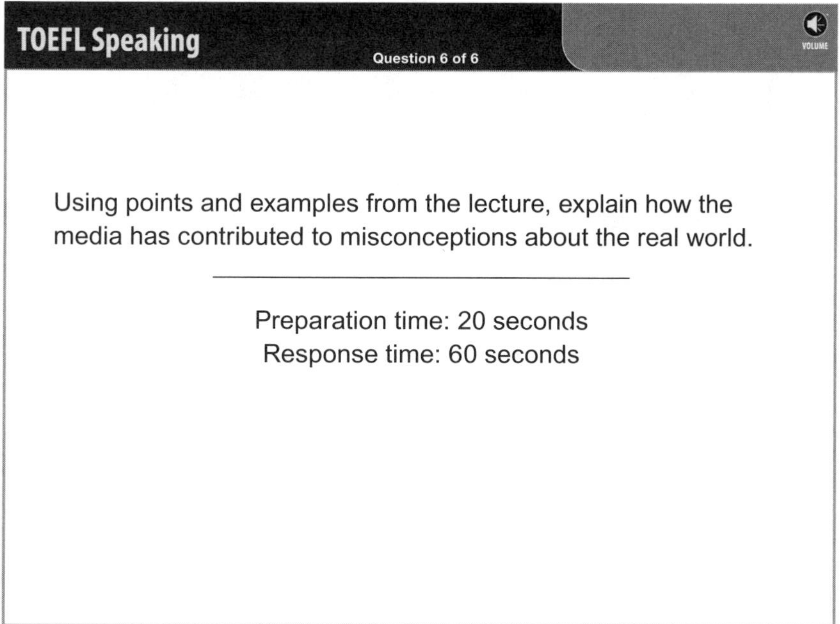
TOEFL Speaking
Question 6 of 6
VOLUME
Using points and examples from the lecture, explain how the media has contributed to misconceptions about the real world.
Preparation time: 20 seconds
Response time: 60 seconds

You may begin to prepare your response after the beep.

Please begin speaking after the beep.

STOP ■

WRITING SECTION

Directions

This section measures your ability to use writing to communicate in an academic environment. There will be two writing tasks.

For the first writing task, you will read a passage and listen to a lecture, and then answer a question based on what you have read and heard. For the second writing task, you will answer a question based on your own knowledge and experience.

Now read the directions for the first writing task.

Writing Based on Reading and Listening

Directions

For this task, you will have three minutes to read a passage about an academic topic. You may take notes on the passage while you read. Then you will listen to a lecture about the same topic. While you listen, you may also take notes.

Then you will have 20 minutes to write a response to a question that asks you about the relationship between the lecture you heard and the reading passage. Try to answer the question as completely as possible using information from the reading passage and the lecture. The question does **not** ask you to express your personal opinion. You can refer to the reading passage again when it is time for you to write. You may use your notes to help you answer the question.

Typically, an effective response will be 150 to 225 words long. Your response will be judged on the quality of your writing and on the completeness and accuracy of the content. If you finish your response before time is up, go on to the second writing task.

On the day of the test, you will be required to type your response into a computer. Therefore, if you are taking this test in the book, practice typing your response on a computer.

INTEGRATED TASK

Directions: You have three minutes to read and take notes from the reading passage. Next, listen to the related lecture and take notes. Then write your response.

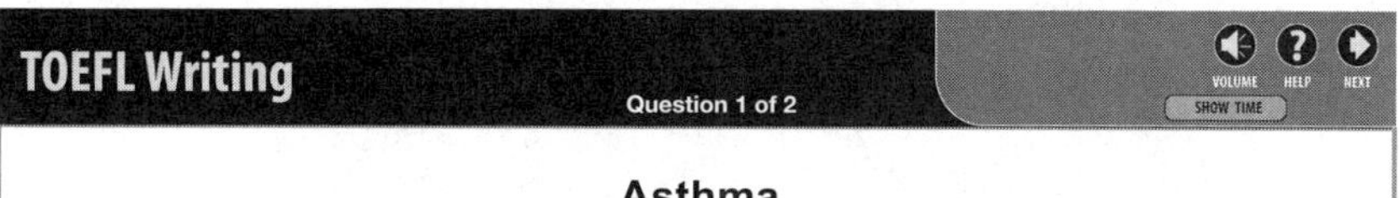

Asthma

Asthma is usually seen as a condition whose symptoms can be adequately controlled with the right medicines. Researchers point out that it is an intermittent disorder, characterized by temporary bouts of inflammation of the airways, which lead to typical symptoms such as wheezing, coughing, and shortness of breath; after each episode (often known as an attack), symptoms subside and the airways return to normal.

Asthmatics tend to be susceptible to certain triggers in the environment. These include but are not restricted to animal fur, pollen, cigarette smoke, house dust mites, and perfumes. Attacks can also be brought on by exercise, emotional stress, or a variety of other factors including respiratory infections such as the common cold.

During an episode of asthma, the bronchial tubes and the smaller tubes dividing off from these, known as bronchioles, become narrow or blocked and as a result air can't get in or out of the lungs easily. There are two basic causes behind bronchial narrowing: either the bronchi and bronchioles are squeezed by muscles wrapped around them rather like elastic bands, or they become blocked by mucus and swelling inside the tubes themselves. When the bronchi are constricted, the condition is called *bronchoconstriction*. Occasional squeezing of the bronchi is normal, but in asthma sufferers these muscles may react too sensitively to environmental triggers. It is also a normal function of the bronchial tubes to produce mucus and, in concert with tiny hairs called cilia, to trap inhaled irritants and remove them from the body, thus protecting the lungs. But some asthmatics produce an overabundance of mucus, and this results in blocked airways and consequent asthmatic symptoms.

START ▶

Now listen to part of a lecture on the topic you just read about.

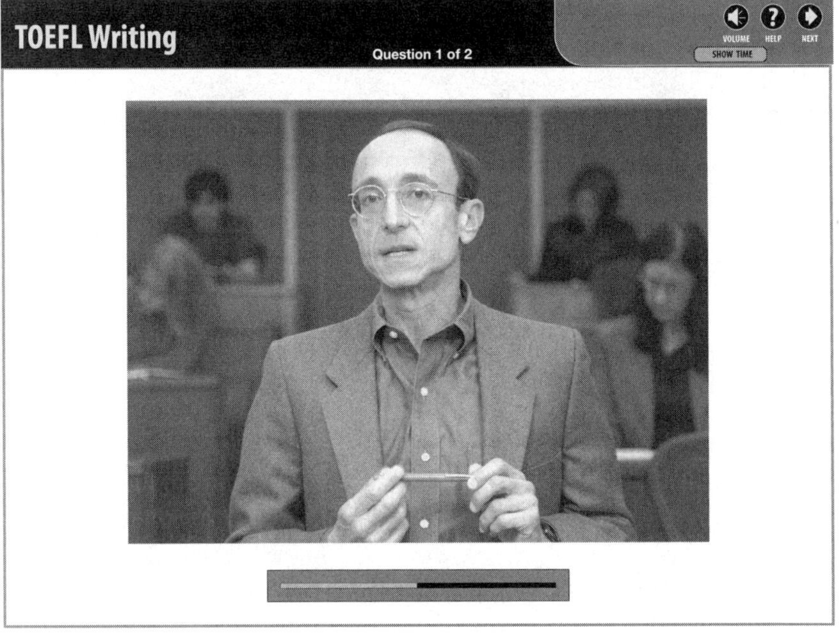
TOEFL Writing
Question 1 of 2
VOLUME HELP NEXT
SHOW TIME

STOP ■

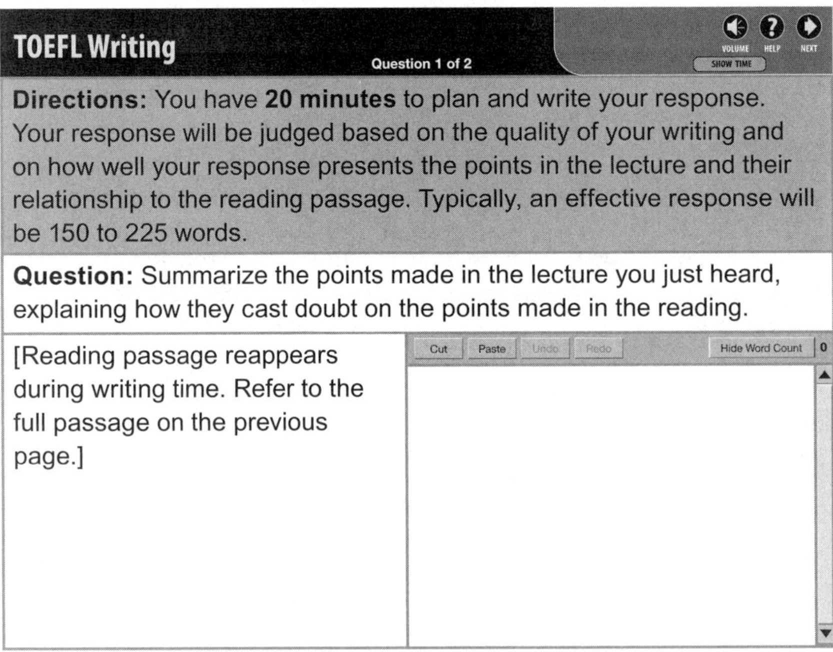
TOEFL Writing
Question 1 of 2
VOLUME HELP NEXT
SHOW TIME
Directions: You have **20 minutes** to plan and write your response. Your response will be judged based on the quality of your writing and on how well your response presents the points in the lecture and their relationship to the reading passage. Typically, an effective response will be 150 to 225 words.
Question: Summarize the points made in the lecture you just heard, explaining how they cast doubt on the points made in the reading.
[Reading passage reappears during writing time. Refer to the full passage on the previous page.]
Cut
Paste
Undo
Redo
Hide Word Count
0

Writing Based on Knowledge and Experience

Directions

For this task, you will write an essay in response to a question that asks you to state, explain, and support your opinion on an issue. You will have 30 minutes to plan, write, and revise your essay.

Typically, an effective essay will contain a minimum of 300 words. Your essay will be judged on the quality of your writing. This includes the development of your ideas, the organization of your essay, and the quality and accuracy of the language you use to express your ideas.

On the day of the test, you will be required to type your response into a computer. Therefore, if you are taking this test in the book, practice typing your response on a computer.

INDEPENDENT WRITING TASK

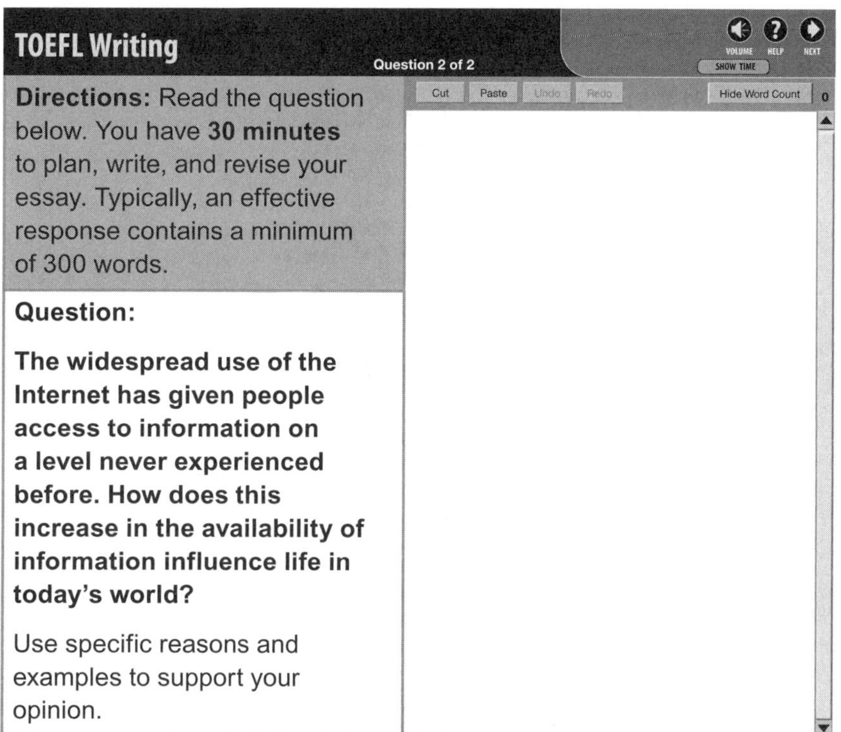

TOEFL Writing
Question 2 of 2
VOLUME HELP NEXT
SHOW TIME
Directions: Read the question below. You have 30 minutes to plan, write, and revise your essay. Typically, an effective response contains a minimum of 300 words.
Question:
The widespread use of the Internet has given people access to information on a level never experienced before. How does this increase in the availability of information influence life in today's world?
Use specific reasons and examples to support your opinion.
Cut
Paste
Undo
Redo
Hide Word Count
0

Practice Test 2

READING SECTION

Directions

In this section, you will read three passages and answer reading comprehension questions about each passage. Most questions are worth one point, but the last question in each set is worth more than one point. The directions indicate how many points you may receive.

You have 60 minutes to read all of the passages and answer the questions. Some passages include a word or phrase followed by an asterisk (*). Go to the bottom of the page to see a definition or an explanation of these words or phrases.

Questions 1–12

Two Atomic Clocks

The nucleus of a radioactive atom disintegrates spontaneously and forms an atom of a different element while emitting radiation in the process. The original atom is called the parent isotope* and its stable product is called the daughter or progeny isotope. For example, rubidium-87 decays by emitting an electron from its nucleus to form a stable daughter called strontium-87. Because the rate of nuclear decay is constant regardless of temperature and pressure conditions, radioactive decay provides a dependable way of keeping time. Radioactive isotopes alter from one type of atom to another at a fixed rate from the moment they are created anywhere in the universe. Since we can calculate the decay rate and also count the number of newly formed progeny atoms and the remaining parent atoms, we can use the ratio as a kind of clock to measure the age of minerals and other materials.

The rate at which a radioactive element decays is known as the half-life of the element. This is the time necessary for one-half of the original number of radioactive atoms in a sample to decay into a daughter product. After two half-lives, the number of atoms remaining after the first half-life will have decayed by half again. Thus, the number of remaining parent atoms is reduced geometrically over time. With some elements, the half-life is very long. Rubidium-87, for example, has a half-life that has been estimated at nearly 48.8 billion years, much longer than the current estimated age of the universe. With other elements, this period can be as short as a few days or even minutes. If we know the half-life of a decaying element, it is possible to calculate the ratio of parent to stable progeny that will remain after any given period of time.

Geologists use a sensitive instrument called a mass spectrometer to detect tiny quantities of the isotopes of the parent and progeny atoms. By measuring the ratio of these, they can calculate the age of the rock in which the rubidium originally crystallized. Because the number of progeny is growing as the parent is decaying and this is occurring at a constant rate, after one-half life the ratio is one parent to one progeny. After two half-lives the ratio is 1 to 3.

Rubidium-87 has often been used to date rocks since it is a widespread element. Various elements including rubidium are incorporated into minerals as they crystallize from magma* or metamorphic rock. During this process the rubidium is separated from any strontium progeny that existed before the rock formed and so we know that the measurable alteration from parent to progeny can be dated from this point. As the radioactive decay of rubidium-87 begins, new progeny atoms of strontium-87 start to accumulate in the rock. In the dating of rocks using these elements, it is important that the rock sample has not been altered subsequent to its formation by other geologic processes or contamination of any kind. Rocks as old as 4.6 billion years can be dated with some degree of reliability using this method.

Another radioactive element useful for dating is carbon-14, which decays into nitrogen-14. With a half-life of 5,730 years, carbon-14 decays much more rapidly than rubidium-87 and so is useful for measuring the ages of objects from the recent historical and geologic past, such as fossils, bones, wood, and other organic materials. Whereas rubidium-87 is incorporated into rocks during their formation, carbon-14, which is an essential element of the cells of organisms, becomes incorporated into living tissues as organisms grow. The ratio of carbon-14 to stable carbon isotopes in the organism is the same as it is in the atmosphere. When a living organism dies, no more carbon dioxide is absorbed and so no new carbon isotopes are added. The daughter nitrogen-14 isotope, existing in gaseous form, leaks out of the dead organism, and thus, we cannot use it to compare the ratio of original to daughter as is done with rubidium-87 and its daughter. However, as the amount of carbon-14 in the dead organism becomes less over time, we can compare the proportion of this isotope remaining with the proportion that is in the atmosphere and from this calculate the approximate number of years since the organism has died. Dating dead organic material by this method is moderately reliable in samples up to about 50,000 years old, but beyond that the accuracy becomes unreliable.

***isotope:** one of the differing forms of an atomic element
***magma:** material that is in liquid form and which cools on the Earth's surface to form rock

1. The word "alter" in the passage is closest in meaning to (A) adapt (B) change (C) revise (D) vary	The nucleus of a radioactive atom disintegrates spontaneously and forms an atom of a different element while emitting radiation in the process. The original atom is called the parent isotope and its stable product is called the daughter or progeny isotope. For example, rubidium-87 decays by emitting an electron from its nucleus to form a stable daughter called strontium-87. Because the rate of nuclear decay is constant regardless of temperature and pressure conditions, radioactive decay provides a dependable way of keeping time. Radioactive isotopes alter from one type of atom to another at a fixed rate from the moment they are created anywhere in the universe. Since we can calculate the decay rate and also count the number of newly formed progeny atoms and the remaining parent atoms, we can use the ratio as a kind of clock to measure the age of minerals and other materials.

2. The rate of nuclear decay in rubidium-87 (A) is always the same (B) changes over time (C) depends on temperature (D) depends on temperature and pressure	[Refer to the full passage.]

3. The word "This" in the passage refers to (A) element (B) half-life (C) rate (D) time	The rate at which a radioactive element decays is known as the half-life of the element. This is the time necessary for one-half of the original number of radioactive atoms in a sample to decay into a daughter product. After two half-lives, the number of atoms remaining after the first half-life will have decayed by half again. Thus, the number of remaining parent atoms is reduced geometrically over time. With some elements, the half-life is very long. Rubidium-87, for example, has a half-life that has been estimated at nearly 48.8 billion years, much longer than the current estimated age of the universe. With other elements, this period can be as short as a few days or even minutes. If we know the half-life of a decaying element, it is possible to calculate the ratio of parent to stable progeny that will remain after any given period of time.

4. The half-life of an element (A) is a reliable way of measuring sample size (B) is a measure of decay rate in radioactive elements (C) is considered an unreliable way of calculating age (D) is approximately half the age of the atoms it contains	[Refer to the full passage.]

5. What can be inferred about the reliability of using radioactive atoms to calculate ages of rock samples? (A) The reliability increases over time. (B) The reliability decreases with older samples. (C) The reliability of the parent atom is greater than the progeny. (D) The reliability of the progeny atom is greater than the parent.	[Refer to the full passage.]

6. According to the passage, from what point can we measure the ages of rocks? (A) From the point at which rubidium-87 became part of the rock structure (B) From the point at which strontium-87 started to decay (C) From the point at which the rocks rubidium-87 and strontium-87 joined (D) From the point at which later contamination entered the rock samples	[Refer to the full passage.]

7. The word "essential" in the passage is closest in meaning to

Ⓐ redundant
Ⓑ stable
Ⓒ dependable
Ⓓ vital

Another radioactive element useful for dating is carbon-14, which decays into nitrogen-14. With a half-life of 5,730 years, carbon-14 decays much more rapidly than rubidium-87 and so is useful for measuring the ages of objects from the recent historical and geologic past, such as fossils, bones, wood, and other organic materials. Whereas rubidium-87 is incorporated into rocks during their formation, carbon-14, which is an essential element of the cells of organisms, becomes incorporated into living tissues as organisms grow. The ratio of carbon-14 to stable carbon isotopes in the organism is the same as it is in the atmosphere. When a living organism dies, no more carbon dioxide is absorbed and so no new carbon isotopes are added. The daughter nitrogen-14 isotope, existing in gaseous form, leaks out of the dead organism, and thus, we cannot use it to compare the ratio of original to daughter as is done with rubidium-87 and its daughter. However, as the amount of carbon-14 in the dead organism becomes less over time, we can compare the proportion of this isotope remaining with the proportion that is in the atmosphere and from this calculate the approximate number of years since the organism has died. Dating dead organic material by this method is moderately reliable in samples up to about 50,000 years old, but beyond that the accuracy becomes unreliable.

8. According to paragraph 5, what happens to an organism after it dies?

Ⓐ It tends to deteriorate rapidly.
Ⓑ The various carbon isotopes decay.
Ⓒ The supply of carbon-14 is no longer replenished.
Ⓓ The stable carbon isotopes deteriorate.

Paragraph 5 is marked with an arrow [➡].

➡ Another radioactive element useful for dating is carbon-14, which decays into nitrogen-14. With a half-life of 5,730 years, carbon-14 decays much more rapidly than rubidium-87 and so is useful for measuring the ages of objects from the recent historical and geologic past, such as fossils, bones, wood, and other organic materials. Whereas rubidium-87 is incorporated into rocks during their formation, carbon-14, which is an essential element of the cells of organisms, becomes incorporated into living tissues as organisms grow. The ratio of carbon-14 to stable carbon isotopes in the organism is the same as it is in the atmosphere. When a living organism dies, no more carbon dioxide is absorbed and so no new carbon isotopes are added. The daughter nitrogen-14 isotope, existing in gaseous form, leaks out of the dead organism, and thus, we cannot use it to compare the ratio of original to daughter as is done with rubidium-87 and its daughter. However, as the amount of carbon-14 in the dead organism becomes less over time, we can compare the proportion of this isotope remaining with the proportion that is in the atmosphere and from this calculate the approximate number of years since the organism has died. Dating dead organic material by this method is moderately reliable in samples up to about 50,000 years old, but beyond that the accuracy becomes unreliable.

9. According to paragraph 5, why can't scientists compare the ratio of carbon-14 to nitrogen-14?
   - (A) The amount of nitrogen-14 is not predictable.
   - (B) The ratio of these two elements doesn't change.
   - (C) Nitrogen-14 has an unpredictable decay rate.
   - (D) Carbon-14 tends to evaporate too quickly.

Paragraph 5 is marked with an arrow [➡].

➡ Another radioactive element useful for dating is carbon-14, which decays into nitrogen-14. With a half-life of 5,730 years, carbon-14 decays much more rapidly than rubidium-87 and so is useful for measuring the ages of objects from the recent historical and geologic past, such as fossils, bones, wood, and other organic materials. Whereas rubidium-87 is incorporated into rocks during their formation, carbon-14, which is an essential element of the cells of organisms, becomes incorporated into living tissues as organisms grow. The ratio of carbon-14 to stable carbon isotopes in the organism is the same as it is in the atmosphere. When a living organism dies, no more carbon dioxide is absorbed and so no new carbon isotopes are added. The daughter nitrogen-14 isotope, existing in gaseous form, leaks out of the dead organism, and thus, we cannot use it to compare the ratio of original to daughter as is done with rubidium-87 and its daughter. However, as the amount of carbon-14 in the dead organism becomes less over time, we can compare the proportion of this isotope remaining with the proportion that is in the atmosphere and from this calculate the approximate number of years since the organism has died. Dating dead organic material by this method is moderately reliable in samples up to about 50,000 years old, but beyond that the accuracy becomes unreliable.

10. According to paragraph 5, the amount of carbon-14 in an organism
   - (A) replaces other carbon isotopes after an organism dies
   - (B) tends to be the same as the other carbon isotopes
   - (C) increases rapidly when an organism dies
   - (D) deteriorates from the moment of death

Paragraph 5 is marked with an arrow [➡].

➡ Another radioactive element useful for dating is carbon-14, which decays into nitrogen-14. With a half-life of 5,730 years, carbon-14 decays much more rapidly than rubidium-87 and so is useful for measuring the ages of objects from the recent historical and geologic past, such as fossils, bones, wood, and other organic materials. Whereas rubidium-87 is incorporated into rocks during their formation, carbon-14, which is an essential element of the cells of organisms, becomes incorporated into living tissues as organisms grow. The ratio of carbon-14 to stable carbon isotopes in the organism is the same as it is in the atmosphere. When a living organism dies, no more carbon dioxide is absorbed and so no new carbon isotopes are added. The daughter nitrogen-14 isotope, existing in gaseous form, leaks out of the dead organism, and thus, we cannot use it to compare the ratio of original to daughter as is done with rubidium-87 and its daughter. However, as the amount of carbon-14 in the dead organism becomes less over time, we can compare the proportion of this isotope remaining with the proportion that is in the atmosphere and from this calculate the approximate number of years since the organism has died. Dating dead organic material by this method is moderately reliable in samples up to about 50,000 years old, but beyond that the accuracy becomes unreliable.

11. Look at the four squares [■] that indicate where the following sentence could be added to the passage.

    Both the unstable carbon-14 and stable carbon isotopes are taken in from the carbon dioxide present in the atmosphere.

Where would the sentence best fit?

Choose the letter of the square that shows where the sentence should be added.

Another radioactive element useful for dating is carbon-14, which decays into nitrogen-14. **A** With a half-life of 5,730 years, carbon-14 decays much more rapidly than rubidium-87 and so is useful for measuring the ages of objects from the recent historical and geologic past, such as fossils, bones, wood, and other organic materials. Whereas rubidium-87 is incorporated into rocks during their formation, carbon-14, which is an essential element of the cells of organisms, becomes incorporated into living tissues as organisms grow. **B** The ratio of carbon-14 to stable carbon isotopes in the organism is the same as it is in the atmosphere. **C** When a living organism dies, no more carbon dioxide is absorbed and so no new carbon isotopes are added. **D** The daughter nitrogen-14 isotope, existing in gaseous form, leaks out of the dead organism, and thus, we cannot use it to compare the ratio of original to daughter as is done with rubidium-87 and its daughter. However, as the amount of carbon-14 in the dead organism becomes less over time, we can compare the proportion of this isotope remaining with the proportion that is in the atmosphere and from this calculate the approximate number of years since the organism has died. Dating dead organic material by this method is moderately reliable in samples up to about 50,000 years old, but beyond that the accuracy becomes unreliable.

12. **Directions:** Select the appropriate phrases from the answer choices and match the dating technique to which they relate. TWO of the answer choices will NOT be used. **This question is worth 4 points.**

Write the letters of the answer choices in the spaces where they belong.
Refer to the full passage.

Answer Choices

(A) Can be used for dating artifacts made of bones or wood
(B) Destroys progeny isotopes
(C) Essential to living organisms
(D) Has a half-life of billions of years
(E) Incorporated into minerals when they crystallized
(F) Progeny cannot be used for dating
(G) Unreliable for dating samples
(H) Used for dating dead trees
(I) Used for dating rocks

Rubidium-87

•
•
•

Carbon-14

•
•
•
•

PRACTICE TEST 2

Questions 13–25

Demographic Transition

Historically, as countries have developed industrially, they have undergone declines in death rates followed by declines in birth rates. Over time they have tended to move from rapid increases in population to slower increases, then to zero growth and finally to population decreases. The model which demographers use to help explain these changes in population growth is known as the *demographic transition model.* In order to properly appreciate the demographic transition model, it is necessary to understand two basic concepts: the crude* birth rate (CBR) and the crude death rate (CDR). The CBR is determined by taking the number of births in a country in a given year and dividing it by the total population of the country and then multiplying the answer by one thousand. So, for example, the CBR of the United States in 2004 was 14 (in other words, there were 14 births per thousand living people in that year). CDR is worked out in a similar way. The CDR for the United States in 2004 was 8 per thousand.

The first stage of the demographic transition model portrays a preindustrial era when both the birth rate and the death rate were high. Typically, women gave birth to a large number of babies. This was partly due to cultural and religious pressures but also because families required a large number of children, since often many didn't survive into adulthood due to the harsh living conditions. Furthermore, children were needed to help adults work the land or perform other chores. The death rate was high due to the high incidence of diseases and famine and also because of poor hygiene. Total population tended to fluctuate due to occasional epidemics, but overall there was only a very gradual long-term increase during this stage.

During the second stage, improvements in hygiene, medical care, and food production led to a decrease in the death rate in newly industrializing regions of Western Europe. However, birth rates remained high due to tradition and because many people were involved in agrarian occupations. The combination of a lowered CDR and a stable CBR led to dramatic increases in population starting at the beginning of the nineteenth century.

In stage three, birth rates also began to fall. In cities there was less incentive to produce large numbers of children, since city dwellers no longer worked the land, and the cost of raising children in an urban environment was greater than in rural districts. Furthermore, more children survived into adulthood due to improved living conditions. These economic pressures led to a lower CBR and over time the numbers of people being born started to approximate the numbers dying.

The final stage, which some demographers have called the *postindustrial stage,* occurs when birth rates and death rates are about equal. In this case there is zero natural population growth. Over time the birth rate may fall below the death rate, and without immigration the total population may slowly decrease. By the early twenty-first century, several European countries were experiencing population declines due to the CDR outstripping the CBR. For example, in Italy in 2004 there were about 9 births per thousand against 10 deaths per thousand.

The demographic transition took about 200 years to complete in Europe. Many developing countries are still in stage two of the demographic transition model: births far outstrip deaths. In these countries, CDR has declined due to improvements in sanitation and increases in food productivity, but the birth rate has still not adjusted downward to the new realities of improved living conditions. This imbalance of births over deaths in the developing world is the fundamental reason for the dramatic population explosion in the latter half of the twentieth century. However, population statistics indicate that in many less developed countries the CBRs have begun to decline over recent decades, giving rise to optimism in some quarters about future trends. The rapid industrialization of many parts of the developing world has meant that these countries have reached stage three of the model much faster than countries in the developed world did during the nineteenth century. This fact has led many demographers to predict that world population will reach an equilibrium level sooner and at a lower total than more pessimistic earlier predictions.

***crude:** not analyzed into specific classes

13. The word "it" in the passage refers to

- (A) population
- (B) year
- (C) country
- (D) number

Historically, as countries have developed industrially, they have undergone declines in death rates followed by declines in birth rates. Over time they have tended to move from rapid increases in population to slower increases, then to zero growth and finally to population decreases. The model which demographers use to help explain these changes in population growth is known as the *demographic transition model.* In order to properly appreciate the demographic transition model, it is necessary to understand two basic concepts: the crude birth rate (CBR) and the crude death rate (CDR). The CBR is determined by taking the number of births in a country in a given year and dividing it by the total population of the country and then multiplying the answer by one thousand. So, for example, the CBR of the United States in 2004 was 14 (in other words there were 14 births per thousand living people in that year). CDR is worked out in a similar way. The CDR for the United States in 2004 was 8 per thousand.

14. According to paragraph 1, what is useful about the demographic transition model?

- (A) It helps explain trends in population growth over time.
- (B) It can be used to measure birth and death rates.
- (C) It clarifies the causes of population increase.
- (D) It predicts the relative speed of population patterns.

Paragraph 1 is marked with an arrow [➡].

➡ Historically, as countries have developed industrially, they have undergone declines in death rates followed by declines in birth rates. Over time they have tended to move from rapid increases in population to slower increases, then to zero growth and finally to population decreases. The model which demographers use to help explain these changes in population growth is known as the *demographic transition model*. In order to properly appreciate the demographic transition model, it is necessary to understand two basic concepts: the crude birth rate (CBR) and the crude death rate (CDR). The CBR is determined by taking the number of births in a country in a given year and dividing it by the total population of the country and then multiplying the answer by one thousand. So, for example, the CBR of the United States in 2004 was 14 (in other words there were 14 births per thousand living people in that year). CDR is worked out in a similar way. The CDR for the United States in 2004 was 8 per thousand.

15. The word "portrays" in the passage is closest in meaning to

   (A) suggests
   (B) represents
   (C) transmits
   (D) associates

The first stage of the demographic transition model portrays a preindustrial era when both the birth rate and the death rate were high. Typically, women gave birth to a large number of babies. This was partly due to cultural and religious pressures but also because families required a large number of children, since often many didn't survive into adulthood due to the harsh living conditions. Furthermore, children were needed to help adults work the land or perform other chores. The death rate was high due to the high incidence of diseases and famine and also because of poor hygiene. Total population tended to fluctuate due to occasional epidemics, but overall there was only a very gradual long-term increase during this stage.

16. In paragraph 2, which of the following is NOT mentioned as relevant to the high birth rates in the preindustrial stage?

   (A) The high level of childhood deaths
   (B) The need for help in work situations
   (C) The pressures of tradition
   (D) The high rate of maternal deaths

Paragraph 2 is marked with an arrow [➡].

➡ The first stage of the demographic transition model portrays a preindustrial era when both the birth rate and the death rate were high. Typically, women gave birth to a large number of babies. This was partly due to cultural and religious pressures but also because families required a large number of children, since often many didn't survive into adulthood due to the harsh living conditions. Furthermore, children were needed to help adults work the land or perform other chores. The death rate was high due to the high incidence of diseases and famine and also because of poor hygiene. Total population tended to fluctuate due to occasional epidemics, but overall there was only a very gradual long-term increase during this stage.

17. What can be inferred from paragraph 2 about the effect of epidemic diseases on population during the preindustrial stage?

   (A) They tended to dramatically lower the population growth.
   (B) They caused the population to decline temporarily.
   (C) They reduced overall population significantly.
   (D) They led to sudden overall increases in the birth rate.

Paragraph 2 is marked with an arrow [➡].

➡ The first stage of the demographic transition model portrays a preindustrial era when both the birth rate and the death rate were high. Typically, women gave birth to a large number of babies. This was partly due to cultural and religious pressures but also because families required a large number of children, since often many didn't survive into adulthood due to the harsh living conditions. Furthermore, children were needed to help adults work the land or perform other chores. The death rate was high due to the high incidence of diseases and famine and also because of poor hygiene. Total population tended to fluctuate due to occasional epidemics, but overall there was only a very gradual long-term increase during this stage.

18. The word "agrarian" in the passage is closest in meaning to

- (A) basic
- (B) menial
- (C) farming
- (D) village

During the second stage, improvements in hygiene, medical care, and food production led to a decrease in the death rate in newly industrializing regions of Western Europe. However, birth rates remained high due to tradition and because many people were involved in agrarian occupations. The combination of a lowered CDR and a stable CBR led to dramatic increases in population starting at the beginning of the nineteenth century.

19. According to paragraph 4, what was one of the main causes of the drop in birth rates?

- (A) The improvements in hygiene
- (B) The lack of agricultural work
- (C) The development of urbanization
- (D) The superior environment

Paragraph 4 is marked with an arrow [➡].

➡ In stage three, birth rates also began to fall. In cities there was less incentive to produce large numbers of children, since city dwellers no longer worked the land, and the cost of raising children in an urban environment was greater than in rural districts. Furthermore, more children survived into adulthood due to improved living conditions. These economic pressures led to a lower CBR and over time the numbers of people being born started to approximate the numbers dying.

20. Which of the sentences below best expresses the essential information in the highlighted sentence in the passage? Incorrect choices change the meaning in important ways or leave out essential information.

- (A) The population gradually declines when there is no immigration and deaths exceed births.
- (B) In time there may be an overall drop in population as the birth rate and death rate fluctuate.
- (C) The relationship between birth and death rates is an important reason for limiting immigration.
- (D) If population losses aren't replaced through immigration, the birth rate may fall below the death rate.

The final stage, which some demographers have called the *postindustrial stage,* occurs when birth rates and death rates are about equal. In this case there is zero natural population growth. Over time, the birth rate may fall below the death rate, and without immigration the total population may slowly decrease. By the early twenty-first century, several European countries were experiencing population declines due to the CDR outstripping the CBR. For example, in Italy in 2004 there were about 9 births per thousand against 10 deaths per thousand.

21. The word "equilibrium" in the passage is closest in meaning to

 (A) economic
 (B) stable
 (C) variable
 (D) fixed

The demographic transition took about 200 years to complete in Europe. Many developing countries are still in stage two of the demographic transition model: births far outstrip deaths. In these countries, CDR has declined due to improvements in sanitation and increases in food productivity, but, the birth rate has still not adjusted downward to the new realities of improved living conditions. This imbalance of births over deaths in the developing world is the fundamental reason for the dramatic population explosion in the latter half of the twentieth century. However, population statistics indicate that in many less developed countries the CBRs have begun to decline over recent decades, giving rise to optimism in some quarters about future trends. The rapid industrialization of many parts of the developing world has meant that these countries have reached stage three of the model much faster than countries in the developed world did during the nineteenth century. This fact has led many demographers to predict that world population will reach an equilibrium level sooner and at a lower total than more pessimistic earlier predictions.

22. According to paragraph 6, what is at the root of the huge population increases during the twentieth century?

 (A) The improvements in health throughout the developing world
 (B) The fact that birth rates are increasing in many countries
 (C) The lack of resources in many developing countries
 (D) The failure of the CDR to respond to economic pressures

Paragraph 6 is marked with an arrow [➡].

➡ The demographic transition took about 200 years to complete in Europe. Many developing countries are still in stage two of the demographic transition model: births far outstrip deaths. In these countries, CDR has declined due to improvements in sanitation and increases in food productivity, but the birth rate has still not adjusted downward to the new realities of improved living conditions. This imbalance of births over deaths in the developing world is the fundamental reason for the dramatic population explosion in the latter half of the twentieth century. However, population statistics indicate that in many less developed countries the CBRs have begun to decline over recent decades, giving rise to optimism in some quarters about future trends. The rapid industrialization of many parts of the developing world has meant that these countries have reached stage three of the model much faster than countries in the developed world did during the nineteenth century. This fact has led many demographers to predict that world population will reach an equilibrium level sooner and at a lower total than more pessimistic earlier predictions.

23. Why does the author mention the optimism felt in some quarters about future population trends? (A) To introduce the fact that birth rates in some developing countries may be declining faster than anticipated (B) To emphasize that most researchers have taken a pessimistic view of population expansion (C) To show that the demographic transition is a valid model of population trends (D) To suggest that some countries have worked hard at reducing birth rates	[Refer to the full passage.]

24. Look at the four squares [■] that indicate where the following sentence could be added to the passage. **Industrialization had led to increased urbanization.** Where would the sentence best fit? Choose the letter of the square that shows where the sentence should be added.	In stage three, birth rates also began to fall. [A] In cities there was less incentive to produce large numbers of children, since city dwellers no longer worked the land, and the cost of raising children in an urban environment was greater than in rural districts. [B] Furthermore, more children survived into adulthood due to improved living conditions. [C] These economic pressures led to a lower CBR and over time the numbers of people being born started to approximate the numbers dying. [D]

25. **Directions:** An introductory sentence for a brief summary of the passage is provided below. Complete the summary by selecting the THREE answer choices that express the most important ideas in the passage. Some sentences do not belong in the summary because they express ideas that are not presented in the passage or are minor ideas in the passage. **This question is worth 2 points.**

Write the letters of the answer choices in the spaces where they belong.
Refer to the full passage.

The demographic transition model links trends in population growth to the level of industrial development.

-
-
-

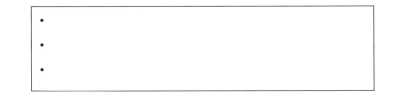

Answer Choices

(A) Preindustrial populations tended to increase due to the large numbers of births and a slowly declining death rate.

(B) Due to economic pressures, the birth rate dropped to match the death rate, leading to zero growth and eventually a decline in population.

(C) High birth and death rates are associated with a preindustrial stage of development when there was only a gradual increase in overall population numbers.

(D) Improvements in medical techniques led to a dramatic drop in death rates, allowing industrialization to increase.

(E) Dramatic increases in population occurred when the death rates declined due to improvements in the quality of life.

(F) The final stage of demographic transition occurs when birth rates outstrip death rates, leading to a new round of population growth.

Questions 26–39

Communicating with the Future

In the 1980s the United States Department of Energy was looking for suitable sites to bury radioactive waste material generated by its nuclear energy programs. The government was considering burying the dangerous waste in deep underground chambers in remote desert areas. The problem, however, was that nuclear waste remains highly radioactive for thousands of years. The commission entrusted with tackling the problem of waste disposal was aware that the dangers posed by radioactive emissions must be communicated to our descendants of at least 10,000 years hence. So the task became one of finding a way to tell future societies about the risk posed by these deadly deposits.

Of course, human society in the distant future may be well aware of the hazards of radiation. Technological advances may one day provide solutions to this dilemma. But the belief in constant technological advancement is based on our perceptions of advances made throughout history and prehistory. We cannot be sure that society won't have slipped backward into an age of barbarism* due to any of several catastrophic events, whether the result of nature such as the onset of a new ice age or perhaps humankind's failure to solve the scourges of war and pollution. In the event of global catastrophe, it is quite possible that humans of the distant future will be on the far side of a broken link of communication and technological understanding.

The problem then becomes how to inform our descendants that they must avoid areas of potential radioactive seepage* given that they may not understand any currently existing language and may have no historical or cultural memory. So, any message dedicated to future reception and decipherment must be as universally understandable as possible.

It was soon realized by the specialists assigned the task of devising the communication system that any material in which the message was written might not physically endure the great lengths of time demanded. The second law of thermodynamics shows that all material disintegrates over time. Even computers that might carry the message cannot be expected to endure long enough. Besides, electricity supplies might not be available in 300 generations. Other media storage methods were considered and rejected for similar reasons.

The task force under the linguist Thomas Sebeok finally agreed that no foolproof way would be found to send a message across so many generations and have it survive physically and be decipherable by a people with few cultural similarities to us. Given this restriction, Sebeok suggested the only possible solution was the formation of a committee of guardians of knowledge. Its task would be to dedicate itself to maintaining and passing on the knowledge of the whereabouts and dangers of the nuclear waste deposits. This so-called atomic priesthood would be entrusted with keeping knowledge of this tradition alive through millennia and in developing the tradition into a kind of mythical taboo forbidding people to tamper in any way with the nuclear waste sites. Only the initiated atomic priesthood of experts would have the scientific knowledge to fully understand the danger. Those outside the priesthood would be kept away by a combination of rituals and legends designed to warn off intruders.

This proposal has been criticized because of the possibility of a break in continuity of the original message. Furthermore, there is no guarantee that any warning or sanction passed on for millennia would be obeyed, nor that it could survive with its original meaning intact. To counterbalance this possibility, Sebeok's group proposed a "relay system" in which information is passed on over relatively short periods of time, just three generations ahead. The message is then to be renewed and redesigned if necessary for the following three generations and so on over the required time span. In this way information could be relayed into the future and avoid the possibility of physical degradation.

A second defect is more difficult to dismiss, however. This is the problem of social exclusiveness brought about through possession of vital knowledge. Critics point out that the atomic priesthood could use its secret knowledge to control those who are scientifically ignorant. The establishment of such an association of insiders holding powerful knowledge not available except in mythic form to nonmembers would be a dangerous precedent for future social developments.

***barbarism:** a state of existence in which the experience, habits, and culture of modern life are absent
***seepage:** an amount of liquid or gas that flows through another substance

26. The word "chambers" in the passage is closest in meaning to
   - (A) cavities
   - (B) partitions
   - (C) openings
   - (D) fissures

In the 1980s the United States Department of Energy was looking for suitable sites to bury radioactive waste material generated by its nuclear energy programs. The government was considering burying the dangerous waste in deep underground chambers in remote desert areas. The problem, however, was that nuclear waste remains highly radioactive for thousands of years. The commission entrusted with tackling the problem of waste disposal was aware that the dangers posed by radioactive emissions must be communicated to our descendants of at least 10,000 years hence. So the task became one of finding a way to tell future societies about the risk posed by these deadly deposits.

27. What problem faced the commission assigned to deal with the burial of nuclear waste?
   - (A) How to reduce the radioactive life of nuclear waste materials
   - (B) How to notify future generations of the risks of nuclear contamination
   - (C) How to form a committee that could adequately express various nuclear risks
   - (D) How to choose burial sites so as to minimize dangers to people

[Refer to the full passage.]

28. In paragraph 2, the author explains the possible circumstances of future societies

Ⓐ to warn us about possible natural catastrophes

Ⓑ to highlight humankind's inability to resolve problems

Ⓒ to question the value of our trust in technological advances

Ⓓ to demonstrate the reason nuclear hazards must be communicated

Paragraph 2 is marked with an arrow [➡].

➡ Of course, human society in the distant future may be well aware of the hazards of radiation. Technological advances may one day provide solutions to this dilemma. But the belief in constant technological advancement is based on our perceptions of advances made throughout history and prehistory. We cannot be sure that society won't have slipped backward into an age of barbarism due to any of several catastrophic events, whether the result of nature such as the onset of a new ice age or perhaps humankind's failure to solve the scourges of war and pollution. In the event of global catastrophe, it is quite possible that humans of the distant future will be on the far side of a broken link of communication and technological understanding.

29. The word "scourges" in the passage is closest in meaning to

Ⓐ worries

Ⓑ pressures

Ⓒ afflictions

Ⓓ annoyances

Of course, human society in the distant future may be well aware of the hazards of radiation. Technological advances may one day provide solutions to this dilemma. But the belief in constant technological advancement is based on our perceptions of advances made throughout history and prehistory. We cannot be sure that society won't have slipped backward into an age of barbarism due to any of several catastrophic events, whether the result of nature such as the onset of a new ice age or perhaps humankind's failure to solve the scourges of war and pollution. In the event of global catastrophe, it is quite possible that humans of the distant future will be on the far side of a broken link of communication and technological understanding.

30. Which of the sentences below best expresses the essential information in the highlighted sentence in the passage? Incorrect choices change the meaning in important ways or leave out essential information.

Ⓐ A message for future generations must be comprehensible to anyone in the world.

Ⓑ A universally understandable message must be deciphered for future generations.

Ⓒ Any message that is globally understandable must be received and deciphered.

Ⓓ The message that future generations receive and interpret must be dedicated.

The problem then becomes how to inform our descendants that they must avoid areas of potential radioactive seepage given that they may not understand any currently existing language and may have no historical or cultural memory. So, any message dedicated to future reception and decipherment must be as universally understandable as possible.

31. In paragraph 4, the author mentions the second law of thermodynamics

 Ⓐ to contrast the potential life span of knowledge with that of material objects
 Ⓑ to give the basic scientific reason behind the breakdown of material objects
 Ⓒ to show that knowledge can be sustained over millennia
 Ⓓ to support the view that nuclear waste will disperse with time

Paragraph 4 is marked with an arrow [➡].

➡ It was soon realized by the specialists assigned the task of devising the communication system that any material in which the message was written might not physically endure the great lengths of time demanded. The second law of thermodynamics shows that all material disintegrates over time. Even computers that might carry the message cannot be expected to endure long enough. Besides, electricity supplies might not be available in 300 generations. Other media storage methods were considered and rejected for similar reasons.

32. The word "Its" in the passage refers to

 Ⓐ knowledge
 Ⓑ guardians
 Ⓒ committee
 Ⓓ solution

The task force under the linguist Thomas Sebeok finally agreed that no foolproof way would be found to send a message across so many generations and have it survive physically and be decipherable by a people with few cultural similarities to us. Given this restriction, Sebeok suggested the only possible solution was the formation of a committee of guardians of knowledge. Its task would be to dedicate itself to maintaining and passing on the knowledge of the whereabouts and dangers of the nuclear waste deposits. This so-called atomic priesthood would be entrusted with keeping knowledge of this tradition alive through millennia and in developing the tradition into a kind of mythical taboo forbidding people to tamper in any way with the nuclear waste sites. Only the initiated atomic priesthood of experts would have the scientific knowledge to fully understand the danger. Those outside the priesthood would be kept away by a combination of rituals and legends designed to warn off intruders.

33. In paragraph 5, why is the proposed committee of guardians referred to as the "atomic priesthood"? (A) Because they would be an exclusive religious order (B) Because they would develop mythical taboos surrounding their traditions (C) Because they would use rituals and legends to maintain their exclusiveness (D) Because they would be an exclusive group with knowledge about nuclear waste sites Paragraph 5 is marked with an arrow [➡].	➡ The task force under the linguist Thomas Sebeok finally agreed that no foolproof way would be found to send a message across so many generations and have it survive physically and be decipherable by a people with few cultural similarities to us. Given this restriction, Sebeok suggested the only possible solution was the formation of a committee of guardians of knowledge. Its task would be to dedicate itself to maintaining and passing on the knowledge of the whereabouts and dangers of the nuclear waste deposits. This so-called atomic priesthood would be entrusted with keeping knowledge of this tradition alive through millennia and in developing the tradition into a kind of mythical taboo forbidding people to tamper in any way with the nuclear waste sites. Only the initiated atomic priesthood of experts would have the scientific knowledge to fully understand the danger. Those outside the priesthood would be kept away by a combination of rituals and legends designed to warn off intruders.

34. The word "sanction" in the passage is closest in meaning to (A) security (B) approval (C) counsel (D) penalty	This proposal has been criticized because of the possibility of a break in continuity of the original message. Furthermore, there is no guarantee that any warning or sanction passed on for millennia would be obeyed, nor that it could survive with its original meaning intact. To counterbalance this possibility, Sebeok's group proposed a "relay system" in which information is passed on over relatively short periods of time, just three generations ahead. The message is then to be renewed and redesigned if necessary for the following three generations and so on over the required time span. In this way information could be relayed into the future and avoid the possibility of physical degradation.

35. According to the author, why did the task force under Sebeok propose a relay system for passing on information? (A) To compensate for the fact that meaning will not be stable over long periods of time (B) To show that Sebeok's ideas created more problems than they solved (C) To contrast Sebeok's ideas with those proposed by his main critics (D) To support the belief that breaks in communication are inevitable over time	[Refer to the full passage.]

36. According to paragraph 7, the second defect of the atomic priesthood proposal is that it could lead to (A) the possible misuse of exclusive knowledge (B) the establishment of a scientifically ignorant society (C) the priesthood's criticism of points concerning vital knowledge (D) the nonmembers turning knowledge into dangerous mythical forms Paragraph 7 is marked with an arrow (➡).	➡ A second defect is more difficult to dismiss, however. This is the problem of social exclusiveness brought about through possession of vital knowledge. Critics point out that the atomic priesthood could use its secret knowledge to control those who are scientifically ignorant. The establishment of such an association of insiders holding powerful knowledge not available except in mythic form to nonmembers would be a dangerous precedent for future social developments.

37. All of the following are mentioned in the passage as difficulties in devising a communication system with the future EXCEPT (A) the loss of knowledge about today's civilization (B) the failure to maintain communication links (C) the inability of materials to endure over time (D) the exclusiveness of a priesthood	[Refer to the full passage.]

38. Look at the four squares [■] that indicate where the following sentence could be added to the passage. **Perhaps scientists will find efficient ways to deactivate radioactive materials.** Where would the sentence best fit? Choose the letter of the square that shows where the sentence should be added.	Of course, human society in the distant future may be well aware of the hazards of radiation. **A** Technological advances may one day provide solutions to this dilemma. **B** But the belief in constant technological advancement is based on our perceptions of advances made throughout history and prehistory. **C** We cannot be sure that society won't have slipped backward into an age of barbarism due to any of several catastrophic events, whether the result of nature such as the onset of a new ice age or perhaps humankind's failure to solve the scourges of war and pollution. **D** In the event of global catastrophe, it is quite possible that humans of the distant future will be on the far side of a broken link of communication and technological understanding.

39. **Directions:** An introductory sentence for a brief summary of the passage is provided below. Complete the summary by selecting the THREE answer choices that express the most important ideas in the passage. Some sentences do not belong in the summary because they express ideas that are not presented in the passage or are minor ideas in the passage. **This question is worth 2 points.**

Write the letters of the answer choices in the spaces where they belong.
Refer to the full passage.

The problem of how to pass on knowledge of the dangers posed by buried radioactive waste was addressed by a commission of experts.

-
-
-

Answer Choices

(A) A task force argued that a select group should be entrusted with passing on knowledge of the dangers of radioactive deposits by using a relay system.

(B) Electricity supplies may not exist in the future, so computers should not be entrusted with storage of vital information.

(C) Technological improvements will possibly allow future generations to decontaminate nuclear waste.

(D) The atomic priesthood proposal has been criticized due to its potential for creating a future society divided into those who hold special knowledge and those who don't.

(E) The atomic priesthood would develop rituals and legends designed to warn off trespassers into the nuclear burial sites.

(F) Various means of storing and passing on information are unreliable over time because of the difficulty of communicating with future societies and the likely physical decay of storage media.

LISTENING SECTION
Directions

This section measures your ability to understand conversations and lectures in English. You will hear each conversation or lecture only one time. After each conversation or lecture, you will answer some questions about it.

The questions typically ask about the main idea and supporting details. Some questions ask about a speaker's purpose or attitude. Answer the questions based on what is stated or implied by the speakers.

You may take notes while you listen. You may use your notes to help you answer the questions. Your notes will not be scored.

In some questions, you will see this icon: 🎧. This means that you will hear, but not see, part of the question.

Some questions have special directions. These directions appear in a gray box.

Most questions are worth one point. A question worth more than one point will have special instructions indicating how many points you can receive.

You will have 20 minutes to answer the questions in this section.

Now get ready to listen. You may take notes.

START ▶

Questions 1–6

Listen to part of a lecture in a biology class.

Now get ready to answer the questions. You may use your notes to help you answer.

1. What is the lecture mainly about?
   - (A) How the tide affects the estuarine environment
   - (B) How the adaptations of estuarine organisms developed
   - (C) How the salinity of water is associated with maintaining the right balance
   - (D) How organisms have adapted to differing concentrations of water and salt

2. Listen again to part of the lecture. Then answer the question.
   What does the professor imply when he says this:
   - (A) The students probably know the term already.
   - (B) The students should have kept better notes.
   - (C) The term is not relevant to the lecture.
   - (D) The term is in their class notes.

3. What two adaptations are mentioned that allow crabs to survive in the estuary environment?

   Choose 2 answers.

   - [A] Their hard shells keep out water and salt.
   - [B] Their gills and skin adjust to changes rapidly.
   - [C] They can burrow into the soft mud.
   - [D] Their internal organs regulate salt intake.

4. Listen again to part of the lecture. Then answer the question.
   Why does the professor says this: 
   - (A) To test the students' understanding of osmoregulators
   - (B) To find out if the students understand how blue crabs breed
   - (C) To show a discrepancy in the behavioral pattern of the crab
   - (D) To give the students an opportunity to ask questions

5. Indicate whether each word or phrase below describes a physiological adaptation or behavioral adaptation.

Check the correct box for each statement.

	Physiological	Behavioral
(A) migrating		
(B) osmoregulating		
(C) dropping leaves		
(D) burrowing into mud		

6. The adaptations of which estuarine creature are NOT discussed in the lecture?
   (A) fish
   (B) birds
   (C) plants
   (D) invertebrates

Questions 7–11

Listen to a conversation between a student and a professor.

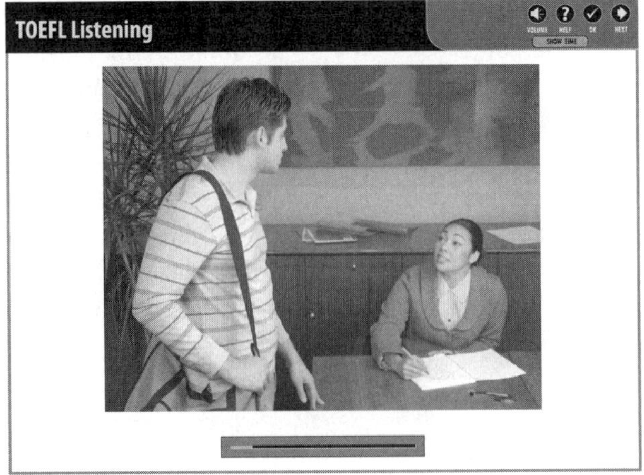

Now get ready to answer the questions. You may use your notes to help you answer.

7. Why does the student go to see the professor?
   (A) To discuss degree requirements
   (B) To get advice about changing degrees
   (C) To ask about American Sign Language
   (D) To inform the professor of changes in his degree program

8. Listen again to part of the conversation. Then answer the question.
   What can be inferred about the professor?
   (A) She does not understand why the student has come to her office.
   (B) She expects the student to have a background in linguistics.
   (C) She advises students getting degrees in linguistics.
   (D) She is not sure why students want to switch majors.

9. Why does the student want to change degree programs?
   (A) He wants to study languages in Peru.
   (B) He's worried about financing his studies.
   (C) He enjoyed his English teaching experience.
   (D) He likes helping people with speech disorders.

10. Listen again to part of the conversation. Then answer the question.
    Why does the professor say this: 
    (A) To avoid giving the student false hopes
    (B) To influence the student's choice of languages
    (C) To suggest that the student may have false information
    (D) To point out to the student the reasons to be cautious

11. What can be inferred about the student?
    (A) He may not be able to finance a change in degree programs.
    (B) He does not intend to take a heavier course load to graduate on schedule.
    (C) He has highlighted all the prerequisites for upper-level courses.
    (D) He wants to look at all the options for other language courses.

Questions 12–17

Listen to a discussion in an education class.

Now get ready to answer the questions. You may use your notes to help you answer.

12. What is the discussion mainly about?
    - (A) The kinds of questions that encourage thought processes
    - (B) The factors that discourage students from asking questions
    - (C) The personality traits of a particular professor in the faculty
    - (D) The way classroom size affects students' abilities to form questions

13. Why does the professor say this: 
    - (A) He is expecting the students to consider an answer to his questions.
    - (B) He is preparing the students for the discussion that he wants them to take up.
    - (C) He is giving an example of the kinds of questions teachers ask students.
    - (D) He is telling the students the kinds of questions students should ask themselves.

14. Listen again to part of the discussion. Then answer the question.
    What can be inferred about the students?
    - (A) They both question the professor's classification of the pressure of feeling stupid.
    - (B) The woman doesn't agree with the man that class size is an aspect of appearing stupid.
    - (C) The man is convinced that it is better to ask questions in a small class.
    - (D) They have different reasons for considering class size as a negative pressure.

15. Why does Lisa mention Professor Clarkson?
    - (A) To make fun of his course
    - (B) To give an example of time pressure
    - (C) To praise his style of answering questions
    - (D) To encourage the others to take his course

16. In the discussion, the professor elicits different reasons why students don't ask questions. Indicate whether each of the following is one of the discussed fears.

Check the correct box for each statement.

	Yes	No
(A) Fear of asking too many questions		
(B) Fear of being considered stupid		
(C) Fear of being the victim of a joke		
(D) Fear of making a mistake		
(E) Fear of wasting a professor's time		

17. Listen again to part of the discussion. Then answer the question.
Why does the professor say this: 
(A) To change the group discussion assignment to a different topic
(B) To challenge the students to reconsider the pressures they have mentioned
(C) To inform the students that they have not done a good job of listing the pressures
(D) To indicate to the students that they are not limited to the pressures written on the board

Questions 18–23

Listen to a lecture in a history of ideas class.

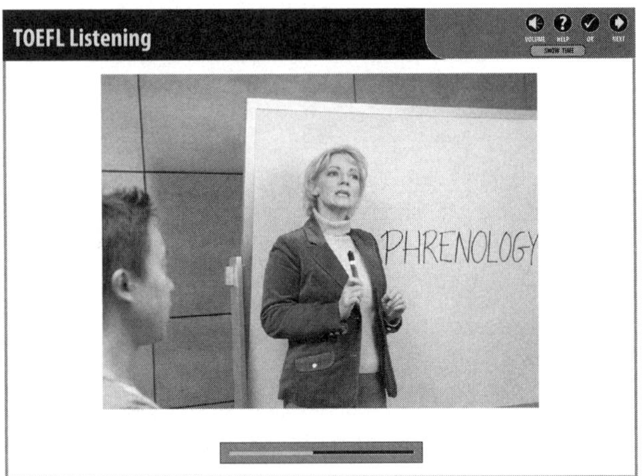

Now get ready to answer the questions. You may use your notes to help you answer.

18. What is the lecture mainly about?
    - (A) A theory about criminal personality development
    - (B) A system for evaluating personality theory
    - (C) A method of psychological analysis
    - (D) A comparison of early psychological theories

19. What points does the professor make about Gall's phrenological theory?

    Choose 2 answers.

    - [A] Abilities were evenly distributed in the brain.
    - [B] Each part of the brain was used for a different ability.
    - [C] The shape of the skull corresponded to brain shape.
    - [D] The shape of the brain was less important than the size.

20. Listen again to part of the lecture. Then answer the question.
    Why does the professor say this: 
    - (A) To express her disagreement with the students' opinions
    - (B) To agree that many people might think this theory is strange
    - (C) To test the students' understanding of the concepts
    - (D) To remind the students of a previous unusual idea

21. According to the professor, how did phrenologists approach evidence?
    - (A) They carefully examined evidence that did not fit with their theory.
    - (B) They were not interested in seeking confirmation of their claims.
    - (C) They only accepted the evidence that seemed to fit their claims.
    - (D) They looked for evidence that they knew was false.

22. What does the professor imply about phrenology?
    - (A) It was once more highly thought of than today.
    - (B) It was mainly a waste of research time.
    - (C) It was never more than a minority interest.
    - (D) It was usually on the receiving end of satirical humor.

23. According to the professor, which of the following modern beliefs was contributed to by phrenology?
    - (A) Certain organs within the brain are responsible for certain kinds of behavior.
    - (B) The power of the brain is related to the size and shape of the organ.
    - (C) The shape of the skull is determined by the shape of the brain.
    - (D) Certain abilities are related to specific areas of the brain.

Questions 24–29

Listen to a discussion in an astronomy class.

Now get ready to answer the questions. You may use your notes to help you answer.

24. What is the discussion mainly about?
    - (A) The differences between conditions on Mars and conditions on Earth
    - (B) The possibility of radically transforming the conditions on Mars
    - (C) The necessity of human migration in the search for new resources
    - (D) The ethical problems arising from the human settlement of Mars

25. Why does the professor say this:
    - (A) To express doubt about the possibility of terraforming
    - (B) To criticize the science community for wasting resources
    - (C) To indicate that terraforming would be a technologically amazing feat
    - (D) To encourage students to think clearly about the need for terraforming

26. Why does the professor mention the migration of Europeans to the Americas?
    - (A) To emphasize that people like to explore new regions
    - (B) To give an example of the fact that population pressures cause migrations
    - (C) To provide background information on the need to terraform Mars
    - (D) To argue that the settlement of the Americas was a valuable use of resources

27. According to the professor, why is Mars the planet that scientists want to terraform?

    Choose 2 answers.

    - [A] It is nearer to Earth than other planets.
    - [B] Its atmospheric conditions are rather similar to those on Earth.
    - [C] The other planets are unsuitable for several reasons.
    - [D] Mars contains water and its surface is solid.

28. Listen again to part of the discussion. Then answer the question.
    Why does the professor say this:
    - (A) He wants to focus on the technological considerations of terraforming.
    - (B) He thinks the ethical considerations are not relevant to classroom discussion.
    - (C) He thinks the students know his opinion about the right way to use Earth's resources.
    - (D) He wants the students to make up their own minds about the ethics of terraforming.

29. Which of the following is NOT mentioned as a method of terraforming Mars?
    - (A) Crashing ammonia-rich asteroids onto the planet's surface
    - (B) Introducing oxygen-releasing plants from Earth
    - (C) Heating the surface with sunlight reflected from orbiting mirrors
    - (D) Building greenhouse gas producing factories on the Martian surface

Questions 30–34

Listen to part of a conversation between a student and a research coordinator.

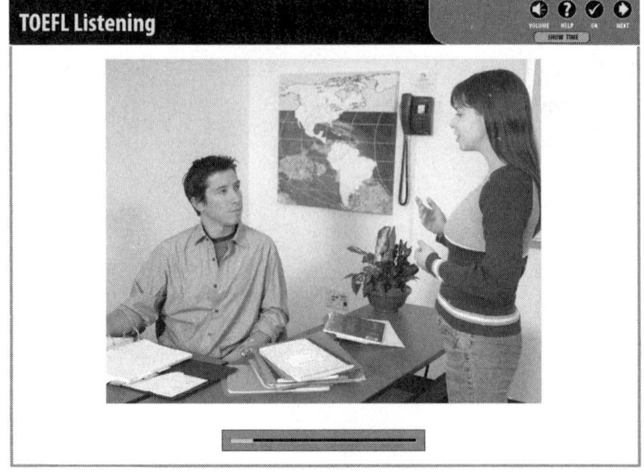

Now get ready to answer the questions. You may use your notes to help you answer.

30. Why has the student gone to see the research coordinator?
    - (A) To investigate food disorders
    - (B) To find out where the Pharmacology Lab is
    - (C) To participate in an experiment
    - (D) To volunteer for making weekly breakfasts

31. Why does the research coordinator ask the student personal questions?
    - (A) To make sure the student fits all the requirements
    - (B) To test if the student has read the announcement correctly
    - (C) To see if the student understands the experiment
    - (D) To help the student decide whether she wants to participate

32. Listen again to part of the conversation. Then answer the question.
    Why does the student say this:
    - (A) Because she gets ill infrequently
    - (B) Because she can only know about her current health
    - (C) Because she intends to stay well for the week
    - (D) Because her bout with flu is over

33. Which of the following topics does the research coordinator NOT ask the student about?
    - (A) Her susceptibility to allergies
    - (B) Her use of medications
    - (C) Her preferences for snacks
    - (D) Her current health situation

34. What example does the research coordinator give of the breakfast that will be provided?
    - (A) Pickled onions or grasshoppers
    - (B) Candy bars or potato chips
    - (C) Yogurt or nuts
    - (D) Eggs or cereal

STOP ■

SPEAKING SECTION

Directions

In this section of the test, you will be able to demonstrate your ability to speak about a variety of topics. You will answer six questions by recording your response. Answer each of the questions as completely as possible.

In questions 1 and 2, you will first hear a statement or question about familiar topics. You will then speak about these topics. Your response will be scored on your ability to speak clearly and coherently about the topics.

In questions 3 and 4, you will first read a short text. You will then listen to a talk on the same topic.

You will be asked a question about what you have read and heard. You will need to combine appropriate information from the text and the talk to provide a complete answer to the question. Your response will be scored on your ability to speak clearly and coherently and on your ability to accurately convey information about what you read and heard.

In questions 5 and 6, you will listen to part of a conversation or a lecture. You will be asked a question about what you heard. Your response will be scored on your ability to speak clearly and coherently and on your ability to accurately convey information about what you heard.

You may take notes while you read and while you listen to the conversations and lectures. You may use your notes to help prepare your response.

Listen carefully to the directions for each question. For each question you will be given a short time to prepare your response. When the preparation time is up, you will be told to begin your response.

START ▶

1. Please listen carefully.

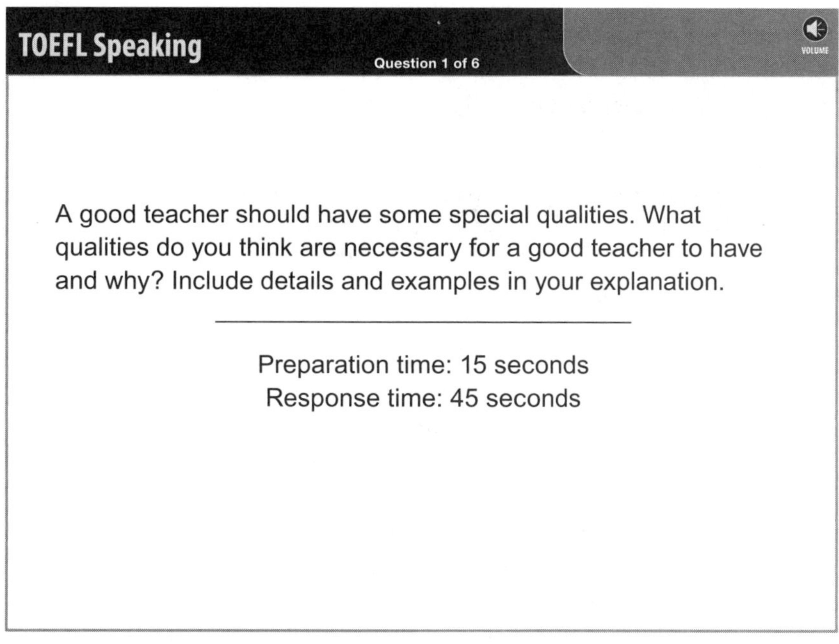

TOEFL Speaking
Question 1 of 6
VOLUME
A good teacher should have some special qualities. What qualities do you think are necessary for a good teacher to have and why? Include details and examples in your explanation.
Preparation time: 15 seconds
Response time: 45 seconds

You may begin to prepare your response after the beep.

Please begin speaking after the beep.

STOP ■

START ▶

2. Please listen carefully.

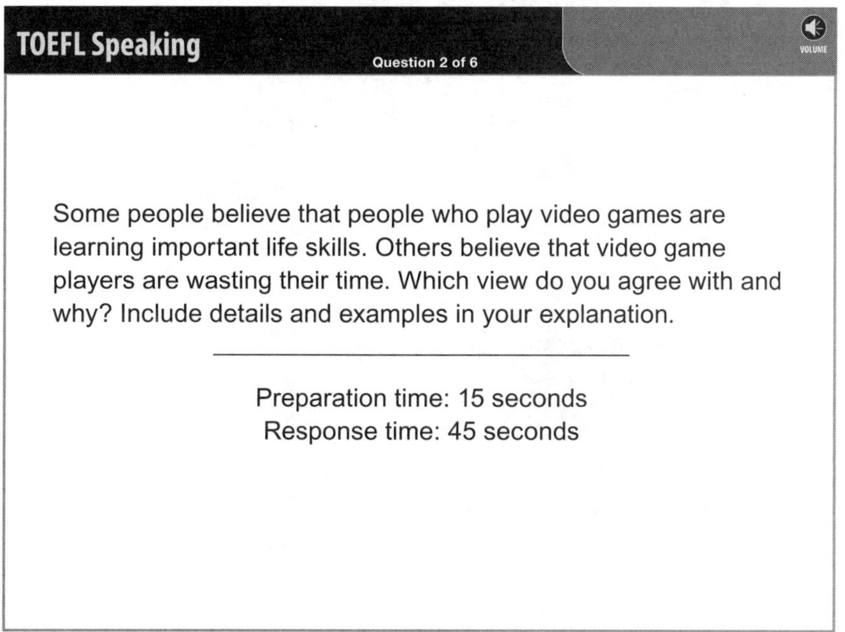

You may begin to prepare your response after the beep.

Please begin speaking after the beep.

STOP ■

START ▶

3. Please listen carefully.

The University of the Rockies newspaper has published a letter to the editor concerning a university policy. Read the letter about the hiring of temporary instructors. You will have 45 seconds to read the letter. Begin reading now.

PAUSE ⏸ (for 45 seconds)

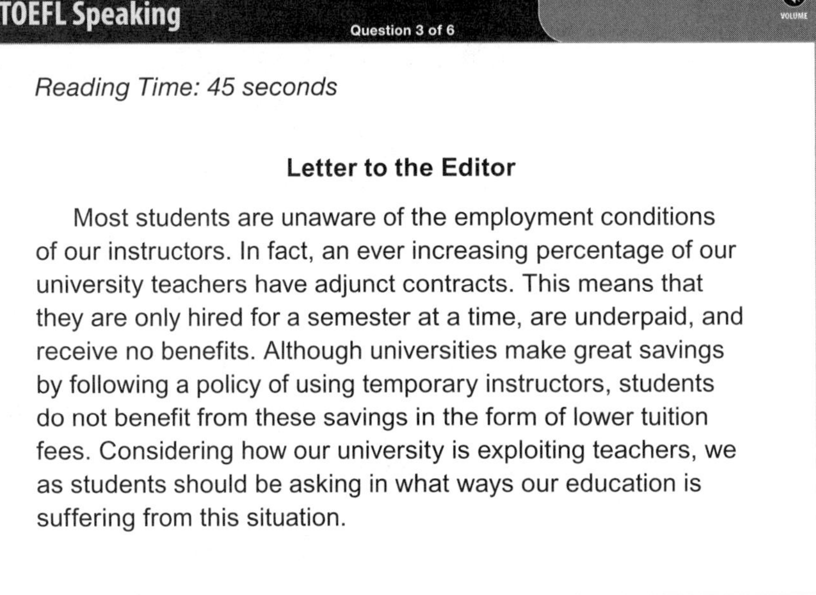

TOEFL Speaking

Question 3 of 6

VOLUME

Reading Time: 45 seconds

Letter to the Editor

Most students are unaware of the employment conditions of our instructors. In fact, an ever increasing percentage of our university teachers have adjunct contracts. This means that they are only hired for a semester at a time, are underpaid, and receive no benefits. Although universities make great savings by following a policy of using temporary instructors, students do not benefit from these savings in the form of lower tuition fees. Considering how our university is exploiting teachers, we as students should be asking in what ways our education is suffering from this situation.

Now listen to two students as they discuss the issue brought up in the letter.

Now get ready to answer the question.

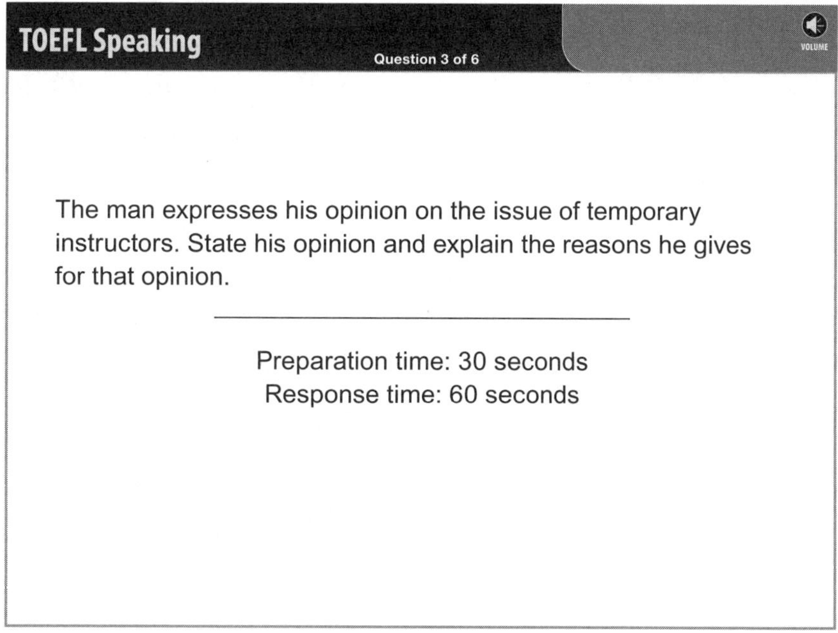

You may begin to prepare your response after the beep.

Please begin speaking after the beep.

STOP ■

START ▶

4. Please listen carefully.

Read the passage about imprinting in baby birds. You have 45 seconds to read the passage. Begin reading now.

PAUSE II (for 45 seconds)

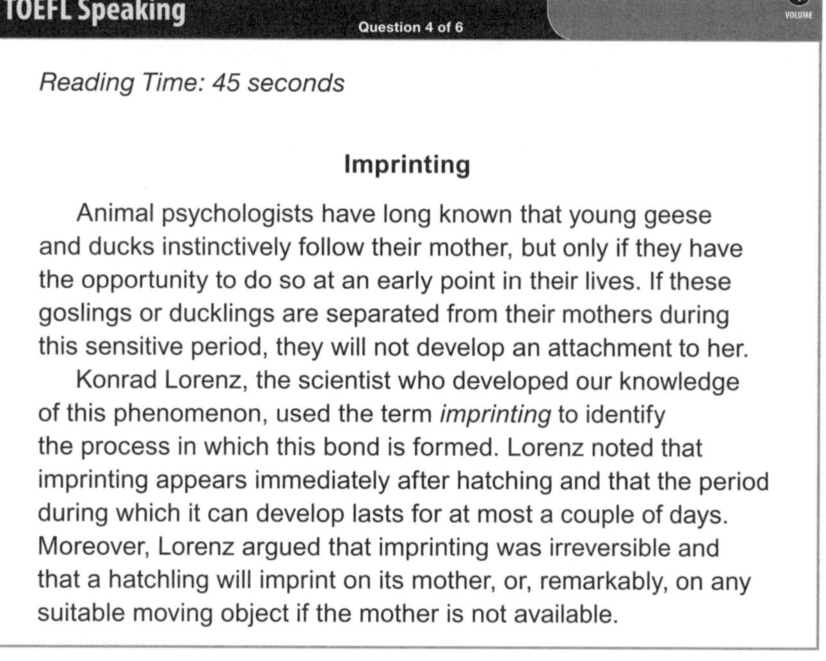

PRACTICE TEST 2

Now listen to part of a lecture on this topic in an ecology class.

TOEFL Speaking
Question 4 of 6
VOLUME

Now get ready to answer the question.

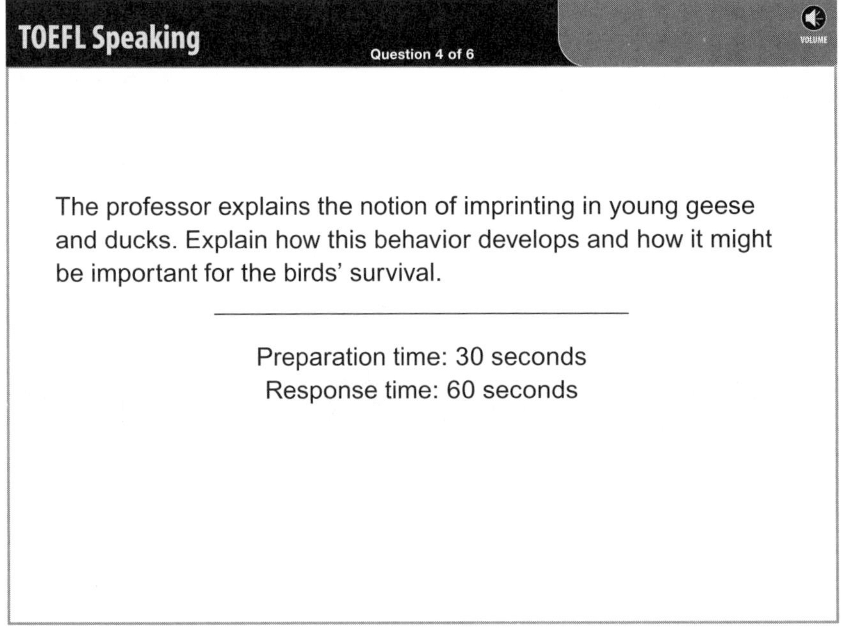
TOEFL Speaking
Question 4 of 6
VOLUME
The professor explains the notion of imprinting in young geese and ducks. Explain how this behavior develops and how it might be important for the birds' survival.
Preparation time: 30 seconds
Response time: 60 seconds

You may begin to prepare your response after the beep.

Please begin speaking after the beep.

STOP ■

START ▶

5. Please listen carefully.

Listen to a conversation between two students.

TOEFL Speaking
Question 5 of 6
VOLUME

Now get ready to answer the question.

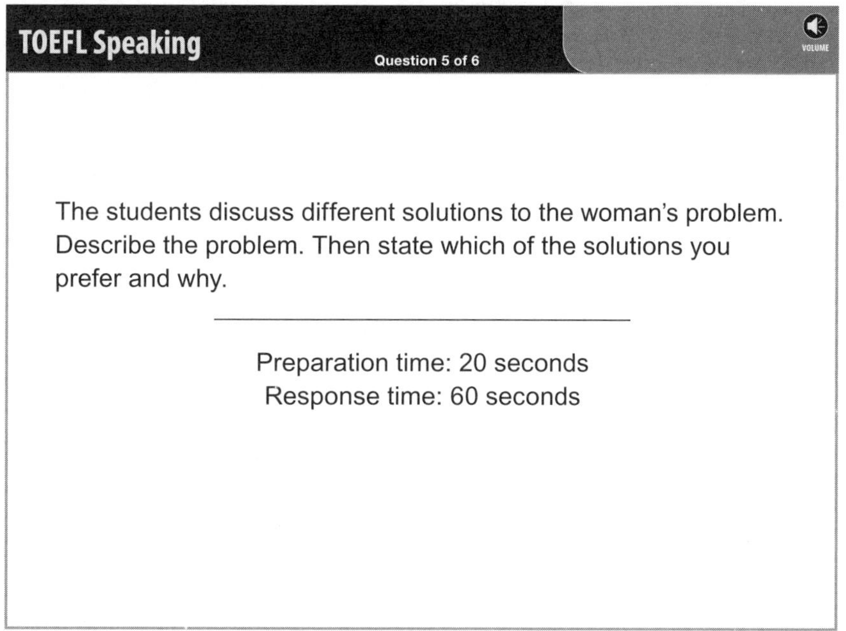
TOEFL Speaking
Question 5 of 6
VOLUME
The students discuss different solutions to the woman's problem. Describe the problem. Then state which of the solutions you prefer and why.
Preparation time: 20 seconds
Response time: 60 seconds

You may begin to prepare your response after the beep.

Please begin speaking after the beep.

STOP ■

START ▶

6. Please listen carefully.

Listen to part of a lecture in an architecture class.

TOEFL Speaking
Question 6 of 6
VOLUME

Now get ready to answer the question.

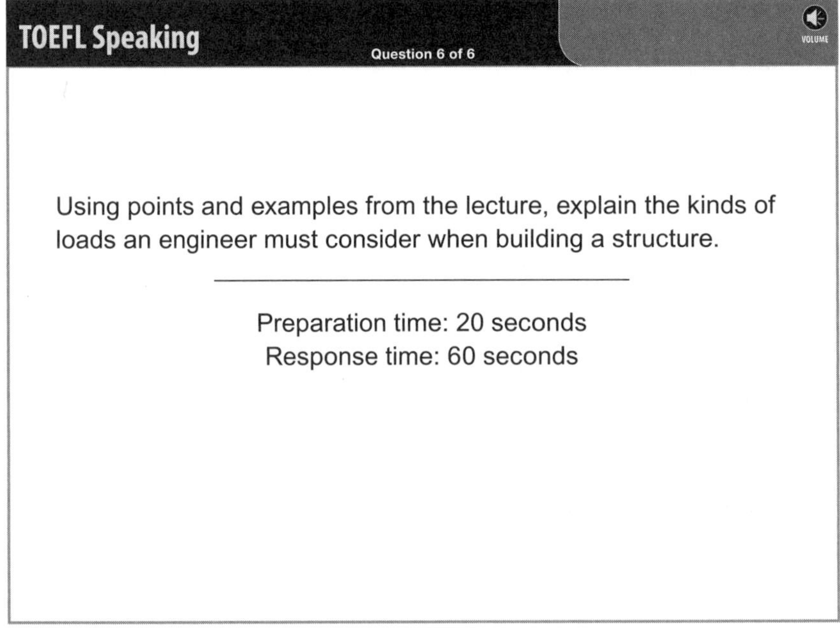
TOEFL Speaking
Question 6 of 6
VOLUME
Using points and examples from the lecture, explain the kinds of loads an engineer must consider when building a structure.
Preparation time: 20 seconds
Response time: 60 seconds

You may begin to prepare your response after the beep.

Please begin speaking after the beep.

STOP ■

WRITING SECTION

Directions

This section measures your ability to use writing to communicate in an academic environment. There will be two writing tasks.

For the first writing task, you will read a passage and listen to a lecture, and then answer a question based on what you have read and heard. For the second writing task, you will answer a question based on your own knowledge and experience.

Now read the directions for the first writing task.

Writing Based on Reading and Listening

Directions

For this task, you will have three minutes to read a passage about an academic topic. You may take notes on the passage while you read. Then you will listen to a lecture about the same topic. While you listen, you may also take notes.

Then you will have 20 minutes to write a response to a question that asks you about the relationship between the lecture you heard and the reading passage. Try to answer the question as completely as possible using information from the reading passage and the lecture. The question does **not** ask you to express your personal opinion. You can refer to the reading passage again when it is time for you to write. You may use your notes to help you answer the question.

Typically, an effective response will be 150 to 225 words long. Your response will be judged on the quality of your writing and on the completeness and accuracy of the content. If you finish your response before time is up, go on to the second writing task.

On the day of the test, you will be required to type your response into a computer. Therefore, if you are taking this test in the book, practice typing your response on a computer.

INTEGRATED TASK

Directions: You have three minutes to read and take notes from the reading passage. Next, listen to the related lecture and take notes. Then write your response.

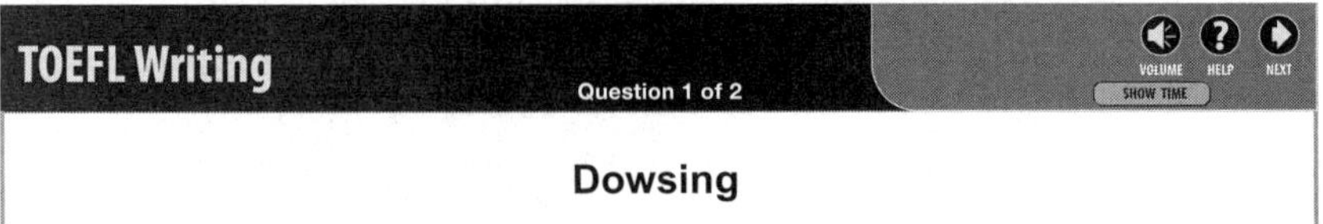

Dowsing

Dowsing is the millennia-old practice of finding hidden things. The most well-known activity of dowsing involves the use of a device such as a forked stick to locate underground water. To this end, the dowser walks slowly back and forth over an area of ground holding the dowsing tool out in front with both hands. It is said that the dowser, by concentrating carefully, is somehow able to feel the energy of the flowing underground streams vibrating through the rod at certain frequencies, and thus is able to tell precisely where to dig or drill to find water. Sometimes the dowsing tool will twist and jerk or suddenly point downward. Some dowsers hold two L-shaped rods, one in each hand. In this case, when he or she walks over an area of underlying water, the rods cross over indicating the place where digging should commence.

In recent years dowsing has gained in popularity not only as a method for finding underground water but also for trying to uncover other objects including buried treasure, oil, or even dead bodies. A recent application has been the search for what some consider harmful energy fields in an attempt to avoid them. Even large businesses and official organizations pay dowsers for their detection skills. Although no one is completely sure how dowsing works, the testimonials of satisfied customers bear witness to the success of this ancient art.

START ▶

Now listen to a professor's response to the reading passage.

TOEFL Writing
Question 1 of 2
VOLUME
HELP
NEXT
SHOW TIME

STOP ■

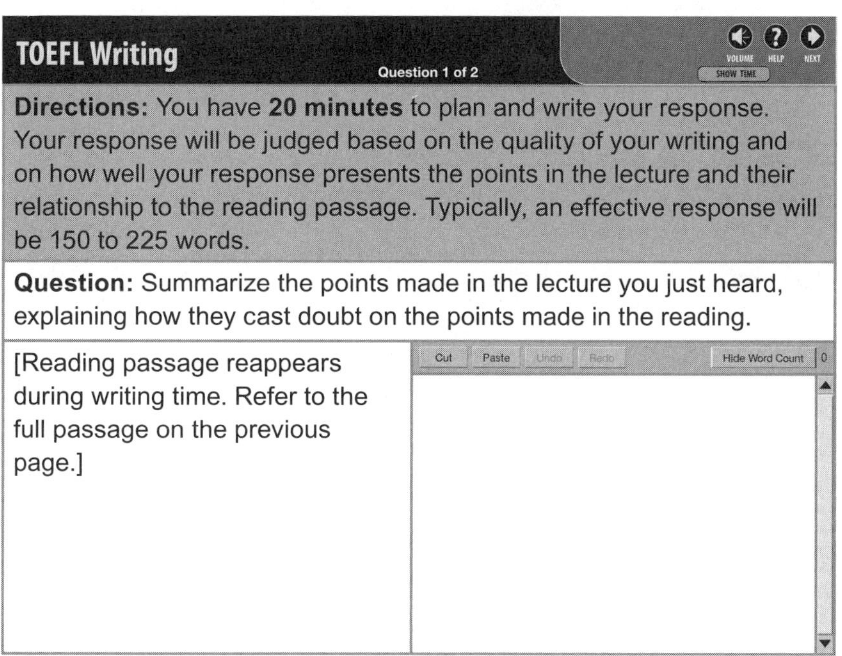
TOEFL Writing
Question 1 of 2
VOLUME
HELP
NEXT
SHOW TIME
Directions: You have **20 minutes** to plan and write your response. Your response will be judged based on the quality of your writing and on how well your response presents the points in the lecture and their relationship to the reading passage. Typically, an effective response will be 150 to 225 words.
Question: Summarize the points made in the lecture you just heard, explaining how they cast doubt on the points made in the reading.
[Reading passage reappears during writing time. Refer to the full passage on the previous page.]
Cut
Paste
Undo
Redo
Hide Word Count
0

Writing Based on Knowledge and Experience

Directions

For this task, you will write an essay in response to a question that asks you to state, explain, and support your opinion on an issue. You will have 30 minutes to plan, write, and revise your essay.

Typically, an effective essay will contain a minimum of 300 words. Your essay will be judged on the quality of your writing. This includes the development of your ideas, the organization of your essay, and the quality and accuracy of the language you use to express your ideas.

On the day of the test, you will be required to type your response into a computer. Therefore, if you are taking this test in the book, practice typing your response on a computer.

INDEPENDENT WRITING TASK

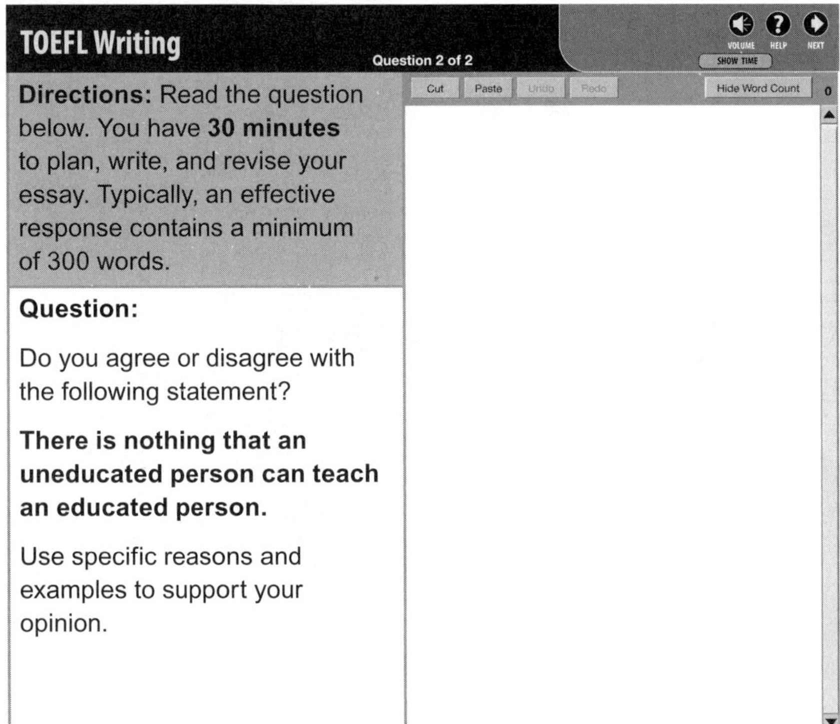
TOEFL Writing
Question 2 of 2
VOLUME HELP NEXT
SHOW TIME
Cut
Paste
Undo
Redo
Hide Word Count
0
Directions: Read the question below. You have **30 minutes** to plan, write, and revise your essay. Typically, an effective response contains a minimum of 300 words.
Question:
Do you agree or disagree with the following statement?
There is nothing that an uneducated person can teach an educated person.
Use specific reasons and examples to support your opinion.

APPENDICES

Answer Keys

DIAGNOSTIC TEST: Reading Section

(p. 1)

Note: If you answered an item incorrectly, complete the exercises listed for that item.

1. (B) To "prevail" means "to exist" or "to occur more prominently or notably." See Exercises R1–R3.
2. (D) The phrase "the three most prominent factors" indicates there are other factors that may not be as prominent. See Exercises R15–R21.
3. (C) The phrase "these eccentricities" refers to the movements of the Earth. The pattern of insolation is not a movement of the Earth. See Exercises R9–R14.
4. (B) The phrase "the match between periods of peak insolation and most intense glaciation were not exact" means that the periods did not occur at the same time. See Exercises R9–R14.
5. (A) The author is using the flat plane image to show the reader how the Earth moves in and out of a plane. See Exercises R15–R21.
6. (D) The Earth, our planet, is plunged into cold periods periodically. See Exercises R4–R8.
7. (D) Space debris reduces the amount of solar energy reaching the Earth. This causes regular cold periods. See Exercises R9–R14.
8. (A) Muller and MacDonald's theory is supported by the fossil record, whereas Milankovitch's theory is not. See Exercises R9–R14.
9. (A) When someone is "persuaded" or "convinced," they have been shown evidence that makes them believe something. See Exercises R1–R3.
10. (C) The problem with Muller and MacDonald's theory is that the amount of debris that reaches Earth in comparison to the debris from volcanoes appears too small to cool temperatures sufficiently. See Exercises R9–R14.
11. [D] The phrase "Earth is at its furthest from the sun" indicates that this is a detail related to the Earth's orbit around the sun. This would follow the sentence that discusses the elliptical nature of the Earth's orbit. See Exercises R4–R8.
12. **Flaws in the Milankovitch Cycles Theory**

    (A) Milankovitch's predicted intervals of sunlight do not coincide with the climate records.

    (B) The Nevada lake temperature increased before Milankovitch's predicted peaks of sunlight.

    (D) Milankovitch's predicted cycles do not always match the periods of most glaciation.

    (H) The data from the ocean sediments does not coincide with Milankovitch's predicted years of glaciation.

    Flaws in the Muller and McDonald Theory

    (E) The mild effect of volcanic eruptions on the climate does not support Muller and MacDonald's theory that interstellar debris affects the amount of sunlight that reaches the Earth.

    (G) There is not enough interstellar debris reaching Earth to support Muller and MacDonald's theory that this dust blocks sunlight.

    (I) Even though the glaciation corresponds to the periods of the Earth's moving through debris, Muller and MacDonald's theory is not supported by much physical evidence of changes in energy levels.

    See Exercises R22–R24.
13. (D) The passage mentions that some species are well-adapted to harsh living conditions. It can be understood that such birds don't migrate south. See Exercises R15–R22.
14. (D) The word "those" refers to the species of birds that find moving south in the winter advantageous. See Exercises R4–R8.
15. (D) According to the passage, "changes in the weather can trigger the start of the journey south." See Exercises R9–R14.
16. (A) When fat "accumulates" under the skin, it "builds up." See Exercises R1–R3.
17. (D) The passage does not mention birds migrating east–west toward a hotter climate. See Exercises R9–R14.
18. (B) "Precisely" refers to an action that is performed "exactly" without error. See Exercises R1–R3.
19. (C) Since the polarization patterns are visible at sunset and the passage mentions patterns in sunlight, we can infer that they are not visible at night. See Exercises R15–R21.
20. (B) The bowtie shape of the pattern has "fuzzy" ends which are reminiscent of a brush. See Exercises R15–R21.

21. (A) The term "subjected" here means that the birds were exposed to the projection on the inside of the planetarium. See Exercises R1–R3.

22. (C) According to paragraph 6, some research using projections on the planetarium ceiling indicates the birds are guided by the constellations. See Exercises R9–R14.

23. (A) The highlighted sentence means the same as "Birds needing to orientate seemed to use the information . . . from the stars that rotate around Polaris." See Exercises R9–R14.

24. (B) The word "this" refers to the fact that when fewer stars are visible on the planetarium ceiling, the birds' sense of direction worsened. See Exercises R4–R8.

25. [B] The particular landscapes such as river valleys and shapes of hills are examples of the topographic features mentioned in the previous sentence. See Exercises R4–R8.

26. (B), (E), and (F) The main ideas from the passage are all theories that scientists have studied in their attempt to understand the methods birds use to migrate. These theories are that birds may determine direction through detection of the gradations of polarization patterns in sunlight, through the rotation of stars around a fixed position, and through knowledge of landscape features. See Exercises R22–R24.

27. (C) The phrase "this element" refers to the parent element, uranium, mentioned in the previous sentence. See Exercises R4–R8.

28. (A) A liquid or gas "seeps" or "leaks" through holes or cracks. See Exercises R1–R3.

29. (A) According to paragraph 2, the health problems are caused by radon after it decays into its radioactive particles. If it has not had time to decay, radon is harmless. See Exercises R9–R14.

30. (A) When a substance "disintegrates" or "breaks down," it changes from one state into its simpler component parts. See Exercises R1–R3.

31. (B) According to the passage, heavy metals such as polonium, lead, and bismuth, which are products of the decay process of radon, are what cause health problems. See Exercises R9–R14.

32. (A) The radon progeny are the products that gather together as the radon disperses. See Exercises R9–R14.

33. (B) According to paragraph 3, products of decay, especially alpha particles, are dangerous because they accumulate into concentrations instead of dispersing throughout the body. In these concentrations, they damage nearby cells. See Exercises R9–R14.

34. (B) Radon is described as a decay product of uranium and, therefore, is a uranium daughter. See Exercises R4–R8.

35. (B) It can be understood that radon is detectable because buildings are tested for the amount of radon that has accumulated. See Exercises R9–R14.

36. (C) According to paragraph 6, a reduction of radon can be achieved by using concrete sealing and active ventilation systems. See Exercises R15–R21.

37. (A) A "prudent" or "sensible" action is one which is wise under the circumstances. See Exercises R1–R3.

38. [C] The phrase "But this research" refers back to the research on radon accumulation and cancer rates. See Exercises R4–R8.

39. (B) After radon enters a building, its decay products form particles that can be breathed into the lungs.

    (D) The alpha particles, in particular, accumulate in the lung tissue and damage cells.

    (F) It is possible to reduce radon exposure, but some of the gas stays in the atmosphere.

    See Exercises R22–R24.

DIAGNOSTIC TEST: Listening Section

(p. 19)

1. (B) The professor explains how the Electoral College works and how it is important for deciding the outcome of a presidential election. See Exercises L9–L12.

2. (C) According to the professor, an elector is a member of a political party who is pledged to that party's candidate for office. See Exercises L13–L17.

3. (A) The professor wants the students to realize that although the number of electors is equal to the number of senators and representatives, the actual people filling these roles are different. The professor thinks that the students might believe they are the same people. See Exercises L18–L23.

4. (A) The professor uses Alaska as an example of a state with a small population and only one representative. The number of electors in any state is equal to the number of senators (two) plus the number of representatives (dependent on population). See Exercises L18–L23.

5. (D) The winner of the election is the candidate whose total Electoral College vote is largest. See Exercises L13–L17.

6. (B) The professor mentions that some people have criticized the Electoral College system. They have raised problems associated with the fairness of the process of choosing a president. See Exercises L18–L23.

7. (D) The student's questioning the professor about his having the chance to look at her proposal and the discussion about ways for her to improve her proposal indicate her reason for going to see the professor. See Exercises L18–L23.

8. (B) The professor suggests that she see a statistician to explain a way to set up her experiment to get meaningful statistics. See Exercises L13–L17.

9. [A] and [C] The professor states that the procedure for getting meaningful statistics should be explained in the proposal and explains that the committee will need to understand how the student plans to select her subjects. See Exercises L13–L17.

10. (A) The professor means that if the student doesn't make it clear to the committee how she will be comparing subjects, they will not understand the relationship. See Exercises L18–L23.

11. (D) The committee will ask questions about those things they don't understand. The professor's discussion of subjects indicates that this is a point that they won't understand and this might affect the student's likelihood of getting the grant. See Exercises L18–L23.

12. (A) The professor and the students mention the different ways to send e-mails in a business situation. See Exercises L9–L12.

13. (C) The professor brings up the situation of sending a message to a large group of customers to get the students to think about the differences in how to deal with different kinds of receivers. See Exercises L18–L23.

14. (B) Both students have opinions about such things as e-mail etiquette and user techniques. This implies they are both experienced. See Exercises L18–L23.

15. (B) The students have not found the best solution of how to keep anonymity when sending group letters. The professor tries to jog their memory by referring to a previous lesson. See Exercises L18–L23.

16. (C) According to the professor, by using the blind-copy function, it is possible to maintain the anonymity of receivers but appear to be sending the message to only one individual. See Exercises L13–L17.

17. [A] and [B] According to the discussion, the customer's identity is protected because the individual addresses are hidden. See Exercises L13–L17.

18. (B) The professor mainly discusses important aspects of London's life and work and how they were related. See Exercises L9–L12.

19. (C) The professor mentions that London felt anxiety because he never knew his father and that this anxiety is reflected in the themes of his books. See Exercises L13–L17.

20. (B) The professor is making a lighthearted reference to the possibility that university life can be difficult at times for students. See Exercises L18–L23.

21. (A) The professor mentions that London read and studied books by other authors in order to learn how to write himself. See Exercises L13–L17.

22. (C) The professor implies that London worked hard to be successful. He mentions that London was a disciplined writer and that he sent many writings to publishers before his work was accepted. See Exercises L18–L23.

23. (C) The professor says that a considerable part of his writing is uninteresting and uninspired. See Exercises L13–L17.

24. (D) The main question the professor addresses is how and why the Neanderthal people became extinct. See Exercises L9–L12.

25. (C) By saying "in other words" followed by an explanation, the professor is providing more information about the meaning of the word *anatomically*. See Exercises L18–L23.

26. (D) The professor mentions that the Neanderthals, like the Cro-Magnon, were able to make and transport fire. This, and their simple art forms, shows they were not as backward as some people have claimed. See Exercises L18–L23.

27. (D) The professor notes that bone remains of Neanderthals suggest that their speech may have been slow and restricted in its range of sounds. See Exercises L13–L17.

28. **Neanderthal**

    (C) The Neanderthals produced simple art forms.

Cro-Magnon

(A) Only the Cro-Magnon developed tools with handles.

(B) Only the Cro-Magnon used bows and arrows.

See Exercises L13–L17.

29. (B) The professor mentions that current research is looking at whether Neanderthal DNA can be found in modern humans. If it were found, this would be evidence that the Neanderthals interbred with the Cro-Magnon. See Exercises L13–L17.

30. (A) The student thinks his car has been stolen and goes to the police to report this. See Exercises L9–L12.

31. (D) Since the student has a car parking problem, he probably drives to campus. Although he is disabled, it cannot be inferred that he uses a wheelchair. See Exercises L18–L23.

32. (B) By saying "I'm sorry to say," the police officer shows that she can see the problem from the student's point of view and that she empathizes about all the costs involved. See Exercises L18–L23.

33. (A) The police officer is finding out if the man knows he has the right to appeal. See Exercises L18–L23.

34. (A) The police offer explains in some detail how the student can appeal the parking fine. The student then thanks the police officer for the information. We can infer that the student will appeal the fine. See Exercises L18–L23.

There is no answer key for the Speaking and Writing sections of the Diagnostic Test. See Calculating Scores for Practice Tests on p. XXIII for information about how to evaluate your responses. Also use the scored sample essays and speaking responses for CD-ROM Test 1 as a guide.

PART 1 BUILDING SUPPORTING SKILLS

Note: An asterisk (*) indicates the correct answer to the question in those places where an explanation is provided for each possible answer.

There is no answer key for **EXERCISES LS1–LS13** *(pp. 42–52)* and **EXERCISE NPS1** *(p. 55)*.

EXERCISE NPS2 *(p. 57)*

Your answers may be stated differently.

1. assoc.
2. WHO
3. e.g.
4. lex'y
5. bldg
6. =
7. conc
8. chaps
9. dev'g
10. w/o

EXERCISE NPS3 *(p. 57)*

Your answers may be stated differently. Make sure you understand your own notes.

1. Fe-work'g Meriotic civ → Afr
2. Fine grnd pigm. + yolk = paint 4 M.A. panls
3. Trade Egp. ↔ Afr, 1st 1460 B.C., Q Hpt's ships → Punt, now Som
4. Free. Info Act, U.S. Congr. '66, = U.S. pers. access Pub. Rcds
5. Sonora D's day temp ↑ 50°C

EXERCISE NPS4 *(p. 58)*

Your answers may be stated differently.

1. likewise: additional information will be presented
2. therefore: a conclusion or result to the previous point or points will be made
3. as an illustration: a longer example will be given
4. granted that: an admission of the truth of an opposing argument will be stated
5. incidentally: something unrelated is going to be said or a regression to something said before will take place
6. previously: a situation that occurred before the given point is going to be discussed
7. conversely: a point that is in contrast to the given point is going to be discussed
8. furthermore: additional information will be presented
9. above all: a point is going to be emphasized
10. to summarize: all the points are going to be repeated in a shortened form

There is no answer key for **EXERCISE NPS5** *(p. 58)*.

EXERCISE NPS6 *(p. 59)*

Your answers may be stated differently.

1. Rube Goldberg, engineer → cartoonist. Best known for crazy inventions. Inventions complex machines do easy thing. Contest, Purdue U. to make R.G. type of machine does tasks in <9 min. + 20 steps. e.g. Turn off alarm clock, peel apple.
2. Animals make sounds/listen for echo to navigate, find food.

   Called echolocation. Way of make out things in obscure places. Used by bats, birds in caves, whales, dolphins in cloudy water

   Toothed whales use Ech.

   Baleen whales have vestigial form, past use?
3. IQ scores rising since '50s

   Why? small families, + food, + living stndrd., + edu or comb?

   IQ ↑ in abstrct reason. Why? kids visual TV, solve prblm video games.

   Emotional Intelligence → self-awareness, understand own emot., manage emot., empathic, social skills.

   A few people ↑IQs ↓EI.

   People ↑EI ↑IQ coz can control emot

   People ↓EI ↓IQ coz emot interfere

EXERCISE NPS7 *(p. 61)*

Your answers may be stated differently.

1. Rube Goldberg was an engineer who changed his career to become a cartoonist. He is best known for the crazy inventions designed by one of his cartoon characters. The inventions are very complex machines that are designed to do easy things. Purdue University runs a contest in which the contestants are required to make a Rube Goldberg invention. The machine has to do the task in less than 9 minutes but with more than 20 steps. Examples of the tasks are to build a machine that turns off an alarm clock or peels an apple.
2. Some animals make sounds and then listen for the echo. They use this to navigate and to find food. This is called echolocation. It is used by creatures that live in dark places. For example, bats and some birds live in caves and dolphins and whales may travel through dark, cloudy water. Not all whales use echolocation. Toothed whales do, but Baleen whales do not. However, Baleen whales have a vestigial form of the mechanisms to use echolocation. This indicates that they may have used it in the past.
3. IQ scores have been rising since the 1950s. The question is why. Perhaps it is because of smaller families, better food, living standards and education, or a combination of those factors. The rise in IQ scores is in abstract reasoning. The reason might be that children since the 1950s are exposed to more visual stimulation such as TVs. They also solve problems set by video games. Besides IQ, there is Emotional Intelligence or EI. EI has to do with one's self-awareness in understanding and managing one's own emotions. People with EI are empathic and have social skills. There seems to be a relationship between IQ and EI. Those people who can control their emotions get higher IQ scores and those who allow their emotions to interfere get lower IQ scores. There are a few people who have high IQ scores and low EI scores.

EXERCISE NPS8 *(p. 61)*

Your answers may be stated differently.

1. Rube Goldberg was a cartoonist famous for depicting very complex machines that were designed to do very easy things, such as turn off an alarm clock. Today university students compete in designing Goldberg machines that meet certain specifications.
2. Echolocation refers to the way some species of bats, birds, dolphins, and toothed whales make sounds and listen for the echo. These creatures use echolocation to navigate and find food in obscure living habitats. Baleen whales have the vestigial forms of the kind of anatomy needed for echolocation, which suggests that they once used it.
3. IQ scores have been increasing, although the reasons for this are not understood. It could be a combination of factors. Today's children have more exposure to TV and video games, which could affect abstract reasoning, an area in the IQ test where scores have increased. Studies have shown that EI, emotional intelligence, or the way one manages one's emotions, can influence IQ scores.

There is no answer key for **EXERCISES NPS9–NPS10** *(p. 62)*.

EXERCISE V1 *(p. 64)*

The words that are specific to biology and biochemistry are shown below. The words you circled depend on your vocabulary needs.

Vacuole, chromosomes, cytoplasm, mitochondria, chloroplasts, glycogen

There is no answer key for **EXERCISES V2–V10** *(p. 64–69)* and **EXERCISES P1–P3** *(pp. 70–71)*.

EXERCISE P4 *(p. 72)*

Since the seventh century, large bells have been used in cathedrals, churches, and monasteries. The greatest bell in the world is in Moscow. This famous "King of Bells" weighs about one hundred ninety-eight tons. The next two largest bells are also located in Russia. One near St. Petersburg weighs one hundred seventy-one tons, and another in Moscow weighs one hundred ten tons. Great Paul, the bell at St. Paul's in London, is the largest bell in England, but weighs a mere seventeen tons.

There is no answer key for **EXERCISES P5–P8** *(pp. 72–74)* and **EXERCISE G1** *(p. 75)*.

EXERCISE G2 *(p. 76)*

The following answers show ways of correcting those sentences that are incorrect. You may have made different changes that also make the sentences correct.

1. A laser cane, which the blind find useful, sends out beams that **detect** obstacles. (incorrect verb form in the adjective clause)
2. This sentence is correct.
3. The most convincing evidence **is** that female chimpanzees in Tanzania use the aspilia plant for medicinal purposes. (incomplete sentence)
4. **That** adults come to night classes eager to learn has been the experience of most adult-education teachers. (incorrect noun clause marker)
5. A vending machine is a kind of robot that automatically **gives** out candy or other items when money is inserted. (incorrect subject/verb agreement)
6. Apprentices sometimes fear that they **might** not be able to master the intricacies of their chosen craft. (incorrect modal)
7. The importance of the Chaco Canyon archaeological site is that **it** reveals insights into a whole civilization. (incorrect referent agreement)
8. Arched roofs were built for **the** first time 2,500 years ago. (incorrect article)
9. Because of financial restrictions, some schools cannot contemplate **staying** abreast of advances in modern technology. (incorrect use of infinitive)
10. Birds that breed on high cliffs have pear-shaped eggs that roll in a tight circle. **Consequently**, that makes them somewhat less likely to roll off the cliff. (incorrect connecting word)
11. This sentence is correct.
12. Butterfly wings have iridescent scales **consisting** of thin, interlaced layers. (incorrect reduced adjective clause)
13. China's first emperor was buried surrounded by 7,000 life-sized clay figures of soldiers standing in battle formation **beside** life-sized ceramic chariots. (incorrect prepositions)
14. Christopher Columbus persuaded the Spanish monarchs Isabel and Fernando **to finance** his expeditions to the Caribbean. (incorrect gerund use)
15. East Coker is where the Anglo-American poet T. S. Eliot **was** buried in 1965. (incorrect use of the active voice)
16. Even though the team of scientists **encountered** snow and strong winds, they continued their excavation. / Even though the team of scientists encounter snow and strong winds, they **continue** their excavation. (incorrect verb tense agreement)
17. Every four years the International Olympic Committee selects **which** city will hold the next games. (incorrect noun clause marker)
18. Filming a wild animal in its habitat requires meticulous preparation, unending patience, and, at times, **courage**. (incorrect parallel structures)
19. George Gershwin gathered motifs for his folk opera *Porgy and Bess* while **he** lived in Charleston. (missing subject in the adverb clause) / George Gershwin gathered motifs for his folk opera *Porgy and Bess* while **living** in Charleston. (incorrect reduced adverb phrase)
20. Having first **been** domesticated for milk production, sheep were then used for wool. (incorrect reduced adverb clause)
21. This sentence is correct.
22. Lucid dreamers are those people who recognize when they are dreaming and thus **control** the plot of their dreams. (incorrect parallel form of verb)
23. Many traditional attitudes and **values** seem to be disappearing under the pressure of global media. (plural form should be used)
24. This sentence is correct.
25. Mice aren't really more attracted to cheese **than** they are to grains. / Mice aren't really **as** attracted to cheese as they are to grains. (incorrect comparison form)
26. Monteverdi, **whose** works were mainly written on commission for the private theaters of wealthy Italian nobility, wrote his final opera in 1642. (incorrect adjective clause marker)
27. **More** pioneers walked across the continent than rode in wagons or on horses. (incorrect comparative form)

28. This sentence is correct.
29. Mount Rainier towers nearly three miles **above** sea level. (incorrect preposition)
30. This sentence is correct.
31. Postwar women had more opportunities to find work than they had had in the prewar days. (the article **the** before "work" should be deleted)
32. This sentence is correct.
33. New Orleans is a city **where** older traditions can still be seen. (incorrect adjective clause marker)
34. This sentence is correct.
35. Of all salmon species, the king salmon is the **rarest**. (incorrect superlative)
36. Only if packages are labeled properly, **will** sufferers be able to avoid severe allergic reactions. (incorrect word order)
37. This sentence is correct.
38. **Putrefaction** is caused by bacteria and not by a chemical process. (incorrect noun form)
39. The diary of Samuel Pepys contains eyewitness **descriptions** of the Great Plague and the Great Fire of London. (incorrect word form)
40. This sentence is correct.
41. Scientists must be willing to change their position when confronted with new and conflicting data as **it** is this openness to change that allows scientific progress to be made. (incomplete sentence because of missing subject)
42. Scissors, a Bronze Age invention **remaining** basically unchanged to this day, consist of two blades linked by a C-shaped spring. (incorrect verb form for reduced adjective clause)
43. This sentence is correct.
44. When telephones were first invented, many business owners refused to have them installed in their offices because **there** were messenger services that they believed to be more efficient. (incomplete sentence because of missing subject)
45. Sixteenth-century mariners called Bermuda the "Isle of Devils" partly because breeding seabirds **were** making horrid sounds in the night. / Sixteenth-century mariners called Bermuda the "Isle of Devils" partly because breeding seabirds **made** horrid sounds in the night. (verb tense agreement)
46. Small animals can **survive** the desert heat by finding shade during the daytime. (incorrect word form)
47. So incredible **were** explorer John Colter's descriptions of the Yellowstone area that people didn't believe in its existence. (incorrect word order)
48. Public lands in many parts of the West may be overgrazed as cattle, sheep, and **wildlife** compete for forage. (incorrect plural form of the noun)
49. This sentence is correct.
50. Swimmers should avoid **entering** ocean areas contaminated by red tide organisms. (incorrect use of infinitive)
51. This sentence is correct.
52. The great stone city Angkor flourished for six centuries **before** it fell in 1431 and lay prey to the jungle for four long centuries. (incorrect adverb clause marker)
53. This sentence is correct.
54. When llamas were first brought into the Colorado wilderness, no one could have predicted how **popular** the animal would become. (incorrect word form)
55. The more technical today's world becomes, the **more** compatible with both humans and machines language needs to be. (incorrect parallel comparison)
56. This sentence is correct.
57. Today, *carpet* refers to floor coverings that reach from wall to wall, **whereas** *rug* refers to a piece of material that covers only one section of the floor. (incorrect connecting word)
58. What we **have** already **learned** about tornadoes has contributed to reducing the casualty rates. (incorrect verb tense agreement)
59. This sentence is correct.
60. While large numbers of eagles have long nested in national parks, only recently **have** the birds **been** generating outside curiosity. (incorrect verb form)

There is no answer key for **EXERCISES G3–G6** *(pp. 80–82)*.

EXERCISE G7 *(p. 86)*

1. This is correct.
2. tolerate
3. cooperative
4. This is correct.
5. symbolizes
6. famous
7. impediment
8. undeniably
9. This is correct.
10. This is correct.
11. tribe
12. hastily

EXERCISE G8 *(p. 88)*

1. This phrase is missing a subject.
2. ✓
3. ✓
4. This phrase is missing a verb.

EXERCISE G9 *(p. 88)*

S V
1. C Soil is highly fertile in volcanic areas, and
S V
volcanic activity offers advantages such as geothermal energy.

S V
2. ____ Women with very narrow pelvises are more likely to experience potentially life-threatening problems during childbirth.

S
3. C On collective farms, land, buildings, and
V S V
equipment are shared, the farmers work together,
S V
and the profits are divided equally.

S
4. ____ Life expectancy, or the average length of an
V
individual life, varies over time within the same community and from community to community at the same time.

EXERCISE G10 *(p. 99)*

IS
ds dv
1. That rent-control laws may inhibit landlords from
IV
repairing properties is unfortunate but true.

IS IV
2. Studies of newborn infants show that some
ds
perceptual processes, such as depth perception,
dv
may be inherited.

IS IV
ds dv
3. How glass is blown in a cylinder was demonstrated at the Stuart Crystal Factory.

IS IV
4. One can easily understand why fast-food
ds dv
restaurants are so popular.

EXERCISE G11 *(p. 100)*

IS ds dv
1. A species of tomato that is adapted to harsh
IV
climatic conditions has been developed.

IS ds dv
2. The date on which Romulus founded Rome
IV
is generally considered to be 753 BCE.

IS IV
3. In the Colosseum in ancient Rome, hoists lifted
ds dv
cages to a level where the animals could enter the arena up a ramp.

IS ds dv
4. The common hedgehog, which has outlived the mammoth an d the saber-toothed tiger,
IV
is now threatened by automobile traffic.

IS IV ds dv
5. Many English villages have churches that date back to Norman times or before.

IS IV ds dv
6. Shakespeare wrote plays people have enjoyed for four centuries.

IS ds dv
7. People who are in charge of ticket reservations
IV
warn travelers to book early during the high seasons.

IS IV ds dv
8. Walt Disney was a man whose creations still bring happiness to many children.

IS ds dv
9. Using low doses of antibiotics that don't kill
IV
bacteria only increases these germs' resistance.

IS ds dv
10. The only U.S. president the people did not choose
IV
in a national presidential election was President Gerald Ford.

EXERCISE G12 *(p. 100)*

1. ✓ trying to overcome severe obstacles
2. ✓ leading into the ancient city of Petra carved out of the sandstone cliffs "that ends in front of an impressive temple" is an adjective clause
3. ____ "who have been raised apart" is an adjective clause
4. ✓ found in the Andes

EXERCISE G13 *(p. 101)*

IS IV ds
1. Hundreds of pandas starved to death when one of
dv
the species of bamboo on which they feed died out.

ds dv
2. While the world population continues to grow,
IS IV
natural resources remain finite.

3. Because the ice crystals from which they form are usually hexagonal, snowflakes often have six sides.

   (ds: the ice crystals; dv: are; IS: snowflakes; IV: have)

4. Antiochus was overthrown by Rome around 34 BCE after he apparently used some of his funds to support a local rebellion backed by the Persians.

   (IS: Antiochus; IV: was overthrown; ds: he; dv: used)

5. The Romans built raised sidewalks of stone in Pompeii so that pedestrians would not get their feet muddy.

   (IS: Romans; IV: built; ds: pedestrians; dv: would not get)

6. Although the existence of germs was verified in about 1600, scientists did not prove the connection between germs and diseases until the mid-nineteenth century.

   (ds: the existence of germs; dv: was verified; IS: scientists; IV: did not prove)

7. Since the search to find and document sites of Native American cave paintings was first begun, several hundred have come to light.

   (ds: the search; dv: was first begun; IS: several hundred; IV: have come)

8. Aphrodisias continued as a Byzantine center until violent earthquakes and invasions brought its prosperity to an end.

   (IS: Aphrodisias; IV: continued; ds: earthquakes and invasions; dv: brought)

EXERCISE G14 *(p. 101)*

1. ____ "when Cartier first discovered them" is an adverb clause
2. ✓ Once covered by thick, solid ice during the last Ice Age
3. ____ "By the time newcomers to the United States had passed through the immigration center on Ellis Island" is an adverb clause
4. ✓ When building Hadrian's Wall

EXERCISE G15 *(p. 111)*

1. The word "recently" indicates a recent past action. Therefore, the verb "will revealed" should be either "has revealed" or "revealed."
2. The verb is used correctly.
3. The phrase "in the future" indicates that a future tense should be used. "May have been measuring" indicates possibility in an undefined past time. "May be measuring" would be correct.
4. The verbs are used correctly.
5. The verb is used correctly. "Have been grown" is the passive voice of the present perfect and indicates that someone has done this action in an undefined past time.
6. The word "now" indicates that the verb should be in the present tense: "are."
7. The verb "has seized" is used correctly. The present perfect tense "has seized" indicates that the action has happened immediately before the second action. The verb "is dragging" is used incorrectly. The present tense "drags" should be used because the crocodile always drags its prey under water. The present tense "seizes" could also be used in the adverb clause indicating that this action is a general fact.
8. The word "since" indicates that this is an action that began in the past and is continuing. Therefore, the verb "harbor" should be in a present perfect tense. Either "have harbored" or "have been harboring" would be correct. The verb "began" is correct.

EXERCISE G16 *(p. 111)*

1. C The verb "has been eliminated" agrees with the subject "difference."
2. C The verb "occurs" agrees with the subject "reorganization."
3. I The verb "is" should be "are" to agree with the plural subject "levels."
4. C The verb "is taking" agrees with the noncount noun "pollution."
5. I The verb "contributes" should be "contribute" to agree with the plural subject "decoration and use."

EXERCISE G17 *(p. 112)*

1. A	6. B
2. A	7. B
3. A	8. A
4. B	9. B
5. A	10. A

EXERCISE G18 *(p. 114)*

1. these qualities: loyal, intelligent, and calm
   them: dogs
2. its: ancient Egypt
   them: hieroglyphics

3. his: Caesar
   they: Caesar and his troops
   their: Caesar and his troops
   they: Caesar and his troops
4. itself: The prickly pear
   those places: rocky, barren hills
5. this bird: The dodo
   that island: Mauritius
   that: around 1600
6. his: Maxie Anderson
   their: Maxie Anderson and his two partners

EXERCISE G19 *(p. 115)*

1. "Were paying homage to pagan gods" is incorrect because the verb is in the past continuous form and the other verbs are in the simple past form. ". . . paid homage . . ." is correct.
2. This sentence is correct.
3. This sentence is correct.
4. "Most importantly medical supplies" is incorrect because it is a noun phrase and the other phrases are gerund phrases. ". . . supply medicines" or "providing medical supplies" is correct.
5. "The small bitter apples make the best cider" is incorrect because it is an independent clause and the other clauses are noun clauses. ". . . that the small bitter apples make the best cider" is correct.
6. This sentence is correct.

EXERCISE G20 *(p. 119)*

1. A	3. A	5. A	7. C	9. B
2. B	4. D	6. D	8. D	10. A

EXERCISE G21 *(p. 123)*

1. "Citizen" should be in its plural form, "citizens."
2. "Motivations" should be in the singular form.
3. "Metalworker" should be in the plural form, "metalworkers," because there is a comparison between Yellin and all the other metalworkers in America.
4. "Children" is the plural form. An "s" should not be added.
5. The use of the plural verb "learn" and the pronoun "their" indicates that the noun "calf" should be in its plural form, "calves."
6. "Advice" does not have a plural form.

EXERCISE G22 *(p. 126)*

1. This article is correct.
2. This article is correct.
3. the eighteenth century
4. Russia: no article
5. This article is correct.
6. nature: no article

EXERCISE G23 *(p. 128)*

1. Had (AUX) Napoleon (S) succeeded (V)
2. are (AUX) federal officials (S) impeached (V)
3. does (AUX) tea (S)
4. should (AUX) he or she (S) start (V)
5. will (AUX) it (S) be able to undertake (V)
6. is (V) the tomato (S)
7. Should (AUX) a medical crisis (S) occur (V)
8. remain (V) the mysterious giant stone heads (S)

EXERCISE G24 *(p. 130)*

1. better than – "Best than" is incorrect because two things are being compared.
2. This sentence is correct.
3. flattest and driest – "The flatter and drier" is incorrect because there are more than two continents.
4. less severe than / not as severe as – "As not severe as" is incorrect because one of two things compared

   does not have as much of the particular quality; incorrect word order.
5. This sentence is correct.
6. tougher – "Tough" is incorrect because it is not in the comparative form.
7. This sentence is correct.
8. the largest sailing ship – The article "the" is used with the superlative.
9. Turkey's largest city – The article "the" should not be used with the possessive form.
10. This sentence is correct.

EXERCISE G25 *(p. 132)*

1. (A) "As" appears to be a clause marker, but there is no verb to complete a clause.
   *(B) "Through" indicates from one point in time to another point in time.
2. *(A) "Full" is the adjective describing the region and "of" is used in the sense of containing.
   (B) "Filled" makes the sentence passive, so the preposition "with" would be needed to complete the sentence correctly.
3. *(A) "That" is a clause marker, "the twenty-first century" is the subject of the clause, and "will bring" is the verb.
   (B) The object of the preposition "from" is the noun "twenty-first century," which cannot also serve as the subject for the verb "will bring."
4. (A) "Because" is a clause marker, but there is no verb to complete the clause.
   *(B) "Because of" is the preposition and "structures" is the object of the preposition.
5. (A) "That" is a clause marker, but there is no verb to complete the clause.
   *(B) "For" is a preposition. The noun "mammal" completes the prepositional phrase.
6. (A) "Was" cannot be used because the sentence is not passive.
   *(B) "Of" indicates the tradition pertains to the spring fertility celebrations.
7. *(A) "For" expresses the object or purpose of the need.
   (B) "Being a new attitude" suggests a reduced adverbial clause, which would not fill the position of describing the noun "need."
8. *(A) "Over" indicates the position of the stones.
   (B) "That" is a clause marker, but there is no position for a clause.

PART 2 BUILDING SKILLS: Reading

Note: An asterisk (*) indicates the correct answer to the question in those places where an explanation is provided for each possible answer.

EXERCISE R1 *(p. 146)*

1. an illness
2. a rodent
3. the smallest part of a chemical element
4. D
5. D
6. B
7. electrical devices
8. a goddess
9. explosions of dying stars
10. B
11. D
12. A
13. ancient burial mounds
14. having a slender body build
15. biting surface of teeth
16. A
17. D
18. B
19. height above sea level
20. specialized bone cells
21. internal walls
22. B
23. B
24. C
25. large fish
26. animals
27. drought-resistant plants
28. D
29. B
30. A
31. a compound used for burns
32. the succession of sounds
33. descended from
34. B
35. D
36. A
37. insects
38. meat-eating animals
39. a marine time-keeping device
40. C
41. D
42. A
43. not deadly
44. flourishes, grows easily, does well
45. high resistance to motion
46. C
47. C
48. B
49. a flower
50. part of a bagpipe
51. made better, lessened
52. A
53. B
54. C

EXERCISE R2 *(p. 155)*

1. B	7. B	13. C
2. D	8. C	14. D
3. A	9. A	15. B
4. D	10. D	16. C
5. C	11. D	17. A
6. A	12. B	18. A

EXERCISE R3 *(p. 159)*

1. B 2. D 3. B 4. A

Reading Mini-test 1 *(p. 160)*

1. (A) The words "scrap" and "waste" can refer to materials that are thrown out because they are damaged or no longer serve their purpose.
2. (C) Something that is "customary" or "regular" is something that is usual or habitual.
3. (A) The word "abatement" means to subside or decrease. The benefit is a reduction of noise.
4. (D) The words "elimination" and "eradication" refer to a complete removal or destruction of something.
5. (A) To be "reclusive" means to deliberately avoid other people, to be "solitary," or to be alone.
6. (D) The word "prolific" means abundant. Dickinson wrote a large number of letters (correspondence).
7. (D) When a feeling is "intense," we can also say it is very "strong."
8. (D) The words "concisely" and "succinctly" refer to something being said clearly, using few words.
9. (C) "Afflictions" and "diseases" refer to illnesses.
10. (A) The word "expire" means to die.
11. (A) The "incidence" of a disease is the number of cases that appear or the "rate of occurrence."
12. (D) To be "susceptible" or "vulnerable" means to be unprotected and open to the possibility of being harmed.
13. (A) When people make a "resolution," they declare their intentions (make a declaration).
14. (C) When people are "bombarded" or "saturated" with information, they are given an overwhelming amount of it.
15. (C) When the experimenter was "claiming to represent a local utility company," that person was pretending to be part of the company in order to hide his or her identity from the homeowners.
16. (A) When people give their "consent" or "permission," they are agreeing to something.

EXERCISE R4 *(p. 167)*

1. themselves: Arctic people
   they: Arctic people
   these natural resources: the environment and wild animals
2. who: individuals
   their: political prisoners
3. when: 1863
   he: a Hungarian count
   the first European variety: wine grapes
   there: California
4. the lawyer and lexicographer: Noah Webster
   who: Noah Webster
   at this time: 1828
   that: English

EXERCISE R5 *(p. 168)*

1. B 2. C 3. D

EXERCISE R6 *(p. 169)*

1. Scientists used to believe that animals scream to startle predators into loosening their grip or to warn their kin. However, now some researchers have concluded that the piercing, far-reaching cries of animals may have another function. Recent studies indicate that these screams may have evolved to attract other predators, which will give the prey a chance to escape during the ensuing struggle between predators.
2. When cartoonists take on the task of drawing real people, they do so by making a caricature. These kinds of cartoon drawings are frequently used to satirize well-known people. Most famous people have several particular characteristics that distinguish them, such as facial features, body posture, or gestures, which are familiar to the general public. Cartoonists can cleverly exaggerate them to the point of ridiculousness.
3. Satellites routinely relay pictures of desert areas. From these pictures, it can be determined where locusts are likely to breed. With information on the locusts' breeding areas, agriculture officials can use pesticides to kill these insects before they become a menace. If not eradicated, a single swarm can devour 80,000 tons of corn a day – sustenance for half a million people for one year.

EXERCISE R7 *(p. 170)*

1. (D) "But" is used to qualify a statement. The statement concerning the value of glass in Egyptian times is qualified by (D) concerning the value of glass today. (A) is added information. (B) and (C) are not related to the fact that glass was valued in Egyptian times.
2. (C) "Such as" is used to introduce examples. An example of "behavior" is (C), sucking a thumb. (A) development, (B) the sex, and (D) structures are not examples of behavior.

3. (D) "Although" is used to qualify a statement. In (D) the fact that desert species are similar is qualified by the contrasting fact that their ancestry is different. (A) gives information that one might assume to be true. However, "Although" indicates that the information is not what one might expect. In (B) the species' not adapting to jungles is not related to their coming from different ancestral stocks. (C) is a repetition of the phrase "the world's various deserts."
4. (C) "In contrast" is used to contrast statements. The informality of Halloween is contrasted with (C), the relative formality of Thanksgiving. (A) doesn't make a contrast but gives another example of a traditional holiday. (B) and (D) don't make contrasts but instead give information that is not related to the topic of Halloween.
5. (C) The main point of the statement is the uses of bamboo in general. "Equally important" introduces another way bamboo is used. In this case, (C), the food that can be made from bamboo and the items that can be made from bamboo are both important. In (A) the importance of grass growing in warm climates is not clear. In (B) the longer cooking time seems to be more of a disadvantage than an aspect of equal importance. (D) does not relate to the importance of making something.
6. (A) "In conclusion" is used to indicate that something is true because the facts lead to this belief. All the facts about satellites lead to the belief that (A) the lives of humankind have been enriched by their existence. The facts given do not lead to any conclusion about (B) the difficulties of satellites, (C) how many TV channels can be picked up, or (D) orbital placement.
7. (B) "In addition" is used to add more information. The lasers and two-way wrist TV in (B) are two additional items Dick Tracy used besides the atomic-powered space vehicle. (A) gives new information about today's astronauts, not added information about space items introduced in a comic strip. Dick Tracy's popularity, (C), is not an addition to his devices. (D) gives new information about items being used by today's astronauts, not the use by Dick Tracy.
8. (D) "Consequently" is used to show the results of an action. The results of a vaccine that reduces the microorganism thought to cause cavities is (D) protection against tooth decay. In (A) a cavity-prevention program for immunizing people against cavity-causing microorganisms would probably be organized instead of eliminated. In (B) there is no inference that test animals were used in the development of this vaccine. In (C) the amount of sweets that children consume is not solely dictated by tooth decay.
9. (A) "In some cases" is used to give information for particular situations. The information in (A) gives the advantages of the nonsurgical method of treating heart disease in the situations where it can be used. In (B) the nonsurgical method cannot replace an artery. In (C) the fact that coronary bypass operations are lucrative does not explain the nonsurgical method. In (D) the fact that the chest is opened up indicates that this information does not relate to the "nonsurgical method."
10. (A) "Indeed" is used to emphasize a fact. In (A) the fact that Einstein's brain contained more glial cells than other people's brains is being emphasized. (B) is added information concerning scientists' studies of brains. (C) is added information concerning where scientists looked for glial cells. (D) is a conclusion concerning the development of Einstein's intellectual processing.

EXERCISE R8 *(p. 172)*

1. B 2. D 3. C 4. C

Reading Mini-test 2 *(p. 173)*

1. (C) "Architects" used techniques to reduce noise.
2. (A) The air is filtered through the air conditioners and furnaces.

   *(B) Because these techniques absorb the sound, there is a lack of sound.

   (C) A filled wall cannot have a reaction.

   (D) These techniques do not distinguish between desirable noise and undesirable noise.
3. [C] A description of the symptoms people suffer when they are in a noiseless environment would support the idea that people react adversely to the lack of sound.
4. (A) "The gambrel roof design" is a feature of Dutch colonial architectural style.
5. (A) The bell-shaped appearance is a description of the roof. There is no suggestion that people want such a roof because it looks like a bell.

   *(B) The spacious interior is an advantage for a growing family.

   (C) The shape would only be traditional for the Dutch, and this does not explain why other homeowners would be attracted to it.

   (D) The angle being shallower at the eaves does not indicate a reason that a homeowner would want it.
6. [D] A second use of a roof that is spacious would follow the detail about the main advantage of a spacious roof.

7. (C) Each point above 1 carat is more valuable than "each point" below 1 carat.
8. (A) The carbon spots, inner flaws, and surface blemishes are imperfections.

   (B) The diamond's rating is based on the number and severity of these imperfections.

   *(C) The imperfections cannot be seen with the naked eye, but they affect the brilliance.

   (D) The diamond might be determined as flawless, but not the imperfections.
9. [C] A sentence that contrasts unprofessionally cut diamonds would follow one that discusses well-cut diamonds.
10. *(A) A contrast is being made between when most people feel drowsy and when narcoleptics doze.

    (B) According to the passage, there are different extremes of narcolepsy. Some sleep most of the time, others just at odd times.

    (C) The two ways narcoleptics suffer is not a contrast to most people feeling drowsy after a meal.

    (D) There is no contrast between feeling drowsy and falling asleep.
11. (C) The "drugs'" administration has unwanted side effects.
12. [A] The estimated number of sufferers would support the sentence that introduces the lack of data on the number of people who have narcolepsy.
13. (B) The crew of the *Dei Gratia* gave a report at the inquiry concerning the finding of the abandoned *Mary Celeste.*
14. (B) "Alien abduction and sea-monster attacks" are outlandish (absurd) explanations concerning the missing crew.
15. [C] A sentence about leaving the hatches open to prevent a blast would come between the sentence that introduces the possibility of an explosion and the sentence that gives other details to support the explanation.

EXERCISE R9 *(p. 180)*

1. A. *T*

   B. *F* The third time the plan was proposed it was accepted.

   C. *T*

   D. *T*

   E. *F* We are not told why the plan was rejected in 1883. ("Bore" has two meanings: "to drill" and "to tire.")

   F. *F* It was not the construction itself but other reasons that led to the tunnel plan being rejected.

   G. *F* The tunnel was not made in 1930.

   H. *T*
2. A. *T*

   B. *F* The animals, not the fossils, were probably 6 to 8 feet long and about 350 pounds in weight.

   C. *F* The middle ear is evidence the ancient whale was a land animal.

   D. *T*

   E. *T*

   F. *F* It is the separation of the ear bones that allows a marine whale to recognize the source of a sound, not the vestigial middle ear.

   G. *T*

   H. *T*
3. A. *T*

   B. *F* The hundreds of varieties of potatoes are ones that the researchers were studying when they discovered the hairy one.

   C. *F* A glue, not a scent, is emitted from the ends of the hairs of the hairy Bolivian potato.

   D. *T*

   E. *T*

   F. *F* A new hybrid potato, not the wild hairy potato, has reduced by 40 to 60 percent the aphid population, not all insects.

   G. *T*

   H. *T*
4. A. *F* It is the quality of a Stradivarius violin that cannot be matched by any other violin.

   B. *T*

   C. *T*

   D. *F* There is no mention of Stradivari having written down his secret for making violins.

   E. *F* It was the type of varnish, not the color, that produced the quality.

   F. *T*

   G. *F* Each Stradivarius violin costs hundreds of thousands of dollars.

   H. *T*
5. A. *F* There are six colors in total. The multicolored one is included in the six.

   B. *F* The kernels were ground into cornmeal.

   C. *T*

   D. *F* There is nothing in the passage to indicate that the colonists' experimentation with cornmeal was related to a dislike of the Native Americans' meal.

E. *F* There is nothing in the passage to indicate that the colonists introduced succotash and mush to the Native Americans.

F. *T*

G. *T*

H. *F* The common forms of cornmeal are found nationwide.

EXERCISE R10 *(p. 183)*

1. D 2. A 3. B 4. D 5. B

EXERCISE R11 *(p. 185)*

1. S	3. S	5. D	7. D
2. S	4. D	6. S	8. S

EXERCISE R12 *(p. 186)*

1. Europa, one of Jupiter's moons, is the only place in the solar system (unequaled in the solar system) – outside of Earth (with one exception) – where enormous quantities of water (vast oceans) are known to exist.
2. . . . A single discharge (a lightning bolt) can actually (it is possible) contain twenty or more successive strokes (a series of bolts). . . . Some seem to stretch for 500 miles (which seems very large).
3. . . . they (porpoises) frequently leap out of the water (travel through the air) to escape the pull of surface drag (air, which creates less drag than water). At that point, leaping out of the water (traveling through the air) actually requires less energy (conserve energy) than swimming.
4. . . . During the flare-up, strong winds blowing off the surface of the star disperse the surrounding dust (scatter the dust particles) and expose the newborn star (allow the birth of a star to be seen) to observers (people who see) on Earth.
5. Perhaps the greatest navigators (expert sailors) in history were the Vikings (the Vikings were).
6. . . . Today, dolphins do such dangerous and necessary work (important task) as locating explosives (find mines) hidden in the sea.
7. . . . trained them (Saint Bernards) to search for travelers lost in snowstorms or avalanches (aided travelers) in the Alps. For hundreds of years, (for centuries) Saint Bernards served this purpose (aided travelers).
8. . . . Out on Lake Biwa, participants attempt to break records by flying (fly) their own inventions (craft they have designed themselves).

EXERCISE R13 *(p. 188)*

1. (A) and (D) It is not the brain that faints.

   *(B)

   (C) It is not the brain that causes the drop in the blood supply.

2. (A) It is not vegetarians that treat gorillas and small animals gently, but gorillas that treat small animals gently.

   (B) All gorillas are vegetarians, not just some.

   (C) Gorillas have been observed behaving in a gentle manner, not the small creatures.

   *(D)

3. (A) The crews do not dig a fire; they dig a fire line.

   (B) It is not the fire that varies the fire line, but the crews who vary the fire line according to the strength and nature of the fire.

   *(C)

   (D) "Depend on" means "rely on." Crews do not rely on fighting fires to dig a line. The result of the fire line is determined by the strength and nature of the fire.

4. (A) It is not the well educated who promise cures, but the medical quacks.

   *(B)

   (C) All people are promised cures, not only the well educated.

   (D) It is not the medical profession that has appealed to the well educated, but the promise of cures that has appeal for even the well educated.

5. (A) It is not the tsetse fly that kills the parasitic protozoa, but the tsetse fly that carries the parasitic protozoa.

   (B) The tsetse fly carries the parasitic protozoa, not the silver compound.

   (C) Parasitic protozoa cause the sleeping sickness, not the tsetse fly.

   *(D)

6. *(A)

   (B) Six out of thirty-seven stories were published, all were written.

   (C) Only six stories were published.

   (D) There is no information concerning the topic of the six accepted stories.

7. (A) It is the convection currents that behave like conveyor belts driving the plates, not the plates.

   *(B)

   (C) It is the convection currents that are in the hot magma and that behave as conveyor belts.

   (D) The earth's crustal plates cannot propose a theory.

8. (A) Medical authorities are reluctant to support the views.

   (B) This statement might be inferred, but it is not a restatement of the sentence that medical authorities are reluctant to support the nutritionists' findings.

   *(C)

   (D) Medical authorities have not supported the findings that vitamin C may prevent the common cold.

9. *(A)

   (B), (C), and (D) Female cowbirds can teach songs by responding to certain chirps.

10. *(A)

    (B) The conflict is of interest not only to those who want to abolish the last remnants of wilderness but to those who want to save it as well.

    (C) There is no information about lawyers' involvement in this conflict.

    (D) The conflict is not about abolishing industry but about abolishing or maintaining wilderness areas.

EXERCISE R14 *(p. 191)*

1. A 2. B 3. B 4. C

Reading Mini-test 3 (p. 193)

1. (A) Borglum was the sculptor.

   (B) The men Borglum trained were not stone carvers.

   (C) The word "hired" indicates that the workers were paid.

   *(D) The passage states that Borglum hired "laid-off workers from the closed-down mines."

2. (A) Although sculpting four presidential faces was an achievement, there is no information concerning Borglum's attitude about it.

   (B) It is stated that this removal took place, but there is no information concerning Borglum's attitude about it.

   *(C) It is stated in the passage that Borglum was proud that no workers were killed or severely injured.

   (D) Although it is stated in the passage that his training of the labor force made the workers skillful at using dynamite, there is no information concerning Borglum's attitude about it.

3. (A) The materials were mixed, not used in separate attempts to cover cracks.

   *(B) Borglum himself invented the mixture to fill the cracks that couldn't be avoided.

   (C) The sentence is discussing how the unavoidable cracks were dealt with, not how Borglum avoided the cracks.

   (D) Borglum did not buy the mixture, he made it himself from a formula he invented.

4. (A) The passage does not discuss air pollution, but natural seasonal climate changes.

   (B) There is no mention of polishing as being part of the maintenance proceedure.

   (C) The work is not restoring the faces, but maintaining them.

   *(D) Mount Rushmore is repaired every autumn, or "periodically."

5. (A) It is stated that the people came from the Black Hills area.

   *(B) The author concentrates on the work involved in making and maintaining the heads but does not mention why Borglum undertook this work.

   (C) It is stated that Borglum dealt with the fissures using a concoction of his own making.

   (D) It is stated that repairs are made to the monument every autumn.

6. (A) The earliest artifacts from over two thousand years ago indicate the existence of an earlier city on the site.

   (B) The size of the population is not related to the finds being dispersed.

   (C) Urbanized areas include residential areas, but this is not related to the finds being dispersed.

   *(D) Dispersed finds are those that are scattered throughout a region. These finds show the influence of surrounding areas.

7. (A) Although the city was abandoned, there is no information as to where the people went.

   (B) Although a depletion of resources is mentioned, there is no information about a famine.

   (C) The sacking by adversaries is stated as a possibility, not a known fact.

   *(D) It is stated in the passage that it is not clear what caused the city's decline.

8. (A) The apartment compounds were on both sides of the avenue.

(B) The avenue passed through the center of the urban area and the Great Compound complexes.

(C) The avenue was a primary axis.

*(D) The symmetrical layout around the avenue indicates planning from the very beginning.

9. (A) The feature is not made up of steps, but looks like steps.

(B) The vertical panels do not give the appearance of steps, it is the series of walls and vertical panels that give the appearance of steps.

(C) The word "taluds" refers to sloping apron walls, and "tableros" refers to vertical panels. This is not the name of the architectural feature.

*(D) The series of *taluds* and *tableros* makes up the steplike appearance of the pyramidal platforms.

10. *(A) There is no mention of market streets.

(B) Finds of the image of the rain god Tlaloc are religious artifacts.

(C) The Pyramids are ceremonial structures.

(D) The apartment compounds made up residential districts.

11. *(A) The first camera obscura was the natural phenomenon of light entering a hole in a wall and creating an image on the opposite wall.

(B) The image projected in a box was a later form of the camera obscura.

(C) The lens made the image clearer within the box. It was not projected onto a wall.

(D) A lens is mentioned as used in a box, not in a hole in the wall.

12. (A) Niépce's pictures were all negative images.

(B) Daguerre was the person who found a way to make positive images.

*(C) Daguerre found a way to reverse the image to make positive prints, but at first he could not keep the images from getting darker.

(D) The fixed image did not need to be reversed.

13. (A) Eastman proposed the use of chemically coated paper film to replace glass plates.

(B) The prints were not light-sensitive. The paper was.

(C) The clear, sharp, positive prints on paper discussed in the passage were those made with the chemically coated glass plates.

*(D) Eastman manufactured the first lightweight camera that people could carry and use.

14. (A) The chemicals are only sensitive to red, green, and blue light.

(B) This information is correct, but it fails to include the important information that all colors can be made from the three mentioned colors.

(C) This information is correct, but it does not include the color film and layers of chemicals.

*(D) The layers of chemicals that are used to make up color film are sensitive to three colors of light, red, green, and blue, and these colors can be used to make all colors.

15. *(A) Although Johann Heinrich Schulze discovered a mixture that became darker when subjected to light, the passage does not indicate that he was working on this mixture to produce photographic images.

(B) Joseph Nicéphore Niépce made the first permanent photographic image.

(C) Louis Daguerre found the way to fix the image.

(D) George Eastman developed the portable camera.

16. (A) The number of lives lost and the number left homeless are facts, not myths.

*(B) The O'Leary cow story has been told to children.

(C) The costs of the fire are facts.

(D) How fast the fire spread and how much of Chicago was destroyed are facts.

17. (A) Some local boys were accused of smoking in the barn.

(B) Other people accused the boys.

*(C) It is stated that Peg Leg's testimony was questionable because his account had inconsistencies and he himself could have been suspected.

(D) Peg Leg invented the cow story. Other people came up with other possible culprits.

18. *(A) Since an asteroid shower could cause fires in many areas, the various fires support the theory.

(B) The fires were in neighboring states, not just the Chicago area.

(C) It is only a theory that asteroids were to blame.

(D) It is not mentioned in the sentence that the number of fires was unusual.

19. (A) The passage mentions near-drought conditions.

(B) The passage mentions densely packed wooden shacks.

(C) The passage mentions the undermanned fire department.

*(D) The populace was described as devastated, not as riotous.

20. (A) Mrs. O'Leary's cow did exist.
    (B) The story is folklore, not the cow.
    *(C) The passage states that the cow was a scapegoat for people to focus their frustrations on.
    (D) Mrs. O'Leary's cow was a real cow.

EXERCISE R15 *(p. 200)*

1. (A) Private individuals must be able to submit reports because two reports came from private individuals.
   (B) The reports were already published. This is understood from the phrase "three of the published reports."
   *(C) Three reports from official investigations and two from private individuals equals a total of five reports.
   (D) There is no information given on what the investigations covered.
2. (A) No information is given concerning how the villages were destroyed.
   *(B) Information must have been collected for the Institute of Anthropology to computerize it, and the villages must be in ruins if the plans are to restore them.
   (C) It is not the Native Americans who have the computers to store data but the Institute of Anthropology.
   (D) It is not the plans that need to be restored but the villages.
3. (A) This statement is contrary to the information given in the statement, which suggests that the European bees will make the African bees gentler. This may be an advantage.
   *(B) If the bees have "devastated" the beekeeping industry, they must be destructive, and if it is believed that the interbreeding might make them "gentler," they must not be gentle now.
   (C) The question of becoming gentler refers to the bees, not the industry.
   *(D) Both kinds of bees must live in Latin America if they are interbreeding there.
4. *(A) If "no partner" helps the male, then the female does not help him.
   *(B) If the nest is floating, it must be on water, and this suggests that the jacana is an aquatic bird.
   (C) The male protects and nurtures its chicks, but whether or not it protects its partner cannot be inferred. A partner probably doesn't need to be nurtured.
   (D) Mating is not mentioned.
5. (A) Elephants are being trapped as a result of farmers' clearing land, not by hunters.
   *(B) It can be inferred by the elephants' being trapped in forest enclaves that these must be their habitat, and these forests are being cleared away for agriculture or farming.
   *(C) Since the land cleared of forests is being used for agriculture, these farms would have to be crossed for an elephant to reach another forest area.
   (D) People are not trapping elephants for use. The elephants are unintentionally being trapped through the process of making space for more cropland.
6. (A) Since it is sunken ships that are being safeguarded, it is understood that they were already sunken and not made to sink by thieves.
   *(B) Sunken ships must contain something valuable for thieves to be interested in plundering them.
   (C) It is not the salvagers who are caught but the salvagers who are trying to protect the ships from adventurers or thieves.
   *(D) There must be more ways than electronic means to protect a ship because "other" means are also used.
7. *(A) The weeds known as gopher plants have been given the name "gasoline plant."
   (B) Although a gasoline substitute can be refined from the gasoline plant, there is no mention of replacing other sources of gasoline.
   *(C) The hydrocarbons in latex can be refined into substitutes for crude oil and gasoline. Therefore, hydrocarbons must contain something that can be made into a substitute for crude oil and gasoline.
   (D) It is the "milky latex" that contains hydrocarbons. It cannot be inferred that milk contains hydrocarbons.
8. (A) Since morphine is still being scraped from the poppy plant and since it has not been profitably synthesized, it must still be profitable to cultivate.
   *(B) If morphine is unsurpassed for controlling pain, it must be more effective than any other drug, including cocaine.
   (C) Although morphine has been used for at least 5,000 years, it cannot be inferred that its use was for controlling pain.
   (D) If morphine is not yet profitably synthesized, then artificial morphine cannot be made economically.

EXERCISE R16 *(p. 202)*

1. Unlike other toads, the male golden toad is nearly voiceless; which is as effective as croaking in luring females during the mating season.
2. Besides earthquakes and volcanos, torrential rains, encroaching tropical vegetation, and time have all taken their toll.
3. medical authorities are skeptical of the treatment
4. powerful legs; lacks the barbules that are needed to lock feathers into a flat vane; head is crowned by a leathery helmet that protects it when it is charging through the jungle.
5. Away from the master carver, who dictated what was to be carved . . .
6. Members of both sexes; learn the art of sword fighting in mock combat
7. Computer-generated motion pictures allow the viewer to see the meaning of data and complex relationships instantly and are a new aid to human understanding.
8. not recommended for beginners
9. Nowhere else, except perhaps in tropical coral reefs, is nature so great in its diversity of organisms.
10. Champion athletes combine new heights of athleticism with the elegance of dance.

EXERCISE R17 *(p. 204)*

1. *Yes* If communities are discovering that they are living near toxic waste dumps, then they must not have known it in the first place because no one told them.
2. *Yes* E. B. White must have been well known if his death was cause for sadness in millions of homes.
3. *No* Although a firestorm may have caused the dinosaurs to disappear, it was not necessarily the cause of their disappearance. Some other catastrophe may have been responsible for the dinosaurs' extinction.
4. *Yes* There were twelve deaths and three were not linked to fresh fruits and vegetables. The remaining nine were linked to fresh foods. The deaths were sulfite-associated and, therefore, the fresh foods must have been contaminated with sulfite.
5. *No* Other antibiotics may still be useful for other kinds of illnesses.
6. *Yes* If actions such as walking and grasping may be impossible for those people who have had nerves damaged, then the nervous system must be important for muscle control.

EXERCISE R18 *(p. 205)*

1. A. _I_ Individuals who have shown outstanding talents in a field must be known. Since these awards are given to such people, it can be inferred that those who are not already known will not receive an award.

   B. _I_ The last sentence in the passage implies that some people might attain success because they worry about money.

   C. _R_ Large grants are given to individuals to allow them time to devote to creative "thinking."

2. A. _I_ The phrase "attempting to solve" suggests that the CDC is not always successful.

   B. _R_ "To crisscross the country" means "to travel back and forth across the nation."

   C. _I_ If patterns and common links among the victims are found during epidemics, it can be inferred that it is through the extra data collected that the patterns emerge.

3. A. _R_ On the basis of the amount of light absorbed and reflected, astronomers determined that comets contain frozen water.

   B. _I_ It can be inferred that since the ice content in Comet Bowell was determined by measuring the light it absorbed and reflected, the ice content in other comets can also be determined.

   C. _R_ The name given for the comet that astronomers were observing was Comet Bowell.

4. A. _R_ "Must be removed" means "not left," and "prevent the spread of disease" means "stop other bees from being sick."

   B. _R_ If the corpses emit a chemical that signals death, then the chemical that is emitted signals to the honeybees that a death has occurred.

   C. _R_ "Within an hour" means "in less than one hour."

5. A. _I_ If the availability of petroleum products is a factor in the reduced demand for seal oil, the implication is that products that were made from seal oil are now made from petroleum.

   B. _I_ Because petroleum products are more available, we can infer that the petroleum to make those products is probably easier to obtain than seal oil.

   C. ___ Although the northern elephant seal has made a dramatic comeback, there is no information concerning how numerous they are.

6. A. _R_ "More than the severe cold [the harsh climate], the lack [scarcity] of resources for food, clothing, and shelter defines [influences] the lifestyles [living conditions]."

B. _I_ It can be inferred from the words "probably descended from" that their ancestry is not known for certain.

C. ___ One cannot make any inference from the information in this passage whether there is more or less sunshine the further north one is.

7. A. _I_ If scientists could tell whether an astronaut who suffers from car sickness will suffer from space sickness, they would not be attempting to find a way to predict who was susceptible.

B. _R_ "It [space sickness] interferes with [causes problems or makes difficult] the important work that must be done [work the astronauts do]."

C. _R_ "Akin to" means "related to."

8. A. _R_ If a white shark belongs to the mackerel shark family, it is a kind of mackerel shark.

B. _I_ If the white shark did not attack people, it would not have a terrifying reputation.

C. _I_ If the shark does not eat people, as the evidence suggests, it must kill them for other reasons. Also, "mindless ferocity" implies that the shark attacks for no discernible reason.

9. A. _R_ An inchworm is a geometrid. "Extends itself forward" means "stretching forward," "draws its back end up to its front legs" means "moving its back to its front," and "repeats the sequence" means "repeating this process."

B. _I_ If only some caterpillars are called *earth measurers*, or *inchworms*, it can be inferred that not all caterpillars are inchworms.

C. _R_ The caterpillars called *geometrids* are commonly know as *inchworms*.

10. A. _I_ The Merlin must be a kind of aircraft because it is compared with a helicopter or small plane and it "takes off and hovers."

B. _I_ If the Merlin is safer than a helicopter or small plane because it has no exposed blades, it must be the exposed blades that make some aircraft unsafe.

C. ___ There is no information given concerning the production of the Merlin. The passage could simply be describing the design or a model of the Merlin, not a Merlin that has actually been produced.

EXERCISE R19 *(p. 208)*

1. D   2. B   3. A   4. C

EXERCISE R20 *(p. 209)*

1.*(A) Along the coast would be at sea level, where the races must be slower if racing is faster at high altitudes.

(B) An indoor track could be in an area at sea level or at a higher altitude.

(C) and (D) A high plateau and near the snowline of a volcano are both high-altitude areas, where the racing would be faster, not slower.

2. (A) While an owner may think it amusing to trick an expert, there would be no need for the owner to do so.

*(B) An owner could hang a copy of a valuable painting so that in the case of a theft, the real painting would not be taken.

(C) If owners want to encourage talented artists, they would do so through other means, such as buying an original work by those artists or encouraging them to paint something special.

(D) If owners enjoyed buying fake paintings, they would probably do this instead of spending a lot of money on valuable paintings.

3. (A), (B), and (C) These are all places where a law enforcement official could use a dog for detecting drugs, but only if he were suspicious that drugs were in use.

*(D) A law enforcement official would always be on the lookout for possible smuggling of drugs into a country and might, therefore, use such a trained dog.

4. (A) There is no information that implies that a Steiner school does not include academic subjects.

(B) A game that is not competitive could be played in a coeducational (boys and girls together) school.

*(C) A contest suggests a competition, and this kind of activity is discouraged in a Steiner school.

(D) A school that is practicing mixed-ability teaching is teaching children with different abilities; therefore, the children are probably at different levels.

5.*(A) If the bacteria can destroy the cyanide, a toxic waste dumped into rivers, then the bacteria can save the water life by getting rid of this poison.

(B) The bacteria destroy cyanide, not fish.

(C) Cyanide is not put into swimming pools; therefore, the bacteria would not serve a purpose there.

(D) The bacteria were exposed to increasing levels of cyanide. An increase of cyanide in the chemical plants is not desirable.

EXERCISE R21 *(p. 211)*

1. (A) The term "chicks" can refer to any baby bird, not just chickens.

   (B) Seals do not build nests in trees.

   *(C) The words "nests," "molts," "chicks," "hatch," and "plumage" all refer to birds.

   (D) Bears do not build nests in trees.

2.*(A) Since the female molts (loses her feathers) inside the nest, the nest is probably lined with those feathers.

   (B) The female probably loses her feathers in order to make the nest, not because the nest is too warm.

   (C) After the female molts, she seals herself into the nest; she does not break it up.

   (D) To lose feathers by molting is different from losing feathers by plucking them out. The female probably uses her feathers to make the nest warm. The passage states she uses mud and dung to seal the nest.

3. (A) There is no information to indicate that the male forces the female into the nest. Both birds seal the opening.

   (B) If sealing the nest happened by accident, it would be exceptional rather than the typical behavior of the species.

   *(C) The female probably seals herself in on purpose for laying her eggs and hatching the chicks.

   (D) There is no information to indicate that the female is protecting her eggs from the male as opposed to other predators.

4. (A) The baby chicks can be fed, but eggs cannot.

   (B) The male helps seal in the female.

   (C) It is not plumage that keeps the chicks safe, but sealing the nest that keeps the chicks safe.

   *(D) Since the male is outside of the sealed nest, he cannot hatch the eggs by keeping them warm.

5. (A) The rivers from two Canadian provinces drain into the Mississippi River. Drainage areas in Canada are not mentioned.

   (B) Thirty-one states out of all the states in the United States have rivers that drain into the Mississippi.

   (C) If only parts of some states have rivers that drain into the Mississippi, there are probably other rivers in other parts of those states that drain elsewhere.

   *(D) If the Mississippi extends to Canada and flows down to the sea carrying sand, silt, and clay, probably some of the silt the river is carrying comes from Canada.

6.*(A) Since the delta system provides shelter and nutrients for the continent's most fertile marine nursery, it must be very important to marine life.

   (B) "Nursery" in the passage means a place where marine life grows, not a nursery for children.

   (C) There is no information about diseases caused by mosquitoes and other insects in the passage.

   (D) There is no information about the United States government establishing nurseries.

7. (A) It is not being destroyed but being built up.

   *(B) If the delta is constantly being built up by the river deposits of sand, silt, and clay, it is probably always changing.

   (C) It is not the sea movement but the river deposits that are building up the delta.

   (D) The delta is being built on the continental shelf. The continental shelf is already there.

8.*(A) The phrase "carries about 5 gallons of fuel" implies that ultralights have an engine that uses fuel.

   (B) If human energy were used, then there would be no need for fuel.

   (C) If an ultralight were powered by remote control, there would be no need for a pilot.

   (D) No mention is made of solar energy in the passage.

9. (A) There is no information given as to where the kits can be bought.

   *(B) If ultralights are sold as kits and take about 40 hours to assemble, people can probably buy their own kit and assemble it.

   (C) Although a person without experience can fly an ultralight, it doesn't mean that people in general who fly ultralights have no experience.

   (D) If a person can buy a kit and assemble it, there is probably no need to have training in aviation to do this.

10. (A) There is no information given as to whether or not ultralights are registered.

   (B) "Rarely fatal" means that they are not frequently fatal.

   *(C) If an accident is rarely fatal or even serious, the pilots can probably walk away from most of the accidents.

   (D) Fatal accidents rarely occur.

Reading Mini-test 4 (p. 213)

1. (A) The author does not discuss whether Epstein's sculpture is good or bad.

   (B) The author does not ridicule or scorn Epstein's work.

   (C) The author does not make any amusing comments.

   *(D) The author states that artists and critics praised his works, that it now receives the recognition it deserves, and that Epstein is considered one of the major sculptors.

2. (A) Although the public tastes were offended, it cannot be inferred that he let their opinions influence him.

   *(B) It is stated in the passage that critics noted the "influence on it of primitive and ancient sculptural motifs from Africa."

   (C) Although Epstein had Russian parents, it cannot be inferred that Russian paintings influenced his work.

   (D) It cannot be inferred that the Rhodesian government's dislike for the sculpture affected Epstein's future work.

3. (A) It is stated in the passage that today Epstein's work has received the recognition it deserves, and therefore, we can conclude that it wouldn't be mutilated.

   (B) It cannot be inferred that because the work has received recognition, it is because it conforms to public tastes. Perhaps public tastes have changed.

   *(C) Because Epstein's work has received the recognition it deserves, it would probably be well received.

   (D) It is stated that Epstein's first commission was of expressive distortion. It cannot not be inferred that all his works are expressive.

4. (A) It is stated that one of Epstein's sculptures was mutilated. The author does not mean that others have been defaced.

   (B) This statement could include all artists' important works of art. The author is only discussing Epstein's works.

   (C) It is stated that the figures of one sculpture offended public tastes because of nudity. The author does not discuss why other works have incited criticism.

   *(D) The author means that other sculptures of Epstein's have been criticized.

5. (A) It cannot be inferred that there is a relationship between small theaters not being able to afford sound effect machines and what they paid their musicians.

   *(B) The word "These" refers to the music and sound effects in the earliest films. These sounds were made by the musicians the author mentions.

   (C) The mentioned musicians were those playing in a pre–*Jazz Singer* era.

   (D) The musicians played to accompany early films. This does not refute any claim about the date of the first film with sound.

6. (A) Some theaters had a pianist, but others had a band or orchestra. There is no information about which was the most common.

   (B) Since only larger theaters could afford sound-effect machines, they were probably not common.

   (C) There is no indication that orchestras were even required to synchronize sound.

   *(D) It is stated that the newly invented gramophone was used as early as 1896 and the earliest public performances of films were in 1896.

7. (A) and (C) The variation in speed was a problem with the projector, not the gramophone.

   (B) The disk for the gramophone is mentioned as being large, but there is no mention of the size of the gramophone itself being too large for theaters.

   *(D) The gramophone was invented in 1896, and there were difficulties with the needle jumping.

8. (A) The sound signals were placed alongside the images, not the system.

   (B) Sound-effect machines were used from the earliest films. The equipment for synchronization was developed in 1922.

   *(C) Since the synchronization system is mentioned as eventually bringing us "talking pictures," it was an important development.

   (D) It was the signal system that guaranteed synchronization, not the synchronization that guaranteed the production of short films.

9. *(A) The sentence "This system [that was used in short films] eventually brought us 'talking pictures'" indicates that short feature films came first.

   (B) There is no mention of what happened to the musicians.

   (C) The optical sensors read the signals for sound.

   (D) The gramophone is mentioned as only being effective for dialogue sequences.

10. (A) The error of the horns effect is slanted toward the negative, whereas that of the halo effect is slanted toward the positive.

    *(B) The misjudgment is the same. It is only the outcome that is different.

(C) Focusing on bad traits does not show how the error is the same

(D) This is the result of the error, not how the error is the same.

11. (A) The halo effect from the very intelligent applicant would affect the interviewer's perception of this person negatively.

(B) The halo effect from the well-dressed and confident applicant would affect the interviewer's perception of this person negatively.

*(C) The applicant with apparent flaws would probably be judged less capable than the well-dressed, confident applicant. This is because of the horns effect.

(D) The primary effect from the applicant who is both confident and well-dressed would affect the interviewer's perception of this person negatively.

12. (A) The author would not agree with this because first impressions have been found to be unrelated to the aptitude of the candidate.

(B) The appearance referred to in the passage concerns the applicant, not the interviewer.

(C) The author would agree to this, but would want the interviewer to do more than just be aware of this fact.

*(D) The author would agree that since the interview is a bad way to decide on an applicant, the interviewer should find a better way to choose an applicant.

13. (A) It is unlikely that the author would return to discussing other misjudgments after introducing the topic of better procedures.

(B) It is unlikely that the author would return to giving more information on kinds of judgments after introducing the topic of better procedures.

*(C) The passage ends with the author introducing the topic of tests designed to measure cognitive ability. The next paragraphs would probably be about these tests.

(D) Since it is stated that interviewing is inadequate, the author probably won't discuss the procedures used in interviewing.

EXERCISE R22 *(p. 217)*

1. A. N	2. A. N	3. A. S	4. A. D
B. S	B. D	B. N	B. N
C. D	C. S	C. D	C. S

EXERCISE R23 *(p. 218)*

1. B, D, F
2. B, C, F
3. A, C, D
4. C, E, F

EXERCISE R24 *(p. 222)*

1. Underground Homes: A, D
   Conventional Homes: B, E
2. Early Forms of Dueling: D, E
   Later Forms of Dueling: A, C
3. Ringtaw: A, D
   Fortification: C, E
4. Artificial Resort: A, D
   Traditional Resort: C, E
5. Creatures Found to Exist: D, E, H
   Creatures That Perhaps Don't Exist: A, B, F, I
6. One of the First Four Stages: A, D, G, I
   Final Stage: C, F, H

Reading Mini-test 5 *(p. 227)*

1. (A) The area that Rogers came from and his origins are details in the passage.

*(B) This was the start of Rogers' climb to fame.

(C) The information about the Ziegfeld Follies is a detail.

*(D) These are characteristics that made Rogers a much loved personality.

*(E) Rogers' being mourned by so many people shows that he was loved and admired.

(F) Rogers' epitaph is a detail.

2.*(A) This is a description of the first way music was made to create a mood.

(B) The information about Camille Saint-Saëns is a detail.

*(C) Synchronization of sound and image is a change that took place in the history of cinema.

(D) These movies are mentioned as examples.

*(E) Music underlying dialogues and being heard in the background were developments that took place.

(F) The characteristics of audiences throughout the growth of the cinema is not mentioned in the passage.

3. **Xerophytes**

   B. Internal characteristics ("internal gums and mucilages") allow water to be held ("water-retaining properties").

   D. Xerophytes "have spines instead of leaves."

   F. The long roots ("extensive root systems") spread out ("radiate out") close to the surface of the ground ("shallow").

   Phraetophytes

   C. Small leaves ("tiny leaves") open to collect water ("open them at night when they can absorb moisture") and close to retain it close their pores during the day to avoid water loss).

   E. The smell and taste of the plant is unpleasant for predators ("some phraetophytes depend on their unpleasant smell and taste for protection").

   G. The roots stretch deep into the ground ("extremely long root systems that draw water from the water table deep underground").

   I. Two sets of root systems ("a double-root system") to collect ground and surface water.

   Not used:

   A. Storage difficulties are not discussed in the passage.

   H. This is a detail about cactus, not about survival tactics.

Reading Section Practice Test (p. 231)

Note: If you answered an item incorrectly, complete the exercises listed for that item.

1. (B) The passage states that slime molds "were regarded as organisms of ambiguous taxonomic status." See Exercises R9–R14.
2. (D) To "ingest" or "consume" bacteria means to eat it as food. See Exercises R1–R3.
3. (C) The passage states that "Their uniqueness lies in an unusual life cycle, which alternates between a feeding stage in which the organism is essentially unicellular and a reproductive stage in which the organism adapts a multicellular structure." See Exercises R9–R14.
4. (A) The passage states that "the organism initiates a new genetic program that permits the cells to eventually find a new, food-rich environment." See Exercises R9–R14.
5. [A] The word "Starvation" refers to "become starved" in the preceding sentence and explains when this occurs. See Exercises R4–R8.
6. (D) An "entity" or "unit" is an assemblage of parts, or as in this case, members. See Exercises R1–R3.
7. (A) There are two distinct kinds of cells. Other cells form prespore cells. See Exercises R4–R8.
8. (C) The author does not mention legs. The organism moves like a slug and then changes to a fungi-like form on a stalk. See Exercises R4–R8.
9. (D) When something bears fruit, it is at the stage where the next generation is produced. The author is referring to the organism as being ready to release its spores. See Exercises R15–R21.
10. (B) After the spores that form the head ("the head develops into spores") are scattered around the area ("are dispersed into the environment"), they develop ("form") into a new generation ("the next generation") of amoebae cells. See Exercises R9–R14.
11. (A) Developmental biologists are interested in this transformation because it is similar "to an important process found in higher organisms in which organs with highly specialized functions are formed from unspecialized stem cells." See Exercises R15–R21.
12. (A) The passage states the DNA approach "has essentially backed up the results of the earlier dye studies." See Exercises R9–R14.
13. **Unspecialized Cells**

    (B) The passage states that the organism is unicellular during the feeding stage.

    (F) The passage states that "This mass [the cells that have come together] sticks together through the secretion of adhesion molecules."

    (G) The passage states that "Once a favorable location has been found with a fresh source of bacteria to feed on, the migration stops."

    (H) The passage states that "a few of the amoebae start to produce periodic chemical pulses that are detected, amplified, and relayed to the surrounding members, which then move toward the pulse origin."

    Specialized Cells

    (D) The passage states that "the back cells climb up the stalk and form a spherical-shaped head, known as the sorocarp."

    (E) The passage states that "The head develops into spores, which are dispersed."

    (I) The passage states that "The front cells turn into a stalk, and the back cells climb up the stalk and form a spherical-shaped head."

    See Exercises R22–R24.
14. (C) The "path" of something is the direction in which it travels. See Exercises R1–R3.

15. (A) "This phenomenon" refers to the movement of icebergs "to the right side of the direction in which the wind blew." See Exercises R4–R8.
16. (A) To "rotate" is to "spin" or "turn" around an axis or central point. See Exercises R1–R3.
17. (C) All points on the planet travel once around the Earth in a single day. Thus the rotational velocity is the same at different latitudes. See Exercises R15–R21.
18. (D) The author points out the linear speed of a point on the Earth depends on its distance from the equator. See Exercises R9–R14.
19. (B) The passage states that an object in the Northern Hemisphere near the equator travels faster than an object further north, where the distance around the Earth is less than at the equator. See Exercises R9–R14.
20. [B] The transitional phrase "And conversely" indicates that the sentence contains some information showing an opposite tendency to the previous sentence. An object traveling northward, away from the equator, travels relatively faster. The converse means that it travels relatively more slowly as it travels southward. See Exercises R4–R8.
21. (D) The passage states that at a depth of about 150 meters water moves in the opposite direction to the surface water. See Exercises R9–R14.
22. (B) Paragraph 4 gives an explanation of how the Coriolis force changes the direction of water flow. See Exercises R9–R14.
23. (A) To "deflect" is to "turn" to one side. See Exercises R1–R3.
24. (D) The information about the movement of icebergs in paragraph 1 and the description of the water deflection in paragraph 4 indicate that it is the Coriolis force that deflects ocean water. See Exercises R15–R21.
25. (A) The passage mentions how the marine ecosystem is affected by water taking the place of water displaced in the Ekman spiral. See Exercises R9–R14.
26. (B), (D), and (E) The Coriolis force results from the Earth's rotation and the fact that the linear speed (distance traveled in a given time) of a point on the Earth's surface is slower the further it is from the equator. This causes an object moving away from (or toward) the equator to be deflected to the right in the Northern Hemisphere and to the left in the Southern Hemisphere. Ocean currents are deflected at an angle with respect to the prevailing wind because of the Coriolis force. Water at successively deeper levels is further deflected in respect to the layers above it, creating a spiral. See Exercises R22–R24.
27. (C) When two armies are "engaged," they are involved in a "battle." See Exercises R1–R3.
28. (B) The passage states that the Confederates' "weaker manufacturing capacity and transportation infrastructure led ultimately to defeat." See Exercises R15–R21.
29. (C) Part of Lee's plan was to lure or entice the Northern army to fight in an exposed or vulnerable position. See Exercises R9–R14.
30. (D) The phrase "aimed at increasing the war weariness of the North" implies that the North was tired of waging war. See Exercises R15–R21.
31. (C) In paragraphs 1 and 2, the invasion of the North by the Confederate army indicates that the Union had to defend itself. In paragraph 3, the passage discusses the defensive positions that the Union took. See Exercises R15–R21.
32. (B) "This crest" refers to the "long rise of land" known as Cemetery Ridge. See Exercises R4–R8.
33. (A) The author is giving a description of what the Union army position may have looked like if it were drawn on a map or seen from the air. See Exercises R15–R21.
34. (D) "Devastating" or "ruinous" means the number of casualties was disastrous. See Exercises R1–R3.
35. (D) The strength of the Confederate infantry was probably great, considering 13,000 men were involved in the charge. See Exercises R9–R14.
36. [D] The word "They" refers to the 13,000 men charging across the open land. See Exercises R4–R8.
37. (D) The passage states that "Both sides had suffered excessive losses of men." See Exercises R9–R14.
38. (C) Because Pickett's Charge failed and the Confederates did not capture Northern territory, they were unable to reach their objectives of weakening the Union army and increasing war weariness, and they had to take on a defensive strategy without adequate manufacturing and transportation infrastructure. See Exercises R9–R14.
39. (B), (E), and (F) The main outlines of the battle were as follows: Two days of fighting failed to lead to a successful outcome for either side. Reinforcements strengthened the positions of both armies, which formed lines facing each other. On the final day, the Confederate army attacked the defensive positions of the Union army, but was unsuccessful. After this failure, the Confederates retreated back to the South. See Exercises R22–R24.

PART 2 BUILDING SKILLS: Listening

EXERCISE L1 *(p. 255, script on p. 592)*

Your answers may be stated differently, but they should contain all the information included here.

1. We need to put alternative medicines under the same investigation as we do to medicines being developed to confirm their efficacy.
2. The brain has the tendency to interpret vague images as specific ones.
3. The savagery of the Mongols was moderated because the tribute they lived on could only come from prosperous subjects.
4. Alliteration, the technique of repeating the initial consonant sounds, is a common poetic device.

EXERCISE L2 *(p. 256, script on p. 592)*

Your answers may be stated differently, but they should contain all the information included here.

1. the endosperm of the seed
2. He doubts that the average person understands the difference between science and pseudoscience.
3. Universal units of time are not accurate enough for modern measurement.
4. When that which is purchased will be worth more than the amount of money borrowed.

EXERCISE L3 *(p. 257, script on p. 592)*

1. B 2. B 3. A 4. A

EXERCISE L4 *(p. 259)*

1. people ← they
   abracadabra ← this word
2. subject matter → frontier life
   her → Willa Cather
   Willa Cather ← her
3. a drying time → 6 to 8 weeks
   nutmeg ← its
   kernels ← their
4. his → Charles duc d'Orléans
   Charles duc d'Orléans ← his
   sending love letters ← this

EXERCISE L5 *(p. 260, script on p. 593)*

1. A. the one who wrote *Uncle Tom's Cabin*: Harriet Beecher Stowe
   B. he: President Lincoln
   C. her: Harriet Beecher Stowe
   D. her: Harriet Beecher Stowe
   E. the little lady who started the Civil War: Harriet Beecher Stowe
2. A. when: 1867
   B. he: William Seward
   C. it: Alaska
   D. the idea: purchasing Alaska
   E. that: that people thought purchasing Alaska was crazy and called it Seward's Folly
3. A. one thing: something interesting
   B. its: the English House of Lords
   C. something: that issue
   D. they: members of the English House of Lords
   E. they: members of the English House of Lords
4. A. it: the Turkish cultural arts exhibition
   B. These: events
   C. one: lecture
   D. that: traditional Turkish music

EXERCISE L6 *(p. 261, script on p. 593)*

1. A. this happening: the breakdown of the traditional family
   B. these people: the elderly
   C. these problems: no home and no family members to help
   D. their ideas: the delegates' ideas
2. A. the dream: to climb Mount Everest
   B. this climb: Mount Everest
   C. <u>these</u> are granted: permits
   D. a few groups: alpine clubs
3. A. He did <u>this</u>: invented the digital calculator
   B. a particular problem: the division of the French currency
   C. such divisions: the divisions of livres, sols, and deniers
   D. <u>which</u> are divisible: today's currencies

EXERCISE L7 *(p. 262, script on p. 594)*

Your answers may be stated differently.

1. <u>In contrast</u> – Large estates have become smaller plots as well as small landholdings becoming larger estates.

2. Consequently – Writers and speakers use connotations to persuade their audience because they have powerful associations.
3. However – Sea defenses built to prevent beach erosion may be the cause of coastal land erosion.
4. first – When the paper is written, follow this order: put it away and do something else.

   then – Go back to the paper.
5. important – Decomposition in organic matter releases and circulates minerals into the environment.

   In particular – Detritus feeders break down dead material.

EXERCISE L8 *(p. 263, script on p. 594)*

Your answers may be stated differently.

1. The dinosaurs were walking on a beach. There are families. The stride and speed, as well as the weight and height, can be calculated.
2. Pests attack a tree. The tree responds by changing its nutritional quality. It is thought that the attacked trees emit a chemical that warns other trees. The surrounding trees change their nutritional quality. This chemical could be used in pest control.
3. The types of caudal fins are rounded fins, soft and flexible, good for maneuvering and acceleration; forked fins, less drag than rounded fins, good for continuous swimming; and lunate fins, rigid, good for traveling long distances, not good for maneuvering.
4. A child riding a tricycle is compared to one riding a bicycle to explain static stability – the tricycle can stand by itself, whereas the bicycle cannot – and dynamic stability – a tricycle is not as stable in motion as a bicycle.

EXERCISE L9 *(p. 265, script on p. 595)*

1. the United Kingdom (The speaker will probably go on to give more facts about the United Kingdom.)
2. the Award for Architecture (The speaker will probably continue his talk by giving more information about the award. He may discuss the qualities an architect must have in order to be considered for the award.)
3. patterns of Irish linen (The speaker will probably continue to talk about the patterns as she displays the Irish linen.)
4. figures carved in hillsides (The speaker will probably talk about specific human- and animal-shaped figures.)
5. Professor Brown's talk on the geology of Mars (The speaker has attended the talk and will probably discuss it.)

EXERCISE L10 *(p. 266, script on p. 595)*

1. (A) Although the discussion may develop into the uses of acupuncture in the West, the talk will probably concentrate on the practice of acupuncture.

   (B) The topic sentence concerns acupuncture in China five thousand years ago, not modern China.

   *(C) The talk has begun with the topic of the practice of acupuncture and will probably continue to discuss the development of acupuncture throughout the centuries.

   (D) There is no mention of arthritis or its cures.
2. (A) Although fabric is made up of threads called fibers, the fibers in the topic sentence concern those of the muscles.

   *(B) The talk begins with a description of muscles and will probably continue with more information about them.

   (C) Although muscle fiber is measured in millimeters, the talk will probably not continue with details about millimeters.

   (D) The length of muscle fiber is mentioned, but the talk will probably not continue with details about lengths in general.
3. (A) The talk mentions satellite-communications technology, not communications technology in general.

   (B) The challenges mentioned are those in education, not in communications.

   (C) The satellites are those of communications, not education.

   *(D) The talk will probably expand on the possibilities and challenges in education that satellites have opened up.
4. (A) This seminar covers a specific period of time in Spanish literature.

   (B) Although this is a Spanish course, it is a specific course.

   (C) Historical events are mentioned in the context of the period of time when the Golden Age of Spanish literature flourished.

   *(D) The professor is probably explaining to the seminar class what the course will be about. He will probably continue to give the students more information concerning the Golden Age of Spanish literature.

5.*(A) Because influenza is emphasized by its being discussed in the main clause, the speaker will probably talk more about its particular characteristics.

(B) and (C) The common cold may be compared to influenza, but the emphasis will probably be on influenza.

(D) The speaker does not mention other diseases.

6. (A) It is not human protein but rather animal protein that is being introduced.

(B) Only one cause of malnutrition will probably be discussed.

(C) Only one world problem – malnutrition – is being introduced.

*(D) The talk will probably discuss the lack of animal protein in the diet of some peoples and the malnutrition that it causes.

EXERCISE L11 *(p. 267, script on p. 595)*

1. *Yes* (topic = magic squares)
2. *No* (topic = public zoos)
3. *No* (topic = the Pony Express)
4. *Yes* (topic = butterfly farm)
5. *No* (topic = gargoyles)

EXERCISE L12 *(p. 268, script on p. 596)*

Your answers may be stated differently.

1. development of a written system to describe dance movements
2. settlement of the New World
3. contemporary photography's lack of historical value
4. no official language in the United States

Listening Mini-test 1 *(p. 268, script on p. 597)*

1. (D) The woman asks the man about his job at the library. The man describes aspects of the job.
2. (B) The man tells the woman that he unpacks boxes of newly purchased books and it is like unwrapping presents. She thinks it would be fun to unpack the books.
3. (B) The man states that the worst thing is to attach the bar code.
4. (C) The talk begins by introducing Buffalo Bill (William Cody) and his Wild West Show. It goes on to discuss the performers in the show and those who saw the show.
5. (A) The given date is the year that William Cody founded the great Wild West Show.
6. (C) Chief Sitting Bull is mentioned as an example of the famous people who joined Buffalo Bill in his tour of Europe.
7. (B) The talk begins by introducing a new musical form in America, called ragtime. It goes on to discuss the musical features of ragtime, important ragtime composers, and how this musical form became popularized.
8. (C) According to the speaker, ragtime was a new musical form that captivated America just before the turn of the twentieth century.
9. (A) The professor discusses the regular beats of waltzes and polkas as a contrast to the main feature of ragtime, its syncopation or irregular beat.
10. (B) The discussion is mainly about the painting featured on the news broadcast.
11. (C) The curator on the news report said that the painting has been "out on unauthorized loan for three years." "Unauthorized loan" is a humorous way of saying it was stolen.
12. (D) Its small size makes it easy to conceal and take out of the museum.

EXERCISE L13 *(p. 275, script on p. 598)*

1. (B) It is not that the people in Homer's time used words from the Kárpathos dialect, but that the Kárpathos dialect of today uses words from the time of Homer.
2. (A) It is not the first hot-air balloon, but the first hot-air balloon flight that was piloted by a person on board.
3. (B) It is not that the word for "beautiful bird" means "tail feather," but that "quetzal," which is the name of a beautiful bird, means "tail feather."
4. (B) Twenty-two men did not cut off the escape route; they secured the escape route.
5. (A) It wasn't the areas themselves that set up the centers; the centers were set up in the areas.
6. (B) It is not our past that has been revolutionized, but our concepts about our past that have been revolutionized.
7. (B) It is not that explorers were unable to locate the island in March 1783, but that the island was described in March 1783.
8. (A) It was not dolphins, whales, and dead fish that were spotted. This suggests that only the fish were dead. Dead fish, dolphins, and whales were spotted. This suggests that creatures from all three groups were dead. Also, the dead creatures were reported by the authorities. The actual spotting could have been either by the authorities or by other people.

EXERCISE L14 *(p. 276, script on p. 598)*

1. [A] , [C] 2. [B], [D] 3. [A], [B] 4. [B], [C]

EXERCISE L15 *(p. 277, script on p. 599)*

1. A, B, D
2. A, B
3. A, D
4. B, C

EXERCISE L16 *(p. 278, script on p. 600)*

1.	2.	3.
A. *Yes*	A. *No*	A. *No*
B. *Yes*	B. *Yes*	B. *No*
C. *No*	C. *Yes*	C. *Yes*
D. *Yes*	D. *Yes*	D. *Yes*
E. *No*	E. *No*	E. *Yes*

EXERCISE L17 *(p. 280, script on p. 602)*

1. A. Prisms
   B. Plates
   C. Stars
2. A. Antiviral
   B. Antibacterial
   C. Antibacterial
3. A. Refrigerator
   B. Icehouse
   C. Icebox
4. A. Drops of water
   B. Drops of water
   C. Drops of water
   D. Flow of water
   E. Flow of water

Listening Mini-test 2 *(p. 281, script on p. 603)*

1. A. *Yes* The artificial chemical CFCs in the production of goods are first released into the atmosphere.

   B. *No* Although it is true that CFCs continue to be used for economic reasons in some parts of the world and that they affect the ozone layer, this is not a step in the process of ozone depletion.

   C. *Yes* The chemical reaction between oxygen atoms of the ozone layer and the CFCs is what is causing the depletion of the ozone layer.

   D. *Yes* This is how the CFCs get into the atmosphere.

   E. *No* This is a result of the depletion of the ozone, not a step in the process.

2. *(A) The professor states that for economic reasons, some countries are not enthusiastic about phasing out the production of CFCs.

   (B) It is not that she doesn't think the CFCs will disperse, but that she is concerned about their being dispersed.

   (C) The professor states that it is hoped the ozone layer will recover by the year 2060.

   (D) The professor states that aerosols are being phased out. This implies that alternatives are acceptable.

3. (A) The chemical reaction is not caused by ultraviolet rays. The reaction allows ultraviolet rays to reach the Earth's surface.

   (B) The CFCs in the atmosphere migrate to the stratosphere, not from the stratosphere.

   (C) The DNA of humans and plants do not contain artificial chemicals.

   *(D) The professor states that CFCs are components of certain products and are produced in various manufacturing processes.

4. *[A] CFCs are mentioned as a main component in dry-cleaning chemicals.

   *[B] CFCs are mentioned as being produced in nitrogen fertilizers.

   [C] Oxygen atoms are mentioned as combining with CFCs, not as being contaminants.

   [D] Ultraviolet light reaching the Earth is discussed as the consequences of the ozone depletion, not as a contaminant.

5. A. Brainwashing – The professor describes brainwashing as forcing someone to accept implanted ideas after losing a sense of reality.

   B. Subception – The experiment that increased the buying of ice cream after an unconscious intrusion was the result of subception.

   C. Hypnosis – The carrying out of a command at a given signal is a feature of post-hypnotic suggestion.

6. (A) There is no mention of this technique being used on unsuspecting people after the end of the experiment.

   *(B) Although the people were not aware that they saw the ad, it did affect them.

   (C) The ad that was shown to the people was not attempting to make people do something unethical. There is no indication that this technique can be used to do this.

   (D) The experiment was given special attention because it was evidence that people are unconsciously aware of things going on around them.

7. (A) People may forget what they were told in hypnosis, but they may never be aware that they were shown anything if exposed to the technique of subliminal perception.

   *(B) According to the speaker, people are not conscious that their minds are being influenced.

(C) People may be given a post-hypnotic suggestion to do something silly after they come out of a hypnotic trance.

(D) People who have been brainwashed are implanted with false ideas that they act upon in a way they would have thought unacceptable before the brainwashing experience.

8. *(A) The professor does not mention drugging in the list of brainwashing techniques used to break down an individual.

(B), (C), and (D) The professor states that the breaking down of an individual "is done through acts such as starving them, preventing them from sleeping, intimidating them, and keeping them in a state of constant fear."

9. A. *Yes* Whether or not they were feasible, they were an attempt to mimic nature.

B. *Yes* These devices mimic the seedpods that grasp animal fur for dispersal.

C. *No* The skeletons that soften to change shape are a feature of a creature whose properties could possibly be mimicked.

D. *No* Antlers are being investigated because of their natural strength. They are not an application of biomimetics.

E. *Yes* A substance that could copy photosynthesis to create energy would be mimicking plants.

10. *(A) The professor states that architects and engineers consciously model buildings on forms found in nature.

(B) The architects and engineers are those who have inventive ideas.

(C) The professor talks about the freedom of birds.

(D) The architects and engineers are not inspired by animals' and plants' problems, but how they have evolved solutions to problems.

11. (A) The professor does not consider the structures to be intelligent but talks about how the structures could be built to appear intelligent.

(B) The professor is discussing the similarity of the structures to intelligence, not to fashion.

*(C) The professor uses the term "smart" because structures that are able to design and repair themselves seem to have intelligence.

(D) The professor is not ridiculing the processes in the natural world but is discussing how those processes could be used effectively.

12. *[A] The high resistance that wood has to impacts would be a useful feature to mimic.

[B] There is no reason that biomimetics researchers would want to study the stimulus for inventive minds.

*[C] The structure that gives antler bone its toughness could be a useful feature to mimic.

[D] Biomimetic researchers would not be interested in studying the impact of their field in the twenty-first century.

13. (A) The professor states that the illegal art trade destroys the integrity of the overall work. She does not compare the illegal art trade with the illegal trade in weapons in terms of which is more devastating.

(B) The professor emphasizes that the illegal art trade equals that of the illegal trade in drugs in economic terms.

(C) The professor does not mention the Mafia.

*(D) The professor states that the illegal art trade equals the trafficking of both weapons and drugs in economic terms.

14. *[A] and *[C] The professor agrees with the man's point that inventories would only be useful if they were available for concerned organizations. The professor then gives examples of several organizations, such as the police, customs agencies, and insurance companies, that would find this information useful for stopping the illegal art trade.

[B] There is no mention of criminals getting into an electronic network to find valuable treasures.

[D] It would be unlikely that a tourist would read an inventory about cultural properties. A tourist would have to be informed in a different way about the illegal art trade.

15. [A] The professor mentions wealthy buyers but does not mention anything about bribery.

[B] Nothing is stated in the discussion about people being afraid of or even having knowledge of illegal art traders.

*[C] The professor states that original owners cannot always furnish an accurate description of their stolen property and, consequently, cannot prove ownership.

*[D] The professor mentions that a criminal could cut up a painting and sell parts of it. This would change the work of art so it might not be recognized.

16. *(A) The professor states that surveillance is not always affordable.

(B) The thieves' possible shrewdness in stealing objects under surveillance is not discussed.

(C) There is no mention of any particular treasures not being worth protecting from theft.

(D) There is no information on any particular government's stand on the issue of the depletion of their cultural treasures. It can be understood that it is an issue because of the mentioned law enforcement officials who are involved in combating the illegal art trade.

EXERCISE L18 *(p. 288, script on p. 606)*

1. *Yes* It is new research that has brought doubt about whether Mata Hari was a spy. Therefore, either a death sentence or prison sentence was probably given at the time of her trial.
2. *No* The woman is showing interest in the man's experience, but there is no indication that she wants to build a mud house herself.
3. *No* A fossil is the remains of a prehistoric creature or organism.
4. *Yes* The speaker's saying that further experiments need to be done before a decision is made concerning use on humans indicates that humans have not yet undergone the operation.

EXERCISE L19 *(p. 289, script on p. 607)*

1. (B) Research into the recurrence of polio may give those involved in medicine new insights in how to treat the disease.
2. (D) The man will probably sign up to take Italian in order to complete his foreign language requirement.
3. (A) Jean Muir's working with her staff to prepare twenty years' of materials suggests she wanted her fashion business to continue after her death.
4. (B) A way to motivate learners and encourage learning would be important for education majors.

EXERCISE L20 *(p. 290, script on p. 608)*

Your answers may be stated differently.

1. She's probably an art major.
2. To contrast the lasting enjoyment that children get from common objects with the short-term enjoyment that they get from high-tech toys.
3. The professor wants the students to take the opportunity to experience Spanish culture and language outside of the classroom.
4. Because there has been a violent incident on campus recently.

EXERCISE L21 *(p. 291, script on p. 609)*

1. A, D
2. B, D
3. B, C
4. A, C

EXERCISE L22 *(p. 292, script on p. 609)*

1. (D) The professor wants the students to think about the different arguments about the relationship between competition and success.
2. (A) The professor is explaining the term *cariogenic* by showing the word *caries* within the term and then stating that it is tooth decay.
3. (D) The professor wants the students to consider the results of tests as an indication of one's natural progress in understanding.
4. (C) The instructor is letting the students know that she is impressed with those people who will be leading the workshop.

EXERCISE L23 *(p. 293, script on p. 610)*

1. (C) The phrase "if that's the case" refers to the situation of students getting so far behind that they can't catch up. The man is concerned that this may be her situation and, if that is true, she should drop out.
2. (D) The man is surprised about what the woman said and wants to confirm his understanding.
3. (A) The professor believes that the relationship between the information written on the board and the statistics shown in the transparency will be understood immediately.
4. (C) The woman gives positive examples of what happens in the pursuit of happiness, and the man gives a negative example.

Listening Mini-test 3 (p. 294, script on p. 611)

1. (A) The professor said that asbestos caused memory loss. She then apologizes and changes the statement to say that asbestos causes lung cancer.
2. (B) The professor means that the situation of synthetic materials causing diseases is very serious.
3. (B) The toxic fumes, which have led to more fire-related deaths, are created when synthetic materials catch on fire. This is another danger of using synthetic materials in houses.
4. (A) Stone is a natural material. The other items are synthetic building materials or use synthetic materials in their processing.
5. (D) Most people cannot move from their homes very easily, but they can remove some of the synthetic materials in their homes and replace them with natural alternatives.
6. (B) The instructor would probably hand out the list of required readings at the beginning of the semester.
7. (D) An out-of-print book would not be available in a bookstore, so a professor might leave a personal copy at the reserve desk.

8. (A) Because the articles are on microfiche and microfiche materials are on reserve, it can be inferred that the articles cannot be taken out.
9. (B) When the professor asks the man to wait after class so that he can explain the procedures, the woman implies that it might be better for the professor to explain to everyone because she thinks that a large number of students need an explanation. The man agrees with her perception.
10. (A) The lecturer has introduced his lecture with a familiar proverb. By stating that this proverb is true in some cases, he indicates that it is not always true or valid.
11. (A) The lecturer has been talking about inventors being dissatisfied people, but he doesn't want those listening to think that they are unhappy or pessimistic.
12. (A) The speaker uses the example of the aspirin bottle to demonstrate that one invention often brings about another invention created to correct a fault of the first one.
13. (A) The speaker asks for the audience to suggest ways to improve the aspirin bottle cap. They may come up with a good improvement.
14. (D) The speaker closes the talk by having the audience discuss their ideas.
15. (D) The students are listening to the lecture about how anthropologists can use garbage to learn about cultures.
16. (A) The professor uses the example of orange peels to demonstrate the various things that can be learned about people by looking at what they discarded.
17. (B) A Stone Age person may have thrown away all of the stated items. However, the broken stone tools would most likely be the only objects that remain today.
18. (C) Since the organic materials that ancient cultures used disintegrated, they no longer exist and, therefore, cannot be studied. The professor regrets that this information has been lost.

Listening Section Practice Test *(p. 299, script on p. 613)*

Note: If you answered an item incorrectly, complete the exercises listed for that item.

1. (B) The professor describes the causes and symptoms of the three main groups of anxiety disorders. See Exercises L9–L12.
2. (D) According to the professor, feeling anxious on a visit to the dentist (and in some other situations) is a normal response and differs from anxiety disorders. See Exercises L18–L23.
3. (A) The professor explains that specific phobias are usually focused on relatively harmless objects, such as spiders. Often the sufferer realizes the irrationality of being fearful of such things. See Exercises L13–L17.
4. (D) The professor mentions some strange anxieties, such as fear of laughter. By saying "I guess that's not a laughing matter for the sufferer," the professor implies that it might seem funny to many people. See Exercises L18–L23.
5. (C) The professor mentions certain social phobias that may include the fear of performing normal everyday activities in front of others. Eating in front of others could be one such activity. See Exercises L18–L23.
6. (A) The term "agoraphobia" is of relatively low usage and the professor probably thinks some students are not familiar with the word or its spelling. See Exercises L18–L23.
7. (D) The professor says there are various medications and therapies that can be used to treat phobias. See Exercises L18–L23.
8. (B) The student reminds the professor that she wrote on his questionnaire "Come and see me." The student wants to know why she wanted to see him. See Exercises L9–L12.
9. (A) The professor used the point about fruit and vegetables to illustrate why *and* questions don't work well on a questionnaire. See Exercises L18–L23.
10. [C] and [D] The professor explains to the student that he may annoy his subjects if he asks questions in a certain way. She also warns against asking questions that he knows how the subjects will answer. See Exercises L13–L17.
11. (D) The professor doesn't have a copy of the questionnaire in front of her and so asks the student if she can see his copy. To jog one's memory means to help someone remember something. See Exercises L18–L23.
12. (A) The professor says that other students in the class have also made mistakes writing their questionnaires. Later she suggests working together with a classmate. This suggests that the task was given as a class assignment. See Exercises L18–L23.
13. (C) The professor discusses with the students various characteristics of tundra plants, such as short plants with short root systems and plant clustering. They also discuss the causes of these characteristics. See Exercises L9–L12.

14. (B) The professor mentions that Alpine tundra has similar characteristics to Arctic tundra, but that it has enough differences to justify spending a separate lesson on its main features. See Exercises L13–L17.

15. [A] and [D] According to the professor, the landscape is flat and treeless – in Finnish the word *tundra* means "treeless plain." A student brings up the fact that the ground is too hard to let melted snow drain through it. See Exercises L13–L17.

16. (C) According to the professor, the plants in the tundra cluster together in depressions to avoid the strong winds, and this helps them to resist the cold arctic temperatures. See Exercises L13–L17.

17. (A) *No* The plant roots are short because the ground is too hard to penetrate.

    (B) *Yes* The snow insulates the plants against the bitter cold.

    (C) *No* Tundra plants use the melted snow that cannot drain as a water source.

    (D) *No* Trees do not grow on the tundra.

    (E) *Yes* Tundra plants take advantage of the long hours of summer sunlight. See Exercises L13–L17.

18. (A) The professor discusses various ways in which Isadora Duncan influenced modern dance stage practice. See Exercises L9–L12.

19. (C) The professor introduces the lecture by noting that artists in various fields were trying to discover new ways of expressing themselves. See Exercises L18–L23.

20. (B) The professor notes that Duncan may have been influenced by folk dancing in her use of the whole body in dance and in her use of costume. See Exercises L13–L17.

21. (D) The professor notes that the use of great concert music to accompany dance movements was an innovation of Duncan's. See Exercises L13–L17.

22. (A) *No* Stiff shoes were used for the dance of her period. She danced barefooted.

    (B) *Yes* Duncan used loose, flowing gowns inspired by Greek models.

    (C) *No* Duncan was concerned with using the whole body for expression

    (D) *No* Duncan chose concert music of classical composers, such as Beethoven, Bach, and Chopin.

    (E) *Yes* Duncan is said to have felt frustrated by the lack of emotional impact and used her movement to express emotions. See Exercises L13–L17.

23. (C) The professor discusses the three ways in which Duncan was an innovator. He also states, "Perhaps all modern dance owes something to Duncan's inventiveness." See Exercises L18–L23.

24. (A) The professor notes that modern audiences may take the achievements made by Duncan for granted and so her originality may not be so obvious today. See Exercises L18–L23.

25. (C) The professor explains the causes of the formation of the layers or stratification inside of the Earth. See Exercises L9–L12.

26. (D) The professor discusses how some scientists are questioning the standard model of planetary formation and mentions that many scientific theories are open to revision. See Exercises L18–L23.

27. (A) The professor says that she knows that some of the students listening have studied Earth formation in other courses. This implies that this topic is familiar to some students. See Exercises L18–L23.

28. (B) The professor mentions that 4.6 billion years ago the material in the Earth was randomly spread around. She concludes by noting how differentiation changed the internal structure from a random mix to a layered structure. See Exercises L13–L17.

29. (D) The professor states that the most important cause of heating was the decay of radioactive elements. See Exercises L13–L17.

30. [A] and [C] The heavier material sinking and the gases escaping and coming out at the surface are two of the aspects of differentiation. See Exercises L13–L17.

31. (B) The man came to the advisor to talk about graduate school. He needs help because he finds the application form "a bit overwhelming." See Exercises L9–L12.

32. (C) The advisor says that they should look in reference books to find universities offering a degree in marine biology. See Exercises L13–L17.

33. (A) The student thinks it would be expensive to apply to a lot of universities. The advisor tells him it would be expensive to apply to all of them on the list. The implication is that an application fee is necessary. See Exercises L18–L23.

34. (A) The advisor makes this statement in order to find out what area the student hopes to specialize in within the field of marine biology. She wants to help the student focus the search more precisely. See Exercises L18–L23.

35. (C) The advisor suggests that the student read published articles in the area he is interested in to find researchers who might be able to help him in his future research. See Exercises L13–L17.

PART 2 BUILDING SKILLS: Speaking

There is no answer key for **EXERCISES S1–S2** *(pp. 313–314)*.

EXERCISE S3 *(p. 315)*

Theaters of the Elizabethan period were open-air constructions in which poorer members of the audience, "the groundlings," stood in a space called "the pit" around three sides of a projecting rectangular platform that formed the main stage. Most of the perimeter of the building comprised covered, tiered galleries, and it is here that the wealthier members of the audience sat. A roof supported on two pillars projected from the back wall and covered part of the stage. The main stage was hollow and could be accessed from below through trapdoors set in the floor. The main stage also had a door on either side at the back, which gave access to the dressing rooms. Between these doors was a small recess, usually curtained off, that could be used for extra stage space. Above this recess was a balcony sometimes used by musicians or, when necessary, by actors in a performance.

EXERCISE S4 *(p. 315)*

It is simply not feasible for every university library in the nation to contain all the books, journals, and resource materials that university students and faculty need for their research. So what have libraries done to meet the needs of their users? Well, several things, in fact. While some money is used for the yearly purchasing of hardbound books and current journals that are recommended by professors, other funds are used to obtain materials that have been put on microfilm and microfiche. These techniques have proved extremely useful for adding informative materials to a library's collection at a low cost and without taking up much space. Another way libraries have increased access has been to invest in computers. Computers are linked to collections in other libraries. Professors and students can perform a computer search to find a library that has the material they need. The material can then be ordered and checked out through the interlibrary loan system, which costs the user a nominal shipping fee.

EXERCISE S5 *(p. 316)*

(Man) Professor Cline?

(Woman) Yes?

(Man) I'm Robert Daley. The work-study office sent me.

(Woman) Oh, I've been waiting for them to send someone. Did you say your name was Robert?

(Man) Yes.

(Woman) What's your major, Robert?

(Man) Zoology.

(Woman) Good. You have some science background then. Let me show you what we're doing in our lab.

(Man) Will I be working in the biology lab?

(Woman) Yes. We're studying the speed of reproduction of paramecia. Uh, paramecia are the most complex single-celled organisms.

(Man) Oh, that sounds interesting.

(Woman) Well, what we need you to do is probably not so interesting.

(Man) And what is that?

(Woman) We'll need you to come in every day at the same time and count the paramecia.

(Man) Count paramecia?

(Woman) Yes. It's very important to keep an accurate count and fill the numbers in on a form. I'll show you where the forms are and explain how to complete it later. After you have completed the form, you need to give it to Nancy. She's the woman that you met in the lab office. She'll feed your numbers into the computer for our statistical analysis. Right now, though, I want to introduce you to the other members of our team so that we can arrange a convenient time for you to come in.

EXERCISE S6 *(p. 316)*

Treasured since ancient times, saffron is obtained from the autumn-flowering *Crocus sativus*. It is the dried flower stigmas – the three slender threads in the center of each flower – that are the source of saffron. This "king of spices" is one of the world's most prized and expensive foodstuffs. The finest variety is grown in La Mancha in the central plateau of Spain. Spain is by far the biggest producer. It contributes seventy percent of the world's output, with India and Iran the only other producers of note. The cultivation of saffron in Spain goes back to the Moorish invasion of the eighth century, when the crocuses were first introduced from the Middle East. Not only is Spain the largest producer of saffron, but it is also the largest consumer. Up to one-third of the crop is bought in Spain, and the remainder is exported. The biggest buyers are Middle Eastern countries, followed by the United States, Italy, and France.

EXERCISE S7 *(p. 319)*

Your answers may be stated differently.

1. I admired my high school history teacher for several reasons. First, he could explain historical events as if he were telling a story.
2. I enjoyed doing quiet activities like playing chess, whereas my brother preferred more physical activities like football.
3. Our teacher would walk around the classroom looking at our work while we were busy on our individual projects.
4. The rain poured down for several days. Consequently, the river banks in my city overflowed.
5. I took as many science courses as I could. For example, I studied biology, chemistry, biochemistry, and physics.
6. Even though the rain forest provides us with many products, the forests are being cleared for crops.

EXERCISE S8 *(p. 320)*

Your answers may be different.

1. Childhood is a time in life before a person has reached an adult state.
2. An avalanche is a great mass of snow that slides quickly down a mountain, destroying everything in its path.
3. Fiction is a literary work that is based on imagination instead of facts.
4. A loan is a sum of money or an object that is given for a period of time and must be returned.
5. An accountant is a person who does bookkeeping for a company or individuals.
6. Whales are air-breathing mammals that live in oceans.

EXERCISE S9 *(p. 320)*

Your answers may be stated differently.

1. Wind and solar energy are alternative forms of energy.
2. To get accepted into some universities you have to send copies of your high school diploma, get letters of recommendation from a teacher who knows your work, and write an essay stating why you want to study there.
3. Students tend to get out of shape because they eat a lot of junk food and spend a lot of time studying.
4. Rivers are polluted both by factories dumping their waste products and by people throwing garbage into the river.

EXERCISE S10 *(p. 321)*

Your answers may be stated differently.

1. Since **I** frequently can't find the definition of words I need in a dictionary, I've had to buy a specialized **one**. I also need to use an encyclopedia that gives more detailed information. Using **these reference books**, I can collect information for my course papers.
2. My grandfather taught me woodcarving when I was young. When I need to relax, I go out into my yard and practice **this hobby**.
3. Many people enjoy reading fantasy stories of imaginary worlds and extraordinary events. **This genre** is also common in popular movies.
4. A pitfall trap can be used to get a sample of small ground-living creatures. To make **this** trap, a glass jar is put into the ground with its rim at ground level. The trapped **animals** can then be counted and identified.

EXERCISE S11 *(p. 321)*

Your answers may be stated differently.

1. I prefer to spend my leisure time with different friends. Since **they** have diverse interests, one or the other is always involving me in different activities.
2. Many children are sent to school at an early age to get a head start in a formal education. That is unfortunate because **they** can learn very important lessons about life through play.
3. The woman believes that the new plan to book study rooms will affect students adversely. Because of the plan, **they** won't be able to book the rooms ahead of time and it is possible that a room will not be available when **it** is needed.
4. The computer program contains activities for dyslexic children. The children work through **these** to help improve reading abilities.

EXERCISE S12 *(p. 322)*

1. Cooking is fun when you are planning a nice meal for visitors. You can make a starter, a main course, a salad, and a dessert. Then, when your guest arrives, you can surprise him with how well you have cooked it. Guests will appreciate all the work one does to make tasty meals.

ANSWER KEYS

2. It is very important for a teacher to be patient because their students don't always understand what they are expected to do. Sometimes one has to guess what the teacher means. It is very upsetting if you guess wrong and then they get angry when it isn't your fault.

3. A movie is never as good as the novel they are based on. Sometimes the novel has two or three subplots. Since all these subplots can't be addressed in a two-hour movie, the main plot is frequently changed. But without the subplot, they don't make sense. In the end, the movie tells a completely different story than that of the novels.

4. The professor talked about the rise and fall of empires. He notes that the conquerors spread through the valleys, the most fertile and accessible parts of a country. However, the people who live in the less accessible areas, like the tropical forests or the high mountain regions, are frequently not affected by the conquerors and continued to maintain languages and traditions throughout the many invasions that will take place over the centuries.

EXERCISE S13 *(p. 323)*
Your answers may be stated differently.

1. Cooking is fun when you are planning a nice meal for visitors. You can make a starter, a main course, a salad, and a dessert. Then, when your guests arrive, you can surprise them with how well you have cooked the various courses. They will appreciate all the work you have done to make a tasty meal.

2. It is very important for a teacher to be patient because his or her students don't always understand what they are expected to do. Sometimes a student has to guess what the teacher means. It is very upsetting if that student guesses wrong and then the teacher gets angry when it isn't the student's fault.

3. A movie is never as good as the novel it is based on. Sometimes the novel has two or three subplots. Since all these subplots can't be addressed in a two-hour movie, the main plot is frequently changed. But without the subplots, the movie doesn't make sense. In the end, the movie tells a completely different story than that of the novel.

4. The professor talked about the rise and fall of empires. He noted that the conquerors spread through the valleys, the most fertile and accessible parts of a country. However, the people who lived in the less accessible areas, like the tropical forests or the high mountain regions, were frequently not affected by the conquerors and continued to maintain languages and traditions throughout the many invasions that took place over the centuries.

There is no answer key for **EXERCISES S14–S26** *(pp. 328–330 and 334–337). You might wish to discuss your recorded responses with a fluent English speaker.*

EXERCISE S27 *(p. 343)*
Your notes may be different.

1. Class cancelled and students should either
   a. accept the opportunity to join another course
   b. officially drop the course

EXERCISE S28 *(p. 343, script on p. 621)*
Your notes may be different.

Man's points	**Woman's points**
Course has good reputation	
	Already read most of the requirements
Easy option	
	Wants a challenge Suspects it will be a large class Likes small classes

EXERCISE S29 *(p. 344)*
Your answers may be stated differently.

1. state the topic – the course replacement
2. state the woman's opinion – She is not interested in the other course.
3. state her reasons for the opinion – already did the reading; wants a challenge; doesn't like large classes

There is no answer key for **EXERCISE S30** *(p. 344)*

EXERCISE S31 *(p. 344)*
Your speech may be different.

The Survey of American Literature course is going to be replaced by the Literature of Minority Groups. The woman is not interested in taking the course replacement for several reasons. First, she has already read most of the books on the required reading list and consequently, does not think that she would find the course a challenge. She would like to take a challenging course. Second, she thinks that when the two classes are joined into one class, there will be too many students in the class. She prefers small classes. She feels that it is easy to discuss ideas in smaller groups. In conclusion, the woman has decided to drop the course instead of taking the course replacement.

EXERCISE S32 *(p. 345)*
Your notes may be different.

Boston Tea Party, 1773 act of defiance
Reason: Br. Parliament imposed taxes
Action: dressed as Native Americans and threw tea overboard

EXERCISE S33 *(p. 345, script on p. 622)*
Your notes may be different.

French/Indian War caused debt and economic crises
Taxation without representation put on colonists who wouldn't pay
Colonists protested
Tea tax not revoked

EXERCISE S34 *(p. 346)*
Your answers may be stated differently.

1. state the topic – the background to the American War of Independence
2. state the events – the French/Indian War, the imposition of taxes
3. state the relationship – the dressing as Indians to represent the French/Indian War, throwing the tea overboard because it was the commodity being taxed

There is no answer key for **EXERCISE S35** *(p. 346)*

EXERCISE S36 *(p. 346)*
Your speech may be different.

The incident of colonists dressing up as Native Americans, boarding British ships and throwing the cargo of tea into the sea was an act of defiance preceded by important events. A war involving the British against the French and Native Americans had left Britain in debt. To pay off this debt, the British imposed a tax on the American colonists. However, the American colonists were suffering an economic crisis because of the same war and could not pay the taxes. In protest of the taxes, the colonists throw the British cargo of tea into the sea. Dressing up as Native Americans was not only a way for the colonists to disguise themselves, but also it represented the French and Indian War. The tea was the only commodity that was still being taxed, but the colonists were making a point about being taxed without representation. The incident became known as the Boston Tea Party and perhaps marked the beginning of the American War of Independence.

There is no answer key for **EXERCISE S37** *(p. 347)*

EXERCISE S38 *(p. 347, script on p. 622)*
The following notes from the reading and listening passages have been made as complete as possible for easier understanding. Your notes may not be as complete.

1. ***Reading***

Old Main building demolished for fine arts center.
Center includes classrooms and facilities for
a. drama – main stage and smaller stages
b. music – concert hall and practice rooms
c. art – exhibition hall and workrooms

Listening

Man's points	Woman's points
Need to stop the demolition	
	Need a fine arts complex
Waste ground better place	
	Waste ground too far away
Old Main a. 1st and only building b. built mid-1800s of stone c. Has historical value d. Preserve heritage	
	Not good for classrooms Expensive to heat
Not expensive to heat Good for graduate student offices	

2. ***Reading***

Lecture by Dr. James Filbert on Restless Leg Syndrome

Restless Leg Syndrome
a. misdiagnosed because difficult to describe
b. probably genetic – runs in families

Dr. Filbert will discuss
a. symptoms
b. ways to relieve pain

Listening

Man's points	Woman's points
	Wants to go to RLS lecture
What is RSL	
	Mother was a misdiagnosed sufferer, thought to be a. growing pains b. strain c. on feet too much d. imagination
Why misdiagnosed?	
	Difficult to describe pain
How diagnosed?	
	Cousin mentioned suffering Runs in families

3. ***Reading***

A decrease in the number of required physical education courses
- a. students responsible for their own physical condition
- b. money saved can be spent on labs/library

Listening

Man's points	**Woman's points**
	Students should take responsibility Money not put into facilities
Money from courses not taught	
	Programs might be affected Women's varsity soccer team
Programs won't be affected	
	Cut in classes means cut in the number of instructors Programs run by those instructors affected

4. ***Reading***

Renovation of classroom building to include state-of-the-art facilities
- a. computers and projection facilities
- b. multimedia labs

Improvements
- a. better access
- b. motion sensor for energy conservation

Listening

Man's points	**Woman's points**
Excited about high-tech classrooms	
	Not excited
Lectures backed up by projected computer images more interesting	
	Technology often fails
Has to be maintained	
	Becomes obsolete Expensive equipment in relation to amount used Many professors not technological Time-consuming to make interesting lecture notes Best teacher doesn't even use old technology
Dr. Rosa is exceptional	

5. ***Reading***

Phytoplankton

what: a. single-celled plants
- b. part of food chain
- c. basis for all marine life

where: a. photic zone
- b. abundant near land masses where nutrients concentrate

Photosynthesis
- a. sunlight
- b. phosphates and nitrates
- c. carbon dioxide
- d. by product – oxygen, 75% of world's oxygen
- e. bloom known as red tide

Listening

Phytoplankton
- a. key nutrient in food chain
- b. important for production of oxygen

Recent study
- a. ocean areas with sunlight and nutrients, but no phytoplankton
- b. analysis of water – no iron
- c. hypothesis–phytoplankton needs iron

1. experiment
- a. added iron sulfate to area
- b. increase of phytoplankton

Possibilities
- a. could be effective for removing carbon dioxide from atmosphere
- b. replenish oxygen
- c. increase of phytoplankton could mean increase of fish

Question
- a. What would be the environmental consequences?

6. ***Reading***

Road sign system
- a. ensures safety of drivers and people
- b. controls car speed and flow
- c. restrictions for parking and stopping
- d. raised sidewalks to separate people and cars
- e. traffic lights and road markings
- f. legal action if drivers don't obey

Listening

Road signs all over cities
- a. to reduce accidents
- b. to inform drivers

Experiment of removing all road markings and signals

results: a significant drop in accidents

why: a. drivers more careful and courteous
- b. signs gave false sense of security

7. ***Reading***

Time – cultural invention

Monochronic
- a. linear
- b. schedules and routines important
- c. efficient and impartial
- d. blind to other people

Polychronic
- a. simultaneous
- b. people more important than schedules
- c. social
- d. deal with many people at the same time
- e. time and schedules not priorities

Listening

Monochronic and polychromic at opposite ends, but most cultures in between

Individual differences within a culture

Monochronic:
- a. linear, predict time for task and follow through
- b. prompt, meet deadlines, dependable

Polychronic:
- a. able to multitask
- b. can move around within a company
- c. become irreplaceable because of this
- d. doesn't get promoted because can't be replaced

8. ***Reading***

Weathering – a process of rock breakdown

Three types
- a. mechanical – physical factors
- b. chemical – reactions between water and minerals in rock
- c. biological – animal or plant factors

Listening

Relation of weathering to climate

Arid areas more mechanical – fluctuations in temperatures

Tropics more chemical – heavy rain

Temperate climates both mechanical and chemical – both fluctuations in temperature and rain

Polar climates show little weathering

Most areas show biological weathering, but less in extreme climates

EXERCISE S39 *(p. 360, script on p. 625)*

Your notes may be different.

Man's points	Woman's points
Best seats $60	
	Too expensive
No student discount Least expensive $15	
	Location of cheap tickets too far away
Middle balcony $40	
	First balcony expensive, but best option

EXERCISE S40 *(p. 360)*

Your answers may be stated differently.

1. state the topic – which seats to purchase for a concert
2. state the problem – the cost and area of the seats
3. explain and support my preference – buy the expensive ones for important concert

There is no answer key for **EXERCISE S41** *(p. 362).*

EXERCISE S42 *(p. 361)*

Your speech may be different.

The students want to purchase seats for a concert and must make a decision on which ones to get. The difficulty in their decision is that the best seats are too expensive for them to buy. Unfortunately, the cheapest tickets are for seats that are too far away for a good view of the stage. The third option is for seats in the middle balcony. Those seats are not as close to the stage, but neither are they as expensive as the best seats. They are more expensive then the cheapest ones, but closer to the stage. The woman believes that they should buy the tickets for the middle balcony, but the man seems hesitant. I would suggest that they get the most expensive tickets. Money can be budgeted and replaced. A special concert may be a once-in-a-lifetime experience that should not be missed.

EXERCISE S43 *(p. 361, script on p. 625)*

Your notes may be different.

A financial crisis is occurring in places where there are low birthrates but a growing number of older people.
Older people are living longer and therefore get benefits for more years.
They need more medical attention that is costly.
Some can't take care of themselves and need expensive intensive care.
Families can't pay for the elderly.

EXERCISE S44 *(p. 361)*

Your answers may be stated differently.

1. state the topic – problem of imbalance of older to younger people
2. explain the points – aging population, live longer, become ill, must be cared for
3. discuss the financial problems – need support longer, need costly medical treatment, need taking care of

There is no answer key for **EXERCISE S45** *(p. 362)*.

EXERCISE S46 *(p. 362)*

Your speech may be different.

The imbalance of older people to younger people is causing financial problems for some governments. Older people are living longer and, therefore, receive a government pension and old-age benefits for more years than ever before. When they get ill, the medical attention that they need is very costly. Some people get too old or ill to take care of themselves. Expensive intensive care may be needed that families cannot pay for, so the government has to provide it for them. The financial situation caused by an aging population is new to many countries. To deal with the situation, those governments have to reconsider their policies concerning the elderly.

There is no answer key for **EXERCISE S47** *(p. 362)*.

EXERCISE S48 *(p. 363, script on p. 625)*

The following notes from the listening passages have been made as complete as possible for easier understanding. Your notes may not be as complete.

1.

Man's points	**Woman's points**
	Instead of GRE results, universities require a. grade point average b. letters of recommendation
Test-anxiety concern	
	Gender bias a. 60 points lower average mean b. higher grade point averages
Wonders about differences	
	Females a. more prone to test anxiety b. approach task differently c. more cautious and analytical d. work slower e. find tricks distracting
	Males a. risk takers b. enjoy finding trick questions
Universities take this into consideration	
	Open-ended tasks better for women, ethnic groups, and nonnative English speakers

2.

Man's points	**Woman's points**
	Needs prerequisite before taking course only offered in autumn Prerequisite offered in summer
Prefers summer courses Summer courses are intensive Can take course online Failed course because a. put off doing assignments b. didn't feel responsible to professor Thinks woman motivated enough for course	

3.

Man's points	**Woman's points**
	Library quiet but can't drink coffee Suggests Student Union
Student Union busy on Monday	
	Book fair
Wants to go to book fair	
	Must work on presentation
Book fair then cafeteria to work over coffee	
	Too noisy with crowds for book fair Long lines in cafeteria

Meet at library	When to reserve study room
If available, can walk in	Risk not reserving Meet in Student Union If too noisy in cafeteria, go to library

4.

Man's points	**Woman's points**
	Wants the course requirements dropped
A bad decision Being fit helps people concentrate	
	Students should be responsible for health
Students involved with studies a. need break b. need stimulation	
	Some students don't like sports
Cuts affect variety offered a. currently something for everyone	
	Not university's responsibility
Money spent wasted Equipment will not get replaced	
	Money better spent on library facilities and labs

5. Goats good for subsistence
   - a. eat plants that are unsuitable for other herd animals
   - b. provide milk and meat

   Goats bad for ecosystems
   - a. overgrazing
   - b. prevents new vegetation by eating young plants
   - c. destroys woody plants that have balance with soil
     - 1. plants
       - a. stabilize soil
       - b. provide biological material to make soil
       - c. hold soil together
     - 2. soil
       - a. provides plants anchor for roots
       - b. provides water and nutrients

   Goats prime cause of deserts
   - a. fault of people's bad management
   - b. educational program needed

6. Justice system principle – children different from adults
   - a. provide individual treatment
   - b. provide services

   System under threat because
   - a. not tough enough, according to critics
   - b. doesn't rehabilitate
   - c. increase of juvenile crime

   Areas of research needed
   - a. accountability
     - 1. how children differ in understanding of behavior
     - 2. how to assess responsibility
   - b. risk evaluation
     - 1. how to determine child at risk
     - 2. how to use this information to prevent a crime
   - c. susceptibility
     - 1. how easy for child to change behavior

   Understanding child
   - a. need experts in all fields
   - b. need input from public
   - c. need to learn more about juvenile crime
   - d. need to spread that knowledge

7. Intermediate technology – people can make with materials around them

   Example – fuel collection
   - a. time-consuming
   - b. causes deforestation
   - c. soil erosion
   - d. ecological imbalances
   - e. not enough for future use

   Answer – solar oven
   - a. made of two boxes, metal or cardboard
   - b. painted black
   - c. insulation rice husks or nut shells
   - d. mirror

   Other advantages
   - a. cheap and energy efficient
   - b. doesn't cause illnesses
   - c. not a fire hazard
   - d. doesn't add to global warming

8. Venice controlled spice trade
   - a. spices brought overland to Constantinople
   - b. shipped from Constantinople to Venice
   - c. sold to northern Europe at high prices

   Late 1400s, early 1500s new methods of navigation
   - a. Spanish and Portuguese challenged Venice monopoly
   - b. Portuguese ships went around Africa
   - c. Spanish ships sailed west

   Consequences
   - a. Portugal made trade directly with India
   - b. Columbus discovered the Americas

Speaking Section Practice Test *(p. 369, script on p. 629)*

The following notes on the reading and listening passages have been made as complete as possible for easier understanding. Your notes may not be as complete.

There is no answer key for **ITEMS 1–2** *(p. 370)*.

3. ***Reading***

Legal Aid Project
- a. non-profit
- b. gives law students experience
- c. part of training
- d. assisted by staff

Listening

Man's points	Woman's points
	Man could get help for housing problem
Just for law students	Service is free and might help get deposit back
Law students are inexperienced	Law students have practice with real case a. study how experienced lawyers managed b. analyze cases
Just classroom exercise	Law students are advised by staff members

4. ***Reading***

Transportation costs factor in agricultural production
- a. heavy items expensive to transport
- b. perishable goods need expensive refrigeration
- c. poor farmers can't get surplus to market

Listening

Model of zones, Von Thünen set out in 17th century

Concentric rings with city at the center
- a. dairy and fresh foods
- b. wood
- c. grain
- d. animals
- e. too far away

5.

Man's points	Woman's points
Needs lots of books Didn't buy all that was required	Textbooks are expensive Can get books at library
Couldn't find them there	Look for individual stories in different texts Look in collections of authors
Didn't look for specific stories	Find individual stories in library Return books to bookstore
Likes to write in books	Go to the used bookstore.
Didn't know there is used bookstore.	Used bookstore on University Avenue. Maybe previous classes had same books. Can own cheaper copy and write in it

6. "Mozart effect" term refers to music and brain experiment

one area of brain
- a. spatial-temporal reasoning
  - reasoning important for some aspects of music
  - reasoning for solving some types of physics and math problems

experiment group, college students, not children,
- a. pretested divided into 3 groups
  1. heard no music
  2. heard variety of music
  3. heard only Mozart
- b. given intelligence test

results of experiment
- a. Mozart group had increased scores on spatial-temporal reasoning
  1. only for 10 minutes
  2. only one type of IQ test used in experiment

public's reaction
- a. media hype of listening to Mozart improving IQ
- b. marketing of products

problems
- a. importance of music for bringing beauty is lost
- b. parents attempting to turn children into geniuses

PART 2 BUILDING SKILLS: Writing

EXERCISE W1 *(p. 379)*

1. C	4. B	7. A	10. A
2. A	5. D	8. D	11. D
3. A	6. B	9. B	12. B

EXERCISE W2 *(p. 381)*

Your answers may be stated differently.

1. Passive smoking is the involuntarily inhalation of cigarette smoke by a person who is in the vicinity of someone who has lit up a cigarette.
2. Subsistence farming is land cultivation in which the food produced is sufficient only to feed the farmer and immediate family without any surplus for sale.
3. An expectorant is a medication that helps to promote the ejection of phlegm from the lungs or chest.
4. Nonfiction is a kind of writing that is based on factual information as opposed to the imagination.
5. A trowel is a tool with an iron blade and wooden handle and is used for digging and cutting soil or turf.

EXERCISE W3 *(p. 381)*

1. **in** the library rather than **at** home
2. **to** read . . . , but also **to** pay attention
3. to **work** . . . , **compare** . . . and then **work** together
4. **of** towering pinnacles **and** grotesque eroded forms
5. **as** working animals and **as** pets
6. **stayed** . . . , **took** . . . and **returned** to Gaul

EXERCISE W4 *(p. 382)*

Your paragraphs will be different. If possible, you should have a fluent English speaker check your paragraphs.

1. Adults tend to cherish soft values that are hard to evaluate monetarily. Such values include family, health, and career satisfaction. In contrast, children take these for granted and place more importance on material objects, such as a favorite toy. Such things become less important to them as interest in relationships increases.

2. The boundary that separates the Earth's crust from the upper mantle is commonly called the Moho. This boundary is like an exaggerated mirror image of the surface profile. So the highest mountain ranges result in the deepest thickness of crust. Beneath these ranges, the crust's thickness can attain 50 miles, while beneath the oceans, it is about 3 miles, and under the continents, 20. The reason for this is that the material making up the upper mantle is denser than the crust, and therefore it floats like an iceberg floats in the sea. You can get an idea of how this works by thinking of different sized ice cubes in a glass of water. The biggest cube extends to the highest point and also to the greatest depth.

EXERCISE W5 *(p. 385)*

Your sentences will be different. If possible, you should have a fluent English speaker check your sentences.

1. If a person is not breathing and if the heart is not beating, it is important to start resuscitation.
2. Inhalation of smoke from a parent's cigarette over a long period may harm a child.
3. I try to give my reader a good impression by making my e-mails clear.
4. Learning and research are fundamentally cooperativc efforts.
5. The car has been a success for people, but not for nature.
6. Because of low birthrates, in the future there may be too few employees to support the increasing number of retirees.
7. My friend was jogging along the riverside when a pack of dogs appeared in his path.
8. My stamp collection even includes stamps from countries that now have different names.

EXERCISE W6 *(p. 386)*

Your paragraphs will be different. If possible, you should have a fluent English speaker check your paragraphs.

1. One of the most important school subjects is mathematics. Although learning to read is important, if we do not know how to do simple sums, we will not be able to keep track of our finances. Besides everyday calculations such as figuring the best prices per weight in the grocery store, we need to understand more complex computation to understand interest rates on our bank accounts and loans for major purchases. People who earn enough sometimes have financial difficulties because they do not understand the mathematics behind finances.

   Mathematics is also important in other parts of our lives. For example, we have to measure and calculate numbers when we cook. We need to know about mathematical functions like fractions or multiplication when we decrease or increase the amounts depending on the number of people who are going to be eating. An error in sums could result in a bad-tasting meal.

2. The electric streetcar was popular in U.S. cities after 1880 when an engineer invented a cable that could run from wire overhead to a streetcar's electric engine. Because of this overhead wire, a dangerous electric rail did not run along the street at ground level. This was a very important feature of the streetcar.

   From 1880 onward, the electric streetcar was very popular in big cities all over the U.S.A. Nonpolluting and very efficient, it carried large numbers of passengers cheaply and at profit for the companies. However, early in the next century, automobile manufacturers and other business interests attempted to replace streetcars with buses and cars. Eventually, cars completely took over the city streets.

EXERCISE W7 *(p. 391)*

Your answers may be stated differently.

1. Topic: ban on smoking in public
   Task: reasons and examples for opinion
2. Topic: advantages of marriage at different ages
   Task: state preference and support it
3. Topic: necessity of university education for success
   Task: reasons and examples for opinion

There is no answer key for **EXERCISES W8–W9** *(pp. 391–393).*

EXERCISE W10–W14 *(pp. 395–397)*

The following introductory paragraphs are modified student-written examples. Your introductory paragraphs will be different. If possible, you should have a fluent English speaker check your paragraphs.

1. Many people are addicted to the nicotine in cigarettes. These people like to smoke whenever or wherever they feel the urge for a cigarette. However, the smoke from the cigarettes disturbs nonsmokers. Because of that, many nonsmokers would like smoking to be banned from public places. Antismokers provide several reasons for the importance for such a ban.
2. Marriage is an important step in a person's life. It is a legal bond between two people and has important social and legal implications. To enter into this bond, a person should have some maturity. To consider the best age to enter into marriage, the advantages of marrying at different ages need to be compared.
3. To be successful is most people's goal. Achieving that goal takes hard work and sometimes education or training. However, a university education is really not necessary for success in many cases. The answer to the question of what success is depends on what one's goals are and the kind of aspirations a person has.

EXERCISE W15 *(p. 399)*

Note: The possible answers for Exercise W15 are so varied that you might wish to discuss your answers with a fluent English speaker.

EXERCISE W16 *(p. 399)*

1. *Yes*
2. *Yes*

Note: The answers for items 3–5 depend on your judgment of your own work. You might wish to discuss your answers with a fluent English speaker.

EXERCISE W17 *(p. 400)*

Note: The possible answers for Exercise W17 are so varied that you might wish to discuss your answers with a fluent English speaker.

EXERCISE W18 *(p. 401)*

Your answers may be different.

1. It is the largest and most interesting city in the country.
2. I read on the bus on my way to class, while I'm waiting for my friends, and before I go to sleep.
3. The university that I want to attend requires that I get a good score.
4. The sound of the water along the shore calms one's nerves.
5. They can be both psychologically and physically addictive.
6. Had my brother been paying attention to the road instead of changing the CD in the CD player while he was driving, he wouldn't have crashed into the tree and broken his leg.
7. The Pompidou Centre in Paris is a building that has provoked controversy.
8. Many city centers are not bustling with shoppers anymore. Instead, the streets are empty except when workers are leaving or returning to their offices.

EXERCISE W19 *(p. 401)*

The following answers illustrate one way that you could add details. Your answers may be different.

1. When you plant a tree, you are helping your environment in many ways. Your tree will provide a home and food for other creatures. Birds may build nests in the branches. The flowers will provide nectar for insects, and the fruits or nuts may feed squirrels

or other small animals. Your tree will hold the soil in place. This will help stop erosion. In addition, your tree will provide shade in the summer. This will give welcome relief on hot days. You can watch your tree grow and someday show your children, or even grandchildren, the tree you planted.

2. Airplanes and helicopters can be used to save people's lives. Helicopters can be used for rescuing people in trouble. For example, when a tall building is on fire, people sometimes escape to the roof, where a helicopter can pick them up. Passengers on a sinking ship could also be rescued by helicopter. Because planes can carry heavy loads, they are useful in transporting food and supplies when disasters strike. This is very important when there is an earthquake, flood, or drought. Both types of aircraft can transport people to hospitals in emergencies. Getting a victim of an accident or heart attack to a hospital quickly could save the person's life. Helicopters and airplanes can be used to deliver medical services to people who live in remote areas. They can also be used as a kind of ambulance service in cases where getting to the hospital by car would take too long.

3. Studying in another country is advantageous for many reasons. The student is exposed to a new culture. This exposure teaches him or her about other people and other ways of thinking, which can promote friendships among countries. Sometimes students can learn a new language. This language may be beneficial for keeping up with research after the student has finished studying. Furthermore, students can often have learning experiences not available in their own countries. For example, an art history student studying in Rome would get to see works of art that can only be seen in Italian museums and churches. A student may also get the opportunity to study at a university where a leading expert in his or her field may be teaching. A leading expert can introduce the student to the most up-to-date findings of the top researchers in the field. Exposure to such valuable knowledge and insights into the field can aid the student in becoming an expert as well.

EXERCISE W20 *(p. 403)*

The following are possible questions to stimulate details.

1. What kind of scenery do you like?

   Why would you want to stop along the road?

   Where and when have you met interesting people on your travels?

   How much luggage can you carry on airplanes?

   Why don't you have to worry about missing flights?

2. What are the poor and inhumane conditions?

   Why don't the animals get exercise?

   What is an example of neurotic behavior?

   Why is it a problem for animals not to breed?

   Why is it a problem for animals to breed with a related animal?

3. Why is knowing the material important?

   Why should teachers be able to explain their knowledge?

   Why are patience and understanding important?

   What should teachers do to show their patience and understanding?

   How can teachers make the subject matter interesting?

EXERCISE W21–W23 *(pp. 403–404)*

The following developmental paragraphs are modified student-written examples. Your developmental paragraphs will be different. If possible, you should have a fluent English speaker check your paragraphs.

1. Smoking has been shown to be harmful to health. The main health effect is that it causes lung cancer. Research now shows that even people who don't smoke themselves are in danger of developing cancer when they are regularly exposed to the smoke of people who do. Besides the danger of cancer, nonsmokers also complain that a smoky environment makes them suffer from a variety of illnesses including sore eyes, headaches, and even asthmatic symptoms.

   Despite the possible dangers and unpleasant side effects of smoking for the general public, we should be cautious about banning smoking in all public spaces. If public space means all areas outside of private homes, then I don't agree with a ban. Such a measure is an infringement of a basic right of enjoyment. But, in places where smoking is a nuisance to nonsmokers, it should be banned completely. It should also be banned in enclosed areas such as railroad carriages, buses, and restaurants, but not in city streets and other open-air places.

2. A young married couple has only a few advantages over a couple who marries later. Because they are young, they are not set in their ways. Therefore, they are more flexible in their relationship than older people. Furthermore, they are probably not yet stable financially, so they share the hardships of starting out together. This can be a bond that brings them closer together.

   A couple that marries at an older age has some important advantages. For one thing, an older couple will tend to have greater emotional stability. They may have more understanding of the difficulties life can bring and thus be more prepared for the ups and downs of married life. By contrast younger people may not have reached their full emotional development and may find that they grow apart due to interests and friendships developing in different directions. Furthermore, older couples are likely to have greater financial or job security. They may also have better jobs since they are more likely to have finished higher education and have better job qualifications. This is particularly important for couples who wish to start a family.

3. For some people success is related to the amount of money earned. Many well-paid jobs are in the area of maintenance or in technical areas. People with skills in construction work, plumbing, or electricity can find well-paid work without spending many years studying at a university. The people in these jobs have important skills that everyone needs to use at some point in their lives, so these people also have good job security.

   Other people relate success to job satisfaction. This does not necessarily require a university education either. A person wanting to help others may find a satisfying career working with people. One who enjoys nature may find an outdoor job. There are many jobs that are not particularly well paid nor require a university education but bring satisfaction to those with an interest in a particular area.

   However, a university education is necessary for people whose goals are to do scientific research or go into different academic fields. These people cannot succeed in their chosen career without getting a university education.

EXERCISE W24–W28 *(pp. 405–406)*

The following concluding paragraphs are modified student-written examples. Your concluding paragraphs will be different. If possible, you should have a fluent English speaker check your paragraphs.

1. In conclusion, there are good reasons to stop people smoking in some public places. If the smoking is in a place where others are exposed to health risks, then it should be banned. However, if smoking is taking place in a public area where the health risk to others is minimal, then smokers should be able to light up. A total prohibition on smoking in all public places is too extreme a solution and violates personal freedoms.

2. The advantages of marrying at an older age outweigh those of marrying young. More mature couples, having better job prospects and a more developed understanding, provide a better environment for raising a family. Although there are some advantages to marrying young, in most cases it is probably better for young people to consider putting off their marriage until a later date.

3. In conclusion, people's goals, whether it is earning money, achieving job satisfaction, or succeeding in academic research, will determine if a university education is necessary. The statement that a university education is a requirement in today's world if one wishes to be successful is only true for certain people. There are many fulfilling, high-paid jobs that do not require a high academic qualification.

EXERCISE W29 *(p. 407)*

Question A

1. *No* The introductory paragraph is incomplete.
2. *No* The restated problem should be in different words, not in the same words as the question.
3. *No* There is no development of the introductory paragraph.
4. *Yes* The thesis statement gives the controlling idea as advantages and disadvantages of small and large cars.
5. *Yes* In the topic sentence of the first developmental paragraph, the topic is "large cars" and the controlling idea is "advantages." In the topic sentence of the second developmental paragraph, the topic is "small cars" and the controlling idea is "advantages and disadvantages."
6. *No* According to the first developmental paragraph, only advantages of large cars will be discussed in that paragraph.
7. *No* The first developmental paragraph discusses both advantages and disadvantages. This supports the thesis statement but not the topic sentence of the paragraph.
8. *Yes* However, more details could be added. For example, how are large cars good for big families? Why is strength important in a bad accident? Has the student had any experiences of crashes in big or small cars?
9. *No* The concluding paragraph is incomplete. The topic and controlling idea are not restated. It is not clear what "for this" refers to or why the student has this preference.
10. *No* A concluding statement should sum up the essay.

11. *No* The reasons the writer likes small cars are not included.

12. *No* The use of transitions would improve this essay. The writer gives the advantages as examples. It would be better to introduce the advantages by using connecting words, such as the *first* advantage or *another* advantage. The writer contrasts the advantages and disadvantages of large cars. Instead of introducing the disadvantages with the phrase "About the disadvantages," the writer could have used a transition, as in "However, large cars cannot get through small streets easily."

    The order in which the ideas are introduced could also be improved. The writer talks about a big car carrying a lot of people, then discusses a large car being stronger in an accident, and then discusses that a large car is good for big families. This third idea relates to the car's being able to carry a lot of people and, therefore, would more logically follow the first point.

13. *No* The sentences are sometime joined in an illogical fashion and sometimes are short and would be better if combined. For example, the sentences "Many people can be carried inside the car. Also, large cars are stronger in bad accidents, and they are very good for big families," could be improved by joining them differently, as in "Large cars are good for big families because they can carry a lot of people. Another advantage is that they protect the passengers better if an accident occurs."

14. *No* There are some grammatical mistakes that may cause confusion.

Question B

1. *Yes*
2. *Yes*
3. *Yes*
4. *Yes* The controlling idea is "pollution problems."
5. *Yes*
6. *Yes*
7. *No* The statements "Public safety does not concern the factory owners, who must know that people don't want to live in pollution that is dangerous for their health" and "Nobody in this world wants to breathe dirty air" are irrelevant.
8. *Yes*
9. *Yes*
10. *Yes* It gives solutions. However, it is weak. A better concluding statement might be "In conclusion, the pollution of our air and seas is a major problem. We must work together to solve it now."
11. *Yes*
12. *No* Throughout the paragraphs there are sentences where cohesion could be improved. For example, the writer is inconsistent in the use of pronouns. In the beginning, the writer uses the pronoun "we," but then changes to using "they." Later the writer uses the pronoun "you" and finishes by going back to the pronoun "we."
13. *No* Throughout the paragraphs, there are sentences that could be more concise. For example, in the introduction, the sentences that narrow the topic would be better combined, as in "Because of this, we must think about these problems and try to find solutions." The thesis statement could be improved by using a different grammar structure, as in "Pollution is one of the more serious problems we need to tackle."
14. *Yes*

EXERCISE W30 *(p. 408)*

1. Score 2: This essay demonstrates some development, but the writer focuses on people who read instead of supporting his or her agreement or disagreement with the given statement. There are insufficient details and a noticeably inappropriate choice of words or word forms (e.g., "emphasize," "imagines," "the read").

2. Score 5: This essay demonstrates competence in writing. It gives a thesis statement that all the paragraphs support. It uses details to illustrate ideas. There is unity, coherence, and progression. Syntactic variety and appropriate word choices are demonstrated.

3. Score 1: This essay contains serious errors in sentence structure. It states an opinion but does not give enough information to support that opinion. There are few details. The specifics are irrelevant (e.g., Helen of Troy).

4. Score 3: This paper demonstrates minimal competence. It lacks a strong thesis statement to give it direction. The first developmental paragraph supports the opinion that reading nonfictional works is beneficial. The second developmental paragraph supports (with only one detail) an implied opinion that reading novels is no longer beneficial. That detail is unnecessarily repeated (TV has taken the place of the novel). There are a number of mistakes in syntax and usage.

5. Score 0: This is not an essay. There is no development of ideas. There are writing errors that make the meaning difficult to understand.

6. Score 4: This paper demonstrates a generally well-organized and well-developed essay. The paper shows unity, coherence, and progression. There are some grammatical errors, but they do not impede understanding. Although the essay is well developed, it does not have the details and the syntactic variety seen on a score 6 paper.

There is no answer key for **EXERCISES W31–W32** *(p. 410 and pp. 413–414).*

EXERCISE W33 *(p. 417)*

Your answers may be stated differently.

1. The Mediterranean monk seal and common gray seal differ in size.
2. Ninety-nine percent of the extinct flora and fauna has not been identified according to figures presented by scientists.
3. Many dangers were encountered by early seafarers sailing to places across unknown seas.
4. In the future, water will be the main cause of disagreements between different countries, according to the UN.
5. It no longer makes good business sense to use sailing ships, because their speed depends on the wind.
6. Chaucer's burial place is marked by a tomb built in the 1500s.
7. As many as 600 species of butterflies called "swallowtails" exist in the world.
8. City parks provide both a venue for celebrations and a hideaway for those seeking escape from everyday noise and disturbance.
9. People who live in places with the right weather conditions and type of food still use their ancestors' method of drying food under the sun.
10. The 1906 San Francisco earthquake destroyed all but a few Victorian structures, most of which are located in the Haight-Ashbury district.

EXERCISE W34 *(p. 419)*

Your answers may be stated differently.

1. *New paraphrase*: Volunteers are given puppies by the Seeing-Eye Puppy-Raising Program to start their training as Seeing-Eye dogs.
2. The paraphrase is correct.
3. *New paraphrase*: In Denmark, a windy country where windmills were once used for pumping water and grinding grain, people have returned to using wind power.
4. *Paraphrase*: It is necessary for an infant to be able to physically react to its surroundings for it to realize its full capabilities.
5. The paraphrase is correct.

EXERCISE W35 *(p. 420)*

Your answers may be stated differently.

1. Shanty towns, found in many cities, are illegal temporary settlements of the poor that eventually become permanent.
2. Arcs of light caused by gravitational pull indicate the existence of dark matter in some galaxies.
3. The Henry Ford Museum offers a variety of exhibitions showing the development of cars and car-related services.

EXERCISE W36 *(p. 420)*

Your answers may be stated differently.

1. The main advantage of herding animals instead of killing them is that they can provide milk and fresh meat. (Note: Although breeding can be done to improve quantities, there is no mention of that in the passage.)
2. Games designed to entertain people by requiring a thinking process have been shown to help people maintain their thinking abilities into older age.
3. Believed to have a religious purpose, the *kiva* was a circular building with pillars, a protected fire pit, and a symbolic entrance into the underworld.

EXERCISE W37 *(p. 421)*

Your answers may be very different.

1. A radio drama about a Martian invasion caused some panic because it included very realistic information. Orson Welles produced the drama, which was based on a novel written by H. G. Wells. The extent of the panic that this play caused was exaggerated by media, and this can be seen as a second deception by the media.
2. A famous engineering feat is that of the Brooklyn Bridge that spans the East River in New York City. There were many difficulties in the building of the bridge. Chambers had to be designed so people could work on the river bottom. They also served as the foundations for the towers. Cables, steel ropes, and stays had to be designed to support the roadway.

Many workers and then the supervisor suffered from the bends due to breathing compressed air, and the supervisor's wife had to take over the management. Despite these problems and financial ones, the bridge finally was opened in 1883.

EXERCISE W38 *(p. 423)*

Your answers may be very different.

1. To help writers find work during the Depression Era, Roosevelt began a controversial program, the Federal Writers Project. Writers interviewed and recorded the personal histories of people from all areas of life. These collections of people's stories are valuable for historians, but sadly the project was never completed. However, the writers involved were able to use this information for their own works.

   Topic sentence: The Federal Writers Project, funded during the Depression, has left collections of people's personal stories, which are important for historians.

2. Test scoring machines were invented by a high school teacher. He knew from his boyhood tricks of using pencil marks to make car engines fail to start that graphite conducts electricity. He realized that pencil marks could be read by a machine. This invention was bought by IBM, which developed the technique. Large numbers of paper tests can be scored quickly and accurately by these machines. Scoring machines will probably be taken over by computers.

   Topic sentence: A high school teacher invented a machine that scored tests quickly and accurately, bringing standardized tests into fashion.

EXERCISE W39 *(p. 423)*

Your notes should include the following outlined points from the readings and lectures in your own note-taking style. Main points are numbered and details are lettered.

1. ***Reading notes***
   1. Fluoride is in all water in varying amounts.
   2. Children in areas of high fluoride had better teeth.
   3. When fluoride was added to areas with low amounts, children's teeth improved.
   4. Fluoride is important for the development of teeth because
      a. makes enamel so it doesn't dissolve easily
      b. keeps plaque organisms from making acids that attack teeth
      c. makes enamel hard and strong so decay is slowed
   5. Fluoride also is good for developed teeth because
      a. helps teeth fight cavities by repairing enamel
      b. added through toothpaste or drops prevents root decay and sensitivity

   Lecture notes
   1. Public treated like test animals with no consent
   2. New studies indicate important results conflicting with original study
      a. no difference between low and high fluoride areas and healthy teeth
      b. better dental hygiene is the real difference, not related to fluoride
   3. Dangers of fluoride
      a. extra amount in water claimed to be environment hazard
      b. side effects seen in test animals
      c. accumulates in the body
      d. is poisonous

2. ***Reading notes***
   1. Belief of animals sensing seismic activity
      a. hear ultrasound from rocks breaking
      b. sense changes in the Earth's magnetic field
   2. Creatures useful for predicting earthquakes
      a. animals and other creatures behave abnormally in advance
      b. quake in China – 7.3 – predicted by animals, evacuation saved thousands

   Lecture notes
   1. weak evidence of animals predicting quakes
   2. all evidence anecdotal and after the fact when impression more vivid
      a. odd behavior common, but unnoticed when not followed by shocking event
      b. animal stories fiction not fact
   3. studies of missing animals reported before a quake show no connection
   4. Chinese city had real warning by shocks preceding quake

There is no answer key for **EXERCISE W40** *(p. 424)*.

EXERCISE W41 *(p. 425)*

Student-written response 1

1. *No* Although the introductory statement is well constructed, the information is incorrect. The lecturer states that people *should* question the addition of fluoride to water. The lecturer's statement implies that most people are not questioning the use of fluoride. The student's statement would be more correct if the writer were to state "Some people are questioning . . .".
2. *Yes*
3. *Yes*

ANSWER KEYS

4. *No* The writer states that fluoride has been shown to accumulate in people's bodies and cause side effects. However, the lecturer states that fluoride has been shown to cause side effects in test animals. The implication might be that it causes side effects in humans, but this has not necessarily been shown and was not stated in the passage.
5. *Yes*
6. *Yes*
7. *Yes*
8. *Yes* For the most part the sentences are concisely written. There are some minor changes that could be made to some sentences to make them more concise.
9. *Yes* However, the concluding statement would be better without the phrase "or toothpaste" since the mention of "toothpaste" was a minor detail. Although it was not discussed in the paragraph, toothpaste tubes indicate their contents so consumers can make their own decisions on buying toothpaste with or without fluoride. In other words, in the case of toothpaste, people are not being used as test animals without consent.
10. *Yes*

Student-written response 2

1. *No* The writer immediately starts the paper with a topic sentence of a paragraph that disputes the use of fluoride.
2. *Yes*
3. *No* There are missing parts, such as the introductory statement. Some irrelevant information has been included.
4. *No* The lecturer doesn't dispute the benefits of fluoride but states that the rates of decay are going down due to other reasons. The concern is that of the dangers. The lecturer ends the lecture with the statement that more research into benefits and dangers needs to be conducted.
5. *No* Although for the most part the writer uses his/her own words, there are places that are copied directly from the reading. "...reduce the solubility of tooth enamel..."
6. *No* The writer adds the opinion about animal testing.
7. *No* The topic sentence of each supporting paragraph does not indicate what the paragraph is about, and the last statement in each of the supporting paragraphs does not add to the topic nor effectively complete the paragraphs.
8. *No* Some sentences are unnecessarily complicated. For example, "It has been found that the teeth of children in areas where there is little fluoride in the water are no different than those of children in areas where there is a lot of fluoride in the water" could be reduced to "The health of children's teeth were similar in areas of differing fluoride amounts."
9. *No* Although the writer has written a concluding statement, it does not summarize the discussion. It gives a personal opinion that does not correspond to the lecturer's conclusion that more research needs to be done. It does agree with the lecturer's statement against widespread experiments without people's consent.
10. *No* There are some grammatical mistakes, such as "like is a poisonous waste in water."

EXERCISE W42 *(p. 425)*

1. Score 3: This response contains important information from the passages. However, the connections between ideas are limited. There are some minor grammatical errors.
2. Score 2: This response contains ambiguities. For example, "they" in the phrase "they do weird things like jump out of the water" should only refer to "fish" and not to "fish and snakes." Points made in both the reading and the lecture are missing. There are grammatical mistakes and misspellings.
3. Score 5: This response covers the main points of the reading and lecture. It is well organized and uses a variety of sentence structures and vocabulary. Errors and occasional inconcise phrases do not detract from the overall presentation of the response.
4. Score 0: This response is too brief. What is written is incomprehensible.
5. Score 4: This response is generally good. It includes the main points from both passages. There is some ambiguity in the first paragraph; and in several places, sentences could be more concise.
6. Score 1: This response contains information from the reading. It is not accurate, and there is insufficient information from the listening to cast doubt on the information of the reading.

EXERCISE W43 *(p. 427)*

Check the main points in the answer key for Exercise W39 to make sure you have covered all points.

EXERCISE W44 *(p. 429)*

The points you should have covered are listed below. Main points are numbered and details are lettered.

1. ***Reading notes***
   1. Apes can communicate
      a. understand language
      b. respond at a human child's level
   2. Can't speak because physically unable, but
      a. can use sign language to show emotions, etc.
      b. can discriminate sounds
      c. can use keyboard of symbols

   Lecture notes
   1. What does acquiring language mean?
      a. use language creatively
      b. take turns
      c. communicate on one's own without a signal from humans
      d. comment on interesting things
   2. Difference in opinion among researchers
      a. people believing in ape communication say those against haven't worked with apes
      b. People skeptical of ape communication say believers are blinded by attachment
   3. Brain scan comparisons might solve dispute

2. ***Reading notes***
   1. Complex life cycle of salmon
      a. salmon leave ocean and swim upstream to lay eggs
      b. smolts swim downstream to ocean
   2. Dams cause problems in the migration
      a. salmon returning must get past them to go upstream
      b. smolts must pass dams without help from current
   3. Attempts to help smolts
      a. barges to transport them
      b. increase flow rate
      c. reduce water level

   Lecture notes
   1. Importance of getting smolts to sea is because of body changes from fresh to saltwater tolerance
      a. changes take 6 to 20 days
      b. slow current takes 60 days, too much time
   2. Solutions unsuccessful
      a. barges kill more fish than they save
      b. flow-rate increase not accepted by power companies
      c. water-level reduction not accepted by power companies

3. ***Reading notes***
   1. DDT crystalline compound used to control diseases
      a. typhus
      b. malaria
   2. DDT used as agricultural insecticide
   3. Environmental consequences on bird population – bald eagle and falcon
      a. accumulation of DDT in bodies
      b. thin egg shells
   4. Humans at risk from cancer
      a. liver cancer
      b. breast cancer
   5. DDT remains in nature for long time

   Lecture notes
   1. Evidence about DDT under question
      a. birds in decline before introduction of DDT
      b. birds almost hunted to extinction
      c. no indication of difficulty in reproducing during time of DDT use
   2. Egg thinning results because
      a. experiments used massive doses
   3. Egg thinning because of other factors
      a. oil spills
      b. lead and mercury poisoning
      c. stress from noise
   4. Other studies show no links between DDT and cancer
   5. Studies showed overuse can cause loss of effectiveness against pests
   6. Conclusion that DDT should be reconsidered as method against malaria

Writing Section Practice Test (p. 433)

There is no answer key to the Writing Section Practice Test. The main points that you should have covered in the integrated writing task are listed below.

Reading notes
1. tides can generate energy through dam-like structure across river entering bay
   a. gates are opened for rising tide and closed at high tide
   b. gates are opened at low tide and the out flow turns turbines
   c. can be used other direction
2. advantages of using tide energy
   a. four periods daily
   b. renewable
   c. nonpolluting
   d. no greenhouse gases

Lecture notes
1. Drawback that tidal power provides small amount toward total needs
   a. aren't enough good locations
2. negative impact as change in water quality, salinity, and the mix up of mud and sediments
   a. provides good conditions for growth of destructive organisms
   b. intertidal zone destroyed

3. causes problems for fish that migrate between river and sea
4. causes problems for finding mooring for fishing boats

PRACTICE TEST 1: Reading Section

(p. 439)

Note: If you answered an item incorrectly, complete the exercises listed for that item.

1. (D) The Greeks were early supporters of the idea that life originated elsewhere and was carried to Earth. See Exercises R9–R14.
2. (D) When something is "propelled" or "thrust," it is pushed onward with great force. See Exercises R1–R3.
3. (D) If it were known for certain that there is no life elsewhere, there would be no hypothesis or debate. See Exercises R9–R14.
4. (B) "Resurrected" and "reintroduced" mean "revived or brought back." See Exercises R1–R3.
5. (D) "Retain" and "keep" mean "to hold in place." See Exercises R1–R3.
6. (B) The phrase "objections . . . can be overcome" indicates that people are seriously looking at the hypothesis again. See Exercises R9–R14.
7. (C) Microscopic studies have been done on the meteorite's ("its") internal structure. See Exercises R4–R8.
8. (A) The phrase "such a trip" refers to a trip from Mars. See Exercises R4–R8.
9. (B) The phrase "many researchers now seem to reject this possibility" indicates that there is some disagreement about whether or not the meteorite contains fossils of microscopic bacteria. See Exercises R15–R21.
10. (C) "The panspermia hypothesis is regarded [judged] with less skepticism [to be less doubtful] than formerly [than was once thought]." See Exercises R9–R14.
11. [C] The word "However" indicates that conflicting information will follow. The facts of being "too heavy to be ejected from a planetary system" conflict with the previous sentence, which introduces the possibility of an organism being ejected. See Exercises R4–R8.
12. **Arguments Against Panspermia Hypothesis**

    (C) Although bacterial spores can survive long enough for interplanetary travel, they cannot for interstellar travel.

    (E) The ultraviolet radiation and cosmic rays would destroy any life-form.

    (F) Any life-form inside a meteorite would not be able to survive these high temperatures.

    Support for Panspermia Hypothesis

    (A) These chemicals may indicate that life can also exist in comets.

    (D) Since comets retain materials that life requires, they could also retain life-forms.

    (I) If bacterial spores can survive in space, the objections to their being destroyed by ultraviolet radiation and cosmic rays is not significant.

    (J) Such an ejecting star would have a high repulsive force.

    See Exercises R22–R24.
13. (B) Something that is "viable" or "feasible" is capable of working successfully. See Exercises R1–R3.
14. (C) The article implies that OTEC energy, despite some drawbacks, is likely to generate electricity in the future. The oceans store energy, and the author mentions that this system could be used to reduce our reliance on nonrenewable sources. See Exercises R15–R21.
15. (D) According to the reading, a temperature difference of at least 20 degrees Celsius between surface and deep water is necessary for efficient energy production. See Exercises R15–R21.
16. (B) According to the passage, both systems use cold water to condense vapor. See Exercises R9–R14.
17. (D) The phrase "other forms" refers to renewable energy directly provided by the sun and wind. See Exercises R4–R8.
18. (A) The fact that OTEC could produce energy that would allow us to reduce our use of fossil fuels and nuclear fission implies that the author thinks we rely too much on these nonrenewable kinds. See Exercises R15–R21.
19. (A) The author mentions that the OTEC technology has other benefits apart from clean energy production. See Exercises R15–R21.
20. (B) No mention is made of the damage that could be caused to fishing grounds. See Exercises R9–R14.
21. (B) The "conventional" alternatives are those that are the more established or accepted as "traditional." Here, it refers to alternatives such as wind power and solar energy. See Exercises R1–R3.

22. (A) Water outflows are water discharges that will raise the water temperature and affect creatures in the marine habitat. See Exercises R9–R14.

23. (C) The author mentions both benefits and disadvantages of OTEC but overall suggests that this energy technology could contribute a portion of the total energy production. See Exercises R15–R21.

24. [C] The sentence gives an explanation of the reason aquaculture is an important spinoff. See Exercises R4–R8.

25. (B) OTEC systems use the variations of water temperature to produce clean, renewable energy.

    (D) A million energy users is a significant number to be supplied with energy.

    (E) The OTEC system can run 24 hours a day for every day of the year.

    See Exercises R22–R24.

26. (B) The word "corollary" is a natural consequence or "result." See Exercises R1–R3.

27. (C) The passage explains that surpluses allow people to use their time in other ways. See Exercises R9–R14.

28. (D) The passage states there was no longer "the need to migrate in search of food supplies." See Exercises R9–R14.

29. (A) Settlements first needed to be established before people could develop their skills. See Exercises R9–R14.

30. (A) When something occurs "independently," it is unrelated or occurs "separately." See Exercises R1–R3.

31. (D) The passage states that "Such tools were certainly used for reaping some grass crop." See Exercises R9–R14.

32. (B) Something that is "fertile" is "productive" in that it provides the environment for productivity. See Exercises R1–R3.

33. (B) The passage states that the sediment was deposited on flood plains and that the fruitfulness of the land was restored annually. See Exercises R9–R14.

34. (A) The passage states that the area was expanded when people learned to draw off the river water into canals and ditches. See Exercises R9–R14.

35. (C) The evaporation of water could lead to an increase in soil salinity. See Exercises R4–R8.

36. (A) The evaporation of water from the irrigation ditches caused an increase of the salt in the soil, and this damaged the land. See Exercises R9–R14.

37. (D) The passage states that "settled agriculture led to the development of property rights and hence to a legal framework . . . to enforce laws." This suggests that an organized government was needed to protect property rights. See Exercises R15–R21.

38. [A] This sentence introduces the topic that the other sentences in the paragraph support. See Exercises R4–R8.

39. (A), (B), and (F) The people who ate the grass began to understand how to cultivate it. With the enriched soil to grow crops, the land sustained more people. Irrigation increased crop-growing areas, but property rights led to the need for a government to enforce laws. See Exercises R22–R24.

PRACTICE TEST 1: Listening Section

(p. 460, script on p. 635)

1. (A) CBA is a system for estimating or evaluating the costs and benefits of the outcomes of decisions. See Exercises L9–L12.

2. **Cost**

   (B) Higher insurance payments are a cost.

   (D) Additional floor space would add to costs since it could increase the rent, maintenance costs, and energy consumption.

   Benefit

   (A) If a new machine lowers energy consumption (a cost), it is a benefit.

   (C) Higher-quality products are a benefit.

   (E) New safety features would be a benefit since they could reduce insurance costs in the long run.

   See Exercises L13–L17.

3. (B) The professor discusses how the purchase of a new machine generates both costs and benefits. She uses the example to show what might be a cost and what, a benefit. See Exercises L18–L23.

4. (A) The professor mentions that in calculating costs and benefits, it is important to take into account the less obvious costs and benefits that are sometimes hidden. See Exercises L18–L23.

5. (D) The professor gives the building of a new road as an example of CBA use in the public domain. See Exercises L18–L23.

6. (B) The professor states that CBA tries to put a value on costs and benefits of subjective things by studying the financial choices people make. See Exercises L13–L17.

7. (C) The student tells the professor that she has come to discuss the research paper. She wants feedback from the professor to improve or correct her paper. See Exercises L9–L12.

8. (D) The student used information from a source that she thought was that of a professor, but in fact, it was that of a student. Her professor wants her to investigate a Web site more thoroughly so that she will understand her source. See Exercises L18–L23.

9. (A) Dr. Johnson points out to the student that the Web site she used was one on which a professor posted students' work, and consequently, the work may not be a good source for research. See Exercises L18–L23.

10. (A) The professor means that the claims may or may not be true, but that they should be questioned because of a possible bias. See Exercises L18–L23.

11. (C) The professor states that the research might be good and not biased, but it has to be repeated by an independent person to ensure that it is not biased toward the company. See Exercises L13–L17.

12. (C) The professor states, "I'd like to focus on the Prairie School of Architecture." See Exercises L9–L12.

13. [A] and [C] The professor explains that the horizontal features are designed to harmonize with the flat prairies. The professor also discusses the many features of the interior that created a living space that was more compatible with human proportions and living requirements. See Exercises L13–L17.

14. (B) The architects' philosophy was to harmonize their buildings with the prairie, but most of the houses were not built on the prairie, so the name isn't really appropriate. See Exercises L18–L23.

15. [B] and [D] The professor discusses the reduction in the number of interior corners and the reduction of the number of rooms to create a feeling of movement and freedom. See Exercises L13–L17.

16. (B) The professor states that ornamentation was only permitted if it complemented the overall expression and feeling of the building. See Exercises L13–L17.

17. (D) The professor states that the architects used geometric or Oriental designs. Then she gives the Japanese turned-up roof design as a feature used in the Prairie School designs. See Exercises L18–L23.

18. (D) The professor lectures on the most important aspect of memes – the fact that they replicate. See Exercises L9–L12.

19. (B) The professor is suggesting that the meme theory is not accepted by all academics. See Exercises L18–L23.

20. (C) The professor discusses how memes are spread among people. See Exercises L13–L17.

21. (B) The professor gives some examples of memes that could be considered unimportant. The meme of how to build a fire is a significant meme. See Exercises L18–L23.

22. (A) According to the professor, our minds are full of thoughts because memes need to be rehearsed and remembered so they can survive and be passed on. See Exercises L18–L23.

23. (A) The professor says that memes behave like genes. They are not part of genes. See Exercises L13–L17.

24. (A) The professor focuses mostly on the possible reasons why the Anasazi abandoned their communities and why their society disappeared. See Exercises L9–L12.

25. (D) The professor points out that some people are not completely happy with the name *Anasazi*. See Exercises L18–L23.

26. (C) When the Anasazi discovered that ceramic ware was better for storing food and liquid, they started making pottery rather than baskets for this purpose. See Exercises L13–L17.

27. (A) The professor was going to talk about the Anasazi buildings and briefly digressed into talking about their road system. She is reminding herself where in the lecture she left off. See Exercises L1–L3.

28. (A) *No* The professor says there is no strong evidence to support the idea that the Anasazi were wiped out by a disease.

    (B) *No* The professor says there is not much evidence to suggest they were invaded.

    (C) *Yes* The professor believes that the Anasazi abandoned their communities because overexploitation of the environment led to a lack of resources.

    See Exercises L13–L17.

29. (B) The professor says that the Anasazi may have caused an environmental disaster by their overexploitation of resources. This implies that they did not take good care of their environment. See Exercises L18–L23.

30. (C) The students are reviewing the definition of some legal terms that a professor discussed in class. See Exercises L9–L12.

31. (B) The woman is in a hurry to meet a roommate. She has only a few minutes to discuss legal terms. See Exercises L18–L23.

32. [A] and [B] The defendant tries to show that the accusation made against him or her is false. According to the woman, the prosecutor usually acts on behalf of the government. See Exercises L13–L17.

33. (C) The man describes how circumstantial evidence can be used to build a case against a defendant. See Exercises L18–L23.

34. (B) According to the woman, most people think that circumstantial evidence is not sufficient to get convictions in court. See Exercises L13–L17.

There is no answer key for the Speaking and Writing sections of Practice Test 1. See Calculating Scores for Practice Tests on p. XXIII for information about how to evaluate your responses. Also use the scored sample essays and speaking responses for CD-ROM Test 3 as a guide.

PRACTICE TEST 2: Reading Section

(p. 481)

Note: If you answered an item incorrectly, complete the exercises listed for that item.

1. (B) When something "alters," it "changes" or takes a different form. See Exercises R1–R3.

2. (A) The passage states that the rate of decay is constant, regardless of conditions. See Exercises R9–R14.

3. (B) The element's half-life is the time necessary for one-half of the original number of radioactive atoms in a sample to decay. See Exercises R4–R8.

4. (B) The rate at which a radioactive element decays, its half-life, is used as a way to calculate its age. See Exercises R9–R14.

5. (B) According to the passage, "Rocks as old as 4.6 billion years can be dated with some degree of reliability." This implies that dating rocks that are older than this is probably less reliable. See Exercises R15–R21.

6. (A) The phrase "from this point" refers to the separation of rubidium and strontium that occurs when the minerals crystallize from magma or metamorphic rock. That point is when the elements are incorporated into the minerals. See Exercises R4–R8.

7. (D) When something is "essential," it is "vital" or necessary. See Exercises R1–R3.

8. (C) According to the passage, when an organism dies, "no more carbon dioxide is absorbed." See Exercises R9–R14.

9. (A) According to the passage, the nitrogen-14 isotope leaks out so it cannot be used for comparisons. See Exercises R9–R14.

10. (D) The passage states that the amount of carbon-14 in the dead organism becomes less over time. See Exercises R9–R14.

11. [C] The information about the kinds of isotopes taken in from the atmosphere would follow the fact that the isotopes are in the same amount in the atmosphere as in the organism. It would precede the information about what happens after an organism dies. See exercises R4–R8.

12. **Rubidium-87**

    (D) Rubidium-87 has a half-life of nearly 48.8 billion years.

    (E) Rubidium-87 is incorporated into minerals as they crystallize from magma or metamorphic rock.

    (I) Rubidium-87 is formed when the rock is formed.

    Carbon-14

    (A) Bones or wood are organic materials.

    (C) Carbon-14 is an essential element of the cells being incorporated into living tissue.

    (F) Carbon-14 has the progeny nitrogen-14, which is a gas that leaks out of the organism and, therefore, is not useful for dating.

    (H) Trees are organic.

    See Exercises R22–R24.

13. (D) The number of births is divided by the total population. See Exercises R4–R8.

14. (A) Demographers use the model because it helps to explain changes in population. See Exercises R9–R14.

15. (B) When something is "portrayed," it is shown or "represented" in a visual or verbal form. See Exercises R1–R3.

16. (D) There is no information given as to the number of women who died while giving birth. See Exercises R9–R14.

17. (B) The fluctuations in total population due to epidemics indicate a drop followed by a rise. There was a gradual rise overall. See Exercises R15–R21.

18. (C) "Agrarian" occupations refer to those that are agricultural, in other words, occupations dealing with "farming." See Exercises R1–R3.

19. (C) The increased urbanization reduced the incentive to have a large number of children. See Exercises R9–R14.

20. (A) The birth rate may fall below the death rate (deaths exceed births) and without immigration (there is no immigration) the total population may slowly decrease (the population gradually declines). See Exercises R9–R14.

21. (B) Something that is at an "equilibrium" level is at a "stable" level or is balanced. See Exercises R1–R3.

22. (A) The improvements in health have caused an imbalance of births over deaths. See Exercises R9–R14.

23. (A) The earlier "pessimistic" predictions were that the population explosion would continue were based on the length of time the demographic transition took place in Europe (200 years). However, the transition in less developed countries seems to be occurring faster then predicted. See Exercises R15–R21.

24. [A] The information about why in cities there was less incentive for large numbers of children would follow the statement that industrialization had led to urbanization. See Exercises R4–R8.

25. (B), (C), and (E) In the preindustrial era, there were high birth and death rates with only a gradual population increase. This was followed by dramatic increases in population as improved health caused a decline in the death rate. Economic pressures reduced the birth rate, bringing the population to zero growth. See Exercises R22–R24.

26. (A) When something is put into an underground "chamber," it is put into a large "cavity" or hole that forms a roomy area. See Exercises R1–R3.

27. (B) The commission understood that the waste may be hazardous for people thousands of years in the future and that these future generations need to be warned of the danger. See Exercises R4–R8.

28. (D) The author mentions different circumstances to help the reader understand that even though we think that future societies may be sophisticated, they may not be, and therefore we cannot leave the matter to chance. See Exercises R15–R21.

29. (C) A "scourge" is a source of extensive "affliction" and devastation. See Exercises R1–R3.

30. (A) The message must be understandable to any person no matter what his or her cultural background or knowledge is. See Exercises R9–R14.

31. (B) The author mentions the second law of thermodynamics to explain why materials can't endure. See Exercises R15–R21.

32. (C) The word "its" refers to the *committee* formed to guard a certain kind of knowledge. See Exercises R4–R8.

33. (D) The committee that guards and passes on specialized knowledge has been called an "atomic priesthood" because it is rather like a priesthood in its exclusiveness and its monopoly of knowledge about nuclear waste sites. See Exercises R15–R21.

34. (D) A "sanction" is a "penalty" used to obtain conformity to someone's wishes. People who do not observe sanctions are punished through legal or moral pressure. See Exercises R1–R3.

35. (A) The idea of a relay system is to pass on information over just a few generations. This would help to prevent the breakdown of communication over long periods of time. See Exercises R9–R14.

36. (A) The author points out that those who have exclusive knowledge could use it to control those who are ignorant. See Exercises R9–R14.

37. (D) While the exclusiveness of the atomic priesthood might lead to other problems, it is not mentioned as a difficulty in devising a communication system with the future. Rather, it is the main proposal put forward for making that communication possible. See Exercises R9–R14.

38. [B] Finding efficient ways to deactivate nuclear waste materials is an example of a technological advance that could be made to solve this problem. See Exercises R4–R8.

39. (A), (D), and (F) All of the various means of storing and passing on information pose a problem in communicating with the future because of the physical decay of storage media. A relay system could be used in which the knowledge is passed by a selected group of people. However, the proposal has potential problems of creating a divided society. See Exercises R22–R24.

PRACTICE TEST 2: Listening Section

(p. 502, script on p. 643)

1. (D) The professor explains the way various creatures deal with the change of water and salt concentrations in the estuarine environment. See Exercises L9–L12.

2. (A) The professor thinks that the students know the definition of osmosis and is confirming that belief. See Exercises L18–L23.

3. [A] and [D] The professor states that crabs keep out both water and salt with their hard shells and that they may have internal organs that can regulate salt intake and excretion. See Exercises L13–L17.

4. (D) The professor has just explained the migration pattern in blue crabs. He is giving the students an opportunity to ask for more explanation if they do not understand. See Exercises L18–L23.

5. **Physiological**

   (B) osmoregulating

   (C) dropping leaves

   Behavioral

   (A) migrating

   (D) burrowing into mud

   See Exercises L13–L17.

6. (B) Although the professor mentions birds as predators of invertebrates in the estuaries, he doesn't talk about any adaptation birds have made in order to live in the estuarine environment. See Exercises L13–L17.

7. (B) The man states that he was told to see the professor to get advice about switching majors. See Exercises L9–L12.

8. (C) The man wants to change majors, and the professor assumes that he is changing to linguistics. Since the man has been sent to this particular professor, it can be inferred that she is an advisor for students in the Linguistics Department. See Exercises L18–L23.

9. (C) The man explains to the professor that he taught English in Peru to earn money. He enjoyed the experience and is considering going into this field of study. See Exercises L13–L17.

10. (A) She does not know if the man's courses in American Sign Language can be used as a second language credit for the Linguistics Department requirements. She would prefer to tell him the wrong answer than to allow him to make a decision based on this point. See Exercises L18–L23.

11. (A) The man's answer to the professor's question indicates that he is concerned about graduating on schedule. He later states that he might be able to get more funding and mentions looking into grant and loan possibilities. This indicates that finances are a factor in his decision on changing majors. See Exercises L18–L23.

12. (B) The professor elicits the kinds of pressures that keep students from asking questions in classroom situations. See Exercises L9–L12.

13. (B) The professor is listing the questions he asks himself after class. He does this in order to set the stage for a discussion on why students don't ask questions in class. See Exercises L18–L23.

14. (D) The woman agrees with the man's reason for considering the class size as a negative pressure but provides her own reason for class size being a negative pressure. See Exercises L18–L23.

15. (B) When the professor asks Lisa to explain what she means by time pressure, she gives the name of Professor Clarkson. Although the professor doesn't understand how this can be an example, the other students do. See Exercises L18–L23.

16. (A) *No* Fear of asking too many questions is not one of the reasons discussed.

    (B) *Yes* The students mention fear of being considered stupid by classmates.

    (C) *Yes* Being the victim of a professor's sarcastic joke is one of the reasons elicited.

    (D) *No* Fear of making a mistake is not discussed in the class.

    (E) *Yes* Fear of wasting a professor's time with a mere question is discussed.

    See Exercises L13–L17.

17. (D) The professor is letting the students know that there are other pressures that did not come up during the conversation but probably will during the discussions. See Exercises L18–L35.

18. (C) The professor discusses the theory of phrenology, an early method of psychological analysis. See Exercises L9–L12.

19. [B] and [C] According to the professor, Gall (the founder of phrenology) said the brain faculties had separate organs placed in a separate part of the brain and that the shape of the brain determined the shape of the skull. See Exercises L13–L17.

20. (B) The professor explains the popularity of the practice and then indicates through the question that nowadays this is considered a strange theory. See Exercises L18–L23.

21. (C) The professor states that the phrenologists looked for confirmation for their hypotheses and ignored anything that went against their hypotheses. See Exercises L13–L17.

22. (A) The professor discusses the widespread practice of phrenology. Today its practice has largely disappeared. See Exercises L18–L23.

23. (D) The professor states that phrenologists were important in arguing that brain functions were localized. See Exercises L13–L17.

24. (B) The professor mentions the differences between the conditions on Mars and Earth, the necessity of human migration, and the ethical problems as part of the issues to be dealt with in radically transforming the conditions on Mars. See Exercises L9–L12.

25. (C) By comparing terraforming to science fiction, the professor is pointing out that technologically it will be a difficult task to undertake. See Exercises L18–L23.

26. (B) The professor states that pressure on resources of a rapidly expanding population has always forced people to migrate in search of new territory. He mentions the migration of Europeans to the Americas as an example of such a migration. See Exercises L18–L23.

27. [C] and [D] The professor states that the other planets are unsuitable and that Mars has water and a solid surface. See Exercises L13–L17.

28. (A) The professor wants to leave aside the ethical considerations and concentrate on the practicalities, which would be those technological considerations. See Exercises L18–L23.

29. (D) The professor mentions greenhouse gas being produced by the ammonia-rich asteroids, not by factories. See Exercises L13–L17.

30. (C) The student has seen an announcement on the bulletin board asking for participants in a research project. She wants to volunteer to participate. See Exercises L9–L12.

31. (A) The coordinator needs to make certain that the student meets the requirements for the experiment. See Exercises L18–L23.

32. (B) The student is indicating that even though she is well this week, no one can be certain about their health later. See Exercises L18–L23.

33. (C) The coordinator does not ask the student her preferences for snacks, but states the snacks will be "typical." See Exercises L13–L17.

34. (D) The coordinator states that the breakfasts will consist of the normal things, and gives eggs and cereal as examples. See Exercises L13–L17.

There is no answer key for the Speaking and Writing sections of Practice Test 2. See Calculating Scores for Practice Tests on p. XXIII for information about how to evaluate your responses. Also use the scored sample essays and speaking responses for CD-ROM Test 4 as a guide.

Audio Scripts

This section contains the audio scripts for all of the exercises and practice tests in this book. Please note the use of the following abbreviations for speaking parts:

(Man S) for Man Student

(Man P) for Man Professor

(Woman S) for Woman Student

(Woman P) for Woman Professor

DIAGNOSTIC TEST: Listening Section

Questions 1–6

Listen to part of a lecture in an American government class.

(Woman P) So today I want to go over the main points about what's called the Electoral College, that is, the way that presidents are chosen in the United States. Also vice presidents too, of course. Now – some of you may think that the president is the candidate who gets the most votes from the voting public. Often that's true. But the way it works, it's not necessarily the one who gets the most votes from the public. In practice, it's the candidate who wins the most votes from the Electoral College. OK. So let me try to make this clear.

First of all, what is an elector? Well, an elector is a person – a member of a political party – who has been chosen by that party in a given state. OK, so this person, this elector, is pledged to his or her party's candidate for president. So in any state there are several electors. The number of electors in a state is equal to the number of U.S. Senators plus the number of U.S. Representatives in that state. Don't get confused here. The senators and representatives are not the same people as the electors. It's just that the numbers are the same. So . . . there are always two senators in each state, as you know, but the number of representatives depends on the population of the state. So a populous state has several representatives and a state without a lot of people will have only a few representatives. Some states, such as Alaska, which has a small population, for example, have only one representative at the current time. That means that Alaska will have three electors chosen by each political party. In total, there are currently 538 electoral votes in the whole country.

OK. So what happens when you vote in the presidential election? Well, what you have when you vote is a ballot – which normally says "Electors for" and then the names of each of the presidential candidates running. So you choose "Electors for" the candidate of your choice.

Here's the interesting part, in a way. Whichever candidate wins the most popular votes in a state also wins all the electors of that state. So back to the case of Alaska: the candidate who wins the greatest share of the vote from the general public wins three electoral votes. Those three electors become the electors of that state. Now, OK, there are a couple of exceptions to that – but we'll have a look at those next week.

Now the election for president, where all the voting public cast their votes, is, as you know, in early November. OK. So, the electors of the state, remember, these are the people who were in effect chosen through popular vote – and who will vote for the candidate of their party – meet in December and they cast their votes, one for the president and one for the vice president.

OK, so the candidate with the most Electoral College votes, provided it's an absolute majority, that is, over half the total of Electoral College votes, is declared president. The same goes for the vice president. If no one gets an absolute majority, then the U.S. House of Representatives chooses the president from among the top candidates.

Well, there are also some problems associated with this system that you will hear raised from time to time. One problem, for example, that I can mention right off the bat, is that it's possible that the person who is declared president through having won the most Electoral College votes may not have won the majority of the general public's votes. This has to do with the fact that the distribution of electoral votes tends to over-represent people in less populous states. Now those who favor this system point out, however, that it more accurately represents all parts of the country, not just the metropolitan populous regions. So, in effect, it balances out rural and urban regions – and contributes to national cohesion. There are several other things that opponents of this system have put forward, but I'd like you to read up on those before we meet next week.

Now get ready to answer the questions. You may use your notes to help you answer.

1. What is the lecture mainly about?
2. According to the professor, who becomes an elector?
3. Why does the professor say this: Don't get confused here. The senators and representatives are not the same people as the electors.
4. Why does the professor use the example of Alaska in the lecture?
5. Which candidate wins the presidential election?
6. What does the professor mean when she says this: There are also some problems associated with this system that you will hear raised from time to time.

Questions 7–11

Listen to a conversation between a student and a professor.

(Woman S) Good morning, Dr. Blake. Sorry I'm running late.

(Man P) Oh, no problem, Angie. It gave me a bit of time to review your research proposal.

(Woman S) Oh, good. Um, so you had a chance to look at my proposal. And what did you think?

(Man P) Well, it's reasonably well presented, but if you really want to get that grant, I think you should explain how you're going to set up, get a more focused statistical analysis.

(Woman S) Oh, I hadn't really given that point much thought, 'cause frankly, I'm not so sure what is the . . . what the best way to go about it is.

(Man P) Well, you really need to clear that up. Why don't you go to the Computer Center? You can tell the woman at the information desk, Miriam, I think her name is. Tell Miriam what you need and she'll direct you to one of the statisticians there, you know, someone who can tell you the best way to set up your experiment in order to get your statistics in a meaningful form. Then that procedure needs to be explained in your proposal.

(Woman S) OK . . . I better do that right away.

(Man P) Yeah, I think that's a good idea. Proposals have to be in before the office closes on Friday, and you're going to want to have a clear idea of how you're going to deal with your data.

(Woman S) Thanks. Bye.

(Man P) Uh, just a minute, Angie?

(Woman S) Yes?

(Man P) Before you go, there are a couple more points. Let's see, I wrote a couple of comments on this draft you gave me . . . Oh, here you are. My concern is how you've defined – or I should say haven't defined – your subjects. You mentioned that you'll be testing nonnative speakers' linguistic recognition of certain English stress patterns . . . but you haven't clearly defined the group of subjects.

(Woman S) Well, I've made contact with a group of international students who are willing to work on the project.

(Man P) Yeah, I know, but there are some issues that the committee will question. The proposal as you have it seems, well, somewhat like comparing apples and oranges. We've talked about your subjects being given an oral fluency test so that you can choose subjects with about the same linguistic level. But you haven't made that clear in your proposal. The committee will say that the data from, let's say, a tonal-language speaker at a high level can't be compared to a romance-language speaker at a beginning level. The data would be ambiguous. You see, you need to explain how you're going to select your subjects.

(Woman S) You mean I should write more about the oral test we talked about?

(Man P) That's right.

(Woman S) Oh, I'm sorry, Dr. Blake. I have a class in 20 minutes and I want to get to the Computer Center – it's on my way to the classroom building – to set up an appointment. So could I come back around 3:30?

(Man P) No. That's not a good time for me. Why don't you read through my comments and work through the explanation about subject selection? And would you have time to bring your next draft in first thing tomorrow morning? We could go over the final details quickly, and that would give you time to make any other necessary changes before turning it in.

(Woman S) Oh, I would really appreciate that, Dr. Blake. Thank you so much for your help. Bye.

Now get ready to answer the questions. You may use your notes to help you answer.

7. Why does the student go to see the professor?
8. Why does the professor suggest that the student go to the Computer Center?
9. According to the professor, what information should the student add in her proposal?
10. Why does the professor say this: The proposal as you have it seems, well, somewhat like comparing apples and oranges.
11. What does the professor imply about the people who will decide on the grant money?

Questions 12–17

Listen to part of a discussion in a business correspondence class.

(Woman P) We've been concentrating on formal letters in business communications, but today I'd like to talk about some issues in using e-mail. Actually, we'll be looking at this topic for the next couple of class sessions, as it's likely much of your written communication in business will be done with e-mail – and the etiquette of using e-mail is extremely important in the business world.

So, OK, there are two types of e-mails that you'll be using in business: internal, those sent within the office, and the external – customers, suppliers, agencies.

Now, we discussed the paper letter and how it could get separated from its envelope. So it's essential for a paper letter to have all the receiver/sender information in the letter itself. Now, most e-mail programs include the receiver/sender information – so the message can't get separated from this information. But, there are a few options that some people are not aware of – and unfortunately, not all programs have all these options. OK. Let's say there are thirty people in the office where you work and you want to tell them about a change in policy. How do you set up your e-mail? I mean, who do you send this message to? What do you put into the box?

(Man S) Well, I'd put the names into the "to" box, you know, the box where I put the names of the people who will get the message.

(Woman P) OK. So you would type all 30 names into the receiver box?

(Man S) Well, probably not type. I might make a mistake. I'd copy them in – or use the "reply to all" icon from another e-mail, and of course, I change the message and the subject.

(Woman P) OK. That is one way. Yes?

(Woman S) Um, yeah, I have to do a lot of official e-mails, and I get really annoyed when people send me a message with lots of names in it. Sometimes I print out the message – and I get three pages of people's addresses for half a page of message.

(Woman P) So what do you suggest?

(Woman S) Well, I usually set up my address book so that I can put all the names of people into one group. And then when I want to send them all a message, I just put the name of the group into the receiver box – and then everyone gets the message. That way, if they print it out, then only the name of the group is on the page.

(Man S) Yeah, I don't like that because . . . well, what annoys me is I need someone's address, right? So, I go to a message to get it and it isn't there – because just the group name is there. Or I want to see if everyone is on the list and that no one has been left out.

(Woman P) OK. So we have two differing opinions on what to put into the receiver box for mail within a company. We'll come back to this point in a moment. Now, let's change the audience. Suppose the message is that you'll be moving to a new office, and you want to tell all your customers the new location.

(Man S) Well, that's different then. 'Cause you can't put all the customers' names and addresses into the receiver box. I mean, that's private information, isn't it? So you gotta use a group name . . .

(Woman S) No, I don't agree. I mean . . . I do agree that it's important to have customer anonymity, but if you put a group name, then it isn't personalized. I really think the customer wants to be addressed by their name, not something like "customer group." Using a name is saying "You are an important individual" instead of "You're just a name on this list."

(Woman P) So what would you do? You don't want to put their names in a list for all to see, and you don't want to address them impersonally.

(Woman S) Well, I guess I would write to them individually so that I could keep, well, . . . maintain privacy and still be sort of personal.

(Woman P) That sounds like a lengthy process – especially if your customers are in the thousands. A lot of work. Any other suggestions? No one? OK. Remember when we were discussing the formal business letter, we talked about a "blind copy"? Remember how you use a blind copy when you don't want the receiver to know who else is receiving copies? Most e-mail systems have a blind-copy function, but it doesn't usually appear automatically. You have to change your settings for it to show up on your screen. I send myself the message, and put everyone's address, including my own as a check, into the blind-copy box. Every individual receives the message, addressed as if he or she was the only recipient of the message.

Now get ready to answer the questions. You may use your notes to help you answer.

12. What is the discussion mainly about?

13. Listen again to part of the discussion. Then answer the question.

(Woman P) OK. So we have two differing opinions on what to put into the receiver box for mail within a company. We'll come back to this point in a moment. Now, let's change the audience.

Why does the professor say this: We'll come back to this point in a moment. Now, let's change the audience.

14. What can be inferred about the students?

15. Listen again to part of the discussion. Then answer the question.

(Woman P) That sounds like a lengthy process – especially if your customers are in the thousands. A lot of work. Any other suggestions? No one? OK. Remember when we were discussing the formal business letter, we talked about a "blind copy"?

Why does the professor ask this: Remember when we were discussing the formal business letter, we talked about a "blind copy"?

16. According to the discussion, which way both protects customer identity and promotes customer personalization?

17. Which of the following are valid points about messages sent to a group address instead of individual addresses?

Questions 18–23

Listen to part of a lecture in a literature class.

(Man P) Before I continue, I want to sketch in some of the significant events of the life of the writer Jack London. This biographical outline is really just to give you a general picture . . . so that you can perhaps appreciate how his life and work were related. It's quite clear, I think you'll agree, that the kind of life London led really did show up in the kinds of stories he wrote. But, before I go on, I want to remind you all that on Tuesday I'll be presenting an overview of London's major works – so in preparation for that I'd like you to read his small masterpiece, *To Build a Fire.*

OK. Now, where was I? London was born in San Francisco in 1876. In fact, he never knew his real father, who had left his mother before Jack was born. Biographers have suggested that the anxiety London felt at not knowing the identity of his real father is clearly shown in the themes of many of his books – which often deal with the struggle for survival and the harshness of the natural and human world. So, I think it's true that we get a feel in his stories that London is often trying to make sense of the difficult events of his childhood.

As a young man, Jack worked at various jobs – some menial and dangerous, and often adventurous. For example, he sailed the Pacific, worked on a fish patrol to catch poachers, raided oyster farms, prospected for gold, joined an army of unemployed workers, and even spent time in jail. Now why is all this so significant? Well, it really comes back to the way London used his life experiences in the characters and themes of his stories. In light of the often harsh experiences he dealt with in these kinds of jobs, I think we can also understand what attracted him to socialism and the struggle for improved social and working conditions.

London's learning was gained largely outside of institutions. In other words, he learned mainly from experience, but was determined to improve himself and enrolled as a student at the University of California. However, he dropped out after one semester due to a lack of money, and perhaps disillusionment with university life. Any of you feel that way?

Of course, it's true that he was always a keen reader and studied the works of other writers in order to learn to become a writer himself. I think we can say that he consciously chose the life of a writer in order to escape the unpleasant prospect of manual work. The adventurous life he led provided him with a great deal of material from which to create imaginative literature. Most writers and intellectuals, of course, know about the struggle for survival only from their readings and observations. London, by contrast, experienced poverty, struggle, and danger first hand. Take, for example, one of his first published stories, *Story of a Typhoon off the Coast of Japan*, which was taken directly from his experience as a sailor in the Pacific when he was just 17. It is clear in this story, as in so many others of London's, that we the readers feel the directness of his writing and this, I think we can say, is because he wrote about what he knew and experienced so deeply.

Now at first, his submissions to publishers met with very little success. However, he was very determined – and he forced himself to write one thousand words per day. This disciplined approach to writing eventually paid off, and he gained international fame, with a large output of writing. In total, he published over 150 stories, 18 novels, and seven books of nonfiction. And many of them were translated into different languages. His novel *The Call of the Wild* was the one that brought him lasting fame, and many of his short stories are considered classics. It's true to say, though, I think we can admit . . . that not all his works are especially good literature. He often wrote carelessly . . . and there's a considerable part of his output which, I think it is fair to say, is uninspired and uninteresting to the modern reader.

In the last period of his life, London tried his hand at agriculture. Much of his later writing, in fact, is concerned with the pleasures of country life and the satisfaction to be gained from earning a living from the land. He pursued this interest with characteristic energy at his ranch in California and he continued a tight work schedule right up to his premature death at the age of 40 in November 1916.

Now get ready to answer the questions. You may use your notes to help you answer.

18. What is the lecture mainly about?

19. According to the professor, what effect did the absence of a father have on London?

20. What does the professor mean when he says this: However, he dropped out after one semester due to a lack of money, and perhaps disillusionment with university life. Any of you feel that way?
21. Why does the professor think that London read so many books?
22. What does the professor imply about London's success?
23. What does the professor think of London's work?

Questions 24–29

Listen to a discussion in an anthropology class.

(Woman P) So I'd like to move on to a discussion of a group of people who vanished from the Earth around 30,000 years ago after having existed successfully for approximately a quarter of a million years. They're known as the Neanderthal people, named by the way, after a place in Germany where their bones, their remains were first found in 1856. Now, let's first look at how these people compared with the other main group of humans existing at that time, known as the Cro-Magnon. Now the remains of Cro-Magnon people show that they were anatomically similar, in other words, their body structure was physically more or less identical to modern humans. OK, does anyone know how our Cro-Magnon ancestors looked different from these Neanderthals?

(Man S) Didn't they have a different skull shape?

(Woman P) Yes. But can you be more precise?

(Man S) Um, well, OK. The Neanderthals had a sloping forehead and no real chin.

(Woman P) OK. Certainly their chins were not prominent and their foreheads sloped backwards. So they looked rather different from the Cro-Magnon. OK. Now, what about their cultural and technological lives? Were they so much different from their Cro-Magnon cousins? Yes?

(Man S) They had the ability to make stone tools – so that was a similarity.

(Woman P) Yes, although their tool-making ability appears to have been less developed than that of the Cro-Magnon. They did know how to make stone into useful tools but they don't appear to have developed fine points or blades. And their wooden spears seem to have been adapted for stabbing but not for throwing. The Cro-Magnon, on the other hand, developed spears with tips carved from bone and stone and other materials. They also used bows and arrows and invented handles for their tools and weapons. Those are things the Neanderthals didn't develop. Yes?

(Woman S) Well, didn't the Neanderthals know how to make fire?

(Woman P) Yes, now that's a very good point. They could make fire and transport it when necessary. And that is an important skill that they shared with the Cro-Magnon. Also, they may have had some simple art forms, but again, fairly undeveloped in comparison with the Cro-Magnon, whose artistic sophistication is well documented. But, you know, there's a recent find – a polished baby mammoth tooth – which suggests that the Neanderthals may have produced items for personal adornment. Both these points show that the Neanderthals may not have been as backward as was once claimed.

(Woman S) Do you think the Neanderthals had the ability to produce language?

(Woman P) Oh, now that's an interesting question. Studies of skull capacity and shape indicate that they probably had similar neurological capacities to modern humans. So, in other words, they certainly had the mental apparatus to produce language. Now, by examining the bone remains of the vocal tract area, we can say that they could produce sounds too, but they would not have been able to produce a large number of sounds and their speech articulation may have been slow. By contrast, the Cro-Magnon would have had the ability to produce language and speech sounds just as modern humans.

OK, so what happened to the Neanderthals? Well, this question has produced a lot of controversy – even division – within the scientific community. So, broadly speaking, we can say that there are two main lines of thought here. First, it's possible that the Neanderthals may have died out due to a relative lack of sophistication in comparison to the Cro-Magnon. The Cro-Magnon people arrived in regions inhabited by Neanderthals about 40,000 years ago. And, then around 30,000 years ago the climate became more severe – and the Cro-Magnons would have been better adapted to survival under these conditions – since they had, as we noted earlier, better weapons and tools and more developed speech. So in competition for territory or in hunting, they would have been more successful. Some people have gone so far as to suggest that the Neanderthals were deliberately destroyed by the newcomers – or perhaps killed off by diseases brought in with them.

So that's one general line of thought. Now, a second approach is to hypothesize that the Neanderthals and the Cro-Magnon interbred – and that over time, the Cro-Magnon genes became more dominant – so that eventually the Neanderthal characteristics disappeared. During the same period, the Neanderthal culture would also have been absorbed into the more dominant Cro-Magnon culture. If they did manage to interbreed, this would mean, of course, that the two types of people were not separate species. And if this scenario is right, it would have appeared as though the Neanderthals had become extinct – whereas in reality they would have merged with the more dominant Cro-Magnon people. Now, I want to emphasize that this issue is still very much debated by anthropologists. A lot of the focus of current research is on trying to determine whether either Cro-Magnon remains or modern humans have any traces of Neanderthal DNA. If they do, then a better case for claiming that the two peoples interbred could be made, and hence, the second of these two hypotheses would be strengthened.

Now get ready to answer the questions. You may use your notes to help you answer.

24. What is the main purpose of the lecture?

25. Why does the professor say this: . . . they were anatomically similar, in other words, their body structure was physically more or less identical to modern humans.

26. Why does the professor refer to the Neanderthal's ability to make and transport fire?

27. What does the professor NOT mention about the Neanderthal's use of language?

28. Indicate whether each sentence below describes Neanderthal or Cro-Magnon characteristics.

29. According to the professor, why is a comparison of Neanderthal and modern human DNA useful?

Questions 30–34

Listen to part of a conversation at a campus police station.

(Woman P) Yes. How can I help you?

(Man S) Yeah. Uh, I think my car has been stolen.

(Woman P) OK. Can you give me the details?

(Man S) Yeah. Uh, it's a 1999 four-wheel-drive blue Subaru.

(Woman P) OK, and when and where did you last see it?

(Man S) Well, this morning I parked it in front of Lacey Hall.

(Woman P) Let me check our records. Ah. It appears your car was in a faculty-only zone.

(Man S) Yeah, I know. But the handicapped parking spaces were all taken, and I had to find a place so I could get easy access to my classes.

(Woman P) Uh-huh, but since you don't have a faculty parking sticker, your car was towed.

(Man S) I was hoping that because I had a handicapped sticker, it would be OK.

(Woman P) There may have been a complaint from a faculty member. Well, sometimes that happens when a professor can't get to work on time because someone who isn't faculty is parked in faculty parking. So the tow truck was called.

(Man S) OK. Um . . . how do I get my car back?

(Woman P) Well, when a vehicle has to be towed, the owner must pay for the towing and storage fees before the car can be taken. And I'm sorry to say, there's also a parking fine.

(Man S) And how much will all that be?

(Woman P) The towing fee is $90 and there's a storage fee of $10 per day. So it'd be a good idea to pick up your car today, if possible. The parking fine is fifty, but if you pay within seven days, the fine is reduced to twenty.

(Man S) I think . . . well, all this is very unfair. If the university's going to charge so much, they should have more spaces. My car gets towed because the handicapped parking spaces are full. One of the cars didn't even have a handicapped sticker.

(Woman P) Uh, well, you know, don't you, that you do have the right to appeal? Since you believe that circumstances exist that may excuse you from certain university regulations.

(Man S) Oh. So how do I go about doing that?

(Woman P) Well, first, you write a letter of appeal – that can be done online. You can go to the university traffic regulations page. You know the university home page?

(Man S) Uh-huh.

(Woman P) OK. In your letter explain the situation and why you believe the ticket was unfair. You'll get a letter immediately, saying that your case is being reviewed. Later, you'll get a reply stating whether or not your appeal is accepted. The fine is put on hold as soon as the letter of appeal has been received. If the charge isn't dropped, then you have seven days to pay up or to make a further appeal.

(Man S) OK. Thank you for your help.

(Woman P) OK. Good luck.

Now get ready to answer the questions. You may use your notes to help you answer.

30. Why did the student go to the campus police?

31. What can be inferred about the student?

32. Listen again to part of the conversation. Then answer the question.

(Woman P) Well, when a vehicle has to be towed, the owner must pay for the towing and storage fees before the car can be taken. And I'm sorry to say, there's also a parking fine.

What does the officer mean when she says this: And I'm sorry to say. . . .

33. Listen again to part of the conversation. Then answer the question.

(Woman P) Uh, well, you know, don't you, that you do have the right to appeal? Since you believe that circumstances exist that may excuse you from certain university regulations.

Why does the officer say this: Uh, well, you know, don't you, that you do have the right to appeal?

34. What will the student probably do?

DIAGNOSTIC TEST: Speaking Section

1. Please listen carefully.

Describe changes in technology that have affected your life, and explain what effect they have had on you as a student. Include details and examples to support your explanation.

You may begin to prepare your response after the beep. [beep]

Please begin speaking after the beep. [beep]

2. Please listen carefully.

What kind of friend is better – one who is very similar to you or one who is very different? Which kind of friend do you prefer and why? Include details and examples in your explanation.

You may begin to prepare your response after the beep. [beep]

Please begin speaking after the beep. [beep]

3. Please listen carefully.

The University of the Rockies is announcing its annual job fair. Read the announcement from the Career Services Center. You will have 45 seconds to read the announcement. Begin reading now.

Now listen to two students as they discuss the announcement.

(Man S) Are you going to register to attend the job fair?

(Woman S) I'm not sure. I'd like the experience of living abroad, but I need a well-paid job to pay back my student loan. Not all the jobs pay that well.

(Man S) Some do.

(Woman S) Yeah, but the ones that pay well want experienced teachers. I've only done my student teaching, and that isn't enough.

(Man S) But you're certified to teach science, so you can probably get a job just about anywhere . . . you know . . . because of the shortage of science teachers.

(Woman S) I still think I need more experience.

(Man S) You also won first prize in the science teaching competition, for your inquiry-based science project. Surely that'd count in the job market.

(Woman S) Maybe, but . . .

(Man S) I think that you ought to register. The service is free. The recruitment people come to campus, so you don't have to travel to an interview. You always said you'd like to work abroad and here's the opportunity. Then, if you aren't offered anything, at least you get the experience of having interviews and you can apply again after you get some teaching experience.

Now get ready to answer the question.

The man expresses his opinion about whether the woman should attend the job fair. State his opinion and explain the reasons he gives for his opinion.

You may begin to prepare your response after the beep. [beep]

Please begin speaking after the beep. [beep]

4. Please listen carefully.

Read the passage about misconceptions in mathematics. You have 45 seconds to read the passage. Begin reading now.

Now listen to part of a lecture on this topic in a math education class.

(Woman P) Misconceptions about simple notions in arithmetic are not readily given up. So for example, a child who believes that 1/4 is larger than 1/2 will not let go of this misconception when he or she gets back an assignment full of red correction marks. The child will let go of this misconception when he or she fully understands fractions. So, how do we develop this understanding?

I think this situation is partly caused by the practice in many schools of teaching mathematics by rote. In other words, children are taught to memorize a formula, to practice using that formula, and then go on to the next one. Children start to believe that math is boring and work through problems without understanding the nature of the concepts. So what happens is that kids can work a problem only if they remember the formula. Using the rote method of teaching doesn't take into account the child's pre-knowledge, or informal knowledge, of mathematics. Even a small child can tell the difference between a whole cookie and a half a cookie. So using this informal knowledge is a very important part of helping children learn fractions – or other math concepts, for that matter. Teachers tend to forget they must put these concepts into daily situations that children can relate to. Using real objects, children can come up with the formula themselves. And having done that, the children learn and understand the formulas better. It's also true that teachers too often assume that children understand the mathematical symbols being used, for example, the symbol for percentages. Unfortunately, too often that is an incorrect assumption.

Now get ready to answer the question.

The professor describes the mistakes that are made in teaching children mathematics. Explain how these mistakes relate to the problems that children have in understanding fractions.

You may begin to prepare your response after the beep. [beep]

Please begin speaking after the beep. [beep]

5. Please listen carefully.

Listen to a conversation between two students.

(Man S) Sally, why the frown?

(Woman S) Oh, John. I've been trying to learn this list of vocabulary words and I'm just getting nowhere. Here, take the list and ask me one of the words. You'll see.

(Man S) OK, how about *arthropoda*?

(Woman S) Those creepy crawly things.

(Man S) But what kind of creepy crawly things? Snakes?

(Woman S) No. Like spiders and scorpions.

(Man S) Right. See? You do know at least one word. So, how did you remember it?

(Woman S) I don't know. I guess it's because it starts with *a* and I've managed to memorize the *a* words. But look at how long the list is.

(Man S) OK. Well I learned it by remembering that *arthro* means joints, like the disease arthritis affects the joints, and *pod* means foot, like a tripod for setting a camera on. I always try to connect new words with the words I already know. So *arthropoda* refers to all those creatures that have lots of jointed feet.

(Woman S) Oh, OK, well that's pretty easy. Although, you know what, now that I think about it, I kind of remember picturing all of the creatures in my mind every time I said the word.

(Man S) Ah, you mean visualizing them. That's a good way of remembering. Making a mental picture. You could try color-coding your words, too. Like a traffic light. That helps me.

(Woman S) OK, what's that? What do you mean by color-coding the words?

(Man S) Go through the list and, for example, color all the words you know well, green, because you can pass by them. And the words you kind of know, yellow, and the words you really don't know, red. Then focus on the red words. You stop at them and think about them. Of course, you don't have to use those colors. That's just my coloring system.

(Woman S) OK, yeah, that sounds like a really good idea. Got any other ideas?

(Man S) Sure. Make a song or a poem out of them – like, let's see, an arthropod with arthritis met a cephalopod with sinusitis . . .

(Woman S) OK, wait. What is a cephalopod, and what does it have to do with sinusitis?

(Man S) Well, *cephalo* has to do with a head, right? Like the disease encephalitis is an inflammation of the brain. And a cephalopod is a big-headed creature like an octopus, for example, so a cephalopod with sinusitis would have a really bad sinus headache.

(Woman S) OK. I see. So finish your poem.

(Man S) Oh, I've forgotten it.

Now get ready to answer the question.

The students discuss several ways to memorize vocabulary. Summarize the ways. Then state which of the ways you prefer and explain why.

You may begin to prepare your response after the beep. [beep]

Please begin speaking after the beep. [beep]

6. Please listen carefully.

Listen to part of a lecture in an earth science class.

(Man P) Of course, you are all familiar with rainbows, perhaps the most beautiful of the atmospheric phenomena. However, there are other interesting, but less common phenomena that I will be speaking about today. These are produced when light from the sun, or sometimes from the moon, passes through hexagonal-shaped, or six-sided, ice crystals.

These ice crystals refract, that is, bend the light in the atmosphere. Imagine that the crystals are prisms bending each wavelength of light at a different angle.

I want to describe three different phenomena that occur depending on the ice crystals' orientation toward the surface of the Earth . . . how the crystals are arranged in relation to the Earth.

OK. So the first phenomenon is a ring called a halo. This happens when the ice crystals are randomly scattered in the atmosphere. If the light enters these crystals . . . randomly scattered crystals . . . the light is dispersed around the sun or moon and is seen as a ring around the light source. So, halos occur when the ice crystals that the light shines through are randomly dispersed in the atmosphere.

OK. Sometimes, however, the ice crystals are oriented horizontally instead of randomly. Now, this causes a different phenomenon. If the sun is low in the sky and its light shines through horizontal ice crystals, we see two bright spots on either side of the sun. These are called "sundogs" and are seen at an angle of 22 degrees from the sun. Both halos and sundogs are caused by refraction of light.

The third phenomenon is a sun pillar. Around sunrise or sunset, you might see a shaft of light stretching either upwards or downwards from the sun, a sun pillar. Unlike halos and sun dogs, though, with sun pillars, sunlight reflects – not refracts – off horizontally aligned ice crystals that are gently falling through the atmosphere.

Now get ready to answer the question.

Using the information in the lecture, explain the three atmospheric phenomena that the lecturer discusses.

You may begin to prepare your response after the beep. [beep]

Please begin speaking after the beep. [beep]

DIAGNOSTIC TEST: Writing Section

Now listen to part of a lecture on the topic you just read about.

(Man P) Today I wanted to question the idea that rewards increase productivity in the workplace. Now, does this approach really work? Well, when people who have experienced a reward system were asked, we found they didn't like it. Most people, it seems, want to be paid, not encouraged through incentives. People want to be given respect for working extra hard.

In fact, I know of no controlled study that has genuinely shown a long-term improvement in work as a result of any productivity reward scheme. On the contrary, there are many studies that show productivity rewards are even counterproductive. Rewards make for less productivity rather than more.

So, why might this be true? Well, in fact, rewards actually punish. Yeah. If we compensate people for high productivity, they may perceive this as being controlled. People understand they're being manipulated and don't like it. But more importantly, people don't necessarily get the expected rewards. So the disappointment for not being rewarded is sort of the same as being punished. Think about it. The more desirable the reward you expect, the more disappointing it is if you fail to get it. Right?

Productivity schemes might even reduce the amount and quality of work. The workers' relationship with the supervisor could be damaged. Instead of trying to work collaboratively with the supervisor, an employee might conceal problems. For example, let's say you had a problem. You might be less likely to ask for help from a supervisor who can withhold rewards. To avoid a negative rating, you keep quiet. Can you see why this would tend to reduce performance rather than improve it?

Summarize the points made in the lecture you just heard, explaining how they cast doubt on the points made in the reading.

PART 1 BUILDING SUPPORTING SKILLS

EXERCISE P3 *Analyzing speech patterns*

(Man) Since the seventh century, large bells have been used in cathedrals, churches, and monasteries. The greatest bell in the world is in Moscow. This famous "King of Bells" weighs about 198 tons. The next two largest bells are also located in Russia. One near St. Petersburg weighs 171 tons, and another in Moscow weighs 110 tons. Great Paul, the bell at St. Paul's in London, is the largest bell in England, but weighs a mere 17 tons.

EXERCISE P4 *Indicating speech patterns*

(Woman) Carnivals, with spectacular parades, masked balls, mock ceremonials, and street dancing, usually last for a week or more before Mardi Gras itself.

(Man) Since the seventh century, large bells have been used in cathedrals, churches, and monasteries. The greatest bell in the world is in Moscow. This famous "King of Bells" weighs about 198 tons. The next two largest bells are also located in Russia. One near St. Petersburg weighs 171 tons, and another in Moscow weighs 110 tons. Great Paul, the bell at St. Paul's in London, is the largest bell in England, but weighs a mere 17 tons.

EXERCISE P5 *Imitating speech patterns*

(Man) Since the seventh century, large bells have been used in cathedrals, churches, and monasteries. The greatest bell in the world is in Moscow. This famous "King of Bells" weighs about 198 tons. The next two largest bells are also located in Russia. One near St. Petersburg weighs 171 tons, and another in Moscow weighs 110 tons. Great Paul, the bell at St. Paul's in London, is the largest bell in England, but weighs a mere 17 tons.

EXERCISE P6 *Listening to accents*

Speaker from the U.K.

(Woman) Since the seventh century, large bells have been used in cathedrals, churches, and monasteries. The greatest bell in the world is in Moscow. This famous "King of Bells" weighs about 198 tons. The next two largest bells are also located in Russia. One near St. Petersburg weighs 171 tons, and another in Moscow weighs 110 tons. Great Paul, the bell at St. Paul's in London, is the largest bell in England, but weighs a mere 17 tons.

Speaker from the U.S.

(Man) Since the seventh century, large bells have been used in cathedrals, churches, and monasteries. The greatest bell in the world is in Moscow. This famous "King of Bells" weighs about 198 tons. The next two largest bells are also located in Russia. One near St. Petersburg weighs 171 tons, and another in Moscow weighs 110 tons. Great Paul, the bell at St. Paul's in London, is the largest bell in England, but weighs a mere 17 tons.

Speaker from Australia

(Man) Since the seventh century, large bells have been used in cathedrals, churches, and monasteries. The greatest bell in the world is in Moscow. This famous "King of Bells" weighs about 198 tons. The next two largest bells are also located in Russia. One near St. Petersburg weighs 171 tons, and another in Moscow weighs 110 tons. Great Paul, the bell at St. Paul's in London, is the largest bell in England, but weighs a mere 17 tons.

PART 2 BUILDING SKILLS: Listening

EXERCISE L1 *Writing what the speaker means*

1. (Man P) Alternative medicine's efficacy has never been, um, confirmed so, uh, obviously we need to put it under the same strict investigation as we would . . . we do with developing medicines, um, medicines under development.
2. (Woman P) So the brain has this tendency and, and this shouldn't surprise you about the brain – you know about infants' recognition of faces, and we're all familiar, of course, with the face we call . . . uh . . . the man in the moon – this tendency is to interpret vague images as specific ones.
3. (Man P) The savagery of the Mongols . . . probably, no doubt exaggerated, um, was moderated . . . moderated because they lived on tribute and, in order to collect tribute . . . only prosperous subjects can provide tribute.
4. (Woman P) The technique, um, the technique of repeating the initial consonant sound, that's alliteration – I don't have to spell that for you, do I? – that's a common poetic device.

EXERCISE L2 *Answering questions about content*

1. (Woman P) Long-term food storage occurs in the ecto-, uh, I mean, endo-, endosperm of the seed.

Where does food storage occur?

2. (Man P) We should be concerned about – as future teachers – does the average person understand the difference between science and pseudoscience . . . um, we seem to be failing in teaching fundamental cri-, critical-thinking skills.

Why does the professor believe teachers have not succeeded in teaching critical-thinking skills?

3. (Woman P) If you take a universal unit of time . . . um, let's say a second. If you take a second, 1/60 of a minute, which is 1/60 of an hour . . . um, 1/24 of a day – you do the math – if you take that universal unit of time, you have to remember that the Earth does not rotate quite regularly . . . not an accurate enough standard for modern measurements.

What is the professor pointing out?

4. (Man P) I think you already know my view on borrowing money. Um, it's good if what you're getting . . . say, a house in an up-and-coming area . . . will ultimately be worth more than, than the money and interest you pay back . . . and bad when you buy, um, a car, for instance, that you can't sell at a profit. Then, you don't want . . . you shouldn't borrow . . . you should never borrow to buy something that depreciates – goes down in value.

Under what conditions does the speaker think it's acceptable to borrow money?

EXERCISE L3 *Identifying the meaning of filler phrases and reductions*

1. (Man S) So if these tribes weren't um, literate, um, how did they send messages?

   (Woman P) Well, let's say that if you wanted to communicate something important and weren't literate, you'd, um, you'd draw a stylized picture, um, a simplified one – something that was agreed upon.

What does the woman mean by "let's say that"?

2. (Man S) Excuse me. Um . . . I've made an appointment – they recommended that students get a flu shot. Um, here's my student ID.

   (Woman S) OK. Hmmm. Lemme see. Uh-huh. Here are your records, Jeff. Go ahead an' take a seat. A nurse will be with you in just a second.

What does the woman mean by "lemme see"?

3. (Man S) I just don't remember how to do this calculus problem.

(Woman S) Oh, come on now. You attended Dr. Brown's lecture . . . you did, didn't you?

What does the woman mean by "come on now"?

4. (Woman S) Well, uh, how does smok-, the mother's smoking actually hurt the baby? How does the smoke get to the fetus, and um, reduce the oxygen to the unborn baby?

(Man P) Well, see, carbon monoxide, instead of oxygen, is absorbed from hemoglobin molecules in the mother's blood.

What does the man mean by "see"?

EXERCISE L5 *Identifying referents in conversation*

1. (Man S) You know the author Harriet Beecher Stowe?

(Woman S) Um, the one who wrote Uncle Tom's Cabin, about slavery, right?

(Man) Yeah, well, when he met her, President Lincoln supposedly called her "the little lady who started the Civil War."

2. (Woman S) Whadja find out about the Alaskan Purchase?

(Man S) Well, when the U.S. Secretary of State . . . who was William Seward then, when he arranged to purchase it from Russia in 1867, people thought the idea was crazy and they started calling Alaska, uh, the Alaskan purchase, Seward's Folly.

(Woman) Oh, I remember reading that.

3. (Man S) Whadja finally decide to do your poli-, political science paper on?

(Woman S) I'm doing a comparative study between the American Congress and the British parliament.

(Man S) Hmmm, find anything interesting?

(Woman S) Well, for one thing, there are no restrictions on debates in the English House of Lords, so if its members think something is really important, they talk the issue through until they are all satisfied.

4. (Woman P) Now I'd like all of you to try to get to the, uh, Turkish cultural arts exhibition at the Metropolitan Museum of Art.

(Man S) D'you know how long it will be on for?

(Woman P) Yes, till November, uh, eighteenth. The museum opening times are ten to five from Tuesday through Saturday and at, uh . . . twelve to five on Sundays. The museum is closed on Mondays. OK? There'll be a number of events to complement the exhibition. These will include three lectures. Of course, I, I realize you have busy schedules, but try to attend at least one.

(Man S) Uh, d'you have the topics and dates of the lectures?

(Woman P) No, I don't, not with me anyway. I'll let you know next week. Also, there will be an evening of traditional Turkish music.

(Man S) Oh, I'd be very interested in that. Could you try to get more information on the music as well?

EXERCISE L6 *Identifying referents in a lecture*

1. (Man P) Because of the disintegration, uh, breakdown of the traditional family in many countries – we have seen this happening here – many elderly people have no, uh, what you could describe as a, a place to call home and there's no one, no family members to help these people if they have . . . in case of an emergency. So, in order to address these problems . . . of the delegates . . . I mean, the elderly, in order to address the problems of the elderly, delegates to the U.N. formed the United Nations Symposium on Population to meet, and to pool their ideas, discuss the different possibilities . . . and make recommendations.

2. (Woman P) To climb Mount Everest is possibly or probably the dream of every mountaineer. But you can't just go out and climb Mount Everest. It takes a lot of planning, expenses to think about, and so on and so forth. One of the things that a club – you have to form a kind of group, an alpine club. You can't go climb Mount Everest by yourself. Anyway, in order for an alpine club to make this climb, it must . . . uh . . . apply to the Nepalese Tourism Ministry for a permit. You need a permit. Normally, these are granted to only a few groups each season.

3. (Man P) Blaise Pascal, uh . . . the guy that's known for Pascal's Law. He also invented the first digital calculator. He did this to help his father. His father was a tax collector. Anyway, a particular problem that he faced was the division of the French currency at the time. Unlike the Euro, or even the French franc, the currency during Pascal's time was more complicated. So, anyway, at that time – Pascal was working on this in the 1640s – the currency was in livres, sols, and deniers. 12 deniers made a sol and 20 made a livre. It was much more difficult technology-wise to build a machine to calculate such divisions of currency than it would have been, say, if the currency was like today's currencies which are divisible by 10.

EXERCISE L7 *Following signals*

1. (Man P) Land reform can involve large estates being parceled out in smaller plots. In contrast, it can also involve small landholdings being consolidated into larger estates.
2. (Man P) Using word connotations that have powerful associations for your reader or listener has the effect of making your facts or opinions appear more attractive or less attractive. Consequently, writers and speakers use connotations to persuade their audience.
3. (Man P) Sea defenses are built to prevent beaches from being washed away. However, these defenses may be the cause of land erosion further along the coastline.
4. (Man P) After the beginning draft of a paper is finished, first put away the paper and do something else and then go back to it later with a clear mind.
5. (Man P) The decomposition in organic matter is important for the release and circulation of minerals into the environment. In particular, detritus feeders, like shrimp in the sea and earthworms on land, have a role in the breakdown of dead material.

EXERCISE L8 *Using signals for understanding conversations and lectures*

1. (Woman P) The importance of these dinosaur tracks that were discovered is how much information about dinosaurs that we can get from them. Uh, first, these tracks are in an area near where, at the time of these animals, there were seas. So they were walking along a beach and sinking into the sand. OK? Second, besides the tracks themselves, giving a location and well, there also appear to be tracks of young dinosaurs near tracks of older ones. So, we can imagine a moving herd, like a herd of elephants. Third, the tracks are in sequences of about eight to ten paces. Now this enables scientists to calculate both the animals' stride and speed. And finally, the depth of the print of the larger animals contrasted with the smaller ones, well, we can use this information to show that the dinosaurs may have weighed as much as 10,000 pounds and been 23 feet tall.
2. (Man P) OK, so this study showed that trees could defend themselves against insects. Pests came and stripped the leaves, OK? Now, as a result of the attack, the trees appeared to defend themselves by undergoing changes in the nutritional quality of their leaves. These changes were directly caused by the pest attack. But an interesting thing about the attack was, what was found was that the leaves of nearby trees underwent the same changes in nutritional quality as the ones that were attacked. Now, why would a pest attack on one tree cause other trees to make these nutritional changes in their leaves as well? So what was happening here? How did the neighboring trees know when they should make these changes? Well, it's hypothesized that the trees that were being studied, the ones attacked, were emitting chemical substances. So the second result of the attack was that the trees under attack seemed to chemically transmit that information to other trees, sort of chemically told the others about the attack. Consequently, the trees that were not under direct attack began to set up their defenses. It's for that reason, that trees can chemically communicate "pest attack," that these same chemical substances are being looked at as a possible way to control pests.
3. (Man S) Are you ready for the marine biology test?

   (Woman S) Well, uh, yeah. Quiz me.

   (Man S) OK. What are the three types of tail fins, uh, caudal fins?

   (Woman S) Right. Caudal fins or tail fins are, um, rounded, forked, and lunate.

   (Man S) Right. And what's the difference?

   (Woman S) Well, rounded fins are soft and flexible.

   (Man S) What are they good for?

   (Woman S) Let's see. Um, they're good for maneuvering and, and effective for speed, no, for acceleration.

   (Man S) OK. And forked fins?

   (Woman S) Oh, rounded fins aren't very efficient for continuous swimming 'cause of the drag and the fish gets tired, but a fish with forked fins can swim quickly without getting tired out. Forked fins have less drag.

   (Man S) That's right. And what about lunate fins?

   (Woman S) Oh, those are are good for going continuously for long distances.

   (Man S) And how is that possible?

   (Woman S) Well, um, they're rigid.

   (Man S) So?

   (Woman S) That makes for high, the book said, high propulsive efficiency and there's very little drag because of a small surface area.

   (Man S) So why don't all fish have lunate fins? If they're so effective?

   (Woman S) Oh, because . . . um, the rigidity. It makes it hard for the fish to maneuver.

   (Man S) Well, it sounds like you know your caudal fins. Let's hope there's a question about them on the test.

4. (Man S) How's the physics class going?

(Woman S) Let's not even talk about it. I'm so confused.

(Man S) Oh. What don't you understand?

(Woman S) Well, all this. Stable or statically stable equilibrium or whatever.

(Man S) OK. Um. You're talking about static stability versus, um, dy-, dynamic stability, I bet.

(Woman S) I don't know. Yeah, I think those are the terms.

(Man S) I think you're getting confused by the terms rather than the ideas.

(Woman S) [sigh]

(Man S) Let me give you a simple illustration, OK?

(Woman S) If you think it'll help.

(Man S) Visualize a kid on a tricycle and one on a bicycle. Got it?

(Woman S) OK.

(Man S) Well, if a child stops and sits on his tricycle with his feet on the pedals, it would stand there. It couldn't be pushed over very easily. Right?

(Woman S) Right.

(Man S) But if a kid stops on a bicycle, he can't just sit there on the bike at a dead stop with his feet on the pedals. He'd topple over, right?

(Woman S) Right.

(Man S) So, physicists say that the tricycle has static stability. That means it balances at a standstill whereas the bicycle doesn't balance at a standstill. Are you with me?

(Woman S) OK. Um, trike stable when standing still, bicycle not.

(Man S) Right. Now think of the kid riding the bicycle. You've seen people speeding along. And then they lean into the corner to go around it. Did you ever go really fast on your trike as a kid and then make a fast turn? What happened?

(Woman S) I can't remember my tricycle days. But I can imagine that the kid on the tricycle will crash.

(Man S) Yeah. Yeah that's right. The kid on the tricycle will crash and the one on the bike won't. And this is called, um, dynamic stability. The bicycle has dynamic stability, and the tricycle doesn't.

(Woman S) So, the bicycle is stable when moving, dynamic stability and the tricycle is stable when not moving, static stability. OK. Yeah. I can understand that.

EXERCISE L9 *Predicting the topic*

1. (Woman P) The United Kingdom is made up of four countries: England, Northern Ireland, Scotland, and . . . uh . . . Wales.
2. (Man P) Architects from around the world vote for one architect, the one architect they believe should receive the Award for Architecture.
3. (Woman P) Let me show you samples of Irish linen to help you get . . . um, a better idea of the various patterns.
4. (Man P) There are a number of human- and uh, animal-shaped figures carved in hillsides around the world.
5. (Woman S) I attended Professor Brown's talk on the geology of Mars last night.

EXERCISE L10 *Identifying the topic from the first statement*

1. (Man P) The practice of acupuncture began in China about five, uh, five thousand years ago.
2. (Woman P) Muscles are made of lots of, uh . . . many fine fibers about twenty-five millimeters long.
3. (Man P) A whole new world of opportunities and, and challenges in education has been opened up by radio . . . uh, I mean satellite, satellite-communications technology has opened up lots of possibilities and challenges in education.
4. (Woman P) We will be concentrating specifically on the Golden Age of Spanish literature in this seminar and . . . uh . . . the historical setting in which the literature flourished.
5. (Man P) Although some of the signs and symptoms of the common cold are similar to those of influenza, influenza is a highly contagious, contagious and potentially life-threatening disease.
6. (Woman P) Lack of animal protein in the human diet is a serious cause of, uh . . . malnutrition in many parts of the world.

EXERCISE L11 *Determining if the topic is stated in the first sentence*

1. (Man P) We have given the name "magic square" to a square-shaped arrangement of numbers, in which the numbers are arranged so that the groups of numbers all add up to the same figure. In other words, if you were to add the horizontal numbers, you would come up with the same answer as you do when you add the numbers vertically or diagonally. Now the largest magic square ever devised has the amazing number, anyway, in my opinion, amazing. The number of boxes is 578,865.

2. (Woman P) The wealthy have kept their own private collections of animals for thousands of years. The first public zoo, however, was not opened until, uh, 1793. That was the zoo at the Jardin des Plantes in Paris. Zoos have not only protected endangered species but they also allow people to see exotic animals without having to travel to distant countries.

3. (Woman P) In the mid-1800s, the Overland Mail stagecoach carried the mail across the American continent. But, uh, because this service was unsatisfactory – kind of slow and not reliable – a freighting firm established a new service called the Pony Express. I'm sure most of you have heard of the Pony Express. The way the Pony Express worked was by use of a relay system. So, these daring young riders made weekly treks on horseback across the rough and dangerous terrain between St. Joseph, Missouri, and Sacramento, California. Although it was very successful, the Pony Express was short-lived. That was because after only sixteen months of being in service, the telegraph came into use. Basically, the telegraph put the Pony Express out of business.

4. (Man P) Penang, Malaysia, is the home of the world's largest butterfly farm. This farm is both a sanctuary and breeding center for something like about 2,000 recorded species of Malaysian butterflies . . . butterflies, which are being driven away from populated areas by pollution and industry, industrialization. So the studies being conducted on the farm are uh, studies into tropical butterflies' habitats, diseases that attack caterpillars, and pest control. Also, research is being done on how the ecological balance would be affected if foreign butterflies were to be imported and bred on the farm.

5. (Woman P) Did you enjoy the architecture excursion to Saint Martin's Cathedral?

   (Man S) Yes, very much, Professor. And uh, we really appreciate your arranging everything for us.

   (Woman P) Thank you. Was there anything special that impressed you?

   (Man S) I especially liked the gar-, gargoyles. But I was wondering, uh . . . Why did stoneworkers put those grotesque heads on cathedrals, anyway? To frighten away bad spirits, or what?

   (Woman P) No, not at all. Nothing like that. They're designed to catch the water that runs off the roof when it rains or when the snow melts.

   (Man S) Ah, I see. That makes sense. The water collects in the gargoyle's mouth and the gargoyle kind of like spits the water out onto the street.

   (Woman P) That's right. That protects the walls from moisture that would otherwise drip down and cause erosion.

EXERCISE L12 *Identifying a change in topic*

1. (Woman P) Folk dances, the steps and movements of the folk dances, have been passed on from one dancer to another over the years. The movements weren't written down. Since this system is not always very accurate, choreographers had to invent ways of writing down the movements. So, at first, they drew little pictures under the music. Then, later, they came up with a system that uses dots on lines. These dots represent hands, feet, and heads.

2. (Man P) It was during his search for a new route to India that Columbus reached America. You may find it surprising that even though he made his discovery in 1492, it took a little over a hundred years for people to finally settle in the New World. So, why did they decide to come? Well, some settlers were hoping to escape from the problems of the Old World by moving to the new. Then, there were reports that excellent crops could be produced in Virginia, especially. That induced many more people to undertake such a long journey across the ocean. So, America was not the sought after India, but it did offer its settlers a new and potentially rich life.

3. (Woman P) It used to be widely accepted that photographs provided a perfect way to document historical events. It seemed that a photographic image preserved – in extraordinary detail – deeds, deeds of both the famous people and, and of the unknown masses. But this is no longer the case, or at least not the case with contemporary photographs, because technological advances in the field of photography in recent years have made it possible to manipulate and alter photographic images – a process you all know as digital imaging. So digital imaging, as fun as it might be or as useful in some fields that it might be, has, in fact, made it increasingly difficult, well, impractical really, to use contemporary photographs as a reliable source of information. We can't conclude anymore that photographic records, for those interested in the historical records, can be used for any serious inquiry. You have to take contents of a contemporary photograph with a grain of salt, so to speak.

4. (Woman P) You hear snatches of Spanish, French, Russian, Chinese, and a dozen other languages which you probably don't recognize on the streets of major cities in America. Right? OK, even though all kinds of languages are heard, the vast

majority of people living in the United States communicate in English. So, the United States is considered an English-speaking country. But is English the official language in the U.S.?

(Man S) Well, sure. All the official stuff – the discussions in the Congress, the official documents – that's all in English.

(Woman P) Can you tell me where in the United States Constitution it says that English is the official language?

(Man S) Uh, no. But maybe it isn't in the Constitution. Maybe it's in a different document.

(Woman P) Well, the fact is that no single language is recognized as an official language in the United States Constitution. Now having said that there's no official language that's written, stated at the federal level. Don't forget that there are also state constitutions.

(Man S) Ahh. OK.

(Woman P) However, like the U.S. Constitution, most state constitutions don't recognize an official language either. Does anyone know of any state constitutions that do recognize an official language?

(Woman S) Well, I'm, I'm from Louisiana, and, and I think that the Louisiana State Constitution recognizes both English and French as official languages.

(Woman P) OK. The state of Nebraska made English its official language sometime early in the twentieth century and, and, from time to time, this issue pops up and is discussed in various states.

Listening Mini-test 1

Questions 1–3

Listen to part of a discussion between two friends.

(Woman S) Hey, Sammy. How's your job at the library working out? You're at the university library aren't you?

(Man S) Yeah. It's great. I've been working in the acquisitions department.

(Woman S) Oh. What d'you do there?

(Man S) Logging in new books, mostly. It's kind of neat 'cause I get to open all the boxes that arrive . . . boxes containing all of the newly purchased books. It's kind of like a birthday, unwrapping presents.

(Woman S) That sounds like fun.

(Man S) That part is, but then I have to enter each book into the computer. I don't mind that too much, but the worst, the worst thing is attaching the bar code on the cover. That can get kind of tedious, you know, just doing the same thing over and over again.

1. What are the people discussing?
2. What is the woman referring to when she states, "that sounds like fun"?
3. Which duty does the man like the least?

Questions 4–6

Listen to part of a lecture from a history class.

(Woman P) William Cody, well . . . you probably know him as Buffalo Bill. OK, so William Cody became an American showman and founded the great Wild West Show. That was in 1883. He traveled around Europe with other famous people that you probably have also heard of, like people such as the sharpshooter Annie Oakley and the Indian chief Sitting Bull. This Wild West Show traveled, as I said, around Europe, and performed for many heads of state, like the queen of England – Queen Victoria . . . the show was featured at her Golden Jubilee celebrations. And the Czar of Russia, that would have been the Czar . . . uh . . . Alexander III. His father, Alexander II, had been assassinated in 1881. So Alexander III would have seen Cody's show.

4. What is the talk mainly about?
5. What is the woman referring to when she states, "That was in 1883"?
6. In addition to Annie Oakley, which other famous person traveled with Buffalo Bill?

Questions 7–9

Listen to part of a lecture from a music class.

(Man P) Just before the turn of the twentieth century, a new musical form captivated America . . . and that was ragtime. I suspect you've all heard of ragtime. The main feature of ragtime is its syncopation. Syncopation – you know how a waltz has a beat of ONE two three ONE two three and a polka has ONE two three four? These beats are regular, but in ragtime there's syncopation, a displaced beat or accent. Traditional strong beats become weak and vice versa, weak become strong or the beat isn't evenly spaced, but comes a little earlier than expected, or later. Although ragtime had its start in 1897 with William Krell's "Mississippi Rag", and I'm going to be playing that for you in a moment – it was Scott Joplin who popularized the rag with his "Maple Leaf Rag." We'll hear that one as well. Now, it was John Philip Sousa, best known for marches actually, who began to feature rags in his band concerts in America and Europe. And by the early 1900s, ragtime was the most popular musical art form in America. OK? Now let's listen to . . . I'd like to play a few of these pieces I've been telling you about.

7. What does the speaker mainly discuss?
8. According to the professor, what is ragtime?
9. What does the professor contrast in his lecture?

Questions 10–12

Listen to a conversation between two students.

(Woman S) Didja hear on the news last night that, that the City Museum had just recovered the missing painting by Rembrandt? They said, um, lemme get this right. The curator said the painting had been returned after being out on unauthorized loan for three years.

(Man S) Yeah, I heard that, but I just got in on the tail end of the story. The part I saw, when I was watching it, I kept wondering . . . why that painting? What's so special, you know, about that particular painting? I mean there are so many more valuable items in the museum. Why was that one stolen?

(Woman S) Yeah, well, they explained that on the news. That same Rembrandt's been taken, stolen, four times in the last twenty years. Thieves seem to favor it . . . and the museum curator believes it may have something to do with its size, you know, it's kind of small – nine inches by eleven.

(Man S) Hmmm. That would make it easy to take. Just put it under your coat and walk out.

(Woman S) Don't get any ideas. [laugh] They do have surveillance cameras.

(Man S) I'd say they need something more.

(Woman S) The museum has taken extra security precautions.

(Man S) How valuable is it, anyway? Did they say?

(Woman S) Yeah, well, the curator said that it's been appraised at five million dollars, but he didn't know what a thief could get for it.

(Man S) That Rembrandt is very well known, isn't it?

(Woman S) Uh-huh.

(Man S) So why would anyone want a stolen painting that's so easily recognized?

(Woman S) The news reporter asked that same question and the curator wasn't sure, but he told a story about the Mona Lisa being stolen and a man painted a bunch of copies and then sold all the fakes as the real stolen one.

10. What are the people discussing?
11. What does the woman mean by the phrase "being out on unauthorized loan for three years"?
12. What reason is given for the painting's popularity among thieves?

EXERCISE L13 *Understanding restatements*

1. (Man P) The dialect spoken in Kárpathos is so old that many words date back to the time of Homer.
2. (Woman P) A Frenchman's 25-minute flight in a hot-air balloon in 1783 was the first manned flight.
3. (Man P) One of the most beautiful birds in the world, the quetzal, takes its name from the Aztec word meaning tail feather.
4. (Woman P) Twenty-two men from Mao Tse-tung's Red Army had to storm the Luding Bridge after an all-night march to capture a needed escape route for Mao's forces.
5. (Man P) Many relief centers were set up in the drought-stricken areas.
6. (Woman P) Recently discovered fossils have revolutionized our concept of the human past.
7. (Man P) Recent explorers have been unable to locate the island that was vividly described in the captain's log in March 1783.
8. (Woman P) The executive secretary of the Protection of the Marine Environment Organization has reported that a large number of dead fish, dolphins, and whales have been spotted off the East Coast.

EXERCISE L14 *Finding two answers*

1. (Man S) You didn't come to art class yesterday, did you?

   (Woman S) Uh-uh. I got out of my chemistry lab late. Anything important I missed?

   (Man S) Yeah. Dr. Mathews has arranged for us to meet at the art museum next week, um, next Tuesday, I think that's the 26th. 'Cause the museum's got a special exhibition on fish rubbings.

   (Woman S) Fish rubbings? Uh, what's that? Not a hands-on exhibition I hope.

   (Man S) No. Well, uh, not exactly. You missed a good lecture, though. Fish rubbings – it's an ancient art form in which fish are used to make prints.

   (Woman S) Sounds slimy. Where was this practiced?

   (Man S) Um, in the Far East and by some native peoples in America.

   (Woman S) Will Dr. Mathews expect us to make some of our own fish rubbings afterwards?

   (Man S) I suppose that's up to you. I think it might be interesting to give it a try.

What can be said about fish rubbings?

2. (Woman P) The world's heaviest gold coin is worth millions of dollars. It was minted in the year 1613 in India. The name of its issuer, Mughal Emperor Jehangir, his name is stamped on the coin. Prior to the reign of this emperor, prior to his reign, rulers in India had to obtain permission to mint coins from the caliph, the ruler in Baghdad. OK? However, Emperor Jehangir changed this tradition. OK? He, uh, started his own policy of issuing coins, coins in his own name. It was during the time of the Mughal dynasty that many art forms were encouraged to flourish, Emperor Jehangir supported the arts. Therefore, it's not surprising that the art of minting coins began and, uh, reached its peak of perfection during his reign.

What is true about Mughal Emperor Jehangir?

3. (Man P) When microscopes are referred to, most people think of optical microscopes. These instruments were developed principally to meet the needs of the biological sciences. They aren't that useful for metallurgists. They, uh, metallurgists have large, and awkwardly shaped specimens. So, those who need to examine metal objects or metal structures use a metallurgical microscope. This is a special . . . the observing and illuminating systems of a metallurgical microscope are mounted in a way that allows adjustment for accommodating odd-shaped samples. Metallurgical microscopes are equipped with devices that provide the capacity to measure an object in the X, Y, and Z axes. These microscopes are frequently used in the field instead of in the laboratory, so they must be, must be more durable.

How is a metallurgical microscope different from an optical microscope?

4. (Woman P) Since people communicate mostly through speech, you can imagine that a defect in speaking or hearing abilities can be an enormous handicap, right? OK. There are three conditions in which communication disorders can result. Any ideas what these may be? Three conditions . . . yes?

(Man S) Well, the obvious condition, I think would be a physical one. Let's say, like, if someone's eardrum has been damaged because of an illness or an injury, that person might not be able to hear. And, um, being deaf or partially deaf not only affects the person's ability to hear, but also deaf people's speech sometimes isn't all that clear, so that makes it difficult for others to understand them.

(Woman P) You bet. If something goes wrong with the speech or hearing mechanisms, communication disorders can result . . . Sue?

(Woman S) Well, I have a cousin who suffered brain damage in an accident and he can't speak very well. And some people are just born with uh, something wrong.

(Woman P) Yes. That's a condition we would classify . . . we classify it under the condition of abnormal functioning of the brain. Besides accidents, people may be born with this condition or it can occur as a result of a stroke or a tumor. And the third condition? Anybody?

(Man S2) Well, some people have been uh, badly shocked, uh, traumatized, and they get kind of emotionally upset, you know. I read about a boy who just stopped talking after he saw this really terrible accident.

(Woman P) Good point. Yes. An unusual emotional or psychological problem can cause communication disorders. OK. So communication disorders can result from uh, one, something going wrong with the speech or hearing mechanisms, uh, two, abnormal functioning of the brain, and finally, an unusual emotional or psychological problem. Now, fortunately, most communication disorders can be improved to-, to some degree, with the help of a speech pathologist.

What is true about communication disorders?

EXERCISE L15 *Getting all the facts*

1. (Man P) So, Victoria C. Woodhull is best remembered as, uh, for being the first woman candidate to run for the U.S. presidency. She did this in 1872 against Ulysses S. Grant. Now, in fact, Woodhull had long been involved in many radical movements, movements including spiritualism, utopian socialism, and women's rights. She was a first, the first woman in other endeavors, as well. Let's see, in 1868 she co-founded the first woman-owned brokerage firm and a couple years later, she established an outspoken political journal, a journal which promoted a variety of extreme views. Although Woodhull lost the presidential election, she continued her political work for several decades, however, over time with less radical views and, uh, with a quieter public profile.

What details about Victoria C. Woodhull's life does the lecture include?

2. (Woman P) OK, now, the coral reef is right below us. So, first, I want all of you to check all your diving equipment. Do you have a full oxygen tank? Is all your equipment functioning properly? OK.

Everyone ready? Now I want everyone, each of you to . . . to find your diving partner. Once you are in the water, remember, stay with your diving partner. Stay together. You should always have someone with you who can signal for help in case of an emergency.

(Man S) Uh . . . my diving partner isn't here today. Is there anyone else who doesn't have a partner, someone who needs a partner?

(Woman P) There doesn't seem to be anyone without a partner so you can join Linda and Jeff. OK? The three of you. Keep an eye on each other. Now, stay together as we descend to the coral reef. It's only about 25 feet below. Follow me as I go along the reef and try to identify the kinds of corals we looked at in class. I'll give a signal when it's time to return to the boat.

What details are included in the diving teacher's instructions to the students?

3. (Woman S) Dr. Jackson, I was reading an article the other day and it referred to a study, uh, a phenomenon called the "hundredth-monkey" phenomenon. It didn't explain the study, but I was curious to know more about it. Are you familiar with it?

(Man P) Yes, I am. Um, this study involved a group of monkeys inhabiting an island off the coast of Japan. The monkeys were shown how to eat sweet potatoes in a particular way, a way that wasn't typical of monkeys. Supposedly, other monkeys living on the island began to copy this behavior, and soon a hundred monkeys were eating sweet potatoes in the new way. At this point, it is claimed that monkeys from another island about two hundred miles away began eating, began the same sweet-potato eating behavior. These monkeys had never been in contact with the monkeys on the first island.

(Woman S) That's really intriguing. Why do you sound so, uh, skeptical?

(Man P) Well, let me me say this. It doesn't sound very likely and I haven't seen the study mentioned in a serious journal. Only in a popular science magazine that . . . might not have investigated the source of the research.

What details about the "hundredth-monkey" study does the professor give?

4. (Man S) OK. Um. For my presentation I decided to talk about puppetry. First, I'm gonna talk about some traditional puppets and then I'm gonna go into some more unusual puppets. So, um, puppetry is an art form used for entertainment and education. It consists of a show in which puppets, figures made to represent humans and other creatures – these can be authentic or mythical representation – they are used to tell a story. So, traditional puppets come in many forms. The most common type of puppet and the easiest to make and use, and one that I'm sure all of you have played with at sometime in your lives, is the hand puppet. So this puppet is like a glove and is worn over the hand of the puppeteer. You, the puppeteer, work the head and arms of the puppet by moving your fingers. OK? So, another common type of puppet is known as the marionette. That's the one that looks kind of like a doll and has all these joints on the body and you control it by moving, uh, manipulating the strings. The puppeteer usually stands on a bridge over the stage and makes the marionette move by pulling the strings. OK. And the last traditional puppet I'm gonna talk about is the third kind of puppet, the shadow puppet. Now, these puppets are controlled by rods. These rods are attached to their hands, the puppets' hands and the puppeteer makes the puppet move by manipulating the rods from below the stage. So, the legs of the figure hang loosely, kind of dangling down, and have freedom of movement. The performance with these kind of puppets takes place behind a screen with lighting set up so that the puppet casts a shadow.

What details about puppetry does the presentation include?

EXERCISE L16 *Recognizing information*

1. (Woman P) The homing instinct of pigeons, uh, pigeons have a homing instinct and this is what makes them popular for racing. But you have to start training a bird when it's young so . . . a bird's training begins when it's about seven year-, uh, excuse me, seven weeks old. At first, this training consists of giving it short exercise flights, teaching the bird to recognize its owner's call. It also has to be taught to enter its cote, uh, a cote, the pigeon's home. Then, the next phase, when the bird is about four months old . . . the next phase of training is started. In this stage, the pigeon is taken short distances from its home and then released. So the distance of these flights is gradually extended from 3 miles up to 100 miles as the bird's stamina increases. And then, when the bird, the pigeon is ready, the owner may enter it in a race, against other trained pigeons. So, the owners take their birds to a central meeting place and all the birds are tagged. The tag is a small metal ring attached to one leg. Then they are released all at once, simultaneously, all these birds take off for home. Now a bird is not considered to be home until it has entered its

cote – that's why it's important to teach it to enter its cote – and . . . its owner removes the tag and this is inserted it into this special kind of clock that records the bird's arrival time. Uh . . . because owners live at different distances from the release point, the first pigeon home may not be the fastest flier. It's the bird that makes the best time in flying the distance home . . . that bird is the winner.

In the lecture, the speaker describes the steps in pigeon training. Indicate whether each of the following is a step in the process.

2. (Man P) I wanted to talk today about the American suffragettes who finally won their battle for the right to vote, when the right to vote in a democratic election was extended to women in 1919. But, because of women's equal rights being harmed by discriminatory legislation, the ERA, um, Equal Rights Amendment was introduced in 1923. This was a special time when the feminist symbolized a young generation of women. It was a time in America's history . . . young women were carefree, exuberant, eager to break out of traditional roles and enjoy personal independence.

All this optimism came to an end during the Great Depression, an economic crisis precipitated by a stock market crash in 1929. OK? At the depth of the Depression, over one-third of the labor force, let me repeat that, one-third of the labor force, that is one out of every three people, was unemployed.

As you can imagine, as men lost their jobs, they became resentment-, uh, resentful, they became resentful, toward those women who had jobs, whose jobs were protected because of the Equal Rights Amendment. This resentment became widespread. And laws were passed that restricted women's rights. One such law was the married-person's clause. OK? The married-person's clause prevented the civil service from hiring more than one member of a family. This law left many women unemployed. Following the assumption that a man is or should be the primary wage earner, many school boards fired married women. Even women in positions of power supported policies that made women's conditions worse rather than improved them.

Now, at the same time that women were losing their rights, there was a propaganda campaign by social workers and public figures which was intended and effectively did its job of convincing women that their responsibility, their duty was to maintain family values. A consequence of this campaign was the strengthening of belief in traditional roles and, uh, an acceptance on the part of women to stay at home instead of pursue a career.

In the lecture, the professor describes events that undermined the gains the suffragettes had made in women's rights. Indicate whether each of the following is an event that hampered the movement.

3. (Woman P) In the natural world, a multitude of symbiotic relationships has developed, uh, between different organisms. In many of these, the partnership is one sided; in other words, one of the symbionts – the two creatures involved in the partnership – one of the symbionts benefits from the association while the other may be harmed by it.

Sometimes two species develop a relationship that is beneficial to both parties. This is called mutualism. OK. So, a symbiotic relationship in which both organisms benefit is called mutualism. Let me give you an example of such an alliance – the relationship of ants and aphids.

Aphids are tiny pear-shaped insects that typically feed exclusively on a particular plant – I think most of you have seen them – they live in crowded clusters on the underside of leaves or on stems. The aphid's mouthparts are adapted to piercing plant tissue and sucking out the sap; they are very efficient at getting the sap, but they can't metabolize it all, so they have to get rid of it. OK? So, from the back of the insects are two cornicles – kind of like a tailpipe of a car – protruding from the back of the insects. The aphids get rid of this sap by secreting it from these tailpipes, these cornicles. Uh . . . this sap, a sticky substance called honeydew, is high in nutritive value. The honeydew falls onto the ground or onto the leaves of the plant and is collected by ants. The ants use this honeydew substance as a food source. Some ant species stroke the back end of aphids, sometimes these aphids are called the ants' cows – the ants stroke the aphids with their legs and antennae in order to stimulate the flow of the honeydew liquid. It's thought that aphids may actually withhold the honeydew . . . waiting until ants caress them. Some ants take care of whole herds of aphids. They build shelters for the aphids and carry them to new plants . . . to new plants when the old plants die.

So the aphid's mouthparts – as I said – are adapted to piercing the leaves and sucking out sap. In contrast, the ants' mouthparts are not well modified for getting the sap from plants. So the ants rely on the aphids to get the sap for them. The aphids are not well adapted for fighting off predators and consequently, they rely on ants to provide this protection service for them. See the mutualism? Both these creatures, ants and aphids, benefit from this arrangement of close cooperation. This relationship is somewhat analogous to the relationship between cattle and human beings.

In the lecture the professor describes a relationship between ants and aphids. Indicate whether each of the following is a benefit that aphids get from ants.

EXERCISE L17 *Organizing information*

1. (Man P) It may be true that no two snowflakes are exactly alike, but they can be classified by their shape, and this is dictated by the way water molecules in the atmosphere react to temperatures. Good snowflake formation needs low temperatures. OK. So what are the different shapes and what influences the final shape that a snowflake takes? Now, there are three different types of snowflakes. The most familiar type of these three basic types is the star, which looks like the common picture-book illustration of a star with six points. The second type, type two, is a solid prism shape, a column, like a section cut through a lead pencil. The third type, the plate, looks like a tiny, hexagonal dinner plate. OK? So how do they get those shapes? Well, extreme conditions like those in the polar areas produce the perfect prisms, but there isn't enough precipitation there, in the polar areas, for stars to form, stars need precipitation in order to form. So you usually don't find stars at the poles. The plates are sort of in-between the prisms and stars. Plates need higher temperatures than those found at the poles where the prisms form, but they need less humidity than is needed for the formation of stars. Now, in places where the temperature is too high or where there's a high wind, snowflakes tend to be irregular. The crystals have not really formed properly or have become damaged by the weather conditions. That's why we frequently don't see nice formations here, and of course, since we don't live at the poles, we never see prisms.

The speaker talks about the shapes of snowflakes. Match each type below with the conditions under which it develops.

2. (Woman P) Many folk cures that have been around for centuries may be more therapeutic, more medically useful than previously suspected. Some home remedies have been found to have antiviral properties and others have antibacterial properties. So, the importance of documenting these . . . remedies and experimenting to see if they really work can't be overemphasized.

A case in point is the wormwood plant. This plant has been used for hundreds of years in China and Vietnam to combat malaria. In fact, an early record of wormwood, of the medicinal use of wormwood, was found in a recipe discovered in a Southeast Asian tomb, a tomb dating from 168 BC. So the properties of the wormwood were closely investigated, and a new anti-malarial drug came out of this study. So, its antiviral properties led to the development of a drug for malaria, because, because the research found that it was, indeed, effective against this virus. So its antiviral properties were found to be correct.

Another case is sugar. See, in parts of South America, a powder obtained from grinding sugar cane is used for healing infections in wounds. And this usage may date back several hundred years. So experiments carried out on several hundred patients indicated that ordinary sugar in high concentrations kills off bacteria. Its suction effect helps by eliminating dead cells and creating a glass-like layer, and this glass-like layer protects the wound and ensures its healing.

Another antibacterial folk medicine that scientists are investigating is one used by Arab fishermen who rub their wounds with a venomous catfish to quicken healing. This catfish excretes a gel-like slime, and this slime has been found to contain not only antibiotics, but a coagulant that helps close injured blood vessels, anti-inflammatory agents, and a chemical that directs production of a glue-like material that aids healing.

Because traditional herbal treatments are often locally available and inexpensive, that makes them ideal for use by local people. Documentation of traditional medicines worldwide needs to be undertaken before those traditions are lost. An analysis of the substances can be made, and artifi-, synthetic substances can be developed for human use around the world.

The speaker talks about folk cures and what they were used for. Match the folk treatment to the properties it supposedly has.

3. (Man P) Today I want to talk about the development of refrigeration. There is evidence that early humans stored food underwater. They, early humans, probably noticed that their meat would last longer if it was kept underwater or stored in a cave or . . . was packed in snow. Later, ice was actively harvested from frozen lakes and rivers, and this ice would be stored in specially constructed buildings called icehouses to preserve food until the following winter. Is anyone familiar with these buildings? Yes, Tom.

(Man S) Well, yeah, in my hometown there's one that's been made into a museum. I think it was used to store ice, um, until the 1920s.

(Man P) Uh-huh. Could you describe the building for us?

(Man S) Uh, well, it's a large, windowless building. A brick and stone building and the ice blocks were packed in straw so that the ice would-, wouldn't melt. The straw kept the ice from melting for a while, anyway.

(Man P) OK, yeah, that's a good description of an icehouse. A later storage container was the icebox. And what would be the advantages of an icebox, an icebox over an icehouse? Susan?

(Woman S) Well, as I understand it, the icebox is a kind of early refrigerator. So, icehouses served whole communities, whereas iceboxes were small enough to put in your house, so it was more private and good for house, uh, domestic use. They kind of look like a cupboard, often with legs, and were made of wood.

(Man P) Uh-huh. That's correct. The inside of the box was lined with tin or zinc, and sawdust was frequently used for insulation purposes. Blocks of ice were delivered to people's homes like morning newspapers. So when do you think this method of refrigeration began to be obsolete?

(Man S) Presumably when modern electric refrigerators were introduced. Iceboxes didn't use electricity, did they?

(Man P) That's right, Tom. That's right. And refrigeration technology didn't stop there. It continues to develop today.

The class discussion is about the development of refrigeration. Match each description with the corresponding form of refrigeration.

4. (Woman P) In underground cave systems, rainfall containing minerals absorbed from carbonate rock and plant debris builds up formations known as speleothems. Let me spell that for you. S-P-E-L-E-O-T-H-E-M-S, speleothems, the formations that build up in caves. So over geological time, a variety of fantastically shaped structures can develop within a cave system. I'd like to talk about the different speleothems and how they're formed, usually by one of two types of water conditions: water dripping or water flowing.

For some speleothems to develop, mineral-laden water drips through the cave roof. The minerals from the dripping water start to build up vertical elongated hollow tubes hanging from the ceiling of the cave. These tubes are known as soda straws. They look like a soda straw and water drips from them, like when you take a straw out of a drink. So drops of water run down the inside of the tube, leaving mineral residues at the opening. Over time these soda straws can build up to several feet in length, and eventually they become plugged up so the water can't run through the straw anymore, so it runs down the outside surface. When this happens – this dripping down the outside of the straw – the formation evolves into an icicle-shaped stalactite.

Of course, this constant dripping of water off the end of the straw, or the stalactite, hits the floor of the cave under the formation and this builds up a vertical formation, rising from the floor, directly underneath, uh, the stalactite, and this formation is known as a stalagmite. Stalagmites typically have rounded ends due to the water splashing down from above, but their shapes vary a lot. Sometimes stalactites and stalagmites grow together to form a column from floor to ceiling.

Other kinds of formations found in caves besides soda straws, stalactites, and stalagmites are those formed by flowing water. OK? So, sometimes the water flows down the inclined ceiling of a cave, and when this happens, the mineral solution is deposited in thin trails. The deposits build up in a series of ripples and folds, and it looks like a layer of cloth. This kind of speleothem is called a drapery. You can visualize this speleothem as a piece of cloth draped over a ramp of some sort. OK. Now, if the water falls down a vertical surface, instead of a slope, the resulting formations take on the appearance of a waterfall, and this is known as flowstone.

Now speleothems are found in a variety of colors as well as shapes. This is due to the impurities – both natural and artificial – that mix with the dripping or flowing water as it seeps underground.

The professor talks about cave formations. Match each cave formation with the corresponding water condition.

Listening Mini-test 2

Questions 1–4

Listen to part of a discussion in an environmental science class.

(Woman P) It's now well established that our planet's protective ozone layer has been thinning in recent decades. This ozone layer lies between 15 and 30 kilometers above the Earth's surface and absorbs ultraviolet rays emitted by the sun. You all know about using skin creams and sunglasses for protection against ultraviolet rays. The thinning of the ozone layer, the loss of ozone is caused because artificial chemicals called chlorofluorocarbons, or CFCs, combine with the oxygen atoms of the ozone. So every oxygen atom that combines with

CFCs, this chemical reaction between CFCs and oxygen is what, is uh, how the amount of ozone is being depleted. Um, this ozone depletion has serious consequences because the more ultraviolet light reaches the Earth, the Earth's surface, the more damage it causes in DNA in humans and animals. The most well-known effect of this is the recent dramatic increase in skin cancers.

(Man S) So who's responsible for creating these CFCs? I mean, we've known about this for a long time. Isn't something being done about it?

(Woman P) Well, to answer your first question, uh, who's responsible, well, in a sense we all are. CFCs are a main component of dry cleaning and refrigerating chemicals. They are also produced in various manufacturing processes, and in nitrogen fertilizers, and aerosols used in products like hair sprays and polishes. Isn't something being done about it, your second question, well, yes. Uh, fortunately, CFCs use in aerosols has been phased out in most countries. But, these chemicals are dispersed in the lower atmosphere where they can linger for years before migrating to the stratosphere where the damage is done.

(Woman S) Dr. Alameda, this all sounds very pessimistic. Haven't there been international agreements to phase out CFCs?

(Woman P) Yes, in fact, since 1985 several international conventions have produced agreements.

(Man S) So, uh, would you say you are optimistic about the future, the future of the ozone layer?

(Woman P) I would say that, that I'm guardedly optimistic for the long-term future. It's true that the various agreements are beginning to take effect. The problem is that it takes many years for the CFCs to disperse, and the fact is, not all countries are enthusiastic about phasing out their production, for economic reasons. However, it's generally hoped that the ozone layer will recover completely by the year 2060 if we all abide by the international agreements.

1. In the discussion, the professor briefly explains the process that breaks down the ozone layer. Indicate whether each of the sentences is a step in the process of ozone depletion.
2. Why is the professor cautious in her prediction of the future?
3. According to the professor, how do CFCs get into the atmosphere?
4. According to the discussion, which of the following are contaminants?

Questions 5–8

Listen to part of a lecture in a psychology class.

(Man P) OK. We all know that people can and do influence each other. However, the real question, the disturbing question is . . . how far can people's minds be influenced against their own will? There are three techniques that have been used in attempts to control other people's behavior, and I'd like to tell you a little about each one of these techniques.

One technique, subliminal perception, is frequently referred to as subception. This technique is based on the observation that people notice a great deal more than they consciously realize. This is not a new observation. We have been aware of it for a long time. But, it has been given special attention since the results of an experiment that took place in a New York movie theater were reported. In this experiment, what they did was, well, an advertisement for ice cream was flashed onto the screen during the feature film. Apparently, the ad was shown for such a brief moment that no one consciously saw the intrusion. Got the picture? Everyone was watching the movie and being shown an ice cream ad so quickly that they weren't aware of it. What was found was that ice cream sales increased dramatically. You could say they soared for the duration of time that the experiment continued. That was subception.

Hypnosis is another technique that can be used for controlling people's minds. OK, so while in a deep trance, people can be told to do something at a specific time or at a certain signal. They can also be told that they won't remember anything when they come out of the trance, what had been said or what they were told to do, at what particular signal, once out of the trance. This is called a post-hypnotic suggestion. It's still unclear whether a subject can be made to carry out an action that otherwise would be unacceptable in that person's mind.

The third technique I want to mention is brainwashing. Brainwashing entails forcing people to believe something, usually something false, by continually telling them or showing them evidence that's supposedly true. The person being brainwashed is, uh, prevented from thinking about whatever it is, thinking about it properly or considering other evidence. Now, brainwashing can take some extreme forms. For example, brainwashing can be done by first causing a complete breakdown of individuals. This is done through acts such as starving them, preventing them from sleeping, intimidating them, and keeping them in a state of constant fear. Eventually, the person, the individual loses their sense of reality . . . and when this happens, new, false ideas can be planted in their minds.

5. In the lecture, the professor describes three types of mind control. Match each behavior with the associated mind-control technique.
6. According to the professor, what is true of subliminal perception?
7. What else is true of subliminal perception?
8. Which of the following did the professor not mention when speaking about brainwashing?

Questions 9–12

Listen to part of a lecture on biotechnology.

(Woman P) Nature has always provided a stimulus for inventive minds. Look at early flying machines, they clearly were an attempt to emulate the freedom of birds. Architects and engineers have often consciously modelled buildings on forms found in nature. A more recent example of inspiration from nature is the invention of that common fastening device, Velcro®. The inventor of Velcro® was out walking his dog and noticed that small burrs – you know, those seedpods that get attached to your clothes? Small burrs had become entangled in his dog's coat by grasping the hairs with tiny hooks. This led him to invent a synthetic fabric, one whose surfaces mimic the clasping properties of these natural seedpods that he was pulling out of his dog's coat.

Animals and plants have evolved solutions to the same kinds of problems that often interest engineers and designers. So lots of current research in material science is concerned with actively examining the natural world, especially at the molecular level, for inspiration to develop materials with novel properties. This is a relatively new field of study, sometimes known as biomimetics, since it consciously attempts to mimic nature. I don't need to write that on the board, do I? Bio from biology, and mimetics from mime or mimic. OK? Biomimetics.

OK. Well, researchers have been investigating several interesting areas, well, what I think are interesting areas. For example, they have studied how the molecular structure of antler bone contributes to its amazing toughness, how the skin structure of a worm contributes to its ability to crawl, how the sea cucumber softens its skeleton and changes shape so that it can squeeze through tiny gaps in rocks, or, uh, what gives wood its high resistance to impact. These investigations have led to several breakthroughs in the development of composite materials with remarkable properties.

Predictions for future inventions that may be developed from these lines of research include so-called smart structures. Those are structures that design and repair themselves in a similar way to a variety of processes in the natural world. For example, engineers have envisaged bridges that would detect areas heavily stressed by vehicle movement or wind. See, the bridge structure would automatically add or move material to the weak areas until the stress is reduced. The same principle might be used to repair damaged buildings.
Other new materials that have been imagined are substances that would copy photosynthesis in green plants. What good is that, you might ask. Well, photosynthesis could be a way to create new energy sources. The potential impact of biomimetic research is so great that we may end up calling the twenty-first century the Age of Materials.

9. In the lecture, the professor explains the field of study called biomimetics. Indicate whether each of the following is an example of biomimetic application.
10. According to the professor, what inspires architects and engineers?
11. When talking about smart structures, what is the professor doing?
12. What are some of the areas that researchers are investigating?

Questions 13–16

Listen to part of a discussion in a criminology class.

(Woman P) Today I'd like to look at the problem of theft . . . theft of cultural antiquities and art. You probably aren't aware . . . what a large problem it is. Let me give you some facts. Illegal trafficking in cultural property has become a massive criminal activity, so massive that today it ranks in economic terms alongside illegal trading in weapons or drugs. Think about that . . . equal to the illegal trade in weapons and drugs. OK, so where do these art treasures come from? Well, in fact, no part of the world is immune from this problem. Works of art are stolen from museums and looted from historic or religious buildings everywhere, and eventually they find their way to wealthy buyers. Frequently, smaller stone or wooden carvings are simply cut or chopped away from a wall or base – sadly, destroying the integrity of the overall work.
In some regions of the world, these thefts have seriously reduced the stock of national treasures. So, what kinds of measures do you think would be most appropriate for dealing with this situation? Anyone? Yes, Luis?

(Man S) Well, electronic surveillance of exhibitions and historical monuments would help.

(Woman P) OK. Electronic surveillance. That, no doubt, would act as a deterrent and would be a very good means of combating some thefts. But, that's not always an affordable or practical option. It can be too expensive and, especially since many cultural objects are located in remote places, not practical at all. Other ideas? . . . for dealing with thefts? Yes?

(Woman S1) Isn't there a move to get owners, uh, countries, to catalog their cultural possessions?

(Woman P) Yes, Mary, there is. Remember that one of the chief problems in policing this kind of crime is that very often, too often, the original owners, whether they are governments, museums, or private collectors, these owners can't furnish an accurate description of the property that has been stolen, and therefore, they can't prove their ownership. So, yes, there are several organizations concerned with combating this illegal trade by stressing the importance of owners' making accurate inventories. These inventories should include relevant data. Data about the object. Data, such as date of fabrication, kind of material, shape, size, the presence of any kind of identifying markings. Of course, these inventories should also include detailed photographic illustrations, so if a thief takes something – let's say a painting, and cuts it up into pieces, selling it as two or three different paintings – a piece can still be identified as coming from the original.

(Man S) But inventories by themselves can't prevent this trade. It just kind of helps in the recovery, and this information can only be really useful if it's widely available to all the people involved in policing – customs agents, border guards.

(Woman P) Yes. Yes. You're absolutely right, Luis. In fact, the development of electronic networks allows the various police forces to use inventories to identify objects and to disseminate information about the objects to any of many official offices worldwide. This information can also be used by customs agencies, the insurance industry, and cultural heritage organizations. Can you think of any other measures that might help stem this illegal trade? Yes?

(Woman S2) Well, I think . . . it seems like a person could buy an artifact without being aware of its historical or cultural value, or that the object may have been stolen. So maybe travelers should be told about this danger. This might go a long way to reducing the trade.

(Woman P) Uh-huh. Uh-huh.

(Man S) Well, I was thinking, not so much about the theft, but how do customs people recognize that something is illegal art as opposed to some cheap trinket? I mean when we, when my family went to Mexico, to see the Mayan pyramids . . . in the Yucatan, well, there were lotsa peddlers selling things like, well, copies of Mayan artifacts, and, uh . . . how would a border official recognize if a particular person is a tourist . . . is crossing with a trinket or someone trying to smuggle in a priceless treasure?

(Woman S2) Yeah . . . say, a farmer finds a Mayan piece in his field and sells it to a tourist without either of them understanding its value. And, of course, there would be no inventory, uh, no record of the item when the tourist crosses the border. How would a border guard recognize that? I mean, if it were stolen, there might be a report and the guard is on the lookout or a smuggler might give himself away through . . . uh . . . body language or something. But a tourist . . .

(Man S) Or . . . think about the long border between Mexico and the States. A smuggler could wade across the Rio Grande.

(Woman S1) And the border guards are more concerned with drug smuggling or illegal immigration, so someone with what looks like a trinket . . . an official might think this is just a guy bringing trinkets into the States.

13. According to the discussion, which of the following is true about the illegal trade in art?

14. What does the professor say about inventories of cultural properties?

15. Which problems in policing the trade in national treasures were discussed?

16. What does the professor say about electronic surveillance?

EXERCISE L18 *Understanding inferences*

1. (Woman P) At her trial, Mata Hari was dubbed the greatest spy of the First World War, of World War I. Her French accusers brought eight charges of spying against her. However, research suggests that she, Mata Hari, was not really a spy.

Mata Hari was probably given a sentence for spying.

2. (Woman S) By the way, Fred, I heard, someone said, that you took an interesting course last summer. Whadja' take?

(Man S) I did. It was a course on building adobe houses. You know, houses made of mud.

(Woman S) What? Houses of mud? Are you joking?

(Man S) No. I'm not. First, we studied the styles of traditional adobe homes in different parts of the world. That was interesting. Then we learned the techniques of mixing sand, straw, and water. Then we put the mixture into molds to dry, and, and when the mud bricks were ready, we built a structure of our own – the class's own structure, not each of us making one. A group effort.

(Woman S) So when are you going to build your house of mud?

(Man S) Well, not in the near future.

(Woman S) (teasing) Well, you'll have to let us know so we can help you. We, well, I, at least, used to like making mud pies as a kid.

The woman will probably sign up for the course.

3. (Woman P) A fossil of an extinct and previously unknown seabird has been excavated. This bird has been identified as history's largest flying seabird. The fossils indicate that it had a wingspan of more than 18 feet and it probably weighed around 90 pounds. Now if we compare that to the largest seabird of today, the albatross, the albatross weighs up to 20 pounds and has a wingspan of about 11 feet. The albatross is the largest living seabird today.

There are probably many fossils of today's albatross.

4. (Man P) The synovial membranes in the body produce fluids that lubricate the areas between the bones. Besides lubricating these areas, they also keep the cartilage tissues in good condition. So, can anyone tell me why it's important to keep the cartilage tissues in good condition?

(Man S) Well, cartilage tissues protect the ends of the bones. They kind of act like elastic shock absorbers.

(Man P) That's right. Now if the cartilage tissues are damaged, regeneration is slowed down or stopped. Yes, Linda?

(Woman S) Yeah, once cartilage has been damaged, is there anything that can be done to repair the damage?

(Man P) Well, there are experiments being conducted to renew damaged cartilage by transplanting synovial membrane cells. And so far, the results have been encouraging, very encouraging in fact, but further experiments need to be conducted before a decision can be made concerning their use on humans.

The transplant operation of synovial membrane cells has probably not been done on humans.

EXERCISE L19 *Drawing conclusions*

1. (Woman P) Polio is a crippling disease that you've all heard about. It reached epidemic proportions during the 1950s. Unfortunately, many sufferers from that decade started experiencing a return of the symptoms thirty years later. Strange, isn't it? The reason behind this recurrence is not yet understood, but it has given scientists further information about the disease.

For what field might the new information about polio be most useful?

2. (Man S) I would really like to get my foreign language requirements out of the way, but I went to register and when I got there to sign up for beginning Spanish, all the Spanish courses were closed. So, do you have any suggestions, Dr. Abbot?

(Woman P) Well, if you are insisting on getting your requirement out of the way, you could sign up for a different language. The Italian teacher on our staff is excellent, and the classes are smaller, so there's more opportunity to practice speaking.

(Man S) Hmmm, I never thought of Italian. Thanks for the advice.

What will the man probably do as a result of this conversation?

3. (Woman S) You were telling us about the famous fashion designer Jean Muir yesterday at the end of the class period. But we had to rush off. I know it wasn't part of your lecture, but we thought it was interesting. Could you finish what you were saying?

(Man P) Sure. What were you interested in?

(Woman S) Well, you were talking about her discovery that she had terminal cancer and how she set about changing the way she managed her fashion business. But you didn't get into those changes. I'd like to know what things she did.

(Man P) I was just saying that she concentrated her time and energy on four women. These women had worked for her over the years. So Muir gradually increased their responsibilities and their training. Together they worked on both Muir's mainline collection and the studio collection using her original ideas and patterns. At the time of her death, she had left enough material for these women to produce collections for twenty years.

(Woman S) She was really passionate about design, wasn't she?

Why might Jean Muir have given so much attention to her staff?

4. (Woman P) Two University of Alaska professors devised a novel way of getting junior high school students interested in the economic history of their state. How many of you are interested in the economic history of your state? No hands up. Uh-huh. OK. So, these professors produced a 120-page comic book that traces the economic history of Alaska from the mid-eighteenth century until the granting of statehood in 1959. Most adolescents seem to find the comic-book format a more entertaining way for learning a subject. So this seems to be the ideal way to pass on information. The writers use fictional and historical characters to illustrate economic concepts and historical events, such as the hunting of whales and the Klondike gold rush of the 1890s. The response from students was overwhelmingly enthusiastic and, as you can imagine, teachers also appreciated the ease with which their students grasped economic concepts taught in this way.

To what group of university students might this talk have been given?

EXERCISE L20 *Inferring reasons*

1. (Woman S) I saw in the course catalog that the university is offering a batik class this semester. Is it still open?

(Man S) I don't know. Do you have the course number?

(Woman S) 309.

(Man S) Lemme see. Yeah, it's open. It meets Monday, Wednesday, and Friday at nine o'clock.

(Woman S) D'you know if it can be used to, as an undergraduate, uh, to meet undergraduate course requirements for art majors?

(Man S) Just a minute . . . uh . . . Yes, it fulfills course requirements for both art and home economics majors.

(Woman S) Good. I'd like to register for it, please.

Why does the woman ask if the course meets the requirements for art majors?

2. (Man P) Sound-activated toys . . . a toy that responds whenever the child talks to it . . . these toys are just one example of how high technology has affected childhood experience. There's a doll on the market that has a memory like a personal computer. It has a soft face that looks alive because it moves when the doll speaks. Its eyes respond to light by blinking, its hands are sensitive to heat, and it has a voice-recognition facility that gives it the ability to respond to the child playing with it. But one of the things we have found . . . uh . . . considering all the high technology that goes into making such expensive toys, you may be surprised, or maybe not be surprised, to find that children become bored with the new toy after its novelty has worn off. What children get the most out of . . . children seem to get the most lasting enjoyment from balls . . . ordinary sticks, uh . . . common cardboard boxes. This is probably because these toys can be turned into anything the child's imaginative play needs, whereas a high-tech doll is just that, a doll. It can never be anything else.

Why does the speaker mention balls, sticks, and boxes?

3. (Woman P) Before we go over those sentences I asked you to translate for today, I want to announce that the Foreign Language Department has set up a foreign-film festival. Uh, it will take place during the first two weeks of November. I'm especially excited about the Spanish-language films they'll be showing. There are two from Spain and three from Mexico. Besides those films, Chile, Argentina, Cuba are represented, and . . . just a minute . . . ah, yes . . . there's a Puerto Rican film that takes place among the New York City Puerto Rican population . . . . These films will give you a wonderful opportunity to listen to regional accents. I've posted a schedule of all the movies outside the door of the Foreign Language Department office. I've also typed up a list of the names, days, and times of just those in Spanish, which I'll pass out at the end of the hour. OK. Now, I realize that some of these showings may conflict with your individual schedules, but I recommend that you try to make every effort to get to as many movies as possible.

Why does the professor encourage students to see the films?

4. (Woman P) I think you all know the reason I'm here. Sadly, well, first of all, I want to say I regret that violent crime has reached our campus, and of course, until the perpetrator is caught, all of you need to take extra precautions. I know some of you are frightened, and I don't mean to frighten you any more. I want to assure you that assault is a very rare occurrence here, and the chances of your becoming a victim are remote. However, as women, we all need to be alert and be cautious here or any other place we go. There are simple procedures we can follow. Try not to be out alone at night, and never use shortcuts, like unlit alleyways or routes across vacant lots. When you're out, walk facing the traffic so a car can't pull up behind you. I know that some of you take night classes. If you don't have anyone to meet you after class, call campus security. They'll send someone to pick you up from your classroom and escort you to your bus, car, or dormitory. At this point I'd like to introduce Mr. Lang, who's going to demonstrate some ways to protect yourselves through body language as well as the best ways to conduct yourselves if . . . if you are confronted. He will also teach you some techniques to break someone's hold on you if it should become necessary. So I'd like you to welcome Mr. Lang.

Why is the speaker giving the talk at this time?

EXERCISE L21 *Identifying attitudes*

1. (Woman S) Aren't you a little old to be reading comic books?

(Man S) Hey, this isn't just any comic book. It's a Walt Disney classic.

(Woman S) Classic or not, this is a university.

(Man S) I'll have you know that this is required reading for my American popular culture course.

(Woman S) What? I can't believe it. Here I am reading stacks of major works by important authors . . . uh . . . Dickens, and Tolstoy for my survey of nineteenth-century literature course, and you're reading comic books!

(Man S) Well, this isn't the only required reading material in the course. We have to read a lot about the events that influenced the comic-book writers, and study contemporary art movements, and how women and minorities are depicted in, uh, comics and other pop art. This course isn't as easy as you think.

2. (Man S) Well, Jane, how was your first day of classes?

(Woman S) Great. I signed up for an American history course. It's about the Revolutionary War period– with Professor Lewis – he's fantastic.

(Man S) Uh, history . . . sounds boring to me. I never did like history.

(Woman S) How can you find history boring when – oh, I guess you never had a teacher like Dr. Lewis. He describes the events so vividly that it seems as though you are actually there, like, caught up in the issues. You would really get into it.

(Man S) Well, maybe.

(Woman S) Oh, come on. Why don't you take it? It's not too late to add a course.

(Man S) Well, I don't need it for my major, and there are other courses I'd rather take as electives.

3. (Woman S) Dr. Reed, are you busy?

(Man P) Hi, Donna. So you've come back to visit your old university, have you?

(Woman S) Yeah, our mid-term break starts a few days earlier than here, so I'm home to see my folks.

(Man P) And how are they?

(Woman S) Oh, just fine.

(Man P) Good. Good. And . . . uh . . . how do you like your program?

(Woman S) Oh, it's great. It's a lot of work, though.

(Man P) Well, now that you are at the doctorate level, you can expect that.

(Woman S) Yes, of course, and Dr. Jennings is – do you know Dr. Jennings?

(Man P) Of him, yes, . . . not personally.

(Woman S) Uh-huh. Well, he's arranging for a field-study group to work in Easter Island over the semester break. I've signed up to go.

(Man P) Fantastic. That'll be a great experience. I'd like to hear more about it, but I have a class in a few minutes. It's good to see you, Donna. Maybe you could pop into my office tomorrow afternoon, say about 2:30?

(Woman S) Sure.

4. (Woman P) Good morning. Can I help you?

(Man S) Yeah. Who do I see about a complaint?

(Woman P) Well, uh, that would be me. What seems to be the problem?

(Man S) [Sigh] Well, we've just moved into student family housing and the apartment is awful, just awful.

(Woman P) Hmmm . . . That's odd. All our units are inspected and decorated before new people move in.

(Man S) I'm sorry, but not in this case. The walls are dirty and the refrigerator doesn't work and—

(Woman P) I see . . . uh . . . that's highly unusual. Could you please tell me the number of your unit?

(Man S) Um. It's 42 in South Court.

(Woman P) 42? Are you sure? Let me look . . . and your name?

(Man S) Anderson. Daniel Anderson.

(Woman P) Ah, I see. Here's the problem. You've been issued the wrong unit. Number 42 hasn't been redecorated yet. I'm really sorry about this. Let's see, you should have been given number 43. It's directly across from number 42.

EXERCISE L22 *Identifying the speaker's purpose*

1. (Man P) So, does competition promote success? Think about it. Does competition promote success? Well, doesn't that depend on what you consider, how you define success? So, if you define success as beating your rival, then yes. But if you define success as finding satisfaction in relationships, possibly, very possibly competition is detrimental to success.

Why does the professor say this: Think about it.

2. (Woman P) In looking at the teeth of skeletons from the, uh, Mesolithic period, it was found that those from Northern Europe had fewer cavities than those from Southern Europe. Why? Simple. Diet. The breakdown of non-carbohydrate foods like

meats and fish does not form acidic by-products, whereas carbohydrates are cariogenic . . . uh . . . you know, caries, cavities, in other words, causing tooth decay. Carbohydrates, especially the sugars, are cariogenic. They produce acids that destroy teeth.

Why does the professor say this: you know, caries, cavities, in other words, causing tooth decay.

3. (Man P) Think about how you prepare for your courses. You read the textbook, take notes during your lectures, you try to learn the concepts. Then, you take a test . . . one that supposedly shows that you've gained that knowledge. But if you get the answer wrong, does that mean you're wrong?

(Woman S) Well, yes. If I get the answer wrong, then I didn't know the concept or didn't understand it. Right? I suppose I could have misread the question.

(Man S) It might mean the question was badly written.

(Man P) It could be any of those things. But I want you to look at this in a different way. When we study the way children gain language, we see certain steps, some of which appear as if the child is regressing in language acquisition instead of progressing. Let me give you an example. When a child has acquired a certain amount of language, she uses the form "I went" correctly. But later in her language development, she starts using the ungrammatical form, "I goed," a word that doesn't exist in English. The child has probably never heard anyone say that. This, by the way, can be very unsettling for parents. But after a while the child goes back to using the correct form. Now this is a natural progression in child language acquisition. So with this in mind, think about a test you didn't do well on. Now the incorrect answers you chose, were they an indication of where you were in the process of understanding particular concepts? In other words, maybe they were correct in terms of the stage of your learning.

(Man S) Does that mean, Dr. Blake, that when I fail your final, I'll get a pass?

(Man P) [laughter] I'm afraid not, Tom.

Why does the professor say this: But I want you to look at this in a different way.

4. (Woman P) Well, we've been rock-climbing together now on several occasions, and I think everyone has made excellent progress. So with that in mind, I thought you might be interested in a special climbing workshop at the State Park Climbing Center. The thing that really strikes me is the people who will be leading the workshop. Jim Brown, for example . . . you know . . . one of the most experienced rock climbers in the world today. I hope that you'll be able to arrange to attend. I'm sure that participants in the course will gain a great deal of confidence, and refine their techniques. So, here are the details: The groups' size will be limited, so everyone will be given lots of personal attention. The cost for the weekend including accommodations and food is $300. There will also be an extra, but small, a small charge for equipment for those participants who don't have their own gear. And, um, a $30 non-refundable deposit is required by the end of next week, with the balance . . . the balance should be paid by July 20th. I do urge everyone here to take advantage of this wonderful opportunity. So, if you can register, I'll be handing out application forms after our climb this morning. Return the form and the deposit to my office as soon as possible.

Why does the professor say this: The thing that really strikes me is the people who will be leading the workshop.

EXERCISE L23 *Identifying the speaker's meaning*

1. (Man P) Sue, you know you missed the deadline, don't you?

(Woman S) Yes. I know, but could I get my report in by early next week?

(Man P) Well, I'm not so concerned about deadlines as such. We all have setbacks from time to time.

(Woman S) Thank you, sir.

(Man P) I'm more concerned about your getting behind in general. I've seen students get so far behind that they can't catch up. If you can't keep up in this course, you're really wasting my time and your time and money. If that's the case, Sue, you should drop now, while you can, before it's too late to drop without penalties.

Listen again to part of the conversation. Then answer the question.

(Man P) If you can't keep up in this course you're really wasting my time and your time and money. If that's the case, Sue, you should drop now, while you can, before it's too late to drop without penalties.

What does the professor mean when he says this: If that's the case, Sue, you should drop now, while you can, before it's too late to drop without penalties.

2. (Man S) I dropped my physics course because I discovered it didn't meet my degree requirements. You wouldn't know anyone in the class who'd like to buy the course book, would you?

(Woman S) Not offhand. But if you bought it new and kept the receipt, I'm sure you could get your money back or exchange it for one you do need.

(Man S) Really? I could do that, could I?

(Woman S) Well, yeah, if it's within a reasonable period of time.

Listen again to part of the conversation. Then answer the question.

(Woman S) Not offhand. But if you bought it new and kept the receipt, I'm sure you could get your money back or exchange it for one you do need.

(Man S) Really? I could do that, could I?

What is the man doing when he says this: Really? I could do that, could I?

3. (Woman P) OK. Now that I have all your decisions . . . your individual and group decisions written on the board, I want to show you this transparency of the, uh . . . each choice has a risk factor. So here are the statistics showing how risky, how much of a gamble each of the alternatives is. So take a moment to compare the risk values with the choices you made. What kind of jumps out at you? Yes, Jason?

(Man S) Well, the individual decisions within each group are, well not always, but they tend to be less risky than the decision the group made.

(Woman P) Right. Do you see how as individuals, most of you were not willing to take the gamble? But as a group you were. The term for this phenomenon is risky shift. Risky shift. A shift in position from less risky to more risky. If we were to average the risk factor of the groups' individual members, it usually, but not always, shows that individuals are more cautious about taking a gamble, while a group decision has a higher risk. So, what implications does this have? Think about business and political decisions in particular.

Listen again to part of the lecture. Then answer the question.

(Woman P) So take a moment to compare the risk values with the choices you made. What kind of jumps out at you?

What does the professor mean when she says this: What kind of jumps out at you?

4. (Woman P) The Declaration of Independence makes the pursuit of happiness a political goal. Life, liberty, and the pursuit of happiness. It's probably true that a country that doesn't have some degree of happiness among its people is going to end up with some sort of strife. But what about the pursuit of happiness? What are the implications of such a goal?

(Woman S) Well, I think it's important that people are free to pursue happiness. I mean . . . if we're free to do that, to follow a dream . . . uh, our interests will lead to development, progress in scientific pursuits, and things like that.

(Man S) Oh, now hold on a minute. Anyone can see what a selfish society we've become in our pursuit of happiness. I think that's clear. Just look at all the materialism here.

Listen again to part of the lecture. Then answer the question.

(Woman S) Well, I think it's important that people are free to pursue happiness. I mean . . . if we're free to do that, to follow a dream . . . uh, our interests will lead to development, progress in scientific pursuits and things like that.

(Man S) Oh, now hold on a minute. Anyone can see what a selfish society we've become in our pursuit of happiness. I think that's clear. Just look at all the materialism here.

What can be inferred about the students?

Listening Mini-test 3

Questions 1–5

Listen to an architecture professor talk about hazards in the home.

(Woman P) It used to be that the safety of a house was judged simply by whether it stood up or not. Well, things have changed. During the twentieth century, people began to build houses with synthetic materials. Unfortunately, these materials have proved over time that they endanger the health of the owners, or the houses' occupants, since the owner doesn't necessarily live in the place. So what are these synthetic materials? Well, asbestos, for example, asbestos, which was used as roofing sheets and paneling. This was found to cause memory loss. No, I'm sorry, it causes lung cancer. Asbestos has been found to cause lung cancer and formaldehyde causes memory loss. Formaldehyde was used in insulating foams, synthetic resins, and glues in things like plywood, chipboard, and hardboard. Formaldehyde used in this way causes damage to the nervous system and as I said before, memory loss, severe memory loss. Then there are wood preservatives. Now they contain, wood preservatives contain potent fungicides and insecticides. These cause cirrhosis of the liver, bone marrow atrophy, and nervous disorders. I'm really painting a bleak picture, aren't I? And that brings us to paints. At one time, lead was the major ingredient in paint. You may think that when lead levels were restricted due to lead poisoning, that was the end of the problem. Now, get this: Paint technologists came up with even more poisonous metals, such as cadmium, to add to paints.

OK. The dangers of synthetic material are most apparent when a fire breaks out. Experts say that today more people are killed by toxic fumes in house fires than by the fire itself. We may have used a lot of synthetic materials in house building, but in fact, for every synthetic material used in a home, there's a biological or natural counterpart. OK, well, we can't all go . . . we can't very well go and tear down our houses and start from scratch. However, there are ways to recognize and safely remove some synthetic material and replace it with natural alternatives.

1. Listen again to part of the lecture. Then answer the question.

(Woman P) Well, asbestos, for example, asbestos, which was used as roofing sheets and paneling. This was found to cause memory loss. No, I'm sorry, it causes lung cancer.

Why does the professor say this: No, I'm sorry, it causes lung cancer.

2. Listen again to part of the lecture. Then answer the question.

(Woman P) These cause cirrhosis of the liver, bone marrow atrophy, and nervous disorders. I'm really painting a bleak picture, aren't I?

Why does the professor say this: I'm really painting a bleak picture, aren't I?

3. Why does the speaker mention fires?
4. What would be an example of a natural building material?
5. What might the listeners do as a result of this lecture?

Questions 6–9

Listen to a discussion between a professor and his students.

(Man P) Are there any questions concerning the required reading list I just passed out?

(Woman S) Yes, I have one. I was wondering . . . I see that some of the book titles have an asterisk by them. Uh . . . could you explain why?

(Man P) Yes, of course. Hmmm, those books are out of print. I asked the library to purchase them, but unfortunately, they can't be purchased. So, I've put my personal copies on reserve at the library. Since you can't take materials on reserve out of the library, you'll have to read them there. You have to go to the reserve desk on the second floor to check out anything on reserve. OK? Anything else?

(Man S) Yeah, I was wondering about the list of articles on the second page. I don't really understand the numbers.

(Man P) Hmmm. Those are articles on microfiche. Have you ever used microfiche?

(Man S) No, I haven't.

(Man P) Could you see me after class and I'll explain it?

(Woman S) Uh, Dr. Burns. I don't know for sure, but I don't think . . . I think that there are a lot of us that don't know about microfiche.

(Man S) Yeah, that's right.

(Man P) Oh. OK. Then I guess I'd better explain. You see, microfiche materials are at the reserve desk as well. You give that number to the librarian at the reserve desk, and the person on duty will give you a small folder containing the articles on microfiche. Then you go to the microfiche room . . . uh . . . it's directly across from the reserve desk, it's where the microfiche machines are. There are instructions beside each machine explaining how to insert the microfiche. It's really very easy.

(Woman S) All right. Thank you.

(Man P) OK. Well, that's all for today. Please be prepared to discuss the first reading in our next class.

6. When would this discussion most likely take place?
7. What would most likely be found at a library reserve desk?
8. What can be inferred about the articles?
9. What can be inferred about the two students?

Questions 10–14

Listen to a talk given by a guest inventor.

(Woman P) It's been said that necessity is the mother of invention, and this may be true in some cases, but most things that people need already exist. We inventors tend to be a group of dissatisfied people. We see the drawbacks of products that are already in existence. I think most people do. Think of something that annoys you . . . your partner leaving the cap off the toothpaste, for instance. Now the difference between most people and an inventor is that while most people grumble, an inventor starts to visualize solutions. We really get swept away with this enthusiasm, this passion for remedying the problem. We aren't grumpy, unhappy people. Let me say this. We may be dissatisfied, but we also tend to be very optimistic problem solvers. One has to be optimistic, extremely optimistic, to persist through the inevitable failures. Why? Because we fail a lot, but inventors thrive on failures. Where most people get discouraged and give up, inventors use failures as stepping stones to new approaches and then to eventual success. I shouldn't say success because once the invention is completed, we often see another fault. Sometimes, in fact, an invention brings about a change that requires another invention. A case in point is the aspirin bottle. Small children managed to get into aspirin bottles with, uh, unfortunately, sometimes fatal results, so the childproof bottle cap was invented. However, arthritis sufferers couldn't open the childproof bottle to get their medicine. In response to this problem, the two-way cap was invented. So now users can choose the most convenient way to close the bottle. Problem solved? No, because a small child and an arthritis sufferer could share the same household. What are we going to do about it? Let's toss some ideas around to get your inventor brains operating.

10. Why does the lecturer say this: It has been said that necessity is the mother of invention, and this may be true in some cases, but most things that people need already exist.

11. Why does the lecturer say this: Let me say this. We may be dissatisfied, but we also tend to be very optimistic problem solvers.

12. Why does the speaker mention aspirin bottles?

13. What might happen as a result of this talk?

14. How does the speaker close the talk?

Questions 15–18

Listen to a discussion in a cultural anthropology course.

(Man P) One way cultural anthropologists can study a culture is by sifting through garbage dumps. Garbage is the remains of what a society used or threw away. Let's take, for example, an orange peel. What can I tell by looking at an orange peel?

(Woman S) Well, uh . . . I think that you could possibly tell whether that orange was eaten or made into juice.

(Man P) OK. Good. Hmmm, let's imagine that we have a pile of orange peels. OK? This pile of orange peels indicates they were squeezed to make juice. What information can I gain from that?

(Man S) You could find out . . . uh . . . count those peels and estimate the number of oranges used. Uh, enough for two glasses may indicate a single person or, or a couple. And enough for a couple of quarts might indicate a family.

(Man P) Good. So we can make estimates on numbers of people. We can make even more assumptions. For example, what could we infer if there's enough for 50 people? Um, what would a seasonal change in the number of peels indicate? As you can see, an analysis of what is discarded can help us map out patterns and give us insights into human behavior. Unfortunately – or fortunately, depending on one's point of view – much of what is thrown away is organic, so when we're sifting through, say, the garbage dump of a Paleolithic village, the remains are limited. Of course, there are places where artifacts are better preserved – areas with dry desert air, such as Egypt, for instance, or with freezing temperatures, such as the Arctic regions. Oh, we've run out of time. OK. I want you to think about – when you pass a pile of garbage – look at it and think about what that garbage can tell you. Tomorrow we'll discuss cultural anthropologists and the issue of grave robbing.

15. What are the students probably interested in?

16. Why does the professor mention orange peels?

17. What would most likely be found in a Stone Age garbage dump?

18. Why does the professor regret that most garbage is organic?

Listening Section Practice Test

Questions 1–7

Listen to part of a lecture in a psychology class.

(Woman P) So today we're going to continue our discussion of various mental disorders. Specifically, I'm going to focus on various anxiety disorders. Now, of course, everyone feels anxious or uneasy now and again. You may feel anxious on your first day of a new job, or when you have to meet someone important, for example. Some people feel anxious when they visit the dentist. Some typical symptoms include a pounding heart, sweaty palms, or a dry mouth. But now – suppose that the anxiety is serious enough to keep you from enjoying life; maybe it interferes with your work or controls much of your daily routine. Or maybe you experience occasional instances of anxiety that are terrifying enough that you become immobilized with fear. Maybe you will take extreme measures to get away from the object or situation causing the fear.

Now these anxieties can be put into three main groups according to what causes the reaction. The first are what we call specific phobias. These are the most common phobias, and their focus is specific objects. In fact, the thing feared is often relatively safe, and also the sufferer usually realizes that and knows that their fear is irrational. A very common specific phobia is fear of heights, for example. This fear is very common. No doubt some of you have felt this fear from time to time. Fear of spiders and insects is another common one. Spiders are not usually harmful. Well, not usually, anyway. But some people break out into a cold sweat and have heart palpitations and become immobile even if they know a spider is on the other side of the room. Some of the less common phobias seem rather bizarre. For example, would you believe some people are afraid of color, say, the color yellow? Another strange one is fear of laughter . . . I guess that's not a laughing matter for the sufferer.

OK. So what causes these specific phobias? Well, we don't know exactly. We do know that they tend to run in families, and they are apparently slightly more common in women. Many of them persist, that is, they don't go away on their own. At least that tends to be the case with phobias that develop in adolescence or adulthood. Specific phobias that develop in childhood are more likely to disappear with time.

Another category of phobia is called social phobia. This fear is really the fear of being embarrassed or humiliated in front of other people. If social phobia is serious enough, it can prevent a person from continuing in school or work, and maybe that person avoids making friends. Now, some social phobics can actually be at ease with other people most of the time except in particular situations. So, for example, a sufferer here may believe that small mistakes they make are more significant than they really are, or feel that everyone is looking at them. They could also be extremely fearful of, for example, using the phone in front of other people, or it may be something really simple and seemingly irrational such as drinking a cup of coffee or even say, buttoning a coat in front of others.

A third category of phobia is known as agoraphobia – do I need to put that on the board? No? OK, fine. OK, so this phobia causes people to suffer anxiety about being in places or situations from which they perceive it might be difficult to escape, or in which it seems help is not available. So agoraphobia might include a fear of traveling alone, being alone in a crowd, or being unable to leave a place easily. People with this condition often develop the disorder after suffering from a panic attack, that is, a feeling of intense terror with symptoms such as sweating and shortness of breath. Such panic attacks may occur randomly and without warning, so this makes it difficult for a sufferer to predict what kind of situation will provoke a panic attack. So then, he or she will try to avoid situations and places where such attacks have happened previously.

OK, to wrap up today . . . well, the good news is that all of these disorders can be treated with some degree of success through various medications and therapies. Tomorrow we'll look in more detail at the kind of treatments that might prove useful in dealing with some of them.

Now get ready to answer the questions. You may use your notes to help you answer.

1. What is the lecture mainly about?
2. Why does the professor say that many people feel anxious when they visit a dentist?
3. What does the professor say about specific phobias?
4. Listen again to part of the lecture. Then answer the question.

(Woman P) Some of the less common phobias seem rather bizarre. For example, would you believe some people are afraid of color, say, the color yellow? Another strange one is fear of laughter . . . I guess that's not a laughing matter for the sufferer.

Why does the professor say this: I guess that's not a laughing matter for the sufferer.

5. Social phobia might include which of the following fears?
6. What does the professor imply when she says this: . . . do I need to put that on the board?
7. What does the professor imply about treatment of phobias?

Questions 8–12

Listen to a conversation between a student and a professor.

(Man S) Uh . . . hello, Dr. Grant. Do you have a minute?

(Woman P) As a matter of fact, I do. So what do you need, Ron?

(Man S) Well, you wrote on my questionnaire "Come and see me."

(Woman P) Ah, yes. Ron, there are a few problems with the way you set your questionnaire up. I'm sorry to say that I don't think you've thought out the statements very well. It was a prime example of why so many people complain about filling out questionnaires. You might even alienate your subjects with a questionnaire like this.

(Man S) Oh. I don't want . . . What did I do?

(Woman P) Don't look so discouraged. Several of your classmates have had similar problems. OK. So, what did you do? Well, for one thing, people get really annoyed with "and" statements.

(Man S) "And" statements? Uh, what do you mean by "and" statements?

(Woman P) Well, let's say you get a questionnaire statement like "I like fruit and vegetables" with the choices of "yes" or "no." Well, if you don't like fruit and vegetables, you check the "no" box and if you do, the "yes" box. No problem. But what do you check if you like fruit, but not vegetables?

(Man S) Oh, I see.

(Woman P) You've several "and" statements in your questionnaire which need to be taken care of.

(Man S) OK. Anything else?

(Woman P) Yes, there was, actually. Can I see your questionnaire to jog my memory?

(Man S) Sure. Here it is.

(Woman P) Thanks. This statement. "Males are better critical thinkers than females." I can tell you now what answers you'll get for that item. Most, if not all males will mark "yes" – and females will mark "no." It's kind of silly to have a statement that you already know how your subjects will answer. And it won't be of much use for collecting data, will it?

(Man S) No, I guess it won't.

(Woman P) Furthermore, women who get this will be really annoyed with the implication that men think more effectively than they do. And, once you've angered your subjects, they won't be very cooperative in answering the rest of the questionnaire. They might sabotage your results by not being truthful or they'll become "critical thinkers" and write their criticism all over your questionnaire. But chances are they'll just dump the questionnaire in the trash.

(Man S) Yeah. I can see that. But, how can I phrase it?

(Woman P) Well, I'm not really sure what you're trying to find out here. Perhaps you want to know if people consider critical thinking to be more prevalent in a particular gender – in which case you could write: "The ability to think critically is gender-based." Is that the information you wanted?

(Man S) Yeah. That's it. Anything else?

(Woman P) Look at this statement, "I'm unable to think critically." That's like saying "I'm stupid." How many people would answer "yes" to that? See?

(Woman P) What I'd like you to do is go through every statement on your questionnaire very critically. Think: what information do I want? How can I phrase my statement to get meaningful results? Maybe you and a classmate could discuss each other's questionnaires.

(Man S) That's a good idea.

(Woman P) Ron, I'd like to look it over once more before you pass it out. OK?

(Man S) OK, Dr. Grant. Thank you for your help.

Now get ready to answer the questions. You may use your notes to help you answer.

8. Why does the student go to see his professor?

9. Why does the professor talk about fruit and vegetables?

10. According to the professor, what should the student avoid in writing his questionnaire?

11. Listen again to part of the conversation. Then answer the question.

(Man S) OK. Anything else?

(Woman P) Yes, there was actually. Can I see your questionnaire to jog my memory?

Why does the professor say this: Can I see your questionnaire to jog my memory?

12. What can be inferred about the questionnaire?

Questions 13–17

Listen to part of a discussion in a geology class.

(Man P) So we've talked about the ecology of grasslands, areas of the world where rainfall is not enough to sustain thick forests, but enough to prevent desertification – that is, the spread of desert lands. I want to turn now to a discussion of a different kind of biome, or natural community, known as the tundra. OK, so as you know, the tundra is a region of the Arctic, lacking in trees, bushes – and covered, for the most part, in short vegetation well adapted to the inhospitable conditions. In fact, the word tundra comes from a Finnish word meaning treeless plain. I guess you could say that's a pretty accurate description of what you find there – flat land and no trees. Today, I'm going to ignore the region known as the Alpine tundra, which is found at higher elevations in mountainous regions all over the world. This has similar characteristics to the Arctic tundra, but also enough differences that I think we can justify spending a separate lesson on its main features.

So, to understand the life systems that exist in the tundra, you have to understand that below the surface is a permanently frozen layer of soil. This is the layer called the permafrost – perma, from permanent, in other words, permanent frost. Anything that grows there has to be able to adapt first to this impenetrable floor of frozen soil. What do you think could be one adaptation to this situation?

(Man S) Well, plants would have to have shallow, I mean, short root systems because the roots wouldn't be able to penetrate the hard layer.

(Man P) OK. That's right. So what about any rain that falls or water from melted snow in the summer? Where does that go?

(Man S) Well, I guess it can't go anywhere if the ground is too hard to soak it up and too flat for it to drain off.

(Man P) Right. So what you get is a kind of shallow waterlogged top layer of soil which freezes and thaws as the seasons change from winter to summer. So on the surface, marshes form and in low-lying areas and depressions small lakes and ponds are common during the periods when the ice and snow melt. This poorly drained water on the surface provides moisture for plants. In fact, there is relatively little annual rain so this marshy wet ground is important for plant growth. So what about the soil itself? What would you guess is the nutrient value for living things?

(Woman S) Well, since it's very cold most of the year, wouldn't that mean that dead organisms break down slowly? So wouldn't that mean a low level of nutrients for plants to use?

(Man P) That's absolutely correct. Just as with the moorland biomes that we were discussing last week, mineral nutrients are in short supply – because cold waterlogged soil slows down the rate of decay of dead plants and other organisms. So the plants that do exist have to adapt to this special environment – a poor, shallow soil and a bitterly cold climate with strong winds. You mentioned the short root systems. But what other kind of plant characteristics do you think might be useful in a region like this?

(Woman S) Well, given the strong winds that blow, wouldn't it be useful to be short? After all, tall plants with shallow roots would be easily blown over.

(Man P) Uh-huh. True. And to add to that, of course, the short roots can only maintain short plants. So that's another reason why the plants are very short. Another adaptation is that the plants cluster together in groups, often taking advantage of depressions in the ground to avoid the strong winds, and that helps them to resist the cold temperatures. Then, also, the snow itself helps them survive in these conditions – since the snow effectively insulates against the bitter cold. When the snow melts in the spring, of course, the plants have a ready supply of moisture, making up for the low levels of precipitation in the region.

So when the summer finally comes, what you get is a time of compensation, you could say. As you know, the summer sun never sets at these high latitudes, so the plants get sunlight for 24 hours a day. It's as though they work overtime to produce essential sugars and the other substances necessary for plant functioning from this continuous light energy. It's like the sudden arrival of summer – as if the vegetation as well as the insect and animal life were hurrying to take advantage of the relatively short time before the onset of the next winter.

Now get ready to answer the questions. You may use your notes to help you answer.

13. What is the discussion mainly about?
14. Why does the professor not want to discuss Alpine tundra?
15. According to the professor, what features are typical of tundra regions?
16. According to the professor, why do tundra plants often cluster together in depressions?
17. In the discussion, various facts about plants in the tundra are mentioned. Indicate whether each of the following describes tundra vegetation.

Questions 18–24

Listen to part of a lecture in a cultural studies class.

(Man P) OK. Let's get started. Now, today I want to continue discussing changes in artistic movements in the late nineteenth and early twentieth centuries. OK, so, now we've seen that in all the arts around that time, there was a strong movement away from what was seen as the restrictions of conventional ideas. Artists of all kinds were searching for more individualistic ways of expressing themselves – trying to break new ground, as it were. Now, this was particularly so in the art form of dance. OK. So remember now that by the late eighteen hundreds dance as an art form had become somewhat stale. There were few people trying to push the boundaries of inventiveness on the stage.

Now, it was right around this point in time that a new free-moving, free-spirited dancer named Isadora Duncan suddenly became influential. Isadora Duncan is known nowadays as the "mother of modern dance" because of her important contributions to theatrical dance, and what I want to do here is take a look at some of the ways in which she was just so different from her contemporaries.

OK. So there are at least three ways in which she was seen as an innovator, as a new force on the stage. First, we have to consider that at the time in dancing, that is, in particular, ballet dancing, it was mostly the feet and leg movements that were highlighted. In other words dancers of the time focused their skills on highly ritualized and complicated movements of the legs.

What Duncan did was to break away from this tradition, from this convention. She was, I think we can say, frustrated by the constrictions of classical dance and by what she felt was its lack of emotional impact. So she took to emphasizing the use of the whole body in dance movement. And this use of the body was inspired by natural forces, as well as folk dancing – and it included skipping, running, and jumping, and twirling – a continuous flowing movement done with skillful abandon and great passion. She believed that the movement of the body could express specific emotions, emotions like anger, joy, and grief. Let me take a moment to mention that it is said that she learned these dance movements as a child – by imitating natural phenomena such as the waves on the beaches near her home in California.

All right, so another of her great contributions was her innovative use of costume. Now, again the dance of the period was notable for its stiff shoes and tunics. Duncan just discarded the restrictiveness of these clothes in favor of loose-flowing gowns inspired by classical Greek models. She danced with loose hair and in bare feet, much to the astonishment of her early audiences. Again, I think we can see the influence here of nature and folk dance, things that conventional dance of the period had ignored, or, I think we can even say, scorned.

So, OK, there was also another way we can consider Isadora as revolutionary in her practice. This is in her use of classical music as an integral part of the performance. She insisted that her art deserved to be performed to great music. For example, Beethoven, Bach, and Chopin and other great concert music accompanied her movements on stage. And this use of music was considered daring and original at the time.

Now, you know, I think, looking back, it may be kind of hard to appreciate Isadora Duncan's achievement since so many of her contributions to modern dance are nowadays, in a sense, well, taken for granted. In truth, she, at first, had to face considerable opposition from traditionalists, as happens to many highly original artists. Her, for the time, unconventional techniques, eventually though, were widely acclaimed. Perhaps, all modern dance technique owes something to Duncan's inventiveness and daring, so perhaps because of that, her deep originality may not be as obvious to us today.

Now get ready to answer the questions. You may use your notes to help you answer.

18. What is the lecture mainly about?

19. What does the professor imply about other artists of Duncan's time?

20. Which of the following may have been an influence on Duncan's art?

21. Which of the following does the professor consider a contribution of Duncan's?

22. In the lecture, the professor describes some of the main contributions made by Isadora Duncan to modern dance. Indicate whether each of the following is a contribution made by this dancer.

23. What is the professor's attitude toward Isadora Duncan's innovations?

24. What does the professor imply about Duncan's current status?

Questions 25–30

Listen to part of a lecture in an astronomy class.

(Woman P) So, I hope you now have an idea about the most accepted theory of how the sun and the solar system were formed. In fact, many new observations are showing major problems with this traditional view of planetary formation. For example, some scientists are now saying that the time frame is all wrong – that planets may have formed much more quickly than the standard theory suggests. And there are other problems too when it comes to the formation of the outer planets, especially about how and where they formed. Some people are saying we may have to revise or even abandon the standard model. As with many theories in science, it's pretty much open to revision.

But now let's move on to an examination of what happened inside the Earth in its early stages. I know some of you have studied Earth formation in other courses, but I want to fill in the gaps for those who haven't got this background. OK. So, about 4.6 billion years ago, the Earth was pretty much organized into a sphere and had a temperature of around 1,000 degrees. Note also that all the material forming the planet was randomly spread around. But at that point three things were happening which caused the planet to heat up further. So, what kind of things would cause the planet to get hotter?

(Man S) All the impacts from rocks and meteorites and other stuff in space. When that stuff hits the Earth, that impact energy would be converted into heat energy. That would heat it up.

(Woman P) OK. Good. Well, sure, that's one of the three main causes of this heating. Certainly at the upper levels – the crust of the planet. Now what else?

(Woman S) Uh, the sun would have heated it.

(Woman P) Well, yes. But I don't just mean warming the surface. We're talking about heating the planet right down to the core, the center. How did the Earth heat up so that iron, for example, could melt? That's at about 2,000 degrees Celsius.

(Man S) What about radiation?

(Woman P) Yes, that's it. That is probably the most important cause of the heating up. Radioactive elements, such as uranium, within the rocks inside the planet decayed, and as they did so heat was generated. In fact, radioactive decay is still going on but at a slower rate than previously – since, of course, well, there isn't nearly as much radioactive material left – due to this decay over time.

OK. A third cause of the heating process was compression due to gravity. As the size of the planet grew due to impacts from space, the gravity increased and the pressure itself contributed to the heating of the Earth's interior.

So, we have three main causes of the heating up of the planet. Now, just to repeat: impacts from the objects outside the planet, radioactive decay of the elements inside, and heating due to pressure caused by gravity. So over the course of a billion years, all these things eventually pushed up the heat until temperatures were hot enough to melt iron and other rocks. Now, as you know, the Earth is composed of a variety of different types of materials – and so these rocks and minerals have different densities. So, that means that heavier, the denser material, tends to sink over time and lighter material tends to rise and float above the heavier stuff. That is what happens in a liquid or molten environment, of course. So iron in particular, being heavy, sank toward the center – and lighter rocky material rose toward the surface. At the same time, gases escaped from the molten rocks and came out at the surface, allowing an atmosphere and oceans to form. When all this sinking and rising – this reshuffling process – eventually slowed down over time with the gradual cooling of the planet – what we find is a stratified Earth; in other words, a series of layers – with the crust – that is, the part we live on – being the lightest, then further down the mantle, then the outer core – and finally at the center, the inner core. So this process, called differentiation, led to the change in the arrangement of the interior structuring of the planet – and the formation of the atmosphere and the oceans. So, while originally, all material was homogeneous, randomly mixed around the planet, eventually we get a planet divided into different layers. This differentiation has been called "perhaps the single most important event in the history of the Earth."

Now get ready to answer the questions. You may use your notes to help you answer.

25. What is the main topic of the lecture?

26. Why does the professor say this: As with many theories in science, it's pretty much open to revision.

27. What does the professor imply about the formation of the Earth?

28. According to the professor, how was rock distributed before differentiation?

29. According to the professor, which is probably the main reason for the heating of the Earth?

30. What two points are true according to the lecture?

Questions 31–35

Listen to part of a conversation between a student and an advisor at the University Learning Center.

(Man S) Ah . . . Hi, Mrs. Douglas. I'm Jack. I made an appointment to talk to you about graduate school.

(Woman P) Yeah, come in, Jack. Um, have a seat.

(Man S) Thanks. I've only just started thinking about going to grad school. And I looked at the application – you know, what you have to do to apply here – and I found it a bit overwhelming . . . . You know, writing a personal statement, asking my professors for letters of recommendation, sending transcripts . . . I've already taken the GRE exams.

(Woman P) OK. So you're applying here?

(Man S) Well, no. I just looked at the application here to see what it was like. I'm finishing up my Bachelor's degree in biology, but I'd like to specialize in marine biology. And they don't offer that here.

(Woman P) So, have you looked around for universities that offer a doctorate in marine biology?

(Man S) No. I was hoping, well, that's why I came to see you.

(Woman P) OK, Jack. The first thing we need to do is look in our reference books on university programs to find which universities offer a degree in marine biology – and make a list.

(Man S) A list? Wouldn't it be kind of expensive to apply to a lot of universities?

(Woman P) Well, yeah, if you applied to all of them. But first you'll want to narrow your choices by finding those offering the kind of program you want. And then, you'll want to consider other aspects – tuition costs, their financial-aid programs, their requirements for entrance.

(Man S) Yeah. I guess I hadn't thought about all that other stuff. Just about the program.

(Woman P) You might want to go to some of the university home pages and find the Biology Department pages. You could find a list of professors and their specializations. That way, you could see if there's anyone doing research in a particular area. . . . Marine biology is a large field. I assume you have a special interest?

(Man S) Yeah, the ecology of the intertidal zone.

(Woman P) The intertidal zone. OK. So when you look at universities, see which ones have professors involved in intertidal-zone studies and read some of the articles they've published. You know, having an idea of the kind of research people are doing might give you an idea of which universities to include on your list and who could advise you in your own research.

(Man S) Hey, yeah. That's a good idea. I can look at some of the articles that I found really interesting and see what university the writer is affiliated with or where that person studied.

(Woman P) Perfect. When you've made your decision, then you can come back for more help if you need it.

(Man S) I'll do that.

(Woman P) Right. Now let's go check those reference books.

Now get ready to answer the questions. You may use your notes to help you answer.

31. What does the student need from the advisor?

32. Where will the student and the advisor look for the information the student needs on university degree programs?

33. What can be inferred about applying to graduate school?

34. Listen again to part of the conversation. Then answer the question.

(Woman P) That way, you could see if there's anyone doing research in a particular area. . . . Marine biology is a large field. I assume you have a special interest?

Why does the advisor say this: I assume you have a special interest?

35. Why does the advisor suggest that the student read some of the published articles about intertidal zones?

PART 2 BUILDING SKILLS: Speaking

EXERCISE S1 *Concentrating on individual consonant sounds*

1. **P**eter called us u**p** and invited us for su**pp**er.

2. The ro**bb**ers escaped in a stolen ca**b** and drove to their hideout, **b**ut they were eventually caught.

3. The children wen**t** on a scavenger hun**t**, and the victorious **t**eam was given a prize.

4. The **d**og followe**d** the ca**dd**y aroun**d** the golf course.

5. Schools **c**an do more to en**c**ourage students to ta**k**e on the responsibilities of learning.

6. The bi**g** lo**gg**ing companies are **g**one from the region.

7. I**f** the **f**ish stocks are depleted, it will be the **f**ishermen who su**ff**er.

8. The **v**ery first editions o**f** the manuscripts are a**v**ailable for e**v**eryone to see.

9. They are re**th**inking the rule of **th**umb that requires people to stay on the pa**th**.

10. **Th**e mo**th**er decided to ba**th**e her baby.

11. A le**ss**on in building a house made of **s**od was offered at the outdoor museum.

12. The **z**oologists u**s**e tranquili**z**ers when tagging the deer that enter the park.

13. Careful land **m**anage**m**ent has saved the ri**m** area fro**m** overgrazing.

14. The judges **n**amed the wi**nn**er as soo**n** as the race was over.

15. Si**ng**i**ng** a favorite so**ng** is a good way to cheer oneself up.

16. The **l**and grant a**ll**ows for fu**ll** use of resources.

17. Coope**r**ative games help children to **r**ealize thei**r** potential in a non-th**r**eatening situation.

18. The people in the to**w**er **w**itnessed ho**w** fast the fire **w**as spreading.

19. The children's **h**ospital **h**as per**h**aps the best doctors to deal with the problem.

20. A la**y**er of **y**ellowish sandstone marks the division between the two geological periods.

21. Since the idea in a demoli**ti**on derby is to demoli**sh** the car, drivers **sh**ould continue until this has been achieved.

22. The **g**enre of art called the colla**g**e is a plea**s**ure to work in.

23. By **ch**ance, a farmer uncovered the ri**ch** burial site that had survived in na**t**ure for several cen**t**uries.

24. According to **J**im, chan**g**ing over to the computerized system led to a sur**g**e in interest.

EXERCISE S2 *Concentrating on consonant clusters*

(Man P) **Sn**ow**fl**a**kes** **sw**i**rled** arou**nd** the makeshi**ft** hu**ts** as the **dr**i**fts**, shi**ft**ed by the howling wi**nds**, mou**nt**ed up agai**nst** the wa**lls**. The **dr**a**ft**y huts **cr**ea**ked** and **gr**oa**ned** in re**sp**o**nse**. Then door hi**ng**es **squ**ea**ked** as abomina**bl**e **sn**owmen **st**e**pped** a**cr**oss the **thr**esho**lds** into the **sp**a**rs**ely furni**shed** roo**ms**. Ma**rg**e **str**ai**ned** her vocal co**rds** as she **scr**ea**med** in an atte**mpt** to **br**ing he**lp**. Her **bl**oodcu**rdl**ing **scr**ea**ms** woke her **fr**om the terri**bl**e **dr**eam.

EXERCISE S3 *Focusing on stress patterns*

(Woman P) Theaters of the Elizabethan period were open-air constructions in which poorer members of the audience, "the groundlings," stood in a space called "the pit" around three sides of a projecting rectangular platform that formed the main stage. Most of the perimeter of the building comprised covered, tiered galleries, and it is here that the wealthier members of the audience sat. A roof supported on two pillars projected from the back wall and covered part of the stage. The main stage was hollow and could be accessed from below through trapdoors set in the floor. The main stage also had a door on either side at the back, which gave access to the dressing rooms. Between these doors was a small recess, usually curtained off, that could be used for extra stage space. Above this recess was a balcony sometimes used by musicians or, when necessary, by actors in a performance.

EXERCISE S4 *Focusing on linking words*

(Man P) It is simply not feasible for every university library in the nation to contain all the books, journals, and resource materials that university students and faculty need for their research. So what have libraries done to meet the needs of their users? Well, several things, in fact. While some money is used for the yearly purchasing of hardbound books and current journals that are recommended by professors, other funds are used to obtain materials that have been put on microfilm and microfiche. These techniques have proved extremely useful for adding informative materials to a library's collection at a low cost and without taking up much space. Another way libraries have increased access has been to invest in computers. Computers are linked to collections in other libraries. Professors and students can perform a computer search to find a library that has the material they need. The material can then be ordered and checked out through the interlibrary loan system, which costs the user a nominal shipping fee.

EXERCISE S5 *Focusing on intonation*

(Man S) Professor Cline?

(Woman P) Yes?

(Man S) I'm Robert Daley. The work-study office sent me.

(Woman P) Oh, I've been waiting for them to send someone. Did you say your name was Robert?

(Man S) Yes.

(Woman P) What's your major, Robert?

(Man S) Zoology.

(Woman P) Good. You have some science background then. Let me show you what we're doing in our lab.

(Man S) Will I be working in the biology lab?

(Woman P) Yes. We're studying the speed of reproduction of paramecia. Uh, paramecia are the most complex single-celled organisms.

(Man S) Oh, that sounds interesting.

(Woman P) Well, what we need you to do is probably not so interesting.

(Man S) And what is that?

(Woman P) We'll need you to come in every day at the same time and count the paramecia.

(Man S) Count paramecia?

(Woman P) Yes. It's very important to keep an accurate count and fill the numbers in on a form. I'll show you where the forms are and explain how to complete it later. After you have completed the form, you need to give it to Nancy. She is the woman that you met in the lab office. She'll feed your numbers into the computer for our statistical analysis. Right now, though, I want to introduce you to the other members of our team so that we can arrange a convenient time for you to come in.

EXERCISE S6 *Putting it all together*

(Man P) Treasured since ancient times, saffron is obtained from the autumn-flowering *Crocus sativus*. It is the dried flower stigmas – the three slender threads in the center of each flower – that are the source of saffron. This "king of spices" is one of the world's most prized and expensive foodstuffs. The finest variety is grown in La Mancha in the central plateau of Spain. Spain is by far the biggest producer. It contributes 70 percent of the world's output, with India and Iran the only other producers of note. The cultivation of saffron in Spain goes back to the Moorish invasion of the eighth century, when the crocuses were first introduced from the Middle East. Not only is Spain the largest producer of saffron, but it is also the largest consumer. Up to one-third of the crop is bought in Spain, and the remainder is exported. The biggest buyers are Middle Eastern countries, followed by the United States, Italy, and France.

EXERCISE S15 *Restating the task and defining your choice*

1. Name a teacher who has influenced you and explain why that teacher was important. Include details and examples to support your explanation.
2. Describe a class you have taken and explain why that class was important to you. Include details and examples to support your explanation.

EXERCISE S18 *Putting it all together*

1. Name a skill you have learned and explain why it is important to you. Include details and examples to support your explanation.
2. Name a hobby you have and explain why it is important to you. Include details and examples to support your explanation.
3. Name a person who has influenced you and explain why that influence was important. Include details and examples to support your explanation.
4. Describe a class you have taken and explain why that class was important to you. Include details and examples to support your explanation.

EXERCISE S21 *Restating the task and stating your position*

Some students would like to have a long vacation during the academic year. Other students would like to have several shorter vacations during the academic year. What is your preference and why? Include details and examples in your explanation.

EXERCISE S24 *Putting it all together*

1. Some students prefer to do group projects. Other students prefer to do individual projects. Which kind of projects do you think produce more learning and why?
2. Some people believe that students should immediately go on to college after completing high school. Others believe that students should take a year off between high school completion and starting college. Which approach do you think is better for students interested in getting a college degree? Include details and examples in your explanation.
3. Some students would like to have a long vacation during the academic year. Other students would like to have several shorter vacations during the academic year. What is your preference and why? Include details and examples in your explanation.

EXERCISE S26 *Practice responding to independent speaking tasks*

1. Name an academic subject that you like and explain why it attracts you. Include details and examples to support your explanation.
2. Describe a personal possession that is special to you and explain why it is important. Include details and examples to support your explanation.
3. Describe a feature of your city that you consider interesting and explain why you think it is interesting. Include details and examples to support your explanation.
4. Some people prefer television programs that present serious issues. Other people prefer those that are for entertainment only. Which kind of program do you consider the most important for people to watch and why?
5. Some people prefer to focus their energy to excel in one activity. Other people prefer to participate in many different activities. Which method do you think is better for the development of a person's intellect and why?
6. Some people believe that children should begin their formal education at an early age (three to five years old). Other people believe that children should begin their formal education later (six to seven years old). Which age do you think is best for a child to begin a formal education and why?

EXERCISE S27 *Identifying important points in a reading passage*

An announcement about a change in one of the University of the Rockies courses is posted on the classroom door. You have 45 seconds to read the announcement. Begin reading now.

EXERCISE S28 *Identifying important points in a conversation*

Now listen to two students as they discuss the announcement.

(Man S) That's a disappointment. I was looking forward to that class.

(Woman S) Me, too. Well, I guess we should hurry on over to the registrar so we can pick up a different course.

(Man S) Oh. Aren't you interested in taking the Literature of Minority Groups? I've heard it's a really good course.

(Woman S) Well, actually it focuses a lot on Hispanic literature and, being Hispanic, I've already done most of the required reading.

(Man S) That would make it an easy option then. Come on. Let's go before we're late.

(Woman S) Sorry. I'd like the challenge of another course. Besides, with the extra students from the survey course, it's going to be a really large class. I prefer smaller groups. I just feel more comfortable discussing ideas when there aren't so many students.

EXERCISE S29 *Analyzing the task that relates to the conversation*

The woman expresses her opinion about the course replacement. State her opinion and explain the reasons she gives for that opinion.

EXERCISE S32 *Identifying important points in a reading passage*

Now read a passage about an incident leading up to the American War of Independence. You have 45 seconds to read the passage. Begin reading now.

EXERCISE S33 *Identifying important points in a lecture*

Now listen to part of a lecture on the background to the American War of Independence.

(Man P) I'd like to address the questions of why the American colonists chose to dress as Indians and why they chose tea to dump overboard. Well, let's go back to why the British had imposed taxes on their colonies. Governments impose taxes to meet expenses. The French and Indian War was over after having doubled the British national debt and leaving the colonists in an economic crisis. Now remember that the French and Indian War consisted of the French and Indians fighting the British and British colonists. To replenish the treasury, a scheme was passed in the British Parliament in which all goods had to be stamped; a stamp that had to be paid for. This was taxation without representation, and the British colonists wouldn't pay it. After a series of different imposed taxes were met by protests, riots, and boycotts, all taxes were eventually revoked except for one on tea. Now I think you can see the significance of dressing as Indians since the taxes stemmed from the French/Indian War, but also why it was tea that was thrown overboard.

EXERCISE S34 *Analyzing the task that relates to the lecture*

The professor gives the background information about the incident that was the prelude to the American War of Independence. Explain how the events were related to the colonists' behavior.

EXERCISE S38 *Responding to the integrated reading/listening/speaking tasks*

1. The University of the Rockies is planning to tear down a building on campus. Read the announcement about the demolition of the building. You have 45 seconds to read the announcement. Begin reading now.

Now listen to two students as they discuss the announcement.

(Man S) Are you gonna join our protest to stop their tearing down Old Main?

(Woman S) You aren't marching about *that*, are you? We need a fine arts complex.

(Man S) I don't disagree with that, but the empty lot behind the sports arena could be used.

(Woman S) Well, that's true, but it's a long distance to walk. So, what's so special about Old Main anyway?

(Man S) Well, Old Main was the first building – actually the only building – on campus in the early days, so it has historical value. We should try to preserve our heritage. You know that it was built in the mid-1800s of stone, so built to last.

(Woman S) I didn't know it was that old. But it doesn't have space for classrooms, and I imagine it's a huge expense to heat in winter.

(Man S) Well, in fact, those heavy walls keep heat in, so it isn't expensive. They could use it for offices. There's a shortage of offices for graduate students who have teaching assistantships.

The man expresses his opinion of the plans being made by the University Board of Trustees. State his opinion and explain the reasons he gives for holding that opinion.

2. The Medical Faculty has announced that a guest speaker will be giving a talk. Read the announcement about the talk. You have 45 seconds to read the announcement. Begin reading now.

Now listen to two students as they discuss the announcement.

(Man S) Hey, Sue. Wanna go for a coffee?

(Woman S) No, thanks. I'm going to the talk about Restless Leg Syndrome. Why don't you join me?

(Man S) Never heard of it. So, what's your interest?

(Woman S) Well, my mom's suffered from it since she was a teenager. At that time, it was diagnosed as growing pains, later as a strained muscle, then, when she began teaching, she was told it was because she was on her feet all day. After she was told it was all in her head, she quit asking and just went on suffering.

(Man S) That sounds awful. So, uh, so why were the doctors so wrong?

(Woman S) Well, she's always described the pain as thousands of microscopic creatures eating away her calf muscles.

(Man S) That's weird. So how did she finally find out what it was?

(Woman S) Oh, a cousin mentioned in passing the medicine that she was taking for Restless Leg Syndrome and went on to describe what Mom had been suffering for over 30 years.

(Man S) Wow.

(Woman S) Yeah. She's on medication now, but I wanna know more about it. It runs in families.

(Man S) So you might get it.

(Woman S) Maybe, but I haven't had any problems yet.

The woman explains her interest in listening to the guest lecturer. State her interest and explain the problems surrounding the syndrome.

3. The University of the Rockies is planning to make a change in the number of required courses in physical education. Read the president's quote, taken from his interview with a reporter from the student newspaper. Begin reading now.

Now listen to two students as they discuss the quote.

(Man S) What do you think about the university dropping its physical education requirement?

(Woman S) I'm torn about it, really. In one way, it's true that students should take the responsibility of keeping fit. But how can we, if money isn't put into the facilities?

(Man S) But, the president didn't say anything about not putting money into the facilities. He said that the money that's saved from courses that will no longer be taught would be put elsewhere.

(Woman S) True, but I can't help but think some of our sports programs are going to be affected.

(Man S) This will only be the loss of some courses. So, what are the programs, what programs are you concerned about?

(Woman S) Well, the women's varsity soccer team, for one. They've worked hard to get any university support at all and are just getting the recognition they deserve.

(Man S) I hardly think that they'll be affected.

(Woman S) Don't be so sure. Fewer classes will result in a cut in the number of instructors, and that can't help but affect the different programs that are run by those particular instructors.

The woman expresses her opinion of what the president was quoted to have said to the reporter. State her opinion and explain the reasons she gives for holding that opinion.

4. The Maintenance Department has announced that the main classroom building will be undergoing some changes. Read the announcement about the renovation. You have 45 seconds to read the announcement. Begin reading now.

Now listen to two students as they discuss the announcement.

(Man S) That'll be really great, won't it? All the classrooms will be high-tech.

(Woman S) Oh, I don't know. Maybe.

(Man S) Maybe? I really like a professor to give a lecture with all sorts of neat computer slides to project on the screen, don't you?

(Woman S) Well, yeah, when it works. But how often have you been excited about doing something special in a lab and the technology failed?

(Man S) Not that often. It does have to be maintained, though.

(Woman S) And upgraded. Technology becomes obsolete very quickly.

(Man S) True.

(Woman S) I've also seen a lot of student presentations using technology that were all showy with animation but no content. It's a big expense, you know, for something that won't be used all that much.

(Man S) Why don't you think it'll be used?

(Woman S) Well, first, lots of professors aren't high-tech minded and won't bother with learning how to use it. Besides it's very time consuming to make a good computer presentation. The best professor I've had here, Dr. Rosa, doesn't even use an overheard projector.

(Man S) Yeah. Well, she *is* kind of exceptional.

The woman expresses her opinion of the announcement made by the University's Maintenance Department. State her opinion and explain the reasons she gives for holding that opinion.

5. Now read the passage about marine organisms known as phytoplankton. You will have 45 seconds to read the passage. Begin reading now.

Now listen to part of a lecture on ocean plants in a marine biology class.

(Woman P) I'd like to discuss an interesting study being done on phytoplankton. I think we all know that phytoplankton is an important nutrient in the ocean's food chain as well as understand its importance in producing oxygen. This study, the study I want to present, was based on the observation that in some areas of the ocean, there's plenty of sunlight and nitrogen compounds for successful photosynthesis. However, there's only a small amount of phytoplankton. So, an analysis was done on the water, and this analysis indicated a lack of iron. We know that iron is a trace mineral that even humans need. It was hypothesized that phytoplankton also need iron. I won't go into full detail, but a small section of one area in the ocean was seeded with iron sulfate. The resulting increase of phytoplankton provided convincing evidence for the hypothesis. Now, this finding opens up several possibilities. Since phytoplankton take carbon dioxide out of the atmosphere, an increase of the plants could remove a significant amount of human-produced carbon dioxide from the atmosphere faster and more effectively than other alternatives. An increase in the plants could also be followed by an increase of marine life along the food chain that ultimately comes to feed people. However, there are unanswered environmental questions that would need to be addressed before phytoplankton farms could be considered.

The professor describes an experiment done on phytoplankton. Explain how the implications of this experiment relate to phytoplankton.

6. Now read the passage about road management. You will have 45 seconds to read the passage. Begin reading now.

Now listen to part of a lecture in a civil engineering class.

(Man P) OK, so we're all familiar with the road markings, signs, and signals cluttering up our cities. They are supposed to reduce accidents – make towns safer for all of us. Accidents still happen, but all these signs surely make accidents fewer. They tell road users where it's safe to be and when. Well, um, experiments have shown something very different. A Dutch traffic engineer named, uh, Hans Monderman has turned this thinking on its head. Monderman removed the traffic signs, markings, and signals from a Dutch town and, uh, guess what! The number of traffic accidents has dropped significantly. In this town there are no center lines separating lanes, no speed limit signs, no stop signs, and even speed bumps have been removed. The thinking behind this radical change is that when drivers have no signs to guide them, they start looking at people and then they drive more carefully, more courteously. This public space makes drivers instinctively understand that cars and pedestrians are equal and drive with this in mind. Supporters of this scheme explain its success by arguing that road regulations give a false sense of security. Regulations also treat road users as irresponsible by continually controlling their behavior, telling them what they can and can't do. When the props supporting this regulation are removed, drivers are given back the responsibility for driving with consideration for other drivers and pedestrians, and then act accordingly.

The professor describes an experimental system of road management. Explain how this experiment is related to road users' behavior.

7. Now read the passage about cultural perceptions of time. You will have 45 seconds to read the passage. Begin reading now.

Now listen to part of a lecture in a cultural studies class.

(Woman P) We were talking about monochronic and polychronic cultures last week, and I wanted to repeat some of the things we discussed. Remember that these are the extremes and most cultures lie somewhere in between. We also discussed that there are monochronic individuals within polychronic cultures and vice versa, polychronic ones within monochronic cultures. Now, one might think that a monochronic society is more efficient because monochronic individuals can make a linear plan, predict how long it will take, and follow through on it. They arrive on time, set deadlines that they meet, and can be depended on to get the work done on time. But how often have you read in job advertisements that they are looking for someone who can multitask? So what does that mean? Someone who can do several things at once, right? And who can do that? A polychronic person. In essence, they are people who can step in and be moved around within a company. These are the people who become irreplaceable on the job because of their ability to juggle several tasks at the same time. Interestingly, while efficient polychronic people are appreciated at the workplace, they frequently don't move up the promotional ladder. Why? Because it isn't easy to replace a person who can multitask effectively.

The professor describes the behavior of monochronic and polychronic people. Explain how their behavior is related to their suitability in the workplace.

8. Now read the passage about weathering. You have 45 seconds to read the passage. Begin reading now.

Now listen to part of a lecture on weathering in a geology class.

(Man P) When we examine rocks in terms of the weathering process, it's obvious that the climatic environments must also be taken into account. Think about the weather conditions in arid areas. In those areas, the frost at night expands along cracks in the rocks, and in the day, the rocks expand in the heat. This mechanical process of weathering due to the fluctuation between frost action and heat expansion is common. Now, in the tropical areas where rainfall is heavy, the chemical process is common. There's less mechanical weathering since the temperature remains high. In temperate climates – where we can see a warm summer with rainfall and a colder winter with frost – both chemical and mechanical weathering are common. What about the polar regions? Well, we're not going to see much weathering in terms of chemical processes since there's little rainfall. Neither will we see many mechanical or biological processes. The arctic conditions allow very little weathering, in fact. Now, what about biological processes: the weathering caused by tree and plant roots wedging into the rocks, animals burrowing into the ground, or, um, the decay of dead organisms causing destructive acids? Well, plants and animals live in all areas, but again, because we see fewer plants and animals in areas of extreme climates, we see less biological weathering there.

The professor describes climatic conditions. Explain how these conditions relate to different weathering processes.

EXERCISE S39 *Identifying important points in a conversation*

Now listen to a conversation between two students.

(Man S) The tickets for the best seats in the concert hall cost $60.

(Woman S) Oh, that's much more than I meant to pay. Don't we get a student discount for these kinds of functions?

(Man S) Not for a concert like this. Look, the least expensive ones are $15.

(Woman S) Where are the $15 seats located?

(Man S) In the top balcony.

(Woman S) That's too far away. We wouldn't be able to see anything on the stage.

(Man S) The middle balcony costs $40.

(Woman S) Well, the $40 seats are still expensive, but I guess if we really want to enjoy the concert, we'd better get them. What do you think?

(Man S) I'm not sure.

EXERCISE S40 *Analyzing the task that relates to the conversation*

The students are discussing the possible choices in a decision they must make. State their problem. Then explain which decision you prefer and why.

EXERCISE S43 *Identifying important points in a lecture*

Now listen to part of a lecture in a cultural geography class.

(Woman P) The problem of aging is taking on new dimensions in many countries. The societies that are faced with this problem are the ones with a large aging population and a low birthrate. They are finding that social security expenditure has become an excessive percentage of the national income. People are living longer and, therefore, are getting benefits for a longer period of time. The aging populations need more medical attention at a time when those costs are skyrocketing. Furthermore, many elderly people can no longer look after themselves and need to be cared for. Frequently, neither they nor their families can pay for this intensive care. Thus, the financial burden falls on the state. Those countries where the problems associated with an aging population are most acute are actively seeking long-term solutions.

EXERCISE S44 *Analyzing the task that relates to the lecture*

Using points and examples from the lecture, explain how the population age distribution is contributing to financial problems for governments.

EXERCISE S48 *Responding to the integrated listening/speaking tasks*

1. Listen to a conversation between two students.

(Man S) Have you signed up for the GRE tests yet?

(Woman S) Yeah. Have to if I wanna get into graduate school.

(Man S) You sound upset.

(Woman S) I am. I don't understand why we've gotta take that test. I mean, the university can tell whether we're up to graduate work by looking at our grade-point average and letters of recommendations.

(Man S) You're just suffering from test anxiety.

(Woman S) Yes, I am. Don't you know those tests are gender biased? Did you know that the average mean scores for women are about 60 points lower than men's on standardized tests, whereas women's grade-point averages are higher?

(Man S) Really? No, I didn't know that. So, uh, what's the deal?

(Woman S) Well, test anxiety may count. Women tend to suffer anxiety levels that negatively affect their scores. You know, there was a study not long ago in which a control group and an experimental group, both with an equal number of men and women, were given a standardized test. The people in the control group were just given the test, and those in the experimental group were told that the researchers were looking at gender differences. The women in the experimental group scored even lower than the women in the control group.

(Man S) And they think the women in the experimental group were more anxious?

(Woman S) Well, that's probably a part of it, but other studies show that men and women approach the tasks differently.

(Man S) So what do we, us guys, do differently?

(Woman S) Uh, for one thing, you guys take risks. We're more cautious and try to analyze the items and check our answers. So we work slower, and that's a disadvantage on a timed test.

(Man S) I can see that. What else?

(Woman S) Men seem to enjoy trick questions, whereas women find them distracting.

(Man S) Well, I guess I can understand your feelings. But don't you think a university takes these differences into account?

(Woman S) I'd hope so. You know, it isn't just women, but ethnic groups and even nonnative English speakers have been shown to do better on open-ended tasks like essay tests.

The students discuss the problem with standardized testing. Describe the woman's concerns. Then state what you think of the woman's concerns and explain why.

2. Listen to a conversation between two students.

(Man S) Hey, Becky, You look kind of . . . uh . . . down.

(Woman S) Yeah, I just discovered that I can't sign up for Research Methodology because I didn't take the prerequisite, Research Writing Skills. Can you believe that Research Methodology is only offered in the fall term? So if I can't take it next fall, it'll be another year before I can take it.

(Man S) I see you have a summer catalog. Is it being offered this summer?

(Woman S) Yeah. But I really need to go home and work this summer.

(Man S) Summer courses aren't so bad. I kind of prefer them. They're so intensive that they're over before you know it. Have you ever done a summer term?

(Woman S) No. But I'll have to this summer if I'm going to graduate in time.

(Man S) Did you know that course is offered as an Internet course? You could go home, hold down a job, and study online after you get off work.

(Woman S) Really? No, I didn't know that. You've signed up for online courses, right?

(Man S) Yeah, once. In fact, it was the Research Writing Skills course.

(Woman S) How was it?

(Man S) I failed.

(Woman S) What? But how is that possible? You're the one that always gets the best grades in class. It must've been really difficult.

(Man S) No, it wasn't. I discovered that when I don't attend a class regularly, I put off doing the assignments. I kept putting them off until it was too late to finish.

(Woman S) I never thought of you as a procrastinator.

(Man S) You know, I think it had a lot to do with not knowing the professor. I couldn't possibly walk into a classroom unprepared and face a professor. But I never met the online professor and didn't feel the embarrassment of not having my assignments ready. But I think you could manage it 'cause you're motivated. I mean, so you can take that other course next fall.

The students discuss two possible solutions to the woman's problem. Describe the problem. Then state which of the two solutions you prefer and explain why.

3. Listen to a conversation between two students.

(Woman S) I think we should meet early next week to finalize our presentation. Whadya think?

(Man S) Yeah. I think you're right. I'm free on Monday at 2:00.

(Woman S) Yeah. That's good for me.

(Man S) D'you want me to book a study room at the library again?

(Woman S) Hmmm. I don't know. It's a nice, quiet place to get work done, but I kind of like to drink coffee while we work. Since they don't allow drinks in the study rooms, whadya think of just meeting at the Student Union?

(Man S) Um, I think there's something going on at the union Monday afternoon. What was it?

(Woman S) Ah, you're right. They're having some sort of book fair.

(Man S) Yeah, that's it. Lots of publishers are going to be setting up displays and everything. I'd really like to go to that.

(Woman S) Me too. But what about our project? Monday is really the last day we can work on it before we have to do the presentation.

(Man S) Well, why don't we meet at the book fair and then go to the cafeteria and make the final preparations over a coffee?

(Woman S) Don't you think it might be pretty noisy?

(Man S) No. I get a lot of studying done in the cafeteria.

(Woman S) Yeah, but with the book fair, there'll be lots of extra people milling around. It could be really chaotic. Just getting a coffee might mean spending half our time waiting for the cafeteria lines.

(Man S) I hadn't thought about that. Maybe we should meet in the library.

(Woman S) D'you know how much ahead of time we have to reserve a study room?

(Man S) I don't think it matters. You can just walk in and if one is available at that moment, you can book it right then and there.

(Woman S) Well, should we take a risk and not reserve a study room? We could meet in the Student Union and if it *is* too noisy to work in the cafeteria, we could walk over to the library.

(Man S) Sounds good to me.

The students are discussing two possible places to meet to finalize their presentation plans. Describe their problem. Then state which of the two solutions you prefer and explain why.

4. Listen to a conversation between two students.

(Woman S) I hope they drop the physical education course requirements soon so that I don't have to take any of those classes.

(Man S) Do you? Personally, I think the decision is a mistake.

(Woman S) Really? Why? I mean–,

(Man S) Well, I guess the president is right about some students not wanting to take them, but lots of different studies have shown that being physically fit helps people to concentrate better.

(Woman S) But, really. Students should take on responsibility for their own health. Don't you think? I mean, they don't need an authority to force them.

(Man S) They should, but they don't. Students frequently get wrapped up in their studies to the detriment of their physical health. Many I've talked to say that they resent having to sign up for the courses, but when they're in the class, they find it stimulating and a good mental break from sitting in the library.

(Woman S) Well, they are probably sports-minded. A lot of students, like me, for instance, I've never been very good at sports. I absolutely dreaded going to my high school gym class and playing basketball.

(Man S) Well, that's a good point in favor of keeping the physical education courses. Currently, the department is able to offer classes in lots of different sports. The variety of classes offers something for everyone. If the requirements are dropped, those classes will be cut, and that hurts people like you who aren't good at competitive sports like basketball, but who could benefit from something noncompetitive like aerobics.

(Woman S) I must admit that I am out of shape, but I still don't think it's the university's job to make me fit.

(Man S) But you probably won't take on the responsibility of getting into shape. And think of all the money that has already been spent on sports equipment and facilities. The equipment will go to waste or break and not get replaced. I think this is a very sad commentary on our university's priorities.

(Woman S) There's nothing wrong with putting library facilities and labs at the top of the priority list.

(Man S) Well, that's true, but I'm still disappointed in this decision.

The man expresses his opinion about the changes in the physical education requirements for students. State his opinion, and explain the reasons he gives for that opinion.

5. Listen to part of a lecture in an agriculture class.

(Man P) Since goats can survive on kinds of vegetation, such as bushes and desert scrub, which are unsuitable for other domesticated herd animals, they're a logical means of subsistence for millions of rural inhabitants the world over. They're a valuable resource for milk and meat and can survive where other animals would starve.

However, goats have also done considerable damage to delicate ecosystems, particularly those areas in danger of turning into deserts. The owners of goats have not kept a balance between goat numbers and the available vegetation, and because of that, overgrazing by goats has destroyed areas of bushes, desert scrub, and herbs as well as woodland in sensitive environments. This animal does not discriminate about where it gets its nourishment and often will eat newly germinated plants, thus preventing the establishment of new vegetation. Also, goats destroy woody plants – in other words, the kind of vegetation whose roots are important for stabilizing the soil. Plants need soil to anchor their roots and to provide them with water and nutrients, and the soil needs plants to provide the biological material from which new soil is created. Plants also hold the soil together, stopping it from being driven away by wind and rain.

We can say that overgrazing by goats is one of the prime causes of the spread of deserts. Of course, it's not the goat itself that is to blame for the spread of desertification; it's the poor management of the animals that's responsible. What is needed is a large-scale educational program on the importance of soil conservation and the spread of techniques for properly managing grazing animals.

Using points and examples from the lecture, explain how goats are related to the spread of desertification.

6. Listen to part of a lecture in a criminal law class.

(Woman P) As you know, the basic principle of the American juvenile justice system is that children are different from adults. And, it follows that the way the justice system deals with children should reflect these differences. When the principle was established, it provided for the individualizing of treatment and services to vulnerable children.

However, this system is under threat. Critics say it's not tough enough. And also it fails to rehabilitate children. And some of you may agree. After all, criminal statistics point to a steadily increasing problem of youngsters committing crimes. But my concern is that young offenders may start to be treated as adults. Before any reforms are made, a rational examination of the whole system needs to be undertaken. As I see it, there are three key areas of research:

The first is accountability. OK, so in other words, how are juveniles different from adults in their understanding of criminal behavior? How do we assess their responsibility?

Secondly, we need to evaluate risk. Risk evaluation. So, this means, how can we determine the chances of a given youth committing a crime and how can we use this information to prevent the crime in the first place?

The third area of research is susceptibility. We need to know how susceptible young people are to change. Can we assess a child's or a young person's likelihood of changing behavior or of responding to treatment?

So, to repeat, accountability, risk evaluation, and uh, susceptibility to change. These three key areas of research should be based on a thorough understanding of child and adolescent development. We need experts from all relevant fields, as well as input from the general public. More needs to be learned about the origins, development, prevention, and treatment of juvenile crime, and that knowledge has to be spread among professionals and the community. In this way, eventual reforms of the system may really be able to tackle the growing problem.

Using specific information from the lecture, explain the professor's concern about changing the justice system and what needs to be done before reforms are made.

7. Listen to part of a lecture in an ecology class.

(Man P) OK. Today I wanted to talk about intermediate technology, which refers to technology individuals can build using the materials at hand. Let me give you an example of the importance of this technology. In parts of the world, collecting fuel for home use, uh, fuel, such as firewood, dung cake, or agricultural waste, is not only time-consuming, but the typical patterns of collection lead to problems like deforestation, soil erosion, and ecological imbalances. Experts predict that even if food supplies are adequate for rural populations, fuel supplies for domestic consumption may not be.

Considering these problems, aid organizations developed a solar oven. These ovens are cheaply constructed, easily operated, and extremely energy efficient. The oven consists of an inner and outer metal or cardboard box, a top cover, and two panes of plain glass. The inner box is painted black to absorb solar radiation. The space between the two boxes is filled with an easily available insulating material, such as rice husks, which, because of their high silicon content, neither attract insects nor rot easily. Other usable materials are, uh, ground nutshells or coconut shells. OK? An adjustable mirror is mounted on one side of the oven box, and this mirror reflects the sunlight into the interior of the box. A sufficiently high temperature can be maintained to cook food gradually but thoroughly.

Apart from being cheap and energy efficient, the solar oven has other advantages over traditional fires. First, indoor wood fires produce smoke that causes respiratory and eye diseases. They're also a fire hazard, especially for small children. Also, the combustion of biofuels produces carbon dioxide, methane, and other greenhouse gases that contribute to global warming. OK? So this intermediate technology, the solar oven, has made a significant improvement in the lives of millions of families in rural societies.

Using points and examples from the lecture, explain how the use of intermediate technology is important for rural societies.

8. Listen to part of a lecture in a world history class.

(Woman P) For hundreds of years, the maritime trading city of Venice had controlled the European spice trade with a firm hand. Various spices including nutmeg, pepper, and cinnamon were hauled overland across Asia to the great trading market of Constantinople, where they were bought up by Venetian merchants and then shipped westward across the Mediterranean to Venice. From here, the spices were sold on, at often excessive prices, to traders from northern Europe. Venice had an almost complete monopoly of the trade, yet many of the spices originated in countries and regions which few, if any, in Europe had visited. As spices became increasingly popular in medieval Europe, Venice's merchants managed the supply to ensure that high prices were maintained.

But in the late fourteenth and early fifteenth centuries, hundreds of other maritime nations attempted to get a share of the spice trade. Until that time, European ships rarely ventured too far from coastal waters due to the lack of navigation technology and knowledge. But gradually as new methods of navigation were developed, the Spanish and Portuguese learned how to successfully send ships onto the open sea. Prince Henry of Portugal set out to challenge the Venetians' grip on the spice trade by sending ships around Africa to India and China, thus avoiding the overland route. The king of Spain sent ships westward across the Atlantic Ocean in the hope of reaching India from the opposite direction. As is well known, the Italian navigator Christopher Columbus eventually reached the American continent by sailing westward but didn't find the spice regions of Asia that had been his goal. Within a few years, the Portuguese explorations paid off when the explorer Vasco da Gama reached the west coast of India and returned to Portugal with spices and jewels as well as the news that the Indians were willing to pursue trade.

Using points and examples from the lecture, explain how maritime nations affected the spice trade in Europe.

Speaking Section Practice Test

1. Please listen carefully.

Some research has indicated that pets are important for a person's mental health. Do you agree or disagree? Explain your point of view. Include details and examples to support your explanation.

You may begin to prepare your response after the beep. [beep]

Please begin speaking after the beep. [beep]

2. Please listen carefully.

If you could donate a large amount of money for scientific or medical research, how would you want the money to be used? Describe one important area in need of more research. Explain how your money could make a difference in that field of research.

You may begin to prepare your response after the beep. [beep]

Please begin speaking after the beep. [beep]

3. Please listen carefully.

The student newspaper has published an article about different services offered on campus. Read the description of the Legal Aid Project. You will have 45 seconds to read the description. Begin reading now.

Now listen to two students as they discuss the Legal Aid Project.

(Woman S) I didn't know that they had a free legal service for students here. You could get help with your housing problem.

(Man S) Oh, I don't know. That project's just set up to help the law students.

(Woman S) Maybe, but you said that you couldn't afford to see a lawyer, and this service is free. You might be able to get your rent deposit back.

(Man S) I don't really trust a student to advise me. I mean, those guys don't have any experience, do they?

(Woman S) Well, I think they do. You know – law students have to take a practicum where they deal with real legal cases that were dealt with in the past. Anyway, they go through old cases as if they were current ones. And then they see how the experienced lawyers dealt with the problems and analyze the ins and outs of the case.

(Man S) But that's just a classroom exercise.

(Woman S) Maybe. But see, it also says that the project staff assists them. The staff probably steps in and gives advice if the student is going in the wrong direction.

Now get ready to answer the question.

The woman expresses her opinion of the Legal Aid Project. State her opinion and explain her arguments in favor of the service.

You may begin to prepare your response after the beep. [beep]

Please begin speaking after the beep. [beep]

4. Please listen carefully.

Read the passage about the transportation of agricultural goods. You have 45 seconds to read the passage. Begin reading now.

Now listen to part of a lecture on this topic in a cultural geography class.

(Woman P) Today I'd like to talk about a German landowner, Johann-Heinrich Von Thünen, who lived in the seventeenth century. After researching ways to make his estate more profitable, Von Thünen developed a model of zones represented by concentric rings to explain market forces. In the center is a city, an imaginary one, to represent the market. As I am talking about these zones, keep in mind that we're talking about the days before refrigeration, electricity, and so on.

OK. So, the first ring around the city represents the zone that includes dairy farming and such crops as fruit and vegetables. Milk and fresh produce tend to spoil and, therefore, have to reach the market quickly. The second ring is the wooded zone, used for growing timber. Logs are heavy to transport but necessary both as a fuel and as a building material. The third ring is the grain zone. Wheat for bread is light and less perishable than fresh produce, so it can be grown further from the market. Next is the livestock zone. People can walk their cows or sheep to market. The livestock zone is the final one. The area beyond that zone is too far from the center to be considered for commercial farming.

Now interestingly, Von Thünen's model is still applicable today in terms of transportation costs and the cost of land.

Now get ready to answer the question.

The professor describes a model of zones relevant for agricultural marketing. Explain how these zones are related to the costs of transportation.

You may begin to prepare your response after the beep. [beep]

Please begin speaking after the beep. [beep]

5. Please listen carefully.

Listen to a conversation between two students.

(Woman S) Hey, you've got your arms full, Ted. Would you like a hand?

(Man S) Nah, I can manage. These are all the books I need for my American short-story course. Quite a load, isn't it?

(Woman S) Um, yeah. Well, literature courses always require a lot of books.

(Man S) Yeah, and you know what? I was supposed to buy a lot more books, but I didn't have the money.

(Woman S) Textbooks are expensive. Hey, did you stop off at the library first to see if you could get any of the books there?

(Man S) Yeah, but I couldn't find any of the titles on the list.

(Woman S) OK, but in literature courses, usually you can find the stories you need in different texts.

(Man S) Yeah?

(Woman S) Yeah, let me see your list. Oh, see this book of stories by Edgar Allan Poe. You can probably find all the stories in other books or collections of famous short stories.

(Man S) But how can I be sure?

(Woman S) Did you check the course syllabus? I bet the professor has stated exactly what stories you need to read before the class meeting – and you can look for them in other books. Do you have the course syllabus?

(Man S) Yeah, right here. See?

(Woman S) OK. Well, see you need to read "Chrysanthemums" by John Steinbeck. That definitely should be in the library in a book of short stories. Did you look?

(Man S) Well, no, I didn't look for individual stories.

(Woman S) Well, I suggest you keep the receipts for all of these books – and then search for the exact stories you need in the library. I'm sure you'll find a lot of them there. Then you can take the books you don't need back to the bookstore.

(Man S) Yeah, I could do that. But you know, I like to own my books, highlight passages and scribble notes in the margins, and whatnot.

(Woman S) Oh, well . . . Oh, hey, here's another thing you could do. Those books look new. Did you go to the used bookstore first?

(Man S) Used bookstore?

(Woman S) Yeah, there's a used bookstore on University Avenue. They buy used textbooks at the end of the semester. If that professor has been requiring that the students read the same books every semester, chances are that you'll find them there. And that way you'll have your own copy and you won't be paying so much.

Now get ready to answer the question.

The woman has two suggestions for the man. Describe the man's problem. Then state which of the two suggestions you prefer and explain why.

You may begin to prepare your response after the beep. [beep]

Please begin speaking after the beep. [beep]

6. Please listen carefully.

Listen to part of a lecture in a music education class.

(Man P) I'm sure you've heard of the Mozart Effect, a term coined to refer to the results of a neuroscience music/brain experiment. In this experiment, researchers were looking at one specific area of the brain, where the ability to think in terms of space and time – or spatial-temporal reasoning – takes place. This kind of reasoning is important in music, but not all aspects of music . . . and it's important in solving some types of physics and mathematics problems. Some types.

The researchers chose Mozart's music because as a child prodigy he used space/time reasoning at an early age. I'm uncertain of the relationship between a child composer's use of this reasoning to create a masterpiece and an adult listener's use when hearing it. Anyway, the experimental group – college students, not children – were given a pretest just in their spatial-temporal reasoning. Then they were divided into three groups: one heard no music; one, a variety of different kinds of music; and one group only heard Mozart. Afterwards, all the subjects took an intelligence test. The results? Well, the Mozart group had increased scores on the spatial-temporal reasoning section. The increase lasted for 10 minutes. Only 10 minutes. Now, there are several types of intelligence tests that could have been used, but only one type was used in the experiment. One wonders if a different IQ test would have had the same results.

The study was interesting, but I'm concerned about the reaction of the general public. The media interest in the belief that listening to Mozart's music can increase one's intelligence was followed by "help your child be a genius" books, popular magazine articles, and the flourishing market of videos, toys, and music products – all aimed at gullible parents. This is unfortunate because the real importance of music, that of bringing beauty into our lives, is being undermined by parents foolishly attempting to turn their children into rocket scientists.

Now get ready to answer the question.

Using points and examples from the lecture, explain how the experiment does not support the public's belief in the Mozart Effect.

You may begin to prepare your response after the beep. [beep]

Please begin speaking after the beep. [beep]

PART 2 BUILDING SKILLS: Writing

EXERCISE W35 *Writing summaries of listening passages*

1. (Woman P) A feature seen in many cities around the world is the shantytown. This is an illegal settlement built on disused city land. The people living in these settlements usually have immigrated to the city from rural areas in hopes of finding jobs. Arriving without enough money to rent housing, they collect scrap materials to build makeshift shelters. The shantytown often lacks public facilities such as water supplies, drainage systems, and electricity. However, in time, these facilities may be added and homes improved until the shantytown becomes a more permanent settlement.

2. (Man P) Astronomers have observed structures of glowing blue arcs of light nearly 2 million trillion miles in length. These arcs are thought to be optical illusions created by light that has been bent due to the immense gravitational pull of a massive galaxy. The arcs are probably formed when the light from a distant galaxy is bent by the gravitational pull of another, less distant, intervening galaxy. Even though such light-bending galaxies contain billions of stars, they still don't contain enough visible stars to exert the pull needed to bend light in this way. Therefore, huge amounts of invisible or dark matter must exist within these galaxies.

3. (Woman P) The Henry Ford Museum was founded in 1929 in Dearborn, Michigan, about 12 miles west of downtown Detroit. This museum has redesigned its display of old cars to show the changes brought about by the automobile. One exhibit, which shows the evolution of roadside services, contrasts a 1940s diner with a 1960s fast-food restaurant. The Getting Away From It All exhibit presents an assortment of recreational vehicles dating from a 1916 camper truck to today's mobile home. Changes in roadside objects such as billboards can be seen along the museum's roadway, where 108 cars are lined up as if traveling. For the car enthusiast, this museum should not be overlooked.

EXERCISE W36 *Revising summaries of listening passages*

1. (Man P) The advantages of herding animals over hunting them are numerous. The most obvious advantage is not having to search for food as the herded animals can provide both milk and meat. Instead of having fresh meat only after the hunt, there's the convenience of keeping the herd animal alive until the meat is needed.

2. (Woman P) Every year game manufacturers introduce many new games to the consuming public. These are designed to entertain millions of fun-seekers who like to roll the dice, pick a card, guess a quote, or buy property depending on the game of their choice. Very popular on the market are the ones that test a player's general knowledge. We shouldn't dismiss these games that puzzle, preoccupy, and, uh, frustrate us as mere entertainment because research is showing that keeping one's mind active is one of the ways to maintain one's thinking capacity into the later years of life.

3. (Man P) One type of structure of the Anasazi people of the southwestern United States that I'd like to discuss today is called a kiva. The kiva is considered to have had a mainly religious and ceremonial purpose. One type of kiva is circular in shape with six stone pillars built into the wall. These pillars were used to support the roof beams. A fire pit in the center of the room has a short wall behind it. The wall served as a deflector for the air intake. Another feature of the kiva is a small round hole in the floor, which was regarded as a symbolic entrance to the underworld.

EXERCISE W38 *Summarizing listening passages*

1. Now listen to part of a lecture.

(Woman P) During the Depression Era in the United States, President Roosevelt's administration started innovative and often controversial cultural programs to ease unemployment among artists and writers, while at the same time give the general public access to the arts. One scheme funded under the Federal Writers Project employed nearly 7,000 writers at its peak in 1936. The funding provided work for both novice and experienced writers, many of whom went on to acquire literary reputations.

Writers interviewed over 10,000 people from different regions, ethnic groups, and occupations about major areas of their life. The wide diversity was encouraged by the administrators, keen to foster tolerance and promote a sense of national identity during the difficult period of the 1930s. People interviewed included those from all walks of life – business executives to vagrants. Many interviewees told of their upbringing in the nineteenth century and included recollections of historic people or important events. Included among the informants were a large number of former slaves whose memories offer a vivid account of conditions before and after the abolition of slavery.

These vivid and often sad accounts of life histories were originally intended for publication in a series that would form a documentary portrait of everyday life in America. Unfortunately, the project was never fully realized, partially due to the redirection of national priorities with the United States entering World War II. However, the raw material collected remains a valuable resource for historians and provides insight into the lives of ordinary people of a bygone era. Furthermore, several of the project writers found that the knowledge and experiences they had gathered from their research was an invaluable source for their own literary creations.

2. Now listen to part of a lecture.

(Man P) You may be interested to know that the first test-scoring machines were developed in the 1930s. The earliest prototype was created by Reynold B. Johnson, a high school teacher from Michigan. His invention was based on the fact that graphite conducts electricity. His inspiration to use graphite came to him when he was recalling one of the boyhood tricks that he played on his sisters' friends. He would scratch pencil marks on the spark plugs of their parked cars. Then, when the drivers tried to start their cars, the graphite in the pencil marks would draw the sparks away from the spark plugs and the engines wouldn't start. Thinking about this prank, Johnson realized that a machine could electrically sense pencil marks made on a sheet of paper and then indicate if these marks were in the right places.

By 1933, Johnson had made a working model of a test-scoring machine. One day he received a telegram from an executive at the IBM Company. Their company had been trying to produce a test-scoring machine for several years and wanted to purchase Johnson's invention. After a few setbacks and interventions within the IBM management, Johnson's machine finally met approval and was improved over the next few years. This machine allowed a large number of exams to be scored efficiently and with no human error. This led to the feasibility of widespread standardized testing.

Nowadays, computerized exams are gradually taking over the role of machine-scored standardized exams. It's likely that the scoring machine will remain around for some time to come before completely being replaced by the computer.

EXERCISE W39 *Linking ideas in reading and listening passages*

1. Now listen to part of a lecture on the topic you just read about.

(Woman P) A lot of evidence seems to underline the need for a more cautious approach to fluoride supplementation. First of all, when we add fluoride to the water supply, we are doing so without the informed consent of the public. Now, you could argue that since the benefits are so obvious to the consumer that no consent is necessary. But several studies have shown that fluoride supplementation may be more hazardous than was once thought. If that's true, then the act of adding fluoride is a kind of large-scale experiment in which the subjects – that is, the general public – have not given their consent to be treated as guinea pigs. Think about it. Would you allow doctors to test medications on you without your knowledge and consent?
In fact, at least one large-scale study carried out recently concluded that average decay rates for children in both fluoridated and non-fluoridated areas were almost identical. Besides this, evidence seems to be coming in that, uh, decay rates are going down in most places for other reasons, unconnected with the use of fluoride. Beyond this, some research has called into question the safety of the supplements. Environmentalists, for example, claim that the supplements are not the same as naturally occurring fluoride since it's derived from a hazardous waste and contains toxic pollutants.

Furthermore, several side effects have been reported from the overexposure to fluoride in animal testing. Remember that fluoride is a cumulative poison; only a percentage leaves the body and the remainder accumulates in different tissues. This can lead to unforeseen health problems. All in all, it seems clear that much more public debate and research into the benefits and potential dangers caused by fluoride supplementation needs to be conducted.

2. Now listen to part of a lecture on the topic you just read about.

(Woman P) Well, the belief in the value of using animals as predictors of earthquakes is, in my opinion, based on very weak evidence. The fact is that no serious scientific research has shown that this actually works. I agree of course that animals have been shown to have different, and often superior, sensory capacities. But all the evidence we've collected about animal behavior prior to earthquakes is anecdotal; in other words, based on what people claim to have observed after the event. So, often after any sudden major event, people focus on things they remember happening just before. Amongst other things, they remember things like animals apparently behaving oddly. It may be that animals from time to time behave in unusual ways but if this is not followed by an impressive event such as an earthquake, then people have no reason to remember this behavior. People often remember vividly all kinds of things that happen prior to any surprising or catastrophic event. Some studies have shown some of the animal stories to be fanciful rather than factual. For example, people have often claimed that many dogs and other family pets go missing just before a quake. The hypothesis that this could be caused by the animals' anticipation of an earthquake has in fact been tested in California by scientists who have studied reports of missing animals in conjunction with earthquake activity. This study, at least, showed no connection between pet behavior and quake occurrence over a three-year period. As for the often-heard success of the evacuation of a Chinese city prior to an earthquake, based on animal behavior, it turns out that, in fact, the real warning was given by a series of foreshocks, shocks that sometimes occur before a major quake.

EXERCISE W44 *Practice responding to the integrated writing task*

1. Now listen to part of a lecture on the topic you just read about.

(Man P) Being able to communicate using language is one of our human species' most important abilities. Some scientists claim that apes, like humans, also use languages. There are many studies into ape acquisition of language, some famous, such as the Koko studies. But are these animals really acquiring language? We really haven't done enough research to address the question of how and when humans started using language, but we can compare human and ape communicative abilities to determine whether the claims about ape language are valid.

First, for behavior to be called "language," it must be communicative; in other words, the signers must be able to use language creatively. They should be able to take turns in conversation, must sign spontaneously rather than as a response to drilling or coercion, and must be able to comment on interesting phenomena. If you think about what the apes have accomplished in communicating, these criteria have not been met.

However, according to the proponents of ape communication, the animals do meet these criteria. They maintain that those of us who question the validity of this research have never worked with apes. However, we wonder how much influence their probable emotional attachment to an animal has on the conclusions they reach.

Is there a solution in sight that would put an end to this controversy? Yes, there might be. Studies are being undertaken at the neurophysiological level. Through the use of modern brain-scanning techniques such as MRI, we may be able to get a better picture of the brain activity of a healthy human during communication and an ape while supposedly communicating. A comparison of these scans should give us an insight into whether apes really do communicate.

Summarize the points made in the lecture you just heard, explaining how they cast doubt on the points made in the reading.

2. Now listen to part of a lecture on the topic you just read about.

(Woman P) The question of why the current is so important to the young salmon was asked and I'd like to respond to this. Smolts, uh, the young salmon, hatch from their eggs in fresh water. Before the large-scale construction of dams, the young fish used the strong current from the spring runoff of melting snow to get to the sea in between six and, uh, twenty days. It's necessary for them to reach the sea within this window of time because during these days the smolts' bodies undergo the physiological changes for adaptation to saltwater. The net result of the slow current is that many of the young fish don't survive the trip, which can now take up to 60 days to reach the sea. What happens is their bodies have adapted to saltwater conditions, but they're still in fresh water. Obviously, with fewer fish surviving the trip to the sea, there are fewer adult salmon to migrate back up the rivers for breeding.

The solutions to the problem that have been presented have not been very successful. Many scientists think that the artificial method of getting the fish to the sea by barge has killed more fish than it saves.

The suggestion some people have made concerning increasing the flow rate temporarily by either releasing water from upstream reservoirs or reducing the water level in all linked reservoirs for the period of smolt migration would be a partial solution to the declining salmon numbers. Unfortunately, both of these proposals have met with criticism from the power companies that manage the dams.

Summarize the points made in the lecture you just heard, explaining how they support the points made in the reading.

3. Now listen to part of a lecture on the topic you just read about.

(Man P) OK, so you all know something about DDT and its apparent environmental risks, but these risks are not necessarily valid. The evidence that DDT led to population declines of various birds of prey – the bald eagle, for instance – has come under criticism. Apparently, the bald eagle populations were in decline well before the widespread use of DDT. On the contrary, in 1960 – that's about 15 years after the introduction of DDT – observers were reporting a rise in bald eagle numbers. Similar results have been found among other high food-chain birds. Brown pelicans, for example, reached their lowest number before the introduction of DDT. The fact is they were hunted to near extinction. I've found studies showing that this bird, as well as the peregrine falcon, actually experienced no difficulty in reproducing during the DDT years.

So, what about the evidence that DDT led to eggshell thinning? Unfortunately, the experiments associating DDT with this phenomenon involved doses massively higher than could ever be encountered in the wild. Even then, the degree of thinning was less than that found in eggs in the wild. In other words, the evidence shows that eggshell thinning and DDT are not correlated. However, other substances are, for example, oil spills, lead and mercury poisoning, and other factors, such as stress from noise, fear, or excitement, may be tied to the eggshell thinning.

Even the human cancer scare seems to have been exaggerated. Again, several studies show that there may be no link between DDT and cancer at all. Research into DDT as a pesticide has indicated that overuse of the pesticide can result in its loss of effectiveness against insect-borne diseases, but responsible use is an effective method of fighting the spread of malaria and its reintroduction should be seriously reconsidered.

Summarize the points made in the lecture you just heard, explaining how they cast doubt on the points made in the reading.

Writing Section Practice Test

Now listen to part of a lecture on the topic you just read about.

(Woman P) OK, now I want to discuss tidal power since I think it's a good example of an alternative energy source that we should look at critically. OK, now let's think about some of the possible drawbacks to the system. For a start, tidal power can never do more than provide a fraction of our total energy needs since there just aren't enough good locations.

However, tidal power could still make some contribution at a regional level. But what about the environmental impact? First of all, the quality of the water in the estuary area will be changed, and this will have an effect, of course, on the local wildlife. Both the increase in salinity, when seawater is mixed with estuary water, and also the amount of mud and sediments churned up in the water will affect the birds and the fish. These conditions could stimulate the growth of the red tide organism, which causes paralysis in shellfish and affects many aquatic creatures. And much of the inter-tidal habitat could be destroyed, and this would have a devastating effect on birds and vegetation types adapted to these conditions.

And what about the fish that naturally migrate between river and sea? Their ability to migrate will be hampered since they won't be able to pass the barrage. Now, it could be possible to make some kind of provision for them to move freely between salt and freshwater environments, but this would lead to expensive design considerations.

Also, there are implications for the people living in the area. For example, fishing boats are normally moored in the estuary for protection from the rougher waters, but they'll no longer be able to navigate between estuary and open sea. In such a case, the economy of the whole area could be affected.

So, all of these things are drawbacks of tidal power and need to be matched against the benefits of alternative energy production.

Summarize the points made in the lecture you just heard, explaining how they cast doubt on the points made in the reading.

PRACTICE TESTS

PRACTICE TEST 1: Listening Section

Questions 1–6

Listen to part of a lecture in a business studies class.

(Woman P) OK, so we've outlined a number of techniques for effective decision-making. Now, let's focus on one approach to figuring out how to make good business decisions. OK, so one way of deciding whether to go ahead with some new investment project is to perform what's known as CBA, or cost benefit analysis. CBA can estimate and total up the money values of both the benefits and costs to a community, institution, or business to establish whether an investment choice is worthwhile.

So let's assume you've generated solutions to a business problem and have thought really carefully about which way to go. You think you have the best solution available. But before going ahead with any investment decision, what you need to do is add up the value of the benefits as well as the costs of this action.

Now what I mean by costs and benefits here is always expressed in monetary terms. So, we find out what the cost is in money terms and also what the benefits might be, also in money terms. Then we subtract the costs from the benefits and we can choose whether to go ahead or not.

All right, in simple terms, costs tend to be what we spend on something, say, for example, a new piece of machinery; and benefits are what advantages – expressed in money units – we get over the lifetime of that machinery because of having purchased it as opposed to, well, not having it, or having some alternative. In such a case, we can figure out a fairly simple CBA just by looking at expenses and then subtracting them from the savings brought about by improved . . . the improvements of introducing the machinery – that would include things like the savings met by not having to pay salaries to employees who previously did the work of the machine. We could add the fact that the machines make fewer mistakes, we hope, than human employees so there will be fewer rejected products. But, on the other hand, we have to factor in the cost of running the machines, such as maybe the increased electricity bill, the cost of repairs, and, of course, the cost of training someone to operate the new equipment.

So that much is pretty straightforward. But we also have to think about less tangible, less visible costs and benefits. Cost benefit analysis really only works if we are careful to add in all the costs and benefits. Costs especially are sometimes hidden. For example, in paying for this new stuff, we're taking liquid money and spending it, right? So we're no longer paid interest from having that money in a bank or otherwise invested. OK, so we have to subtract that loss from the benefit side. Then suppose also that the new machines are noisy. That means soundproofing. That's a cost. Or will it take up more space than the replaced workers, and therefore require an addition to the building? These are less obvious costs, but they should be factored in to get an accurate picture.

When we do CBA in a more public domain – say, on the building of a new road – the calculations can become even more tricky, although there's some impressive software nowadays that helps us out, of course. So, how do we measure the benefits here? Does the road improve or worsen people's lives? A new road may, for example, damage some wildlife habitat or some residential community may be inconvenienced by the noise or air pollution. On the other hand, the new road could improve property values by decreasing commuting times. It could also save human lives, since it's safer than the old road.

In practice, CBA tries to put a value on all these things, although a lot of people may not like what it says. What it does is try to find out how people really value these apparently subjective things – by looking at the financial choices they're prepared to make to gain a benefit, or to avoid something on the cost side. In this way, we can put a monetary figure on all benefits and costs. Of course these calculations can be complex, and sometimes controversial, but I want to point out that CBA is a powerful tool – and perhaps the most rational way of choosing whether to go ahead with a complex investment decision.

Now get ready to answer the questions. You may use your notes to help you answer.

1. What is the lecture mainly about?
2. In the lecture, the professor describes some costs and benefits of investing in new machinery. Indicate whether each of the following is a cost or a benefit for a company planning on making an investment decision.
3. Why does the professor mention the introduction of machinery?

4. Why does the professor say this: So that much is pretty straightforward. But we also have to think about less tangible, less visible costs and benefits.

5. Listen again to part of the lecture. Then answer the question.

When we do CBA in a more public domain – say, on the building of a new road – the calculations can become even more tricky, although there's some impressive software nowadays that helps us out, of course.

Why does the professor say this: . . . say, on the building of a new road . . .

6. According to the professor, how does CBA evaluate subjective things?

Questions 7–11

Listen to a conversation between a student and a professor.

(Woman S) Hi, Dr. Johnson. I came by to discuss my research paper. I dropped it by on Monday . . . about the nutritional value of chocolate.

(Man P) Oh, yes, Lisa. That's right.

(Woman S) Have you had a chance to look at it yet?

(Man P) Yeah, I sure have. Let me dig it out of my files . . . Yeah. Here it is. OK, well, Lisa, you've done a fine job of citing your sources and writing up your reference page. But, you used a lot of Internet resources for your information.

(Woman S) That's right. You said we could, didn't you?

(Man P) Oh, yeah. But I also said to be sure to evaluate the site to make sure that it's worthwhile before you used it. This one here . . . that I've circled, I don't think this is what I'd call a good source.

(Woman S) But it has the university address of a professor. Isn't it OK to use sites with the *.edu* domain in the address?

(Man P) Well, you have to look beyond just the address. Yes, you are correct that this site is that of a professor, a professor at a very prestigious university, in fact. But did you notice this particular set of Web pages were student papers that the professor had uploaded for the class to read and critique? You happened to have used one of the student papers. Well, that particular student may have done a fine job in his or her research, but a student is hardly an expert in the field.

(Woman S) Oh, I hadn't realized that it was a student's work. I just noticed that it was on the Web site of a professor and thought . . . well, that it would be his work.

(Man P) You really need to investigate a bit deeper before you use online material. You could have checked the sources that the student had used. There might have been some useful papers by experts in that student's reference page.

(Woman S) OK.

(Man P) Now the study here that you've cited looks very good. But did you notice that the person who did the study works for a laboratory that's funded by a major chocolate company?

(Woman S) Oh . . . so it's biased.

(Man P) Well, perhaps. At least it should be taken with a grain of salt. But it might also be very good research. So with data like that – data which may be biased – you should try to find an independent person who's run the same kind of experiment. Remember that a good experiment should be . . . you should be able to replicate it. So if a major chocolate company comes out with a study, we should have other people looking at that research with a critical, but open mind.

(Woman S) So, it might be a good source. I don't have to throw it out.

(Man P) Right, but I think you should try to find more studies to back up the results. OK, so has that been helpful?

(Woman S) Yes, oh, yeah, very, Dr. Johnson. Thank you. I really appreciate your help.

Now get ready to answer the questions. You may use your notes to help you answer.

7. Why does the student go to see her professor?

8. Listen again to part of the conversation. Then answer the question.

(Woman S) But it has the university address of a professor. Isn't it OK to use sites with the *.edu* domain in the address?

(Man P) Well, you have to look beyond just the address. Yes, you are correct that this site is that of a professor, a professor at a very prestigious university, in fact.

Why does the professor say this: Well, you have to look beyond just the address.

9. Why does Dr. Johnson criticize the student's use of a university Web site?

10. Listen again to part of the conversation. Then answer the question.

(Man P) Now the study here that you've cited looks very good. But did you notice that the person who did the study works for a laboratory that's funded by a major chocolate company?

(Woman S) Oh . . . so it's biased.

(Man P) Well, perhaps. At least it should be taken with a grain of salt.

Why does the professor say this: . . . it should be taken with a grain of salt.

11. What does the professor say about the research sponsored by a company?

Questions 12–17

Listen to part of a lecture in an architecture class.

(Woman P) So, now I'd like to focus on the Prairie School of Architecture, which developed the most significant architectural style in North America in the first decades of the twentieth century. The main influences on this style came from several places, for example, the philosophy and practice of the architect Louis Sullivan. Now, you may remember that Sullivan liked to say that form follows function. In other words, the shape and structure of a building should follow, should depend on the purpose, the intended use of the building. There was also the English Arts and Crafts movement – that was important around this time, too. That was a second important influence. And I should mention traditional Oriental themes, which also played an important part in the Prairie School ideas. Now the students and followers of Sullivan, the most famous of whom was Frank Lloyd Wright, developed these themes and ideas into a truly American style; a style expressing a belief in the unity of mankind and nature.

Now, when people think of architecture, they often think of large public buildings, but most of the effort of the Prairie School was devoted to domestic buildings, mainly houses for well-to-do private citizens. So, can anyone here describe to me any of the important features of Prairie School houses?

(Man S) Didn't they mostly have long horizontal lines, rather than a vertical appearance?

(Woman P) Yes, they did. That's certainly part of it. We can say that the most visible external features of this architecture were horizontal lines and heavy roofs projecting away from the walls. The shapes were designed to both harmonize with and reflect the broad, flat prairies of the Midwestern United States. But, somewhat ironically, I suppose, most of these houses were actually built in more urban areas, especially in the Chicago suburbs, rather than on the prairies themselves. OK. Now, what about the insides, the interiors?

(Man S2) Didn't they want to do away with small rooms?

(Woman P) Well, in a sense, yes. There was certainly an emphasis on keeping the number of separate rooms to a minimum, opening up living space, and designing internal walls so that the light and view created a sense of unity. The idea was to reduce the number of interior corners typical of traditional European houses. See, Prairie School architects thought of this traditional home as confining, both physically and also spiritually. So by ridding the inside of houses of so many rooms and corners and walls, they hoped to create a feeling of movement and freedom. Their ideal of beauty was to try to make the living space more compatible with human proportions and living requirements. Often, large fireplaces were built at the center of the overall design rather than attached to an outside wall. And this gave additional structural support to the building, so it further allowed the building to get by with fewer interior walls.

Now, let me add that, in line with their belief in the importance of nature, these architects related the interiors to the surrounding natural landscape by their use of windows that were continuous ribbons of glass. So, in that way, the outside and inside of the houses were more closely related. Other ways they suggested the importance of nature were in designing terraces projecting from the external walls with parapets, walls that were used as planting boxes for flowers and shrubs, and deep roof overhangs that led the eye toward the horizon. Of course, not all Prairie School houses had all these features, but certainly we can say that there was a general tendency among these architects to provide their designs with many of them. OK, so now we've discussed overall structure; now what about ornamentation?

(Man S2) Didn't they reject almost all decorative elements?

(Woman P) Well, not entirely, although, it's true they liked to keep things simple. Again, this was in line with their opposition to what they perceived as the fussiness of more traditional housing styles. We can say that ornamentation was only permitted if it complemented, if it blended in with the overall expression and feeling of the building. So, to this end, the Prairie School architects tended to use simple, unmixed, natural materials, sometimes with geometric or Oriental designs. For example, many of the Prairie houses had a "turned-up" roof edge reminiscent of traditional Japanese houses.

OK. So, finally, I'd like to mention that these architects usually designed all the furniture that went with each house. Each piece of furniture, whether built-in or freestanding, was carefully crafted to fit in with the overall feeling of the house. Again, natural materials were preferred and restful horizontal lines were emphasized.

Now get ready to answer the questions. You may use your notes to help you answer.

12. What is the lecture mainly about?

13. What can be said about the nature of Prairie School architecture?

14. Listen again to part of the lecture. Then answer the question.

(Woman P) The shapes were designed to both harmonize with and reflect the broad, flat prairies of the Midwestern United States. But, somewhat ironically, I suppose, most of these houses were actually built in more urban areas, especially in the Chicago suburbs, rather than on the prairies themselves.

Why does the professor say this: . . . somewhat ironically, I suppose, most of these houses were actually built in more urban areas . . .

15. According to the professor, how did the Prairie School architects make living space more compatible with human needs?

16. What does the professor say about the use of ornamentation by Prairie School architects?

17. Why does the professor mention traditional Japanese houses?

Questions 18–23

Listen to part of a lecture in a psychology class.

(Man P) OK. Now I'd like to present an idea that has recently become much talked about in the fields of biology and psychology, and also in studies of cultural transmission. I should point out that some of what this is is not fully accepted by some academics, but I'm bringing this up today just to, well, hopefully, whet your appetite.

OK. Now, you are all familiar, of course, with the term "gene," and how it's considered as the unit of inheritance. As you know, we inherit our genes from our parents, and then we pass them on to our kids. What genes do is replicate, that is, they make copies of themselves. Some scientists even like to claim that animals and plants and all organisms are just essentially systems for the transmission of genes from one generation to the next. Now, sometimes genes make mistakes and the mutant forms that result may make new life forms, at least if they succeed. If the environment in which they find themselves is suitable, they will succeed and thrive and reproduce. Now, of course, environments differ from place to place, and successful genes, which inhabit various organisms, themselves change the environment. The pressures of the changing environment lead to variation in the organisms, and this eventually creates the vast complexity of life.

All right, so now I want to bring in here something that is kind of like a gene in the way it behaves. This thing is called a *meme*. Now, it's spelled M-E-M-E. The term "meme" was invented by the zoologist Richard Dawkins to refer to a unit of information in our minds which influences events so that copies of itself are passed on to other minds. Some people have described memes as patterns of information that spread just like viruses or bacteria and which alter the behavior – even if in a very subtle, very small, or hardly noticeable way – causing the host to pass on the pattern. In a sense they're parasites, because they use us, or at least our brains, as a springboard for their transmission to other brains. The essential point is that a meme replicates, that is, it's capable of imitation, just like a gene. A meme can be an idea, a song, a joke, a food recipe, or even a way of constructing bridges. "How to make a fire" could be considered another one. What is important here is that memes are imitated and thus passed on from one person to another. Also, they don't even have to be true; they just have to, in some way, make sense to us.

Memes seem to come in all sizes; they can be as small as, say, a new slang term, to very large, that is to say, a whole way of looking at the world, say a political ideology. Some people who write about memes would probably call such a large meme a "meme complex," – a whole set of memes clustered together – for, as it were, mutual protection.

All right. So the useful thing about this idea is that it enables us to explain certain things about behavior and even our physical makeup that are difficult to explain without it. At the most simple level, it helps us to understand why some ideas survive and some just drop out of sight. The memes that are transmitted are the survivors. And just as genes group together, so to speak, to form organisms that can reproduce, so memes may cluster together in human brains and pass on to other brains complex systems of thought such as political ideas or even scientific theories.

Now if we ask why our minds always appear to be active and full of thoughts, we can answer using this meme idea, that it is because memes need to get repeated over and over in our heads. They need to be rehearsed and remembered. If they're not thought about and transferred to another brain, they'll die out, disappear. So from the meme's point of view, it's necessary to be practiced, then passed on to another mind.

According to some theorists in this field, the reason our minds are continually filling up with ideas, is that the memes force us to. One person has even suggested that the human brain, with all its complexity, was in some way designed by memes in order to promote their own success.

Furthermore, surprisingly, it's claimed that we ourselves are not the ones who benefit from our ideas, it's – you guessed it – the memes themselves. The "self" itself is a meme. In other words, at least some theorists seem to be saying, we are nothing but temporary groupings of memes that have come together in order to be protected and passed on to other minds, in order that they can survive and prosper.

Now get ready to answer the questions. You may use your notes to help you answer.

18. What aspect of a meme's behavior does the professor mainly discuss?

19. Why does the professor say this: I should point out that some of what this is is not fully accepted by some academics. . . .

20. What does the professor say about memes?

21. Listen again to part of the lecture. Then answer the question.

(Man P) A meme can be an idea, a song, a joke, a food recipe, or even a way of constructing bridges. "How to make a fire" could be considered another one.

Why does the professor say this: "How to make a fire" could be considered another one.

22. What does the professor imply about the importance of memes in our minds?

23. Which of the following is NOT true about memes?

Questions 24–29

Listen to part of a lecture in an anthropology class.

(Woman P) So we've had a look at the general distribution of Native American peoples throughout the continent and before the arrival of the Spaniards. Today, I wanted to focus on a particular culture, which inhabited the Southwest of what is today the United States. This was a remarkable group of agricultural people generally referred to as the "Anasazi." By the way, I'm going to continue to use that term even though some people are not completely happy with it. It's the best term we've got at the moment, and all the proposed alternative names are less accurate.

OK. So these people arrived in the Southwest area approximately 2,000 years ago and engaged in hunting and gathering. Over time they developed an agricultural economy with corn, squash, and beans as their primary crops. During the earlier periods, they made waterproof basketware, and today these periods are known as the "Basketmaker" cultures. We'll take a more detailed look at these cultures later on in the course. So, anyway, eventually the Anasazi discovered that pottery was more effective for storing foodstuffs and liquids. So they developed ceramic work often patterned with bold, brightly colored designs. This pottery was good enough to be traded throughout the region. In fact, there is evidence that trade extended into central Mexico.

Now, as well as highly skilled pottery techniques, the Anasazi also developed remarkable building techniques. They also developed a kind of road system. Well, perhaps "system" is the wrong word, since the roads didn't really go anywhere. They were mostly just sections extending out from their larger houses, possibly to emphasize their status. Some authorities have said their purpose was really symbolic, rather than practical. OK. Where was I? Oh, yeah. The buildings. Their dwellings and ceremonial structures were often built in inaccessible locations on cliffs or protected by caves. A well-known example of an Anasazi building is the so-called "Cliff Palace" in Mesa Verde National Park. I'm sure some of you have seen pictures of this site. This large structure – oh, it contains over 200 rooms – was built on a cliff in the 1200s. It consisted of homes made of blocks of rock – varying from simple structures to large, multi-storied buildings. The Cliff Palace has generated the perception of the Anasazi as "cliff dwellers." This extraordinary structure, along with other dwellings in the area, was deserted around AD 1300. Only about 100 years after it was built. Yes, did you have a question?

(Woman S) Why did the Anasazi build such a large city and then abandon it?

(Woman P) OK. I was coming to that. The reason for the abandonment has been the source of much debate. Can anyone here think of any reason why an entire population would abandon its city?

(Man S) Well, the Southwest is a rather dry part of the country. Perhaps there was a drought that led to mass starvation.

(Woman P) OK. That is a possibility. And, in fact, tree rings from this area have been studied, and, as you know, sections through trees indicate a lot about climate patterns. These tree rings do indicate that there was a drought in the last quarter of that century. Having said that, however, it was no more severe than previous droughts, and those were not bad enough to force the people to leave.

Some researchers have argued that warfare could have been a factor in the abandonment of the area. And there is evidence that by this time people were crowded into a smaller area, and some villages were moved away from lowland areas up to higher ground. This might suggest the presence of invaders, but there's not much other evidence to support this theory. Later sites appear to be built for defense, and excavation at other sites in the region indicates some violent struggles. The best we can say here is that warfare was a factor but probably not the underlying factor.

(Woman S) What about a plague? After all, there were diseases in Europe around that time that really wiped out a large part of the population.

(Woman P) That's a possibility. But again, there's no strong evidence to support that theory. Myself, I'm coming around to the idea that there was some kind of environmental disaster which affected the area. We now know that the Anasazi were not living harmoniously with nature. That's a rather naïve viewpoint. They exploited their environment like most human groups. Research has shown, in fact, that the Anasazi destroyed most of the larger animals through over-hunting. So they were forced to hunt for smaller game animals. That would have meant less efficient use of their time. In other words, they would have found less food for the same amount of work. And another thing, they had to collect wood for cooking and for heat, and so the surrounding areas became deforested. Both of these environmental causes must have played a large part in their eventual disappearance from the region. OK. So this is my thinking about this mystery. I'd have to say, though, that the general consensus today appears to be that there was a combination of factors, including environmental ones, that led to the abandonment of the communities in the region, and eventually to the decline of the whole culture.

Now get ready to answer the questions. You may use your notes to help you answer.

24. What is the main topic of the lecture?

25. What does the professor imply about the term *Anasazi*?

26. According to the professor, why did the Anasazi start making pottery?

27. Why does the professor say this: Where was I? Oh, yeah. The buildings.

28. Based on the information in the discussion, indicate whether each of the following is accepted by most scientists.

29. What does the professor imply about the Anasazi's use of their environment?

Questions 30–34

Listen to part of a conversation between two students.

(Man S) OK, so do you want to review that legal terminology that Dr. Bryant went over in class?

(Woman S) OK. Yeah. But I was going to meet my roommate at the Union. We planned to jog around campus for some exercise. You can come along too if you feel up to it.

(Man S) Great. Thanks. I'd like that. But shouldn't we review the terms first?

(Woman S) OK. We've got a few minutes I guess. So what was the first one?

(Man S) It's *burden of proof.* What do you remember about that?

(Woman S) OK. Well, this one has to do with the fact that in law cases, every person is presumed to be innocent until they're proven guilty, right?

(Man S) Well, yeah. But what else? What's the important thing?

(Woman S) And, it means that the party that brings the case, that's the plaintiff, has to prove the allegations in order to win the case. OK?

(Man S) OK. And the defendant, that's the person who is being accused, has the right, or the opportunity, to disprove the accusation. That is, the defendant can show, or try to show, that the accusation is false and that the evidence used against him or her is weak.

(Woman S) So, that means that the burden of proof is always – always rests on the party, the person making the accusation, because the defendant is presumed innocent and so has to be proven guilty. So in a criminal case it's up to the prosecutor to convince the judge or the jury that the allegations are true. The burden of proof rests with him or her.

(Man S) The prosecutor, that's the government lawyer, right?

(Woman S) Usually, but as far as I can remember anyone can act as a prosecutor except in certain types of cases. Anyway, what was the next term you wanted to review?

(Man S) Well, what exactly is meant by *circumstantial evidence*?

(Woman S) OK. Circumstantial evidence. Lemme think. Yeah, well, that's like indirect evidence.

(Man S) Yeah, OK. So it kind of implies someone could have been involved in a crime. It's not – it doesn't in itself directly prove who did it.

(Woman S) So what about evidence from a witness who says they heard or saw a person commit the crime?

(Man S) No, that's not circumstantial. That's called direct evidence. It has to be more indirect than that. Just about everything that is not direct is called circumstantial.

(Woman S) Remember Dr. Bryant gave an example. What was it now?

(Man S) Yeah, OK. He gave a couple of examples. One was, suppose a man earns a certain, known salary and then makes some big purchases way beyond what someone on his salary could afford. He might buy a luxury yacht or a new beachfront apartment or something. And this happens around the time he is alleged to have stolen a large sum of money. This is not direct proof, but it is circumstantial. It would help build a case against him.

(Woman S) Right. And it could be used in a court of law, right?

(Man S) Yeah, right. Unless the connection is really weak. Didn't Dr. Bryant say that, in fact, most convictions in court are based on circumstantial evidence?

(Woman S) Yeah, I remember him saying that. Most people have the opposite idea, maybe from watching too many TV dramas. But in real life, circumstantial evidence is considered very persuasive. A strong circumstantial case is often better than an eyewitness description.

Now get ready to answer the questions. You may use your notes to help you answer.

30. What are the students mainly discussing?

31. Why does the woman say this: But I was going to meet my roommate at the Union. We planned to jog around campus for some exercise.

32. According to the conversation, which of the following statements are correct?

33. What can be inferred about the value of circumstantial evidence for prosecutors?

34. According to the conversation, what do most people think about circumstantial evidence?

PRACTICE TEST 1: Speaking Section

1. Please listen carefully.

Describe a skill you have that will be important for your success in the modern world, and explain why this skill is so important. Include details and examples to support your explanation.

You may begin to prepare your response after the beep. [beep]

Please begin speaking after the beep. [beep]

2. Please listen carefully.

Some people work for a business, and some people work in their own business. Which would you prefer to do and why? Include details and examples in your explanation.

You may begin to prepare your response after the beep. [beep]

Please begin speaking after the beep. [beep]

3. Please listen carefully.

The University of the Rockies Financial Aid Office has posted information about work-study grants. You will have 45 seconds to read the announcement. Begin reading now.

Now listen to two students as they discuss the announcement.

(Woman S) Hey, do you know anything about the work-study program?

(Man S) A bit. You know that guy Jim? In our philosophy class? Well, he got a grant. You have to fill in papers about your financial needs, and then you're allotted an amount of money that you can earn and told how much you get per hour.

(Woman S) Oh, do you know how much he was paid?

(Man S) He was allotted the full amount. You know, Jim's from a big family, so money's tight.

(Woman S) Uh-huh. Hey, I heard there's an opening in the Astronomy Department, . . . that would give me some good job experience. You applying for something?

(Man S) Well, it'd be nice to get some job experience, and be able to work on campus, but I'm not eligible. You have to really need financial aid, and between my summer job and my parents helping me out, well . . .

(Woman S) Oh, you know what, I earned some money last summer. I wonder if I'll qualify.

(Man S) Maybe not for the full amount. Why don't you just go fill out the financial needs assessment form and find out? No harm in trying.

Now get ready to answer the question.

The woman expresses her desire for a work-study job. State the requirements necessary for taking part in the program and explain the advantages discussed.

You may begin to prepare your response after the beep. [beep]

Please begin speaking after the beep. [beep]

4. Please listen carefully.

Read the passage about symbiotic relationships. You have 45 seconds to read the passage. Begin reading now.

Now listen to part of a lecture on this topic in a biology class.

(Man P) We've been discussing the three symbiotic relationships between species: mutualism, in which both organisms benefit; parasitism, in which one benefits and the other is harmed; and commensalism, where one benefits while neither benefiting nor harming the other. Now, of course, these relationships are not always clear cut. For example, there is a plant called the bee orchid. Its flowers look like female bees – to the male bee anyway. The bee orchid tricks the male bee into mating with the flower, thus pollinating it. However, we don't know if, in fact, the relationship between this particular plant and the bee is mutualism, parasitism, or commensalism.

Sometimes the relationship actually changes. Let me give you some examples. We have bacteria on our skin, for instance. These colonies of bacteria don't harm us. So we can say that at this point the relationship is commensal. But what happens if we get burned? The bacteria on our skin can take advantage of the burn and cause infections. The bacteria turn into what we call an *opportunistic pathogen*. A pathogen, by the way, is parasitic.

Here's another example. Shrimp and crabs take advantage of colonies of coral, which provide a nice home. They neither harm nor benefit the coral colonies. So the relationship here is also commensal. But sometimes a coral-eating sea star attacks the coral. At that point, the shrimp and crabs defend the coral. Without these creatures to protect it, the coral would be eaten. So in this case the relationship becomes mutual. The coral and its defenders are now in a relationship in which both organisms benefit.

Now get ready to answer the question.

The professor gives two examples of symbiotic relationships that change. Explain both examples in terms of what the original symbiotic relationship was and what symbiotic relationship it became.

You may begin to prepare your response after the beep. [beep]

Please begin speaking after the beep. [beep]

5. Please listen carefully.

Listen to a conversation between two students.

(Woman S) Hey, Steve, I heard you've moved out of the dorms.

(Man S) Well, no. I haven't. I'd like to, but . . .

(Woman S) Yeah? What's the problem?

(Man S) Well, the places close to campus are expensive and the ones I can afford are too far to walk. So I've got to figure out what transportation's going to cost me.

(Woman S) Buses and trains aren't that expensive, are they?

(Man S) Nah. The problem is schedules. Sometimes I have to stay on campus late, after things stop running, so I'd have to take a taxi or get a car.

(Woman S) What's wrong with getting a car? Gets you where you want to go at your convenience.

(Man S) A car? In the city? No thanks. Besides, insurance rates are high for my age group and, you know, other costs, maintenance, parking . . .

(Woman S) That's a point for being close to campus. Also, it's easy to get home if you forget something.

(Man S) Yeah, and sometimes I like to take an afternoon nap, 'cause of the late hours I'm in the lab. It'd be nice to be able to do that.

(Woman S) Uh-huh. Can't if you live out in some suburb. Maybe it's best to stay in the dorms, right on campus.

(Man S) Yeah. Well, one of my complaints about the dorms is they're too noisy in the daytime. Can't sleep 'cause everyone's got their music going.

(Woman S) You get your meals and don't have to clean up afterwards.

(Man S) I think I could save a lot, doing my own shopping.

(Woman S) So what's the difference in costs of . . . a dorm, a place near campus, one on the train line or, oh, on the bus route?

(Man S) I don't know.

(Woman S) You don't know? Well, if I were you, I'd get all the figures and make a, you know, hypothetical budget. A budget showing you taking a taxi three times a week, and a budget for the costs of a car . . . And just put all the possibilities on paper. I think you'd make a better decision doing that and also make a list of advantages and disadvantages.

Now get ready to answer the question.

The students discuss the man's options. Describe his problem. Then state which of the options you prefer and explain why.

You may begin to prepare your response after the beep. [beep]

Please begin speaking after the beep. [beep]

6. Please listen carefully.

Listen to part of a lecture in a cultural studies class.

(Woman P) Although the entertainment industry is concerned with telling a good story, it has had a profound effect on people's conceptions and misconceptions of the world around them. Let me give you an example. There are many films and TV programs in which a serious crime takes place and a police detective solves or maybe doesn't solve the crime. It appears that these fictional crimes – added to news reports of real crime – cause viewers' perception of the rate of criminal behavior to outrank, to exaggerate reality. In other words, the actual, let's say, murder rate is probably well below people's perception of the murder rate.

I've just been talking about misconceptions of crime rates, but there are other misconceptions, which may be more harmful. Now, I'm not saying that believing in an exaggerated level of criminality, say a high murder rate, isn't harmful. It could cause a lot of people undue stress, for example, but what I mean is misconceptions about race and gender stereotypes – a person of a different race or a female being typecast into certain roles. Think about, for example, the portrayal of a person in a wheelchair. He or she is either portrayed as overcoming incredible odds to do heroic deeds or, on the other hand, being a helpless victim. Does this promote understanding or misconceptions?

In the movies, doctors perform miracles, lawyers win cases, and crime scene investigators find the evidence. People in these actual professions often get clients with unreasonable expectations. Professional people comment that the reality of their daily routine – their job – is seldom like that portrayed in the media. Students are sometimes disillusioned about their career choice because the job seemed much more interesting in the television program than in reality.

Unfortunately, we make these judgmental mistakes about our own society knowing full well the existence of the fantasy created by the media industry.

Now get ready to answer the question.

Using points and examples from the lecture, explain how the media has contributed to misconceptions about the real world.

You may begin to prepare your response after the beep. [beep]

Please begin speaking after the beep. [beep]

PRACTICE TEST 1: Writing Section

Now listen to part of a lecture on the topic you just read about.

(Man P) Often in medical research, new evidence makes us take a fresh look at causation. Now, the immediate causes of asthma are not in doubt, but there is some new thinking about the fundamental causes of this condition. It's been said that after an asthma attack, the airways of the sufferer return to normal. But what about in between attacks? Until recently, it was assumed that bronchial function returned to normal until the onset of a new attack.

But it has become clear in some asthmatics that the airways can become permanently narrowed and the walls of the airways thickened. These abnormalities in asthmatics' airways are due to what is called "remodeling." It used to be thought that remodeling was the result of long-term inflammation, a kind of scarring from repeated episodes over a long period.

But more recently, it has been suggested that remodeling of the tubes is not only a result of this scarring, but also may be the primary cause of the condition. In other words, remodeling may be fundamental to the disease. This idea has gained acceptability recently due to evidence from studies of young children. This research shows that many asthmatic children already have remodeled airways. So, according to this view, remodeling is not just a consequence of asthma, it may also be an underlying cause.

So, what causes the remodeling in the first place? Certainly, genetic factors play a role, but it seems that a combination of genetics and the environment are to blame. In other words, certain individuals may develop remodeled, vulnerable airways due to the environment affecting them even before birth.

Summarize the points made in the lecture you just heard, explaining how they cast doubt on the points made in the reading.

PRACTICE TEST 2: Listening Section

Questions 1–6

Listen to part of a lecture in a biology class.

(Man P) OK, so today we're going to continue with a discussion about the aquatic environment. Specifically, I'm interested here in some of the adaptations that make survival possible in estuary conditions. Now, as you know, the thing about the estuarine environment is that because the tide washes in and out twice a day, the salinity, that is, the amount or proportion of salt in the water, varies or can vary considerably throughout any 24-hour period. When the tide is out, the water may be near freshwater levels and when the tide is in, the levels of salt may be more like seawater. When the water is in between seawater and freshwater, it's called "brackish" water. By this term, we mean water that is typically less than 30 parts per thousand of salt. So, plants and animals that live in this environment must be able to adapt to these constant changes in the saltiness of the estuary waters.

So, what are the kinds of adaptations that estuarine organisms have developed? Well, the most important are either physiological and/or behavioral. Regarding the first, the physiological, the bodily adaptations tend to be associated with maintaining the right balance of salinity within the body. Some organisms, generally known as osmoregulators, control their internal concentrations of water salinity when the external environment changes. This word, of course, refers to osmosis, which . . . you don't need me to define osmosis, do you? Good, OK. Usually this kind of creature is less permeable to water and salt. Crabs are a very good example. Crabs that live in the estuarine environment keep out both water and salt with their hard shells. But, in addition, they may have internal organs and cell functions, which can regulate salt intake and excretion. Also, certain species of fish, which adjust to differing saline conditions have specialized kidneys, gills, and skin. Specialized kidneys and gills are able to switch between excreting more or less water and also between absorbing more or less salt, as conditions permit. So, the combined properties of gills, kidneys, and an impermeable skin allow them to live in conditions of varying salinity.

Plants as well as animals may use osmoregulation to survive since, in saline habitats, salt levels can reach deadly levels. A common species of grass known as smooth cordgrass has adapted through its complex root system. These roots are able to remove salts from the water they take in. Such plants can also expel salt through their leaves, and in some species, they can also shed leaves that become loaded with excess salt.

OK. So, what about the behavioral factors that help creatures exist in the estuary? Well, a common adaptation, especially among invertebrates, that is, creatures without backbones, is the ability to dig or burrow into the soft mud. Of course, this helps them avoid being eaten by predators such as birds or fish. But it's also an important advantage for species that cannot osmoregulate – cannot control the concentration of salt solution in their bodies. This is because below the surface of the mud the concentration of salt is less than in the open water above – and what's more, the temperature is less variable, which is also beneficial for creatures that don't tolerate changes of temperature. On the other hand, creatures such as oysters and clams don't like to have too low a level of salt. So these organisms simply close their shells tightly when the level of salt becomes too low, during low tides. At this point, they stop feeding and stop breathing through their gills. When the high tide returns and the oxygen and salt levels increase, they open their shells and feed and breathe oxygen again.

Other creatures are more mobile, and this too, by the way, is a behavioral adaptation. They can move upstream or downstream as conditions require. Certain crabs live in low salt areas because they can osmoregulate, but their young may not have developed this ability. So during breeding season, such species may move to areas in the sea with higher levels of saline. In the blue crab, for example, the females migrate to water of high salinity to hatch their young. Then the new generation of crabs moves back to fresher water as they develop into adults. So, does that make sense?

Now get ready to answer the questions. You may use your notes to help you answer.

1. What is the lecture mainly about?

2. Listen again to part of the lecture. Then answer the question.

(Man P) Some organisms, generally known as osmoregulators, control their internal concentrations of water salinity when the external environment changes. This word, of course, refers to osmosis, which . . . you don't need me to define osmosis, do you?

What does the professor imply when he says this: This word, of course, refers to osmosis, which . . . you don't need me to define osmosis, do you?

3. What two adaptations are mentioned that allow crabs to survive in the estuary environment?

4. Listen again to part of the lecture. Then answer the question.

(Man P) Certain crabs live in low salt areas because they can osmoregulate, but their young may not have developed this ability. So during breeding season, such species may move to areas in the sea with higher levels of saline. In the blue crab, for example, the females migrate to water of high salinity to hatch their young. Then the new generation of crabs moves back to fresher water as they develop into adults. So, does that make sense?

Why does the professor say this: So, does that make sense?

5. Indicate whether each word or phrase below describes a physiological adaptation or behavioral adaptation.

6. The adaptations of which estuarine creature are NOT discussed in the lecture?

Questions 7–11

Listen to a conversation between a student and a professor.

(Man S) Professor James?

(Woman P) Yes.

(Man S) I was told that I should talk to you about . . . well, I'm interested in switching majors, and I wanted some advice.

(Woman P) OK. So I assume you're switching to a degree in linguistics. Could you give me some background on your previous studies?

(Man S) Yeah, I was studying speech pathology, specializing in phonological disorders. But I went to Peru last summer, and, well, I ran out of money, and to pay for my expenses, I did some English teaching, and I really enjoyed it.

(Woman P) OK, um, so are you thinking about a degree in applied linguistics?

(Man S) Well, yeah, you know, with my background in phonology, I was able to help people improve their pronunciation, and I thought that perhaps I'd be more interested in that aspect of language.

(Woman P) OK. Well, some of your courses will probably fulfill linguistic requirements, and many of them will be advantageous for you as far as the knowledge is concerned, but not necessarily for course transfer.

(Man S) OK.

(Woman P) Let me find our, oh, here it is. This is an overview of the course requirements. Do you have a copy of your transcripts with you?

(Man S) Uh, yeah. Here you go.

(Woman P) Thank you. OK. Hmmm, well, besides the courses you've had in phonology, your Language Development course will transfer . . . Sociolinguistics and Psycholinguistics, and of course, all your general electives.

(Man S) Excuse me. Could you hang on a second? I want to mark the courses that will transfer.

(Woman P) Here's a pen.

(Man S) Oh, thank you. OK . . . Language Development, Sociolinguistics, Psycholinguistics . . . OK.

(Woman P) Now, the Linguistics Department requires two foreign languages. I see you have Spanish. The second language should be one that is not so commonly used.

(Man S) What about the courses I've taken in American Sign Language? We had to be fluent in signing in order to communicate with people who have hearing disabilities.

(Woman P) I'm not sure if we can count your sign language courses, and at this point I'd rather err on the side of caution and tell you that it doesn't fulfill the requirement.

(Man S) That seems reasonable. So Spanish will transfer – and I'll put a question mark beside the American Sign Language courses.

(Woman P) Hmmm. Well, just at a glance, I would say that this change of major may only set you back by a semester or two.

(Man S) Are you calculating that based on the average number of classes that students take per term?

(Woman P) Well, yes. Would graduating later be a problem?

(Man S) It might be.

(Woman P) I suppose that if you were to carry a heavier course load, you might be able to finish on schedule. But since some of the higher level courses have prerequisites, your taking on more courses per semester may not necessarily enable you to graduate as soon as you'd like.

(Man S) Well, I need to look into all options. I might be able to get more funding.

(Woman P) OK. Well, why don't you take the overview I gave you and continue crossing out the courses you won't have to take. Then check the courses that you must take and see which ones have prerequisites – and which ones you could take at the same time. Circle the ones you have questions about, and feel free to come back to see me during my office hours.

(Man S) OK. I guess, I'll have to see if I can get another grant or a loan or something as well. Do I need to make an appointment to see you?

(Woman P) No, just show up during my office hours. And in the meantime, I'll try to find out if the American Sign Language course can be used to fulfill your language requirement.

(Man S) OK. Thank you. Oh, here's your pen.

(Woman P) Thank you.

Now get ready to answer the questions. You may use your notes to help you answer.

7. Why does the student go to see the professor?

8. Listen again to part of the conversation. Then answer the question.

(Woman P) OK. So I assume you're switching to a degree in linguistics. Could you give me some background on your previous studies?

What can be inferred about the professor?

9. Why does the student want to change degree programs?

10. Listen again to part of the conversation. Then answer the question.

(Woman P) I'm not sure if we can count your sign language courses, and at this point I'd rather err on the side of caution and tell you that it doesn't fulfill the requirement.

Why does the professor say this: . . . at this point I'd rather err on the side of caution . . .

11. What can be inferred about the student?

Questions 12–17

Listen to a discussion in an education class.

(Man P) OK, up until now, we've been discussing the questions we as teachers construct for our students in order to encourage their thought process. But today, I want to look at the issue of asking questions from a different direction. Now, young children are full of questions. But once they're in the school system, the role reverses and the teacher becomes the primary questioner. Now, according to various studies, teachers ask between 300 and 400 questions a day in the average elementary school. Unfortunately, as children get older, they stop asking their own questions. By the time students are in a university . . . Well, last week I walked out of the Elementary Literacy course I teach, feeling kind of discouraged because not one of my students had asked me a question. Did they know it all, and consequently, was I wasting my time and theirs? Were they so lost that they found it impossible to ask questions? Was I such a great lecturer that they understood everything perfectly? What is it that keeps students from asking questions? Anybody? Annie.

(Woman S1) Well, you know, I think it's hard for us to admit in front of our classmates that we don't understand something. I mean, nobody wants to feel stupid.

(Man P) So in other words, you look around at your classmates and think, "Everybody else understands this, so I must be a real idiot"?

(Woman S1) Well, sometimes I think that, even though I know that if I don't understand a concept, well, probably several of my classmates don't understand it either.

(Man P) OK. What Annie is describing is the primary negative pressure that we as teachers need to constantly try to help students overcome. So, let me write that on the board: "negative pressures." And for item number one, I'll write "the fear of appearing stupid." OK. Can you think of other factors that keep students from asking questions?

(Man S) Well, maybe this is another aspect of feeling stupid, but I think class size counts. This is a small class, and we all know each other. I don't feel as intimidated asking a question in front of a small group of people I trust.

(Woman S1) You know, I can see why Tony might think class size is relevant to feeling stupid, but I think there's more to it than that. I mean . . . well, when you ask a question in one of the large lecture halls, sometimes you have to repeat it several times 'cause the professor can't hear you . . . and, well, that is embarrassing.

(Man S) Yeah, and sometimes a question is asked that the professor heard, but the students in the back of the class couldn't hear and so the professor's answer is meaningless.

(Man P) OK. So, in other words, large class size discourages meaningful dialog, both in terms of the room size and the number of students. I'm going to write this as "large class size pressure." Lisa?

(Woman S2) It's not just large class sizes that make one feel uncomfortable. Sometimes it's more difficult to ask a question, just because everyone knows everyone else. But lost in the crowd, it might, in fact, be easier to talk.

(Man P) OK. I can see that. So let me erase "large." There . . . "class size pressure." Anything more to add?

(Woman S2) Time pressure.

(Man P) "Time pressure"? Can you expand on that?

(Woman S2) Professor Clarkson. [laughter]

(Man P) Professor Clarkson? I seem to have missed the joke.

(Man S) Professor Clarkson is . . . sort of . . . the epitome of time pressure.

(Woman S2) Yeah, he dashes through his lectures like, well as if he were trying to cram the entire field of child development into one class session.

(Woman S1) Yeah, it's like he doesn't even stop to breathe. I feel intimidated about stopping his lecture with a mere question.

(Man P) OK. I think we have two negative pressures going on here. "Time pressure," as Lisa said, and personality. A teacher's personality seems to deter students from asking questions.

(Woman S2) It's not exactly personality. I mean Professor Clarkson is a really nice man and a good lecturer.

(Man P) OK, but isn't it the signal he sends of being in a hurry that keeps you from asking questions?

(Woman S2) Yes, but . . . Well, when someone does get the courage to ask Professor Clarkson a question, he never gives the impression that his time is being wasted. I think the type of teacher personality that keeps students from asking questions is . . . well, sometimes a teacher makes a sarcastic joke at the student's expense.

(Man P) OK. So you do agree that personality may keep students from asking questions, even though you don't think it applies to Professor Clarkson. So "personality." Does anyone have any more to add? No? OK. So now I'd like you to split into groups of three. In your groups, I'd like you to discuss possible ways teachers can promote question-asking in the classroom. Keep in mind the negative pressures we've discussed, oh, and by the way, there are other pressures that were not mentioned, but I think you'll come up with them in your discussions. I'll ask you to share your thoughts in, say, 20 minutes.

Now get ready to answer the questions. You may use your notes to help you answer.

12. What is the discussion mainly about?

13. Why does the professor say this: . . . Did they know it all, and consequently, was I wasting my time and theirs? Were they so lost that they found it impossible to ask questions? Was I such a great lecturer that they understood everything perfectly?

14. Listen again to part of the discussion. Then answer the question.

(Man S) Well, maybe this is another aspect of feeling stupid, but I think class size counts. This is a small class, and we all know each other. I don't feel as intimidated asking a question in front of a small group of people I trust.

(Woman S1) You know, I can see why Tony might think class size is relevant to feeling stupid, but I think there's more to it than that. I mean . . . well, when you ask a question in one of the large lecture halls, sometimes you have to repeat it several times 'cause the professor can't hear you . . . and, well, that is embarrassing.

What can be inferred about the students?

15. Why does Lisa mention Professor Clarkson?

16. In the discussion, the professor elicits different reasons why students don't ask questions. Indicate whether each of the following is one of the discussed fears.

17. Listen again to part of the discussion. Then answer the question.

(Man P) . . . In your groups, I'd like you to discuss possible ways teachers can promote question-asking in the classroom. Keep in mind the negative pressures we've discussed, oh, and by the way, there are other pressures that were not mentioned, but I think you will come up with them in your discussions.

Why does the professor say this: . . . by the way, there are other pressures that were not mentioned . . .

Questions 18–23

Listen to a lecture in a history of ideas class.

(Woman P) I want to talk about what was once a very popular way of studying character based on the shape of the skull. This theory, what was known as "phrenology," was started by a German doctor named Franz Gall around the year 1800. What Gall proposed was that it was possible to determine character by feeling or "reading" the bumps on a person's head. I want to discuss here the basic principles of this theory, what it claimed to be able to do – and then why it became unfashionable and disappeared. Finally, I want to ask whether it contributed anything to our knowledge about the brain.

So, what were some of the important features of phrenology? Gall said that the brain is the organ of the mind; that our talents and mental abilities stem from the brain. Furthermore, he said that the brain is composed of several distinct organs – and that each of the brain's faculties has a separate organ in a separate part of the brain. What's more, the size of any organ is a reflection of its power – and hence importance in the makeup of an individual's character. He also claimed that the overall shape of the brain is determined by the development of the organs which it contains. He argued that the outside skull takes on the shape of the brain which it encloses – and therefore the surface of the skull can be taken as an accurate reflection of the shape of the brain and thus of a person's psychological tendencies and aptitudes.

So how did it work? Well, a phrenologist would run his fingers over a person's head, examining every bump or indentation. So, for example, a protuberance – a bump, in say, the forehead – would indicate that the person had a pronounced tendency to be benevolent, since the organ of benevolence was supposedly in that location. An indentation somewhere else would mean a weakly developed attribute, say a poor memory.

Now, these things were the basic ideas of phrenology as practiced throughout the early nineteenth century. So widespread was this theory that many people would consult phrenologists before, oh, for example, hiring an employee, or even, say, finding a marriage partner. Proponents also tried to determine a person's predisposition to crime or dishonesty, and unfortunately, at one stage some scientists tried to justify notions such as criminal tendency or racial superiority through skull readings. At the peak of its popularity, phrenology was widely practiced in both North America and Europe. So, you're probably thinking all this is really bizarre, right? Well, so did some people back then! In truth there had always been dissenting voices. The theory was made fun of and criticized by various individuals from its earliest appearance.

So what happened to phrenology? Well, educated people lost interest as more academic approaches to psychology became common. It was noticed by some that phrenologists tended to seek confirmation for their hypotheses – while ignoring counterexamples. Suppose a person was said after a reading to have a marked tendency towards, let's say, honesty, but then exhibited strongly dishonest personality traits; it would be clear that the analysis was not accurate. Phrenologists tended to dogmatically reject or explain away falsifying evidence, such as this example shows.

Have we learned anything from this theory? Well, I would like to argue that there was some value in it. First of all, it was an important step historically to emphasize that the brain was the organ of the mind, that thinking and feeling were done through the brain. Furthermore, phrenologists were important in arguing that brain functions were localized – that some parts of the brain were specialized for certain abilities. Nowadays, of course, we know that this is only partly true. Some parts of the brain appear to be very much involved with certain functions, whereas many abilities seem to be distributed throughout the brain rather than in one location. So, to sum up, we can say that phrenology was of some scientific value although many, if not most, of its ideas have been superseded.

Now get ready to answer the questions. You may use your notes to help you answer.

18. What is the lecture mainly about?

19. What points does the professor make about Gall's phrenological theory?

20. Listen again to part of the lecture. Then answer the question.

(Man P) At the peak of its popularity, phrenology was widely practiced in both North America and Europe. So, you're probably thinking all this is really bizarre, right?

Why does the professor say this: So, you're probably thinking all this is really bizarre, right?

21. According to the professor, how did phrenologists approach evidence?

22. What does the professor imply about phrenology?

23. According to the professor, which of the following modern beliefs was contributed to by phrenology?

Questions 24–29

Listen to a discussion in an astronomy class.

(Man P) Today I'd like to discuss an interesting research area for space scientists. So, I think most of you have heard of the term *terraforming*. For those of you who haven't, let me just repeat that terraforming is the name given to the process of transforming a planet from its current conditions into a planet something like the Earth. That is, changing the temperature and the atmospheric conditions so that it is livable for humans and other life forms found on Earth. I know this sounds a lot like science fiction. But a lot of scientists are beginning to take this idea seriously. So, why would we want to do this, go to such an immense expenditure in terms of money, resources, time . . .

(Man S) Excuse me, Professor, are you serious? What a waste. That's assuming it's possible.

(Woman S) Well, it could be very useful in the future if the population of the world got so out of hand that the resources on Earth couldn't support the number of people here. I think some people would say that we've already reached that point.

(Man P) OK. Yeah. The pressure on resources of a rapidly expanding population has always forced people to migrate in search of new territory. We could say that human migrations have, historically and even prehistorically, occurred when populations have grown too much for the available space. Think of the migrations to the Americas from Europe and elsewhere.

But let's get back to the problem of terraforming. How could this possibly be done? Let's take Mars. This is the planet most scientists think of when talking about terraforming. It's certainly the best candidate, at least in our solar system. The other planets are much less suitable for all kinds of reasons. At least Mars has water in ice form and a solid surface. But, remember, it has a very thin atmosphere, made up largely of carbon dioxide and almost no oxygen, its temperature averages about -60 degrees Celsius, and as far as we can tell, it's completely lifeless.

(Man S) So wait a minute. You're saying we could change this into an Earth-like environment? That's a total waste of resources. What about using that money to improve the Earth? And don't we have to ask ourselves whether we have the right to tamper with unspoiled environments?

(Woman S) I don't agree with you there. I mean, if we can do it, it would be worth it to have so much more living space, and no one actually lives there, on Mars. We wouldn't be spoiling it for any life form. Mars is lifeless. If we could turn it into a habitable planet, I think it's worth a shot.

(Man P) OK. There are certainly ethical considerations. And they are sure to lead to heated debate. But let's just think about the practicalities for now. What kind of technology could make this possible anyway? Several suggestions have been made on how we could raise the temperature. One suggestion is that we put up huge orbital mirrors to reflect sunlight onto the surface. Another one is that asteroids, containing great amounts of ammonia, could be forced to smash into the planet. Ammonia is a greenhouse gas, so that would also have the effect of raising the temperature. Those are just two of the ideas which have been discussed. Now, once the temperature has been raised, the ice at the poles would melt – and the water could be used to sustain life. At first this could be plant life introduced from Earth. Finally, after perhaps thousands of years, the plants would have given off enough oxygen to transform the atmosphere into one in which animals and eventually humans could survive.

Now get ready to answer the questions. You may use your notes to help you answer.

24. What is the discussion mainly about?

25. Why does the professor say this: I know this sounds a lot like science fiction.

26. Why does the professor mention the migration of Europeans to the Americas?

27. According to the professor, why is Mars the planet that scientists want to terraform?

28. Listen again to part of the discussion. Then answer the question.

(Man P) OK. There are certainly ethical considerations. And they are sure to lead to heated debate. But let's just think about the practicalities for now.

Why does the professor say this: But let's just think about the practicalities for now.

29. Which of the following is NOT mentioned as a method of terraforming Mars?

Questions 30–34

Listen to part of a conversation between a student and a research coordinator.

(Man) Yes. Can I help you?

(Woman S) Uh, yes, I'm here about that announcement on the bulletin board about your needing participants in an experiment.

(Man) OK. We have several doctoral projects needing participants. Which one in particular are you interested in?

(Woman S) Oh, I didn't realize there was more than one. The one I saw was about a food experiment . . . one about how food affects mood.

(Man) Oh, that's Kenny's experiment. Yeah, can I ask you some questions . . . personal ones . . . to see if you meet the requirements?

(Woman S) Sure, why not.

(Man) First, are you diabetic or do you have any allergies to any common foods or food additives?

(Woman S) No. Not that I know of.

(Man) OK. Are you currently on any type of diet or taking any medication?

(Woman S) No. These are the questions on the notice that's on the bulletin board, aren't they?

(Man) Yeah, but we have to go through all of them with volunteers because some people don't read the notices carefully and really aren't suitable for the experiment. We also need you to sign an agreement of participation stating that you've understood all the requirements and are willing to take part in the study.

(Woman S) OK. That makes sense.

(Man) Are you suffering from any cold, flu, or respiratory problems?

(Woman S) Well, not this week.

(Man) OK, if you do come down with a cold next week while the experiment's going on, we would like you to notify us and drop out.

(Woman S) OK. That sounds reasonable.

(Man) Have you ever been diagnosed with an eating disorder?

(Woman S) No.

(Man) OK. Now, let me explain what we need you to do. You're not supposed to eat anything in the morning before coming into the lab. That's the Pharmacology Lab, on the second floor of the red brick building behind the Student Center. So, every morning all next week you're to come to the lab for breakfast.

(Woman S) Great.

(Man) And you are expected to eat it, whether you like the breakfast or not.

(Woman S) It won't be too strange, will it? Like pickled onions or grasshoppers?

(Man) No, there won't be anything like that. Now, where was I?

(Woman S) Eating all my breakfast whether I like it or not.

(Man) Oh. Right. Breakfast will consist of the normal things, like eggs or cereal – different each day though. After breakfast, you'll be given some tests that look at your responses to certain interactive stimuli on a computer. Then you're free to go, but we need you back about two hours later for a snack. And you're not supposed to have any outside snacks before coming back for our snack. The snacks are yogurt or nuts, candy bars, potato chips . . . typical snacks really, followed by some more interactive tests.

(Woman S) OK. Sounds fun.

(Man) Yeah, I've volunteered for it myself. Now, let's look at the schedule. It's very important that you can make all the sessions.

(Woman S) Does it have to be exactly the same time every morning? That could be a problem for me.

(Man) No. Uh, well, uh . . . yeah. I mean you can have breakfast at a different time every day, but the snack has to be two hours after the breakfast. We've tried to set times so participants could have breakfast before going off to class and get back for the snack.

(Woman S) Oh, OK. Yes, I can fit into your schedule times every day.

(Man) Great. Can you mark the times that you'll be coming on this schedule and, oh, sign this consent form?

(Woman S) Sure.

Now get ready to answer the questions. You may use your notes to help you answer.

30. Why has the student gone to see the research coordinator?

31. Why does the research coordinator ask the student personal questions?

32. Listen again to part of the conversation. Then answer the question.

(Man) Are you suffering from any cold, flu, or respiratory problems?

(Woman S) Well, not this week.

Why does the student say this: Well, not this week.

33. Which of the following topics does the research coordinator NOT ask the student about?

34. What example does the research coordinator give of the breakfast that will be provided?

PRACTICE TEST 2: Speaking Section

1. Please listen carefully.

A good teacher should have some special qualities. What qualities do you think are necessary for a good teacher to have and why? Include details and examples in your explanation.

You may begin to prepare your response after the beep. [beep]

Please begin speaking after the beep. [beep]

2. Please listen carefully.

Some people believe that people who play video games are learning important life skills. Others believe that video game players are wasting their time. Which view do you agree with and why? Include details and examples in your explanation.

You may begin to prepare your response after the beep. [beep]

Please begin speaking after the beep. [beep]

3. Please listen carefully.

The University of the Rockies newspaper has published a letter to the editor concerning a university policy. Read the letter about the hiring of temporary instructors. You will have 45 seconds to read the letter. Begin reading now.

Now listen to two students as they discuss the issue brought up in the letter.

(Woman S) Hmm, I thought university teachers were well paid. I mean they have to have advanced degrees and be experienced to teach here, don't they?

(Man S) Yeah, but I've heard that over 60 percent of our teachers are temporary.

(Woman S) Really? Well, I don't think my education is suffering because of it. Do you?

(Man S) Well, it's kind of hard to know, isn't it? I mean part-timers have to hold down another job, so they can't concentrate on course development.

(Woman S) That's true, but I still think my teachers are pretty well prepared.

(Man S) Yeah, me too. But, there are other drawbacks to having part-time teachers, too. Like, well, I needed to see my literature instructor, but arranging a time was difficult 'cause she also works at the city library, and then our meeting wasn't private 'cause temporary staff members share offices.

(Woman S) Really?

(Man S) Uh-huh. And they don't have a voice in departmental issues or access to university funding.

(Woman S) Wow. I can't imagine they feel any loyalty to the university at all.

Now get ready to answer the question.

The man expresses his opinion on the issue of temporary instructors. State his opinion and explain the reasons he gives for that opinion.

You may begin to prepare your response after the beep. [beep]

Please begin speaking after the beep. [beep]

4. Please listen carefully.

Read the passage about imprinting in baby birds. You have 45 seconds to read the passage. Begin reading now.

Now listen to part of a lecture on this topic in an ecology class.

(Woman P) So, we've been looking at animal behavior and especially the process of imprinting in young birds. Of course, the first thing a young gosling sees when it hatches is its mother. Now, birds that walk almost immediately after hatching, as opposed to those who are helpless and can't get around for several weeks, have to follow their mother for their own safety, for their survival. It seems that walking birds will follow just about anything that moves and has eyes. In fact, we've seen that they will easily imprint on human beings. But some researchers have gone even further. One set of experiments, for example, has found that young geese will imprint on inanimate objects, such as plastic milk bottles that are attached to a moving object like an electric toy train.

Now, it seems that in some species of birds, and this includes nesting birds, which are helpless after hatching, imprinting can affect later learning and social behavior, for example, territorial behavior. If a human takes on the role of the parent, the bird's social behavior becomes directed at the wrong object or species. A bird that sees a human as one of its own kind – and follows or accompanies a human – will not understand the importance of keeping to its own territory. This is why wildlife specialists tell us not to try to raise young birds that we find outside a nest. If the bird becomes attached to us, it can't learn to associate with its own species and would quickly be rejected.

Now get ready to answer the question.

The professor explains the notion of imprinting in young geese and ducks. Explain how this behavior develops and how it might be important for the birds' survival.

You may begin to prepare your response after the beep. [beep]

Please begin speaking after the beep. [beep]

5. Please listen carefully.

Listen to a conversation between two students.

(Man S) I just finished my history project.

(Woman S) That must feel nice. It takes me so long to do Professor Madison's assignments.

(Man S) Really? Well, what do you think the problem is? Do you have trouble understanding the task?

(Woman S) It's not a matter of understanding the material. My problem is technical. You know how he wants us to turn in the projects on disk? Well, I'm just computer illiterate. I write out all my assignments by hand.

(Man S) Wow. Well, you could pay someone to type up your handwritten work. There are always ads on the bulletin board of people willing to do that for a fee.

(Woman S) That's an idea, but it could get too expensive after a while.

(Man S) Yeah, I imagine it would. Oh, why don't you go on over to the Study Skills Center? Maybe they could direct you to some online sites that give typing lessons you can do on your own time. You know, they may even hold some beginning word-processing classes.

(Woman S) Do you think so?

(Man S) Well, I don't know for sure, but it's worth a try. And another thing you should do is sign up for a beginning computer course. You know – the world is getting more technical everyday – and if you really want to fit into the job market, you should learn everything you can about computers while you're here and have all these available resources.

(Woman S) Yeah, I guess you're right.

Now get ready to answer the question.

The students discuss different solutions to the woman's problem. Describe the problem. Then state which of the solutions you prefer and why.

You may begin to prepare your response after the beep. [beep]

Please begin speaking after the beep. [beep]

6. Please listen carefully.

Listen to part of a lecture in an architecture class.

(Man P) When planning a structure, engineers must consider the internal and external forces the structure must withstand. These are called *loads.* Broadly speaking there are two types of loads, static and dynamic. Now, static loads concern those forces that don't change, and dynamic loads are those that change abruptly.

First, let's look at static loads, which can be broken down into dead loads and live loads. Dead loads concern the weight distribution that the structure itself must bear. These would include beams, walls, floors, ceilings, and roofs. Calculating dead loads is quite straightforward. Now, live loads are those other weights that a structure must support. Live loads can be people, furniture, or, in the case of a bridge, cars and trucks. You may wonder why live loads like people or cars are considered static – since we move around all the time. Well, we can calculate how many people will fit into this classroom, say, or how many trucks can be on a bridge at the same time. Our comings and goings flow, they do not happen abruptly. Imagine that your family is sitting in different parts of a room and someone says, "Oh, look, northern lights," so everyone rushes to the same window to look outside. The live load changes from the weight being evenly distributed to its being concentrated at one point. Like dead loads, live-load calculations can be computed.

Now, remember that I said dynamic loads are those in which the forces change suddenly, for example, a gust of wind. Extreme examples of dynamic loads are tidal waves, hurricanes, or earthquakes. Think about earthquake zones. Here the engineer must consider features that allow the building to withstand or, let's say, counteract a sudden change of force, a force that is unpredictable.

Now get ready to answer the question.

Using points and examples from the lecture, explain the kinds of loads an engineer must consider when building a structure.

You may begin to prepare your response after the beep. [beep]

Please begin speaking after the beep. [beep]

PRACTICE TEST 2: Writing Section

Now listen to a professor's response to the reading passage.

(Woman P) Now, in this course we've focused on the need for judging unusual claims with strong empirical evidence. I want you to take a fresh look at the claims here. Many people will accept dowsing without question, just assuming that, somehow, underground water does or can be detected because it gives off invisible frequencies. Can we accept this? On the face of it this is an unusual claim since it seems to go against the laws of physics. Now, I've said before, and I'll repeat it here, extraordinary claims require extraordinary evidence.

But first of all, these forces or whatever that are supposed to be given off by objects are . . . are unknown to science. Attempts made with very sensitive instruments have not been able to detect them. Think about it. We have instruments that can detect weak radio signals from distant objects in space, but we can't detect signals from a nearby material that is claimed to exert a strong pull on dowsing tools. Furthermore, there have been numerous attempts to test what we might call the dowsing hypothesis: to test whether under strict scientific conditions it still works. It's been found that, when the experiment is . . . when all the variables are controlled, that dowsing doesn't work. The results it gives are no better than random luck. In other words, if you dig for water anywhere at all, you would have a chance of finding it – the same kind of chance that a dowser would have. So under strict conditions dowsers have about the same chance as anyone with a hunch. Now, when experiments have been performed without strict conditions attached, it seems that dowsing can be successful. I'd like you to think about this and come with your own ideas tomorrow on how this could be possible.

Summarize the points made in the lecture you just heard, explaining how they cast doubt on the points made in the reading.

Index

Instructions for Installing the CD-ROM

On Windows computers

Insert the CD-ROM into your CD-ROM drive. The program will start automatically. If it does not start by itself, click on "My Computer" on your desktop or in the Start menu. Next, click on the CD-ROM icon ("Cambridge Prep").

A dialog box will give you two options:

1. Install the application on your hard drive
2. Run the application off the CD-ROM (limited functionality)

We recommend that you install the application on your hard drive. If you run the application off the CD-ROM, you will not be able to create or manage a user account, save your test results, or send your scores and responses to your teacher.

If you choose to install the application, select that option in the dialog box, click on "OK," and follow the instructions on the following screens to complete the installation process. A program folder and a desktop shortcut ("Cambridge TOEFL® Prep") will be created. Once the application has started, you can choose to create a user account or log in as a guest. If you choose to log in as a guest, you will not be able to save your test results or send your scores and responses to your teacher.

Whether you install the application on your hard drive or run the application off the CD-ROM, the CD-ROM needs to be in the CD-ROM drive for the application to work.

On Macintosh computers

Insert the CD-ROM into your CD-ROM drive. On most computers the CD-ROM folder will automatically open. If it doesn't open by itself, click on the CD-ROM icon ("Cambridge TOEFL® Prep") on your desktop. In the CD-ROM folder, you can choose to install the application on your hard drive or run the application off the CD-ROM.

We recommend that you install the application on your hard drive. If you run the application off the CD-ROM, you will not be able to create or manage a user account, save your test results, or send your scores and responses to your teacher.

If you choose to install, follow these steps:

1. Drag the Cambridge Install Folder to the Applications folder.
2. Open the Applications folder.
3. Open the Cambridge Install Folder.
4. Click on the Cambridge TOEFL® Prep program icon to start the application.

Once the application has started, you can choose to create a user account or log in as a guest. If you choose to log in as a guest, you will not be able to save your test results or send your scores and responses to your teacher.

Whether you install the application on your hard drive or run the application off the CD-ROM, the CD-ROM needs to be in the CD-ROM drive for the application to work.

Terms and Conditions of Use

This is a legal agreement between you ("the customer") and Cambridge University Press.

1. License
   (a) Cambridge University Press grants the customer the license to use one copy of this CD-ROM (i) on a single computer for use by one or more people at different times, or (ii) by a single person on one or more computers (provided the CD-ROM is only used on one computer at one time and is only used by the customer), but not both.
   (b) The customer shall not: (i) copy or authorize copying of the CD-ROM, (ii) translate the CD-ROM, (iii) reverse-engineer, disassemble, or decompile the CD-ROM, (iv) transfer, sell, assign, or otherwise convey any portion of the CD-ROM, or (v) operate the CD-ROM from a network or mainframe system.
2. Copyright
   All material contained within the CD-ROM is protected by copyright and other intellectual property laws. The customer acquires only the right to use the CD-ROM and does not acquire any rights, express or implied, other than those expressed in the license.
3. Liability
   To the extent permitted by applicable law, Cambridge University Press is not liable for direct damages or loss of any kind resulting from the use of this product or from errors or faults contained in it, and in every case, Cambridge University Press's liability shall be limited to the amount actually paid by the customer for the product.